FIDE (the International Federation for European Law) brings together National Associations for European Law and their members and serves as a forum for the study, development, critical appraisal and renewal of European law.

Written for the XXI FIDE Congress taking place in Dublin in June 2004, this book explores EU policy on migration and asylum, and the manner in which this policy is being implemented at a national level. With national reports from 20 EU, EEA and EFTA Member States, it is the most wide ranging and comprehensive international survey of this issue to date. Each report was prepared by a national expert and focuses on: the national implementation of existing EU legislation in the field of migration and asylum law; the compatibility of national migration and asylum law and policies with pending EC legislation on asylum procedure, legal status of third country nationals, and definition of refugees; national attitudes to European Commission proposals on the future development of European migration and asylum law; and long term perspectives for EU legislation in the field of migration and asylum law and policy.

IMELDA HIGGINS is a practising barrister at the Bar of Ireland. She is also a part-time lecturer in European law at the Faculty of Law, Trinity College Dublin and at the Faculty of Law, University College Dublin. Before coming to the bar, Ms Higgins worked as a Legal Secretary to Judge D.A.O. Edward at the Court of Justice of the European Communities, and prior to that was engaged as a Lecturer by the European Institute of Public Administration, where her central role was the training of judges and lawyers in the accession countries, mainly in the context of Community training programmes. Ms Higgins has published numerous articles in the field of European Law.

PROFESSOR DR. KAY HAILBRONNER, LL.M. is Professor of public law, international law and European law at the University of Konstanz. He obtained his Master of Laws from McGill University in Montreal, and, in 1971, his Doctorate in law from the University of Heidelberg. From 1988 to 1992, Professor Hailbronner was Judge at the Administrative Appeal Court of Baden-Württemberg. Since 1990, he has been Legal Counsel for the Federal Government in asylum and immigration law, and European law. He is Director of the Centre for International and European Law on Immigration and Asylum at the University of Konstanz, which was established in 1994. He is widely published in the area of Immigration and Asylum Law, and is co-editor of the leading journal in aliens law in Germany.

MIGRATION AND ASYLUM LAW AND POLICY IN THE EUROPEAN UNION

FIDE 2004 National Reports

Editor
IMELDA HIGGINS

General Rapporteur
KAY HAILBRONNER

CAMBRIDGE
UNIVERSITY PRESS

CAMBRIDGE UNIVERSITY PRESS
Cambridge, New York, Melbourne, Madrid, Cape Town, Singapore, São Paulo

Cambridge University Press
The Edinburgh Building, Cambridge CB2 2RU, UK

Published in the United States of America by Cambridge University Press, New York

www.cambridge.org
Information on this title: www.cambridge.org/9780521605588

First published 2004

A catalogue record for this publication is available from the British Library

ISBN-13 978-0-521-60558-8 paperback
ISBN-10 0-521-60558-X paperback

Transferred to digital printing 2005

CONTENTS

Welcome from the President of FIDE vi
THE HON. MR JUSTICE NIAL FENNELLY
Judge of the Supreme Court of Ireland

Foreword by the FIDE Secretary General vii
MR PATRICK McCANN

General Rapporteur Bio xi
PROFESSOR KAY HAILBRONNER

Editor Bio xiii
MS IMELDA HIGGINS

Editor's Note xiv

TEXT OF QUESTIONNAIRE 1

National Reports

Austria 33
Croatia 45
Denmark 65
Estonia 89
Germany 111
Greece 135
Hungary 161
Ireland 179
Italy 205
Latvia 221
Luxembourg 245
Malta 267
The Netherlands 291
Norway 305
Poland 321
Portugal 343
Spain 371
Sweden 383
Switzerland 393
United Kingdom 431

General Rapporteur Report 455

WELCOME TO XXI FIDE CONGRESS

FIDE PRESIDENT
The Hon. Mr Justice Nial Fennelly

It has been a great honour for Ireland to be asked to host the XXI Congress of FIDE. It has equally been a great honour for me personally to have been asked to act as President of FIDE during this very important year for the European Union.

The topics for the Congress were chosen after much debate and wide consultation. The choice was not easy. There are several other topics worthy of debate. The Congress debates will cover both old and new ground.

There are two special features of this year's Congress.

First, on the virtual eve of our meetings in Dublin, ten new Member States will join the European Union. Words are not adequate to express the great happiness which I share with my colleagues at the Irish Society for European Law at being able to welcome the delegates from these States to Dublin and to the Union at the same time.

Second, even as I write, the Constitution for Europe remains under discussion, though the outcome is shrouded in uncertainty. I express the hope that, whatever the state of political discussions, delegates to the Congress will grasp the opportunity for a lively exchange of views.

Finally, I offer a hearty welcome to all delegates, rapporteurs, spouses and others. I hope that you enjoy your stay in Dublin.

FOREWORD

PATRICK McCANN
FIDE Secretary General

The XXI FIDE Congress takes place in Dublin, Ireland between the 2nd and 5th of June, 2004. The Congress is the biennial meeting of Fédération Internationale de Droit Européene (FIDE – the International Federation for European Law).

FIDE brings together National Associations for European Law and their members and serves as a forum for the study, development, critical appraisal and renewal of European law.

The FIDE Congress has a special place among the many conferences and seminars on European law. First, it is a not for profit venture organised on behalf of FIDE by different National Associations in rotation as a matter of professional solidarity between lawyers interested in European law. Secondly, the Congress brings together the full range of lawyers – Judges, Practitioners and Academic Lawyers – across the breadth of Europe.

The Irish Presidency of FIDE is particularly pleased to have been able to develop relationships with lawyers in the new Member States of the Union. Also, the Irish Presidency of FIDE is very pleased to have delegates and Rapporteurs from potential or future Member States as well as the continued participation and representation by Rapporteurs and Delegates of Lawyers from EU EFTA and EEA Member States.

This will be the second time the FIDE Congress has taken place in Dublin. The 10th FIDE Congress took place in Dublin in June 1982. The late Mr. Justice Brian Walsh, formerly of the Irish Supreme Court and the European Court of Human Rights, was the President of FIDE on that occasion. Mr. Finbarr Murphy B.L. was the chairman of the host National Association, the Irish Society for European Law, and Mr. Eoghan P. Clear Solicitor was Honorary Secretary. As with the present Congress, it is worth noting that there were delegates from Finland, Spain, and Sweden, then prospective Member States, as well as delegates from the then Member States.

The President of FIDE for the present Congress is the Honourable Mr. Justice Nial Fennelly, a member of the Irish Supreme Court and a former Advocate General at the European Court of Justice.

For the XXI Congress, the Presidency of FIDE has selected, in consultation with FIDE's National Associations, three topics for the Congress. The three topics which will be discussed are: –

Topic 1: "Criminal Law in the European Union: a giant leap or a small step?"
Topic 2: "European Union Competition Law and Policy: The Reform of Competition Law Enforcement will it work?"
Topic 3: "European Union and Member State Migration and Asylum Law and Policy."

The Irish Presidency is delighted that Professor Mario Chiavario of the University of Turin has agreed to act as General Rapporteur for Topic 1; that Judge John Cooke of the European Court of First Instance has agreed to act as General Rapporteur for Topic 2; and that Professor Kay Hailbronner of the University of Konstanz has agreed to act as General Rapporteur for Topic 3.

The working method of the Congress began with the preparation by the General Rapporteurs of detailed Questionnaires on each of the Topics. The Questionnaires are addressed to Rapporteurs in the existing and future Member States of the European Union and other affected States with a view to exploring the transposition and reception of European Law into the domestic legal systems, its effectiveness and the problems the domestic legal systems might have to face in dealing with Community law.

The Questionnaires from the General Rapporteurs were then translated and disseminated among the existing National Associations and the embryonic National Associations in the new Member States and potential future Member States.

The Irish Presidency of FIDE is particularly pleased that Rapporteurs have been designated by each of the existing and new Member States, as well as Rapporteurs from EFTA and EEA States. We are also very pleased that lawyers in Albania and Croatia also nominated Rapporteurs for participation in the FIDE process. As a result, some twenty-nine States have nominated approximately one hundred and six National and Assistant National Rapporteurs. Also, we are delighted to have Institutional Rapporteurs from the Council, the Commission and the Université Libre de Bruxelles.

The National Reports were prepared by the National Rapporteurs or teams of National Rapporteurs and delivered to the General Rapporteurs, their Dublin based National Report Co-Ordinators and to the Institutional Rapporteurs. The General Rapporteurs wrote the General Reports, which offer a synthesis on the development of European Law in their chosen Topic, and an assessment of the dynamic relationship between European Law and the National legal systems. The Institutional Reports offer a thematic response to the Questionnaire from a European Union perspective.

The Congress itself does not take the format of a conference. Apart from the opening address by the President of the Court of Justice there will be no formal set piece presentations. Rather, the General Rapporteurs, in conjunction with various chairpersons of working sessions, will moderate a debate and discussion. Each delegate, having been informed by the publication of this volume and the Reports' earlier appearance on the FIDE website (www.fide2004.org), will be able to participate and discuss different aspects of each Topic. The tradition of FIDE has been participation by all Delegates.

As well as the formal Congress Topics, the Irish Presidency intends to host a debate and discussion on the Constitution for Europe on the morning of Saturday the 5th of June, 2004.

The Presidency of FIDE is again pleased to welcome the Presidents of the European Court of Justice and the Court of First Instance to Dublin for the FIDE Congress. Their participation and that of their colleague Judges from the Courts as well as Référendaires and the permanent staff of the Court, contributes to the unique quality of the Congress.

The FIDE Congress also offers an opportunity for Delegates to meet up with old friends and to make new ones. The accession of the new Member States is a very particular opportunity to make new friends and to re-orientate our conception of Europe.

The Presidency has arranged an extensive and varied social programme with the assistance of the Congress' sponsors, and it is hoped that these social gatherings will facilitate the continuation of the Congress' debates in informal settings and allow for the development of friendships and professional ties.

The Irish Presidency of FIDE is very appreciative of the work and professionalism of Finola O' Sullivan and Jane O'Regan of Cambridge University Press in preparing and printing these volumes. The Irish Presidency would also like to express its appreciation to the three Dublin Co-Ordinators who looked after the considerable task of collating the National Reports and doing verification and pre-publication editing on each of the volumes. This immense and invaluable work was carried out by Mr Anthony Moore B.L. (Criminal Law), Mr Dermot Cahill (University College Dublin) (Competition Law) and Ms Imelda Higgins B.L. (Immigration and Asylum Law).

The Irish Presidency would like to thank its predecessor National Associations, the United Kingdom National Association, the Finnish National Association and the Swedish National Association in particular, for all their help and assistance in organising this Congress.

The venue for the next Congress, the XXII FIDE Congress, will be decided at the Dublin Congress. The Irish National Association hopes that it will relinquish its Presidency with both pride and anticipation; pride at the success of the Congress and anticipation for the future success of the XXII Congress.

GENERAL RAPPORTEUR

Prof. Dr. Kay Hailbronner, LL.M.

Professor Dr. Kay Hailbronner was born in Ulm/Germany in 1943 and has held a professorial chair for public law, international law and European law at the University of Konstanz since 1979. After his education in law at the universities of Tübingen, Freiburg and Heidelberg he received his Master of Laws from McGill University in Montreal pursuant to graduate studies at the Institute of Air and Space Law in Montreal, and, in 1971, his Doctorate in law from the University of Heidelberg. Subsequent to his work as a legal assistant at the Max-Planck-Institute for Comparative Public Law and International Law in Heidelberg, he was appointed senior legal officer at the Ministry of Justice, Rheinland-Pfalz. After two years as assistant to the vice-president of the Federal Constitutional Court, Professor Hailbronner received a call to the University of Konstanz in 1979. From 1988–1992, Professor Hailbronner was Judge at the Administrative Appeal Court of Baden-Württemberg. Since 1990, he has been Legal Counsel for the Federal Government in asylum and immigration law and European law. In 1992, Professor Hailbronner was elected Foreign Member of the Academy of Arts and Sciences, Erfurt/Thüringen. He is Director of the Center for International and European Law on Immigration and Asylum at the University of Konstanz, which was established in 1994. Moreover, Professor Hailbronner was Chairman of the ILA (International Law Association) Committee on Refugee Procedures and has been a member of the German Advisory Council on Science (Wissenschaftsrat) since 1999. From 2000 until 2001, he was a member of the Governmental Commission on Immigration Issues. Since 2000, Professor Hailbronner has been a member of the Advisory Board of the German Federal Office for the Recognition of refugees.

The main emphasis of his scientific activities is on national and international aliens and asylum law, citizenship, university legislation, regulation for awarding contracts as well as on European law.

Among his principal publications, the following should be mentioned; his monograph *Immigration and Asylum Law and Policy of the European Union*; his commentary on aliens law (*Kommentar Ausländerrecht*); and the commentary on citizenship (*Kommentar zum Staatsangehörigkeitsrecht*, together with G. Renner). Moreover, he is co-editor of the leading journal in aliens law in Germany.

VOLUME EDITOR

Imelda Higgins is a practising barrister at the Bar of Ireland. She is also a part-time lecturer in European law at the Faculty of Law, Trinity College Dublin and at the Faculty of Law, University College Dublin. Before coming to the bar, Ms Higgins worked as a Legal Secretary to Judge D.A.O. Edward at the Court of Justice of the European Communities. Prior to working at the Court of Justice, she was engaged as a Lecturer by the European Institute of Public Administration. In this capacity Ms Higgins primarily focused on the training of judges and lawyers from the accession countries in European Community Law, mainly in the context of Community training programmes. Ms Higgins has published numerous articles in the field of European Law and is an editor (Ireland) for the *European Law Reports of cases in the United Kingdom & Ireland.*

EDITOR'S NOTE

Collating the National Reports on the topic of "Migration and Asylum Law & Policy in the European Union" on behalf of the Irish Society for European Law and FIDE was both an honour and a privilege. The Reports contain a wealth of information supplied by eminent practitioners and academics from all over Europe in response to a comprehensive and challenging questionnaire devised by Prof. Hailbronner. Prof. Hailbronner is a renowned expert in the field of EU migration and asylum law and policy, and the questionnaire reflected his expertise in this respect. Fortunately, as can be seen from the high standards of the National Reports, the National Rapporteurs proved themselves both able and willing to meet the challenge set. The result is a fascinating overview of the current state of the law and policy of both Member States and affected countries in this area. The General Rapporteur's Report draws together many of the main developments and perspectives identifiable from the National Reports.

The quality of the National Reports is all the more impressive given the very short time limits within which the National Rapporteurs were required to operate. In this respect, the reader should bear in mind, that the National Reports reflect the position at the time the reports were submitted, namely 26 January 2004. Most of the Reports follow the layout of the General Rapporteur's Questionnaire, although a small number preferred a more thematic approach. In all cases the Reports are very readable and the information contained therein is easily accessible.

I very much look forward to meeting the faces behind the Reports and to a lively discussion on Migration and Asylum Law & Policy in the European Union with my FIDE colleagues.

Imelda Higgins,
Law Library,
Four Courts,
Dublin
8 February 2004

FIDE CONGRESS DUBLIN 2–5 JUNE 2004

Topic 3: Migration and Asylum Law and Policy

QUESTIONNAIRE

Introduction

The aim of the Congress on this topic is to explore EU and Member States' law and policy on migration and asylum. It will consider the policies in the light of international obligations concerning refugees and migrants from third countries. It will explore the scope for improvement, taking account of the labour market requirements of the Member States. In addition, the topic will explore whether the policies of the Member States undermine or maintain EU-policy.

The topic of migration and asylum law and policy embraces a wide range of different subjects, such as: illegal entry; border control; relations with sending countries; integration issues; admission for labour and other purposes; reception of asylum seekers; asylum procedure; exclusive competence to process asylum claims; burden-sharing; re-admission agreements; return policies; etc. National reports should concentrate upon issues which relate to EU-migration and asylum policy as reflected in the directives and proposals for directives. Therefore, national reports may differ in their structures concerning the compatibility or incompatibility of national law with EU law. In some Member States some aspects will raise major problems while in other Member States such problems do not arise. It is quite obvious that the national reports cannot deal with all issues raised in this questionnaire in detail. It is not the intention of the questionnaire to provide the basis for a comprehensive comparative account of Member States' law and policy in migration and asylum issues. National reports may rely on a number of comparative studies which have been made in preparation for the Commission's Proposals on directives, for instance on the reception of asylum seekers, the legal status of third country nationals, the regularization of illegal aliens, Member States' law and policy on expulsion and deportation, the feasibility of single asylum procedures, etc. I suggest that national rapporteurs briefly review the outcome of these studies or refer to more details of these studies – provided they are correct – in answering the questionnaire if they consider it appropriate.

The focus of the general report equally will not consist of a repetition of already existing comparative surveys, but on a critical examination of the state of national law and policies in relation to the EU. Therefore particular emphasis will be laid on the following points:

- Implementation of existing EU legislation in the field of migration and asylum law;
- Compatibility of national migration and asylum law and policies with pending EC directives and regulations, particularly on asylum procedure, legal status of third country nationals and definition of refugees;
- Prospects and conflicts concerning draft directives and communications of the European Commission on the future development of a European migration and asylum law on which no agreement has yet been achieved in council;
- Long term perspective of EU legislation in the field of migration and asylum law and policy.

The Questionnaire is divided into four major subjects:

1 Entry, visa regime and border control
2 Admission and residence of third country nationals
3 Asylum and refugee law
4 Termination of illegal residence, return and repatriation.

PART I (ENTRY, VISA REGIME AND BORDER CONTROL)

In this section each national rapporteur should give a brief account of the national law and policy concerning measures undertaken against illegal entry and stay of third country nationals (return and readmission will be dealt with under 4) relating to the EU-visa regime and the Schengen rules on border control and issuance of Schengen visas. It might also be useful to have a brief factual account of visa issuance and illegal entries, respectively arrests in relation to illegal border crossing.

1.1 What national authorities are competent to deal with visa applications (Schengen visas and long-term visas)? Are there any procedures to avoid duplication or successive visa applications at different EU-consulates? On what substantive criteria, other than the

Schengen minimum requirements, are visas granted or refused? How many visas have been issued or refused?

1.2 Is there a visa tracking procedure in order to identify visa overstayers? What data are collected from visa-applicants (fingerprints)? Admissibility of visa data to alien and police authorities?

1.3 Have courts ever decided on the refusal of a Schengen visa based upon Schengen blacklisting by other Member States?

1.4 What measures have been undertaken in the implementation of the action programme for administrative cooperation in the field of external borders, visa, asylum and immigration following the Council Decision of 13 June 2002?

1.5 What measures have been undertaken to implement the Directive 2001/51 EC supplementing the Schengen rules concerning carrier sanctions? How often have carrier sanctions been used?

1.6 In your judgement, does the visa law and policy of your country live up to EU standards or are adjustments needed? Do you consider that there is need for further EU-harmonization of visa policies concerning:
   - common criteria for granting visas aiming at harmonizing visa obligations among states participating in the Budapest Process;
   - establishment of a European visa identification system (VIS and SIS II)?

To what extent will the EU enlargement process present an opportunity or challenge for tackling issues of illegal entry and border control?

PART II (ADMISSION AND RESIDENCE OF THIRD COUNTRY NATIONALS)

In this section national rapporteurs should identify the basic rules of admission and residence of third country nationals as compared with:

- Proposal for a Directive on conditions of entry and residence of third country nationals for the purpose of paid employment and self-employed activities, COM 2001, 386 final
- Proposal for a Directive on the conditions of entry and residence of third country nationals for the purpose of studies, vocational training or voluntary service, COM 2002, 548 final

- Proposal for a Directive concerning the status of third country nationals who are long-term residents, COM 2001, 127
- Amended Proposal for a Council directive on the right to a family reunion, COM 2002, 227 final, as agreed upon by Council in a modified version on June 5, 2003 (Council Doc 10214/03).

The focus should be upon a description of the differences between the approach taken by the European Commission and the national approaches as reflected in the law and policy of your country.

It will not be necessary to describe in detail the national laws and procedures on admission of third country nationals. It would however be useful to identify major "philosophical" differences concerning the admission of third country nationals. As to the Family Reunion Directive, national rapporteurs may wish to engage in a debate on the constitutional and public international law issues relating to the standards required under the family Reunion Directive as agreed upon by Council in June 2003.

Concerning the status of third country nationals with long-term residence, national rapporteurs should identify problems relating to the definition of long-term residents, the conditions under which such nationals may take residence in your home country and issues relating to the loss of status, renewal or deportation and the possibility of naturalization.

2.1 What are the basic principles in your country concerning:
   - admission of third country nationals for labour purposes or self-employed activities;
   - admission of third country nationals for study and vocational training;
   - legal status of third country nationals in possession of a long-term residence permit of another Member State?

   To what extent do these principles differ from the European Commission's proposals?

2.2 What are the legal requirements and procedures for obtaining a residence permit for third country nationals for the purpose of employment? Which procedures are used in maintaining the preferred access of EU-citizens and Turkish nationals (association agreement) to the labour market? Do special programmes exist for highly qualified professionals facilitating access to the labour market? To what extent are trade unions and employers involved in such programmes? Is there a procedure to calculate the demand for foreign labour? How is the EU-enlargement taken into consideration? To what extent has the recent economic recession and unemployment influenced the concepts on admission of third country nationals?

2.3 To what extent do existing national laws and practices differ substantially from the approach taken in the Commission's Proposal on admission for the purpose of paid employment and self-employed activities relating to:
- admission of third country nationals for study and vocational training;
- on legal status of third country nationals in possession of a long-term residence permit of another Member State?

To what extent do these principles differ from the European Commission's proposals?

2.4 What measures have been taken to implement the Directive of 29th June 2000, implementing the principle of equal treatment between persons irrespective of racial or ethnic origin and Council Directive 2000/78/EC of 27th November 2000, establishing a general framework for equal treatment in employment and occupation? Have legislative changes been undertaken? To what extent is "affirmative action" considered as necessary to promote equal opportunities for migrant workers from third countries?

2.5 Concerning the proposal for a directive on the right to family reunion agreed upon by the Council in February 2003:
- Do you consider the proposed standards below the principles of family reunification applicable in your country?
- Will the implementation of the directive, once it is adopted, lead to changes in the national law on family reunification downgrading the standard of protection? If so, what changes are envisaged?

2.6 The proposal for a directive on the rights of long-term third country nationals as agreed upon by the Council on 5 June 2003, provides for a number of rights approximating the situation of long-term residents to the status of EU-citizens. Will the implementation of the directive involve major legal and policy changes in your country? What are the major points of concern if any, concerning the approximation concept of the directive relating to:
- non-discrimination in social rights;
- the concept of "civic citizenship" (see also extended impact assessment on the Communication on Integration of June 11, 2003);
- family reunification and access of family members to the labour market;
- security of stay?

2.7 Considering the perspective of a future common migration policy as developed by the Commission in the Open Coordination Communication (COM 2001, 387) and the Communication on a Migration policy of the European Union (COM 2000, 757 final), how do you assess the role of the Community organs in determining a European migration policy in terms of competences of the Member States to decide on residence rights and admission to the labour market and integration? Should harmonization of legislation go further, and if so, in what respect?

PART III (ASYLUM AND REFUGEE LAW)

In this section national rapporteurs should describe primarily the impact of EU asylum legislation adopted or pending upon national laws and practices. Three major topics arise from the directives that have been adopted or are about to be adopted:

- reception of asylum seekers
- asylum procedure
- exclusive competence and burden sharing.

Again, one may rely upon the EU-commissioned studies in order to characterize the present legal situation in Member States. The focus should be on an implementation of EU legislative action and the prospects of a further development of a common European asylum procedure including matters like external processing.

3.1 Have the Dublin Rules worked satisfactorily and what is expected of the Dublin II Regulation No. 343, 2003 of 18 February 2003?

3.2 Has the Eurodac Regulation No. 2725/2000 of 11th December 2000, concerning the establishment of Eurodac for the comparison of fingerprints for an effective application of the Dublin Convention, operative since 15 January 2003, resulted in an increase of Dublin cases? Has Eurodac become effective in your country or is it expected to become effective eventually?

3.3 What major changes, if any, will the implementation of the amended proposal for a directive on minimum standards on procedures in Member States for granting and withdrawing refugee status, on which the Council has reached political agreement on most points in June 2003, bring for the legislation and practice in your country in particular relating to:

- rights of applicants in the procedure;
- administrative and judicial appeal procedures;
- the use of safe third country and safe country of origin concepts;
- detainment of asylum seekers;
- airport and border procedures?

3.4 What measures have been undertaken to implement Directive 2003/9 of 27 January 2003, on reception of asylum seekers in your country relating to
- the flexibility clauses in the Directive;
- restriction of free movement;
- access to the labour market;
- rights of migrant workers under Article 11 § 2 of the Directive?

3.5 What steps have been undertaken to implement the Directive on temporary protection, COM 2001, 55 in national law? Are there any procedures for burden sharing arrangements? Is there a legal basis for the admission of refugees for the purposes of receiving temporary protection in a mass-movement situation?

3.6 The Council has reached political agreement on the principles for a Directive on minimum standards for the qualification and status of third country nationals as refugees or persons who otherwise need international protection, COM 2001, 510 final (see Council documents of June 2003). What measures are envisaged to implement the Directive, once it is adopted, in your country relating to:
- the definition of refugee;
- the definition of persons entitled to subsidiary protection;
- status of persons entitled to subsidiary protection;
- the issue of internal flight alternative as defined by the Directive;
- exclusion clauses, particularly issues of terrorism?

To what extent are the refugee policies as reflected in the law and jurisprudence of your country in accordance with the proposal for the directive?

3.7 In the Commission's Communication of 22 November, 2000, COM 2000, 755 (see also 2nd Commission Report COM 2003, 152 final) the Commission's concept of a common European asylum procedure and a uniform status for those who are granted asylum valid throughout the Union is set out. Do you consider that the concept is generally in line with your country's asylum policy? Are the concerns of refugee organizations, such as Amnesty International and other organizations, of an undermining of the international regime for the protection of refugees shared in the political circles responsible for decision-making of your country?

3.8 The open coordination-mechanism, as suggested by the Commission, provided for first stage and second stage legislation in which the flexibility provisions in some of the directives on migration and asylum are to be replaced by full harmonization. Is this concept discussed in your country and what are the perceptions relating to the gradual establishment of a European asylum policy which might eventually replace national procedures and national decision-making?

3.9 The Communication of June 2003, towards a more accessible, equitable and managed asylum system – in reaction to the UK paper – develops some ideas on new approaches to pursue an orderly and managed arrival of persons in need of international protection. What is the political reaction in your country to the concept of an outside accessed asylum procedure, distribution of refugees and responsibility-sharing and other new concepts and ideas in coping with mass refugee movements?

PART IV (TERMINATION OF ILLEGAL RESIDENCE, RETURN AND REPATRIATION)

In this section national rapporteurs should provide information on national measures concerning sanctions against illegal entry, other measures against illegal trafficking, problems related to the termination of residence of third country nationals, not disposing of a valid residence permit, cooperation with other EU Member States in return and expulsion issues (common return programmes; enforcement of expulsion decisions and efforts to cooperate with sending countries in curbing illegal immigration (efficiency of bilateral re-admission agreements, typical problems of enforcement). It may also be useful to give a brief description of the crucial issues of enforcement and the actual situation (number of deportations, typical reasons of failure; lack of documentation, residence, etc.) It may not be necessary to give a detailed description of the existing laws on expulsion and deportation. However, remarks on the major gaps and deficits for an efficient return policy may be useful as well as ideas and suggestions on further harmonization needed in enforcement procedures and human rights implications of return procedures.

4.1 How many third country nationals without a valid residence permit are currently, according to estimates, staying in your country? How many deportations have actually been made in previous years? Is the whole enforcement process considered as acceptable?

4.2 What has been undertaken to implement the Directive of 28 November 2002, dealing with the facilitation of unauthorized entry, transit and residence?

4.3 How many illegal applicants have been apprehended at or near the border? How many criminal procedures for human trafficking have been instituted in the last year?

4.4 What efforts have been undertaken in your country regarding the Budapest June 2003 recommendations concerning the harmonization of penalty scales with regard to the crime of the smuggling of migrants and trafficking of persons, in line with Council Directive 2002/90 of 28th November 2002? Did your country sign the relevant UN protocols on the smuggling of migrants?

4.5 What measures have been taken to implement the Council Directive of 28 May 2001, on the mutual recognition of decisions on the expulsion of third country nationals? What, if any shortcomings or gaps of the Directive should be corrected in a further directive on cooperation on expulsion or deportation of third country nationals?

4.6 Do readmission agreements or other international treaties or arrangements with the aim of controlling and curbing illegal immigration and facilitating return exist in your country? Have they functioned satisfactorily?

4.7 To what extent have EU-standards and recommendations influenced your country's return policy? Have efforts been undertaken to cooperate with other EU Member States in enforcing return decisions by common deportation actions, exchange of information, facilitation of air and land transit, common principles on flight security, etc.?

4.8 Do you consider that there is a need to elaborate a common legal regime for air deportations (legal status of armed guards on board of the aircrafts, rights of the aircraft commander, legal rules in case of transit stops, applicability of national police law on board of aircraft on flight, etc.)?

FIDE KONGRESS DUBLIN 2.–5. JUNI 2004

Thema 3: Auswanderungs- und Asylrecht und -politik

FRAGEBOGEN

Einleitung

Das Ziel des Kongresses für dieses Thema ist es, das Recht und die Politiken der Gemeinschaft und der Mitgliedstaaten zu erforschen. Die Politiken werden im Licht der internationalen Verpflichtungen in Bezug auf Flüchtlinge und Migranten aus Drittländern betrachtet. Die Verbesserungsmöglichkeiten werden erforscht werden, wobei die Arbeitsmarktbedingungen von Mitgliedstaaten in Betracht gezogen werden. Zusätzlich wird dieses Thema erforschen, ob die Politiken der Mitgliedstaaten die Politik der Gemeinschaft untergraben oder unterstützen.

Das Thema des Migrations- und Asylrechts und -politik umschließt eine Bandbreite von verschiedenen Dingen, z.B. illegale Einreise, Grenzenkontrolle, Beziehungen mit Versandländern, Integrationsfragen, Zugang zur Arbeit und anderen Zwecken, Aufnahme von Asylbewerbern, Asylrichtlinien, die ausschließliche Befugnis Asylanträge zu bearbeiten, das Teilen von Belastungen, Wiederaufnahmeverträge, Rücksenderichtlinien, etc. Nationale Berichte sollten sich auf die Dinge konzentrieren, welche in Bezug zu der Migrations- und Asylpolitik der Gemeinschaft, die in den Richtlinien und Vorschlägen von Richtlinien wiedergespiegelt ist, stehen. Nationale Berichte können sich daher in deren Struktur unterscheiden im Anblick der Vereinbarkeit oder Unvereinbarkeit mit dem Recht der Gemeinschaft. In manchen Mitgliedstaaten werden manche Aspekte große Probleme bereiten, während solche Probleme in anderen Mitgliedstaaten nicht entstehen.

Es ist offensichtlich, dass die nationalen Berichte sich nicht mit allen Dingen, die in diesem Fragebogen genannt werden, im Detail befassen können. Es ist nicht die Absicht dieses Fragebogens, eine Basis für einen vollständigen vergleichenden Bericht des Migrations- und Asylrechts- und der -politik in den Mitgliedstaaten darzustellen. Nationale Berichte können sich auf eine Anzahl von vergleichenden Studien stützen, welche in der Verfassung von Kommissionsvorschlägen für Richtlinien hergestellt worden sind, z.B. in Bezug auf die Aufnahme von Asylsuchenden, den rechtlichen Status von Drittstaatsangehörigen, die Regularisierung von illegalen Einwanderern, das Recht und die Politik der Mitgliedstaaten bezüglich Ausweisung und Deportation, die Durchführbarkeit von einzelnen Asylrichtlinien, usw. Ich schlage vor, dass nationale Berichterstatter das Ergebnis dieser Studien in Kürze untersuchen oder auf die Details dieser Studien verweisen – vorausgesetzt sie sind korre Der Fokus des Hauptberichtes wird gleichermaßen nicht eine Wiederholung der schon bestehenden vergleichenden Umfragen darstellen, sondern eine kritische Überprüfung des Status des nationalen Rechts und der Politiken in Bezug auf die Gemeinschaft. Daher wird auf die folgenden Punkte besonderen Wert gelegt:

1 Durchführung von bestehendem EU Recht im Bereich des Migrations- und Asylrechts
2 Vereinbarkeit von nationalen Migrations- und Asylrechten und -politik mit schwebenden EU Verordnungen und Richtlinien, insbesondere Asylrichtlinien, der rechtliche Status von Drittstaatsangehörigen und der Definition von Flüchtlingen.
3 Aussichten und Konflikte in Bezug auf Vorschläge von Richtlinien und Mitteilungen der EU Kommission über die zukünftige Entwicklung eines europäischen Migrations- und Asylrechts über das noch keine Vereinbarung in dem Ministerrat getroffen worden ist.
4 Langzeitperspektive des EU Rechtes in Bezug auf das Migrations- und Asylrechts und -politik.

Der Fragebogen ist in vier Hauptthemen aufgeteilt:

1 Einreise, Visaregime und Grenzkontrolle
2 Aufnahme und Aufenthalt von Drittstaatsangehörigen
3 Asyl- und Flüchtlingsrecht
4 Beendigung von illegalem Aufenthalt, Rücksendung und Rückführung

TEIL I (EINREISE, VISAREGIME UND GRENZKONTROLLE)

In diesem Teil sollte jeder nationale Berichterstatter einen kurzen Bericht über das nationale Recht und die Politik betreffend der Maßnahmen erstellen, die gegen die illegale Einreise und den Aufenthalt von Drittstaatsangehörigen in Bezug auf das Visaregime der Gemeinschaft und die Schengenregeln über Grenzkontrolle und die Austellung von Schengenvisas, unternommen wurden (Rücksendung und Wiederaufnahme werden in dem 4.Teil behandelt). Es wäre auch nützlich, einen kurzen faktischen Bericht über die Austellung von Visas, illegale Einreisen und Verhaftungen für illegale Grenzübertritte zu bekommen.

1.1 Welche nationalen Behörden sind dafür zuständig, Visaanmeldungen zu bearbeiten (Schengenvisas und Langzeitvisas)? Gibt es Verfahren, um die Duplikation von Visaanmeldungen oder aufeinanderfolgende Visaanmeldungen bei verschiedenen EU Konsulaten zu vermeiden? Welche materiellen Kriterien sind ausschlagebend für die Vergabe oder Nichtvergabe von Visas, mit Ausnahme der minimalen Schengenerforderungen? Wie viele Visas sind ausgestellt oder abgeschlagen worden?
1.2 Gibt es ein Visatrackingverfahren, um herauszufinden, wer länger bleibt, als das Visa erlaubt? Welche Daten werden von Visabewerbern ersucht (Fingerabdrücke)? Dürfen die Visadaten an dritte und Polizeibehörden weitergegeben werden?
1.3 Haben die Gerichte jemals ein Schengenvisa abgelehnt aus dem Grund, dass derjenige in anderen Mitgliedstaaten auf der schwarzen Liste steht?
1.4 Welche Maßnahmen sind unternommen worden in der Ausführung des Aktionsprogrammes für administrative Kooperation im Bereich der Außengrenzen, Visa, Asyl und Einwanderung im Anschluß an die Ratsentscheidung vom 13. Juni 2002?
1.5 Welche Maßnahmen sind unternommen worden, um Richtlinie 2001/51 EC auszuführen, zusätzlich zu den Schengenregeln für Sanktionen für Beförderer? Wie often sind Sanktionen für Beförderer benutzt worden?
1.6 Ist das Visarecht und die -politik ihres Landes ihrer Meinung nach im Einvernehmen mit dem EU Standard oder sind Veränderungen benötigt? Glauben Sie, dass eine weitere unionsweite Harmonisierung von Visarichtlinien für folgende Punkte benötigt wird:
   a) Gemeinsame Kriterien für die Ausgabe von Visas mit dem Ziel, die Visapflichten der Teilnehmer des Budapester Prozesses zu harmonisieren
   b) Gründung eines europäischen Visaidentifizierungssystems (VIS and SIS II)

In welchem Maße wird die Erweiterung der Gemeinschaft eine Chance oder eine Gefahr darstellen, um Probleme mit illegalen Einreisen und Grenzkontrollen anzugehen?

TEIL II (AUFNAHME UND AUFENTHALT VON DRITTSTAATSANGEHÖRIGEN)

In diesem Teil sollten die nationalen Berichterstatter die Grundregeln der Aufnahme und des Aufenthaltes von Drittstaatsangehörigen identifizieren im Vergleich mit:

1 Vorschlag für eine Richtlinie über die Bedingungen für die Einreise und den Aufenthalt von Drittstaatsangehörigen zur Ausübung einer unselbstständigen oder selbständigen Erwerbstätigkeit, KOM 2001, 386 endg.
2 Vorschlag für eine Richtlinie über die Bedingungen für die Einreise und den Aufenthalt von Drittstaatsangehörigen zur Aufnahme eines Studiums, einer Berufsbildung oder eines Freiwilligendienstes, KOM 2002, 548 endg.
3 Vorschlag für eine Richtlinie betreffend den Status der langfristig aufenthaltsberechtigten Drittstaatsangehörigen, KOM 2001, 127 endg.
4 Geänderter Vorschlag für eine Richtlinie des Rates betreffend das Recht auf Familienzusammenführung, KOM 2002, 227 endg., wie er von dem Rat in einer geänderten Version am 5. Juni 2003 angenommen wurde, Dokument des Rates 10214/03

Der Fokus sollte eine Erklärung der Unterschiede zwischen der Methode der EU Kommission und den nationalen Methoden, wie sie in dem Recht und der Politik ihres Landes wiedergespiegelt ist, sein.

Es ist nicht nötig, im Detail die nationalen Rechte und Verfahren für die Aufnahme von Drittstaatsangehörigen zu erklären. Es wäre jedoch hilfreich, die wichtigsten 'philosophischen' Unterschiede bezüglich der Aufnahme von Drittstaatsangehörigen zu identifizieren. Nationale Berichterstatter möchten vielleicht an einer Debatte über die Grundgesetzprobleme und Probleme des internationalen öffentlichen Rechts in Bezug auf die Normen, die in der Richtlinie betreffend das Recht auf Familienzusammenführung, welche von dem Ministerrat im Juni 2003 angenommen worden ist, gefordert werden, teilnehmen.

In Bezug auf den Status von langfristig aufenthaltsberechtigten Drittstaatsangehörigen sollten nationale Berichterstatter die

Definitionsprobleme von langfristig aufenthaltsberechtigten, die Bedingungen unter welchen solche Angehörigen sich in Ihrem Land aufhalten dürfen und Probleme über den Verlust von Status, Erneuerung oder Ausweisung und die Möglichkeit der Naturalisierung identifizieren.

2.1 Was sind die Grundprinzipien in Ihrem Land betreffend:
  1 Aufnahme von Drittstaatsangehörigen für unselbstständige oder selbstständige Erwerbstätigkeit
  2 Einlass von Drittstaatsangehörigen zum Studium und zu einer Berufsausbildung
  3 Der rechtliche Status von Drittstaatsangehörigen, die in einem anderen Mitgliedsstaat langfristig aufenthaltsberechtigt sind
  4 In welchem Ausmaß unterscheiden sich diese Prinzipien von den Vorschlägen der Europäischen Kommission?

2.2 Was sind die rechtlichen Vorraussetzungen und Verfahren für Drittstaatsangehörige, um eine Aufenthaltserlaubnis für eine Erwerbstätigkeit zu bekommen? Welche Verfahren werden benutzt, um den bevorzugten Zugang von EU Einwohnern und Türken (Beitrittsvereinbarung) zum Arbeitsmarkt zu erhalten? Bestehen spezielle Programme, um den Zugang von hochqualifizierten Facharbeitern zum Arbeitsmarkt zu erleichtern? In welchem Maße sind Gewerkschaften und Arbeitgeber in solchen Programmen involviert? Gibt es ein Verfahren, um die Nachfrage für ausländische Arbeiter zu kalkulieren? Wie wird die Erweiterung der Gemeinschaft in Betracht gezogen? In welchem Maße hat die kürzliche wirtschaftliche Rezession und Arbeitslosigkeit die Konzepte über die Aufnahme von Drittstaatsangehörigen beeinflusst?

2.3 In welchem Ausmaß unterscheiden sich bestehende Rechte und Praktiken wesentlich von der Methode, die von der Kommission gewählt wurde in ihrem Vorschlag über die Aufnahme zum Zweck von unselbständiger oder selbstständiger Erwerbstätigkeit betreffend:
  1 Aufnahme von Drittstaatsangehörigen zum Studium und zu einer Berufsausbildung
  2 Der rechtliche Status von Drittstaatsangehörigen, die in einem anderen Mitgliedstaat langfristig aufenthaltsberechtigt sind
  3 In welchem Ausmaß unterscheiden sich diese Prinzipien von den Vorschlägen der Europäischen Kommission?

2.4 Welche Maßnahmen sind getroffen worden, um die Richtlinie vom 29. Juni 2000 zur Anwendung des Gleichbehandlungsgrundsatzes ohne Unterschied der Rasse oder der ethnischen Herkunft und die Richtlinie 2000/78 EC des Rates vom 27. November 2000 zur Festlegung eines allgemeinen Rahmens für die Verwirklichung der Gleichbehandlung in Beschäftigung und Beruf umzusetzen? Sind Veränderungen des Rechts unternommen worden? In welchem Maß werden positive Aktionen ('affirmative action') als notwendig angesehen, um die Gleichbehandlung staatenlose Arbeiter aus Drittländern zu fördern?

2.5 In Bezug auf den Entwurf für eine Richtlinie betreffend das Recht zur Familienzusammenführung, welches von dem Rat im Februar 2003 genehmigt wurde:
   1 Glauben Sie, dass die vorgeschlagenen Normen der Familienzusammenführung niedriger sind als die, die in Ihrem Land gültig sind?
   2 Wird die Umsetzung der Richtlinie, wenn sie angenommen worden ist, zu Veränderungen in Ihrem nationalen Recht zur Familienzusammenführung führen, die den Standard des Schutzes zurückstufen? Falls dies der Fall ist, welche Veränderungen sind vorgesehen?

2.6 Der Vorschlag für eine Richtlinie über die Rechte von Langzeitstaatsangehörigen von Drittländern, der vom Rat am 5. Juni 2003 genehmigt wurde, beinhaltet eine Anzahl von Rechten, die die Standarde für Langzeiteinwohner auf den Status von EU Bürger angleichen. Wird die Umsetzung dieser Richtlinie wichtige rechtliche und politische Veränderungen in Ihrem Land beinhalten? Was sind die wichtigsten Belange, falls es welche gibt, betreffend des Annäherungskonzepts der Richtlinie in Bezug auf:
   1 Keine Diskriminierung von sozialen Rechten
   2 Das Konzept der zivilen Staatsbürgerschaft ('civic citizenship') (siehe auch die erweiterte Auswirkungsbeurteilung der Mitteilung über die Integration vom 11. Juni 2003)
   3 Familienzusammenführung und Zugang von Familienmitgliedern zum Arbeitsmarkt
   4 Aufenthaltssicherheit

2.7 Im Angesicht der Perspektive einer gemeinsamen Migrationspolitik, wie sie von der Kommission in der Mitteilung über den offenen Koordinierungsmechanismus (KOM 2001, 387) und die Mitteilung über eine Migrationspolitik der Gemeinschaft (KOM 2000, 757 endg.) entwickelt worden ist, welche Rolle werden Ihrer Meinung nach die EU Organe haben bezüglich der Befugnisse, welche die Mitgliedstaaten haben werden, um Aufenthaltsrechte, den Zugang zum

Arbeitsmarkt und Integration zu entscheiden? Sollte Harmonisierung des Rechtes weitergehen und, falls dies der Fall ist, in welcher Hinsicht?

TEIL III (ASYL- UND FLÜCHTLINGSRECHT)

In diesem Teil sollten nationale Berichterstatter hauptsächlich die Auswirkung des EU Asylrechts, welches angenommen worden ist oder welches noch nationale Rechte und Praktiken erwartet, beschreiben. Drei wichtige Themen ergeben sich von den Richtlinien, die angenommen worden sind oder die in Kürze angenommen werden:

1 Aufnahme von Asylsuchenden
2 Asylverfahren
3 Ausschließliche Kompetenz und Teilen von Lasten

Man kann sich hier noch einmal auf die Studien, die von der Gemeinschaft kommissioniert worden sind, stützen, um die jetzige rechtliche Situation in den Mitgliedstaaten zu charakterisieren. Der Fokus sollte die Annahme von EU Rechtsakten und die Aussicht auf eine weitere Entwicklung eines gemeinsamen europäischen Asylverfahrens sein, inklusive Sachen wie äußerliche Verfahren (external processing).

3.1 Sind die Dubliner Regeln zufriedenstellend und was wird von der Dublin II Verordnung Nr. 343, 2003 vom 18. February, 2003 erwartet?
3.2 Hat die Eurodac Verordnung Nr. 2725/2000 vom 11. Dezember 2000 über die Einrichtung von 'Eurodac' für den Vergleich von Fingerabdrücken zum Zwecke der effektiven Anwendung des Dubliner Übereinkommens, die seit dem 15. Januar 2003 in Kraft ist, zu einem Anstieg von Dubliner Fällen geführt? Ist Eurodac in Ihrem Land effektiv oder wird es erwartet, dass es letztendlich effektiv wird?
3.3 Welche wichtigen Veränderungen, falls es welche gibt, wird die Annahme von dem geändertem Vorschlag der Richtlinie über Mindestnormen für Verfahren in Mitgliedstaaten für die Anerkennung oder die Wegnahme vom Flüchtlingsstatus, über die der Rat in den meisten Punkten im Juni 2003 politisches Einvernehmen erreicht hat, für das Recht und die Praxis in Ihrem Land bringen, insbesondere in Bezug auf die folgenden Punkte:
   1 Rechte von Bewerbern in dem Verfahren
   2 Administratives and richterliches Revisionsverfahren
   3 Die Benutzung von Konzepten von sicheren Drittländern und sicheren Ursprungsländern

4 Inhaftierung von Asylbewerbern
5 Verfahren an Flughafen und Grenzen?

3.4 Welche Maßnahmen sind unternommen worden, um die Richtlinie 2003/9 vom 27. Januar, 2003 über die Aufnahme von Asylsuchenden in Ihrem Land umzusetzen?
1 In Bezug auf die Flexibilitätsparagraphen in der Richtlinie
2 Behinderung des freien Verkehrs
3 Zugang zum Arbeitsmarkt
4 Die Rechte von Migranten laut Artikel 11 § 2 der Richtlinie

3.5 Welche Schritte sind unternommen worden, um die Richtlinie über vorübergehenden Schutz, KOM 2001, 55 in nationales Recht umzusetzen? Gibt es Verfahren für Vereinbarungen, die die Teilung von Lasten vorsehen? Gibt es eine rechtliche Basis für die Aufnahme von Flüchtlingen für einen vorübergehenden Schutz im Falle eines Massenzustroms?

3.6 Der Rat hat eine politische Vereinbarung getroffen über die Grundsätze für eine Richtlinie über Mindestnormen für die Anerkennung und den Status von Drittstaatsangehörigen und Staatenlosen als Flüchtlinge oder als Personen, die anderweitig internationalen Schutz benötigen, KOM 2001, 510 endg. (siehe Ratsdokument vom Juni 2003). Welche Maßnahmen sind vorgesehen, um die Richtlinie in Ihrem Land umzusetzen wenn sie in Kraft tritt, bezüglich:
1 Die Definition von Flüchtlingen
2 Die Definition von Personen die einen Anspruch auf subsidiaren Schutz haben
3 Der Status von Personen die einen Anspruch auf subsidiaren Schutz haben
4 Das Problem von Alternativen zu Inlandsflügen, wie es in der Richtlinie definiert ist
5 Auschlußparagraphen, inbesondere ein Problem mit Terrorismus?
In welchem Ausmaß ist die Flüchtlingspolitik, die in dem Recht und der Rechtssprechung Ihres Landes wiedergespiegelt ist, im Einvernehmen mit dem Vorschlag der Richtlinie?

3.7 In der Mitteilung der Kommission vom 22. November, 2000, KOM 2000, 755 (siehe auch der 2. Kommissionsbericht KOM 2003, 152 endg.) ist das Konzept der Kommission für ein gemeinsames europäisches Asylverfahren und einen unionsweit geltenden Status für die Personen, denen Asyl gewährt wird, enthalten. Glauben Sie, dass das Konzept generell mit der Asylpolitik Ihres Landes übereinstimmt? Teilen politische Kreise in Ihrem Land, die

Entscheidungen treffen, die Bedenken von Flüchtlingsorganisationen wie z.B. Amnesty International und anderen Organisationen, dass das internationale Regime für den Schutz von Flüchtlingen untergraben wird?

3.8 Der von der Kommission vorgeschlagene Koordinationsmechanismus sieht eine erste und zweite Rechtsstufe vor, in der die Flexibilitätsvorkehrungen in manchen Richtlinien über die Migration und das Asyl mit voller Harmonisierung ersetzt werden. Ist dieses Konzept in Ihrem Land diskutiert worden und was sind die Auffassungen über die schrittweise Erstehung von einer europäischen Asylpolitik, die letztendlich nationale Verfahren und nationale Entscheidungen ersetzen könnte?

3.9 Die Mitteilung vom Juni, 2003 für ein zugänglicheres, gleichberechtigteres und besser organisiertes Asylsystem – als Reaktion zu dem UK Bericht – entwickelt manche Ideen über neue Versuche, eine geordnete und organisierte Ankunft von Personen, die internationalen Schutz benötigen, zu verfolgen. Was ist die politische Reaktion in Ihrem Land zu dem Konzept eines Asylverfahrens, dass von außen zugegriffen werden kann, die Verteilung von Flüchtlingen und das Teilen von Verantwortungen und anderen neuen Konzepten und Ideen, die helfen sollen, mit Massenflüchtlingsbewegungen fertig zu werden?

TEIL IV (BEENDIGUNG EINES ILLEGALEN AUFENTHALTS, RÜCKSENDUNG UND RÜCKFÜHRUNG)

In diesem Teil sollten nationale Berichterstatter Informationen über nationale Maßnahmen in Bezug auf Sanktionen für illegalen Eintritt, andere Maßnahmen für illegales Handeln, Probleme in Bezug auf die Beendigung von Aufenthalten Drittstaatsangehöriger, das Versagen, eine gültige Aufenthaltserlaubnis zu verfügen, die Kooperation mit anderen EU Mitgliedstaaten in Problemen der Rücksendung und Ausweisung (gemeinsame Rücksendeprogramme; Durchsetzen von Ausweisungentscheidungen und Versuche mit Sendeländern illegale Einreisen zu verhindern (Effektivität von bilateralen Wiederaufnahmevereinbarungen, typische Probleme der Durchsetzung). Es könnte auch hilfreich sein, einen kurzen Überblick über die wichtigsten Probleme der Durchsetzung und die aktuelle Situation (Anzahl der Deportationen, typische

Gründe für ein Versagen, das Fehlen von Dokumenten, Aufenthalt, usw.) zu geben. Es ist nicht notwendig, eine detaillierte Beschreibung der bestehenden Rechte über

1.1 Wie viele Drittstaatsangehörige ohne eine gültige Aufenthaltserlaubnis sind momentan nach Schätzungen in Ihrem Land? Wie viele Deportationen sind in den letzten Jahren tatsächlich vorgenommen worden? Wird das gesamte Durchsetzungsverfahren als akzeptabel angesehen?
1.2 Was ist unternommen worden, um die Richtlinie vom 28. November, 2002, die sich mit der Erleichterung von unerlaubter Einreise, Transit und Aufenthalt befasst, umzusetzen?
1.3 Wie viele illegale Bewerber sind an, oder in der Nähe, der Grenze festgenommen worden? Wie viele strafrechtliche Verfahren für das Handeln von Personen sind im letzten Jahr eingeleitet worden?
1.4 Welche Bemühungen sind in Ihrem Land betreffend der Empfehlungen von Budapest im Juni 2003 in Bezug auf die Harmonisierung von Sanktionen für das Schmuggeln von Migranten und das Handeln von Personen im Einklang mit der Richtlinie des Rates 2002/90 vom 28. November 2002 unternommen worden? Hat Ihr Land das UN Protokoll über das Schmuggeln von Migranten unterschrieben?
1.5 Welche Maßnahmen sind unternommen worden, um die Richtlinie des Rates vom 28. Mai 2001 über die gegenseitige Anerkennung von Entscheidungen zur Ausweisung von Drittstaatsangehörigen umzusetzen? Welche Mangel oder Lücken der Richtlinie sollten verbessert werden in einer weiteren Richtlinie über die Kooperation in der Ausweisung und Deportation von Drittstaatsangehörigen?
1.6 Gibt es Wiederaufnahmevereinbarungen oder andere internationale Verträge oder Vereinbarungen mit dem Ziel der Kontrolle und dem Verhindern von illegaler Einwanderung und der Erleichterung von Rücksendungen in Ihrem Land? Sind diese zufriedenstellend?
1.7 In welchem Ausmaß haben EU-Normen und Empfehlungen die Rücksendepolitik Ihres Landes beinflusst? Welche Versuche sind unternommen worden, mit anderen EU Mitgliedstaaten zu kooperieren in der Durchsetzung von Rücksendeentscheidungen gemeinsamer Deportationsaktionen, dem Austausch von Informationen, der Erleichterung von Luft und Landtransit, gemeinsamen Prinzipien der Flugsicherheit, usw.?

1.8 Ist es Ihrer Meinung nach notwendig, ein gemeinsames Rechtssystem für Luftdeportationen zu entwickeln (rechtlicher Status von bewaffneten Sicherheitsleuten in einem Flugzeug, Rechte des Flugkapitäns, rechtliche Regeln für Transitstops, Anwendbarkeit von nationalem Polizeirecht in einem fliegenden Flugzeug, usw.)?

FIDE CONGRÈS DUBLIN 2–5 JUIN 2004

Sujet 3: Immigration et droit d'asile

QUESTIONNAIRE

Introduction

L'objet de ce Congrès porte sur l'étude du droit et des politiques de l'Union européenne et des Etats membres en matière d'immigration et d'asile. Il s'agira d'examiner ces politiques à la lumière des obligations internationales relatives aux réfugiés et immigrants des Etats tiers, ainsi que les possibilités d'amélioration de ces politiques en prenant en compte les exigences du marché du travail des Etats membres. En plus, il s'agira de savoir si les politiques des Etats membres contribuent ou portent atteinte à la politique de l'Union européenne en ce domaine.

Le sujet du droit et des politiques des Etats membres en matière d'immigration et d'asile, comprend de nombreux aspects tels que ceux de l'immigration clandestine, le contrôle aux frontières, les rapports avec les Etats de provenance, la questions d'intégration, la question d'admission sur le marché du travail dans les Etats d'accueil, les procédures d'admission et de traitement des demandeurs d'asile, ainsi que la question de compétence exclusive pour processer les demandes d'asile, la répartition des efforts consentis par les Etats dans ces types de procédures, les accords de réadmission, les politiques favorisant le retour des immigrants, etc.

Les rapports nationaux devront se concentrer sur les questions relatives à l'immigration et au droit d'asile au sein de l'Union européenne telles qu'elles apparaissent dans les directives communautaires et les propositions de directives. Par conséquent, la structure des différents rapports nationaux pourra être différente et varier en fonction de la compatibilité ou non de chacun des droits nationaux avec le droit de l'Union européenne. Dans certains Etats membres, certains aspects, ci-dessus mentionnés, poseront problème, alors que dans d'autres ils ne soulèveront pas de difficulté particulière.

Il est évident que les rapports nationaux ne pourront pas traiter en détail de toutes les questions soulevées dans ce questionnaire. D'ailleurs, ce n'est pas l'objet de celui-ci d'amener à une analyse exhaustive et comparative des législations et politiques des Etats membres en matière d'immigration et d'asile. Les rapports pourront s'appuyer sur les différentes études comparées qui ont été réalisées dans le cadre de la préparation des propositions de directives de la Commission concernant par exemple l'accueil des demandeurs d'asile, le statut juridique des nationaux d'Etats tiers, la régularisation des immigrés clandestins, la législation des Etats membres relative aux mesures d'éloignement, la faisabilité d'une procédure d'asile unique etc. Je suggère que les rapporteurs nationaux s'y réfèrent brièvement au résultat de ces études ou s'y réfèrent de façon plus approfondie dans leurs réponses aux questions ci-après soulevées s'ils le jugent opportun et dans la mesure de la pertinence de l'analyse fournie.

De même, l'objet du rapport général ne consistera pas en une répétition de l'étude du contenu des rapports comparés existants, mais portera sur une analyse critique de l'état du droit et des politiques nationaux en relation avec le droit et les politiques de l'Union européenne. Par conséquent, il est demandé d'insister sur les points particuliers suivants:

- mise en œuvre de la législation existante de l'Union européenne dans le domaine de l'immigration et du droit d'asile;
- compatibilité du droit et des politiques nationaux en la matière avec les futures directives et règlements communautaires, portant notamment sur la procédure d'asile, le statut juridique des ressortissants de pays tiers et la définition de la notion de réfugiés;
- les perspectives et les conflits qu'impliquent ces propositions de directives ainsi que les communications de la Commission européenne sur l'évolution future du droit européen en ce domaine sur lequel aucun accord réel n'a vu le jour au sein du Conseil de l'Union européenne;
- enfin, les perspectives à long terme de la législation de l'Union européenne en ce domaine.

Le questionnaire est divisé en quatre parties principales qui sont les suivantes:

I L'entrée sur le territoire, le régime des visas et le contrôle aux frontières;
II L'accueil et le droit de séjour des ressortissants des pays tiers;
III La législation relative aux demandeurs d'asile et aux réfugiés;

IV Les procédures visant à mettre fin à une résidence illégale, les procédures de retour et rapatriement.

PARTIE I ENTRÉE SUR LE TERRITOIRE, RÉGIME DES VISAS ET CONTRÔLE AUX FRONTIÈRES

Dans cette section, chaque rapporteur exposera brièvement son droit national et la politique concernant les mesures prises en matière d'entrée illégale et séjour des ressortissants de pays tiers sur le territoire national (les questions du retour et de la réadmission seront traitées dans la quatrième partie). Concernant la réglementation de l'Union européenne relative aux visas ainsi que les règles applicables dans l'espace Schengen en matière de contrôle aux frontières et d'octroi des visas, il serait aussi utile d'avoir un bref exposé sur la délivrance des visas et l'entrée illégale ou détention en cas de franchissement illégal des frontières.

1.1 Quelle sont les autorités nationales compétentes en matière de demandes de visas (dans le cadre de l'espace Schengen et pour les visas de longue durée)? Existe-t-il des procédures permettant d'éviter une duplication des demandes de visas ou d'éviter le dépôt de demandes successives dans les différents consulats dans l'Union européenne? En fonction de quels critères substantiels, autres que les exigences minimum requises dans le cadre de l'espace Schengen, les visas sont-ils accordés ou refusés? Combien de demandes de visas ont été satisfaites, combien ont été rejetées?
1.2 Existe-t-il une procédure permettant de tracer les personnes dont le visa a expiré? Quel genre de données sont recueillies lors du dépôt d'une demande de visas (empreintes digitales, par exemple)? Les données recueillies peuvent-elles être communiquées aux autorités policières ou étrangères?
1.3 Les juridictions se sont-elles déjà prononcées sur un refus de demande de visa dans le cadre de Schengen au motif qu'elle provenait d'un ressortissant d'un pays figurant sur la "liste noire" des Etats membres?
1.4 Quelles ont été les mesures prises afin de mettre en œuvre le programme d'action en matière de coopération administrative dans le domaine du contrôle aux frontières extérieures, des questions de visas, d'immigration et de demandes d'asile en application de la décision du Conseil du 13 juin 2002?
1.5 Quelles démarches ont été entreprises afin de transposer la directive communautaire 2001/51/CE du Conseil du 28 juin 2001 visant à

compléter les dispositions de la Convention d'application de l'accord de Schengen relativement aux sanctions imposées aux transporteurs? Ces sanctions ont-elles souvent été appliquées?

1.6 Selon vous, le droit et les politiques relatifs aux visas en vigueur dans votre pays respectent-ils les exigences de l'Union européenne en la matière ou des ajustements sont-ils nécessaires? Pensez-vous qu'une harmonisation communautaire des réglementations en matière de visas soit indispensable concernant notamment:
   - les critères communs d'octroi des visas visant à harmoniser les obligations pesant en ce domaine sur les Etats participant au processus de Budapest;
   - la création d'un système européen d'identification des visas (VIS et SIS II).

1.7 Dans quelle mesure le processus d'élargissement de l'Union européenne représente-t-il une opportunité ou, au contraire, un danger dans la lutte contre l'immigration clandestine et le contrôle des frontières?

PARTIE II LES PROCÉDURES D'ACCUEIL ET LE DROIT DE SÉJOUR DES RESSORTISSANTS DES PAYS TIERS

Dans cette partie, les rapporteurs nationaux devront faire une comparaison entre leurs règles nationales fondamentales concernant l'accueil et le séjour des ressortissants des pays tiers et des dispositions des textes suivants:

- la proposition de directive du Conseil relative aux conditions d'entrée et de séjour des ressortissants des pays tiers aux fins d'un emploi salarié ou de l'exécution d'une activité économique indépendante (COM 2001/386, version finale);
- la proposition de directive sur les conditions d'entrée et de séjour des ressortissants des pays tiers aux fins d'études, de formation professionnelle ou de volontariat (COM 2002/548, version finale);
- la proposition de directive relative au statut des ressortissants des pays tiers résidents de longue durée (COM 2001/127);
- la proposition d'amendement d'une directive sur le droit au regroupement familial dans la version adoptée par le Conseil le 5 juin 2003 (Doc 10214/03).

Les rapporteurs devront insister sur les différences d'approche entre la Commission européenne et leur législation nationale. Il ne sera pas nécessaire cependant de décrire dans le détail la réglementation et les procédures nationales sur l'admission des ressortissants des pays tiers, mais simplement d'identifier les grandes divergences conceptuelles. Concernant la directive sur le droit au regroupement familial, les rapporteurs pourront amorcer un débat sur les questions de droit constitutionnel et de droit international public qu'impliquent les obligations posées par ce texte tel qu'adopté par le Conseil en juin 2003. Enfin, concernant le statut des ressortissants des pays tiers bénéficiant d'un titre de séjour de longue durée, les rapporteurs devront se concentrer sur les problèmes liés a la définition de résidents de longue durée, les conditions en vertu desquelles des ressortissants des pays tiers peuvent résider dans votre pays et celles dans lesquelles ils perdent ce droit, le renouvellent ou sont expulsés, ainsi que la question de la naturalisation.

2.1 Quels sont les principes fondamentaux dans votre pays concernant:
   - l'entrée des ressortissants des pays tiers afin d'exercer une activité salariée ou une activité économique indépendante;
   - l'entrée des ressortissants des pays tiers afin de faire des études ou de suivre une formation professionnelle;
   - le statut juridique des ressortissants qui bénéficient d'un droit de séjour de longue durée dans un autre Etat membre;
   - dans quelles mesure ces principes diffèrent-t-ils des propositions de la Commission européenne?

2.2 Quels sont les exigences juridiques et les procédures requises en vertu du droit national pour obtenir un titre de séjour permettant aux ressortissants des pays tiers de travailler dans le pays d'accueil? Quelles sont les procédures utilisées afin de maintenir la préférence en faveur des citoyens de l'Union européenne et des nationaux de Turquie (en application de l'accord d'association) dans leur accès au marché du travail? Existe-t-il des programmes spécifiques en faveur des professionnels qualifiés leur facilitant l'accès au marché du travail? Quelle est le degré d'implication des syndicats et des employeurs dans ce genre de programmes? Y-a-t-il une procédure visant à évaluer la demande pour des travailleurs étrangers? Dans quelle mesure l'élargissement de l'Union européenne est-il pris en considération? Quel a été l'impact de la récession économique récente et de l'augmentation corrélative du chômage sur le concept de l'admission des ressortissants des pays tiers?

2.3 Dans quelle mesure les droits et pratiques nationaux en vigueur diffèrent-ils substantiellement de l'approche adoptée par la

Commission dans sa proposition sur la politique d'admission à des fins de l'exercice d'une activité salariée ou d'une activité professionnelle indépendante, concernant notamment:

- l'entrée des ressortissants des pays tiers aux fins d'études et de formation professionnelle;
- le statut juridique des ressortissants des pays tiers qui ont un titre de séjour de longue durée accorder par un autre Etat membre;

2.4 Quelles démarches ont été entreprises afin de transposer en droit national la directive du 29 juin 2000 relative au principe de non-discrimination en fonction de la race ou de l'origine ethnique et la directive du Conseil du 27 novembre 2000 établissant un cadre général d'égalité de traitement sur le lieu de travail? Est-ce que des réformes législatives ont été entrepris? Dans quelle mesure le recours à la notion de "discrimination positive" est-il jugé nécessaire afin de promouvoir l'égalité des chances en faveur des travailleurs immigrés en provenance des pays tiers?

2.5 Concernant la proposition de directive sur le droit au regroupement familial présentée par le Conseil en février 2003,

- pensez-vous que les critères proposés soient en deça des principes relatifs au regroupement familial actuellement en vigueur dans votre pays?
- la mise en œuvre de cette directive, une fois adoptée, va-t-elle conduire à des changements dans votre système juridique national sur le droit au regroupement familial et qui abaissent le niveau de protection existant? Si c'est le cas, quels changements sont envisagés?

2.6 La proposition de directive sur les droits des résidents de longue durée telle que présentée par le Conseil le 5 juin 2003 prévoit un certain nombre de droits visant à approximer le statut des résidents de longue duré avec celui des citoyens de l'Union européenne. L'application de ce texte communautaire va-t-elle conduire à des réformes juridiques et politiques importantes dans votre pays? Quelles seront les questions essentielles soulevées, le cas échéant, par le processus d'approximation envisagée par la directive à l'égard notamment:

- du principe de non-discrimination dans le domaine des droits sociaux;
- du concept de "citoyen civique" (voir aussi l'évaluation de l'impact de la communication sur l'intégration du 11 juin 2003);
- du droit au regroupement familial et de l'accès des membres de la famille au marché du travail;
- de la garantie du droit de rester sur le territoire.

2.7 En ayant à l'esprit la perspective d'une future politique commune en matière d'immigration telle qu'élaborée par la Commission dans sa communication sur la coordination ouverte (COM 2001/387) et sa communication sur la politique de l'immigration de l'Union européenne (COM 2000/757, version finale), comment envisagez-vous le rôle des institutions communautaires dans la définition d'un telle politique concernant notamment les compétences des Etats membres pour décider du droit de séjour, de l'accès au marché du travail et de l'intégration? L'harmonisation des législations nationales doit-elle aller plus loin, et si oui, dans quelle mesure?

PARTIE III LA RÉGLEMENTATION APPLICABLE AUX DEMANDEURS D'ASILE ET AUX RÉFUGIÉS

Les rapporteurs nationaux devront ici s'attacher essentiellement à décrire l'impact de la législation, en vigueur ou en voie d'adoption, de l'Union européenne sur l'asile à l'égard du droit et des pratiques en vigueur au niveau national. Trois aspects principaux se dégagent des directives et des propositions de directives en ce domaine:

- les procédures d'admission des demandeurs d'asile;
- la procédure de demande d'asile;
- la question des compétences, exclusives ou partagées.

Encore une fois, il peut être fait appel aux études commandés par l'Union européenne afin de caractériser le régime juridique actuellement en vigueur dans les différents Etats membres. Il faudra insister sur la mise en œuvre de l'action législative de l'Union européenne et les perspectives d'un développement futur d'une procédure communautaire en matière de droit d'asile comprenant les questions relatives aux le traitement externe.

3.1 Les règles de Dublin ont-elles fonctionné de facon satisfaisante jusqu'à présent et qu'attend-on du règlement 343/2003 du 18 février 2003 (Dublin II)?

3.2 Le règlement 2725/2000 du Conseil du 11 décembre 2000 relatif à la création du système Eurodac pour la comparaison des empreintes digitales aux fins de l'application efficace de la Convention de Dublin, et en vigueur depuis le 15 janvier 2003, a-t-il eu pour résultat une augmentation des affaires en ce domaine? Eurodac est-il déjà effective dans votre pays ou, sinon, le sera-t-il dans l'avenir?

3.3 Quels changements significatifs impliquent la transposition de la directive (telle qu'amendée et pour la majorité de quelle le Conseil a obtenu un accord politique en juin 2003) relative aux normes minimales applicables dans le cadre des procédures nationales d'octroi et de retrait du statut de réfugié, pour la législation et la pratique dans votre pays, en termes notamment:
- de droits procéduraux des demandeurs;
- de recours administratifs ou judiciaires;
- d'utilisation des concepts de "*safe third country*" et "*safe country of origin*" (Etats tiers ou Etats d'origine garantissant les droits des demandeurs);
- de la détention des demandeurs d'asile;
- des procédures de contrôle dans les aéroports et aux frontières.

3.4 Quelles ont été les mesures prises dans votre pays afin de transposer la directive communautaire 2003/9/CE du Conseil du 27 janvier 2003 relative à l'accueil des demandeurs d'asile dans les Etats membres? Vous insisterez sur les points particuliers suivants:
- les clauses de flexibilité dans la directive;
- les restrictions à la libre circulation;
- l'accès au marché du travail;
- les droits des travailleurs immigrés en vertu de l'article 11 paragraphe 2 de la directive.

3.5 Quelles démarches ont été entreprises en droit national afin de transposer la directive 2001/55/CE du Conseil du 20 juillet 2001 relative à l'octroi d'une protection temporaire en cas d'afflux massif de personnes déplacées? Existe-t-il des procédures visant à la répartition des efforts consentis par les Etats membres en ce domaine? Y-a-t-il un fondement juridique ouvrant droit à des mesures de protection temporaire pour des réfugiés dans le contexte d'une immigration de masse?

3.6 Les membres du Conseil se sont mis d'un accord politique sur les principes d'une directive relative aux normes minimales requises en matière de qualification et de statut des ressortissants des Etats tiers en tant que réfugiés ou personnes exigeant une protection internationale (proposition COM 2001/510, voir les documents du Conseil de juin 2003). Quelles sont les mesures envisagées au niveau national afin de transposer cette directive en ce qui concerne:
- la définition du réfugié;
- la définition des personnes ayant droit à une protection complémentaire;

- le statut des personnes ayant droit à une protection complémentaire;
- la question de l'alternative d'un vol interne telle que défini par la directive;
- les dispositions relatives aux exceptions, notamment liées au terrorisme (*exclusion clause*).

Dans quelle mesure les politiques internes visant les réfugiés telles que reflétées dans le droit et la jurisprudence de votre pays sont-elles conformes à la proposition de directive?

3.7 Dans la communication de la Commission du 22 novembre 2000 (COM 2000/755; voir aussi le second rapport de la Commission, COM 2003/152), on trouve l'idée d'une procédure communautaire commune d'asile et un statut uniforme à travers l'Union des personnes bénéficiaires d'un droit d'asile. Considérez-vous que cette idée soit généralement en accord avec votre politique nationale en matière de droit d'asile? Les craintes émises par certaines organisations de protection des droits des réfugiés, telle qu'Amnesty International, concernant une diminution éventuelle du niveau international de protection des réfugiés sont-elles partagées par les cercles politiques chargés de prendre les décisions dans votre pays?

3.8 La méthode de coordination ouverte telle que suggérée par la Commission prévoyait un premier et un deuxième étape dans le processus d'adoption de la législation au cours desquelles les dispositions offrant une certaine discrétion aux autorités nationales figurant dans certaines des directives sur l'immigration et le droit d'asile devaient être remplacées par une harmonisation totale. Cela est-il discuté dans votre pays et quelle est la perception de la mise en place progressive d'une politique communautaire relative au droit d'asile qui remplacera, au bout du compte, les procédures et les mesures adoptées au niveau national?

3.9 La Communication de juin 2003 visant à organiser un système plus accessible et équitable en matière de droit d'asile – en réaction notamment à la proposition britannique – envisage de nouvelles approches afin d'assurer une arrivée mieux organisée des personnes nécessitant une protection internationale. Quelle a été la réaction politique dans votre pays à l'égard d'une politique d'asile commune, de la répartition des réfugiées entre les Etats membres ainsi que du partage des responsabilités et autres nouvelles approches et idées qu'implique la prise en charge d'un afflux massif de réfugiés?

PARTIE IV SANCTIONS DES RESSORTISSANTS EN SITUATION IRRÉGULIÈRE, RETOUR ET RAPATRIEMENT

Dans cette partie, les rapporteurs nationaux devront fournir des informations sur les réglementations nationales applicables en ce qui concerne les sanctions contre l'entrée illégale et autres moyens de lutte contre le trafic des clandestins, les problèmes relatives à la termination du droit de séjour des ressortissants des pays tiers qui ne disposent pas d'un titre de séjour valable, la coopération avec les autres Etats membres sur les questions du retour et d'expulsion du territoire national. Vous pourrez vous pencher notamment sur l'existence de programmes communs de retour, sur l'application des mesures d'expulsion, sur les efforts de coopération entre les Etats membres et les Etats de provenance dans la lutte contre l'immigration clandestine, et sur l'efficacité des accords bilatéraux de réadmission ainsi que les problèmes typiques rencontrés lors de leur mise en œuvre.

Il serait également intéressant de donner une brève description de la situation actuelle relative au nombre d'expulsions et de reconduites à la frontière, aux principales causes d'échec des procédures d'entrée sur le territoire (absence de papiers, de titre de séjour, etc.), sans pour autant décrire en détail la législation existante sur ces mesures d'éloignement. Cependant, quelques remarques sur les principaux défauts affectant l'efficacité d'une véritable politique favorisant le retour seraient les bienvenues, ainsi que des idées et suggestions quant à la nécessité d'une plus grande harmonisation dans les procédures de mise en œuvre du retour et de leurs implications en matière de droits de l'homme.

4.1 Combien, selon les estimations fournies, de ressortissants de pays tiers sans titre de séjour valable sont-ils dans votre pays? Combien d'expulsions ont-été ordonnées ces précédentes années? L'ensemble du processus de mise en œuvre de ces mesures est-t-il considéré comme acceptable?

4.2 Quelles démarches ont été entreprises afin de transposer la directive du 28 novembre 2002 relative aux mesures facilitant l'entrée non autorisée sur le territoire, le transit et le droit de séjour?

4.3 Combien de clandestins ont-ils été appréhendés aux frontières ou dans un périmètre proche des frontières? Combien de procédure pour trafic illégal de clandestins ont-elles été mises en œuvre l'année passée?

4.4 Quels efforts ont été entrepris dans votre pays concernant les recommandations de Budapest de juin 2003 sur l'harmonisation des échelles de peines applicables aux délits de trafic des immigrés et de traite des êtres humains en accord avec les dispositions de la directive du 28 novembre 2002? Votre pays a-t-il- signé les protocoles des Nations Unies relatifs au trafic des clandestins?

4.5 Quelles démarches ont-elles été entreprises afin de mettre en œuvre la directive 2001/40/CE du Conseil du 28 mai 2001 sur la reconnaissance mutuelle des décisions d'éloignement des ressortissants des pays tiers? Quels seraient, le cas échéant, les améliorations à apporter afin de remédier aux défauts et combler les lacunes de la directive en question en vue de l'adoption d'une nouvelle mesure sur la coopération des Etats membres en la matière?

4.6 Existe-t-il dans votre pays des accords de réadmission ou autres arrangements internationaux visant à contrôler et limiter l'immigration clandestine et faciliter le rapatriement? Si c'est le cas, ces accords ont-ils fonctionné de façon satisfaisante?

4.7 Dans quelle mesure les critères et recommandations adoptés dans le cadre de l'Union européenne ont-ils influencé la politique du retour en vigueur dans votre pays? Des efforts de coopération ont-ils été entrepris avec d'autres Etats membres de l'Union européenne afin de mettre en œuvre les mesures d'expulsion et d'éloignement du territoire dans le cadre d'actions communes, d'échanges d'informations, de mesures visant à faciliter le transit aérien ou terrien, de principes communs sur la sécurité dans les avions, etc.?

4.8 Pensez-vous qu'il soit nécessaire d'élaborer un régime commun juridique de déportation aérienne, avec notamment la nécessité de déterminer le statut juridique des agents de sécurité armés à bord des avions, les droits du pilote de l'avion, les règles applicables en cas d'arrêt de transit, l'applicabilité des règles nationales de police à bord de l'appareil en cours de vol, etc.?

AUSTRIA

MAG. WOLFGANG TAUCHER
Head of federal Asylum office

MAG. THOMAS MARTH
Ministry for the interior
Legal department

DR. ANDREA JELINEK
Head of the federal Police of the 3rd district in Vienna

Einleitung

Das Ziel des Kongresses für dieses Thema ist es, das Recht und die Politiken der Gemeinschaft und der Mitgliedstaaten zu erforschen. Die Politiken werden im Licht der internationalen Verpflichtungen in Bezug auf Flüchtlinge und Migranten aus Drittländern betrachtet. Die Verbesserungsmöglichkeiten werden erforscht werden, wobei die Arbeitsmarktbedingungen von Mitgliedstaaten in Betracht gezogen werden. Zusätzlich wird dieses Thema erforschen, ob die Politiken der Mitgliedstaaten die Politik der Gemeinschaft untergraben oder unterstützen.

Das Thema des Migrations- und Asylrechts und -politik umschließt eine Bandbreite von verschiedenen Dingen, z.B. illegale Einreise, Grenzenkontrolle, Beziehungen mit Versandländern, Integrationsfragen, Zugang zur Arbeit und anderen Zwecken, Aufnahme von Asylbewerbern, Asylrichtlinien, die ausschließliche Befugnis Asylanträge zu bearbeiten, das Teilen von Belastungen, Wiederaufnahmeverträge, Rücksenderichtlinien, etc. Nationale Berichte sollten sich auf die Dinge konzentrieren, welche in Bezug zu der Migrations- und Asylpolitik der Gemeinschaft, die in den Richtlinien und Vorschlägen von Richtlinien wiedergespiegelt ist, stehen. Nationale Berichte können sich daher in deren Struktur unterscheiden im Anblick der Vereinbarkeit oder Unvereinbarkeit mit dem Recht der Gemeinschaft. In manchen Mitgliedstaaten werden manche Aspekte große Probleme bereiten, während solche Probleme in anderen Mitgliedstaaten nicht entstehen.

Es ist offensichtlich, dass die nationalen Berichte sich nicht mit allen Dingen, die in diesem Fragebogen genannt werden, im Detail befassen können. Es ist nicht die Absicht dieses Fragebogens, eine Basis für einen vollständigen vergleichenden Bericht des Migrations- und Asylrechts- und der -politik in den Mitgliedstaaten darzustellen. Nationale Berichte können sich auf eine Anzahl von vergleichenden Studien stützen, welche in der Verfassung von Kommissionsvorschlägen für Richtlinien hergestellt worden sind, z.B. in Bezug auf die Aufnahme von Asylsuchenden, den rechtlichen Status von Drittstaatsangehörigen, die Regularisierung von illegalen Einwanderern, das Recht und die Politik der Mitgliedstaaten bezüglich Ausweisung und Deportation, die Durchführbarkeit von einzelnen Asylrichtlinien, usw. Ich schlage vor, dass nationale Berichterstatter das Ergebnis dieser Studien in Kürze untersuchen oder auf die Details dieser Studien verweisen – vorausgesetzt sie sind korrect.

Der Fokus des Hauptberichtes wird gleichermaßen nicht eine Wiederholung der schon bestehenden vergleichenden Umfragen darstellen, sondern eine kritische Überprüfung des Status des nationalen Rechts und der Politiken in Bezug auf die Gemeinschaft. Daher wird auf die folgenden Punkte besonderen Wert gelegt:

1 Durchführung von bestehendem EU Recht im Bereich des Migrations- und Asylrechts
2 Vereinbarkeit von nationalen Migrations- und Asylrechten und -politik mit schwebenden EU Verordnungen und Richtlinien, insbesondere Asylrichtlinien, der rechtliche Status von Drittstaatsangehörigen und der Definition von Flüchtlingen.
3 Aussichten und Konflikte in Bezug auf Vorschläge von Richtlinien und Mitteilungen der EU Kommission über die zukünftige Entwicklung eines europäischen Migrations- und Asylrechts über das noch keine Vereinbarung in dem Ministerrat getroffen worden ist.
4 Langzeitperspektive des EU Rechtes in Bezug auf das Migrations- und Asylrechts und -politik.

Der Fragebogen ist in vier Hauptthemen aufgeteilt:

1 Einreise, Visaregime und Grenzkontrolle
2 Aufnahme und Aufenthalt von Drittstaatsangehörigen
3 Asyl- und Flüchtlingsrecht
4 Beendigung von illegalem Aufenthalt, Rücksendung und Rückführung

TEIL I (EINREISE, VISAREGIME UND GRENZKONTROLLE)

1.1 Welche nationalen Behörden sind dafür zuständig, Visaanmeldungen zu bearbeiten (Schengenvisas und Langzeitvisas)? Gibt es Verfahren, um die

Duplikation von Visaanmeldungen oder aufeinanderfolgende Visaanmeldungen bei verschiedenen EU Konsulaten zu vermeiden? Welche materiellen Kriterien sind ausschlagebend für die Vergabe oder Nichtvergabe von Visas, mit Ausnahme der minimalen Schengenerforderungen? Wie viele Visas sind ausgestellt oder abgeschlagen worden?

Zu 1.1. Zur Visabearbeitung sind die österreichischen Berufsvertretungsbehörden im jeweiligen Antragsland berufen; sowohl für Schengenvisa, als auch für Visa für den längerfristigen Aufenthalt. Ein Einreisetitel kann einem Fremden auf Antrag erteilt werden, wenn er ein gültiges Reisedokument besitzt und kein Versagungsgrund wirksam wird. Visa dürfen nur erteilt werden, wenn ihre Gültigkeitsdauer nicht die Gültigkeitsdauer des Reisedokuments übersteigt. Die Gültigkeitsdauer des Reisedokuments soll jene des Visums um mindestens drei Monate übersteigen. Der Fremde benötigt darüber hinaus einen alle Risken abedeckenden Versicherungsschutz, ausreichende eigene Mittel zur Deckung seines Unterhalts für die Dauer seines Aufenthaltes im Bundesgebiet (in eventu die Verpflichtung eines auf Dauer im Bundesgebiet lebenden Menschen für die Kosten des Fremden für die Dauer dessen Aufenthaltes im Bundesgebiet aufzukommen). Es werden keine Visaerteilungsstatistiken geführt.

Darüber hinaus sind bestimmte Grenzübergangsstellen ermächtigt (Verordnung), Visa zu erteilen.

1.2 Gibt es ein Visatrackingverfahren, um herauszufinden, wer länger bleibt, als das Visa erlaubt? Welche Daten werden von Visabewerbern ersucht (Fingerabdrücke)? Dürfen die Visadaten an dritte und Polizeibehörden weitergegeben werden?

Zu 1.2. Es werden keine Fingerabdrücke genommen. Siehe 1.1. Soweit Visadaten zentral gespeichert werden, haben die Polizeibehörden darauf direkten Zugriff.

1.3 Haben die Gerichte jemals ein Schengenvisa abgelehnt aus dem Grund, dass derjenige in anderen Mitgliedstaaten auf der schwarzen Liste steht?

Zu 1.3. Nach österreichischem Fremdenrecht entscheiden die Berufsvertretungsbehörden im Ausland über die Erteilung von Visa.

1.4 Welche Maßnahmen sind unternommen worden in der Ausführung des Aktionsprogrammes für administrative Kooperation im Bereich der Außengrenzen, Visa, Asyl und Einwanderung im Anschluß an die Ratsentscheidung vom 13. Juni 2002?

Zu 1.4. Es gibt mannigfache Sicherheitspartnerschaften, die sich nicht nur auf die Nachbarstaaten Österreichs beschränken.

1.5 Welche Maßnahmen sind unternommen worden, um Richtlinie 2001/51 EC auszuführen, zusätzlich zu den Schengenregeln für Sanktionen für Beförderer? Wie often sind Sanktionen für Beförderer benutzt worden?

Zu 1.5. Im österreichischen Fremdenrecht gab es bereits vor der RL 2001/51 EC eine Norm, die Sanktionen für Beförderungsunternehmer vorsah. Im Oktober 2001 wurde durch Initiativantrag das Fremdengesetz novelliert und die Richtlinie umgesetzt (§§ 53 iVm 103 Abs. 3 FrG 1997, idgF).

1.6 Ist das Visarecht und die -politik ihres Landes ihrer Meinung nach im Einvernehmen mit dem EU Standard oder sind Veränderungen benötigt? Glauben Sie, dass eine weitere unionsweite Harmonisierung von Visarichtlinien für folgende Punkte benötigt wird:
a) Gemeinsame Kriterien für die Ausgabe von Visas mit dem Ziel, die Visapflichten der Teilnehmer des Budapester Prozesses zu harmonisieren
b) Gründung eines europäischen Visaidentifizierungssystems (VIS and SIS II)
In welchem Maße wird die Erweiterung der Gemeinschaft eine Chance oder eine Gefahr darstellen, um Probleme mit illegalen Einreisen und Grenzkontrollen anzugehen?

Zu 1.6. Das österreichische Visarecht und die Visapolitik sind im Einvernehmen mit dem EU-Standard. Eine weitere unionsweite Harmonisierung ist sicher sinnvoll und geboten. Es wurde in in mannigfachen Projekten auf bi- und multilateraler Ebene im Rahmen von EU-Projekten (ua. TWINNINGS) in der Vorbeitrittszeit mit den Staaten, die ab 1. Mai 2004 Mitgliedstaaten der Europäischen Union sein werden, Maßnahmen (legistisch und praxisbezogen) getroffen und Unterstützung gewährt. Die gemeinsame eu-weite Herangehensweise wird sicher in weiterer Folge sehr sinnvoll sein, um nicht rechtmäßgie Einreisen hintanzuhalten.

TEIL II (AUFNAHME UND AUFENTHALT VON DRITTSTAATSANGEHÖRIGEN)

2.1 Was sind die Grundprinzipien in Ihrem Land betreffend:
1 Aufnahme von Drittstaatsangehörigen für unselbstständige oder selbstständige Erwerbstätigkeit

Zu 2.1.1: In Österreich ist grundsätzlich ein Quotensystem vorgesehen. Der Antrag ist vor der Einreise im Ausland zu stellen; da seit 1. Jänner 2003 nur mehr Schlüsselkräfte nach Österreich zuwandern können, wird in einem sogenannten One-Stop-Shop Prinzip verfahren. Wenn die beschäftigungsrechtlichen und die fremdenrechtlichen Voraussetzungen gegeben sind, wir eine Niederlassungsbewilligung als Schlüsselkraft erteilt. Die Familienangehörigen dürfen sich auch in

Österreich niederlassen. Auch sie erhalten auf Antrag eine Niederlassungsbewilligung, wenn die fremdenrechtlichen Voraussetzungen gegeben sind.

2 Einlass von Drittstaatsangehörigen zum Studium und zu einer Berufsausbildung

Zu 2.1.2.: Drittstaatsangehröige, die in Österreich ein Studium aufnehmen oder fortsetzen wollen, erhalten bei Vorliegen der Voraussetzungen eine nicht quotenpflichtige Aufenthaltserlaubnis.

3 Der rechtliche Status von Drittstaatsangehörigen, die in einem anderen Mitgliedsstaat langfristig aufenthaltsberechtigt sind

Zu 2.1.3.: Wer in einem andere EU-Staat langfrisitg aufenthaltsberechtigt ist, ist zum bis zu dreimonatigen sichtvermerksfreien Aufenthalt in Österreich berechtigt. Diese Drittstaatsangehörigen sind in diesem Zeitraum nicht zur Ausübung einer Erwerbstätigkeit berechtigt.

4 In welchem Ausmaß unterscheiden sich diese Prinzipien von den Vorschlägen der Europäischen Kommission?

Zu 2.1.4. Kompatibilität gegeben

2.2 Was sind die rechtlichen Vorraussetzungen und Verfahren für Drittstaatsangehörige, um eine Aufenthaltserlaubnis für eine Erwerbstätigkeit zu bekommen? Welche Verfahren werden benutzt, um den bevorzugten Zugang von EU Einwohnern und Türken (Beitrittsvereinbarung) zum Arbeitsmarkt zu erhalten? Bestehen spezielle Programme, um den Zugang von hochqualifizierten Facharbeitern zum Arbeitsmarkt zu erleichtern? In welchem Maße sind Gewerkschaften und Arbeitgeber in solchen Programmen involviert? Gibt es ein Verfahren, um die Nachfrage für ausländische Arbeiter zu kalkulieren? Wie wird die Erweiterung der Gemeinschaft in Betracht gezogen? In welchem Maße hat die kürzliche wirtschaftliche Rezession und Arbeitslosigkeit die Konzepte über die Aufnahme von Drittstaatsangehörigen beeinflusst?

Zu 2.2. Wer sich in Österreich zur Ausübung einer Erwerbstätigkeit auf Dauer niederlassen möchte : siehe 2.1.1. Für kurzfristige Arbeitsaufnahme (ohne Niederlassungsabsicht) wird das Modell der kurzfristigen Erwerbstätigkeit gewählt, die an zeitliche Obergrenzen gebunden ist. Es erfolgt in beiden Fällen eine enge Verschränkung zwischen Ausländerbeschäftigungsrecht und Fremdenrecht.

EU-Staatsangehörige unterliegen weder einer Titelpflicht im Fremdenrecht noch im Ausländerbeschäftigungsrecht. Bei der Aufnahme einer Erwerbstätigkeit sind sie Österreichern gleichgestellt. Ihre fremdenrechtliche Position ergibt sich aus den Grundfreiheiten der

Union. Die durch das Assoziationsabkommen aus dem Jahre 1964 und dem AB Beschluß 1/80 privilegierten türkischen Staatsbürger unterliegen zwar der Quotenpflicht, sind aber in der Folge am Arbeitsmarkt privilegiert.

Die Frage der hochqualifizierten Facharbeiter und den Zuzug dieser nach Österreich hat Österreich mit der Neuregelung der Zuwanderung von Schlüsselkräften sinnvoll beantwortet. In Österreich sind die Interessenvertretungen in den legistischen Prozeß im Rahmen eines Begutachtungsverfahrens involviert. Die Kalkulationd es Bedarfs erfolgt über eine jährlich zu erstellende Studie (wird bereits seit mehr als 10 Jahren erstellt) des Wirtschaftsforschungsinstituts, in diese Studie fließen die in der Fragestellung genannten Kriterien ein.

2.3 In welchem Ausmaß unterscheiden sich bestehende Rechte und Praktiken wesentlich von der Methode, die von der Kommission gewählt wurde in ihrem Vorschlag über die Aufnahme zum Zweck von unselbständiger oder selbstständiger Erwerbstätigkeit betreffend:

1 Aufnahme von Drittstaatsangehörigen zum Studium und zu einer Berufsausbildung

2 Der rechtliche Status von Drittstaatsangehörigen, die in einem anderen Mitgliedstaat langfristig aufenthaltsberechtigt sind

3 In welchem Ausmaß unterscheiden sich diese Prinzipien von den Vorschlägen der Europäischen Kommission?

2.4 Welche Maßnahmen sind getroffen worden, um die Richtlinie vom 29. Juni 2000 zur Anwendung des Gleichbehandlungsgrundsatzes ohne Unterschied der Rasse oder der ethnischen Herkunft und die Richtlinie 2000/78 EC des Rates vom 27. November 2000 zur Festlegung eines allgemeinen Rahmens für die Verwirklichung der Gleichbehandlung in Beschäftigung und Beruf umzusetzen? Sind Veränderungen des Rechts unternommen worden? In welchem Maß werden positive Aktionen ('affirmative action') als notwendig angesehen, um die Gleichbehandlung staatenlose Arbeiter aus Drittländern zu fördern?

2.5 In Bezug auf den Entwurf für eine Richtlinie betreffend das Recht zur Familienzusammenführung, welches von dem Rat im Februar 2003 genehmigt wurde:

1 Glauben Sie, dass die vorgeschlagenen Normen der Familienzusammenführung niedriger sind als die, die in Ihrem Land gültig sind?

Zu 2.5.1. nein

2 Wird die Umsetzung der Richtlinie, wenn sie angenommen worden ist, zu Veränderungen in Ihrem nationalen Recht zur Familienzusammenführung führen, die den Standard des Schutzes zurückstufen? Falls dies der Fall ist, welche Veränderungen sind vorgesehen?

Zu 2.5.2.: nein

2.6 Der Vorschlag für eine Richtlinie über die Rechte von Langzeitstaatsangehörigen von Drittländern, der vom Rat am 5. Juni 2003 genehmigt wurde, beinhaltet eine Anzahl von Rechten, die die Standarde für Langzeiteinwohner auf den Status von EU Bürger angleichen. Wird die Umsetzung dieser Richtlinie wichtige rechtliche und politische Veränderungen in Ihrem Land beinhalten? Was sind die wichtigsten Belange, falls es welche gibt, betreffend des Annäherungskonzepts der Richtlinie in Bezug auf:

1 Keine Diskriminierung von sozialen Rechten
2 Das Konzept der zivilen Staatsbürgerschaft ('civic citizenship') (siehe auch die erweiterte Auswirkungsbeurteilung der Mitteilung über die Integration vom 11. Juni 2003)
3 Familienzusammenführung und Zugang von Familienmitgliedern zum Arbeitsmarkt
4 Aufenthaltssicherheit

In Österreich gibt es das Prinzip der Aufenthaltsverfestigung von auf Dauer niedergelassenen Fremden seit 1997 im Fremdenrecht. Je länger jemand in Ö rechtmäßig niedergelassen ist, umso gesicherter sein Aufenthalt. Die Stufen der Aufenthaltsverfestigung sind 5, 8 und 10 Jahre. Wer als Kleinkind nach Österreich zuwandert oder hier geboren und aufgewachsen ist, unterfällt dem Aufenthaltsverbot-Verbot, d.h. diese Menschen können nicht mehr des Landes verwiesen werden.

2.7 Im Angesicht der Perspektive einer gemeinsamen Migrationspolitik, wie sie von der Kommission in der Mitteilung über den offenen Koordinierungsmechanismus (KOM 2001, 387) und die Mitteilung über eine Migrationspolitik der Gemeinschaft (KOM 2000, 757 endg.) entwickelt worden ist, welche Rolle werden Ihrer Meinung nach die EU Organe haben bezüglich der Befugnisse, welche die Mitgliedstaaten haben werden, um Aufenthaltsrechte, den Zugang zum Arbeitsmarkt und Integration zu entscheiden? Sollte Harmonisierung des Rechtes weitergehen und, falls dies der Fall ist, in welcher Hinsicht?

TEIL III (ASYL- UND FLÜCHTLINGSRECHT)

3.1 Sind die Dubliner Regeln zufriedenstellend und was wird von der Dublin II Verordnung Nr. 343, 2003 vom 18. February, 2003 erwartet?

Zu 3.1. Dublin-VO seit September 2003 in Anwendung, erwartet wird Beschleunigung der Verfahren. Dies gilt insbesondere auch in Zussammenhang mit der Aufnahme der elektronischen Kommunikation unter DUBLINET. Eine weitergehende Evaluierung der Inhalte ist erst nach längerer Anwendung der VO sinnvoll.

3.2 Hat die Eurodac Verordnung Nr. 2725/2000 vom 11. Dezember 2000 über die Einrichtung von 'Eurodac' für den Vergleich von Fingerabdrücken zum Zwecke der effektiven Anwendung des Dubliner Übereinkommens, die seit dem 15. Januar

2003 in Kraft ist, zu einem Anstieg von Dubliner Fällen geführt? Ist Eurodac in Ihrem Land effektiv oder wird es erwartet, dass es letztendlich effektiv wird?

Zu 3.2. Eurodac hat zu einem Anstieg der Dublin Verfahren geführt, gleichzeitig aber auch zu einer Beschleunigung der Zuständigkeitsverfahren nach Dublin II; Eurodac ist in Österreich effektiv und trägt zur Unterstützung bei.

3.3 Welche wichtigen Veränderungen, falls es welche gibt, wird die Annahme von dem geändertem Vorschlag der Richtlinie über Mindestnormen für Verfahren in Mitgliedstaaten für die Anerkennung oder die Wegnahme vom Flüchtlingsstatus, über die der Rat in den meisten Punkten im Juni 2003 politisches Einvernehmen erreicht hat, für das Recht und die Praxis in Ihrem Land bringen, insbesondere in Bezug auf die folgenden Punkte:

1 Rechte von Bewerbern in dem Verfahren
Der Asylwerber erhält nicht nur die gebotenen Informationen sondern darüber hinaus im Zulassungsverfahren (Trennung in Zulassungsverfahren und materielles Verfahren erfolgte) einen Rechtsberater zur Seite gestellt.
2 Administratives and richterliches Revisionsverfahren
Das Berufungsverfahren wird seit dem 1. Jänner 1998 von einer unabhängigen Behörde mit richterlichem Einschlag, dem unabhängigen Bundesasylsenat – geführt.
3 Die Benutzung von Konzepten von sicheren Drittländern und sicheren Ursprungsländern
Es gibt eine Liste der sicheren Drittstaaten: Schweiz und Liechtenstein Es gibt eine Liste der sicheren Herkuftsstaaten: EU-MS, Australien, Island, Neuseeland, Kanada, Liechtenstein, Schweiz, Norwegen Es gilt in beiden Fällen die widerlegliche Regelvermutung
4 Inhaftierung von Asylbewerbern
Es wurden Sondernormen in der Asylgesetznovelle 2003 geschaffen, um der Besonderheit von Asylverfahren Rechnung zu tragen. Asylwerber werden nur in Ausnahmefällen in Schubhaft genommen.
5 Verfahren an Flughafen und Grenzen?
Es gibt seit 1998 ein Sonderverfahren am Flughafen unter Einbeziehung von UNHCR. Ab 1. Mai 2004 wird es die Möglichkeit der Zurückweisung an der Landgrenze im Verhältnis zu Schweiz und Liechtenstein geben.

Österreich hat im Jahr 2003 eine umfassende Asylgesetznovelle erlassen (BGBl. I Nr. 101/2003), die am 1. Mai 2004 in Kraft tritt, die – unter anderen – alle 5 genannte Bereiche umfasst.

3.4 Welche Maßnahmen sind unternommen worden, um die Richtlinie 2003/9 vom 27. Januar, 2003 über die Aufnahme von Asylsuchenden in Ihrem Land umzusetzen?

1 In Bezug auf die Flexibilitätsparagraphen in der Richtlinie
2 Behinderung des freien Verkehrs
3 Zugang zum Arbeitsmarkt
4 Die Rechte von Migranten laut Artikel 11 § 2 der Richtlinie

Die Richtlinie wird bis 6. Februar 2005 schrittweise umgesetzt, ein Teil der Umsetzung erfolgte durch die Asylgesetznovelle 2003, ein weiterer wesentlicher Umsetzungsschritt ist die Art. 15a Vereinbarung zwischen Bund und Ländern betreffend die Grundversorgung hilfs- und schutzbedürftiger Fremder, die ebenfalls mit 1. Mai 2004 in Kraft treten wird. Den letzten Schritt wird die noch zu erfolgende Novelle des Bundesbetreuungsgesetzes darstellen.

3.5 Welche Schritte sind unternommen worden, um die Richtlinie über vorübergehenden Schutz, KOM 2001, 55 in nationales Recht umzusetzen? Gibt es Verfahren für Vereinbarungen, die die Teilung von Lasten vorsehen? Gibt es eine rechtliche Basis für die Aufnahme von Flüchtlingen für einen vorübergehenden Schutz im Falle eines Massenzustroms?

Bereits vor Erlassung dieser Richtlinie befand sich eine Norm im österreichischen Fremdenrecht, die es ermöglichte, diesen Menschen rasch und vorübergehend Schutz zu gewähren. § 29 des Fremdengesetzes sieht die Möglichkeit der Erlassung einer Verordnung in solchen Fällen vor. Von dieser Norm wurde insbesondere im Zuge der Balkankriege mehrfach Gebrauch gemacht. Lastenteilungsvorschriften enthält die österreichische Gesetzgebung in diesem Bereich nicht.

Von der in der RL vorgesehenen Möglichkeit, das Asylverfahren für die Dauer des vorübergehenden Schutzes auszusetzen – wurde in der Asylgesetznovelle 2003 Gebrauch gemacht.

3.6 Der Rat hat eine politische Vereinbarung getroffen über die Grundsätze für eine Richtlinie über Mindestnormen für die Anerkennung und den Status von Drittstaatsangehörigen und Staatenlosen als Flüchtlinge oder als Personen, die anderweitig internationalen Schutz benötigen, KOM 2001, 510 endg. (siehe Ratsdokument vom Juni 2003). Welche Maßnahmen sind vorgesehen, um die Richtlinie in Ihrem Land umzusetzen wenn sie in Kraft tritt, bezüglich:
1 Die Definition von Flüchtlingen
2 Die Definition von Personen die einen Anspruch auf subsidiaren Schutz haben
3 Der Status von Personen die einen Anspruch auf subsidiaren Schutz haben
4 Das Problem von Alternativen zu Inlandsflügen, wie es in der Richtlinie definiert ist
5 Auschlußparagraphen, inbesondere ein Problem mit Terrorismus?
In welchem Ausmaß ist die Flüchtlingspolitik, die in dem Recht und der Rechtssprechung Ihres Landes wiedergespiegelt ist, im Einvernehmen mit dem Vorschlag der Richtlinie?

Eine Beantwortung dieser Fragen setzt die förmliche Annahme der gegenständlichen Richtlinie voraus.

3.7 In der Mitteilung der Kommission vom 22. November, 2000, KOM 2000, 755 (siehe auch der 2. Kommissionsbericht KOM 2003, 152 endg.) ist das Konzept der Kommission für ein gemeinsames europäisches Asylverfahren und einen unionsweit geltenden Status für die Personen, denen Asyl gewährt wird, enthalten. Glauben Sie, dass das Konzept generell mit der Asylpolitik Ihres Landes übereinstimmt? Teilen politische Kreise in Ihrem Land, die Entscheidungen treffen, die Bedenken von Flüchtlingsorganisationen wie z.B. Amnesty International und anderen Organisationen, dass das internationale Regime für den Schutz von Flüchtlingen untergraben wird?

3.8 Der von der Kommission vorgeschlagene Koordinationsmechanismus sieht eine erste und zweite Rechtsstufe vor, in der die Flexibilitätsvorkehrungen in manchen Richtlinien über die Migration und das Asyl mit voller Harmonisierung ersetzt werden. Ist dieses Konzept in Ihrem Land diskutiert worden und was sind die Auffassungen über die schrittweise Erstehung von einer europäischen Asylpolitik, die letztendlich nationale Verfahren und nationale Entscheidungen ersetzen könnte?

3.9 Die Mitteilung vom Juni, 2003 für ein zugänglicheres, gleichberechtigteres und besser organisiertes Asylsystem – als Reaktion zu dem UK Bericht – entwickelt manche Ideen über neue Versuche, eine geordnete und organisierte Ankunft von Personen, die internationalen Schutz benötigen, zu verfolgen. Was ist die politische Reaktion in Ihrem Land zu dem Konzept eines Asylverfahrens, dass von außen zugegriffen werden kann, die Verteilung von Flüchtlingen und das Teilen von Verantwortungen und anderen neuen Konzepten und Ideen, die helfen sollen, mit Massenflüchtlingsbewegungen fertig zu werden?

TEIL IV (BEENDIGUNG EINES ILLEGALEN AUFENTHALTS, RÜCKSENDUNG UND RÜCKFÜHRUNG)

1.1 Wie viele Drittstaatsangehörige ohne eine gültige Aufenthaltserlaubnis sind momentan nach Schätzungen in Ihrem Land? Wie viele Deportationen sind in den letzten Jahren tatsächlich vorgenommen worden? Wird das gesamte Durchsetzungsverfahren als akzeptabel angesehen?

1.2 Was ist unternommen worden, um die Richtlinie vom 28. November, 2002, die sich mit der Erleichterung von unerlaubter Einreise, Transit und Aufenthalt befasst, umzusetzen?

1.3 Wie viele illegale Bewerber sind an, oder in der Nähe, der Grenze festgenommen worden? Wie viele strafrechtliche Verfahren für das Handeln von Personen sind im letzten Jahr eingeleitet worden?

1.4 Welche Bemühungen sind in Ihrem Land betreffend der Empfehlungen von Budapest im Juni 2003 in Bezug auf die Harmonisierung von Sanktionen für das Schmuggeln von Migranten und das Handeln von Personen im Einklang mit der

Richtlinie des Rates 2002/90 vom 28. November 2002 unternommen worden? Hat Ihr Land das UN Protokoll über das Schmuggeln von Migranten unterschrieben?

1.5 Welche Maßnahmen sind unternommen worden, um die Richtlinie des Rates vom 28. Mai 2001 über die gegenseitige Anerkennung von Entscheidungen zur Ausweisung von Drittstaatsangehörigen umzusetzen? Welche Mangel oder Lücken der Richtlinie sollten verbessert werden in einer weiteren Richtlinie über die Kooperation in der Ausweisung und Deportation von Drittstaatsangehörigen?

Diese Richtlinie wurde im Rahmen der Fremdengesetznovelle 2003 in innerstaatliches Recht umgesetzt. (§ 34a FrG)

1.6 Gibt es Wiederaufnahmevereinbarungen oder andere internationale Verträge oder Vereinbarungen mit dem Ziel der Kontrolle und dem Verhindern von illegaler Einwanderung und der Erleichterung von Rücksendungen in Ihrem Land? Sind diese zufriedenstellend?

Es gibt eine Vielzahl von Vereinbarungen; der Vollzug ist unterschiedlich

1.7 In welchem Ausmaß haben EU-Normen und Empfehlungen die Rücksendepolitik Ihres Landes beinflusst? Welche Versuche sind unternommen worden, mit anderen EU Mitgliedstaaten zu kooperieren in der Durchsetzung von Rücksendeentscheidungen gemeinsamer Deportationsaktionen, dem Austausch von Informationen, der Erleichterung von Luft und Landtransit, gemeinsamen Prinzipien der Flugsicherheit, usw.?

Es wurde und wird immer wieder bilateral kooperiert.

1.8 Ist es Ihrer Meinung nach notwendig, ein gemeinsames Rechtssystem für Luftdeportationen zu entwickeln (rechtlicher Status von bewaffneten Sicherheitsleuten in einem Flugzeug, Rechte des Flugkapitäns, rechtliche Regeln für Transitstops, Anwendbarkeit von nationalem Polizeirecht in einem fliegenden Flugzeug, usw.)?

Ein gemeinsames EU-weites Vorgehen ist sinnvol, allerdings durch das Tokioter Abkommen bereits ohnedies völkerrechtlich vorgesehen, da alle EU-MS Mitgliedstaaten der genannten Konvention sind.

CROATIA

IRIS GOLDNER
Faculty of Law, University of Zagreb

INTRODUCTION

Croatia is not an EU Member State, but has started the process of alignment of its legislation with the *acquis* with the aim of future integration into the European Union. Croatia signed a Stabilisation and Association Agreement on 29 October 2001. The Agreement is not yet in force. Instead an Interim Agreement, covering trade and trade-related measures was concluded parallel with the Agreement and entered into force on 1 March 2002.

PART I ENTRY, VISA REGIME AND BORDER CONTROL

1.1 What national authorities are competent to deal with visa applications (Schengen visas and long-term visas)? Are there any procedures to avoid duplication or successive visa applications at different EU-consulates? On what substantive criteria, other than the Schengen minimum requirements, are visas granted or refused? How many visas have been issued or refused?

Continuing alignment with the Community visa regime has been recognised as one of Croatia's priorities in the European Commission Stabilisation and Association Report 2002.[1] The 2003 Stabilisation and Association Report[2] no longer identifies it as a priority, due to the fact that a number of relevant issues had in the meantime been addressed by the then newly drafted Act on Foreigners, whose aim is to provide the highest possible level of harmonisation of the Croatian visa regime with the Community visa regime and the Schengen *acquis.*

The Act on Foreigners[3] has in the meantime been passed by the Croatian Parliament and, together with subordinate legislation, determines the visa regime in the Republic of Croatia. It was adopted on 2 July and entered into force on 17 July 2003. The Act on Foreigners is being implemented as of 1 January 2004, and replaces many of the provisions of the previous Act

[1] COM (2002) 163, p. 31. [2] COM (2003) 139 final, p. 31.
[3] Official Gazette of the Republic of Croatia No. 109/03.

on the Movement and stay of Foreigners.[4] It provides the legal basis for the adoption of implementing regulations that had to be adopted within ninety days from the date of entry into force of the Act.[5]

National authorities competent to deal with visa applications are the diplomatic missions and consular offices of the Republic of Croatia.[6] Exceptionally, the body in charge of the control of border crossings may issue a single travel or a transit visa to a foreigner in case this is required by humanitarian, serious professional or personal reasons, and the foreigner, due to time constraints, cannot apply for a visa at the diplomatic mission/consular office of the Republic of Croatia abroad, and there are no reasons for its rejection specified by Article 24 of the Act on Foreigners.[7]

The Act on Foreigners lists substantive criteria for granting/refusing a visa. Article 24 of the Act provides that a foreigner shall not be granted a visa if there are grounds for rejecting his/her entry into the Republic of Croatia,[8] or if a foreigner does not personally respond to the invitation of a diplomatic mission or a consular office. Article 29 of the Act prescribes that a foreigner shall not be permitted to enter Croatia in case:

- he/she does not have a valid travel document, including a visa or an approval of stay, unless otherwise provided by the Act or an international agreement;
- he/she does not have sufficient funds for sustenance for the period of his/her stay in Croatia and return to the country from which he/she has arrived or for travelling to a third country;
- he/she is in transit and does not fulfil the conditions set for the entry into a third country;
- a protective or a safety measure of expulsion is in effect;

[4] Official Gazette of the Republic of Croatia No. 53/91, 22/92, 26/93 and 29/94.

[5] Implementing regulations adopted on the basis of the Act on Foreigners are: Rule Book on the Travel Documents for Foreigners, Visas, Border Passes and the Treatment of Foreigners (Official Gazette of the Republic of Croatia No. 202/03); Rule Book on the Issuing of Travel Documents, Visas and Special Identity Cards to Foreigners (Official Gazette of the Republic of Croatia No. 303/03); Decision on Determining the Annual Quota of Work Permits for Employing Foreigners for Calendar Year 2004 (Official Gazette of the Republic of Croatia No. 194/03); Rule Book on the Status of Foreigners in the Republic of Croatia (Official Gazette of the Republic of Croatia No. 202/03).

[6] Article 6 of the Rule Book on the Issuing of Travel Documents, Visas and Special Identity Cards to Foreigners (Official Gazette of the Republic of Croatia No. 303/03).

[7] Article 12 of the Rule Book on the Travel Documents for Foreigners, Visas, Border Passes and the Treatment of Foreigners (Official Gazette of the Republic of Croatia No. 202/03).

[8] These grounds are listed in Article 29 of the Act on Foreigners.

- he/she does not possess an immunisation certificate and comes from a territory affected by an epidemic of infectious disease;
- this is required on the grounds of protecting the legal system, national security or public health;
- there is a reasonable belief that his/her stay will be connected with committing criminal acts prosecuted ex officio;
- he/she has been entered in the records of a competent body as an international offender;
- there is reasonable doubt that his/her stay will not be used for the intended purpose.

1.2 Is there a visa tracking procedure in order to identify visa overstayers? What data are collected from visa-applicants (fingerprints)? Admissibility of visa data to alien and police authorities?

Diplomatic missions/consular offices of the Republic of Croatia keep a record of visa applications and visas being issued.[9] The record contains the following data: number; class; the date of submitting the application; name and surname of the applicant; date and place of birth; nationality; type, number and period of validity of the travel document; information as to whether the visa has been granted or rejected; serial number, issuance date and period of validity of the visa; type of visa and the purpose of its issuance; additional remarks.[10]

Since 1995 the Ministry of Interior has been keeping a register of all visa applications forwarded to the Ministry for processing by diplomatic missions/consular offices. The register includes information on visa applications both granted and rejected by the Ministry, as well as on visa applicants. It does not contain any information on visa applications in cases where no consent by the Ministry was needed and visas were issued independently by diplomatic missions/consular offices. Presently, work is being done on establishing a new and complete online national visa register containing information on all visa applications and visa applicants. This information-communication system (IKOS) is expected to be finalised by the end of 2004. Online connections between a number of Croatian diplomatic missions/consular offices and the Ministry of Foreign

[9] Article 54 of the Rule Book on the Issuing of Travel Documents, Visas and Special Identity Cards to Foreigners (Official Gazette of the Republic of Croatia No. 303/03).

[10] Article 56 of the Rule Book on the Issuing of Travel Documents, Visas and Special Identity Cards to Foreigners (Official Gazette of the Republic of Croatia No. 303/03) and Article 81 of the Rule Book on the Travel Documents for Foreigners, Visas, Border Passes and the Treatment of Foreigners (Official Gazette of the Republic of Croatia No. 202/03).

Affairs started in May 2002. Diplomatic missions/consular offices have been recording all visa applications into the IKOS system since 1 January 2003. Additionally, the Ministry of Interior receives all visa applications needing prior consent, as well as all notifications of the intent to issue visas and all the information on issued visas through IKOS.

1.4 What measures have been undertaken in the implementation of the action programme for administrative cooperation in the field of external borders, visa, asylum and immigration following the Council Decision of 13 June 2002?

In the field of border management, the establishment of the new Border Police Directorate within the General Police Directorate in January 2002, was an important step in creating an efficient system of state border protection. Generally speaking, at present there is no overall national strategy of integrated border management in Croatia. However, implementation of a new project entitled "Enhancing Inter-Agency Co-operation – Development and Implementation of Croatia's Integrated Border Management Strategy", within the framework of CARDS, is supposed to start by the beginning of 2004, with the participation of the Republic of Austria as a partner country in the project. The aim of the project is the creation of an overall integrated border management strategy in accordance with the European Union standards in the protection of the existing and future EU external borders. Further specialisation and training of border police officers is needed. To this end the project "Continued Support and Capacity Building for the Border Directorate", within the framework of the CARDS programme and representing a follow-up of a previous twinning project, is expected to begin in the first half of 2004.

1.5 What measures have been undertaken to implement the Directive 2001/51 EC supplementing the Schengen rules concerning carrier sanctions? How often have carrier sanctions been used?

The new Act on Foreigners imposes carrier obligations and sanctions in line with the *acquis*. Article 25 of the Act imposes a duty on a carrier or a travel agency to take a foreigner, who does not fulfil the conditions to enter the Republic of Croatia, out of the state without delay and to carry the financial burden of the foreigner's stay in Croatia. Additionally, Article 105 of the Act imposes fines on legal persons or self-employed individuals who transport foreigners to the territory of the Republic of Croatia or refuse to take them away contrary to the provision of Article 25 of the Act. Apart from the fine in such cases, the Act gives room for the additional sanction of banning further professional activity in this field by a legal person.[11]

1.6 In your judgement, does the visa law and policy of your country live up to EU standards or are adjustments needed? Do you consider that there is need for further EU-harmonization of visa policies concerning:
- **common criteria for granting visas aiming at harmonizing visa obligations among states participating in the Budapest Process;**
- **establishment of a European visa identification system (VIS and SIS II)?**

To what extent will the EU enlargement process present an opportunity or challenge for tackling issues of illegal entry and border control?

The enforcement of the new Act on Foreigners brought a number of adjustments of Croatian legislative framework, bringing it closer to the Community visa law and policy. The Act adjusts Croatia's visa regime and types of visas to the Community framework. It distinguishes the visa regime for travel purposes from residence and work permits and determines competent bodies and deadlines for issuing documents.

The Croatian visa list[12] is similar to the Community visa list,[13] as defined by Council Regulation 539/2001.[14] The only difference is that citizens of Bosnia and Herzegovina, former Yugoslav Republic of Macedonia, Jamaica and Turkey need a visa to enter the European Union, while they are exempt from visa obligations when entering Croatia.[15]

Croatia took part in the Rhodes Ministerial Conference (as part of the Budapest Process) on the prevention of irregular migration in the wider European region, held on 25–26 June 2003. The Recommendations resulting from the Conference support further harmonisation of visa policies and procedures among all participating states as a necessary precondition for a more efficient reduction of irregular immigration. Adjustments should encompass both the establishment of common criteria for granting visas and harmonisation of visa obligations among participating states.

[11] Artilce 105(2) of the Act on Foreigners.

[12] The list of countries whose citizens require a visa for entry into the Republic of Croatia.

[13] The list of countries whose citizens require a visa for entry into the EU Member States.

[14] OJ L 81/1 of 15 March 2001.

[15] Additionally, according to a decision of the Croatian Government on temporary suspension of the visa regime with Serbia and Montenegro, citizens of Serbia and Montenegro may enter the Republic of Croatia without a visa for visits not extending 90 days, in the period between 10 June 2003 and 31 January 2004. On the other hand, Serbia and Montenegro is on the EU visa list.

PART II ADMISSION AND RESIDENCE OF THIRD COUNTRY NATIONALS

2.1 What are the basic principles in your country concerning:
- **admission of third country nationals for labour purposes or self-employed activities;**
- **admission of third country nationals for study and vocational training;**
- **legal status of third country nationals in possession of a long-term residence permit of another Member State?**

To what extent do these principles differ from the European Commission's proposals;

Provisions determining the right of third country nationals to employment and self-employment on the territory of the Republic of Croatia are stipulated by the Act on Foreigners. They mostly comply with the approach taken by the Proposal for a Council Directive on the conditions of entry and residence of third country nationals for the purpose of paid employment and self-employed economic activities.[16] According to the Act, third country nationals are entitled to employed activities based on a work permit, and to self-employed activities based on a business permit.[17] The Government of the Republic of Croatia issues the annual quota of work permits in Croatia, based on the proposal of the ministry in charge of labour activities[18] and in accordance with the migration policy and the labour market situation in Croatia.[19] The policy of setting quotas is in line with the approach taken by the Proposal for a Council Directive, which does not allow for an unconditional immigration right of third country nationals but acknowledges the Member States' right to limit their admission by setting ceilings or suspending/halting the issuing of work permits for a defined period.[20] According to the Act on Foreigners, a work permit is issued within fifteen days upon the application of the employer whose intention is to employ a third country national.[21] The Act does not provide for the possibility of a third country national submitting the application himself/herself and, in this respect, differs from

[16] COM (2001) 386 final. [17] Article 85 of the Act on Foreigners.

[18] The proposal is based on the opinion of the Croatian Employment Service.

[19] Further on, in accordance with Article 86 of the Act on Foreigners, the Government determines the quota by taking into consideration prior opinions of the ministries in charge of specific activities falling within the quota system and the opinion of the Economic and Social Committee.

[20] Article 26 of the Proposal for a Council Directive, COM (2001)386 final.

[21] Article 88 of the Act on Foreigners.

the Proposal for a Council Directive.[22] Further on, apart from the application, the employer is obliged to submit specified information on the third country national concerned, the type of job and working conditions, the registration of the company, payment of taxes and the justification for employing the third country national concerned.[23] A third country national is obliged to sign the employment contract prior to commencing work, or within fifteen days from the date of the issuance of the work permit at the latest.[24] The Proposal for a Council Directive sets a more extensive list of documents necessary to accompany the application for a work permit, among them being the evidence that the third country national has sufficient resources to support himself/herself and his/her family members and of having a sickness insurance covering all risks in the host Member State.[25] The aim of this requirement is to avoid a situation where the third country national would become "a burden on the social assistance system of the host Member State for the duration of his/her stay".[26] According to the Croatian Act on Foreigners, a work permit is issued for a predetermined period, identical to the period of validity of a third country national's employment contract, but for no longer than two years, with the possibility of renewal.[27] A business permit is issued for a period of two years and can be renewed.[28] Both provisions comply with the wording of the Proposal for a Council Directive, stipulating that permits for employed and self-employed activities of third country nationals within Member States are valid "for a period of up to three years to be determined in accordance with national legislation" and can be renewed.[29]

Third country nationals coming to the territory of the Republic of Croatia for the purpose of study have to apply for temporary residence.[30] Temporary residence permits are normally issued for a period of up to one year and can be renewed for up to two years.[31] However, the Act states that "temporary residence permits issued for the purpose of study can be renewed for up to two years upon the expiry of the period prescribed for

[22] Article 5(1) of the Proposal stipulates that the application must be submitted by the third country national concerned, while the future employer has the right to submit the application on behalf of the third country national.

[23] Article 89 of the Act on Foreigners. [24] Article 91(1) of the Act on Foreigners.

[25] Article 5(3) of the Proposal for a Council Directive.

[26] Article 5(3)(h) of the Proposal for a Council Directive.

[27] Articles 92 and 93 of the Act on Foreigners. [28] Article 98 of the Act on Foreigners.

[29] Articles 7(1) and 20(1) of the Proposal for a Council Directive.

[30] Article 37 of the Act on Foreigners. [31] Article 35 of the Act on Foreigners.

studying",[32] meaning that "student" residence permits can be renewed for the whole period prescribed for studying and two years afterwards. This provision complies with wording of the Proposal for a Council Directive on the conditions of entry and residence of third country nationals for the purposes of studies, vocational training or voluntary service,[33] according to which a "student" residence permit is issued for a period of one year and renewed for the period of the student's enrolment in the course of study. Additionally, the Proposal for a Council Directive states that where the duration of the course of study is less than one year, the permit is valid only for the duration of the course of study. Apart from submitting evidence that he/she has enough resources to maintain himself/herself, has accommodation and sickness insurance, in case of applying for a temporary residence permit for the purpose of study in Croatia, a third country national has to submit a letter of certification proving his/her enrolment in a course of study.[34] The same conditions are imposed by the Proposal for a Council Directive, with a slight difference that the Proposal does not expressly mention accommodation as a condition, but requires "sufficient resources to cover subsistence, study and return travel costs".[35]

For the analysis of the legal status of third country nationals in possession of a long-term residence permit in Croatia and the comparison with the approach taken by the Proposal for a Council Directive concerning the status of third country nationals who are long-term residents,[36] see 2.6.

2.2 What are the legal requirements and procedures for obtaining a residence permit for third country nationals for the purpose of employment? Which procedures are used in maintaining the preferred access of EU-citizens and Turkish nationals (association agreement) to the labour market? Do special programmes exist for highly qualified professionals facilitating access to the labour market? To what extent are trade unions and employers involved in such programmes? Is there a procedure to calculate the demand for foreign labour? How is the EU-enlargement taken into consideration? To what extent has the recent economic recession and unemployment influenced the concepts on admission of third country nationals?

For the analysis of the legal requirements and procedures for obtaining a residence permit for third country nationals for the purpose of employment, see 2.1. The procedure for calculating the demand for foreign labour is, likewise, examined in 2.1.

[32] Article 41(2) of the Act on Foreigners.
[33] COM (2002) 548 final. [34] Article 41(1) of the Act on Foreigners.
[35] Article 6(1)(b) of the Proposal for a Council Directive. [36] COM (2001) 127 final.

The Act on Foreigners facilitates access to the labour market for some categories of highly qualified professionals from third countries, by exempting them from the work permit requirement at all. Some of the categories having preferential treatment are university professors invited by Croatian universities, scientists coming to Croatia for the purpose of vocational training or to take part in a research project important for Croatia, artists and technical staff engaged in opera, ballet, theatre, concerts, art galleries and other cultural events, etc.[37]

2.3 To what extent do existing national laws and practices differ substantially from the approach taken in the Commission's Proposal on admission for the purpose of paid employment and self-employed activities relating to:
- **admission of third country nationals for study and vocational training;**
- **on legal status of third country nationals in possession of a long-term residence permit of another Member State?**

To what extent do these principles differ from the European Commission's proposals?

See 2.1 and 2.6.

2.4 What measures have been taken to implement the Directive of 29th June 2000, implementing the principle of equal treatment between persons irrespective of racial or ethnic origin and Council Directive 2000/78 EC of 27th November 2000, establishing a general framework for equal treatment in employment and occupation? Have legislative changes been undertaken? To what extent is "affirmative action" considered as necessary to promote equal opportunities for migrant workers from third countries?

Article 2 of the amended Croatian Employment Act[38] bans direct and indirect discrimination of employees and persons applying for employment, on the basis of race, colour of skin, sex, sexual orientation, marital status, family commitments, age, language, religion, political or other beliefs, national or social origin, financial status, birth, social status, membership or non-membership in a political party or trade union, and physical or psychological difficulties. Non-discrimination applies to conditions for access to employment including selection criteria and recruitment conditions, promotion, access to vocational training, employment and working conditions including equal pay, dismissal and the right to membership and involvement in workers' or employers' organisations including the benefits provided by such organisations. It therefore complies with the principles set out in Council Directive 2000/43/EC implementing the

[37] Article 95 of the Act on Foreigners.
[38] Official Gazette of the Republic of Croatia No. 114/03.

principle of equal treatment between persons irrespective of racial or ethnic origin, and Council Directive 2000/78/EC establishing a general framework for equal treatment in employment and occupation.

2.5 Concerning the proposal for a directive on the right to family reunion agreed upon by the Council in February 2003:
- **Do you consider the proposed standards below the principles of family reunification applicable in your country?**
- **Will the implementation of the Directive, once it is adopted, lead to changes in the national law on family reunification downgrading the standard of protection? If so, what changes are envisaged?**

Matters of family reunion of third country nationals are stipulated by the Croatian Act on Foreigners in the chapter on temporary residence of foreigners, which can lead further to permanent residence. Generally speaking, the scope of the Act in the field of family reunification is broader than the one of Council Directive 2003/86/EC (Family Reunification Directive). Unlike the Directive, which covers only cases where both the "sponsor" i.e. the person already residing lawfully in the EU Member State and his/her family member are third country nationals, the Act covers both cases of family reunification between Croatian citizens and third country nationals, as well as third country nationals residing lawfully in Croatia and their third country national family members. Additionally, the Act also encompasses the family reunification of asylum seekers as "sponsors", while the Family Reunification Directive expressly excludes its application in such cases.[39]

As prescribed by the Act, family reunification is one of the bases for granting temporary stay to foreigners[40] and can lead to the further granting of permanent stay.[41] Generally speaking, temporary stay can be granted to a foreigner only in case he/she has enough resources to maintain himself/herself, has accommodation and sickness insurance, and his/her stay is not contrary to public policy/public security/public health requirements.[42] In this respect, the Croatian Act on Foreigners is in line with the Community criteria for family reunification of third country nationals set out in Article 7 of the Family Reunification Directive. The Act sets an additional requirement to a foreigner applying for temporary stay the first time. He/she needs to provide a certificate proving he/she has not been

[39] See Article 42 of the Act on Foreigners and Article 3(2) of the Family Reunification Directive.

[40] Article 37 of the Act on Foreigners. [41] Article 47 of the Act on Foreigners.

[42] Article 38(1) of the Act on Foreigners.

previously criminally sanctioned in the state of his/her nationality or permanent residence.[43] This requirement can be viewed as being close to public policy/public security/public health requirements stipulated both by the Act on Foreigners and the Family Reunification Directive, which can arguably be seen as a weakness due to their possible misuse.

According to the Croatian Act on Foreigners, family members eligible for reunification are the spouse, minor unmarried children and parents of minor children. The last category (parents of minor children) authorises entry and residence of a sponsor's unmarried partner in case they have a minor child. In this respect, the Croatian Act on Foreigners goes beyond the stipulation of the Family Reunification Directive which leaves the decision on the family reunification of unmarried partners to Member States' national law.[44] Exceptionally, family reunification in Croatia can also apply to other relatives, adoptees and adopters in case of special personal or humanitarian reasons.[45] In this respect Croatian legislation slightly departs from the wording of the Directive which does not allow a discretion in case of the adopted children of the sponsor or his/her spouse, including them among the family members eligible for family reunification.[46]

In some aspects it could be argued that the Croatian Act on Foreigners goes beyond the standards set by the Community Directive. Unlike the Directive which gives EU Member States the right to require the sponsor to have stayed lawfully in their territory for a period of up to two years before having his/her family members join him/her, the Croatian Act allows family reunification of temporarily/permanently resident third country nationals, without any reference to the period of their prior residence in Croatia. On the other hand, while the Directive grants family members the right to have access to employment and self-employment,[47] the Croatian Act on Foreigners expressly states that temporary residence granted on the basis of family reunification does not entitle the family member to have access to employment on the territory of the Republic of Croatia.[48] However, in case a family member fulfils the criteria for being granted

[43] Article 38(2) of the Act on Foreigners.

[44] Article 4 of the Family Reunification Directive.

[45] Article 42 of the Act on Foreigners.

[46] Article 4(1)(b), (c) and (d) of the Family Reunification Directive.

[47] Article 14(1)(b) of the Family Reunification Directive.

[48] Article 42(4) of the Act on Foreigners. This applies only to cases where both the sponsor and the family member are third country nationals. In case the sponsor has Croatian nationality, his/her spouse and children residing on the territory of the Republic of Croatia have access to employment without a work permit (see Article 95(1), indent 12 of the Act on Foreigners).

permanent residence, he/she has access to employment and does not need a work permit.[49]

2.6 The proposal for a directive on the rights of long-term third country nationals as agreed upon by the Council on 5 June 2003, provides for a number of rights approximating the situation of long-term residents to the status of EU-citizens. Will the implementation of the directive involve major legal and policy changes in your country? What are the major points of concern if any, concerning the approximation concept of the directive relating to:
- **non-discrimination in social rights;**
- **the concept of "civic citizenship" (see also extended impact assessment on the Communication on Integration of June 11, 2003);**
- **family reunification and access of family members to the labour market;**
- **security of stay?**

The Croatian Act on Foreigners determines the status of long-term third country nationals in the Republic of Croatia (the Act refers to them as permanently resident foreigners). Article 47 of the Act states that permanent residence will be granted to a foreigner who, by the date of submission of his/her permanent residence application, has had temporary residence approved for five consecutive years. The five-year requirement coincides with the provisions of Article 5(1) of the Proposal for a Council Directive concerning the status of third country nationals who are long-term residents,[50] granting long-term residence status "to third country nationals who have resided legally and continuously for five years in the territory of the Member State concerned". Additionally, both the Croatian Act and the Community Proposal set extra requirements for the approval of permanent residence. Both pieces of legislation require the third country national to have sufficient resources[51] and sickness insurance,[52] and are subject to public policy/public security/public health exceptions.[53] The Croatian Act also requires the third country national to have accommodation and not to have been previously sentenced to prison.[54]

[49] Article 95(1), indent 22 of the Act on Foreigners.

[50] COM (2001) 127 final.

[51] Unlike Article 49, indent 2 of the Croatian Act which requires "resources sufficient to maintain himself/herself", Article 6(1)(a) of the Community Proposal is stricter requiring "stable resources corresponding to the level of resources below which social assistance may be granted in the Member State" sufficient for maintaining himself/herself and dependent family members.

[52] Article 49, indent 4 of the Act on Foreigners and Article 6(1)(b) of the Community Proposal.

[53] Article 49, indent 5 of the Act on Foreigners and Articles 7 and 20 of the Community Proposal.

[54] Article 49 of the Act on Foreigners.

Additionally, the Croatian Act allows approval of permanent residence to a foreigner who has been granted temporary residence in Croatia and who has been married for three years to a Croatian citizen or to a foreigner with approved permanent residence in the Republic of Croatia. A minor child with temporary residence in the Republic of Croatia will be granted permanent residence if one of the parents is a foreigner with approved permanent residence, with the prior consent of the other parent.[55] According to the Croatian Act on Foreigners, third country nationals who are granted permanent residence have access to employment and do not need a work permit.[56]

PART III ASYLUM AND REFUGEE LAW

3.1 Have the Dublin Rules worked satisfactorily and what is expected of the Dublin II Regulation No. 343, 2003 of 18 February 2003?

Due to the fact that Croatia is not an EU Member State, neither the currently valid Articles 31–38 (chapter on refugees) of the Act on the Movement and Stay of Foreigners,[57] nor the new Asylum Act,[58] entering into force on 1 July 2004, contains provisions determining the service in charge for the application of the provisions on determining the state responsible for the examination of asylum applications submitted by citizens of third countries to one of the Member States. However, the process of further association of the Republic of Croatia to the European Union will require legal adjustments in this field.

3.2 Has the Eurodac Regulation No. 2725/2000 of 11th December 2000, concerning the establishment of Eurodac for the comparison of fingerprints for an effective application of the Dublin Convention, operative since January 15, 2003, resulted in an increase of Dublin cases? Has Eurodac become effective in your country or is it expected to become effective eventually?

According to the current system, a service within the General Police Directorate records and keeps databases of the fingerprints of each asylum

[55] Article 47 of the Act on Foreigners. [56] Article 95(1), indent 22 of the Act on Foreigners.

[57] Official Gazette of the Republic of Croatia, Nos. 53/91, 26/93, 29/94. Apart from a specified list of provisions from the Act on the Movement and Stay of Foreigners, including provisions 31–38 on refugees, the Act is no longer in force from 1 January 2004, as the date of the implementation of the Act on Foreigners.

[58] Official Gazette of the Republic of Croatia No. 103/03. By coming into force of the Asylum Act, all provisions on refugees from the Act on the Movement and Stay of Foreigners will no longer be valid.

seeker. Fingerprinting is performed by taking prints of all ten fingers and both palms. With the coming into force of the new Asylum Act, an improved system will start to operate whereby fingerprints and palm prints could be sent to the central database, thus making the system compatible with Eurodac.

3.3 What major changes, if any, will the implementation of the amended proposal for a directive on minimum standards on procedures in Member States for granting and withdrawing refugee status, on which the Council has reached political agreement on most points in June 2003, bring for the legislation and practice in your country in particular relating to:
- **rights of applicants in the procedure;**
- **administrative and judicial appeal procedures;**
- **the use of safe third country and safe country of origin concepts;**
- **detainment of asylum seekers;**
- **airport and border procedures?**

According to the currently valid Act on the Movement and Stay of Foreigners, a third country national who has left the country of his/her citizenship, or the country in which he/she had been permanently residing as a stateless person, in order to flee from persecution on the grounds of his/her political opinions, or national, racial or religious origin, may be granted refugee status in Croatia.[59] The third country national is required to submit an application to the competent body immediately upon arrival to Croatia. Unless food and accommodation have been provided otherwise, the third country national will be accommodated in the reception centre for foreigners until the procedure has been completed.[60] Upon receiving the opinion of the Ministry of Labour and Social Welfare, the Ministry of the Interior will reach a positive or a negative decision on the asylum application.[61] The asylum seeker is not entitled to an appeal, but can initiate a dispute before the Administrative Court of the Republic of Croatia.

With the coming into force of the new Asylum Act, the procedure is going to change. The asylum application will be submitted to the Reception Centre for Asylum Seekers, while the asylum seeker will have the right to declare his/her intention to apply for asylum upon border control at a border crossing or at a police station. A third country national who has expressed his/her intention to apply for asylum will then be directed to the Reception Centre for Asylum Seekers, where he/she will be entitled to

[59] Article 31 of the Act on the Movement and Stay of Foreigners.
[60] Article 32 of the Act on the Movement and Stay of Foreigners.
[61] Article 35 of the Act on the Movement and Stay of Foreigners.

stay until the completion of the procedure.[62] In cases where the asylum seeker is an unaccompanied minor, the asylum application shall be processed in the shortest possible period.[63] The new Asylum Act prescribes a three-instance procedure. The Ministry of Interior reaches a decision on the asylum application. An appeal, postponing the Ministry's decision, may be submitted to the Commission of the Government of the Republic of Croatia for Processing Appeals by Asylum Seekers. Finally, an administrative dispute against the Commission's decision, which does not postpone its enforcement, may be initiated before the Administrative Court of the Republic of Croatia.[64]

The currently valid Act on the Movement and Stay of Foreigners does not apply the concepts of a "safe third country" and "safe country of origin". However, the new Asylum Act will use the concept of a "safe third country". According to the Asylum Act, a safe third country is a country in which a foreigner stayed prior to his/her arrival in Croatia provided that in this country he/she has been safe from persecution or violation of human rights on the grounds listed in the Act; the country abides by international principles with regard to the protection of refugees as listed in the Geneva Convention and the Protocol; the foreigner may legally return to this country and seek asylum without fear of deportation to a country where his/her life, safety or freedom would be jeopardised. The Government of the Republic of Croatia will publish a list of safe third countries in the Official Gazette of the Republic of Croatia.[65] The Asylum Act does not contain the concept of a "safe country of origin", but of "country of origin", which is the country of the foreigner's citizenship, or the country in which a stateless person had his/her previous residence. If a foreigner is a citizen of more than one country, the country of origin is each of the countries of citizenship.[66]

3.4 What measures have been undertaken to implement Directive 2003/9 of 27 January 2003, on reception of asylum seekers in your country relating to:
- **the flexibility clauses in the Directive;**
- **restriction of free movement;**
- **access to the labour market;**
- **rights of migrant workers under Article 11 § 2 of the Directive?**

According to Article 20 of the new Asylum Act, coming into force on 1 July 2004, asylum seekers will be entitled to residence, sufficient

[62] Article 8 of the Asylum Act.
[63] Article 15 of the Asylum Act.
[64] Article 6 of the Asylum Act.
[65] Article 2 of the Asylum Act.
[66] Article 2 of the Asylum Act.

resources for subsistence and accommodation, sickness insurance, primary schooling, financial assistance, access to courts and legal aid, humanitarian aid, religious beliefs and religious education of their children. The rights will be valid until the termination of the procedure concerning the asylum application. These rights are narrower in scope than the ones listed under Council Directive 2003/9/EC laying down minimum standards for the reception of asylum seekers. Apart from the rights listed by the Croatian Asylum Act, the Directive also provides for the rights to schooling and education of minors[67] (unlike the Croatian Asylum Act granting the right to primary schooling only, which finishes at the age of fourteen), employment and vocational training.[68] The reasons given by the Croatian authorities for not granting the right to education to minor asylum seekers and the right to access the labour market at this stage have been the need for a specific type of education for minor asylum seekers and the high unemployment rate in Croatia.

According to Article 22 of the Croatian Asylum Act, asylum seekers are accommodated in the reception centre during the procedure for granting/withdrawing asylum status. They are not allowed to leave the territory of the Republic of Croatia during the procedure and their free movement within the territory of Croatia can be restricted.[69] Both provisions fully comply with Articles 7 and 14 of the Council Directive.

3.5 What steps have been undertaken to implement the Directive on temporary protection, COM 2001, 55 in national law? Are there any procedures for burden sharing arrangements? Is there a legal basis for the admission of refugees for the purposes of receiving temporary protection in a mass-movement situation?

Temporary protection is stipulated by Articles 56–65 of the Croatian Asylum Act, coming into force on 1 July 2004. Provisions of the Act generally comply with the wording of Council Directive 2001/55/EC on minimum standards for giving temporary protection in the event of a mass influx of displaced persons and on measures promoting a balance of efforts between Member States in receiving such persons and bearing the consequences thereof. According to the Asylum Act, temporary protection is approved to persons coming to Croatia from a country in which, due to war or similar situation, violence or internal conflicts, there is a violation of human rights, in case such persons cannot be protected by their country of origin. Temporary protection is provided by the Ministry

[67] According to the Directive, minors are person below the age of 18 (see the definition of "unaccompanied minors" in Article 2(h) of the Directive).

[68] Articles 10, 11 and 12 of the Directive.

[69] Article 21 of the Asylum Act.

of Interior for a period of six months and can be extended for periods of six months, but altogether cannot be longer than three years.[70] The Government of the Republic of Croatia decides upon the need of providing temporary protection and, based on economic and other abilities of Croatia and reasons of national security, public policy, peace and similar reasons, determines the number of persons that will be provided temporary protection and the reasons for not extending that number.

3.6 The Council has reached political agreement on the principles for a Directive on minimum standards for the qualification and status of third country nationals as refugees or persons who otherwise need international protection, COM 2001, 510 final (see Council documents of June 2003). What measures are envisaged to implement the Directive, once it is adopted, in your country relating to:
- **the definition of refugee;**
- **the definition of persons entitled to subsidiary protection;**
- **status of persons entitled to subsidiary protection;**
- **the issue of internal flight alternative as defined by the Directive;**
- **exclusion clauses, particularly issues of terrorism?**

To what extent are the refugee policies as reflected in the law and jurisprudence of your country in accordance with the proposal for the directive?

The definition of refugees provided by the Croatian Asylum Act complies with the definition prescribed by the Proposal for a Council Directive on minimum standards for the qualification and status of third country nationals as refugees or persons who otherwise need international protection.[71] However, the Asylum Act does not distinguish refugees from persons entitled to subsidiary protection as a separate category of third country nationals entitled to international protection.

PART IV TERMINATION OF ILLEGAL RESIDENCE, RETURN AND REPATRIATION

4.1 How many third country nationals without a valid residence permit are currently, according to estimates, staying in your country? How many deportations have actually been made in previous years? Is the whole enforcement process considered as acceptable?

The number of third country nationals staying illegally in Croatia amounted to 4060 in 2002, and to 1566 in the first six months of 2003.

[70] The duration of temporary protection provided by the Croatian Asylum Act is different from the one stipulated by Article 4(1) of the Council Directive stating that "the duration of temporary protection shall be one year" and "may be extended automatically by six monthly periods for a maximum of one year".

[71] COM (2001) 510 final.

4.2 What has been undertaken to implement the Directive of 28 November 2002, dealing with the facilitation of unauthorized entry, transit and residence?

and

4.4 What efforts have been undertaken in your country regarding the Budapest June 2003 recommendations concerning the harmonization of penalty scales with regard to the crime of the smuggling of migrants and trafficking of persons, in line with Council Directive 2002/90 of 28th November 2002? Did your country sign the relevant UN protocols on the smuggling of migrants?

Croatia is a party to the UN Convention against Transnational Organised Crime and its two Protocols (the Protocol to Prevent, Suppress and Punish Trafficking in Persons, Especially Women and Children, and the Protocol against the Smuggling of Migrants by Land, Sea and Air), as well as to the UN Convention on Eliminating All Forms of Discrimination against Women (CEDAW) and its Optional Protocol. The amendments to the Croatian Criminal Code,[72] which came into effect on 1 December 2003, introduced provisions on trafficking in persons into the Croatian legal system, in accordance with Article 3 of the Protocol to Prevent, Suppress and Punish Trafficking in Persons, Especially Women and Children. They generally comply with Council Directive 2002/90/EC defining facilitation of unauthorised entry, transit and residence. Article 175 of the amended Criminal Code, entitled "Trafficking in Persons and Establishment of Slavery", states that trafficking in persons means the "recruitment, transportation, transfer, purchase, sale, harbouring or receipt of persons by various forms of coercion, fraud or abuse of power with a view to exploitation either through forced labour or sexual exploitation, servitude, begging or the unauthorised removal of organs". According to the Act, such a person will be sentenced to one to ten years of imprisonment. Trafficking in children, trafficking committed within an organised group, or affecting a wider number of persons, or trafficking causing the death of one or more persons, is considered a more serious form of the same criminal act and, therefore, results in a more severe sentence.

4.3 How many illegal applicants have been apprehended at or near the border? How many criminal procedures for human trafficking have been instituted in the last year?

Charges against 5415 persons were brought in 2002, and against 1605 persons in the first six months of 2003, under Article 3 (Evasion of border

[72] Official Gazette of the Republic of Croatia No. 111/03.

control) and Article 5 (Border crossing outside the designated place and time, i.e. illegal border crossing) of the previously valid State Border Protection Act.[73] In comparison to previous years, the data indicate a decline in illegal immigration, which can be attributed to the post-war stabilisation of the whole region.

4.5 What measures have been taken to implement the Council Directive of 28 May 2001, on the mutual recognition of decisions on the expulsion of third country nationals? What, if any shortcomings or gaps of the Directive should be corrected in a further directive on cooperation on expulsion or deportation of third country nationals?

Croatia is not an EU Member State.

4.6 Do readmission agreements or other international treaties or arrangements with the aim of controlling and curbing illegal immigration and facilitating return exist in your country? Have they functioned satisfactorily?

The Republic of Croatia has signed readmission agreements with the following EU Member States: Austria, Benelux countries, France, Greece, Italy and Sweden. Negotiations with Denmark, Finland and Spain are on the way. The Member States with whom Croatia has not yet started negotiations on readmission agreements are Germany,[74] Ireland, Portugal and the UK. Croatia has signed readmission agreements with the following accession countries: Czech Republic, Estonia, Hungary, Latvia, Lithuania, Poland, Slovakia and Slovenia. Readmission agreements are currently being negotiated with Cyprus, Slovenia (a new agreement according to EU standards in order to replace the existing agreement) and Turkey. Additionally, readmission agreements have been signed with Albania, Bulgaria, Bosnia and Herzegovina, Iceland, Macedonia, Romania, Serbia and Montenegro[75] and Switzerland. Since illegal migration is moving from the east to the west, and the readmission agreement with Serbia and Montenegro is not yet in force, the best readmission cooperation has been

[73] Official Gazette of the Republic of Croatia No. 34/95. The Act became invalid with the coming into force of the new State Border Protection Act (Official Gazette of the Republic of Croatia No. 173/03), which came into force in November 2003. Under the new State Border Protection Act, the provision of evasion of border control is now stipulated by Article 26(1) of the Act and the provision on border crossing outside the designated place and time by Article 8(2) of the Act.

[74] However, on 25 April 1994 Croatian and German Governments signed the Agreement on the Readmission of Returnees and its implementing protocol. The agreement was joined in August 2001 by Luxembourg and the Netherlands.

[75] The readmission agreement with Serbia and Montenegro was signed in April 2002, but is still not in force since it has not been ratified by the Parliaments of Serbia and Montenegro.

exercised with Bosnia and Herzegovina and Slovenia. 1035 third country nationals were returned to Bosnia and Herzegovina in 2002 and 448 in the first six months of 2003. Under the readmission agreement with Slovenia, 1830 third country nationals were returned to Croatia in 2002 and 565 in the first six months of 2003.

4.7 To what extent have EU-standards and recommendations influenced your country's return policy? Have efforts been undertaken to cooperate with other EU Member States in enforcing return decisions by common deportation actions, exchange of information, facilitation of air and land transit, common principles on flight security, etc.?

The most important mode of return policy in Croatia is based on readmission agreements, if there is one existing with the country the illegal immigrant came from. The other mode of return policy is deportation to the country of origin. In 2002, 1025 persons were returned to their countries of origin, and in the first six months of 2003 the number amounted to 234. In case the illegal migrant does not leave the territory of the Republic of Croatia voluntarily, he/she will be deported (compulsory return).[76] The illegal migrant will be accommodated in the Reception Centre for Foreigners pending his/her deportation.[77] The illegal immigrant may not be deported to a country where his/her life or freedom might be endangered due to his/her race, religious or national origin, belonging to a special social group, or due to political beliefs, or where he/she could be exposed to torture, inhuman or degrading treatment or punishment.[78] Return is preferably performed in cooperation with the Mission of International Organisation for Migration in Zagreb. If possible, illegal immigrants are deported without a police escort to their country of origin. However, if required, due to security reasons, a police escort is provided.

[76] Article 56(1) of the Act on Foreigners.
[77] Article 58(2) of the Act on Foreigners.
[78] Article 57(1) of the Act on Foreigners.

DENMARK

JENS VEDSTED-HANSEN
University of Aarhus Law School

01 SPECIFIC ASPECTS RELATING TO EU MIGRATION AND ASYLUM LAW IN THE DOMESTIC LEGAL ORDER

As an introduction to the more detailed presentation on the impact of the EU harmonisation of migration and asylum law on Danish law and policy, and in particular the varying degrees of transposition of the EC directives on migration and asylum in the domestic legal order, it is necessary to outline the special features relating to Denmark's participation in the EU harmonisation process within this area of legislation and, consequently, the status of certain legislative acts in the domestic legal order. As it will be known, Denmark has a special arrangement with regard to EU legislation under TEC Title IV, according to the Protocol on the position of Denmark, adopted by the 1997 Amsterdam Treaty and annexed to the TEU and the TEC.[1]

Referring to the 1992 Edinburgh Decision of the European Council concerning certain problems raised by Denmark on the Treaty on European Union, Article 1 of the Protocol provides that Denmark shall not take part in the adoption by the Council of proposed measures pursuant to Title IV of the TEC. According to Article 2, none of the provisions of Title IV of the TEC, no measure adopted pursuant to that Title, no provision of any international agreement concluded by the Community pursuant to that Title, and no decision of the Court of Justice interpreting any such provision or measure shall be binding upon or applicable in Denmark. That Article further provides that no such provision, measure or decision shall in any way affect the competences, rights and obligations of Denmark, and no such provision, measure or decision shall in any way affect the acquis communautaire nor form part of Community law as they apply to Denmark. These exemptions, however, do not apply to measures determining the third countries whose nationals must be in

[1] Protocol (5) on the position of Denmark, annexed to the TEU and the TEC pursuant to the Treaty of Amsterdam Amending the Treaty on European Union, the Treaties Establishing the European Communities and Related Acts (OJ 1997, C 340).

possession of a visa when crossing the external borders of the Member States, or measures relating to a uniform format for visas, cf. Article 4 of the Protocol.

In further modification of Denmark's exemption from participating in the EU harmonisation of asylum and immigration legislation, Article 5 of the Protocol sets up a special procedure relating to the development of the Schengen acquis within the First Pillar cooperation under TEC Title IV. Under this procedure, Denmark shall decide within a period of 6 months after the Council has decided on a proposal or initiative to build upon the Schengen acquis under the provisions of Title IV of the TEC, whether it will implement this decision in its national law. If it decides to do so, this decision will create an obligation under international law between Denmark and the other Member States referred to in Article 1 of the Protocol integrating the Schengen acquis into the framework of the European Union[2] as well as Ireland or the United Kingdom if those Member States take part in the areas of cooperation in question. If Denmark decides not to implement such a Council decision, the other Member States will consider appropriate measures to be taken.[3]

As will be illustrated in the following parts of this report, the special position under the 1997 Protocol does not imply that Denmark generally fails to implement EU harmonisation measures within the field of migration and asylum. Experience from previous years suggests that Danish implementation of such legislative measures depends on a combination of legal and political considerations.

First, Denmark can be expected to adjust its domestic legislation so as to keep it in conformity with those legislative measures which are a development of the Schengen acquis under TEC Title IV. This results from the

[2] Protocol (2) integrating the Schengen *acquis* into the framework of the European Union, annexed to the TEU and the TEC pursuant to the Treaty of Amsterdam Amending the Treaty on European Union, the Treaties Establishing the European Communities and Related Acts (OJ 1997 C 340). Article 3 of this Protocol can be considered a kind of *stand-still clause* regarding Denmark's position under the Schengen rules: Following the Council's determination according to Article 2(1) of the legal basis for each of the provisions or decisions which constitute the Schengen *acquis*, Denmark shall maintain the same rights and obligations in relation to the other signatories to the Schengen agreements, as before the said determination with regard to those parts of the Schengen *acquis* that are determined to have a legal basis in Title IV of the TEC. With regard to those parts of the Schengen *acquis* that are determined to have a legal basis in Title VI of the TEU, Denmark shall continue to have the same rights and obligations as the other signatories to the Schengen agreements.

[3] Cf. Article 5 (2) of the Protocol on the position of Denmark.

fact that in this area of harmonisation Denmark is indirectly bound under the aforementioned Article 5 of the 1997 Protocol to enter into intergovernmental agreements adhering to the EC legislative measures adopted, and to align domestic legislation to these measures notwithstanding the formal Danish "reservation" against this First Pillar cooperation. Second, Denmark is likely to adjust domestic legislation if this appears necessary in order to conclude intergovernmental parallel agreements associating Denmark with other legislative measures under TEC Title IV which are considered as being of vital interest to the country.[4] Third, there may be some areas of harmonisation where it is considered appropriate, for purely political reasons, to amend Danish legislation in accordance with general EU developments, either because more restrictive domestic rules could be seen as incompatible with perceived state interests, for instance regarding labour market policies, or because EU legislative tendencies can be invoked as a pressure or a legitimisation for restricting Danish domestic law.[5]

1 ENTRY, VISA REGIME AND BORDER CONTROL

1.1 What national authorities are competent to deal with visa applications (Schengen visas and long-term visas)? Are there any procedures to avoid duplication or successive visa applications at different EU-consulates? On what substantive criteria, other than the Schengen minimum requirements, are visas granted or refused? How many visas have been issued or refused?

First instance decisions under the Aliens Act relating to third country nationals are normally taken by the Danish Immigration Service.[6] Refusal of entry at the border can be decided by the police, provided that the alien is not seeking asylum.[7] For asylum seekers, decisions on refusal of entry, transfer or retransfer under the Dublin Convention, and the

[4] For instance, the Danish government has informed the Parliament of its intention to forward a Draft Bill amending the Aliens Act in order to allow for Danish association, on an intergovernmental basis, to the Eurodac and the Dublin II Regulations, cf. below at 3.1-2.

[5] Cf. R. Byrne, G. Noll and J. Vedsted-Hansen, *Understanding Refugee Law in an Enlarged European Union*, IIIS Discussion Paper No. 11, IIIS, Trinity College, Dublin 2003, pp. 14–15, for an analysis of such legitimacy-creating mechanisms in domestic policy-making.

[6] Cf. Section 46 (1) of the Aliens Act, Consolidation Act No. 685 of 24 July 2003. Pursuant to Section 47, Danish diplomatic and consular representations abroad can be authorised to issue visas and residence permits. Similar authorisation may, by agreement with the Ministry of Foreign Affairs, be given to other states' diplomatic and consular representations abroad.

[7] Section 48 of the Aliens Act.

subsequent decision to deport the alien without substantive examination of the asylum application must be taken by the Danish Immigration Service.[8]

Appeal against these decisions of the Danish Immigration Service and the police can be lodged with the Ministry of Refugee, Immigration and Integration Affairs.[9] Such an appeal does not suspend the enforcement of the refusal of entry or the deportation.[10] Under certain circumstances, appeal to the Ministry of Refugee, Immigration and Integration Affairs against negative Immigration Service decisions concerning the issue of residence permits (long-term visas) carries suspensive effect.[11] In narrowly specified types of cases, the Ministry's decision on the appeal can be brought before the courts under a special facilitated procedure allowing for full judicial review.[12]

Following Danish accession to the 1990 Schengen Convention in December 1996, the Aliens Act was amended in order to secure implementation of the Convention.[13] The most important elements of the initial implementing legislation concern: free travel for third country nationals holding a visa or residence permit for another Schengen state;[14] rejection at the border;[15] revocation of residence permits;[16] and the exchange of information with relevant authorities under the Schengen Convention.[17] Decisions to enter an alert into the Schengen Information System for the purpose of refusal of entry of a third country national are taken by the National Police Commissioner,[18] while consultations under Article 25 of the Schengen Convention are conducted by the Danish Immigration Service.[19]

[8] Section 48 a (1) of the Aliens Act.

[9] Section 46 (2) of the Aliens Act. As an important exception, appeals against substantive decisions on asylum applications shall be lodged to the Refugee Appeals Board, cf. Section 53 a.

[10] Sections 48 and 48 d of the Aliens Act.

[11] Section 33 (3) of the Aliens Act.

[12] Section 52 (1) (i)–(iv) of the Aliens Act.

[13] Act No. 410 of 10 June 1997 amending the Aliens Act. The Schengen-related parts of the Amendment Act entered into force on 25 March 2001 pursuant to Ministry of Interior Regulation No. 170 of 13 March 2001.

[14] Section 2 b of the Aliens Act.

[15] Section 28 (1) (vi)–(vii) and Section 28 (2), (3) and (6) of the Aliens Act.

[16] Section 19 (3) of the Aliens Act. Section 19 (4) was adopted in 2002 in order to implement Directive 2001/40/EC, cf. below at 4.2.

[17] Section 58 b (2), Section 58 d, and Sections 58 g–h of the Aliens Act.

[18] Section 58 g of the Aliens Act.

[19] Section 58 h of the Aliens Act.

According to Article 4 of the 1997 Protocol on the position of Denmark, as outlined in the introduction, the exemptions under this Protocol shall not apply to measures determining the third countries whose nationals must be in possession of a visa when crossing the external borders of the Member States, or measures relating to a uniform format for visas. Hence, Denmark participates fully in EU harmonisation on these elements of visa policies pursuant to TEC Article 62 (2) (b) (i + iii).[20] Moreover, the EC Visa Regulation is being implemented with direct effect in Danish law.[21]

As regards free travel within the Schengen area, aliens holding a residence permit for another Schengen country may enter and stay in Denmark for up to 3 months per 6-month period reckoned from the date of their first entry into Denmark or another Schengen country other than the state which issued the residence permit. Aliens holding a visa valid for all Schengen countries may enter and stay in Denmark within the period of validity of the visa, provided that the duration of a continuous stay or the total duration of several consecutive stays in Denmark does not exceed 3 months per 6-month period from the date of first entry into the Schengen area.[22]

The substantive criteria for granting visa vary, depending on the applicant's country of nationality. In addition to the general criteria (that the applicant poses no security risk, has the necessary economic means, and that there is no alert in the Schengen Information System), the application will be considered under more or less restrictive criteria based on a four-group division of the states whose citizens are required to have a visa. The overriding consideration of this division appears to be the likelihood that applicants might intend to seek permanent or long-term residence in Denmark, not least by way of lodging an asylum claim upon arrival.

[20] It might nonetheless be questioned whether Article 4 of the Protocol allows for Danish participation in visa policies with regard to countries whose nationals are *exempt* from visa requirement, cf. TEC Article 62 (2) (b) (i) *in fine*. Cf. K. U. Kjær, "How Many Borders in the EU?", in E. Guild & P. Minderhoud (eds.), *In Search of Europe's Borders*, Kluwer Law International 2002, p. 179.

[21] Council Regulation (EC) No. 539/2001 of 15 March 2001 listing the third countries whose nationals must be in possession of visas when crossing the external borders and those whose nationals are exempt from that requirement (OJ 2001, L 81/1), amended by Council Regulation (EC) No. 2414/2001 of 7 December 2001 (OJ 2001, L 327/1), and by Council Regulation (EC) No. 453/2003 of 6 March 2003 (OJ 2003, L 69/10).

[22] Section 2 b (1)–(2) of the Aliens Act. Section 2 b (3)–(4) regulates the entry, stay and transit of aliens pursuant to Articles 18 and 5 (3) of the Schengen Convention.

As every application is to be examined individually, the division of the visa-required countries provides only general guidance. Nonetheless, as a general rule, the following criteria apply:

> **Group 1** is the so-called asylum group, which presently consists of citizens from Afghanistan, Algeria, Armenia, Bosnia-Herzegovina, Eritrea, Ethiopia, Gambia, Ghana, India, Iran, Iraq, Lebanon, Pakistan, Serbia and Montenegro, Syria, Sierra Leone, Somalia, Sri Lanka, Sudan, Uganda and Yemen as well as stateless Palestinians.
>
> As a rule, visas for citizens of these countries are only granted to spouses, underage children and parents.
>
> Iraqi and Somali citizens are only eligible for visas in extraordinary circumstances, for example if a family member living in Denmark has a life-threatening illness or has died.
>
> Stateless individuals other than stateless Palestinians are evaluated with respect to the country where they permanently reside.
>
> **Group 2** is the so-called immigration group, which presently consists of citizens from Albania, Bangladesh, Benin, the Ivory Coast, Jordan, Kenya, China, Macedonia, Morrocco, Niger, Rwanda, Tunisia, Turkey, Togo and Vietnam.
>
> As a rule, visas for citizens of these countries are only granted to spouses, children, siblings and parents.
>
> **Group 3** consists of citizens from Azerbaijan, Belarus, Burundi, Congo, Egypt, Georgia, Libya, Moldova, Mongolia, Nigeria, Russia, Tanzania, Thailand and Ukraine.
>
> As a rule, citizens of these countries are eligible to receive a visa if they can demonstrate a connection to an individual living in Denmark. Visas are not granted to citizens of these countries for tourist visits.
>
> **Group 4** consists of citizens from all other visa-requisite countries. Citizens from these countries are generally eligible to receive a visa for any variety of reasons, including tourist visits.[23]

In statistical terms, Danish visa issuance practices can be illustrated as follows:[24]

[23] Danish Immigration Service, Fact sheet on visa (http://www.udlst.dk/english/Visa/Default.htm, 22 February 2004).

[24] Danish Immigration Service, Statistical Overview 2002 (http://www.udlst.dk/english/Statistics/statistical_overview_2002.htm, 17 February 2004).

	Positive decisions	Negative decisions
1994	16.880	8.049
1995	21.786	6.145
1996	20.157	6.719
1997	20.767	7.689
1998	17.357	7.586
1999	17.288	8.340
2000	20.083	7.957
2001	16.986	10.723
2002	14.084	9.182

1.2 Is there a visa tracking procedure in order to identify visa overstayers? What data are collected from visa-applicants (fingerprints)? Admissibility of visa data to alien and police authorities?

No formal visa tracking procedure is known to exist in Denmark. The information submitted by visa applicants will normally be accessible to both the alien authorities (Danish Immigration Service and, if an appeal was lodged, the Ministry of Refugee, Immigration and Integration Affairs) and the police authorities.

1.3 Have courts ever decided on the refusal of a Schengen visa based upon Schengen blacklisting by other Member States?

There is no information available about court decisions on the refusal of Schengen visas, and it is hardly probable that such judicial review has ever been attempted.

1.4 What measures have been undertaken in the implementation of the action programme for administrative cooperation in the field of external borders, visa, asylum and immigration following the Council Decision of 13 June 2002?

In accordance with Article 5 of the 1997 Protocol, Denmark has decided to implement the action programme under this decision.[25] However, as such implementation requires administrative cooperation, and legislative measures are unnecessary, no concrete information about the measures undertaken to this effect is publicly available.

[25] Cf. survey of existing EU rules on asylum and immigration adopted since the entry into force of the Amsterdam Treaty on 1 May 1999, which are subject to the Danish reservation relating to Justice and Home Affairs (Annex 1 to Note of 5 December 2003 to the Europe Committee of the Danish Parliament from the Ministry of Foreign Affairs, the Ministry of Justice and the Ministry of Refugee, Immigration and Integration Affairs).

1.5 What measures have been undertaken to implement the Directive 2001/51 EC supplementing the Schengen rules concerning carrier sanctions? How often have carrier sanctions been used?

No particular measures have been taken or proposed in order to implement the Directive concerning carrier sanctions.[26] As this Directive builds upon the Schengen acquis, Denmark was required to decide whether it will implement this legislative measure in its domestic law: it decided to do so. However, the Danish government considers the existing carrier sanctions legislation compatible with the provisions of the Directive, and therefore has found no need for formal transposition measures.[27]

The assessment of compatibility between domestic legislation and the requirements of the Directive is based on the following provision in Section 59 a of the Aliens Act:

> (1) Any person that brings to Denmark an alien who upon his entry is not in possession of the requisite travel document and visa, cf. section 39, is liable to a fine.
> (2) The provision of subsection (1) does not apply on entry from a Schengen country.

In considering formal transposition unnecessary, the government has presumably found the level of fines under Section 59 a to live up to the minimum requirements in the Directive. Given that only very little court practice under this provision has been published it is difficult to verify this assessment. In any event, it will be possible for the prosecutor in future carrier liability cases to utilise the Directive as a reference in support of maintaining the required level of fines.

In addition to a few court decisions on carrier sanctions it is likely that a considerable number of administrative fines have been issued to air carriers without being submitted to judicial proceedings.

2 ADMISSION AND RESIDENCE OF THIRD COUNTRY NATIONALS

2.1 What are the basic principles in your country concerning:
- **admission of third country nationals for labour purposes or self-employed activities;**
- **admission of third country nationals for study and vocational training;**

[26] Directive 2001/51/EC of 28 June 2001 (OJ 2001, L 187/45).

[27] Cf. survey of existing EU rules on asylum and immigration (note 25).

- **legal status of third country nationals in possession of a long-term residence permit of another Member State?**
- **To what extent do these principles differ from the European Commission's proposals?**

2.2 What are the legal requirements and procedures for obtaining a residence permit for third country nationals for the purpose of employment? Which procedures are used in maintaining the preferred access of EU-citizens and Turkish nationals (association agreement) to the labour market? Do special programmes exist for highly qualified professionals facilitating access to the labour market? To what extent are trade unions and employers involved in such programmes? Is there a procedure to calculate the demand for foreign labour? How is the EU-enlargement taken into consideration? To what extent has the recent economic recession and unemployment influenced the concepts on admission of third country nationals?

2.3 To what extent do existing national laws and practices differ substantially from the approach taken in the Commission's Proposal on admission for the purpose of paid employment and self-employed activities relating to:
- **admission of third country nationals for study and vocational training;**
- **on legal status of third country nationals in possession of a long-term residence permit of another Member State?**
- **To what extent do these principles differ from the European Commission's proposals?**

Even while Denmark has, as a point of departure, a policy of non-immigration for third country nationals, there are significant exemptions from this main rule. Hence, a residence permit may be issued to an alien if essential employment or business considerations make it appropriate, in particular if the applicant can obtain employment within a professional field short of specially qualified labour.[28] Under this rule the so-called job-card scheme has been introduced with a view to facilitating access to the Danish labour market for certain groups of highly qualified professionals, in particular within the IT sector and research-based sectors of the industry such as medico-science companies. This scheme has streamlined the procedure for issuing residence and work permits, so that the Danish Immigration Service is not bound to consult with the relevant trade unions or other labour market organisations, as is normally the case.[29] Due to the increase in unemployment for Danes with relevant qualifications that has occurred within some of these sectors of the labour market, however, criticism has been voiced against too liberal practices under this

[28] Section 9 a of the Aliens Act. Transitional rules relating to the EU enlargement on 1 May 2004 have been proposed by the Minister's Draft Bill No. L 157 of 6 February 2004.

[29] Draft Bill No. L 152 of 28 February 2002, Minister for Refugee, Immigration and Integration Affairs, pp. 35–37 and pp. 61–62.

scheme, and the procedures and the criteria for issuing job-cards seem to have been partly restricted within certain sectors.

The issuance of residence permits for the purpose of study and vocational training is not expressly regulated by the Aliens Act, and the immigration authorities therefore have a considerable amount of discretion in these matters. Certain general criteria have been laid down in the Aliens Regulation, implying rather important liberalisation of admission practices for educational purposes, not least for students from the Central European countries.[30]

The issuance of work permits will raise no separate policy issue in cases concerning refugees and family members, because aliens holding a residence permit for the purpose of asylum or family reunification are among those who are exempt from the requirement of a work permit.[31] For aliens who are admitted to Denmark for the purpose of taking up employment or self-employment pursuant to the abovementioned Section 9 a of the Aliens Act, the same reasons as those favouring the grant of a residence permit imply that a work permit be issued automatically. Accordingly, these aliens are entitled to a work permit without the imposition of any further conditions.[32]

As regards the Directive's proposals on conditions of entry and residence for third country nationals for the purposes of paid employment and self-employed economic activities,[33] and of studies, vocational training or voluntary service,[34] these EU legislative measures are subject to the Danish reservation under the 1997 Protocol. According to the government's official assessment, amendments to domestic legislation will be necessary in the event that Denmark were to participate in these areas of EU harmonisation, assuming that the proposals in the Directive are adopted by the Council.[35]

[30] Sections 28–30 of the Aliens Regulation, Ministry of Refugee, Immigration and Integration Affairs Regulation No 581 of 10 July 2002.

[31] Cf. Section 14 (1) (i)–(vii) of the Aliens Act, enumerating such exemptions. Further exemptions have been laid down in Section 33 (1) and (2) of the Aliens Regulation.

[32] Section 34 (1) of the Aliens Regulation.

[33] Commission Proposal of 12 September 2001 for a Council Directive, COM (2001) 386 final.

[34] Commission Proposal of 7 October 2002 for a Council Directive, COM (2002) 548 final.

[35] Cf. survey of proposed EU legislative measures on asylum and immigration presently being negotiated, which are subject to the Danish reservation relating to Justice and Home Affairs (Annex 2 to Note of 5 December 2003 to the Europe Committee of the Danish Parliament from the Ministry of Foreign Affairs, the Ministry of Justice and the Ministry of Refugee, Immigration and Integration Affairs).

2.5 Concerning the proposal for a directive on the right to family reunion agreed upon by the Council in February 2003;
- **Do you consider the proposed standards below the principles of family reunification applicable in your country?**
- **Will the implementation of the Directive, once it is adopted, lead to changes in the national law on family reunification downgrading the standard of protection? If so, what changes are envisaged?**

The Directive on the right to family reunification[36] is subject to the Danish reservation under the 1997 Protocol. According to the government's official assessment, amendments of domestic legislation will be necessary in the event that Denmark were to participate in EU harmonisation within this policy area. Such amendments would, in particular, concern the minimum age required for issuing residence permits to a spouse, the waiting-period for resident aliens' access to reunification with a spouse, the affiliation requirement and certain parts of the economic requirements for family reunification with spouses.[37]

As a background to this assessment of the potential impact of the Directive, the existing Danish rules on family reunification will be summarised. The general conditions for the issuance of residence permits to family members are set up in Section 9 (1) of the Aliens Act, covering spouses, cohabiting partners, under-age children, and foster children etc:

> (1) Upon application, a residence permit will be issued to:
> (i) an alien over the age of 24 who cohabits at a shared residence, either in marriage or in regular cohabitation of prolonged duration, with a person permanently resident in Denmark over the age of 24 who:
> (a) is a Danish national;
> (b) is a national of one of the other Nordic countries;
> (c) is issued with a residence permit under section 7 or 8; or
> (d) has held a permanent residence permit for Denmark for more than the last 3 years,
> (ii) an unmarried, under-age child of a person permanently resident in Denmark or of that person's spouse, provided the child lives with the person having custody of it and has not started its own family through regular cohabitation, and provided the person permanently resident in Denmark:
> (a) is a Danish national;
> (b) is a national of one of the other Nordic countries;

[36] Council Directive 2003/86/EC of 22 September 2003 (OJ 2003, L 251/12).
[37] Cf. survey of existing EU rules on asylum and immigration (note 25 above).

(c) is issued with a residence permit under section 7 or 8; or
(d) is issued with a permanent residence permit or a residence permit for the purpose of permanent residence,

(iii) an under-age alien for the purpose of residence with a person permanently resident in Denmark other than the person having custody of it, provided the residence permit is issued for the purpose of adoption, residence as a result of a foster relationship or, if particular reasons make it appropriate, residence with the child's closest family, and provided the person permanently resident in Denmark:
(a) is a Danish national;
(b) is a national of one of the other Nordic countries;
(c) is issued with a residence permit under section 7 or 8; or
(d) is issued with a permanent residence permit or a residence permit for the purpose of permanent residence.

As a principal rule, the spouses' or the cohabitants' aggregate ties with Denmark must be stronger than their aggregate ties with another country.[38] Furthermore, a residence permit cannot be issued if it is considered doubtful that the marriage was contracted at both parties' desire, or if there are definite reasons for assuming that the decisive purpose of contracting the marriage was to obtain a residence permit.[39] In addition to these conditions regarding the family members' personal situation and relationship, the Aliens Act stipulates that certain conditions relating to housing must be fulfilled,[40] as well as a number of economic conditions. Most of these additional requirements are likely to be incompatible with the EC Directive on family reunification.

The 1992 Amendment of the Aliens Act introduced the possibility of imposing income requirements on spouses or partners being either Danish citizens, refugees, or settled immigrants, even though it was stipulated in the preparatory works that refugees and Danish citizens were susceptible to dispensation under liberal conditions. However, it caused administrative difficulty as well as political controversy that Danish citizens in a number of cases were prohibited from having their spouse live with them in their own country, due to insufficient income. The 1998 Amendment Act therefore exempted Danish citizens from the income

[38] Section 9 (7) of the Aliens Act. This provision was modified by Amendment Act No. 1204 of 27 December 2003.

[39] Section 9 (8) and (9) of the Aliens Act. The former provisions was restricted by Amendment Act No. 1204 of 27 December 2003.

[40] Section 9 (6) of the Aliens Act. The housing requirement has been specified in Ministry of Refugee, Immigration and Integration Affairs Regulation No. 579 of 10 July 2002.

requirement connected to reunion with spouses, while it could still be dispensed with for refugees under liberal criteria. However, the 2002 Amendment Act reintroduced the income requirement for Danish citizens.

Since the introduction of the income requirement for family reunification it has been understood – on the basis of the preparatory remarks accompanying the 1992 Amendment Act – that the income has to be above the level of social welfare assistance to which the members of the united family would otherwise be entitled. Hence, given that the spouses already earn more than this minimum, they will not be eligible for cash benefits under the ordinary social welfare legislation. In recent years, the income requirement has been specified in administrative rules.[41]

In each individual case, the municipality council must issue a statement to the Danish Immigration Service as to whether the person living in Denmark is able to maintain the applicant(s) for family reunion.[42] In the standard evaluation of the resident's ability to fulfil the maintenance requirement, the following primary sources of income are taken into account by the Danish Immigration Service, on the basis of the municipality's statement:

- wage or salary income;
- positive income earned from an independent business;
- public and private pension income;
- sick leave or maternity leave benefits, in certain cases.[43]

Additional restrictions adopted by the 2002 Amendment Act include the following economic requirements:

- the person resident in Denmark must provide an economic guarantee of 50,000 DKK to cover any future public expenses to support the spouse or partner;[44]
- the person resident in Denmark must not have received social welfare assistance for a period of one year prior to submission of the application for the spouse's residence permit, nor during the time it may take for the permit to be issued. For this purpose, welfare assistance is defined

[41] Ministry of Refugee, Immigration and Integration Affairs Regulation No. 580 of 10 July 2002 on the assessment of maintenance ability in family reunion cases.

[42] Section 9 (16) of the Aliens Act.

[43] Social welfare assistance paid out under the Act on Active Social Policy, or unemployment benefits as defined by the Law on Unemployment Assistance, are not considered adequate sources of income when assessing the maintenance ability of the spouse or partner already living in Denmark.

[44] Section 9 (4) of the Aliens Act.

as economic benefits paid out under the Integration Act or under the Act on Active Social Policy.[45]

2.6 The proposal for a directive on the rights of long-term third country nationals as agreed upon by the Council on 5 June 2003, provides for a number of rights approximating the situation of long-term residents to the status of EU-citizens. Will the implementation of the Directive involve major legal and policy changes in your country? What are the major points of concern if any, concerning the approximation concept of the directive relating to:
- **non-discrimination in social rights;**
- **the concept of "civic citizenship" (see also extended impact assessment on the Communication on Integration of June 11, 2003);**
- **family reunification and access of family members to the labour market;**
- **security of stay?**

As the Directive Proposal on the rights of long-term resident aliens[46] is subject to the Danish reservation under the 1997 Protocol, it will not be binding upon or applicable in Denmark, if adopted. According to the government's assessment, the proposed Directive would require amendment of domestic legislation, in case Denmark were to participate in this part of the EU harmonisation.[47]

According to Section 11 (1) of the Aliens Act, a residence permit may be issued for a limited period of time, the duration depending on the type and purpose of residence.[48] The principal rule on the issuance of permanent residence permits stipulates that the alien must have lived lawfully in Denmark for more than the last 7 years and has, throughout this period, been issued with a residence permit on the same basis.[49] The waiting period can be reduced to 5, or even 3 years, for aliens who are particularly well-integrated into the Danish society and labour market.[50] In case of non-compliance with either of these conditions, a permanent residence permit may be issued at an earlier point in time if essential considerations conclusively make it appropriate.[51]

In addition to these conditions regarding the period of residence and its legal basis, the issuance of a permanent residence permit depends

[45] Section 9 (5) of the Aliens Act.

[46] Proposal for a Council Directive concerning the status of third country nationals who are long-term residents, COM (2001) 127 final.

[47] Cf. survey of proposed EU legislative measures on asylum and immigration (note 35 above).

[48] Cf. Section 23 of the Aliens Regulation, laying down detailed rules on the duration of time-limited residence permits.

[49] Section 11 (3) of the Aliens Act.

[50] Section 11 (4)–(5) of the Aliens Act.

[51] Section 11 (6) of the Aliens Act.

on various conditions relating to the alien's general integration. These integration-related conditions were introduced by the 1998 Amendment Act[52] and expanded into a quite restrictive system in 2002:

- the alien having committed no serious crime within a specified period of time, and never having been sentenced to 2 years of imprisonment or more for any serious crime;[53]
- the completion of an introduction programme pursuant to the Integration Act, or a comparable course offered to the alien;
- the passing of a test in the Danish language;
- the alien having no overdue debts to public authorities.[54]

The most important impact of the issuance of a permanent residence permit is the significantly increased security of residence. While time-limited residence permits may be revoked, or renewal upon expiration may be refused, if any kind of change of circumstances might result in the non-compliance with the initial conditions of the permit,[55] aliens holding a permanent residence permit can only loose their residential rights if the residence permit was obtained by fraud, or in case of criminality, threat against national security or violation of public order.[56]

Traditionally, long-term or permanently resident third country nationals have been entitled to social welfare benefits on an equal footing with Danish citizens, even while an important exemption regarding the accrual of old-age pension rights has existed for decades. In recent years, however, rather significant exemptions from this equality tradition have been introduced, most notably the policy of reduced welfare benefits for newly arrived immigrants and refugees. Reduced cash benefits were first introduced in the 1998 Integration Act, but abolished after about a year due to the fact that the underlying labour-market assumptions appeared to fail. As part of the general restrictions on immigration and asylum in 2002, the policy of non-equality for aliens was reintroduced with an even larger differentiation between the levels of normal and reduced benefits,

[52] Cf. Ministry of Interior Regulation No. 1065 of 17 December 1999, specifying the requirements under the 1998 Amendment Act.

[53] Section 11 (7) (i)–(iii), Sections 11 (8) and 11 a of the Aliens Act.

[54] Section 11(9) (i)–(iii) of the Aliens Act. Not least the latter integration-related condition would seem incompatible with the Directive Proposal.

[55] Section 19 (1) (i)–(vii) of the Aliens Act.

[56] Section 19 (2) (i)–(iii), and Sections 22–26 of the Aliens Act. Cf. J. Vedsted-Hansen, "Abolition of Border Controls within the Nordic Region and Security of Residence in Denmark", in E. Guild & P. Minderhoud (eds.), *Security of Residence and Expulsion. Protection of Aliens in Europe*, Kluwer Law International 2001, pp. 99–101.

yet now in a less manifestly discriminatory manner because the reduction formally applies to aliens and Danish citizens alike. Under the present system the right to normal cash benefits is conditional on the applicant having stayed in Denmark for a total period of 7 years out of the most recent 8 years,[57] a condition that is evidently more readily met by Danish citizens than by aliens.

Further exemptions stem from the rules regarding expulsion on economic grounds. If a third country national who has not been lawfully staying in Denmark for the purpose of permanent residence during more than 7 years is found in need of long-term welfare benefits, it can be decided to expel the alien so that the country of origin takes care of his/her needs.[58]

3 ASYLUM AND REFUGEE LAW

3.1 Have the Dublin Rules worked satisfactorily and what is expected of the Dublin II Regulation No. 343, 2003 of 18 February 2003?

3.2 Has the Eurodac Regulation No. 2725/2000 of 11th December 2000, concerning the establishment of Eurodac for the comparison of fingerprints for an effective application of the Dublin Convention, operative since January 15, 2003, resulted in an increase of Dublin cases? Has Eurodac become effective in your country or is it expected to become effective eventually?

Apart from some dissatisfaction with the time-limits for processing requests for transfer or retransfer under the Dublin Convention, Denmark appears to have a clear interest in continuing its participation in the Dublin mechanism, as amended by the Regulation,[59] and to join the Eurodac system.[60] Hence, the Danish government has requested the Commission to enter into negotiations with a view to concluding parallel agreements that allow for Danish association, on an intergovernmental basis, to the

[57] Section 11 (3) and (5) of the Act on Active Social Policy, Consolidation Act No. 709 of 13 August 2003. The residence requirement does not apply to EU and EEA nationals, in so far as they are entitled to welfare benefits under EU law, cf. Section 11 (4). Hence, the requirement appears discriminatory against third country nationals, not least refugees, in violation of Article 23 of the Refugee Convention and possibly other non-discrimination rules in international law.

[58] Cf. Section 3 (4) of the Act on Active Social Policy. Section 3 (3) defines long-term benefits as assistance that has been, or is assumed likely to be, extended to more than 6 months. The possibility to expel on economic grounds was originally limited to the first 2 years of lawful residence, then to 3 years, and in 1998 and 2002 further extended.

[59] Council Regulation (EC) No. 343/2003 of 18 February 2003 (OJ 2003, L 50/1).

[60] Council Regulation (EC) No. 2725/2000 of 31 October 2000 (OJ 2000, L 316/1).

Eurodac and the Dublin II Regulations. Such agreements are necessary since these Regulations are not considered an expansion of the Schengen acquis, in which case Denmark would have been able to 'opt in' under Article 5 of 1997 Protocol.

The Commission was authorised by the Council on 8 May 2003, to negotiate such parallel agreements, and negotiations are currently taking place. In case of a positive outcome, the Danish government intends to forward a Draft Bill amending the Aliens Act as necessary in order to comply with the two Regulations.[61]

3.3 What major changes, if any, will the implementation of the amended proposal for a directive on minimum standards on procedures in Member States for granting and withdrawing refugee status, on which the Council has reached political agreement on most points in June 2003, bring for the legislation and practice in your country in particular relating to:
- **rights of applicants in the procedure;**
- **administrative and judicial appeal procedures;**
- **the use of safe third country and safe country of origin concepts;**
- **detainment of asylum seekers;**
- **airport and border procedures?**

As the Directive Proposal on minimum standards for asylum procedures[62] is subject to the Danish reservation under the 1997 Protocol, it will not be binding upon or applicable in Denmark, if adopted. According to the government's assessment, the proposed Directive would require amendment of domestic legislation, in case Denmark were to participate in this part of the EU harmonisation.[63] In particular, such amendments would seem necessary in respect of the appeal system, and possibly also the special procedure for manifestly unfounded applications for asylum.

Under the present Danish system, appeals concerning the determination of refugee status and the granting of asylum – as opposed to admissibility issues – can be brought before the Refugee Appeals Board, which is an administrative appeals body, although quasi-judicial in terms of procedure.[64] When examining concrete cases, the Refugee Appeals Board consists of the chairman and two other members, one of whom is appointed by the Minister of Refugee, Immigration and Integration

[61] Cf. the Prime Minister's statement to the Parliament, 7 October 2003, and survey of existing EU rules on asylum and immigration (note 25).

[62] Amended Proposal for a Council Directive on minimum standards on procedures in Member States for granting and withdrawing refugee status, COM (2002) 326 final.

[63] Cf. survey of proposed EU legislative measures on asylum and immigration (annex 35).

[64] Sections 53 a and 54–56 of the Aliens Act.

Affairs, and the other one is nominated by the General Council of the Bar.[65] Despite the administrative nature of the Refugee Appeals Board, its decisions can generally not be brought before the ordinary courts, due to a finality clause from which the Supreme Court has allowed exemption only in very extraordinary circumstances.[66] This is one of the points on which the existing appeal system is hardly compatible with the Directive Proposal.

A special accelerated procedure was established in Danish asylum law in 1986, in order to deal more expeditiously with manifestly unfounded applications. The concept of "manifestly unfounded" here refers to cases being examined on the merits, but in an accelerated procedure with no appeal.[67] Hence, the procedure for manifestly unfounded cases is fundamentally different from the admissibility procedure applied to "safe third country" cases, the latter being a formal one involving no substantive examination of the asylum application.[68]

3.4 What measures have been undertaken to implement Directive 2003/9 of 27 January 2003, on reception of asylum seekers in your country, relating to
- **the flexibility clauses in the Directive;**
- **restriction of free movement;**
- **access to the labour market;**
- **rights of migrant workers under Article 11 § 2 of the Directive?**

As the Directive on minimum standards for the reception of asylum seekers[69] is subject to the Danish reservation under the 1997 Protocol, it is not binding upon or applicable in Denmark. According to the government's assessment, the Directive would require amendment of domestic legislation, in case Denmark were to participate in this part of the EU harmonisation.[70] Such amendments would, in particular, concern access to the labour market and educational rights for adolescents. So far no measures have been taken to align domestic legislation to the standards of the Directive.

3.5 What steps have been undertaken to implement the Directive on temporary protection, COM 2001, 55 in national law? Are there any procedures for burden

[65] Section 53 (1) and (3) of the Aliens Act. The chairman and his deputies must be judges, cf. Section 53 (7).
[66] Section 56 (8) of the Aliens Act. [67] Section 53 b of the Aliens Act.
[68] Section 48 a of the Aliens Act, cf. above at 1.1.
[69] Council Directive 2003/9/EC of 27 January 2003 (OJ 2003, L 31/18).
[70] Cf. survey of existing EU rules on asylum and immigration (note 25).

sharing arrangements? Is there a legal basis for the admission of refugees for the purposes of receiving temporary protection in a mass-movement situation?

No measures have been taken to implement the Directive on minimum standards for giving temporary protection.[71] Formally, this is in line with the Danish reservation under the 1997 Protocol, as the Directive is not binding upon or applicable in Denmark. According to the government's assessment, the Directive would require amendment of domestic legislation, in case Denmark were to participate in this part of the EU harmonisation.[72] No legislative proposals are known to have been prepared with a view to Denmark's de facto implementation of the standards of the Directive.

The special legislation providing for temporary protection of Bosnian refugees was abolished in December 2002.[73] Special legislation on temporary protection of Kosovars is still in force, albeit in practice being phased out, cf. section 9 e of the Aliens Act. No general legislative reform concerning temporary protection or similar asylum schemes seems to be contemplated by the Danish government at present. Temporary protection became a policy issue in the mid-1990s, and a committee was asked to explore the issue against the background of the ad hoc legislation introduced in 1992 in order to provide for temporary protection of Bosnian refugees. However, these reform contemplations were suspended in 1998, in connection with the increasingly restrictive asylum and immigration policy then introduced, and in 1999 yet another ad hoc legislation was put in place relating to Kosovar refugees.

3.6 The Council has reached political agreement on the principles for a Directive on minimum standards for the qualification and status of third country nationals as refugees or persons who otherwise need international protection, COM 2001, 510 final (see Council documents of June 2003). What measures are envisaged to implement the Directive, once it is adopted, in your country relating to:
- **the definition of refugee;**
- **the definition of persons entitled to subsidiary protection;**
- **status of persons entitled to subsidiary protection;**
- **the issue of internal flight alternative as defined by the Directive;**
- **exclusion clauses, particularly issues of terrorism?**

[71] Council Directive 2001/55/EC of 20 July 2001 (OJ 2001, L 212/12).

[72] Cf. survey of existing EU rules on asylum and immigration (note 25).

[73] Act No. 1044 of 17 December 2002, abolishing the Act on Temporary Residence Permits for Certain Persons from Former Yugoslavia etc.

To what extent are the refugee policies as reflected in the law and jurisprudence of your country in accordance with the proposal for the directive?

As the Directive Proposal on the qualification and status of refugees and persons in need of subsidiary protection[74] is subject to the Danish reservation under the 1997 Protocol, it will not be binding upon or applicable in Denmark, if adopted. According to the government's assessment, the proposed Directive would not require amendment of domestic legislation, in case Denmark were to participate in this part of the EU harmonisation.[75] While this may well hold true for the interpretation of the 1951 Refugee Convention definition of refugees, it may be questionable in respect of subsidiary protection, as the existing Danish provision on this issue does not seem to comply fully with the proposed definition of serious harm, for the purpose of granting subsidiary protection, in Article 15 of the Directive Proposal.

Pursuant to Section 7 (2) of the Aliens Act, protection outside the scope of the 1951 Refugee Convention can be extended to persons as defined with reference to ECHR Article 3, Protocol 6 Article 1, and CAT Article 3:

> Upon application, a residence permit will be issued to an alien if the alien risks the death penalty or being subjected to torture or inhuman or degrading treatment of punishment in case of return to his country of origin.

4 TERMINATION OF ILLEGAL RESIDENCE, EXPULSION AND RETURN

4.1 How many third country nationals without a valid residence permit are currently, according to estimates, staying in your country? How many deportations have actually been made in previous years? Is the whole enforcement process considered as acceptable?

Danish law does not provide any official definition of illegality as regards the entry and presence of aliens. Some ex contrario inferences can be drawn from the Aliens Act as regards the modalities of entry and residence in the country, even while this may result in too formalistic definitions

[74] Proposal for Council Directive on minimum standards for the qualification and status of third country nationals and stateless persons as refugees or as persons who otherwise need international protection, COM (2001) 510 final.

[75] Cf. survey of proposed EU legislative measures on asylum and immigration (note 35).

of situations constituting illegality. The most relevant basis for defining such situations seems to be the provisions setting up the time-limit for an alien's departure and eventual deportation upon expulsion or refusal or revocation of a residence permit.[76] It is, however, quite conceivable that an alien cannot be legally deported despite having passed the time-limit for voluntary departure, due to the prohibition of refoulement.[77] In such cases the alien will consequently have a right to remain in Denmark for the time being, hence his/her continued presence cannot be considered illegal. At most, the alien can be said to be in an irregular position, and the stay will often have the legal nature of "tolerated presence" in the country.[78]

4.5 What measures have been taken to implement the Council Directive of 28 May 2001, on the mutual recognition of decisions on the expulsion of third country nationals? What, if any shortcomings or gaps of the Directive should be corrected in a further directive on cooperation on expulsion or deportation of third country nationals?

The Directive on mutual recognition of decisions on the expulsion of third country nationals[79] has been transposed by the insertion of a number of new provisions into the Aliens Act on the revocation of residence permits and the enforcement of expulsion decisions made by administrative authorities of other Schengen or EU countries.[80] This method of transposition was necessary because such administrative decisions need to have a formal legislative basis, and the Aliens Act already contains provisions stipulating the conditions under which revocation and deportation may take place.

It appears from the explanatory remarks that these amendments were being suggested by the government in order to enable Denmark to comply with the Directive which is considered a development of the Schengen

[76] Section 33 (2)–(7) and (9)–(10) of the Aliens Act.

[77] Cf. Section 31 (1) and (2) of the Aliens Act, referring to the *non-refoulement* rules in ECHR Article 3, Protocol 6 Article 1, CAT Article 3, and Article 33 of the 1951 Refugee Convention, respectively.

[78] Cf. J. Vedsted-Hansen, "Regularization of Illegal Immigrants in Denmark", in P. De Bruycker (ed.), *Les régularisation des étrangers illégaux dans l'Union européenne. Regularisations of illegal immigrants in the European Union*, Bruylant 2000, pp. 401–06.

[79] Council Directive 2001/40/EC of 28 May 2001 (OJ 2001, L 149/34).

[80] Amendment Act No. 134 of 20 March 2002 which was to enter into force on 2 December 2002 unless the Minister for Refugee, Immigration and Integration Affairs should decide on earlier entering into force.

acquis.[81] Therefore the implementation of the Directive was stipulated in Article 5 of the 1997 Protocol.

The main element of the amendment was three new provisions on the enforcement of final administrative decisions made by authorities of other Schengen countries or of Member States of the European Communities on the return of aliens, inserted as a new Part IV a of the Aliens Act.[82] In addition, the following provision was inserted into Section 19 of the Aliens Act on the revocation of residence permits:

> (4) A time-limited or permanent residence permit can be revoked if an administrative authority of another Schengen country or of a Member State of the European Communities has made a final decision on the return of an alien who is not a national of a Schengen country or a Member State of the European Community because of circumstances which, in Denmark, could lead to expulsion under sections 22 to 25 or section 25 a(1) or (2)(iii). If the decision on return has been made on the basis of a criminal offence, the residence permit can only be revoked if the alien was sentenced in respect of an offence which, in the country in question, may result in a punishment of at least one year's imprisonment. Subsection (3), second sentence, applies correspondingly. No decision on revocation can be made under the first sentence hereof if the alien is a member of the family of a national of a Member State of the European Communities who has made use of his right to freedom of movement, cf. section 2(4).

The adoption of these rules on the enforcement of decisions made by administrative authorities of other Schengen or EU countries was particularly important, because it introduced a new and so far unseen mechanism allowing for deportation on the basis of decisions made by other states' authorities. In a more technical sense, it is a novelty in the Danish Aliens Act to issue such separate enforcement decisions, as deportation in consequence of expulsion is normally decided as an integral element of the expulsion order.[83]

While the enforcement rules in Sections 27 b-d of the Aliens Act were clearly necessary in order to transpose the Directive, it is questionable

[81] Draft Bill No. L 34 of 12 December 2001, Minister for Refugee, Immigration and Integration Affairs, pp. 4–9. This Draft Bill was a restatement of the initial Draft Bill No. L 42 that had been put before Parliament on 23 October 2001, but lapsed as a result of the Parliamentary elections in November 2001.

[82] See Sections 27 b–27 d of the Aliens Act.

[83] Draft Bill No. L 34 of 12 December 2001, pp. 7–8.

whether the adoption of an extended legal basis for revocation of residence permits in Section 19 (4) was actually required under the Directive. Notably, Article 3(1) (a) of the Directive only allows for the residence permit to be withdrawn if this is authorised by national legislation, hence there is no requirement under EC law to authorise such revocation. This issue does not seem to have been clearly brought out in the explanatory remarks of the Draft Bill.[84]

[84] Ibid., pp. 12–14.

ESTONIA

DR. ANNELI ALBI
Lecturer in European Law in the University of Kent (UK)

DR. JULIA LAFFRANQUE
Deputy Secretary General on Legislative Drafting
Ministry of Justice of Estonia

PART I (ENTRY, VISA REGIME AND BORDER CONTROL)

1.1 What national authorities are competent to deal with visa applications (Schengen visas and long-term visas)? Are there any procedures to avoid duplication or successive visa applications at different EU-consulates? On what substantive criteria, other than the Schengen minimum requirements, are visas granted or refused? How many visas have been issued or refused?

In the European Union, the most developed regulations about the current topic can be found in the Schengen *acquis*. Much of the Schengen *acquis* will not apply to the acceding countries, including Estonia, until a separate Council Decision to be taken at a later stage. However, the Schengen Implementation Action Plan aims to prepare for this on the basis of a credible schedule for the introduction of the Schengen provisions. Binding rules which must be put in place as from the date of accession include, among others, part of the rules on visas, rules on external borders and the *acquis* on migration and asylum. Estonia needs not only to adopt the relevant legislation, but also to be equipped to meet adequate standards of administrative capacity, as well as independent, reliable and efficient judiciary and police.

The main legislation to regulate entry, visa regime and border control in Estonia consists of the following acts: Aliens Act (passed on 8 July 1993[1] and entered into force on 12 July 1993, with several modifications); Obligation to Leave and Prohibition on Entry Act (passed on 21 October 1998[2] and entered into force on 1 April 1999); the Government of the Republic Regulation on the Procedure for Application, Issue, Extension, Revocation and terms of Residence and Work Permits and the List of

[1] RT I 1993, 44, 637 (RT = Riigi Teataja = State Gazette). [2] RT I 1998, 98/99, 1575.

the Evidence and Data to be Presented by Applying for the Residence and Work Permits, and the Procedure of inserting the Data on Residence Permit into the Travel Document of a Foreign State and the Registration of Absence of the Alien from Estonia (passed on 26 November 2002[3] and entered into force on 1 January 2003); the Government of the Republic Regulation on the Approval of Visa Rules (passed on 16 January 1998[4] and entered into force on 1 March 1998); the Government of the Republic Regulation on the Establishment of the Visa Record and on the Statutes for Maintenance of the Register (passed on 30 August 2000[5] and entered into force on 8 September 2000); State Border Act (passed on 30 June 1994[6] and entered into force on 31 July 1994); Border Guard Act (passed on 30 June 1994[7] and entered into force 31 July 1994); and the Government of the Republic Regulation on the Maintenance of the Boundary Construction and Boundary Marker (passed on 14 November 2002[8] and entered into force on 1 January 2004).

Estonia has not issued any Schengen visas since it is not a Signatory State of the Schengen Treaty. However, Estonia fully applies the main criteria of the Schengen rules (relevant amendments to the Aliens Act will be adopted by May 1, 2004). This progress has been confirmed by the European Commission in its Comprehensive Monitoring Report, of November 2003, on Estonia's preparations for membership, which overall was satisfied with Estonia's alignment with the EU visa *acquis*.

The authorities responsible for dealing with visa applications are the Ministry of Foreign Affairs (Estonian diplomatic missions and consular posts) and the Ministry of Internal Affairs (Citizenship and Migration Board, Board of Border Guard).

Estonia has introduced visa requirements for all countries with EU visa obligations. As Estonian authorities use a common visa register, the duplication of visa applications (or successive visa applications) at different Estonian missions abroad or at the border is excluded.

According to preliminary statistics for the year 2003, the Estonian diplomatic representations abroad received approximately 96,000 visa applications and issued approximately 95,500 visas. The visa refusal rate was 0.5%. The Estonian Consulates with the highest workload are those in the Russian Federation, Belarus and the Ukraine. The Board of Border Guard issued, as an exception at border checkpoints, 561 visas in 2003.

[3] RT I 2002, 98, 574. [4] RT I 1998, 8, 87. [5] RT I 2000, 71, 444.
[6] RT I 1994, 54, 902. [7] RT I 1994, 54, 903. [8] RT I 2002, 95, 553.

The Citizenship and Migration Board extended 499 visas and confirmed 42,253 visa invitations in 2003.

1.2 Is there a visa tracking procedure in order to identify visa overstayers? What data are collected from visa-applicants (fingerprints)? Admissibility of visa data to alien and police authorities?

The authorities responsible for identifying visa overstayers are the Citizenship and Migration Board, the Board of Border Guard and police prefectures. Visa applicants must submit only paper-based documents (incl. recent photo). No biometric data is collected. Data about aliens who have entered into the territory of Estonia by using a visa but have not left after the expiration of the visa will be available due to the improvements in the Visa Register (by creating a connection with the border crossing database). Access to this information is guaranteed to the appropriate authorities.

1.3 Have courts ever decided on the refusal of a Schengen visa based upon Schengen blacklisting by other Member States?

Since Estonia does not issue Schengen visas, Estonian embassies and consular posts have issued and issue only national (Estonian) visas. According to the national legislation, decisions on the refusal of a national visa are not subject to review by the courts.

1.4 What measures have been undertaken in the implementation of the action programme for administrative cooperation in the field of external borders, visa, asylum and immigration following the Council Decision of 13 June 2002?

Estonia has participated in and received different kinds of benefits from the ODYSSEUS program which is the predecessor of ARGO. However, Estonia did not participate in the 2003 annual programme for administrative cooperation in the field of external borders, visa, asylum and immigration (ARGO) following the Council Decision of June 13, 2002.

1.5 What measures have been undertaken to implement the Directive 2001/51 EC supplementing the Schengen rules concerning carrier sanctions? How often have carrier sanctions been used?

As concerns the approximation of the Directive 2001/51 EC supplementing the Schengen rules concerning carrier sanctions, paragraph 16.1 (2) of the Estonian Aliens Act provides that a person who transports or whose representative (hereinafter carrier) transports an alien who, upon arrival at the Estonian border, lacks a legal basis to stay in Estonia or a document necessary for crossing the border, is required to transport the alien, upon such alien being returned from the Estonian border, back to the same place where the alien boarded the means of transport of the carrier or back to the country of his or her habitual residence. If this is impossible, the carrier is required to compensate the state for the costs related to the stay of the alien in Estonia and his or her departure from Estonia. According to paragraph 16.7 of the Aliens Act (entered into force 01.03.2003), a fine of up to 50,000 Kroons can be imposed on a legal person engaged in transport operations, who has directly delivered an alien without legal basis to stay in Estonia or in the transit zone, to the transit zone, state border or temporary border line.

The Board of Border Guard has required carriers to transport back aliens, but the sanction of the fine has not yet been implemented.

1.6 In your judgement, does the visa law and policy of your country live up to EU standards or are adjustments needed? Do you consider that there is need for further EU-harmonization of visa policies concerning:
– common criteria for granting visas aiming at harmonizing visa obligations among states participating in the Budapest Process;
– establishment of a European visa identification system (VIS and SIS II)?
To what extent will the EU enlargement process present an opportunity or challenge for tackling issues of illegal entry and border control?

Overall, the visa law and policy of Estonia essentially live up to EU standards. After the accession to the European Union, immigration pressure on Estonia will probably increase, because Estonia is seen as presenting an opportunity to move on to more developed European countries.

PART II (ADMISSION AND RESIDENCE OF THIRD COUNTRY NATIONALS)

2.1–2.3; 2.5–2.6.

2.1 What are the basic principles in your country concerning:
– admission of third country nationals for labour purposes or self-employed activities;
– admission of third country nationals for study and vocational training;
– legal status of third country nationals in possession of a long-term residence permit of another Member State?
– To what extent do these principles differ from the European Commission's proposals?

2.2 What are the legal requirements and procedures for obtaining a residence permit for third country nationals for the purpose of employment? Which procedures are used in maintaining the preferred access of EU-citizens and Turkish nationals (association agreement) to the labour market? Do special programmes exist for highly qualified professionals facilitating access to the labour market? To what

extent are trade unions and employers involved in such programmes? Is there a procedure to calculate the demand for foreign labour? How is the EU-enlargement taken into consideration? To what extent has the recent economic recession and unemployment influenced the concepts on admission of third country nationals?

2.3 To what extent do existing national laws and practices differ substantially from the approach taken in the Commission's Proposal on admission for the purpose of paid employment and self-employed activities relating to:
- **admission of third country nationals for study and vocational training;**
- **on legal status of third country nationals in possession of a long-term residence permit of another Member State?**
- **To what extent do these principles differ from the European Commission's proposals?**

2.4 Concerning the proposal for a directive on the right to family reunion agreed upon by the Council in February 2003:
- **Do you consider the proposed standards below the principles of family reunification applicable in your country?**
- **Will the implementation of the Directive, once it is adopted, lead to changes in the national law on family reunification downgrading the standard of protection? If so, what changes are envisaged?**

2.5 The proposal for a directive on the rights of long-term third country nationals as agreed upon by the Council on 5 June 2003, provides for a number of rights approximating the situation of long-term residents to the status of EU-citizens. Will the implementation of the Directive involve major legal and policy changes in your country? What are the major points of concern if any, concerning the approximation concept of the directive relating to:
- **non-discrimination in social rights;**
- **the concept of "civic citizenship" (see also extended impact assessment on the Communication on Integration of June 11, 2003);**
- **family reunification and access of family members to the labour market;**
- **security of stay?**

In Estonia, the entry and residence of third country nationals for the purpose of paid employment and self-employed activities are regulated by the Aliens Act. Recent amendments to the Aliens Act, which were adopted on 18 December 2002[9] and entered into force partly on 1 March 2003 and mostly on 1 May 2003, have taken into consideration the Proposal for a Directive on the conditions of entry and residence of third country nationals for the purpose of paid employment and self-employed activities.[10] Compared to the Proposal, the Estonian legislation provides that in order to work in Estonia, a third country national must hold a work permit. However, there also exist residence permits for employment (comparable

[9] RT I 2003, 4, 20. [10] COM 2001, 386 final.

with the "residence permit- worker") and residence permits for enterprise (comparable with the "residence permit- self-employed person").

A work permit shall not be issued to a third country national to whom a residence permit has been issued on the condition that his or her legal income is sufficient to ensure his or her subsistence. A work permit can be extended if a third country national holds a valid residence permit or if his/her residence permit is extended and (s)he has an employer at the time of the extension of his/her work permit.

The following persons do not require a work permit in order to work in Estonia: third country nationals with permanent residence permits; third country nationals who have residence permits for employment; third country nationals who have applied for a residence permit before July 12, 1995 and who have obtained such a permit; imprisoned persons during their stay in prison; members of locomotive crews; staff serving in locomotives and trains; drivers for taking passengers or cargo over state borders.

Activities as a sole proprietor, employment with an employment contract or any other contract, or any activity which may result in gaining profit or any other benefit, irrespective of the type or form of the contract, or the location or place of residence of the other party to the contract, shall be deemed to be employment unless an international agreement stipulates otherwise.

A third country national can be granted a residence permit for employment if an open competition has been carried out to staff the post and if, within two months, it has not been possible to recruit anybody through the state employment mediation service. The Labour Market Board has to give its consent before a third country national can be employed. A residence permit is issued only if the wages of a third country national are sufficient for his/her subsistence in Estonia.

According to the information available from the Ministry of Social Affairs, there are currently no special programmes for highly qualified professionals facilitating access to the labour market. There are also no procedures for calculating the demand for foreign labour. However, this issue will be dealt with in the field of governance of the Ministry of Education and Research by facilitating mutual recognition of certain professional qualifications. For example, the development plan of the University of Tartu, which was approved by the decision of the Council of the University on 19 December 2003 and entered into force on 20 December 2003, foresees the internationalization of the university *inter alia* by increasing the number of foreign teaching staff. In addition, a Draft Act on the

Working Conditions of Workers posted to Estonia is currently in the legislative proceedings of the Estonian Parliament (*Riigikogu*). The Act will regulate the work of workers posted by an employer to Estonia under the following conditions: 1) where the work is performed at the expense of the employer under his management and inspection and subject to a contract which has been concluded between the employer and the contracting entity resident in Estonia; 2) where the work is performed in a branch of the employer or in a company which, together with the employer, belongs to the same group of undertakings; 3) if the employer is a legal person who intermediates temporary labour force or self-employed persons. The Draft Act also regulates the settlement of disputes according to which the posted worker has the right of recourse to the courts in Estonia. It is envisaged that the Act will enter into force upon Estonia's accession to the EU.

A third country national who has been issued a residence permit for study may take up employment in Estonia without a work permit in order to participate in practical training pursuant to the curriculum. Otherwise (s)he may take up employment in Estonia only on the basis of a work permit and only outside of school hours, on the condition that such employment does not interfere with his or her studies.

To conclude, the Estonian Aliens Act is to a great extent in line with the Proposal for a Directive on the conditions of entry and residence of third country nationals for the purpose of studies, vocational training or voluntary service;[11] however no provision is made for unremunerated trainees and volunteers in the Estonian Aliens Act.

According to the Estonian Aliens Act, a permanent residence permit may be issued to a third country national who has resided in Estonia on the basis of a temporary residence permit for at least three years within the last five years and who has a valid residence permit, a residence in Estonia and legal income for subsistence in Estonia. As regards the legal status of the third country nationals in possession of a long-term residence of an EU Member State, it is not yet regulated in Estonia but regulations are under preparation in the light of the Proposal for a Directive concerning the status of third country nationals who are long-term residents.[12]

The regulations on family reunification in Estonia, in case one of the spouses is an alien, were introduced by Amendments to the Aliens Act, which were passed on 12 June 2002[13] and entered into force on

[11] COM 2002, 548 final. [12] COM 2001, 127. [13] RT I 2002, 56, 351.

1 October 2002. The main purpose of these amendments was to safeguard the rights and freedoms of the individual stemming from Articles 26 and 27 of the Constitution and Articles 8 and 12 of the European Convention on Human Rights. At the same time, these amendments also aimed at approximating Estonia's legislation to the EU Resolution of 4 December 1997 on marriages of convenience[14] and the Resolution of 1 June 1993 on harmonization of Family Reunification,[15] thus fulfilling the obligations assumed during the accession negotiations. Pursuant to these amendments, the list of aliens who will not be subject to the immigration quota was increased. A residence permit cannot be denied solely on the grounds that an immigration quota has been filled where the alien lives a family life in Estonia in the meaning of the Constitution of Estonia.

According to Estonian law, an Estonian citizen who lives in Estonia, or a third country national who is permanently resident in Estonia, may invite his or her spouse to settle in Estonia if the spouses share close economic ties and a psychological relationship, their family is stable and the marriage is not a marriage of convenience.

If a person has been married for less than three years, the validity of a temporary residence permit shall not exceed one year. The residence permit can be extended by one year at a time up to a maximum of three years, unless the marriage is dissolved. If the person has been married for more than three years, the validity of a residence permit shall not exceed three years.

If the spouse is a third country national residing in Estonia and wishes to invite his or her spouse to settle with him or her, the family's legal income must meet the rates established by the government. The family must have a registered place of residence, an actual domicile in Estonia, and an insurance certificate which assures the costs of treatment of an illness or injury during the duration of the residence permit.

If a third country national receives a residence permit to settle with a spouse who is permanently resident in Estonia, (s)he needs a work permit in order to take up employment in Estonia.

The Aliens Act also lays down the conditions under which a residence permit may be issued for the purposes of settling with a close relative residing in Estonia. By issuing the residence permit to a minor child in order to settle with a parent who permanently resides in Estonia, the interests and rights of the child are taken into primary consideration. If

[14] OJ C 328 of 16 December 1997. [15] WGI 1497 REV 1.

the child has attained the age of majority, the residence permit will no longer be related to the residence permit of the parent. There is also a possibility of issuing a residence permit to an adult child in order to settle with a parent who permanently resides in Estonia, if the child is unable to cope independently due to health reasons or disability. In addition, there is a possibility to issue a permanent residence permit after five years of issuing the first temporary residence permit to a parent or grandparent to whom a residence permit was issued in order to settle with his or her adult child or grandchild who permanently resides in Estonia. This is in cases where the parent or grandparent needs care s/he is not able to receive in the country of his or her location or in another country, and if his or her permanent legal income or the permanent legal income of his or her child or grandchild who legally resides in Estonia ensures that the parent or grandparent can be maintained in Estonia.

As seen from the above, there are differences between Estonian legislation and the approach taken by the European Commission, albeit not significant in substance. This is also why the implementation of the proposal for a directive on the rights of long-term third country nationals, as agreed upon by the Council on 5 June 2003, will not involve any major changes in Estonia's law or policy.

2.4 What measures have been taken to implement the Directive of 29th June 2000, implementing the principle of equal treatment between persons irrespective of racial or ethnic origin and Council Directive 2000/78 EC of 27th November 2000, establishing a general framework for equal treatment in employment and occupation? Have legislative changes been undertaken? To what extent is "affirmative action" considered as necessary to promote equal opportunities for migrant workers from third countries?

In order to implement the Directive of 29th June 2000 implementing the principle of equal treatment between persons irrespective of racial or ethnic origin and the Council Directive 2000/78 EC of 27th November 2000 establishing a general framework for equal treatment in employment and occupation, a draft Act on the Equality between Women and Men was submitted by the government to the legislative proceedings of the Parliament. As a next step, legislation will be prepared in order to prevent discrimination on the ground of racial, ethnic, religion or other beliefs, disability, age or sexual orientation.

2.7 Considering the perspective of a future common migration policy as developed by the Commission in the Open Coordination Communication (COM 2001, 387) and the Communication on a Migration policy of the European Union (COM 2000, 757 final), how do you assess the role of the Community organs

in determining a European migration policy in terms of competences of the Member States to decide on residence rights and admission to the labour market and integration? Should harmonization of legislation go further, and if so, in what respect?

With regard to the perspective of a future common migration policy as developed by the Commission in the Open Coordination Communication[16] and the Communication on Migration Policy of the European Union,[17] it can be said that the principles of Estonian migration policy are in accordance with the European Union migration policy. These will continue to take into consideration the developments and changes in the EU's migration policy.

PART III (ASYLUM AND REFUGEE LAW)

3.1 Have the Dublin Rules worked satisfactorily and what is expected of the Dublin II Regulation No. 343, 2003 of 18 February 2003?

3.2 Has the Eurodac Regulation No. 2725/2000 of 11th December 2000, concerning the establishment of Eurodac for the comparison of fingerprints for an effective application of the Dublin Convention, operative since January 15, 2003, resulted in an increase of Dublin cases? Has Eurodac become effective in your country or is it expected to become effective eventually?

3.7 In the Commission's Communication of 22 November, 2000, COM 2000, 755 (see also 2nd Commission Report COM 2003, 152 final) the Commission's concept of a common European asylum procedure and a uniform status for those who are granted asylum valid throughout the Union is set out. Do you consider that the concept is generally in line with your country's asylum policy? Are the concerns of refugee organizations, such as Amnesty International and other organizations, of an undermining of the international regime for the protection of refugees shared in the political circles responsible for decision-making of your country?

3.8 The open coordination-mechanism, as suggested by the Commission, provided for first stage and second stage legislation in which the flexibility provisions in some of the directives on migration and asylum are to be replaced by full harmonization. Is this concept discussed in your country and what are the perceptions relating to the gradual establishment of a European asylum policy which might eventually replace national procedures and national decision-making?

3.9 The Communication of June 2003, towards a more accessible, equitable and managed asylum system – in reaction to the UK paper – develops some ideas on new approaches to pursue an orderly and managed arrival of persons in need of international protection. What is the political reaction in your country to the

[16] COM 2001, 387. [17] COM 2000, 757 final.

concept of an outside accessed asylum procedure, distribution of refugees and responsibility-sharing and other new concepts and ideas in coping with mass refugee movements?

The Refugees Act came into force in July 1997 and it was substantially amended in January 2003 in order to comply with EU requirements.[18] Estonia has also ratified the 1951 United Nations Convention relating to the Status of Refugees and its 1967 Protocol, in February 1997.[19] In addition, Estonia is a party to the main international human rights treaties, including the United Nations Convention against Torture and Other Cruel, Inhuman or Degrading Treatment or Punishment.[20]

Under Articles 2 and 3 of the Accession Treaty, Estonia has undertaken to adopt and apply the EU asylum *acquis* without exemptions or a transition period.[21] Estonia's Refugees Act covers mainly the minimum standards of procedure for granting and withdrawing the status of a refugee. It is estimated that Estonia's legislation needs some amendments to harmonise it with the EU asylum law and policy.

The development of the asylum system forms a priority area for the Ministry of Internal Affairs for the year 2004.[22] This includes the development of fast and effective asylum proceedings, appeals mechanisms and the enhancement of general administrative capacity. Mechanisms are to be developed for an operative data collection and a data exchange system with the institutions in Estonia, other countries and EU institutions, as well as for participation in the EU's common asylum system.[23]

The Dublin Convention, Dublin II Regulation No. 343 of 2003 and Eurodac Regulation No 2725/2000 are currently being implemented by Estonia; relevant national acts are expected to be in force by the time of accession. In order to prepare the technical infrastructure for implementing the Eurodac Regulations 2726/2000/EC and 407/2002/EC, the Ministry of Internal Affairs, the Forensic Service Centre, the Citizenship

[18] Refugees Act, adopted 18.02.1997, RT I 1997, 19, 306; 18, 301; 25, 365; 2001, 16, 68; 2002, 42, 266; 61, 375; 2003, 13, 65; see also Chapter: 24 Justice and Home Affairs (version of 18 July 2003), in *Monitoring Report for the Commission Review – Estonia*, June 2003, available at www.eib.ee.

[19] RT II 1997, 6, 26. [20] RT II 1994, 14/15, 44.

[21] See Liitumislepingu seletuskiri [Explanatory letter to the Accession Treaty], http://www.mfa.ee.

[22] Siseministeeriumi prioriteedid 2004. aastaks [The priorities of the Ministry of Internal Affairs for year 2004], available at http://www.sisemin.gov.ee/atp/index.php?id=6317.

[23] Kodakondsus- ja Migratsiooniameti Arengusuunad 2003–2007 [Trends in the developments in the Board of Citizenship and Migration 2003–2007], available at http://www.sisemin.gov.ee/atp/failid/KMA_arengusuunad.doc.

and Migration Board and the Border Guard Administration are participating in a joint project to renew the Automated Fingerprint Identification System and to provide necessary training for the respective officials.[24]

According to the data of the Citizenship and Migration Board, the total amount of applications during the period of 09.07.1997–30.09.2003 was 82. The majority of these applications were rejected. Estonia has granted asylum to 4 persons and issued a residence permit to 9 others on subsidiary protection grounds. 11 applicants have received a residence permit on other grounds, mainly on the basis of the right to family life. Asylum application proceedings have been suspended or terminated in 18 cases, 35 applicants have left Estonia, and 8 applications are currently being processed. Out of the total number of applications, 57 were from male applicants, 12 from female applicants and 13 from children. In 2003, 13 applications were submitted, of which 3 were submitted at the border and 10 inside the state. The main countries of origin of the applicants are Iraq (17 applications), Pakistan (8), Afghanistan (8), Russia (7) and African countries (several applications).[25] Most of these applicants have come to Estonia by chance rather than on a pre-planned basis.[26] The average rate of positive decisions is approximately 35% of the overall applications, which meets the EU average.[27]

Although the number of asylum applications and the amount of positive decisions has been modest, an increase in applications and in the amount of work is predicted,[28] taking into account the enforcement of the Dublin system and the loss of internal borders: Estonia will form part of the future EU's external borders. Since Estonia has undertaken to apply the EU asylum legislation without exemptions or a transition periods, there are some concerns about the likely increase in migration and asylum applications. However, this topic has not yet been the subject of major political debate.

The authorities dealing with asylum applications in Estonia are the Citizenship and Migration Board, the Border Guard Administration, the local offices of the regional Border Guards and the police authorities (all these bodies are designated by the Ministry of Internal Affairs), as well as the Ministry of Social Affairs.

[24] Liitumislepingu seletuskiri . . . , supra note 21.

[25] This statistics is available at the website of the Reception Centre of Refugees, http://www.vastuvotukeskus.ee/?res=4 (25.01.2004).

[26] Kodakondsus- ja Migratsiooniameti Arengusuunad 2003–2007, supra note 23.

[27] *Ibid.* [28] *Ibid.*

3.3 What major changes, if any, will the implementation of the amended proposal for a directive on minimum standards on procedures in Member States for granting and withdrawing refugee status, on which the Council has reached political agreement on most points in June 2003, bring for the legislation and practice in your country in particular relating to:
– rights of applicants in the procedure;
– administrative and judicial appeal procedures;
– the use of safe third country and safe country of origin concepts;
– detainment of asylum seekers;
– airport and border procedures?

The main aspects of the Refugees Act meet the requirements of the Amended Proposal for a Council Directive on minimum standards on procedures in Member States for granting and withdrawing refugee status.[29] As a general rule, the procedural safeguards also apply to applications for a residence permit on the ground of need for subsidiary protection.

The Refugees Act provides that an applicant has a right to receive information concerning his or her rights and duties related to asylum proceedings in a language which he or she understands, and a right to be in contact with the Office of the United Nations High Commissioner for Refugees. She or he also has a right to a representative during asylum proceedings, with the exception of the provision of explanations or the performance of other procedural acts which, by virtue of their nature, must be carried out personally. Applicants have also a right of recourse to the courts if their rights and freedoms are infringed.

An asylum application can be submitted at the border or on the territory of the State. Inland applications have to be submitted to the Citizenship and Migration Board immediately after entering Estonia. An alien who has no legal basis for crossing the State border and for entry into Estonia must submit an asylum application immediately to the Border Guard authority, before his or her entry into Estonia.

If an asylum application is submitted to the Border Guard authority, the Border Guard shall immediately perform the following acts: 1) examination of the person and his or her personal effects; 2) admission for deposit of personal effects and documents; 3) identification; 4) receipt of standard asylum application form; 5) collection of explanations concerning the arrival to Estonia and the circumstances which constitute the basis for the application for asylum; 6) fingerprinting and photographing;

[29] COM 2002, 326 final.

7) medical examination if necessary. The applicant shall be detained while these acts are being performed; he or she is required to stay in the assigned premises. If the performance of the acts lasts longer than forty-eight hours, the permission of an administrative court judge is required for further detention.

If the person is refused entry, with the approval of the Citizenship and Migration Board, he or she is immediately turned away from the border where the refusal to grant asylum is based on the following grounds: (1) the applicant has arrived to Estonia through a country which can be considered as a safe country; (2) asylum, or other international protection has been accorded to the applicant in another country, and such protection is still accessible to the applicant; or (3) there is a reason to consider the applicant's country of nationality or country of permanent residence to be a safe country of origin.

After performing the above acts with regard to the asylum application, the Border Guard Authority sends the applicant to an initial reception centre and forwards the asylum application, together with the deposited personal effects and documents, to the Citizenship and Migration Board which will conduct the relevant proceedings.

An alien who wishes to apply for asylum during his or her stay in Estonia must submit a corresponding application to the Citizenship and Migration Board. After the submission of an asylum application, the applicant is sent to an initial reception centre. The Citizenship and Migration Board performs the above-mentioned acts with regard to the asylum application.

Thus, Estonian legislation incorporates the concepts of a safe country of origin and safe third country. A safe country is a country which observes the requirements set out in Articles 32 and 33 of the Convention, Article 3 of the United Nations Convention against Torture and Other Cruel, Inhuman or Degrading Treatment or Punishment and Article 3 of the European Convention on Human Rights and Fundamental Freedoms. A safe country also means any other country where an applicant would be accorded protection against persecution or deportation to his or her country of origin or to another country where the applicant would not be accorded such protection. A safe country of origin is defined as a country where, as a general rule, there exists no serious threat of being persecuted. When determining the safety of a country of origin, account must be taken of whether or not such country has acceded to the main international agreements related to human rights and if, as a general rule, it adheres to their provisions. Whether or not a country is safe is determined by the Citizenship and Migration Board.

An applicant is obliged to co-operate in every way in the clarification of the circumstances of the asylum application. This includes the provision of information and explanations, the submission of documents and other evidence in his or her possession, enabling the performance of a medical examination and of fingerprinting, co-operation in the collection of information needed for personal identification, cooperation for verification purposes, and fulfillment of other duties stipulated by law. The Estonian Refugees Act does not require personal interviews to be conducted, if the application is found to be inadmissible.

The practice of the applicable standard in asylum proceedings may need to be revised in the light of Article 16 of the Proposal of the Council Directive. Paragraph 3 of this Proposal requires that the determining authority give the applicant the benefit of the doubt, even in circumstances where there is a lack of evidence for some of the applicant's statements, provided that the required conditions are met.

A decision to reject an asylum application is prepared in writing and it is accompanied by an order to leave Estonia immediately. An order to leave Estonia, which is issued to an alien with the decision to reject the asylum application on the basis of the safe country of origin, safe third country or obligation of another state to provide international protection, is subject to immediate execution. The alien is deported from Estonia pursuant to the procedure provided by the Obligation to Leave and Prohibition on Entry Act,[30] without prior permission of an administrative court. Rejection on other grounds is subject to compulsory execution by deporting the alien from Estonia, with the permission of an administrative court.

It is important to note that an appeal against the rejection of an asylum application, by an alien even if permitted by an administrative court does not postpone the deportation. However, the court can provide for preliminary protection, which suspends the deportation until the end of the proceedings. The decision to refuse a residence permit and an order to leave Estonia issued thereby may be contested in an administrative court within ten days of the date of the adoption of the decision. An order is not subject to compulsory execution before the entry into force of the corresponding judicial decision.

[30] RT I 1998, 98/99, 1575; 2001, 68, 407; 2002, 53, 336; 61, 375; 102, 599; 2003, 4, 21; 13, 56.

If another state party to the Refugee Convention is responsible for the review of the asylum application pursuant to an international agreement or legislation of an international organisation, the alien shall be deported from Estonia without the prior issuing of an order to leave Estonia and without the prior permission of an administrative court. He or she shall be sent to another country party to the Convention, pursuant to an international agreement or legislation of an international organisation, which country will then be responsible for reviewing the asylum application.

3.4 What measures have been undertaken to implement Directive 2003/9 of 27 January 2003, on reception of asylum seekers in your country relating to
- **the flexibility clauses in the Directive;**
- **restriction of free movement;**
- **access to the labour market;**
- **rights of migrant workers under Article 11 § 2 of the Directive?**

Although Estonia's legislation corresponds with the main provisions of Council Directive 2003/9/EC of January 2003 laying down the minimum standards for the reception of asylum seekers, it is estimated that some adjustments and specifications are necessary for the transposition of the directive; this is currently been analysed by the relevant national authorities. Harmonisation has not yet started as the deadline for implementing the Directive is in February 2005.[31] By way of example of areas needing improvement, the Board of Citizenship and Immigration deems it necessary to create a data centre for the faster and better performance of asylum proceedings; to create interviewing rooms with relevant technical equipment, to equip a primary reception room, and to ensure speedy documentation of asylum seekers by systematic photographing, fingerprinting and processing of pertinent data.[32] In order to establish whether an asylum application is justified, it is necessary to develop linguistic analysis to ascertain the origin of applicants, to develop DNA-analysis for ascertaining family links, and to verify the applicant's age. In order to respond to the expected increase in the number of asylum applications and Estonia's relatively small previous experience in the field, more human capital and financial investment will be needed for dealing with asylum applications.[33]

Currently, it is stipulated that an applicant who has submitted an application during his or her stay in the country is required to stay in an initial

[31] Liitumislepingu seletuskiri . . . , supra note 21.

[32] Kodakondsus- ja Migratsiooniameti Arengusuunad 2003–2007, supra note 23.

[33] *Ibid.*

reception centre. The initial reception centre shall, as necessary, arrange for the assistance of the aliens, such as temporary accommodation, food, essential clothing and other necessities and toiletries, emergency care and medical examination, essential translation services, information regarding their rights and duties and other essential services.

As a general rule, an applicant is required to stay at the reception centre during the asylum proceedings. The applicant may reside outside the reception centre with the written permission of the Citizenship and Migration Board, provided that the accommodation and support of the applicant is ensured by a person legally residing in Estonia, the applicant has sufficient financial resources to provide for his or her accommodation and support or it is necessary for the applicant to reside outside the reception centre in order to ensure his or her safety. The reception centre has obligations similar to the initial reception centre, including the provision of essential translation services and provision of information regarding the applicant's rights and duties. At the request of an applicant, these services may be substituted by a monetary benefit, which corresponds to the size of the applicable subsistence limit.

Applicants are not allowed to undertake employment or engage in enterprise in Estonia during the course of asylum proceedings. Infringement of the prohibition to contract employment or to engage in enterprise is dealt with under the provisions of the Aliens Act. This regulation needs to be revised in the light of the obligations deriving from Council Directive 2003/79/EC.

3.5 What steps have been undertaken to implement the Directive on temporary protection, COM 2001, 55 in national law? Are there any procedures for burden sharing arrangements? Is there a legal basis for the admission of refugees for the purposes of receiving temporary protection in a mass-movement situation?

Directive 2001/55/EC on temporary protection has not yet been implemented in Estonia; it is expected to be implemented by the time of accession.[34] The Board of Citizenship and Immigration has declared that the establishing of the mechanism of temporary protection, including the possibility of applying so-called "group-decision" to certain categories of persons, forms the priority for forthcoming years.[35]

3.6 The Council has reached political agreement on the principles for a Directive on minimum standards for the qualification and status of third country nationals

[34] Liitumislepingu seletuskiri . . . , supra note 21.

[35] Kodakondsus- ja Migratsiooniameti Arengusuunad 2003–2007, supra note 23.

as refugees or persons who otherwise need international protection, COM 2001, 510 final (see Council documents of June 2003). What measures are envisaged to implement the Directive, once it is adopted, in your country relating to:
- **the definition of refugee;**
- **the definition of persons entitled to subsidiary protection;**
- **status of persons entitled to subsidiary protection;**
- **the issue of internal flight alternative as defined by the Directive;**
- **exclusion clauses, particularly issues of terrorism?**

To what extent are the refugee policies as reflected in the law and jurisprudence of your country in accordance with the proposal for the directive?

According to the Refugees Act, a refugee is an alien who has been issued a residence permit on the grounds that he or she is deemed to be a refugee pursuant to the Refugee Convention. This definition replaces earlier more restrictive regulation, which envisaged that asylum may be granted to a person who has applied for asylum in Estonia and who has a reason to fear persecution in his or her country of permanent residence or nationality as laid out in Article 1 of the Convention, provided that the applicant had arrived directly from the country of his or her permanent residence or nationality or indirectly from another country in which the person is also threatened by the above-mentioned persecution or by deportation to a country where such persecution is threatened.[36] A refugee was defined as a person who met the requirements of the Refugee Convention and its Protocol, and to whom Estonia had granted asylum. The new regulation takes into account the shortcomings of the earlier provisions and incorporates the idea that the recognition of refugee status is a declaratory act.

Estonian law also provides protection to persons who are not deemed to be refugees pursuant to the Convention but who are in need of protection due to the existence of reasons for considering that his or her return or deportation could give rise to the consequences specified in Article 3 of the European Convention on Human Rights and Fundamental Freedoms or Article 3 of the United Nations Convention against Torture and Other Cruel, Inhuman or Degrading Treatment or Punishment, or lead to the application of the death penalty in his or her country of nationality or country of permanent residence. By establishing the definition of a person in need of subsidiary international protection, Estonia has eliminated a

[36] See the study about Estonia by A. Potisepp, in R. Byrne (ed), New Asylum Countries? Migration Control and Refugee Protection in an Enlarged European Union (The Hague: Kluwer Law International, 2002) p. 291.

lacunae in its national regulation. The earlier regulation in the Aliens Act only provided for the possibility to issue a temporary residence permit to a person on the basis of an international agreement, without specifying which international agreements would qualify for the purposes of that provision.[37] Nevertheless, the grounds for issuing subsidiary protection seem to be narrower than the grounds enlisted in Article 15 of the Proposal for the Council Directive on minimum standards for the qualification and status of third country nationals and stateless persons as refugees or as persons who otherwise need international protection.[38]

Unlike the Proposal for the Council Directive on minimum standards, Estonian legal acts do not stipulate the criteria for the assessment of the applicant's fear of being persecuted or exposed to other forms of serious and unjustified harm, the sources of harm and protection, nor the nature and reasons for persecution. The law does not provide explicitly for the needs of international protection arising *sur place*, although it does not exclude such an option either.

Estonian law incorporates the idea of the internal flight alternative; this ground is invoked in practice with regard to asylum applications and applications for subsidiary protection. Accordingly, a residence permit is not issued if the persecution threatening the applicant is limited to a particular geographical area, and sufficient protection can be accorded to the applicant in another area of his or her country of nationality or country of permanent residence.

In the context of asylum proceedings, a residence permit may be issued to a minor child and to the married spouse of the applicant.

The issuing of a residence permit is refused if the alien has committed a criminal offence of first degree in Estonia, or otherwise poses a threat to national security, public safety or public order.

PART IV (TERMINATION OF ILLEGAL RESIDENCE, RETURN AND REPATRIATION)

4.1 How many third country nationals without a valid residence permit are currently, according to estimates, staying in your country? How many deportations have actually been made in previous years? Is the whole enforcement process considered as acceptable?

[37] A. Potisepp, supra note 36, p. 297. [38] COM 2001, 510.

4.2 What has been undertaken to implement the Directive of 28 November 2002, dealing with the facilitation of unauthorized entry, transit and residence?

4.3 How many illegal applicants have been apprehended at or near the border? How many criminal procedures for human trafficking have been instituted in the last year?

4.4 What efforts have been undertaken in your country regarding the Budapest June 2003 recommendations concerning the harmonization of penalty scales with regard to the crime of the smuggling of migrants and trafficking of persons, in line with Council Directive 2002/90 of 28th November 2002? Did your country sign the relevant UN protocols on the smuggling of migrants?

4.5 What measures have been taken to implement the Council Directive of 28 May 2001, on the mutual recognition of decisions on the expulsion of third country nationals? What, if any shortcomings or gaps of the Directive should be corrected in a further directive on cooperation on expulsion or deportation of third country nationals?

4.6 Do readmission agreements or other international treaties or arrangements with the aim of controlling and curbing illegal immigration and facilitating return exist in your country? Have they functioned satisfactorily?

4.7 To what extent have EU-standards and recommendations influenced your country's return policy? Have efforts been undertaken to cooperate with other EU Member States in enforcing return decisions by common deportation actions, exchange of information, facilitation of air and land transit, common principles on flight security, etc.?

4.8 Do you consider that there is a need to elaborate a common legal regime for air deportations (legal status of armed guards on board of the aircrafts, rights of the aircraft commander, legal rules in case of transit stops, applicability of national police law on board of aircraft on flight, etc.)?

The issues of termination of illegal residence, return and repatriation are regulated under the Obligation to Leave and Prohibition on Entry Act.[39] The State Borders Act[40] establishes the border regime, and the liability for violation of the border regime and illegal crossing of the state border. Violation of the border regime and the illegal crossing of the state border or temporary border line of the Republic of Estonia are

[39] Obligation to Leave and Prohibition of Entry Act, adopted 21.10.1998, RT I 1998, 98/99, 1575; 1999, 84, 762; 2000, 40, 254; 58, 376; 2001, 16, 68; 58, 352; 2002, 53, 336; 61, 375; 102, 599; 2003, 4, 21; 13, 65.

[40] State Borders Act, adopted 30.06.1993, RT I 1994, 54, 902; 1997, 77, 1315; 1999, 25, 365; 2000, 86, 550; 2001, 23, 126; 2002, 58, 363; 63, 387; 90, 516; 102, 599; 2003, 23, 138; 26, 156; 51, 350; 88, 591; 2004, 2, 4.

punishable under the Code of Misdemeanor Procedure. The illegal crossing of the state border or temporary border line is punishable as a criminal offence by a pecuniary punishment, or up to one year of imprisonment if it is committed: in disregard of a stop signal or order given by a Border Guard official; by a group; or by a means of transport in a location not intended for crossing; and a punishment for a misdemeanor has been imposed on the offender for the same act. The illegal transportation of an alien across the state border or temporary border line is punishable by pecuniary punishment or up to one year of imprisonment.

A stay of an alien in Estonia without a legal basis is punishable by a fine of up to 300 fine units or by detention. An alien who stays in Estonia without a legal basis at least twice within a year shall be punished by a pecuniary punishment or up to one year of imprisonment. The direct delivery by a legal person engaged in transport operations of an alien who has no legal basis to stay in Estonia or the transit zone, state border or temporary border line is punishable by a fine of up to 50 000 Kroons.

The Board of Citizenship and Immigration has declared amongst it priorities for 2003–2007 the development of structures for the detention system, in order to ensure that aliens whose stay in Estonia is illegal or who have submitted unfounded asylum applications leave the country. In addition, it is envisaged that the existing centre for deportation needs to be further developed and a primary reception centre needs to be built in order to meet the increasing needs.[41]

The need to deal with the problems of human trafficking has recently become a priority in Estonia. Relevant ministries and state agencies are analysing the sufficiency of the legislative framework and assessing the need for amendments in their field of responsibility and for steps needed to achieve better law enforcement. In addition, the International Organisation for Migration is carrying out a project of mapping and analysing the situation in Estonia. According to the Ministry of Internal Affairs, 12 criminal charges were initiated in 2001 with regard to human trafficking, 13 charges in 2002 and 8 charges in the first eight months of 2003.[42]

Estonia has concluded readmission treaties with Latvia and Lithuania, Finland, Norway, Sweden, Iceland, Slovenia, Italy, Switzerland, France, Germany, Spain, Croatia, Hungary, Austria and Portugal. Further

[41] Kodakondsus- ja Migratsiooniameti Arengusuunad 2003–2007, supra note 23.

[42] Elustransiit [Human trafficking]. *Molodjop Estonii*, 15.10.2003.

readmission agreements are to be signed with Ukraine, Hungary and Poland and are being negotiated with Russia, Belarus and Azerbaijan.[43] In cases of negative decisions on asylum applications, the applicants have been returned on the basis of the readmission treaties to Latvia and Lithuania.

[43] Chapter: 24 Justice and Home Affairs . . . , supra note 18.

GERMANY

PROF. DR. THOMAS GROß
Universität Gießen

VORBEMERKUNG*

Zur Zeit wird eine grundlegende Neuordnung des deutschen Ausländer- und Asylrechts beraten. Das von der Bundesregierung vorgeschlagene Zuwanderungsgesetz wurde bereits im Jahr 2002 verabschiedet. Es ist jedoch im Dezember 2002 vom Bundesverfassungsgericht wegen eines Verfahrensfehlers für nichtig erklärt worden[1]. Daraufhin ist es im Mai 2003 erneut vom Bundestag beschlossen worden[2]. Im Juni 2003 wurde es jedoch vom Bundesrat, der zweiten Parlamentskammer, abgelehnt. Das Vermittlungsverfahren, in dem ein politischer Kompromiss gesucht wird, konnte im Jahr 2003 nicht abgeschlossen werden, so dass noch unklar ist, ob das Gesetz in Kraft treten wird. Der folgende Bericht legt die Rechtslage im Dezember 2003 zugrunde.

I EINREISE, VISA UND GRENZKONTROLLE

1.1 Welche nationalen Behörden sind dafür zuständig, Visaanmeldungen zu bearbeiten (Schengenvisa und Langzeitvisa)? Gibt es Verfahren, um die Duplikation von Visaanmeldungen oder aufeinanderfolgende Visaanmeldungen bei verschiedenen EU-Konsulaten zu vermeiden? Welche materiellen Kriterien sind ausschlaggebend für die Vergabe oder Nichtvergabe von Visa, mit Ausnahme der minimalen Schengen-Anforderungen? Wie viele Visa sind ausgestellt oder abgelehnt worden?

Ausländer bedürfen für die Einreise und den Aufenthalt im Bundesgebiet grundsätzlich einer Aufenthaltsgenehmigung (§ 3 I 1 AuslG[3]). Diese Aufenthaltsgenehmigung ist vor der Einreise in Form eines Sichtvermerks (Visum) einzuholen (§ 3 III 1 AuslG). Dabei sind Schengen-Visa

* Für Hilfe danke ich meinen Mitarbeitern Dennis Graf und Dr. Timo Hebeler. Die angegebenen Internet-Seiten wurden zuletzt am 15.1.2004 aufgerufen.

1 BVerfGE 106, 310. 2 BT-Drs. 15/420, BR-Drs. 343/03.

3 Gesetz über die Einreise und den Aufenthalt von Ausländern im Bundesgebiet vom 9. Juli 1990.

eines anderen Staates den deutschen Visa gleichgestellt[4]. Staatsangehörige eines anderen Mitgliedstaates der Europäischen Gemeinschaft können dagegen im Rahmen der Freizügigkeit ohne Visum in die Bundesrepublik einreisen (§ 2 III AufenthG/EWG[5]). Weitere Ausnahmen bestehen für verschiedene Personengruppen, insbesondere entsprechend der Visums-Verordnung Nr. 539/2001 für Staatsangehörige von bestimmten Staaten, sofern ihr Aufenthalt bis zu drei Monate dauert und sie keine Erwerbstätigkeit aufnehmen (§ 1 DVAuslG[6]), für Staatsangehörige im Alter unter 16 Jahren der EG- und EWR-Mitgliedstaaten, der Schweiz sowie Ecuadors (§ 2 DVAuslG), sowie für Staatsangehörige der EG- und EWR-Mitgliedstaaten, der Schweiz, von Australien, Israel, Japan, Kanada, Neuseeland und der Vereinigten Staaten von Amerika, die eine erforderliche Aufenthaltsgenehmigung nach der Einreise einholen können (§ 9 I DVAuslG).

Ausländer ohne erforderliches Visum werden beim Versuch der Einreise zurückgewiesen (§ 60 I AuslG). Sie können, wenn die Einreise bereits erfolgt ist, zurückgeschoben werden (§ 61 I AuslG). Wer ohne erforderliches Visum eingereist ist, kann keine Aufenthaltsgenehmigung erhalten (§ 8 I Nr. 1 AuslG).

Verantwortlich für die Visumerteilung im Ausland sind die Botschaften und Generalkonsulate der Bundesrepublik (§ 63 III AuslG). Sofern sich der Ausländer jedoch mehr als drei Monate im Bundesgebiet aufhält, eine Berufstätigkeit ausüben will oder einer unter Terrorismusverdacht stehenden Gruppe angehört, bedarf die Auslandsvertretung zur Erteilung des Visums der vorherigen Zustimmung der für den vorgesehenen Aufenthaltsort zuständigen Ausländerbehörde (§ 11 I DVAuslG). Für Staatsangehörige bestimmter Problemstaaten besteht nach Art. 17 II des Schengener Durchführungsübereinkommens ein Konsultationsverfahren mit den anderen Schengen-Staaten[7]. Zur Vermeidung von Mehrfachanträgen wird gemäß der Gemeinsamen konsularischen Instruktion ein Stempel in den Pass eingetragen, wenn ein Visum erteilt wurde. Die Ablehnung eines Visums wird den Vertretungen der anderen Staaten mitgeteilt. In besonderen Fällen können Ausnahme-Visa von den Grenzkontrollbehörden

[4] Dazu *Westphal/Stoppa*, ZAR 2003, 211 ff.

[5] Gesetz über Einreise und Aufenthalt von Staatsangehörigen der Mitgliedstaaten der Europäischen Wirtschaftsgemeinschaft in der Fassung vom 31. Januar 1980.

[6] Verordnung zur Durchführung des Ausländergesetzes vom 18. Dezember 1990.

[7] Vgl. *Westphal/Stoppa*, ZAR 2003, 211 ff., 213.

ausgestellt werden, sofern sie hierzu vom Bundesinnenministerium ermächtigt worden sind (§ 58 II AuslG).

Die Voraussetzungen für die Erteilung eines Visums sind nicht eigenständig geregelt, sondern ergeben sich aus den allgemeinen ausländerrechtlichen Bestimmungen über den Aufenthalt (vgl. unten II.). In diesem Rahmen steht die Erteilung des Visums im Regelfall im Ermessen der zuständigen Auslandsvertretung[8]. Dabei können bereits vor der Einreise Auflagen und Bedingungen beigefügt werden, sofern sie im öffentlichen Interesse erforderlich sind[9]. Die Versagung oder Beschränkung eines Visums bedarf in Abweichung von den allgemeinen Regelungen des Verwaltungsverfahrensrechtes keiner Begründung (§ 66 II AuslG)[10].

Nach der Statistik des Auswärtigen Amtes für das Jahr 2002 (2001)[11] wurden insgesamt 3.037.315 (3.232.626) Anträge bearbeitet. 2.203.028 (2.349.724) Visa für kurzfristige Aufenthalte und 394.423 (399.975) Visa für längerfristige Aufenthalte bzw. Erwerbstätigkeit wurden erteilt. 218.929 (195.575) Visumanträge wurden schriftlich abgelehnt.

1.2 Gibt es ein Visaverfolgungsverfahren, um herauszufinden, wer länger bleibt, als das Visum erlaubt? Welche Daten werden von Visabewerbern erfasst (Fingerabdrücke)? Dürfen die Visadaten an Dritte und Polizeibehörden weitergegeben werden?

Folgende Daten werden in einer besonderen Datei des Ausländerzentralregisters von allen Personen gespeichert, die ein Visum beantragen (§ 29 I AZRG[12]): das Geschäftszeichen der Registerbehörde (Visadatei-Nummer), die Auslandsvertretung bzw. bei einem Antrag auf Erteilung eines Ausnahmevisums die mit der polizeilichen Kontrolle des grenzüberschreitenden Verkehrs betraute Behörde, die Grundpersonalien und die weiteren Personalien, das Lichtbild, das Datum der Datenübermittlung, die Entscheidung über den Antrag, das Datum der Entscheidung und das Datum der Übermittlung der Entscheidung, die Art, Nummer und Geltungsdauer des Visums, bei Erteilung eines Visums das Datum der Verpflichtungserklärung nach

[8] *Kloesel/Christ/Häußer*, Deutsches Ausländerrecht (Stand Juli 2003), § 3 AuslG Rn. 21a.
[9] BVerwG, NVwZ 1986, 1027.
[10] Dazu näher *Lipski*, ZAR 2002, 196 ff.; krit. *Teipel*, ZAR 1995, 162 ff., 165 m.w.N.
[11] http//www.auswaertiges-amt.de/www/de/willkommen/einreisebestimmungen/visumangelegenheiten_html
[12] Gesetz über das Ausländerzentralregister vom 2. September 1994.

§ 84 I, § 82 II des Ausländergesetzes und die Stelle, bei der sie vorliegt, bei Vorlage ge- oder verfälschter Dokumente im Visaverfahren die Bezeichnung der vorgelegten ge- oder verfälschten Dokumente (Art und Nummer des Dokuments, im Dokument enthaltene Angaben über Aussteller, Ausstellungsdatum, Gültigkeitsdauer). Ein spezielles Verfahren zur Überprüfung, ob eine Aufenthaltsgenehmigung abgelaufen ist, gibt es nicht.

Auf Ersuchen werden diese Daten an folgende öffentliche Stellen zur Erfüllung ihrer Aufgaben übermittelt (§ 32 AZRG): die Grenzschutzdirektion und die mit grenzpolizeilichen Aufgaben betrauten Stellen, das Bundesamt für die Anerkennung ausländischer Flüchtlinge, das Bundeskriminalamt, die Landeskriminalämter, sonstige Polizeivollzugsbehörden des Bundes und der Länder, die Ausländerbehörden, die Träger der Sozialhilfe und die für die Durchführung des Asylbewerberleistungsgesetzes zuständigen Stellen, die Verfassungsschutzbehörden des Bundes und der Länder, den Militärischen Abschirmdienst und den Bundesnachrichtendienst, die Gerichte und Staatsanwaltschaften. Es kann sogar ein Abruf im automatisierten Verfahren zugelassen werden (§ 33 AZRG). Eine Übermittlung an Behörden anderer Staaten kann auf Ersuchen erfolgen, wenn ein berechtigtes Interesse glaubhaft dargelegt wird, doch ist im Regelfall die Einwilligung des Betroffenen erforderlich (§ 26 AZRG).

1.3 Haben die Gerichte jemals entschieden über die Ablehnung eines Schengenvisums aus dem Grund, dass der Antragsteller in anderen Mitgliedstaaten auf der schwarzen Liste steht?

Entsprechende Gerichtsentscheidungen sind nicht veröffentlicht worden.

1.4 Welche Maßnahmen sind unternommen worden zur Ausführung des Aktionsprogrammes für administrative Kooperation im Bereich der Außengrenzen, Visa, Asyl und Einwanderung im Anschluss an die Ratsentscheidung vom 13. Juni 2002?

Im Rahmen des ARGO-Programmes wurde im Bundesinnenministerium ein Zentrum Landgrenzen gegründet, in dem Grenzpolizeien verschiedener Länder zusammenarbeiten. Es hat bereits mehrere gemeinsame Einsätze der Grenzpolizeien koordiniert, u.a. Kontrollen von einreisenden Bussen aus Mittel- und Osteuropa, die von gemischten Teams an großen Straßenübergängen in Deutschland, Österreich und Italien durchgeführt wurden. Zu Beginn des Jahres 2003 gab es insgesamt 17 Projekte mit dem Ziel, grenzpolizeiliches Handeln (Arbeitsmethoden, operative Vorgehensweisen, Lageanalysen etc.) aufeinander abzustimmen.

1.5 Welche Maßnahmen sind unternommen worden, um die Richtlinie 2001/51/EG auszuführen, zusätzlich zu den Schengen-Regeln für Sanktionen für Beförderer? Wie oft sind Sanktionen gegen Beförderer erlassen worden?

Beförderungsunternehmer dürfen Ausländer nur dann auf dem Luft- oder Seeweg in das Bundesgebiet befördern, wenn sie im Besitz eines erforderlichen Passes und Visums sind (§ 74 I 1 AuslG). Auch kann Beförderungsunternehmern im Einzelfall untersagt werden, Ausländer ohne ein erforderliches Visum in das Bundesgebiet zu befördern (§ 74 I 2, II 1 Nr. 1 AuslG). Bei Zuwiderhandlungen kann ein Zwangsgeld pro befördertem Ausländer (§ 74 II 2 AuslG) sowie eine Geldbuße bis zu 10.000 EURO (§ 93 III Nr. 2 AuslG) festgesetzt werden. Bei der Einreise an der Grenze zurückgewiesene Ausländer müssen von dem Beförderungsunternehmer, mit dessen Luft-, See- oder Landfahrzeug der Ausländer einreisen will, unverzüglich außer Landes gebracht werden (§ 73 I AuslG). Der Unternehmer haftet neben dem Ausländer für alle Kosten der Rückbeförderung und für alle Kosten, die von der Ankunft des Ausländers an der Grenzübergangsstelle bis zum Vollzug der Entscheidung über die Einreise entstehen (§ 82 III AuslG). Hierunter fallen auch die Kosten für Dolmetscher[13]. Diese Rechtsvorschriften bestanden bereits vor dem Erlass der Richtlinie 2001/51/EG.

Nach Auskunft des Bundesinnenministeriums wurden in den Jahren 2000 und 2001 jeweils 10 Untersagungsverfügungen mit Zwangsgeldandrohungen gegen Luftfahrtunternehmen erlassen. Über die Durchführung der Rückbeförderungspflicht werden keine Statistiken geführt.

1.6 Ist das Visarecht und die -politik ihres Landes ihrer Meinung nach im Einvernehmen mit dem EU-Standard oder sind Veränderungen nötig? Glauben Sie, dass eine weitere unionsweite Harmonisierung von Visarichtlinien für folgende Punkte benötigt wird:

1 gemeinsame Kriterien für die Ausgabe von Visa mit dem Ziel, die Visapflichten der Teilnehmer des Budapester Prozesses zu harmonisieren,

2 Gründung eines europäischen Visaidentifizierungssystems (VIS and SIS II)?

In welchem Maße wird die Erweiterung der Gemeinschaft eine Chance oder eine Gefahr darstellen, um Probleme mit illegalen Einreisen und Grenzkontrollen anzugehen?

Die deutschen Rechtsvorschriften über die Ausstellung von Visa und ihre Durchführung in der Verwaltungspraxis entsprechen den EU-Standards. Eine weitergehende Harmonisierung der nationalen Rechtsvorschriften

[13] BVerwG, DVBl. 2003, 1276.

erscheint mir nur dann sinnvoll, wenn auch das Aufenthaltsrecht vereinheitlicht wird. Eine vollständige Vergemeinschaftung der Regeln für Einreise und Einwanderung wäre die Konsequenz aus dem Ziel der ausnahmslosen Durchsetzung der Freizügigkeit innerhalb der Europäischen Union. Hierzu besteht jedoch in der Bundesrepublik im Augenblick bei den meisten politischen Kräften keine Bereitschaft.

Das im Rahmen von SIS II für 2006 geplante gemeinsame Visa-Identifikationssystem ist dagegen weniger am Ziel der Erleichterung der Freizügigkeit als an dem Ziel der Verbesserung der Kooperation bei der Kontrolle der Außengrenzen orientiert. Eine solche Datenbank, die bald Hunderte von Millionen Personen mit sensiblen persönlichen Daten erfassen und zudem dem Zugriff der Sicherheitsbehörden offen stehen würde, wirft gravierende datenschutzrechtliche Bedenken auf. Problematisch ist v.a. die Vermischung von allgemeinen ausländerrechtlichen Aufgaben mit polizeilichen Funktionen durch die Aufnahme in ein integriertes Informationssystem. Diese Bedenken können nach meiner Auffassung auch durch eine strenge Datenschutzkontrolle nicht ausgeräumt werden. Die Bundesregierung befürwortet dagegen die Pläne zur Einführung von SIS II.

Im Rahmen der Diskussion über die Erweiterung der Europäischen Union wurden Befürchtungen geäußert, dass die Kontrollen an den nach Osten verschobenen Außengrenzen weniger effektiv sein würden als an der deutschen Schengen-Außengrenze nach Polen und Tschechien. Es gibt jedoch inzwischen eine intensive Kooperation mit den zuständigen Behörden der Beitrittsstaaten, durch die Maßnahmen gegen eine mögliche Verstärkung der illegalen Einwanderung vorbereitet werden. Das Schengener Durchführungsabkommen und damit die Kontrollfreiheit im Personenverkehr mit Polen und Tschechien wird erst nach einer Evaluierung der Durchführung des Schengen-Besitzstandes in Kraft gesetzt werden[14].

II EINREISE UND AUFENTHALT VON DRITTSTAATSANGEHÖRIGEN

2.1 Was sind die Grundprinzipien in Ihrem Land betreffend:

1 Aufnahme von Drittstaatsangehörigen für unselbständige oder selbständige Erwerbstätigkeit,

[14] BT-Drs. 15/722.

2 Einreise von Drittstaatsangehörigen zum Studium und zu einer Berufsausbildung,
3 rechtlicher Status von Drittstaatsangehörigen, die in einem anderen Mitgliedsstaat langfristig aufenthaltsberechtigt sind?
In welchem Ausmaß unterscheiden sich diese Prinzipien von den Vorschlägen der Europäischen Kommission?

Das deutsche Ausländergesetz aus dem Jahr 1990 unterscheidet mehrere verschiedene Formen der Aufenthaltsgenehmigung. Durch das Zuwanderungsgesetz soll die Rechtslage vereinfacht werden, da es nur noch die befristete Aufenthaltserlaubnis und die unbefristete Niederlassungserlaubnis geben soll[15].

Eine Aufenthaltserlaubnis wird erteilt, wenn keine Bindung an einen bestimmten Aufenthaltszweck vorliegt (§ 15 AuslG). Sie wird zunächst befristet erteilt, ist nach fünf Jahren jedoch unbefristet zu verlängern, wenn eine Arbeitsberechtigung oder sonstige Erlaubnis zur Erwerbstätigkeit, einfache deutsche Sprachkenntnisse und ausreichender Wohnraum vorliegen und kein Ausweisungsgrund gegeben ist (§ 24 AuslG). Nach frühestens acht Jahren Aufenthalt und dem Nachweis einer hinreichenden sozialen Absicherung besteht ein Anspruch auf eine Aufenthaltsberechtigung, die nicht beschränkt werden kann (§ 27 AuslG).

Eine Aufenthaltsbewilligung wird für einen bestimmten, seiner Natur nach nur vorübergehenden Aufenthalt erteilt (§ 28 AuslG). Sie wird auf höchstens zwei Jahre befristet und nur verlängert, wenn der Zweck des Aufenthalts noch nicht erreicht ist, aber in angemessener Frist noch erreicht werden kann.

Die Aufenthaltsbefugnis kann aus humanitären Gründen gewährt werden (§ 30 AuslG). Sie wird grundsätzlich für längstens zwei Jahre erteilt bzw. verlängert (§ 34 AuslG).

Keine Aufenthaltsgenehmigung, sondern eine zeitweise Aussetzung der Abschiebung stellt die Duldung dar, die erteilt wird, wenn die Abschiebung rechtlich oder tatsächlich nicht möglich ist oder andere dringende Gründe vorliegen (§§ 55 f. AuslG). Durch das Zuwanderungsgesetz soll dieser besondere Status abgeschafft werden[16].

Der Aufenthalt zur Ausübung einer unselbständigen Tätigkeit ist grundsätzlich unzulässig, sofern nicht ausnahmsweise eine Arbeitsgenehmigung erteilt wird (§ 10 AuslG). Für Arbeitnehmer aus Drittstaaten besteht entsprechend im Sozialrecht ein Beschäftigungsverbot, sofern nicht besondere Erlaubnistatbestände vorliegen (§ 284

[15] Vgl. dazu *Davy*, ZAR 2002, 171 ff.

[16] Dazu näher *Duchrow*, ZAR 2002, 269 ff., 276 f.

SGB III[17]). Diese Ausnahmefälle sind in der Arbeitsgenehmigungsverordnung aufgeführt. Ein Arbeitsplatz kann in jedem Fall nur dann an einen Ausländer aus einem Drittstaat vermittelt werden, wenn kein geeigneter deutscher bzw. gleichgestellter Bewerber zur Verfügung steht (§ 285 I SGB III).

Die Voraussetzungen für die Ausübung einer selbständigen Tätigkeit durch einen Ausländer sind nicht explizit gesetzlich geregelt, so dass die Erteilung einer Aufenthaltsgenehmigung zu diesem Zweck im Ermessen der Behörde liegt. Die Einzelheiten sind in Verwaltungsvorschriften geregelt, die auf ein besonderes örtliches Bedürfnis, ein überregionales Interesse oder ein sonstiges öffentliches Interesse abstellen[18]. Wer eine Aufenthaltsberechtigung besitzt, kann allerdings keinen Beschränkungen im Hinblick auf eine selbständige Erwerbstätigkeit unterworfen werden. Durch das Zuwanderungsgesetz sollen diese Voraussetzungen gesetzlich geregelt werden.

Ein Aufenthalt zu Ausbildungszwecken, insbesondere zur Durchführung eines Studiums, ist typischerweise vorübergehend, so dass nur eine Aufenthaltsbewilligung erteilt werden kann. Im Rahmen des Ermessens ist insbesondere zu berücksichtigen, ob eine Zulassung zum Studium erfolgt ist und ob ausreichende Mittel zum Bestreiten des eigenen Lebensunterhaltes zur Verfügung stehen[19].

Die Tatsache, dass ein Drittstaatsangehöriger seit längerer Zeit in einem anderen EG-Mitgliedstaat wohnhaft ist, ist kein gesetzliches Kriterium für die Erteilung einer Aufenthaltsgenehmigung. Vielmehr gelten die allgemeinen Regeln. Der Aufenthalt in einem anderen Mitgliedstaat kann folglich lediglich im Rahmen der Ermessensausübung berücksichtigt werden.

2.2 Was sind die rechtlichen Voraussetzungen und Verfahren für Drittstaatsangehörige, um eine Aufenthaltserlaubnis für eine Erwerbstätigkeit zu bekommen? Welche Verfahren werden benutzt, um den bevorzugten Zugang von EU-Einwohnern und Türken (Beitrittsvereinbarung) zum Arbeitsmarkt zu erhalten? Bestehen spezielle Programme, um den Zugang von hochqualifizierten Facharbeitern zum Arbeitsmarkt zu erleichtern? In welchem Maße sind Gewerkschaften und Arbeitgeber in solchen Programmen involviert? Gibt es ein Verfahren, um die Nachfrage für ausländische Arbeiter zu kalkulieren? Wie wird die Erweiterung der Gemeinschaft in Betracht gezogen? In welchem Maße hat die kürzliche wirtschaftliche Rezession und Arbeitslosigkeit die Konzepte über die Aufnahme von Drittstaatsangehörigen beeinflusst?

[17] Sozialgesetzbuch Drittes Buch vom 24. März 1997.
[18] *Welte*, Ausländerrecht, 2000, S. 64; *Renner*, Ausländerrecht in Deutschland, 1998, S. 412 f.
[19] *Renner*, aaO, S. 529.

Drittstaatsangehörige benötigen für die Ausübung einer unselbständigen Tätigkeit eine Aufenthaltsgenehmigung. Die Kriterien für die Erlaubnis des Aufenthalts zu diesem Zweck sind in der Arbeitsaufenthalteverordnung geregelt. Daneben ist eine Arbeitsgenehmigung erforderlich. Arbeitnehmer, die Staatsangehörige eines EU-Mitgliedstaates sind, benötigen für Arbeitsaufenthalte von mindestens drei Monaten eine Aufenthaltsgenehmigung-EG (§ 3 AufenthG/ EWG), auf deren Erteilung jedoch ein Anspruch besteht. Für türkische Staatsangehörige sind die Beschlüsse zur Durchführung des Assoziationsabkommens bei der Entscheidung über den Aufenthalt zu berücksichtigen, ein besonderes Verfahren besteht hierfür jedoch nicht[20]. Durch das Zuwanderungsgesetz soll das Verfahren zur Erlangung einer Aufenthalts- und Arbeitsgenehmigung vereinfacht werden[21].

Nach einer intensiven öffentlichen Diskussion wurde im Jahr 2000 die Verordnung über die Arbeitsgenehmigung für hochqualifizierte ausländische Fachkräfte der Informations- und Kommunikationstechnologie erlassen, auf deren Grundlage als Ausnahme vom allgemeinen Anwerbestopp auf drei Jahre befristet bis zu 10.000, bei erhöhtem Bedarf maximal 20.000 Arbeitserlaubnisse erteilt werden durften[22]. Gewerkschaften und Arbeitgeberverbände sind nur mittelbar durch die Teilnahme an der Selbstverwaltung der Arbeitsämter, die die Arbeitsgenehmigungen erteilen, an diesem Programm beteiligt. Aufgrund der wirtschaftlichen Rezession ist die Inanspruchnahme dieser Möglichkeit des Zugangs zum deutschen Arbeitsmarkt jedoch weit hinter den Erwartungen zurückgeblieben[23].

Die zu erwartende Zuwanderung aus den östlichen Beitrittsstaaten hat in der politischen Diskussion der letzten Jahre eine wichtige Rolle gespielt[24], doch haben wissenschaftliche Studien betont, dass Vorhersagen über ihren Umfang sehr schwierig zu treffen sind. Insbesondere darf von einer grundsätzlichen Abwanderungsbereitschaft nicht auf die tatsächlichen Wanderungsbewegungen rückgeschlossen werden[25]. Die Bundesregierung erwartet keine Zunahme der Einwanderung im unmittelbaren Zusammenhang mit der Erweiterung der Union[26].

Im Rahmen der politischen Beratungen über das Zuwanderungsgesetz sind insbesondere die Regelungen über den Zugang zum Arbeitsmarkt

[20] Dazu ausführlich *Renner*, aaO, S. 211 ff. [21] Vgl. *Feldgen*, ZAR 2003, 132 ff.

[22] Dazu näher *Moll/Reichel*, RdA 2001, 308 ff.

[23] Vgl. *Kolb*, ZAR 2003, 231 ff. [24] Vgl. *Wollenschläger/Pietsch*, ZAR 2003, 259 ff.

[25] Dazu *Fassmann/Münz*, in: Bade/Münz (Hrsg.), Migrationsreport 2002, 2002, S. 61 ff.; *Heilemann/v. Loeffelholz/Sieveking*, Arbeitsmarktgesteuerte Zuwanderung, 2003, S. 43 f.

[26] BT-Drs. 15/1458.

heftig umstritten[27]. Eingeführt werden soll ein Auswahlverfahren für Arbeitsimmigranten im Rahmen einer festgesetzten Höchstzahl.

2.3 In welchem Ausmaß unterscheiden sich das bestehende Recht und die Praxis wesentlich von der Methode, die von der Kommission gewählt wurde in ihrem Vorschlag über die Aufnahme zum Zweck von unselbständiger oder selbständiger Erwerbstätigkeit betreffend:
1 Aufnahme von Drittstaatsangehörigen zum Studium und zu einer Berufsausbildung,
2 rechtlicher Status von Drittstaatsangehörigen, die in einem anderen Mitgliedstaat langfristig aufenthaltsberechtigt sind?
In welchem Ausmaß unterscheiden sich diese Prinzipien von den Vorschlägen der Europäischen Kommission?

2.6 Der Vorschlag für eine Richtlinie über die Rechte von Langzeiteinwohnern aus Drittländern, der vom Rat am 5. Juni 2003 genehmigt wurde, beinhaltet eine Anzahl von Rechten, die die Standards für Langzeiteinwohner an den Status von EU-Bürgern angleichen. Wird die Umsetzung dieser Richtlinie wichtige rechtliche und politische Veränderungen in Ihrem Land beinhalten? Was sind die wichtigsten Belange, falls es welche gibt, betreffend des Annäherungskonzepts der Richtlinie in Bezug auf:
1 keine Diskriminierung bei sozialen Rechten,
2 das Konzept der zivilen Staatsbürgerschaft ('civic citizenship') (siehe auch die erweiterte Auswirkungsbeurteilung der Mitteilung über die Integration vom 11. Juni 2003),
3 Familienzusammenführung und Zugang von Familienmitgliedern zum Arbeitsmarkt,
4 Aufenthaltssicherheit?

Studierende und Auszubildende aus Drittstaaten können eine befristete Aufenthaltsbewilligung erhalten (§ 28 AuslG). Ihre Gewährung steht im Ermessen der Behörden, wobei bei der Entscheidung insbesondere zu prüfen ist, ob eine Hochschulzulassung bzw. ein Ausbildungsplatz vorliegt, die Sprachkenntnisse ausreichen und ausreichende Mittel zur Verfügung stehen, um den Lebensunterhalt zu bestreiten[28]. Für die Aufnahme einer Erwerbstätigkeit bedürfen sie einer besonderen Genehmigung im Rahmen des Ausbildungsaufenthaltes[29]. Dies entspricht den Anforderungen des Richtlinienentwurfs der Kommission, so dass keine grundlegenden gesetzlichen Änderungen erforderlich werden.

Die geplanten Privilegien für Drittstaatsangehörige, die bereits längere Zeit in einem anderen Mitgliedstaat wohnhaft sind und rechtmäßig

[27] Vgl. zu den Szenarien *Heilemann/v.Loeffelholz/Sieveking*, aaO, S. 28 ff.; *Bogai*, SF 2003, 126 ff.

[28] Vgl. *Renner*, aaO, S. 529. [29] *Renner*, aaO, S. 527 f.

Tätigkeiten als Arbeitnehmer ausgeübt haben, sind bisher im deutschen Recht nicht vorgesehen. Aufgrund der Heterogenität der sozialen und materiellen Lebensbedingungen wird eine Annäherung des Aufenthaltsrechtes für Drittstaatsangehörige an das von Unionsbürgern zum Teil kritisch beurteilt[30]. Wenn man dagegen ein stärker grundrechtlich orientiertes Verständnis der Freizügigkeit zugrunde legt[31], ist diese Tendenz positiv zu bewerten. Nach der Verabschiedung der Daueraufenthalts-Richtlinie muss im deutschen Recht ein neuer europäischer Aufenthaltstitel und ein Recht auf Weiterwanderung eingeführt werden. Die inhaltlichen Kriterien unterscheiden sich jedoch nicht grundlegend von den bestehenden Anforderungen des deutschen Ausländerrechts.

2.4 Welche Maßnahmen sind getroffen worden, um die Richtlinie vom 29. Juni 2000 zur Anwendung des Gleichbehandlungsgrundsatzes ohne Unterschied der Rasse oder der ethnischen Herkunft und die Richtlinie 2000/78/EG des Rates vom 27. November 2000 zur Festlegung eines allgemeinen Rahmens für die Verwirklichung der Gleichbehandlung in Beschäftigung und Beruf umzusetzen? Sind Veränderungen des Rechts vorgenommen worden? In welchem Maß werden positive Maßnahmen ('affirmative action') als notwendig angesehen, um die Gleichbehandlung von Arbeitskräften aus Drittländern zu fördern?

Die beiden Anti-Diskriminierungs-Richtlinien der EG sind noch nicht in das deutsche Recht umgesetzt worden. Ein von der Bundesregierung vorbereiteter Gesetzentwurf wurde in der Öffentlichkeit sehr kontrovers beurteilt, so dass er bisher noch nicht in das Parlament eingebracht worden ist. Nach Ablauf der Umsetzungsfrist müssen allerdings die hinreichend bestimmten Vorschriften der Richtlinien bei der Auslegung zivilrechtlicher Generalklauseln berücksichtigt werden, so dass sie bereits eine begrenzte Wirkung entfalten können[32].

2.5 In Bezug auf den Entwurf für eine Richtlinie betreffend das Recht zur Familienzusammenführung, welcher vom Rat im Februar 2003 genehmigt wurde:

1. **Glauben Sie, dass die vorgeschlagenen Normen der Familienzusammenführung niedriger sind als die, die in Ihrem Land gültig sind?**
2. **Wird die Umsetzung der Richtlinie, wenn sie angenommen worden ist, zu Veränderungen in Ihrem nationalen Recht zur Familienzusammenführung führen, die den Standard des Schutzes zurückstufen? Falls dies der Fall ist, welche Veränderungen sind vorgesehen?**

Einem ausländischen Familienangehörigen eines in Deutschland lebenden Ausländers kann eine Aufenthaltserlaubnis für die Herstellung

[30] *Hägel/Deubner*, ZAR 2001, 154 ff., 155; *Hauschild*, ZAR 2003, 266 ff., 267 f.

[31] Vgl. *Groß*, KJ 2001, 100 ff.

[32] Dazu näher *Thüsing*, NJW 2003, 3441 ff.

und Wahrung der familiären Lebensgemeinschaft erteilt und verlängert werden (§ 17 AuslG). Voraussetzung ist generell, dass der Ausländer eine Aufenthaltserlaubnis oder Aufenthaltsberechtigung besitzt, ausreichender Wohnraum zur Verfügung steht und der Lebensunterhalt des Familienangehörigen aus eigener Erwerbstätigkeit des Ausländers, eigenem Vermögen oder sonstigen eigenen Mitteln gesichert ist oder durch andere Familienangehörige gewährleistet wird. Lediglich bei Ehegatten und minderjährigen Kindern von Asylberechtigten kann von diesen Voraussetzungen abgewichen werden.

Die weiteren Bedingungen differenzieren zwischen Ehegatten bzw. Lebenspartnern, Kindern und sonstigen Familienangehörigen. Ein Anspruch auf Ehegattennachzug besteht nur, wenn der Ausländer eine Aufenthaltsberechtigung besitzt oder als Asylberechtigter anerkannt ist oder wenn er eine Aufenthaltserlaubnis besitzt, die Ehe schon zum Zeitpunkt seiner Einreise bestanden hat und von ihm angegeben wurde, oder wenn der Ausländer im Bundesgebiet geboren oder als Minderjähriger eingereist ist, eine unbefristete Aufenthaltserlaubnis besitzt, sich acht Jahre rechtmäßig im Bundesgebiet aufgehalten hat und volljährig ist (§ 18 I AuslG). Die gleichen Regeln gelten seit 2001 auch für Lebenspartner (§ 27a AuslG). Einen Anspruch auf Nachzug haben minderjährige ledige Kinder von Asylberechtigten und bis zu 16jährige Kinder, wenn beide Eltern in der Bundesrepublik leben (§ 20 AuslG). Liegen diese Voraussetzungen bei Ehegatten, Lebenspartnern oder Kindern dagegen nicht vor, liegt die Gewährung der Aufenthaltserlaubnis im Ermessen. Sonstige Familienangehörige können nur dann eine Aufenthaltserlaubnis erhalten, wenn es zur Vermeidung einer außergewöhnlichen Härte erforderlich ist (§ 22 AuslG).

Im Rahmen der Verhandlungen über die Familiennachzugs-Richtlinie 2003/86/EG konnte die deutsche Regierung ihre tendenziell restriktiven Vorstellungen, wie sie dem geltenden deutschen Recht entsprechen, weitgehend durchsetzen[33]. Eine Absenkung der deutschen Standards zuungunsten des Schutzes von Ehe und Familie ist in keinem Fall ersichtlich. Soweit Art. 4 Abs. 1 der Familiennachzugs-Richtlinie allen minderjährigen Kindern einen Anspruch auf Familiennachzug einräumt, wird diese Ausweitung gegenüber der bisherigen Altersbegrenzung im deutschen Recht dadurch relativiert, dass nach Art. 4 Abs. 1 UAbs. 3 der Familiennachzugs-Richtlinie die Möglichkeit besteht, bei über

[33] *Hauschild*, ZAR 2003, 266 ff., 273.

12jährigen die Erfüllung eines Integrationskriteriums zu verlangen, und dass nach Art. 4 Abs. 6 der Familiennachzugs-Richtlinie die Verpflichtung besteht, den Antrag vor Vollendung des fünfzehnten Lebensjahres zu stellen[34].

2.7 Angesichts der Perspektive einer gemeinsamen Migrationspolitik, wie sie von der Kommission in der Mitteilung über den offenen Koordinierungsmechanismus (KOM 2001, 387) und der Mitteilung über eine Migrationspolitik der Gemeinschaft (KOM 2000, 757 endg.) entwickelt worden ist, welche Rolle werden Ihrer Meinung nach die EU-Organe haben bezüglich der Befugnisse der Mitgliedstaaten, um über Aufenthaltsrechte, den Zugang zum Arbeitsmarkt und Integration zu entscheiden? Sollte die Harmonisierung des Rechtes weitergehen und, falls dies der Fall ist, in welcher Hinsicht?

In den 90er Jahren hat sich die deutsche Bundesregierung energisch für eine gemeinsame europäische Einwanderungs- und Ausländerpolitik eingesetzt[35]. Nach der Erweiterung der EG-Kompetenzen im Vertrag von Amsterdam erhoben sich aber bald Bedenken, dass eine Europäisierung der Einwanderungspolitik das nationale Sozialsystem unangemessen belasten könnte[36]. Die Bundesregierung hat deshalb großen Wert auf die Beibehaltung des Einstimmigkeitsprinzips gelegt[37]. Sie stimmt einer Harmonisierung nur zu, wenn sie nicht mit einer spürbaren Erleichterung der Bedingungen für die Einwanderung verbunden ist. Humanitäre und langfristige demographische Gesichtspunkte spielen demgegenüber kaum eine Rolle.

III ASYL UND FLÜCHTLINGE

3.1 Sind die Dubliner Regeln zufriedenstellend und was wird von der Dublin II-Verordnung Nr. 343/2003 vom 18. Februar 2003 erwartet?

Im Jahr 1993 wurde mit Art. 16a V GG eine ausdrückliche Regelung in die Verfassung aufgenommen, um klarzustellen, dass das Grundrecht auf Asyl dem Abschluss von völkerrechtlichen Abkommen über Zuständigkeitsregelungen für die Prüfung von Asylbegehren und die gegenseitige Anerkennung von Asylentscheidungen nicht entgegensteht.

34 Zur Vereinbarkeit mit Art. 8 EMRK vgl. *Davy*, ZAR 2002, 171 ff., 176; *Langenfeld/Mohsen*, ZAR 2003, 398 ff., 401 ff.

35 Vgl. *Schoch*, DVBl. 1992, 525 ff., 526; *Weber*, ZAR 1993, 11 ff., 17.

36 So z.B. der CSU-Politiker *Beckstein*, ZAR 1999, 151 ff., 152.

37 So der SPD-Innenminister *Schily*, NVwZ 2000, 883 ff., 885.

Damit wird die Berufung auf das Grundrecht im Anwendungsbereich des Dubliner Abkommens ausgeschlossen[38].

Nachdem die deutschen Behörden am Anfang nur zurückhaltend Übernahmeersuchen gestellt haben[39], sind die Zahlen inzwischen angestiegen. Im Jahr 2002 (2001) hat Deutschland 4.729 (4.255) Übernahmeersuchen gestellt, von denen die meisten an Italien, Österreich und Frankreich gerichtet wurden[40]. Die Zahl der Rückübernahmeersuchen von anderen Mitgliedstaaten betrug im Jahr 2002 (2001) 8.649 (6.838), wobei hier zuletzt Schweden, Norwegen und Großbritannien führend waren.

Als problematisch wurde beim Dubliner Übereinkommen v.a. die dreimonatige Antwortfrist des Aufnahmestaates und der Beweisaufwand für die Zuständigkeit angesehen[41]. Von der Dublin II-Verordnung Nr. 343/2003 erwartet man sich eine Beschleunigung des Verfahrens und Klarstellungen für verschiedene strittige Fragen wie die Behandlung von Familienangehörigen und das Selbsteintrittsrecht der Mitgliedstaaten[42]. Auch das neue Verfahren wird jedoch als kompliziert kritisiert[43].

3.2 Hat die Eurodac-Verordnung Nr. 2725/2000 vom 11. Dezember 2000 über die Einrichtung von EURODAC für den Vergleich von Fingerabdrücken zum Zwecke der effektiven Anwendung des Dubliner Übereinkommens, die seit dem 15. Januar 2003 in Kraft ist, zu einem Anstieg von Dubliner Fällen geführt? Ist EURODAC in Ihrem Land effektiv oder wird erwartet, dass es letztendlich effektiv wird?

EURODAC wurde am 15.1.2003 in Betrieb genommen und hat bis Ende August 2003 bereits zu etwa 1.300 Treffern geführt[44]. Daraus ist zu schließen, dass zukünftig eine größere Zahl von Asylbewerbern bekannt werden wird, die bereits in einem anderen Mitgliedstaat einen Asylantrag gestellt haben, so dass auch die Anzahl der Übernahmeverfahren steigen wird[45].

3.3 Welche wichtigen Veränderungen, falls es welche gibt, wird die Annahme des geänderten Vorschlages der Richtlinie über Mindestnormen für Verfahren in Mitgliedstaaten für die Anerkennung oder den Entzug des Flüchtlingsstatus, über die der Rat in den meisten Punkten im Juni 2003 politisches Einvernehmen erreicht

[38] BVerfGE 94, 49, 86. [39] Vgl. *Hailbronner/Thiery*, ZAR 1997, 52 ff., 64 ff.

[40] Vgl. Bundesamt für die Anerkennung ausländischer Flüchtlinge, Der Einzelentscheider-Brief 09/2003.

[41] *Löper*, ZAR 2000, 16 ff., 24; *Schröder*, ZAR 2001, 71 ff., 71 f.

[42] Vgl. *Schröder*, ZAR 2003, 126 ff. [43] *Piotrowicz*, ZAR 2003, 383 ff., 385.

[44] Bundesamt für die Anerkennung ausländischer Flüchtlinge, Der Einzelentscheider-Brief 09/2003.

[45] So auch *Schröder*, ZAR 2001, 71 ff., 75.

hat, für das Recht und die Praxis in Ihrem Land bringen, insbesondere in Bezug auf die folgenden Punkte:
1 Rechte von Bewerbern im Verfahren,
2 administratives und richterliches Rechtsmittelverfahren,
3 Verwendung von Konzepten von sicheren Drittländern und sicheren Ursprungsländern,
4 Inhaftierung von Asylbewerbern,
5 Verfahren an Flughäfen und Grenzen?

Die deutschen Vorschriften über die Rechte der Asylbewerber im Anerkennungsverfahren entsprechen weitgehend den Anforderungen des Richtlinien-Vorschlages[46]. Nicht ausreichend gesichert ist jedoch bisher die Unterrichtung des Asylbewerbers über seine Rechte und Pflichten in einer als ihm bekannt vorauszusetzenden Sprache. Auch eine spezielle Entscheidungsfrist für beschleunigte Verfahren gibt es noch nicht. Die Sonderregelungen für das verwaltungsgerichtliche Verfahren in Asylsachen entsprechen bereits den Vorgaben des Richtlinien-Entwurfs[47].

Ob die deutschen Vorschriften über die Bestimmung sicherer Drittstaaten (Art. 16a II 2 GG i.V.m. § 26a AsylVfG[48]), die abstrakt vom Gesetzgeber festgelegt werden[49], den stärker einzelfallbezogenen Kriterien des Richtlinien-Entwurfs entsprechen, ist fraglich[50]. Allerdings besteht bereits eine Möglichkeit der Abweichung durch Verordnung (§ 26a III AsylVfG). Die bisherigen Regelungen über die anderweitige Sicherheit vor Verfolgung (§ 27 AsylVfG) garantieren keinen ausreichenden Schutz vor Verfolgung, da bei der Entscheidung nicht berücksichtigt wird, ob die Möglichkeit der Rückkehr in den Aufnahmestaat besteht[51].

Die Regelungen über das Verfahren bei der Einreise an der Grenze bzw. über einen Flughafen entsprechen ebenfalls den Anforderungen des Richtlinien-Entwurfs. Die zwingende Unterbringung auf dem Flughafengelände (§ 18a I AsylVfG) stellt nach der Auffassung des Bundesverfassungsgerichtes keine Freiheitsentziehung dar, da eine Ausreise jederzeit möglich sei[52]. Es ist deshalb strittig, ob eine weitergehende gesetzliche

[46] Vgl. zum folgenden *Renner*, ZAR 2003, 88 ff.; *Hailbronner*, ZAR 2003, 299 ff.
[47] *Renner*, ZAR 2003, 88 ff., 95 f.; kritisch zum "Sonderprozessrecht" *Geiger*, BayVBl. 2003, 673 ff.
[48] Asylverfahrensgesetz vom 26. Juli 1992.
[49] Vgl. zum Konzept der "normativen Vergewisserung" BVerfGE 94, 49, 87 ff.; *Groß/Kainer*, DVBl. 1997, 1315 ff., 1318 f.
[50] *Hailbronner*, ZAR 2002, 259 ff., 262; *Renner*, ZAR 2003, 88 ff., 89 f.
[51] *Renner*, ZAR 2003, 88 ff., 89 f.; vgl. dazu BVerwGE 75, 181.
[52] BVerfGE 94, 166, 198 f.

Regelung des Gewahrsams und seiner gerichtlichen Kontrolle künftig erforderlich sein wird[53].

3.4 Welche Maßnahmen sind unternommen worden, um die Richtlinie 2003/9/EG vom 27. Januar 2003 über die Aufnahme von Asylsuchenden in Ihrem Land umzusetzen
1 in Bezug auf die Flexibilitätsparagraphen in der Richtlinie,
2 Beschränkungen des Aufenthalts,
3 Zugang zum Arbeitsmarkt,
4 die Rechte von Migranten laut Artikel 11 § 2 der Richtlinie?

Der Aufenthalt von Asylbewerbern ist räumlich auf den Bezirk einer Ausländerbehörde, also regelmäßig einen Stadt- oder Landkreis beschränkt (§ 56 AsylVfG). Sie dürfen ihn zum persönlichen Erscheinen vor Behörden und Gerichten verlassen, im übrigen bedarf es hierfür einer einzelfallbezogenen Genehmigung (§§ 57 f. AsylVfG). Diese Beschränkungen sind vom Bundesverfassungsgericht als verhältnismäßig gebilligt worden[54] und dürften auch den Anforderungen von Art. 7 der Aufnahme-Richtlinie 2003/9/EG entsprechen.

Das Arbeitsverbot für Asylbewerber ist bereits im Jahr 2000 gelockert worden, so dass sie wie auch ihre Angehörigen nunmehr nach einem Jahr Wartezeit eine Arbeitserlaubnis erhalten können[55]. Dies entspricht den Anforderungen von Art. 11 der Aufnahme-Richtlinie.

3.5 Welche Schritte sind unternommen worden, um die Richtlinie über vorübergehenden Schutz in nationales Recht umzusetzen? Gibt es Verfahren für Vereinbarungen, die die Teilung von Lasten vorsehen? Gibt es eine rechtliche Basis für die Aufnahme von Flüchtlingen für einen vorübergehenden Schutz im Falle eines Massenzustroms?

Ausländer aus Kriegs- oder Bürgerkriegsgebieten können aufgrund einer Vereinbarung von Bund und Ländern vorübergehend Schutz in Deutschland erhalten, wobei eine Aufenthaltsbefugnis nur erteilt wird, wenn die aufgenommene Person keinen Asylantrag stellt (§ 32a AuslG). Außerhalb der Instrumente des Ausländergesetzes können Personen nach dem Gesetz über Maßnahmen für im Rahmen humanitärer Aktionen aufgenommene Flüchtlinge aufgenommen werden. Diese Kontingentflüchtlinge sind weitgehend den anerkannten Asylbewerbern gleichstellt.

[53] Dafür *Renner*, ZAR 2003, 88 ff., 94 f.; *Zimmermann*, ZAR 2003, 354 ff., 355; dagegen *Hailbronner*, ZAR 2002, 259 ff., 261; anders jetzt *ders*., ZAR 2003, 88 ff., 89 f.

[54] BVerfGE 96, 10, 20. [55] Vgl. *Marschner*, DB 2001, 385 f.

Regelungen zur Umsetzung der Richtlinie 2001/55/EG sind bisher nicht erlassen worden. Jedoch soll in das Zuwanderungsgesetz eine Vorschrift zur Erteilung einer Aufenthaltserlaubnis an Ausländer, denen aufgrund eines Beschlusses des Rates vorübergehender Schutz gewährt wird, aufgenommen werden.

3.6 Der Rat hat eine politische Vereinbarung getroffen über die Grundsätze für eine Richtlinie über Mindestnormen für die Anerkennung und den Status von Drittstaatsangehörigen und Staatenlosen als Flüchtlinge oder als Personen, die anderweitig internationalen Schutz benötigen, KOM 2001, 510 endg. (siehe Ratsdokument vom Juni 2003). Welche Maßnahmen sind vorgesehen, um die Richtlinie in Ihrem Land umzusetzen, wenn sie in Kraft tritt, bezüglich:

1 die Definition von Flüchtlingen,
2 die Definition von Personen, die einen Anspruch auf subsidiaren Schutz haben,
3 der Status von Personen, die einen Anspruch auf subsidiaren Schutz haben,
4 das Problem von internen Fluchtalternativen, wie es in der Richtlinie definiert ist,
5 Ausschlussparagraphen, insbesondere im Zusammenhang mit Terrorismus?

In welchem Ausmaß ist die Flüchtlingspolitik, die in dem Recht und der Rechtsprechung Ihres Landes widergespiegelt ist, im Einklang mit dem Vorschlag der Richtlinie?

Das deutsche Recht unterscheidet zwischen Asylberechtigten, denen das Grundrecht auf Asyl nach Art. 16a I GG zuerkannt worden ist, und sonstigen Personen, die lediglich Abschiebungsschutz genießen (§§ 51, 53 AuslG).

Nach der Rechtsprechung entspricht der Begriff der "politischen Verfolgung" als Voraussetzung für die Gewährung von Asyl weitgehend den Anforderungen der Genfer Flüchtlingskonvention[56]. Unterschiede zur Definition im Richtlinienentwurf bestehen allerdings insoweit, als die deutsche Rechtsprechung nichtstaatliche Verfolgung nicht als Asylgrund anerkennt[57]. Im Gegensatz zur überwiegenden Auffassung auf internationaler Ebene gehen die Gerichte davon aus, dass nur die Staatsgewalt selbst eine politische Verfolgung vornehmen kann, vor der das Asylrecht schützt. Allerdings hat das Bundesverfassungsgericht mittlerweile entschieden, dass dies auf "staatsähnliche Organisationen" auszuweiten ist[58]. Außerdem kann die Verfolgung durch Privatpersonen dem Staat zugerechnet werden, wenn er dem Verfolgten keinen Schutz gewährt[59]. Die Aufnahme der nichtstaatlichen Verfolgung ist ein wesentlicher Grund für den Widerstand der Bundesregierung im Ministerrat gegen

[56] BVerfGE 54, 341, 358; 76, 153, 157. [57] BVerwGE 95, 42, 45.
[58] BVerfG, NVwZ 2000, 1165. [59] BVerwG, NVwZ 1996, 85.

den Richtlinienvorschlag der Kommission, obwohl eine entsprechende Regelung in das Zuwanderungsgesetz aufgenommen werden soll[60].

Nicht eindeutig geklärt und politisch umstritten ist, ob geschlechtsspezifische Verfolgung als Asylgrund anzuerkennen ist[61]. Die Pflicht zur Beachtung der islamischen Bekleidungsvorschriften in Afghanistan wurde z.B. nicht als politische Verfolgung im Sinne des Asylrechts gewertet, da es sich nicht um eine Verletzung der Menschenwürde handele[62]. Höchstrichterliche Rechtsprechung liegt zu dieser Frage noch nicht vor, doch soll eine entsprechende Regelung in das Zuwanderungsgesetz aufgenommen werden[63].

Die in der Richtlinie genannten Voraussetzungen für die Gewährung subsidiären Schutzes entsprechen weitgehend den deutschen Regelungen zum Abschiebungsschutz. Die Gefahr individueller nichtstaatlicher Verfolgung wird allerdings von der deutschen Rechtsprechung nicht als zwingendes Abschiebungshindernis nach § 53 IV AuslG, der auf Art. 3 EMRK verweist, aufgefasst, sondern nur als fakultatives Abschiebungshindernis nach § 53 VI AuslG[64]. Diese Auslegung steht allerdings in Konflikt mit der Rechtsprechung des Europäischen Gerichtshofs für Menschenrechte[65].

Ein Asylantrag ist bereits nach geltendem Recht als offensichtlich unbegründet abzulehnen, wenn der Antragsteller aus schwerwiegenden Gründen als eine Gefahr für die Sicherheit der Bundesrepublik Deutschland oder für die Allgemeinheit anzusehen ist (§ 30 IV AsylVfG i.V.m. § 51 III AuslG).

3.7 In der Mitteilung der Kommission vom 22. November 2000, KOM 2000, 755 (siehe auch den 2. Kommissionsbericht KOM 2003, 152 endg.) ist das Konzept der Kommission für ein gemeinsames europäisches Asylverfahren und einen unionsweit geltenden Status für die Personen, denen Asyl gewährt wird, enthalten. Glauben Sie, dass das Konzept generell mit der Asylpolitik Ihres Landes übereinstimmt? Teilen politische Kreise in Ihrem Land, die Entscheidungen treffen, die Bedenken von Flüchtlingsorganisationen, wie z.B. Amnesty International und andere Organisationen, dass das internationale Regime für den Schutz von Flüchtlingen untergraben wird?

[60] Dazu *Duchrow*, ZAR 2002, 269 ff., 270 ff.

[61] Vgl. *Hailbronner*, ZAR 1998, 152 ff.; *Bumke*, NVwZ 2002, 423 ff.; relativierend zur Bedeutung als Anerkennungsgrund *Lehnguth*, ZAR 2003, 305 ff., 306.

[62] OVG Koblenz, NVwZ-Beil. I/2002, 100 f.

[63] *Duchrow*, ZAR 2002, 269 ff., 272.

[64] BVerwGE 99, 331; 104, 265; 105, 187.

[65] Vgl. dazu *Frowein*, DÖV 1998, 806 ff.; *Groß*, KJ 2001, 100 ff., 105 f.; relativierend *Hailbronner*, ZAR 2003, 299 ff., 299.

3.8 Der von der Kommission vorgeschlagene Koordinationsmechanismus sieht eine erste und zweite Rechtsstufe vor, in der die Flexibilitätsvorkehrungen in manchen Richtlinien über die Migration und das Asyl durch eine volle Harmonisierung ersetzt werden. Ist dieses Konzept in Ihrem Land diskutiert worden und was sind die Auffassungen über die schrittweise Schaffung einer europäischen Asylpolitik, die letztendlich nationale Verfahren und nationale Entscheidungen ersetzen könnte?

Die Bundesregierung setzt sich zwar für eine Harmonisierung des Asylverfahrens und der Anerkennungsvoraussetzungen ein, legt aber großen Wert darauf, dass die gemeinschaftsrechtlichen Regelungen nicht wesentlich großzügiger als die bisherigen deutschen Vorschriften sind. Eine vollständige Europäisierung der Asylpolitik wird von ihr nicht befürwortet, während dies nach meiner Auffassung die Konsequenz einer vollständigen Herstellung der Freizügigkeit sein müsste, da diese auch anerkannte Asylbewerber genießen.

Die politischen Parteien verfolgen dabei unterschiedliche Linien. Nur die an der Bundesregierung beteiligten Grünen teilen die Bedenken von Flüchtlingsorganisationen, dass die internationalen Schutzstandards nicht ausgehöhlt werden dürfen. Dagegen befürwortet die in der Opposition zur Bundesregierung stehende CDU/CSU, die aber in der zweiten Parlamentskammer die Mehrheit führt, eine noch restriktivere Regelung. Diese Differenzen sind ein wesentlicher Grund für die Schwierigkeit der Kompromisssuche im Vermittlungsausschuss bei der Beratung des Zuwanderungsgesetzes.

3.9 Die Mitteilung vom Juni 2003 über ein zugänglicheres, gleichberechtigteres und besser organisiertes Asylsystem – als Reaktion auf den britischen Bericht – entwickelt manche Ideen über neue Versuche, eine geordnete und organisierte Ankunft von Personen, die internationalen Schutz benötigen, zu verfolgen. Was ist die politische Reaktion in Ihrem Land zu dem Konzept eines Asylverfahrens mit Zugang im Ausland, die Verteilung von Flüchtlingen und das Teilen von Verantwortung und anderen neuen Konzepten und Ideen, die helfen sollen, mit Massenflüchtlingsbewegungen fertig zu werden?

Die Bundesregierung hat den Vorschlag der britischen Regierung zur Einrichtung von Flüchtlingslagern außerhalb der EU-Grenzen abgelehnt. In einer gemeinsamen Stellungnahme zum Konzept des regionalisierten Flüchtlingsschutzes der Organisationen amnesty international, Sektion der Bundesrepublik Deutschland e.V., Arbeiterwohlfahrt Bundesverband e.V., Arbeitsgemeinschaft Ausländer- und Asylrecht im Deutschen Anwaltverein, Deutscher Caritasverband (Referat Migration und Integration), Deutscher Paritätischer Wohlfahrtsverband, Diakonisches Werk der EKD, Neue Richtervereinigung und PRO ASYL, Bundesweite Arbeitsgemeinschaft für Flüchtlinge, wird der Vorschlag ebenfalls deutlich abgelehnt[66]. Nach meiner Auffassung ist der Vorschlag mit der Funktion des Asylrechts, Zuflucht vor Verfolgung zu gewähren, nicht vereinbar. Davon unabhängig besteht die Notwendigkeit, Fluchtursachen durch außen- und wirtschaftspolitische Maßnahmen zu beseitigen. Verfahren zur Verteilung von Flüchtlingen auf die Mitgliedstaaten in Krisensituationen über die Regelungen der Richtlinie 2001/55/EG hinaus können sinnvoll sein. Sie werden von der Bundesregierung befürwortet[67].

IV BEENDIGUNG DES ILLEGALEN AUFENTHALTS, RÜCKKEHR UND AUSREISE

4.1 Wie viele Drittstaatsangehörige ohne eine gültige Aufenthaltserlaubnis sind momentan nach Schätzungen in Ihrem Land? Wie viele Abschiebungen sind in den letzten Jahren tatsächlich vorgenommen worden? Wird das gesamte Durchsetzungsverfahren als akzeptabel angesehen?

Die Zahl der sich illegal in der Bundesrepublik aufhaltenden Personen entzieht sich naturgemäß der Erfassung durch eine amtliche Statistik. Vermutlich ist die Zahl derjenigen, deren Aufenthalt nachträglich illegal geworden ist, größer als die derer, die bereits illegal eingereist sind[68]. In den 1990er Jahren wurde die Zahl der sich illegal aufhaltenden Ausländer zwischen 150.000 und 1.000.000 geschätzt[69]. Auch der damit zusammenhängende Sektor der informellen Schattenwirtschaft ist schwer zu quantifizieren. Da der illegale Aufenthalt die Betroffenen jedes sozialen Schutzes beraubt, wurde wiederholt die Forderung erhoben, eine Möglichkeit zur Legalisierung unter bestimmten Voraussetzungen zu schaffen[70] oder zumindest die grundlegenden sozialen Rechte zu sichern[71]. Die Bundesregierung hat jedoch umfangreiche Legalisierungsaktionen nach dem Vorbild anderer europäischer Länder aus migrationspolitischen Gründen abgelehnt[72].

[66] Abrufbar unter http://www2.amnesty.de/internet/Gutachte.nsf/AlleDok/9EC802BCD900EB1AC1256D4B00391974?Open

[67] *Schily*, NVwZ 2000, 883 ff., 886; *Klos*, ZAR 2000, 202 ff., 209.

[68] *Alt/Cyrus*, in: Bade/Münz (Hrsg.), Migrationsreport 2002, 2002, S. 141 ff., 143.

[69] Vgl. *Lederer*, in: Eichenhofer (Hrsg.), Migration und Illegalität, 1999, S. 53 ff., 62.

[70] Z. B. Bade, in: Blum/Hölscher/Kampling (Hrsg.), Die Grenzgänger, 2002, S. 25 ff., 32.

[71] *Alt*, ZAR 2003, 406 ff., 410 f.

[72] Vgl. die Antwort der Bundesregierung in BT-Drs. 14/1678.

Nach 27.902 Abschiebungen im Jahr 2001 erfolgten 29.036 im Jahr 2002[73]. Die meisten Abschiebungen erfolgen auf dem Luftweg über den Flughafen Frankfurt/Main.

4.2 Was ist unternommen worden, um die Richtlinie vom 28. November 2002, die sich mit der Beihilfe zu unerlaubter Einreise, Transit und Aufenthalt befasst, umzusetzen?

4.4 Welche Bemühungen sind in Ihrem Land betreffend der Empfehlungen von Budapest im Juni 2003 in Bezug auf die Harmonisierung von Sanktionen für das Schmuggeln von Migranten und das Handeln von Personen im Einklang mit der Richtlinie des Rates 2002/90 vom 28. November 2002 unternommen worden? Hat Ihr Land das UN-Protokoll über das Schmuggeln von Migranten unterschrieben?

Das organisierte Einschleusen von Ausländern wird mit Freiheitsstrafe bis zu fünf Jahren oder mit Geldstrafe bestraft, in schweren Fällen des gewerbs- oder bandenmäßigen Handelns mit Freiheitsstrafe von sechs Monaten bis zehn Jahren (§ 92a AuslG). Versuch, Anstiftung und Beteiligung sind strafbar. Diese bereits seit 1994 geltende Strafvorschrift erfüllt die Anforderungen der Richtlinie 2002/90/EG. Von der Möglichkeit in Art. 1 Abs. 2 der Richtlinie, keine Sanktionen zu verhängen, wenn das Ziel der Handlungen die humanitäre Unterstützung der betroffenen Person ist, hat der deutsche Gesetzgeber keinen Gebrauch gemacht[74]. Nur Flüchtlinge selbst können sich auf das Grundrecht des Art. 16a I GG als persönlichen Strafausschließungsgrund berufen, nicht aber diejenigen, die sie einschleusen[75].

Die Bundesrepublik hat das UN-Protokoll über das Schmuggeln von Migranten am 12. Dezember 2000 unterzeichnet, aber noch nicht ratifiziert[76].

4.3 Wie viele illegale Bewerber sind an oder in der Nähe der Grenze festgenommen worden? Wie viele strafrechtliche Verfahren für das Schleusen von Personen sind im letzten Jahr eingeleitet worden?

Die Zahl der vom Bundesgrenzschutz und den anderen Behörden der Grenzkontrolle aufgegriffenen illegal Einreisenden hat sich zwischen 1990 und 1998 verfünffacht[77], wofür in erster Linie eine Erhöhung

[73] Bundesgrenzschutz, Jahresbericht 2002, S. 18; abrufbar unter http://www.bundesgrenzschutz.de/downloads/jahresberichte/2002/2002.pdf.

[74] Für eine entsprechende Ausnahme *Alt*, ZAR 2003, 406 ff., 411.

[75] *Aurnhammer*, Spezielles Ausländerstrafrecht, 1996, S. 159; *Heinrich*, ZAR 2003, 166 ff., 173.

[76] http://www.unodc.org/unodc/en/crime_cicp_signatures_migrants.html

[77] *Lederer*, aaO, S. 65.

der Effektivität der Grenzkontrollen v.a. an den Ostgrenzen als Ursache anzusehen ist. Seither ist die Zahl der Aufgegriffenen rückläufig, sie ging von 28.560 im Jahr 2001 auf 22.638 Fälle im Jahr 2002 zurück[78]. Die meisten Fälle traten an der deutsch-tschechischen Grenze auf, aber auch an den Grenzen zu den Schengen-Mitgliedstaaten wurden Tausende von Fällen illegaler Einreise festgestellt. An den Seehäfen wurden 481, an den Flughäfen 848 unerlaubte Einreisen festgestellt. Die Zahl der aufgegriffenen Schleuser ist von 2.463 im Jahr 2001 auf 1.844 im Jahr 2002 zurückgegangen.

Nach der Polizeilichen Kriminalstatistik für das Jahr 2002 wurden 7.004 Fälle mit 6.187 Tatverdächtigen eines Verstoßes gegen § 92a AuslG erfasst.

4.5 Welche Maßnahmen sind unternommen worden, um die Richtlinie des Rates vom 28. Mai 2001 über die gegenseitige Anerkennung von Entscheidungen zur Ausweisung von Drittstaatsangehörigen umzusetzen? Welche Mängel oder Lücken der Richtlinie sollten verbessert werden in einer weiteren Richtlinie über die Kooperation in der Ausweisung und Abschiebung von Drittstaatsangehörigen?

Die Richtlinie 2001/40/EG ist noch nicht umgesetzt worden, da die entsprechende Vorschrift Teil des noch nicht verabschiedeten Zuwanderungsgesetzes ist.

4.6 Gibt es Rücknahmevereinbarungen oder andere internationale Verträge oder Vereinbarungen mit dem Ziel der Kontrolle und dem Verhindern von illegaler Einwanderung und der Erleichterung von Rückführungen in Ihrem Land? Sind diese zufriedenstellend?

Die Bundesrepublik Deutschland hat mittlerweile 27 bilaterale Rückübernahmeabkommen mit anderen Staaten geschlossen. Sie regeln v.a. das Verfahren bei der Durchführung von Abschiebungen. Vom Bundesinnenministerium werden sie als weitgehend erfolgreich eingeschätzt. Eine unabhängige wissenschaftliche Untersuchung ist nicht erfolgt.

4.7 In welchem Ausmaß haben EU-Normen und -Empfehlungen die Rückführungspolitik Ihres Landes beeinflusst? Welche Versuche sind unternommen worden, mit anderen EU-Mitgliedstaaten zu kooperieren in der Durchsetzung von Rückführungsentscheidungen, gemeinsamen Abschiebungsaktionen, dem Austausch von Informationen, der Erleichterung von Luft- und Landtransit, gemeinsamen Prinzipien der Flugsicherheit usw.?

Der innenpolitische Druck zur Durchsetzung der Ausreisepflicht von Ausländern, die sich nicht oder nicht mehr legal in Deutschland aufhalten,

[78] Bundesgrenzschutz, Jahresbericht 2002, S. 14.

ist bereits so groß, dass nicht anzunehmen ist, dass die gemeinsame EU-Politik in diesem Bereich einen wesentlichen Einfluss hat. Im Rahmen der Zusammenarbeit der Grenzpolizeien gibt es auch gemeinsame Projekte im Bereich Rückführungen[79].

4.8 Ist es Ihrer Meinung nach notwendig, ein gemeinsames Rechtssystem für Abschiebungen auf dem Luftweg zu entwickeln (rechtlicher Status von bewaffneten Sicherheitsleuten in einem Flugzeug, Rechte des Flugkapitäns, rechtliche Regeln für Transitstops, Anwendbarkeit von nationalem Polizeirecht in einem fliegenden Flugzeug usw.)?

Die Bundesregierung hat im Jahr 2002 den Vorschlag für eine Richtlinie über die Unterstützung beim Transit im Rahmen von Rückführungsmaßnahmen auf dem Luftwege in den Rat eingebracht[80], der zur Verabschiedung der Richtlinie 2003/110/EG geführt hat. Nach den Kriterien des Subsidiaritätsprinzips nach Art. 5 Abs. 2 EGV ist allerdings schwer erkennbar, warum darüber hinaus eine einheitliche Regelung von Mindeststandards bei Abschiebungen auf dem Luftweg erforderlich sein sollte. Dass die Menschenrechte auch bei Abschiebungen gelten, ist selbstverständlich. Die Ergebnisse der in der Mitteilung der Kommission KOM 2002, 564 vorgeschlagenen Kooperation und der Erfahrungsaustausch bzgl. der Ausreise von Ausländern sollten nach meiner Meinung zunächst abgewartet werden. Diese Auffassung wird auch von der Bundesregierung vertreten.

[79] Bundesgrenzschutz, Jahresbericht 2002, S. 23. [80] BR-Drs. 864/02.

GREECE

PARTS I, II AND IV: GEORGIA PAPAGIANNI
Researcher, European University Institute, Florence, Italy

PART III, DR. PAROULA NASKOU-PERRAKI

PART I ENTRY, VISA REGIME AND BORDER CONTROL

1.1 What national authorities are competent to deal with visa applications (Schengen visas and long-term visas)? Are there any procedures to avoid duplication or successive visa applications at different EU-consulates? On what substantive criteria, other than the Schengen minimum requirements, are visas granted or refused? How many visas have been issued or refused?

1.2 Is there a visa tracking procedure in order to identify visa overstayers? What data are collected from visa-applicants (fingerprints)? Admissibility of visa data to alien and police authorities?

1.3 Have courts ever decided on the refusal of a Schengen visa based upon Schengen blacklisting by other Member States?

As is the case for the other Member States participating in Schengen, Greece issues, on the one hand, Schengen uniform visas, and on the other, national long-stay visas for stays exceeding three months.

Schengen visas are issued in accordance with the relevant provisions of the EU *acquis*, meaning the Schengen Convention, the Schengen Common Consular Instructions and the various EU acts developing the Schengen *acquis*. The Greek authorities involved are: the Greek consular authorities, the Ministry of Foreign Affairs and the Ministry of Public Order, which is responsible for checking the relevant databases of undesirable persons. Greek courts have not yet pronounced on the issue of the refusal of a Schengen visa based upon Schengen blacklisting by another Member State.

National visas are granted according to the provisions of Law 2910/2001, the currently applicable basic Immigration Act, which establishes in detail the various purposes for entry as well as the procedure and the documents to be submitted with regard to the issuing of the relevant visas.[1] The Greek authorities involved are, on the one hand, the Greek consular authorities, the Ministry of Foreign Affairs and the Ministry of Public Order, and on the other, the Ministry of Interior as well as the Ministries of Labour or Education, depending on the specific purpose of entry concerned. At this stage, no fingerprints are collected nor is there a visa tracking procedure at national level.

In so far as statistics on the issuing of visas are concerned, for 2002, the Greek Consular Authorities issued in the region of 430,000 Schengen visas. The rejection rate was around 9%. During this same period, around 36,000 national visas were issued.[2]

1.4 What measures have been undertaken in the implementation of the action programme for administrative cooperation in the field of external borders, visa, asylum and immigration following the Council Decision of 13 June 2002?

Given its special geographical position, Greece is deeply interested in developments regarding the EU policy on external borders. Within the framework of the implementation of the relevant EU plan, Greece has been the leader country for two projects. These projects concerned, respectively, an operation on migration pressure at the Eastern external land borders of the EU and an operation on sea border control in the South-eastern Mediterranean. Greece has also participated in a series of other projects led by other Member States. Moreover, Greece has submitted a proposal for the establishment of a Joint Sea Borders Co-ordination Centre in Greece. Finally, Greece, during the course of its Presidency, has closely followed

[1] Government Gazette A No 91, 21.5.2001. According to Article 71 (4) of Law 2910/2001 "all visas granted for non tourist purposes are national visas and have to be granted in accordance with the provisions of this Law".

Despite its short life Law 2910/2001 has been already amended several times. For the subsequent amendments of Law 2910/2001, *see* Articles 19 to 25 of Law 3013/2002, Government Gazette A No 102, 1.5.2002; Article 82 of Law 3057/2002, Government Gazette A No 239, 10.10.2002; Article 11 of Law 3074/2002, Government Gazette A No 296, 4.12.2002; Article 23 of Law 3103/2003 Government Gazette A No 23, 29.1.2003; Article 8 of Law 3146/2003, Government Gazette A No 125, 23.5.2003; Article 37 of Law 3153/2003, Government Gazette A No 153, 19.6.2003; Article 10 of Law 3169/2003, Government Gazette A No 189, 24.7.2003 and Article 32 of Law 3202/2003, Government Gazette A No 284, 11.12.2003. Moreover, Law 2910/2001 has been complemented by Article 15 of Law 3068/2002 – Government Gazette No A No 274 – establishing a right of appeal in cases of rejection of an application for visa or residence permit, and Law 3064/2002 – Government Gazette A No 248, 15.10.2002 – regarding trafficking in human beings.

[2] Statistical data provided by the Ministry of Foreign Affairs.

the implementation of the relevant EU plan and prepared a special report in that respect in view of the European Council of Thessaloniki.

1.5 What measures have been undertaken to implement the Directive 2001/51 EC supplementing the Schengen rules concerning carrier sanctions? How often have carrier sanctions been used?

Directive 2001/55/EC on carriers' liability has already been transposed into Greek law *via* an amendment of the relevant provision of the basic Immigration Act – Article 55 of Law 2910/2001 – by Article 37 of Law 3153/2003.

1.6 In your judgement, does the visa law and policy of your country live up to EU standards or are adjustments needed? Do you consider that there is need for further EU-harmonization of visa policies concerning:
– common criteria for granting visas aiming at harmonizing visa obligations among states participating in the Budapest Process;
– establishment of a European visa identification system (VIS and SIS II)?
To what extent will the EU enlargement process present an opportunity or challenge for tackling issues of illegal entry and border control?

Both the implementation of the relevant Schengen *acquis* in Greece and co-operation at EU level regarding visa policy are considered generally satisfactory. However, one should highlight, on the one hand, the lack of effective procedures for avoiding duplicate or successive visa applications at different EU Consulates, and on the other, the fact that the level of local consular co-operation among EU consular authorities is seen as an area where co-operation needs to be further reinforced. Indeed, the issue of closer consular co-operation as well as the establishment of a Visa Information System and the introduction of biometric data in both visas and residence permits of third country nationals are currently being discussed at EU level. The Greek position on both issues is positive.

With regard to the challenge that the forthcoming enlargement represents for the management of the EU's external borders, it is worth highlighting the following: on the one hand, according to the Schengen Protocol, the new Member States will have to apply the entire Schengen *acquis* without any possibility of "picking and choosing", whereas on the other, according to the Schengen *acquis* the Schengen two-step implementation process will have to be applied, meaning that controls at internal borders will only be lifted following an intense screening of the level of controls at the new external borders. Indeed, these two factors constitute safety nets for the correct and smooth application of the relevant Schengen *acquis* guaranteeing a high level of controls at the EU's external borders.

PART II ADMISSION AND RESIDENCE OF THIRD COUNTRY NATIONALS

2.1 What are the basic principles in your country concerning:
- admission of third country nationals for labour purposes or self-employed activities;
- admission of third country nationals for study and vocational training;
- legal status of third country nationals in possession of a long-term residence permit of another Member State?
- To what extent do these principles differ from the European Commission's proposals?

2.2 What are the legal requirements and procedures for obtaining a residence permit for third country nationals for the purpose of employment? Which procedures are used in maintaining the preferred access of EU-citizens and Turkish nationals (association agreement) to the labour market? Do special programmes exist for highly qualified professionals facilitating access to the labour market? To what extent are trade unions and employers involved in such programmes? Is there a procedure to calculate the demand for foreign labour? How is the EU-enlargement taken into consideration? To what extent has the recent economic recession and unemployment influenced the concepts on admission of third country nationals?

2.3 To what extent do existing national laws and practices differ substantially from the approach taken in the Commission's Proposal on admission for the purpose of paid employment and self-employed activities relating to:
- admission of third country nationals for study and vocational training;
- on legal status of third country nationals in possession of a long-term residence permit of another Member State?
- To what extent do these principles differ from the European Commission's proposals?

2.5 Concerning the proposal for a directive on the right to family reunion agreed upon by the Council in February 2003:
- Do you consider the proposed standards below the principles of family reunification applicable in your country?
- Will the implementation of the Directive, once it is adopted, lead to changes in the national law on family reunification downgrading the standard of protection? If so, what changes are envisaged?

2.6 The proposal for a directive on the rights of long-term third country nationals as agreed upon by the Council on 5 June 2003, provides for a number of rights approximating the situation of long-term residents to the status of EU-citizens. Will the implementation of the Directive involve major legal and policy changes in your country? What are the major points of concern if any, concerning the approximation concept of the directive relating to:
- non-discrimination in social rights;
- the concept of "civic citizenship" (see also extended impact assessment on the Communication on Integration of June 11, 2003);

– family reunification and access of family members to the labour market;
– security of stay?

Right to family reunification

The admission of third country nationals for the purpose of family reunification is regulated by Articles 28 to 33 of Law 2910/2001, as amended by Law 3074/2002 and Law 3202/2003.

Despite the fact that the mandatory provisions of the definitive version of the Directive are in general terms compatible with Greek legislation – apart from certain limited exceptions – it is interesting to summarise not only the changes to which the Greek legislator will have to proceed in view of the implementation of the Directive, but also the position of Greece with regard to the optional clauses of the Directive.

First, with respect to the definition of "family", whereas Greek legislation is compatible with the mandatory provisions of Article 4 (1) of the Directive, it does not provide for the admission of any of the categories falling under the optional clauses of the second and third paragraph of Article 4. Nonetheless, it does not include provisions regarding any of the derogations provided expressly in Article 4 either.

Second, regarding the procedural aspects linked to the exercise of the right, according to Greek legislation the application for family reunification is submitted exclusively by the sponsor and at a time when the family member is outside the territory of the country. Moreover, there is usually a waiting period of two years.[3]

Third, as far as the requirements for the exercise of the right and the documentary evidence that needs to be submitted are concerned, Greek legislation expressly provides that the sponsor needs to submit a copy of his tax review and that the application for a residence permit needs to be accompanied by a medical certificate issued by a domestic hospital or health centre. Despite the fact that neither of these documents is expressly mentioned in the Directive, both provisions could eventually be considered compatible with the Directive in the light of Articles 5 (2) and 6 (1) of the Directive. Greek legislation does not provide for an obligation for

[3] The exceptions to the two-year waiting period concern specific categories of workers such as members of administrative boards and personnel of specific companies, athletes and training staff and persons employed by diplomatic missions in Greece. See Article 35 of law 2910/2001 as well as Articles 19 and 20 of Law 3013/2002.

compliance with integration measures. It remains to be seen whether such provisions will be included.

Fourth, as far as entry and residence are concerned, according to a recent amendment of Law 2910/2001, the duration of the residence permit of the family member is the same as that of the sponsor, whereas previously it was provided that it was of one year's duration.[4] Moreover, as far as the renewal of residence permits is concerned, Greek legislation does not provide for an obligation to take into account the contributions of the family members. Whilst, it is worth noting that the basic immigration act did not include any provision establishing expressly a right of appeal, this has been provided at a later stage by Law 3068/2002.

Furthermore, according to Greek legislation an autonomous residence permit is granted only under special circumstances, such as the death of the sponsor, divorce or family violence. The duration of this permit is of one year, renewable for one year. Further renewal is only allowed for reasons provided by national law.[5] Despite the fact that *prima facie* Greek legislation is not compatible with the rule established by Article 15 (1), it is though rendered compatible with the Directive *via* the optional derogation of the second subparagraph of paragraph 1 and the provisions of Article 15 (3) and (4).

Fifth, as far as the rights of family members are concerned, according to Greek legislation family members have access to the labour market after having been granted a work permit, whereas there are no provisions regarding access to vocational training or access to education for adults. Such provisions most probably need to be included when transposing the Directive.

Sixth, as far as the family reunification of refugees is concerned, it is important to underline the fact that, in contrast to the provisions of the Directive, according to Greek legislation refugees are required to provide evidence that they fulfil the relevant requirements and an application can be rejected due to the lack of documentary evidence.

[4] Article 32 (5) of Law 3202/2003. Given that in general according to Greek legislation residence permits have one-year's duration, the family member's first residence permit might following this recent amendment have a duration of less than a year. However, it needs to be stressed that even according to the Directive itself the duration of the family member's residence permit shall in principle not go beyond the date of expiry of the residence permit of the sponsor.

[5] According to a recent amendment the residence permit can only be renewed until the family member reaches the age of 21 years old (*see* Article 11 (4) of Law 3074/2002). Most probably the Greek legislator was envisaging exclusively the case of children, since the application of this age limit to other categories of family members would not make any sense.

Last but not least, one of the major changes to be made to Greek legislation regards the limitation of the discretionary power of the administration with respect to the exercise of the right of family reunification, since the Directive clearly establishes an obligation for Member States to authorise the entry of the persons concerned once the conditions of the Directive are fulfilled.

Status of long-term residents

In contrast to the case of the Directive on family reunification, the Directive on the status of long-term residents is expected to require major changes in Greek law. There are two reasons for this: first, the lack of special provisions on the mobility of third country nationals having acquired such a status in another Member State – indeed, the Directive establishes for the first time a long-term resident status at EU level – second, the lack of detailed rules on the status of long-term residents in general. The relevant provisions are not only limited but also extremely restrictive.

According to the current legislative framework, a permanent residence permit is granted after ten years of continuous stay and is completely dependent on the discretionary power of the administration. A permanent residence permit may be issued exclusively to third country nationals who have been admitted for purposes either of paid employment, provision of services or self-employed activities, or to third country nationals who have entered for no specific purpose but because they dispose of the necessary financial means to stay in Greece.[6]

Moreover, the current legislative framework does not provide any special rights for third country nationals having acquired the status of long-term resident nor any special protection against expulsion. The only rights expressly provided – not for long-term residents specifically but for immigrants in general – concern access to social security, social assistance and the access of minors to education. However, it needs to be underlined that the Greek Constitution guarantees the access of foreigners to a series of fundamental and social rights.

Finally, Greek legislation does not provide for any special provisions regarding the integration of migrants. Integration policy in Greece is at a rather primitive stage not only from a legislative point of view but also from a policy making one. Furthermore, Greece is rather reticent with regard to concepts such as "civic citizenship" since this issue is often seen through the lenses of certain sensitive foreign policy issues.

[6] See respectively Articles 22 (2), 23 (1), 27 (4) and 37 (3) of Law 2910/2001.

Admission for the purpose of employment

The Greek legal framework differs in quite a few aspects from the system proposed by the Commission in the relevant Directive.[7] The main elements of the Greek system regarding admission for paid-employment, as compared to the system proposed by the Commission, could be summarised as follows. First, in contrast with the Commission proposal which provides for a single national application procedure, Greek legislation distinguishes among visas, work permits and residence permits. Subsequently, the documents that the third country national has to present are submitted at different stages. Moreover, according to the Greek system the application is submitted by the employer and cannot be accepted if the person concerned has already entered Greek territory.

Second, Greek legislation is based on a system of annual quotas. These quotas are established at regional level by a special Committee composed of the Secretary-General of the Region and representatives of the Manpower Employment Organisation (OAED) as well as by representatives of both employers and employees and representatives of trade unions. The decision of the Committee is based on an examination of the interests of the Greek economy as well as on the labour possibilities offered by Greek nationals or foreigners legally residing in Greece.

Whereas previously the work permit and the residence permit were granted on an annual basis, a recent amendment of the relevant provisions provides that after the lapse of a two-year period after the issuing of the first residence permit, their renewal will take place on a two-year

[7] The present analysis is based on the system provided by Articles 19 to 23 of Law 2910/2001 – as subsequently amended, mainly by Law 3203/2003 – as for the admission of third country nationals for the purpose of paid employment. Nevertheless, it needs to be underlined that this system has not been applied in practice, due to the fact that the "labour offices", which according to Law 2910/2001 had to be established within the framework of the Greek consulates, have not been established yet. Currently, another system, similar to the "pre-approval system" of the former Law, is applied in practice. According to this system employers "invite" foreign labour and their application is accepted under the condition that the relevant post is publicised but not fulfilled for a certain period of time by a Greek national or a foreigner residing legally in Greece.

It is worth clarifying that admission for self-employed activities is regulated by Articles 25 to 27 of Law 2910/2001, whereas Greek legislation provides a special framework for specific categories of immigrants, such as members of the administrative boards of certain companies, athletes and training staff, journalists as well as a fast track procedure for foreigners whose admission is considered necessary for reasons of "public interest". In view of the character of the information requested by the questionnaire and the limited space available these issues will not be discussed.

basis. Moreover, the work permit is now valid throughout Greece and the employee is free to change his employer.[8]

Greek legislation does not include any special provisions establishing a preference for Community citizens or Turkish nationals. However, it is expressly stated that Law 2910/2001 applies without prejudice to any bilateral or international agreements containing more favourable clauses.[9] Moreover, Greek legislation neither includes any strong special clauses for highly qualified employees nor establishes any particular incentives for that category of immigrants. According to one specific provision, the Minister of Interior may grant a residence permit, valid for no more than one year, to "distinguished foreign scientists" as well as to "foreign scientists of the new technologies, informatics in particular".[10]

Finally, as far as seasonal workers are concerned it is worth noting that Greece has already signed relevant bilateral agreements with Bulgaria and Albania.[11] Greece has also signed an agreement on bilateral co-operation regarding employment matters with Egypt.[12]

Admission for the purposes of studies, vocational training or voluntary service

Admission for the purposes of study, vocational training and participation in special exchange programmes is regulated by Articles 10 to 18 of Law 2910/2001 as amended by Article 19 of Law 3013. Third country nationals are admitted for study purposes on the basis of annual quotas – meaning the number of posts per faculty, department or educational institution that can be occupied by third country nationals – which are established by a Decision of the Minister for Education. Greek legislation does not include any special provisions for the entry of volunteers or the exchange of pupils.

The main points of eventual incompatibility between the Commission proposal and Greek legislation could be summarised as follows. First, in contrast to the relevant Community proposal, the entry and residence of students in Greece is clearly a two-step process, inasmuch as the persons concerned need to obtain first the relevant entry visa and subsequently

[8] Article 32 of Law 3202/2003. [9] Article 2 of Law 2910/2001.

[10] *See* Article 37 (4) (c) and (d) of Law 2910/2001.

[11] Ratified respectively by Law 2407/1996, Government Gazette A No 103, 4.6.1996 and Law 2482/1997, Government Gazette A No 73, 16.5.1997.

[12] Ratified by Law 1453/1984, Government Gazette A No 88, 16.6.1984.

enter the national territory and apply for the relevant residence permit. In addition, most of the relevant documentary evidence needs to be submitted when lodging the application for the relevant visa. Furthermore, Greek legislation does not provide for a fast track procedure such as the one described in Article 21 of the Commission's proposal.

Second, as far as the procedure and the documents to be submitted are concerned, apart from the conditions and the documents that are mentioned in the Commission's proposal, in accordance with Greek legislation students have to prove that they have accommodation in Greece, and the decision on the issuing of the residence permit lies within the discretionary power of the administration. Furthermore, in contrast with the Commission's proposal, Greek legislation provides for a maximum total period of residence. This maximum period cannot exceed the total period of studies increased by half, however, there is also the possibility of adding a further year for learning Greek. In as much as the rights of students are concerned, according to Greek legislation students have the right to work part-time once they obtain a part-time work permit. Finally, as this is the case in most Member States, there are no special provisions for the mobility of third country nationals studying in another Member State.

Last but not least, it is interesting to highlight the level of fees that immigrants have to pay for the issuing of residence permits, which varies between 147 and 881 euros. If one takes into consideration the fact that residence permits are usually renewed on an annual basis it becomes clear that this constitutes a considerable burden for immigrants. However it needs to be mentioned that the Directive on family reunification does not regulate the matter expressly and that the relevant clause has been deleted from the Commission's proposal on the status of long-term residents. The final outcome of the negotiations on this point with regard to the two latter proposals remains to be seen.

2.4 What measures have been taken to implement the Directive of 29th June 2000, implementing the principle of equal treatment between persons irrespective of racial or ethnic origin and Council Directive 2000/78 EC of 27th November 2000, establishing a general framework for equal treatment in employment and occupation? Have legislative changes been undertaken? To what extent is "affirmative action" considered as necessary to promote equal opportunities for migrant workers from third countries?

It is worth stressing that the Greek legal framework regarding the fight against racism dates from 1979. However, it needs to be noted that despite the fact that the deadline for the implementation of the relevant EC

Directives has already lapsed, these have not yet been implemented. However, the Ministries of Justice and Labour have prepared a draft Law that is expected to be submitted to the Parliament soon.

2.7 Considering the perspective of a future common migration policy as developed by the Commission in the Open Coordination Communication (COM 2001, 387) and the Communication on a Migration policy of the European Union (COM 2000, 757 final), how do you assess the role of the Community organs in determining a European migration policy in terms of competences of the Member States to decide on residence rights and admission to the labour market and integration? Should harmonization of legislation go further, and if so, in what respect?

In contrast to the major developments with regard to visa policy and most of the security aspects of migration policy – which had nevertheless already been extensively elaborated within the Schengen framework – one could convincingly argue that policy making with regard to legal migration at EU level is still in its infancy phase. The implementation of the Tampere agenda so far has clearly shown that Member States are not yet ready to hand over their sovereign powers regarding entry and residence of third country nationals. A comprehensive EU response to the migration challenge should definitely include further harmonisation of legislation. Nevertheless, this stage has not yet been reached.

PART III (ASYLUM AND REFUGEE LAW)

The impact of asylum legislation adopted or pending upon national laws and practices

Reception of asylum seekers

The main legislative instruments for the granting of refugee status to an applicant for asylum are relatively recent. Few changes have to be made in order for Greece to comply with EU legislation. The major Greek legislation is the Presidential Decree(PD) 61/1999 on refugee status recognition; the PD 189/1998 providing for the right to employment of asylum seekers and refugees; and PD 266/1999 providing for free hospital and medical care and for reception centers.[13] As soon as the applicant enters Greek territory, the relevant authorities give him an information booklet in a language he understands. This booklet contains information regarding the procedure for the examination of the asylum request and the applicant's rights and duties, with special emphasis on his obligation

[13] Government Gazette A No 63,140,217.

to cooperate closely with the authorities, during the examination of his claim. The applicant is also informed of the NGOs which assist refugees and about the UNHCR and its function in the country. In the case that such a booklet does not exist in a language understood by the claimant, the authorities find an interpreter.[14]

The Police officers who examine the applicant must be specially trained and experienced.[15] The interview must be conducted in a suitable place, which will guarantee the secrecy of the procedure.[16]

The claimant can request the assistance of a lawyer who will help him throughout the whole procedure.[17] If the claimant is a woman who has difficulties in expressing the reasons for her application, the interview will be held by a woman trained for such interviews with the assistance of a female interpreter.[18] In general terms, Greek legislation is in alignment with the directive. A draft PD is now pending,[19] waiting for the finalization of the first major phase of European immigration and asylum legislation. It amends provisions of the PD 61/1999, aiming to ameliorate the procedure before the competent authority (Ministry of Public Order) from the moment the refugee enters into Greek territory.

Asylum Procedure

The normal procedure[20] requires the asylum seekers to be present for an interview before the police officer in order to develop their claims orally and to submit all relevant written evidence in their possession. An interpreter can help the applicant if needed. The Secretary General of the Ministry of Public Order is the decisive authority on the basis of the recommendation of the Directorate of State Security of the Ministry.

[14] Art. 1 § 6 of the P. D 61/1999. See also P. Naskou Perraki, The procedure for recognition of refugee status according to the PD 61/1999, Revue Hellenique de Droit Européenee, 1994:4. p. 725 (in Greek).

[15] Ibid., Art. 2 § 1. [16] Ibid., Art. 2 § 2 and 3.

[17] Ibid. See also N. Sitaropoulos, Issues pertaining to the reception and access of asylum seekers to the asylum procedure, 50 Nomiko Vima (Greek law journal) 2002, 1598–1603, and the same author in Greek National Commission for Human Rights, Report 2002, Athens, National Printing Office, 2003, 143–152 (in Greek).

[18] Ibid. [19] Since 8.11.02.

[20] Art. 3 § 1 of the P.D., op. cit. See also N. Sitaropoulos, Study on the asylum single procedure – National Report on Greece, in K. Hailbronner (ed), Study on the Asylum Single Procedure (One-Stop Shop» Against the Background of the Common European Asylum System and the Goal of a Common Asylum Procedure, Brussels, European Commission, Directorate for Justice and Home Affairs, 2002, 381–420.

Upon recognition of refugee status, the refugee is given an identity card which is valid for five years with the possibility of being renewed for another five years.[21]

If the application is refused, the applicant has a right to appeal to the Minister of Public Order within 30 days from the date he received the decision. The Minister pronounces his decision within 90 days, taking into consideration the opinion of a Committee. The Committee, which has six members, is composed of the Legal Advisor of the Ministry of Public Order, as president, a member of the Diplomatic Corps of the Ministry of Foreign Affairs, the Legal Advisor of the same Ministry, a High Officer of the Police, a member of the Athens Bar Association and a Legal Counsel of the UNHCR.[22] In the event the Minister rejects the appeal, the applicant can apply to the Council of State.[23] If that application is rejected, the applicant has the right to request residence for humanitarian reasons before the Minister of Public Order. The Minister can permit his stay for one year with the possibility of being renewed for another year.

Few of the dispositions of the P.D. require review due to the draft directive and the ones that do mainly deal with deadlines and procedural matters. Apart from these, the Greek legislation is more progressive, both compared to the legislation of other Member States and to the draft directive. The gradual weakening of the text of the directive, following the various modifications at the negotiating table of the Council undermines the claim that the text lays down common standards and emphasises the "minimum" element of the draft directive. The danger for the Greek situation is the potential that there will be a weakening of the rights and procedures currently provided for in the P.D., in a number of areas allowed for by the draft directive.

Exclusive competence and burden sharing

Until recently there was no legislative framework for temporary protection in the event of a mass influx or imminent mass influx of displaced persons from third countries, unable to return to their country of origin. Greece

[21] Ibid., Art. 3 § 2. [22] Ibid., Art. 3 §5.

[23] According to Articles 20 and 95 § 1 of the Greek Constitution 1975/86/2001. For positive remarks, mainly for the participation of the UNHCR in the Committee, See M. Stavropoulou, A «Jump» to the protection of refugees in Greece. The Committee of Art. 3 § 5 of the P.D. 61/1991, Yearbook of Refugees and Aliens Law, Ant. N. Sakkoulas, Athens 2001, p. 17 (in Greek).

has deposited a draft P.D.[24] incorporating Directive 2001/55/EC of 20 July 2001.

It is worth mentioning that the above draft incorporates the directive word for word.

3.1 Have the Dublin Rules worked satisfactorily and what is expected of the Dublin II Regulation No. 343, 2003 of 18 February 2003?

The Dublin rules have worked rather satisfactorily. After the entry into force of the Convention, Greece received a large number of returned asylum seekers. In particular, Greece received 818 requests to readmit asylum seekers from other countries, accounting for over 17% of all asylum applications registered. Of the above number, Greece accepted only 220 requests. This fact can be explained by the geographic location of the country and its particular coastline. A substantial number of third country nationals choose Greece as a point of entry into the EU, in order to apply for asylum. In addition, a number of Schengen entry visas were issued by Greek consular authorities, in particular in the former Soviet Union countries, valid for all EU countries. The Regulation stipulates that the asylum applications lodged by the holder of such a visa, should be examined by Greece.[25]

On the other hand, Greece has very rarely requested other countries to readmit asylum seekers on the basis of the Dublin Convention. A total of 14 requests have been made, of which 7 were accepted by the other countries concerned. In general terms, Dublin II is expected to further facilitate and expedite the relevant procedures among EU Member States.

3.2 Has the Eurodac Regulation No. 2725/2000 of 11th December 2000, concerning the establishment of Eurodac for the comparison of fingerprints for an effective application of the Dublin Convention, operative since January 15, 2003, resulted in an increase of Dublin cases? Has Eurodac become effective in your country or is it expected to become effective eventually?

The Eurodac Regulation No 2725/2000 has been allegedly applied in an effective way by the competent Greek authorities.

[24] The Draft was deposited by the Ministry of Public Order to the Ministry of Foreign Affairs, General Directorate C, European Affairs – Section European Community Law, Athens November 19, 1993 (No 4866/2/15).

[25] See I. F. Papageorgiou, The Dublin-II Regulation (establishing criteria and mechanisms for determining the Member State responsible for examining an asylum application, lodged in one of the Member States by a third-country national) and its implications on Greek policies and practice in asylum, in *Revue Hellenique de Droit Européenne* 2004:1 (in Greek).

It has increased Dublin requests both in quantity and in substance. The quantity of requests has increased as asylum seekers entering the EU through Greece and then seeking asylum in another EU country, are sent back to Greece as the country of first entry: fingerprints assist in determining this issue. The substance of requests has increased because the procedure for the identification of the alien is quicker and safer.

3.3 What major changes, if any, will the implementation of the amended proposal for a directive on minimum standards on procedures in Member States for granting and withdrawing refugee status, on which the Council has reached political agreement on most points in June 2003, bring for the legislation and practice in your country in particular relating to:
- **rights of applicants in the procedure;**
- **administrative and judicial appeal procedures;**
- **the use of safe third country and safe country of origin concepts;**
- **detainment of asylum seekers;**
- **airport and border procedures?**

The implementation of this directive is expected to further and improve the status of legal protection of asylum seekers and refugees.

Rights of applicants in the procedure

The applicant has a right to stay in Greece until the final decision on his application,[26] receiving from the relevant authority an "identity for request of asylum" for a 6 month duration which can be renewed for another 6 months, until the final decision is made. The same identity is given to the members of his family. The applicant has the right to be informed about the procedure, to ask for an interpreter, to consult a lawyer, to be in touch with the UNHCR, to discuss his application with an expert on refugee issues in the administration, to receive a well-founded decision, and to be informed about his rights for appeal in case of a negative decision.[27] The reception directive provides that information about his rights must be given to the asylum seeker within a maximum of 15 days from his arrival/registration as an asylum seeker. Relevant documentation must be given within three days. The P.D. 61/99 provides for documentation of the asylum seeker following the first interview and within a period of three months after his request for asylum.

[26] Art. 2 § 7 of the P.D. 61/1999.

[27] Art. 1 § 1, ibid. See also P. Naskou-Perraki op.cit. p. 39.

The legal status of asylum applicants has been criticised by the National Committee on Human Rights, since the Greek legislation doesn't provide any special protection for fundamental social rights and often creates problems due to the malfunction of the asylum procedure in the Ministry leading to significant delays for the first interview.

The National Committee for Human Rights proposed that the examination of asylum requests be transferred to the Ministry of Interior as is the case in most EU countries.[28]

Administrative and judicial appeal Procedure

Article 38 of the proposed directive[29] is not compatible with the Greek system for granting asylum, the latter being strictly administrative. The implementation of this provision requires a profound change in the legislative framework, something which is extremely difficult to accomplish. Greece provides for an examination before a court only at the latest stage. This examination is before the Council of State and concerns applications to annul decisions of the Minister. Before this point, the procedure takes place only before the administrative authority (Ministry of Public Order).[30] The latter agrees the appeal procedure to be conducted by an independent body,[31] which differs from the first degree examination which is conducted by officers of the Aliens Directorate. The Ministry is of the opinion that it would be much easier if we could proceed to a system where the appeal procedure will be examined by a "quasi-judicial body" and not by a Court, noting among others that this possibility was included in the Council's Conclusions of JHA, December 2001. The Ministry has deposited a relevant document to the Ministry of Justice waiting for its opinion.

The use of safe third country and safe country of origin concepts

The arrival of a refugee from a safe third country does not constitute a reason to deny entrance to Greek territory or the examination of his

[28] Proposals for an effective framework for the protection of refugees (asylum) in Greece I. Sakelaropoulou and N. Sitaropoulos, National Committee for Human Rights, in *Revue Hellenique des droits de l' homme*, 14, 2002 p. 455 et seq. (in Greek).

[29] COM (2002) 326 final 10279/02 10–6–2002.

[30] As defined by the Presidential Decree 61/1999.

[31] See «Note» of the Ministry of Public Order Directorate of Aliens, Section Asylum dated 9.12.2002, p. 2. This Independent Body will have the prerequisites required, as they were defined by the ECJ in the Case *Dorsch Consult v. Bundisbaugesellschaft Berlin* 17/9/97 (54/1996).

claim.[32] This examination can be processed by way of the accelerated procedure and manifestly unfounded claims can be rejected.[33]

This provision is considered to be unclear for legal and political reasons. Firstly, there is no definition of a safe third country. Secondly, it is the Administration that judges every particular case taking into consideration the Decision of 30/11–1/12/1992 of the Ministers of Immigration of the EU and Conclusions Nos. 30 and 58 of the Executive Committee of the UNHCR.

The issue has been discussed among the EU Member States over the last years, although, as yet, no agreement has been reached. However, among the proposals made to the relevant asylum working party[34] Member States have reached agreement on the following: a safe third country is considered a country a) bound by the provisions of the Geneva Convention and observes its provisions with respect to the principle of non-refoulement and the rights of persons who are recognised and admitted as refugees, b) has in place an asylum procedure prescribed by law and c) has ratified the European Convention for the Protection of Human Rights and Fundamental Freedoms, and observes its provisions including the standards relating to effective remedies. Greece agrees with the above, based on general principles for the protection of refugees.

Detainment of asylum seekers

Greek Courts do not punish aliens for illegal entry into Greek territory as soon as they declare that they are refugees.[35] The jurisprudence of the penal courts is rather rich in this respect and it's been a practice in the last years,[36] to apply inter alia, the benefit of the doubt.

The lack of evidence with regard to some of the statements of aliens as well as lack of proof do not lead to the conclusion that the accused are not telling the truth before the Court in cases where they are arrested for

[32] According to Art. 4 § 1 of the P.D. 61/1999 in conjunction with Art. 25 § 2 of the Law 1975/1991 and Art. 2 of the Law 2452/1996. The same opinion was stated by the Council of State in its decision 830/1985, See H. Spathana, Legal Assistence in Asylum seekers and rafugees in Greece, Greek Council of Refugees, rev. edition 2003 pp. 17–18.

[33] According to Articles 24 and 24 of the Law 2452/1996, op.cit.

[34] COM (2002) 326 final 2, 15198/03 ADD1 Asile 66 4 December 2003.

[35] N. Sitaropoulos, Illegal entry of refugees into a country of refuge and judicial syllogisms ab absurdo – A contribution to the interpretation of Article 31(1) of the 1951/1967 UN Refugee Convention, Yearbook of Refugee and Aliens Law – 1998, Athens, UNHCR / Ant. N. Sakkoulas Publishers, 1998, 135–146 (in Greek).

[36] The jurisprudence of the Penal Courts is rich but not homogeneous.

illegal entry: sometimes the lack of evidence can be justified by the special situation in which the accused were found.[37] The directive is not different in this respect.

Airport and border procedures

The accelerated procedure is being applied for asylum applications lodged in transit zones in ports or airports.[38] This procedure requires the creation of particularly arranged areas in the above transit zones where the asylum seekers can stay during the time of the examination of the application, which cannot exceed two weeks.[39] In practice, this procedure exceeds the required time, creating problems for the detention of the applicants in the transit zones.

The new directive will offer the applicants the right to appeal to a court against administrative decisions on detention in the transit zone.[40]

It is worth mentioning that the new directive extends the time in which to adopt a decision on an asylum application to 3 weeks time, offering more time than the national Greek law.[41]

3.4 What measures have been undertaken to implement Directive 2003/9 of 27 January 2003, on reception of asylum seekers in your country relating to:
- **the flexibility clauses in the Directive;**
- **restriction of free movement;**
- **access to the labour market;**
- **rights of migrant workers under Article 11 § 2 of the Directive?**

The Directive 2003/9/2003[42] aiming to harmonise the reception conditions in all Member States has not been implemented in Greece yet. The Ministry of Public Order has not reported any relevant measures. In any case, Member States have until January 2005 to transpose the Directive.

Relating to the flexibility clauses in the Directive

Greece will need some time to adopt this Directive. Time is not required for legislative changes but for changes at the level of reception infrastructure,

[37] Nikos Sitaropoulos, The detention of refugees and asylum seekers in Greece, in Perrin-Martin, J.-P. (ed.), Europe Barbelée, Paris, L'Harmattan, 1998, 110–113.

[38] Art. 25 § 3 of Law 1975/1991 as was amended by Art. 2 of Law 2452/96.

[39] In the Draft P.D. the 2 weeks time limit was changed to 24 hours.

[40] Ibid., art. 35 § 1. [41] Ibid., art. 35 § 4.

[42] Directive 2003/9/EC EE L 31 6.2.2003 p. 18–25.

staffing and establishing adequate and appropriate reception centres. Among others, emphasis should be placed on the provision of information to asylum seekers (language) and housing.

Although there are 11 reception centres all over Greece,[43] the personnel is not adequate and not properly trained. The reasons for Greece's inadequacy with regard to its reception obligations are mainly financial and logistic, there is a limited budget for funds for the reception of asylum seekers. At this point we should emphasise the important role played by NGOs in collaboration with the Ministry of Health and the European Fund for Refugees. These offer great relief to refugees in general and, in collaboration with the National Youth Foundation, to unaccompanied minor refugees in particular.

Restriction of free movement

Greece has made a reservation on Article 26 of the Geneva Convention on the right of refugees to free movement. This reservation has not yet been withdrawn, thus creating problems for the implementation of the Directive.

Access to labour market

According to P.D. 189/1998, recognised refugees have immediate access to the labour market on the same conditions as Greek citizens. Refugees with disabilities, over 67%, receive the same benefits, as well as mothers with more than three children, according to the legislation for the protection of families.

The above benefits don't include applicants who are temporarily resident for humanitarian reasons or living in "Centers of temporary residence".[44] Although the above provision is not in contradiction with the Directive it could be amended only for social reasons. In general terms, Greek legislation is wide enough to offer refugees access to the labour market.

[43] See P.D. 266/1999 "for the functioning of Lavrion Center for reception of refugees and social protection of recognized refugees, applicants and residence for humanitarian reasons" op.cit.

[44] Art. 4, § a of the P.D. 189/1998.

Rights of migrant workers under Art. 11 § 2 of the Directive

Greek legislation offers rights to refugee workers equal to those available to Greek nationals. There is no restriction on time such as is foreseen by the Directive. In this respect, Greek laws are wider in scope than the Directive.

3.5 What steps have been undertaken to implement the Directive on temporary protection, COM 2001, 55 in national law? Are there any procedures for burden sharing arrangements? Is there a legal basis for the admission of refugees for the purposes of receiving temporary protection in a mass-movement situation?

Temporary protection has been provided for by Article 25 § 6 of the Aliens Law 1975/1991, as amended by Law 2452/1996.[45] This provision has actually provided for the promulgation of an Inter-Ministerial Decision that would regulate the issue of a "special status of temporary protection with regard to a specific category of aliens who enter Greece for reasons of force majeure".

The draft of the P.D. transposing Directive 2001/55/EC has been deposited by the Ministry of Public Order to the Ministry of Foreign Affairs,[46] but has not yet been incorporated into Greek legislation.

In any case, asylum and refugee protection are in need of a radical overhaul, given the existence of chronic, serious structural problems[47] occasionally recognised by the Greek administration. In 2002–2003, the Ministry of Public Order initiated a review procedure, through the drafting of a P.D., for asylum procedure. This seems to have been reviewed by the above Ministry. The Ministries competent for asylum and refugee welfare currently seem to be waiting for the first phase of European Union immigration and asylum legislation to be finalised before they proceed to any major revisions and/or amendments of asylum legislation.

3.6 The Council has reached political agreement on the principles for a Directive on minimum standards for the qualification and status of third country nationals

[45] For an interpretation of this provision, see P. Naskou-Perraki, Application for asylum request and procedure for recognition refugee identity. A global examination in the light of new developments, Arts 24 and 25 of the Law 1975/91 as amended by Art. 1 and 2 of the Law 2452/96, *Revue Hellenique de Droit Européenne*, 1998:1, p. 39 (in Greek).

[46] General Directorate C, European Affairs-Section European Community Law, Athens, November 19, 2003 (No 4866/2/15-).

[47] See UNHCR BO for Greece, The Protection of Refugees and Asylum Seekers in Greece in 2002, Athens, May 2003, N. Sitaropoulos, Comparative legal study on subsidiary protection – Greece in D. Bouteillet-Paquet (ed.), Subsidiary Refugee Protection in the EU: Complementing the Geneva Convention?, Brussels, Bruylant, 2002, pp. 529–568.

as refugees or persons who otherwise need international protection, COM 2001, 510 final (see Council documents of June 2003). What measures are envisaged to implement the Directive, once it is adopted, in your country relating to:
- **the definition of refugee;**
- **the definition of persons entitled to subsidiary protection;**
- **status of persons entitled to subsidiary protection;**
- **the issue of internal flight alternative as defined by the Directive;**
- **exclusion clauses, particularly issues of terrorism?**

To what extent are the refugee policies as reflected in the law and jurisprudence of your country in accordance with the proposal for the directive?

The draft directive is considered as one of the most important directives for the protection of refugees in the European Union. We do regret the delay in its adoption by the Member States.

The definition of refugee

The harmonisation of the interpretation of the Geneva Convention, of Article 1A2, and the determination of cases on the so-called subsidiary forms of protection are probably the most important elements in the creation of "a Common European Asylum System". In this context, it could be suggested that the draft directive should have been examined in priority, before the EU Member States dealt with other aspects of the asylum policy.

The definition of the term refugee in the above Convention is, still today, thorough, complete and flexible enough to ensure international protection to all persons falling within its remit. Any attempt to differentiate this definition may create doubtful and uncertain situations.

This definition is applied to non EU nationals or stateless persons, limiting the universal scope and character of the Convention. In Greece, worries have been expressed for not including in the definition the EU nationals.

The definition of persons entitled to subsidiary protection

This definition resembles the so-called "humanitarian reasons" in Greece, provided for by the national legislation.[48] It must be considered as a positive initiative on condition, that it provides guarantees for the protection

[48] Art. 8 § 2, P.D. 61/1999.

and decent living of persons in need of international protection[49] in the EU.

Status of persons entitled to subsidiary protection

The protection provided to a third country national or stateless person is distinct but complementary to that provided by refugee status. In Greece, it falls in the category of persons receiving humanitarian protection. The treatment of persons entitled to subsidiary protection is not the same as that of refugees. For example, they cannot have access to employment and to travel documents. The exclusion clauses for refugee status are specifically regulated by the 1951 Convention. However, using the same legal basis for the exclusion of persons from subsidiary protection status is contrary to the principles of this form of international protection as well as Article 3 of the ECHR and the Convention Against Torture. These texts represent the reference provisions for the determination of subsidiary protection beneficiaries. In general terms though the two P.D. provide broader protection.

The issue of internal flight alternative as defined by the directive

On this issue, Greek legislation is also broader than the draft directive.

Exclusion clauses, particularly issues of terrorism

The draft directive repeats Article 1D, E and F of the 1951 Convention. Consequently, the exclusion clauses remain the same. The matter of terrorism should not be considered or fall within the scope of the draft directive as it will lead to endless discussions without leading to any results.

3.7 In the Commission's Communication of 22 November, 2000, COM 2000, 755 (see also 2nd Commission Report COM 2003, 152 final) the Commission's concept of a common European asylum procedure and a uniform status for those who are granted asylum valid throughout the Union is set out. Do you consider that the concept is generally in line with your country's asylum policy? Are the concerns of refugee organizations, such as Amnesty International and other organizations, of

[49] See draft directive on minimum standards for the qualification and status of third country nationals and stateless persons as refugees or as persons who otherwise need international protection, Greek Council for Refugees, NICE p. 4.

an undermining of the international regime for the protection of refugees shared in the political circles responsible for decision-making of your country?

The concept of asylum valid throughout the territory of the EU area is viewed favourably by Greek authorities. There has not been any open political discussion on these issues in Greece so far.

3.8 The open coordination-mechanism, as suggested by the Commission, provided for first stage and second stage legislation in which the flexibility provisions in some of the directives on migration and asylum are to be replaced by full harmonization. Is this concept discussed in your country and what are the perceptions relating to the gradual establishment of a European asylum policy which might eventually replace national procedures and national decision-making?

No discussion has thus far taken place in Greece on the open coordination mechanism proposed by the Commission. In general Greece has viewed favourably the "Europeanisation" of the asylum regime (potentially improving national procedures).

3.9 The Communication of June 2003, towards a more accessible, equitable and managed asylum system – in reaction to the UK paper – develops some ideas on new approaches to pursue an orderly and managed arrival of persons in need of international protection. What is the political reaction in your country to the concept of an outside accessed asylum procedure, distribution of refugees and responsibility-sharing and other new concepts and ideas in coping with mass refugee movements?

It is well established in international law that granting asylum to an applicant falls within the discretion of the relevant authorities of a state according to national legislation and international norms that the state has ratified. States which have ratified the Geneva Convention must be very careful in implementing its provisions, mostly Articles 31, 32 and above all Article 33. In Greece, the unofficial reaction to the UK proposal stressed the fact that the proposal will lead to the disappearance of the notion of territoriality in asylum matters. Some NGOs went even further and claimed the above proposal would result in the non-application of the above Articles of the Geneva Convention. One could also see the disappearance of all NGOs dealing with the matter in the country.[50]

So, in general terms Greek opinion is not in favour of the UK proposal, although responsibility sharing has been a main preoccupation of the Greek state for many years due to the geographical situation of the country as a European entry point.

[50] As for example the Greek Council for Refugees, etc.

PART IV TERMINATION OF ILLEGAL RESIDENCE, RETURN AND REPATRIATION

4.1 How many third country nationals without a valid residence permit are currently, according to estimates, staying in your country? How many deportations have actually been made in previous years? Is the whole enforcement process considered as acceptable?

The number of illegal migrants deported during the last years varies between 10,000 and 13,000 persons per year, whereas there has been a considerable increase in 1999 and 2000.[51] The whole enforcement process is considered as satisfactory, mainly due to the fact that illegal immigrants are in most cases detained. Moreover, deportees are usually registered in the national list of undesirable persons, and eventually also in the SIS. Finally, illegal residents that are apprehended either in the country or during their exit from the country have to pay a penalty, the level of which varies according to the length of their illegal stay in the country.[52]

4.2 What has been undertaken to implement the Directive of 28 November 2002, dealing with the facilitation of unauthorized entry, transit and residence?

4.4 What efforts have been undertaken in your country regarding the Budapest June 2003 recommendations concerning the harmonization of penalty scales with regard to the crime of the smuggling of migrants and trafficking of persons, in line with Council Directive 2002/90 of 28th November 2002? Did your country sign the relevant UN protocols on the smuggling of migrants?

Despite the lack of any specific implementation measures regarding Directive 2002/90, it is worth highlighting the fact that Greek legislation already provides a detailed set of penalties for a series of public and private persons who facilitate either the entry or residence of illegal migrants.[53]

Furthermore, special attention is paid to the cases of victims of trafficking and especially those of prostitution networks. Following recent legislative developments, penal sanctions have been substantially increased,

[51] Statistical data provided by the Ministry of Public Order. There are no data available as for the number of illegal residents present in the country.

[52] Article 41 of Law 2910/2001.

[53] *See* Articles 51 to 54 of Law 2910/2001. According to Articles 51 and 52 of Law 2910/2001 all public services and persons under public law, the local self-administration authorities, public utilities ventures, social security ventures, as well as notaries are obliged to refrain from offering their services to illegal immigrants. This obligation is also extended to hospitals and clinics, unless there is a case of emergency or children need medical care, a provision that has been severely criticised by the National Authority for Human Rights.

assistance is granted to the victims, expulsion orders may be suspended and a residence permit is granted to victims co-operating with the authorities.[54] Moreover, Greece has signed the UN Palermo Protocols on human trafficking, albeit these have not yet been ratified.

4.3 How many illegal applicants have been apprehended at or near the border? How many criminal procedures for human trafficking have been instituted in the last year?

The number of third country nationals that are apprehended at the border while attempting to enter illegally varies between 35,000 and 150,000 persons per year. Moreover, between 500 to 1200 traffickers are arrested by Greek authorities every year.[55]

4.5 What measures have been taken to implement the Council Directive of 28 May 2001, on the mutual recognition of decisions on the expulsion of third country nationals? What, if any shortcomings or gaps of the Directive should be corrected in a further directive on cooperation on expulsion or deportation of third country nationals?

A draft Presidential Decree aiming at the implementation of Directive 2001/40 has already been prepared and is expected to be submitted to the Greek Parliament soon.

4.6 Do readmission agreements or other international treaties or arrangements with the aim of controlling and curbing illegal immigration and facilitating return exist in your country? Have they functioned satisfactorily?

Greece has signed readmission agreements with Bulgaria, France, Italy, Croatia, Lithuania, Latvia, Hungary, Poland, Romania and Slovenia, and it has also signed a Protocol for the implementation of the readmission clause of the police co-operation agreement with Turkey. Moreover, readmission clauses are included in a series of police co-operation agreements. Most of the readmission agreements are not extensively used in practice: the ones mostly used are those concluded with neighbouring countries, namely Bulgaria, Italy and Turkey.

4.7 To what extent have EU-standards and recommendations influenced your country's return policy? Have efforts been undertaken to cooperate with other EU Member States in enforcing return decisions by common deportation actions, exchange of information, facilitation of air and land transit, common principles on flight security, etc.?

[54] *See* Article 44 (7) as complemented by Law 3064/2002 and Presidential Decree No 233.

[55] Statistical data provided by the Ministry of Public Order for the last five years.

4.8 Do you consider that there is a need to elaborate a common legal regime for air deportations (legal status of armed guards on board of the aircrafts, rights of the aircraft commander, legal rules in case of transit stops, applicability of national police law on board of aircraft on flight, etc.)?

Greece's return policy has unavoidably been influenced initially by Schengen and subsequently by EU relevant standards. For the moment there is no substantive co-operation with other Member States in enforcing return decisions by common deportation actions or any other form of co-operation at bilateral level. Nevertheless, the Greek position regarding relevant initiatives at EU level such as the organisation of joint flights for removal and the establishment of a legal regime for air deportations is positive.

Given its geographical position and the strong migration pressure it receives, Greece is deeply interested in measures regarding the fight against illegal migration, trafficking in human beings and return policy as well as in reinforcing co-operation at EU level on these issues.

HUNGARY

DR. SUZANNE VEGH

PART I (ENTRY, VISA REGIME AND BORDER CONTROL)

1.1 What national authorities are competent to deal with visa applications (Schengen visas and long-term visas)? Are there any procedures to avoid duplication or successive visa applications at different EU-consulates? On what substantive criteria, other than the Schengen minimum requirements, are visas granted or refused? How many visas have been issued or refused?

Initially, a visa application should be made at the foreign missions of Hungary. In some special cases, when national (e.g. economic or cultural) interests need to be taken into account, the border guards at the border crossing point may take the application. Where there are special personal conditions, an application may be made in Hungary at the regional branch of the OIN.

In the case of a short-term visa, the mission decides. In the case of persons who are citizens of nations listed in the Consular Instructions, the OIM deals with the application. The border guard should decide in all cases dealt with at the border. The branch of OIM which takes the application is responsible for it.

In 2003, a total of 418,014 visas were granted while 4,043 visa applications were refused.

Hungary has no standard procedures to avoid duplication or successive visa applications at different consulates. Practically, there are regional consular checking sections to prevent duplicate or successive applications, but these operate on an ad hoc basis. Our N-VIS is able to check an attempt, but only at national level; this checking will be available at international level when C-VIS comes on line.

The Hungarian Aliens Act has implemented the Schengen criteria, so all the requirements have been taken into account.

1.2 Is there a visa tracking procedure in order to identify visa overstayers? What data are collected from visa-applicants (fingerprints)? Admissibility of visa data to alien and police authorities?

Random police checks are carried out as a means of identifying visa overstayers.

Visa data is made available to both alien as well as police authorities.

1.3 Have courts ever decided on the refusal of a Schengen visa based upon Schengen blacklisting by other Member States?

Hungary has not yet joined the Schengen area, consequently there have been no cases dealing with this issue.

1.4 What measures have been undertaken in the implementation of the action programme for administrative cooperation in the field of external borders, visa, asylum and immigration following the Council Decision of 13 June 2002?

Hungary has not yet joined the Schengen area.

1.5 What measures have been undertaken to implement the Directive 2001/51/EC supplementing the Schengen rules concerning carrier sanctions? How often have carrier sanctions been used?

Hungarian border guards carry out these checks at the airports to prevent illegal migration. Border Guards have the right to sanction those carriers. Altogether, 58 offences were detected in 2003.

1.6 In your judgement, does the visa law and policy of your country live up to EU standards or are adjustments needed? Do you consider that there is need for further EU-harmonization of visa policies concerning:
- **common criteria for granting visas aiming at harmonizing visa obligations among states participating in the Budapest Process;**
- **establishment of a European visa identification system (VIS and SIS II);**
- **To what extent will the EU enlargement process present an opportunity or challenge for tackling issues of illegal entry and border control?**

All the common criteria connected to visa cases will be accepted and introduced in connection with the EU enlargement. Neither C-VIS nor C-SIS have been set up, so no further information is available on this field.

Illegal migration has been a problem in this region. As Hungarian border guards have had exemplary training on technical and personal issues relating to illegal immigration, our country is able to carry out effective counter-measures.

PART II (ADMISSION AND RESIDENCE OF THIRD COUNTRY NATIONALS)

2.1 What are the basic principles in your country concerning:
- **admission of third country nationals for labour purposes or self-employed activities;**

– admission of third country nationals for study and vocational training;
– legal status of third country nationals in possession of a long-term residence permit of another Member State?
To what extent do these principles differ from the European Commission's proposals?

According to Hungarian law, third country nationals, in possession of a valid residence visa ("D" type visa), are entitled to multiple entries and to stay for a period not exceeding one year in Hungary for the purpose of permanent or seasonal employment or of gainful activities. Upon the request of a foreigner staying in Hungary with a valid residence visa, the alien policing authority may issue a temporary residence permit in order to extend the period of stay. Extended-stay visas/temporary residence permits for employment may be issued to foreign nationals holding a valid work permit for the purpose of taking up employment in Hungary. Extended-stay visas/temporary residence permits for gainful activities may be issued to foreign nationals wishing to enter Hungary to engage in economic, intellectual or artistic activities, or to perform work that is not subject to an employment permit. The temporary residence permit shall be valid for the period defined in the application. The temporary residence permit for the purpose of employment is valid for the period defined in the work permit issued by the Employment Centre. At present the validity of work permits does not exceed one year. The temporary residence permit for the purpose of gainful activities is generally valid for two years.

An extended-stay visa for scholarship or other scientific or professional training purposes may be issued to foreign nationals wishing to enter for the purpose of studying in an institution of higher education or in a scientific research facility, or for participating in continuing professional training, provided the applicant holds a certificate or statement of admission from the educational institution or the research facility in question. Before the date of expiry of this visa, the third country national can apply for a temporary residence permit at the regional aliens policing authority. The validity of the residence permit issued for a foreigner studying in higher education or participating in vocational training or practice, shall not exceed one year when issued for the first time. It may be extended on an annual basis until the studies or the practice are completed.

According to Hungarian law, there is no difference between the legal status of third country nationals who are in possession of a long-term residence permit issued by one of the Member States and third country nationals who are not in possession of such a permit. Third country nationals in possession of a long-term residence permit issued by one of the Member States enjoy equal treatment to other third country nationals in the territory of the Hungarian Republic.

There are some differences between the Hungarian legislation, and the principles laid down in the Commission's proposal. The purpose of the Directive is to make the conditions under which third country nationals may enter a Member State's labour market easier and clearer. The exact text of the Directive is currently the subject of discussion and the new text will determine the extent of the correspondence between Hungarian law and the principles set out in the Directive. The main principles in the Commission's Proposal for a Council Directive on the conditions of admission of third country nationals for the purposes of studies, pupil exchange, unremunerated training or voluntary service correspond with the main principles of the relevant Hungarian rules. The text of the proposal though is still flexible and in the future is likely to be the subject of numerous modifications.

2.2 What are the legal requirements and procedures for obtaining a residence permit for third country nationals for the purpose of employment? Which procedures are used in maintaining the preferred access of EU-citizens and Turkish nationals (association agreement) to the labour market? Do special programmes exist for highly qualified professionals facilitating access to the labour market? To what extent are trade unions and employers involved in such programmes? Is there a procedure to calculate the demand for foreign labour? How is the EU-enlargement taken into consideration? To what extent has the recent economic recession and unemployment influenced the concepts on admission of third country nationals?

Unless otherwise provided by an international agreement, third country nationals may enter and reside on the territory of Hungary for employment purposes with either a work permit and a residence type visa or a residence permit for employment purposes. Work permits and residence visas/residence permits are issued by two separate authorities under separate procedures.

At the moment, EU citizens and Turkish nationals are treated equally to other third country nationals regarding access to the Hungarian labour market. Following EU enlargement, citizens of Member States applying TEC without restrictions on the access of Hungarian workers to their labour market will be entitled to work in Hungary without requiring a work permit. The present regulation will continue to apply to the citizens of Member States who restrict the access of Hungarian workers to their labour market.

There are no existing special programmes for facilitating the access of highly qualified professionals to the Hungarian labour market.

Yes, there is an existing procedure to calculate the demand for foreign labour. There is no intention to modify that procedure in order to take account of EU enlargement.

The recent economic recession and unemployment have not had a significant influence on the concepts on the admission of third country nationals.

2.3 To what extent do existing national laws and practices differ substantially from the approach taken in the Commission's Proposal on admission for the purpose of paid employment and self-employed activities relating to:
- **admission of third country nationals for study and vocational training;**
- **on legal status of third country nationals in possession of a long-term residence permit of another Member State?**

To what extent do these principles differ from the European Commission's proposals?

Existing laws and practices are in line with the approach taken in the Commission's Proposal on admission for the purpose of paid employment and self-employed activities relating to the admission of third country nationals for study and vocational training. Third country nationals admitted for study and vocational training are regarded as regular students and do not require a work permit to take up work at the same time.

In the case of third country nationals in possession of a long-term residence permit of a Member State, present regulations continue to apply and there are no preferences. In this second category, there are some differences between the principles applied under Hungarian law and those contained in the European Commissions proposal.

2.4 What measures have been taken to implement the Directive of 29th June 2000, implementing the principle of equal treatment between persons irrespective of racial or ethnic origin and Council Directive 2000/78/EC of 27th November 2000, establishing a general framework for equal treatment in employment and occupation? Have legislative changes been undertaken? To what extent is "affirmative action" considered as necessary to promote equal opportunities for migrant workers from third countries?

On 1 January 2004, the Hungarian Government established the Office for Equal Opportunities. The Office's main pursuits are facilitating the integration of ethnic minorities and supporting programmes to promote social cohesion. In the field of equal treatment and equal opportunities, a large number of laws have already been amended, and a draft legislative provision on equal treatment and equal opportunities is before the Parliament at present.

2.5 Concerning the proposal for a directive on the right to family reunion agreed upon by the Council in February 2003:

- **Do you consider the proposed standards below the principles of family reunification applicable in your country?**
- **Will the implementation of the Directive, once it is adopted, lead to changes in the national law on family reunification downgrading the standard of protection? If so, what changes are envisaged?**

In relation to the family reunification Directive, the principles in that Directive are in accordance with the principles laid down in Hungarian legislation. Implementation of the Directive will not require any vital changes in national law, because during the preparatory work for the Aliens Act, all the effective multilateral agreements on family reunification were taken into consideration.

2.6 The proposal for a directive on the rights of long-term third country nationals as agreed upon by the Council on 5 June 2003, provides for a number of rights approximating the situation of long-term residents to the status of EU-citizens. Will the implementation of the Directive involve major legal and policy changes in your country? What are the major points of concern if any, concerning the approximation concept of the directive relating to:

- **non-discrimination in social rights;**
- **the concept of "civic citizenship" (see also extended impact assessment on the Communication on Integration of June 11, 2003);**
- **family reunification and access of family members to the labour market;**
- **security of stay?**

Hungary has begun preparations for a comprehensive amendment of the current Aliens Act. This amendment is in accordance with our commitment regarding EU harmonization, which includes the provisions of the Directives concerning family unification and long-term residents. At the same time, in order to ensure full harmonization, the amendment of other laws relating to the Aliens Act has begun, or has already finished. The regulations concerning third country nationals, who are permanent residents/long-term residents have been partly modified. As far as social rights are concerned, the above mentioned category of persons has almost the same rights as Hungarian nationals. An extension of those rights is expected in the near future pursuant to further modifications of the existing laws.

Concerning the concept of so called "civic citizenship" recent amendments to the various laws have made it possible for third country citizens to vote in both municipal and European Parliament elections. Regarding the entrance of family members on the labour market, a proposed amendment to the Aliens Act is currently being considered. This amendment would make it possible for family members to enter the labour market subject to the application of general rules but on easy terms. Effectively, family members would not require a visa to take up a job. It is proposed to include provisions in the Hungarian laws, which provide more guarantees concerning the security of stay of third country nationals.

2.7 Considering the perspective of a future common migration policy as developed by the Commission in the Open Coordination Communication (COM 2001, 387) and the Communication on a Migration policy of the European Union (COM 2000, 757 final), how do you assess the role of the Community organs in determining a European migration policy in terms of competences of the Member States to decide on residence rights and admission to the labour market and integration? Should harmonization of legislation go further, and if so, in what respect?

From our point of view, the present degree of harmonization of national legislation is necessary and useful. However, some fields should remain under national competency as economic figures and productivity indicators are quite different in the different Member States, thus labour market and social integration have different indicators in each state.

PART III (ASYLUM AND REFUGEE LAW)

3.1 Have the Dublin Rules worked satisfactorily and what is expected of the Dublin II Regulation No. 343, 2003 of 18 February 2003?

The creation of a Dublin Unit under the auspices of the Office of Immigration and Nationality is an ongoing process. The Office is formulating the internal regulations concerning the operation of DubliNet, data-transmission, and the working methodology of Dublin officials. A twinning-light project will be put in place from February till June 2004, to enable OIN officials to act in line with the Dublin II Regulation.

In general, Hungarian Asylum experts expect an increase in the inflow of asylum seekers, taking into consideration the external EU border situation of the country.

3.2 Has the Eurodac Regulation No. 2725/2000 of 11th December 2000, concerning the establishment of Eurodac for the comparison of fingerprints for an effective application of the Dublin Convention, operative since January 15, 2003, resulted in an increase of Dublin cases? Has Eurodac become effective in your country or is it expected to become effective eventually?

Not applicable yet.

3.3 What major changes, if any, will the implementation of the amended proposal for a directive on minimum standards on procedures in Member States for granting and withdrawing refugee status, on which the Council has reached political agreement on most points in June 2003, bring for the legislation and practice in your country in particular relating to:
– rights of applicants in the procedure;
– administrative and judicial appeal procedures;
– the use of safe third country and safe country of origin concepts;
– detainment of asylum seekers;
– airport and border procedures?

The present asylum legislation is in line with the EU asylum directives as they have been approved. However, an amendment to the Act on Asylum which would have reflected the position agreed in the negotiations regarding minimum standards on procedures was postponed until the entire directive had been finally approved. The present regulation on airport procedure must be changed.

Access to the procedure – In Hungary everyone has the right to make an application for asylum either on his/her own behalf or on behalf of his/her dependants. Applications by minors and unaccompanied minors are regulated by special rules of law. Administrators are obliged to give applicants all the information regarding the application and this is constantly checked by the superior authorities.

Right to remain in the Member State pending the examination of the application – This is a basic element of Hungarian practice.

Requirements for the examination of applications – The applications are examined at first by public administrative organs (one inferior and one superior body) and in the event of a negative decision, the applicants can turn to the court and after to an appellate body. There are four levels which involve professional as well as administrative and judicial control.

Requirements for a decision by the determining authority – The applicant has a right to a clear, written decision, based on the facts, including information regarding possible legal remedies.

Guarantees for applicants for asylum – At the beginning of the procedure, all the applicants get a written guide – in a language they understand – about their rights and obligations. During the procedure, every applicant has a right to an interpreter and to free legal assistance. If the applicant has a legal representative, the decisions of the authorities are sent to those representatives as well.

Persons invited to a personal interview – A personal interview is required before the first administrative decision, and it is possible for a hearing to be conducted at every level. In so far as minors are concerned, the authorities guarantee more rights in the context of a special procedure. The authorities cooperate with medical and psychological experts in any case in which such expertise is needed.

Status of the report of a personal interview in the procedure – A written report of the interview is made and the requirement of a guaranteed hearing is examined by the supervisory authorities in every case.

Right to legal assistance and representation – There is a possibility of obtaining free legal aid, which is guaranteed by the state, but also applicants can choose alternate assistance.

Scope of legal assistance and representation – Legal advisers are allowed to visit applicants in detention, and they are informed about all the relevant information of the case upon which the decision of the authorities is based.

Guarantees for unaccompanied minors – The authorities handle these cases with special treatment and with a special expedited procedure that guarantees a quick decision. In those cases, legal representation is obligatory.

Detention – Speedy judicial review and legal representation is guaranteed.

Procedure in case of an implicit withdrawal or abandonment of the application – No one can be deported contrary to the principle of non-refoulment: the application of this principle is always examined.

The role of the UNHCR – The UNHCR is informed about every case, all of the decisions are sent to them and the UNHCR has the right to send a representative to any hearing.

Collection of information on individual cases – The authorities in cases of family members decide on the applications in the context of a single procedure for request.

Examination procedure – The application must be decided within 60 days. In cases in which it is established that the application is manifestly unfounded, an expedited procedure is used.

Specific procedure – the only special procedure is the expedited procedure which is used in manifestly unfounded cases. The airport, as a special place, has alternate rules with shorter deadlines (8 days).

Cases of inadmissible applications – Hungary does not have this practice, only the expedited procedure.

Application of the concept of first country of asylum – The principle of non-refoulement is always examined by the authorities.

Unfounded application cases – Manifestly unfounded applications are dealt with by way of the expedited procedure.

Safe countries of origin – The applicant's particular circumstances are examined in every case and the principle of non-refoulement is always analysed by the authorities.

Cases of subsequent applications – There are four levels of authorities, two administrative and two judicial.

Procedural rules – Aside from the guarantees provided by procedural rules, both professional and judicial control is also available (superior authority, Appellate body).

Cases of border procedures – At the airport in the transit sector the public administration organs are required to make a decision on an application within 8 days. All the procedural rights are guaranteed.

Right to remain during review and appeal procedures – Every applicant has the right to remain in Hungary during the entire application procedure.

The present Hungarian appeal system provides three possible legal remedies. After the first administrative decision, the applicant can appeal to the superior public administrative organ. The next two levels are judicial instances, the Capital Court and the Regional Court of Appeal. The requirements of a fair and equal system of remedies are fulfilled. The amendment under preparation intends to reduce the number of instances to the number in existence prior to 2002, because the asylum procedures are too lengthy.

3.4 What measures have been undertaken to implement Directive 2003/9 of 27 January 2003, on reception of asylum seekers in your country relating to:
- **the flexibility clauses in the Directive;**
- **restriction of free movement;**
- **access to the labour market;**
- **rights of migrant workers under Article 11 § 2 of the Directive?**

The flexibility clauses (Art. 4.): In the field of the free movement of asylum seekers, the Hungarian regulations are more flexible than the provisions of the Directive in the sense that an asylum seeker may move freely within the whole territory of the country if he or she fulfils his or her obligations under the Asylum Act. At the same time the Hungarian regulations may be considered somewhat stricter than the Directive's requirements, because the free movement of the asylum seeker is restricted on the grounds of public health. The regulations provide that an asylum seeker is to be isolated until the certificate issued by the Institute of the State Public Health and Medical Administration attests that the applicant does not suffer from an infectious disease, and is not virulent or host for the diseases listed in the Asylum Act. Under the Directive, the public health exception allows for such restrictions.

Restriction of free movement: (Art.7.) According to the Hungarian Asylum Act, the asylum seeker is obliged to stay and live at the reception centre, or in any other place of accommodation designated by the refugee authority. The Hungarian Executive Decree of the Asylum Act (hereinafter Executive Decree) contains the detailed rules of this obligation. Pursuant to the Executive Degree, the rules of continuous stay at a place of accommodation are deemed to be violated if the place of accommodation is left for 24 hours without the permission of the refugee authority. In practice, the refugee authority never rejects an application for such a permission, but despite this fact, our experiences show that asylum seekers usually violate this obligation. This means that, in many cases, effectively they do not live at the reception centres.

Under the Executive Decree, upon the request of the asylum seeker, private accommodation may also be designated by the refugee authority as the place of accommodation. In relation to this provision, the practical experience is that asylum seekers usually give fictitious addresses to the refugee authority, and they fail to inform the authority about changes of address in cases of private accommodation.

Access to the labour market (Art.11): The existing Hungarian regulations in this field provide that an asylum seeker may not engage in employment, other than employment at the reception centre, but our intention is to change this regulation. According to the proposed Asylum Act amendment, which will be debated by Parliament in the 2nd half of 2004, this prohibition only applies for a period of one year from the time the application has been lodged. After this period, the asylum seeker may engage in employment under the conditions determined by a government decree, provided that the delay in the asylum process is not caused by the asylum seeker him- or herself.

Concerning the rights of migrant workers, we are of the opinion that the notion of "migrant worker" cannot be interpreted under the Directive in question, because a migrant worker in general is not an asylum seeker. If the question refers to an asylum seeker's right of access to work, than the answer is that the Hungarian regulation, as it stands now, does not yet comply with the Directive, however a proposed amendment will introduce the right to work after the expiry of 1 year from the time of lodging the asylum claim.

3.5 What steps have been undertaken to implement the Directive on temporary protection, COM 2001, 55 in national law? Are there any procedures for burden sharing arrangements? Is there a legal basis for the admission of refugees for the purposes of receiving temporary protection in a mass-movement situation?

The draft amendment, we have referred to above (see the 3rd point in 3.4), provides in its final provisions that the measure is in compliance with the Directive on temporary protection (COM 2001, 55).

According to this provision, the draft amendment

- modifies the definition of persons receiving temporary protection in a mass-movement situation (hereinafter: TP),
- modifies the legal conditions of admission of a TP,
- modifies the legal conditions of withdrawal of TP status,
- is completed with the rules of family unification in the case of those families which have been split up due to mass-movement circumstances.

As the present Hungarian regulation stands, there is no compliance with the Directive in question, but there will be once the draft amendment of the Hungarian Asylum Act is adopted, which is to be done by the end of 2004. The sole reason for not submitting the draft amendment earlier is that Hungary is waiting for the adoption of the qualification Directive, in order to be able to establish a comprehensively harmonized asylum-legislation.

Under the current Hungarian regulation, there are no specific procedures for burden sharing arrangements, but crises management regulations for handling the possible mass influx do exist.

According to the current provisions of the Hungarian Asylum Act, refugee and TP status are not mutually exclusive and a person who is under temporary protection can apply for refugee status. The draft amendment regulates this matter in detail and in compliance with the Directive of 2001 on temporary protection. Under the draft regulation, the application of a TP for refugee status must be lodged before the day of expiry of the temporary protection. The provisions provide that the applicant is always under the protection of either of the statuses until his or her application is decided and his or her position becomes certain.

3.6 The Council has reached political agreement on the principles for a Directive on minimum standards for the qualification and status of third country nationals as refugees or persons who otherwise need international protection, COM 2001, 510 final (see Council documents of June 2003). What measures are envisaged to implement the Directive, once it is adopted, in your country relating to:

- **the definition of refugee;**
- **the definition of persons entitled to subsidiary protection;**
- **status of persons entitled to subsidiary protection;**
- **the issue of internal flight alternative as defined by the directive;**
- **exclusion clauses, particularly issues of terrorism?**
- **To what extent are the refugee policies as reflected in the law and jurisprudence of your country in accordance with the proposal for the directive?**

Hungary plans to comply with its harmonization obligations in advance so as to be well-prepared for becoming a Member State.

The Hungarian Asylum Act has the same definition following the Geneva Convention of refugee as the draft directive in question.

In the Hungarian terminus technicus, the notion of subsidiary protection is equal to the notion of "a person authorized to stay" (hereinafter: PAS), and the definition of PAS is to be found in the Aliens Act instead of in the Asylum Act. The definition complies with that of the directive in question.

The regulation of the status of PAS also falls under the Aliens Act. According to this Act, a PAS has the following rights and obligations:

- right to be informed about his or her rights and obligations;
- right to maintain family unity, which complies with the draft directive;
- right to a residence permit: in Hungary the residence permit is issued on humanitarian grounds, and can be valid up to a maximum of one year, while under EU legislation this period of validity is a minimum of one year;
- right of access to employment: access to employment for a PAS in Hungary is easier than for other third country nationals, because the Office of Immigration and Nationality support them by assuring an accelerated permission procedure, so a PAS can obtain an employment permit faster;
- right of access to education and also diploma qualification complies with the draft directive
- right to social welfare: the present system does not grant access to social welfare on the same grounds as for nationals, but special subsidies are provided for by an executive decree of the 170/2001 Aliens Act;
- the right to health care: under the provisions 25/1998 Government Decree on Care and Maintenance, the right to health care of a PAS is restricted to basic health care; in- and outpatient healthcare in the case of emergency, including emergency dental treatment; prenatal and

obstetric care and medicine which can be ordered with a 90% or 100% social security subsidy. There will be no change in this regulation due to the large number of PAS;

- right to access to integration facilities: the present system does not allow for access to integration programmes for PAS but there are efforts to integrate them;
- right to repatriation: repatriation subsidies can be claimed by PAS;
- the right to travel documents is not regulated yet.

The Hungarian regulations are in compliance with the provisions of Art. 10(1) and 10(2) of the draft directive on qualification. According to these provisions, Member States may determine that an applicant is not in need of international protection if in a part of the country of origin there is no well-founded fear of being persecuted or no real risk of suffering serious harm, and the applicant can reasonably be expected to stay in that part of the country.

The Hungarian Asylum Act complies with the draft directive in question in relation to the exclusions, and considers the matter of terrorism within the category of national security.

The permanently evolving Hungarian asylum policy is in line with the comparatively stricter EU legislation. The role of the UNHCR in the field of protection must be stressed, because in Hungary it is of a higher standard than in many Member States.

3.7 In the Commission's Communication of 22 November, 2000, COM 2000, 755 (see also 2nd Commission Report COM 2003, 152 final) the Commission's concept of a common European asylum procedure and a uniform status for those who are granted asylum valid throughout the Union is set out. Do you consider that the concept is generally in line with your country's asylum policy? Are the concerns of refugee organizations, such as Amnesty International and other organizations, of an undermining of the international regime for the protection of refugees shared in the political circles responsible for decision-making of your country?

With regard to 2000/755 (COM); 152/2003 (COM), Hungarian asylum policy corresponds to the common rules of the EU, and the asylum procedure is in accordance with the common policy. As a professional administrative organ, the Office of Immigration and Naturalization share the Commission's opinion on the question of harmonization. On the other hand the OIN is an administrative body, thus it is not in a position to represent or evaluate political decisions/opinions. Regarding the question of concerned refugee organizations, the representatives of the Hungarian political parties can give you a more authentic standpoint.

3.8 The open coordination-mechanism, as suggested by the Commission, provided for first stage and second stage legislation in which the flexibility provisions in some of the directives on migration and asylum are to be replaced by full harmonization. Is this concept discussed in your country and what are the perceptions relating to the gradual establishment of a European asylum policy which might eventually replace national procedures and national decision-making?

Hungary, as an acceding country is ready to accept and apply approximated common EU law. However, the OIN is of the opinion that a comprehensive and exclusive EU asylum policy and procedure will not be easy to reach or, subsequently, to at a later stage implement unless the guarantees of fair burden sharing take into consideration not only the number of inhabitants but also the objectively expected productivity of the states (see: acceding countries with a historical and fiscal backlog).

3.9 The Communication of June 2003, towards a more accessible, equitable and managed asylum system – in reaction to the UK paper – develops some ideas on new approaches to pursue an orderly and managed arrival of persons in need of international protection. What is the political reaction in your country to the concept of an outside accessed asylum procedure, distribution of refugees and responsibility-sharing and other new concepts and ideas in coping with mass refugee movements?

The concepts of managed arrival and the equal distribution of asylum seekers has not provoked a high-profile political or public debate, yet. In general, the establishment of a common approach towards mass influx situations is a desirable solution, if a political consensus can be built up.

PART IV (TERMINATION OF ILLEGAL RESIDENCE, RETURN AND REPATRIATION)

For illegal migrants, Hungary is a transit country, but EU accession may transform our country into a destination. The prevention of the entry of illegal migrants takes place primarily at the state border. The provisions of the alien Policing law which entered into force 1 January 2002, harmonizes Hungarian law with the EU law norms adopted in December 2000. Recently, we have introduced an obligatory visa system with many countries who are the source of illegal migrants. We have also concluded readmission agreements, which are effective in helping to combat the migration of undesirable aliens to the territory of Hungary and in assisting in their removal from that territory.

A complex and profound monitoring system was introduced and is being operated to improve public security and increase the effectiveness of actions against third country nationals entering into or residing or working illegally in Hungary as well as against other unlawful acts related to illegal migration.

In the framework of coordinated cooperation, the Migration Office implements complex and profound monitoring with the Border Guard and the Police, customs authorities, and labor inspectorates. Cooperation with Austria, Germany, and the Benelux States in the course of the implementation of the readmission agreements is correct and constructive.

4.1 How many third country nationals without a valid residence permit are currently, according to estimates, staying in your country? How many deportations have actually been made in previous years? Is the whole enforcement process considered as acceptable?

The aliens policing Register does not contain data regarding the number of illegal migrants staying in the territory of the Republic of Hungary without valid residence permit. The following numbers of persons were expelled for violating entry rules: 1,753 persons in the year 2002; and 547 persons up to the end of October 2003. The following numbers of persons were expelled for violating residence rules: 735 in the year 2002; and 352 up to the end of October 2003. The expulsion process, which takes places within the framework of readmission agreements aiming to eliminate illegal migration, is quick, without unnecessary formalities, economic and effectively ensures the repatriation of the migrants to their own countries. In the case of countries, with whom no valid readmission agreements are in existence, the expulsion process takes more time due to the need to verify the identity of the foreigners. In some cases the expulsion process even fails.

In the year 2002, Hungarian authorities ordered the deportation of 1,759 expelled foreigners and in 2003, of 1,605 expelled foreigners.

4.5 What measures have been taken to implement the Council Directive of 28 May 2001, on the mutual recognition of decisions on the expulsion of third country nationals? What, if any shortcomings or gaps of the Directive should be corrected in a further directive on cooperation on expulsion or deportation of third country nationals?

The modifications of the Act XXXIX 2001, on the entry and stay of foreigners and its implementation orders are ready and currently are under public administration coordination. These modifications, which harmonize Hungarian law with Community norms, entered into force from December 2000, to 30 December 2003. The detailed rules on the recognition and implementation of expulsion orders made by the EU

Member States, will be regulated according to the legislative amendments in the government degree.

4.6 Do readmission agreements or other international treaties or arrangements with the aim of controlling and curbing illegal immigration and facilitating return exist in your country? Have they functioned satisfactorily?

The Government of the Republic of Hungary concluded readmission agreements with 23 countries of Europe and there are professional negotiations being carried on with many countries aimed at signing further agreements.

Hungary is part of the Agreement created by 9 countries in order to authorize the transit of Yugoslavian citizens, who are obliged to return. In order to support the voluntary return of migrants, the Ministry of the Interior of the Republic of Hungary and the International Organization for Migration (IOM) have concluded an Agreement. The above mentioned agreements are effective tools for the repatriation of migrants to their countries of origin.

4.7 To what extent have EU-standards and recommendations influenced your country's return policy? Have efforts been undertaken to cooperate with other EU Member States in enforcing return decisions by common deportation actions, exchange of information, facilitation of air and land transit, common principles on flight security, etc.?

As part of the preparation for joining the EU, we are continuously incorporating EU standards and recommendations into the migration laws. EC recommendations and directives form the basis of numerous readmission agreements and the modification of former agreements.

4.8 Do you consider that there is a need to elaborate a common legal regime for air deportations (legal status of armed guards on board of the aircrafts, rights of the aircraft commander, legal rules in case of transit stops, applicability of national police law on board of aircraft on flight, etc.)?

Harmonizing with the Recommendation 1547(2002), in order to ensure that expulsion procedures are in conformity with human rights and enforced with respect for safety and dignity, we urge the elaboration of a common law system of deportation by air.

IRELAND

JOHN HANDOLL
Partner, William Fry, Solicitors

GENERAL REMARKS

As a country of emigration for much of the 19th and 20th Centuries, Ireland has only relatively recently had to address the challenge of accommodating significant numbers of asylum seekers and other immigrants.

In the field of asylum, Ireland participates in the Geneva Convention System and is bound by the international legal obligations arising out of that regime. It is also bound by international obligations on non-refoulement. Initially dealing with refugee applications on an administrative basis, specific refugee legislation – the Refugee Act 1996 – was adopted in 1996 and, after a rather fitful start, this legislation as amended (most recently by the Immigration Act 2003) provides the basis for a comprehensive system of refugee protection. The costs involved in processing a large number of claims and providing support during the process – where a substantial proportion of applications are judged to be unfounded – has resulted in a tightening-up of procedures, which has arguably led to a reduction in the "pull" factor.

In the field of immigration, there is, in contrast to the asylum regime, a considerable element of ministerial discretion reflecting the judicially-endorsed belief that the "State must have very wide powers in the interest of the common good to control aliens, their entry into the State, their departure and their activities within the State". Subject always to international legal obligations, entry and stay entail executive discretion, subject to the prohibition of refoulement and to the observance of procedural and other conditions set out in the legislation and requirements of constitutional justice. Legislative change has been patchy, reflecting specific concerns (such as trafficking) or the need to replace constitutionally impugned legislation dating back from the days of the Irish Free State. Despite proposals to introduce new legislation on immigration and residence, the principal legislation governing entry and residence is the Aliens Act 1935 and – until very recently – the Aliens Order 1946 (as periodically amended). Following a 1999 Supreme Court ruling in the *Laurentiu* case that the deportation provisions under the 1935 Act were unconstitutional, the Immigration Act 1999 was passed, providing a new framework for deportation. This was followed by the Illegal Immigrants (Trafficking) Act 2000, designed to combat the growing phenomenon of smuggling of migrants. The Immigration Act 2003 introduced carrier sanctions amongst other matters and the Employment Permits Act 2003 imposed sanctions on those employing persons without the requisite work permit.

In a controversial Supreme Court judgment in early 2003, which involved cases of rejected asylum seekers and asylum seekers covered by the Dublin Convention each with Irish citizen children born in Ireland, it was held – by a five to two majority of the judges – that non-national parents do not have the right to remain in the State by virtue of the residence rights of their Irish national children (*L & O v Minister for Justice*). Rather, the Minister for Justice, Equality and Law Reform was entitled to deport the parents (to be accompanied by the citizen child) where he considered that this was in the common good on the basis of the need to preserve respect for the integrity of the asylum and immigration system. As a result of the judgment, the Minister no longer accepts applications for residency for persons on the basis of their parentage of an Irish-born (and hence Irish citizen) child. Of the estimated 11,000 persons subject to the possibility of deportation following the ruling, only around 1,000 have to date been given notice of deportation and a small number actually deported.

In January 2004, the High Court declared that certain provisions of the Aliens Act 1935, of the Aliens Order 1946 and of the Immigration Act 1999 were unconstitutional (case of *Leontava and Chang*). This resulted in the swift presentation of the Immigration Bill 2004, which may best be characterised as emergency legislation. Reflecting the belief that no aspect of the Aliens Orders would, as secondary legislation, be safe from challenge, the Immigration Act 2004 expresses in primary statute the main elements of the law governing the State's operation of controls on entry and presence in the State of non-nationals (see, generally, the clear Explanatory and Financial Memorandum with the Bill). In essence, the Act reflects the content of the Aliens Orders as they stood immediately prior to the High Court judgment, with certain changes and additional provisions consistent with modern legislative practice. The Bill was subject to criticism from various NGOs and others, and it was suggested that adoption of the Act would result in Ireland being in breach of its international human rights obligations. This debate will doubtless resurface in the forthcoming Immigration and Residence Bill.

Ireland does not fully participate in the EU immigration and asylum regime, and did not participate in the precursor Schengen system. In a number of Protocols agreed in the Amsterdam Treaty, Ireland (as is the UK): (a) is able to retain border controls – notwithstanding Article 14 of the EC Treaty – as long as it retains the Common Travel Area; (b) does not participate in measures under the Title on Freedom, Security and Justice, although it may opt in completely or to particular measures; and (c) is not bound by the Schengen *Acquis*, though it may request to take part in some or all of the *Acquis.* At least as far as Ireland is concerned, the stated reason for this "flexibility" or "variable geometry" is the need to protect the integrity of the Common Travel Area. Ireland has thus "reluctantly" gone this route and in a Declaration to the Final Act, it has declared its readiness to participate to the maximum extent compatible with the maintenance of the Common Travel Area.

Ireland has signed up to four adopted asylum measures – on the European Refugee Fund, on Eurodac, on temporary protection and the Dublin II Regulation (replacing, save with respect to Denmark, the Dublin Convention). It is also participating in the proposed qualification and status and procedures Directives. It has, up to now, not opted in to the proposed reception conditions Directive (although the UK has opted in).

In relation to immigration, it has, together with the UK, not opted in to the forthcoming Directive on the status of legally-resident third-country nationals, apparently because the free movement provisions in Chapter III of that Directive could affect the integrity of the Common Travel Area. It has, however, opted in to proposed Directives on the conditions of entry and residence for employment and on the facilitation of unauthorised entry, transit and residence. Ireland has requested and been allowed to participate in some elements of the Schengen *Acquis.* It is, with the exception of carrier sanctions, not participating in the measures relating to borders, including visas.

Up to now, the Irish courts have tended to see fundamental rights protection in the context of the Irish Constitution rather than the ECHR. Ireland has, after a long delay, incorporated the ECHR into Irish law, albeit in a somewhat indirect way reflecting the specific characteristics of the Irish Constitution (European Convention on Human Rights Act 2003). This, and the increasing involvement of Ireland in the European Union regime, could result in a less insular regime than that which has evolved up to now.

PART I (ENTRY, VISA REGIME AND BORDER CONTROL)

Ireland does not participate in Schengen/European Community measures which concern entry, visa policy and borders, although – reflecting its concerns about illegal immigration – it does participate in the Schengen measures on organised travel and measures building on these provisions.

1.1 What national authorities are competent to deal with visa applications (Schengen visa and long-term visa)? Are there any procedures to avoid duplication or successive visa applications at different EU- consulates? On what substantive criteria other than the Schengen minimum requirements are visas granted or refused? How many visas have been issued or refused?

Overall responsibility for visa policy lies with the Minister for Justice, Equality and Law Reform as part of his general responsibility for immigration matters. Section 17 of the Immigration Act 2004 empowers the Minister, "for the purposes of ensuring the integrity of the immigration system, the maintenance of national security, public order or public health or the orderly regulation of the labour market or for the purposes of reciprocal immigration arrangements with other states or the promotion of tourism" by order to declare that members of specified classes of non-nationals are not required to have a valid Irish visa or are required to possess a valid Irish travel visa.

Within this general visa policy, the Department of Foreign Affairs processes visa applications through its embassies and consular representations. Problematic cases are referred back to the Department of Justice.

1.2 Is there a visa tracking procedure in order to find out visa over-stayers? What data are collected from visa applicants (fingerprints)? Admissibility of visa data to alien and police authorities?

The issue of a visa gives the person concerned the right to present himself or herself at the frontier of the State in order to request leave to enter and remain for a period of up to 90 days. Persons wishing to remain for longer must register with the Garda National Immigration Bureau and apply for further permission to remain before the expiry of the initial period of leave: this will generally not be given to persons on short-visit category visas.

There is no visa tracking procedure as such and no fingerprinting. However, a new computerised system for registering non-nationals introduced in 2001 contains details of more than 100,000 legally-resident non-EEA nationals and this is accessible to immigration officers at major points of entry. The Garda Registation Certificate – which is issued to persons on initial registration or renewal – is a high security document in bank card format with a digitised photograph and security features.

1.3 Have courts ever decided on the refusal of Schengen visas based upon Schengen blacklisting of other Member States?

This is not relevant in the Irish context.

1.4 What measures have been undertaken in implementation of the action programme for administrative cooperation in the field of external borders, visa, asylum and immigration following the Council Decision of 13 June 2002?

This is not relevant in the Irish context.

1.5 What measures have been undertaken to implement Directive 2001/51 EC supplementing the Schengen rules concerning carrier sanctions? How often have carrier sanctions been used?

Section 5 of the Immigration Act 2003, containing provisions on removal from the State of persons refused leave to land, contains provisions on carrier's liability implementing at the same time Article 26 of the 1990 Schengen Convention and the supplementing provisions contained in Directive 2001/51.

The new provisions came into effect in September 2003. It is too early to make any meaningful assessment how they have been, or are likely to be, applied. However, the Garda National Immigration Bureau is charged with implementing effective strategies to combat trafficking in illegal immigrants and will become better equipped to pursue carriers.

1.6 According to your judgement, does the visa law and policy of your country live up to EU standards or are adjustments needed? Do you consider that there is need of further EU-harmonization of visa policies concerning:
- **common criteria for granting visas aiming at harmonizing visa obligations among States participating in the Budapest Process;**
- **establishment of a European visa identification system (VIS and SIS II)?**

This is not relevant in the Irish context.

1.7 To what extent will the EU enlargement process present a chance or danger for tackling with issues of illegal entry and border control?

No specific comments as far as Ireland is concerned.

PART II (ADMISSION AND RESIDENCE OF THIRD COUNTRY NATIONALS)

2.1 What are the basic principles in your country concerning:
– admission of third country nationals for labour purpose or self-employed activities

With certain exceptions, third country nationals require a work permit and, unless citizens of States not requiring Irish visas, must have visas. Such work permits are issued to employers, are non-transferable and limited in time. A more liberal regime applies to persons in sectors where there are skill shortages. A person wishing to carry out self-employed activity must apply for business permission and, where required, apply for a visa. There is a general requirement to register with the Garda National Immigration Bureau where there is an intention to stay more than 90 days.

– admission of third country nationals for study and vocational training

Third-country nationals may be admitted for study and vocational training and there is a policy of openness to genuine students. Where a visa is required, a "C" study visa may be issued for a period of up to 3 months and a "D" study visa for longer periods. If the student intends to remain for more than three months, he/she must register with the Garda National Immigration Bureau. Those registered as full-time students are permitted to work for up to 20 hours a week to support themselves.

– legal status of third country nationals in possession of a long-term residence permit of another Member State

There is no special legal status attaching to a third country national possessing a long term residence right in another EU Member State. Ireland is not participating in the 2003 Long-Term Residents Directive.

– To what extent do these principles differ from the European Commission's proposals?

In relation to access to economic activity, the developing policy in Ireland is broadly consistent with the Commission's approach. There is an increasing level of transparency, with clear and detailed guidance given by the Department of Enterprise, Trade and Employment. Application procedures are relatively simple and clear. Preferential access is given to EEA nationals, and nationals of the Accession States. Increased efforts have been made to identify sectors where there are skill shortages justifying a more flexible regime. There are nonetheless differences from the

Commission's approach. Employed and self-employed persons are dealt with under substantially different regimes and there are separate requirements for work permits and residence permits, access to economic activity by third-country nationals is generally seen as a discretionary matter, rather than of entitlement. The idea of an open coordination method is a novel one (which has not received explicit endorsement by the Council of Ministers/European Council).

In relation to admission for study purposes, the general openness to genuine students is consistent with the Commission's proposals. However, there are certain differences in the operation of Irish policy. There are no specific published rules/guidelines addressing the position of school children, unremunerated trainees and volunteers from third countries. Although the need to show adequate resources is clearly stated, no figure setting out the minimum required is published. The opportunity for part-time work is consistent with the Commission's proposals. Efforts are being made to increase transparency.

2.2 What are the legal requirements and procedures for obtaining a residence permit for third country nationals for the purpose of employment? Which procedures are used in maintaining the preferred access of EU-citizens and Turkish nationals (association agreement) to the labour market? Do special programmes exist for highly qualified professionals facilitating access to the labour market? To what extent are trade unions and employers involved in such programmes? Is there a procedure to calculate the demand for foreign labour? How is the EU-enlargement taken into consideration? To what extent has the recent economic recession and unemployment influenced the concepts on admission of third country nationals?

Under Section 2 of the Employment Permits Act 2003, a non-national may not be employed except in accordance with an employment permit granted by the Minister for Enterprise Trade and Employment. Penalties apply to non-nationals who work, and those who employ them, without such a permit. The requirement does not apply to refugees, those entitled to enter and be employed in the State pursuant to the European Communities Treaties and those permitted to remain by the Minister for Justice without the need for an employment permit.

The work permit system is administered by the Department of Enterprise, Trade and Employment which distinguishes between two main methods for acquiring permits. First, the standard Work Permit can be applied for by employers in Ireland, who are required to have demonstrated that they have made every attempt to employ an EEA national – and Accession State nationals. The Minister for Enterprise, Trade and Employment has designated, on a rolling basis, certain occupational sectors as ineligible for work permit application purposes, reflecting the belief that these jobs can be filled by workers from the EEA and Accession States. Those wishing to employ workers in eligible occupational sectors must be registered with the State employment agency – FÀS – for a four week period to see if the position can be filled by an EEA/Accession State worker and it must be shown that every effort has been made to source nationals from these States. Second, there is the Working Visa/Work Authorisation scheme which is designed to attract third-country nationals to sectors where skill shortages are acute – covering information technology workers, construction professionals and medical/healthcare professionals. Applications for such workers can be made and processed at Irish embassies and Consulates abroad.

Ireland has decided to allow access to work by nationals of all eight of the acceding States from the date of their accession in May 2004, although it now appears that access to social welfare benefits may be restricted. Section 3 of the Employment Permits Act 2003 provides that the requirement for employment permits will not apply to nationals of such States after enlargement, although – in accordance with the Treaty of Accession – the Minister for Enterprise, Trade and Employment may re-impose the requirement for a limited period after accession, if labour market circumstances so require.

2.3 To what extent do existing laws and practices differ substantially from the approach taken in the Commission's Proposal on admission for the purpose of paid employment and self-employed activities relating to:
- **admission of third country nationals for study and vocational training;**
- **on legal status of third country nationals in possession of a long-term residence permit of another Member State?**
- **To what extent do these principles differ from the European Commission's proposals?**

See the response to Section 2.1, above.

2.4 What measures have been taken to implement Council Directive 2000/43/EC of 29 June 2000 implementing the principle of equal treatment between persons irrespective of racial or ethnic origin and Council Directive 2000/78 EC of 27 November 2000 establishing a general framework for equal treatment in employment and occupation? Have legislative changes been undertaken? To what extent is "affirmative action" considered as necessary to promote equal chances for migrant workers from third countries?

The Equality Bill 2004, presented on 13 January 2004, contains a series of amendments to the Employment Equality Act 1998 and the Equal Status Act 2000, to give effect to the two 2000 Directives. Both the 1998 and 2000 Acts currently allow positive action measures in relation to gender, people with disabilities, older people and Travellers. A proposed amendment to the 1998 Act will allow, in line with Article 5 of Directive 2000/43 and Article 7 of Directive 2000/78, positive action measures to be taken to prevent or compensate for disadvantages linked to other grounds, including race. The Equality Authority (see www.equality.ie), amongst other bodies, has sought to encourage positive action measures in relation to the existing grounds and would be expected to continue this approach in relation to migrant workers faced with discrimination on grounds of race.

2.5 Concerning the proposal of a directive on the right to family reunion agreed upon by Council in February 2003:
- **Do you consider the proposed standards below the principles of family reunification valid in your country?**
- **Will the implementation of the Directive once it is adopted lead to changes in the national law on family reunification downgrading the standard of protection? If so, what changes are envisaged?**

Ireland did not participate in the adoption of Council Directive 2003/86 on the right to family reunification and is not bound by or subject to its application.

The question of family reunification for the general class of third-country nationals is largely dealt with on an administrative basis. There is no policy objection to family reunion where the legally resident non-national is able to support family members without recourse to public funds. In the case of family members requiring visas, there is an additional general requirement that the worker be in the State for twelve months and be offered a further twelve month contract before being joined by family members: this waiting period may be considerably reduced in the case of certain highly-skilled professionals.

2.6 The proposal for a directive on the rights of long-term third country nationals as agreed upon by the Council on June 5, 2003 provides for a number of rights approximating the standards of long-term residents to the status of EU-citizens. Will the implementation of the Directive involve major legal and policy changes in your country? What are the major points of concern if any, concerning the approximation concept of the directive relating to:
- **non-discrimination in social rights;**
- **the concept of "civic citizenship" (see also extended impact assessment on the Communication on Integration of June 11, 2003);**
- **family reunification and access of family members to the labour market;**
- **security of stay?**

Ireland has not opted in to this Directive. Its reservations appear to relate to the free movement provisions contained in Chapter III of the Directive rather than to any serious conceptual difficulties relating to the rights of long-term residents under that Directive.

The fact that Ireland has not opted in means that the legal and policy implications of the Directive for the status of long-term resident third-country nationals will not need to be addressed, at least for the present. The treatment of the residual class of long-term third-country national residents is addressed in national immigration rules applied in the light of national constitutional requirements and the State's international obligations.

It should be noted that Ireland has for long extended local political rights to resident non-nationals. Local elections are to be held later in the year and a number of non-nationals have already signalled their intention to stand for election. In the context of "civic citizenship," Ireland would thus seem to be ahead of many of the other Member States.

2.7 Considering the perspective of a future common migration policy as developed by the Commission in the Open Coordination Communication (COM 2001, 387) and the communication on a migration policy of the European Union (COM 2000, 757 final), how do you assess the role of the Community organs in determining a European migration policy in terms of competences of the Member States to decide on residence rights and admission to the labour market and integration? Should harmonization of legislation go further, and if so, in what respect?

The Commission's approach to immigration policy, as seen in its 2000 Communication on migration policy, its 2001 Communication on an open method of coordination in immigration policy and, more recently, its June 2003 Communication on immigration, integration and employment, recognises Member States' concerns that Community action should not trespass into areas of national competence. The Commission's concern has, however, been to develop a Union "umbrella" to promote consistency between Community and national policies, by proposing the use of the open coordination method. At the same time, it has sought to be pragmatic in its proposals (witness, for example, its decision not to propose a Directive on the admission of third-country nationals who are not gainfully employed, on the basis that this can be dealt with adequately by domestic law at the current stage of approximation of immigration legislation) without fettering the possibility of proposing new harmonising measures in the future.

The open method of coordination has not proved attractive to the Member States, with the Thessaloniki European Council pointedly not accepting the Commission's approach and pointing to the fact that primary responsibility for immigration policies remains with the Member States. In legislating, the Council has accommodated national sensitivities at the expense of uniform and clear rules (witness the 2003 Long-Term Residents Directive). In relation to promoting the integration of legally-resident third-country nationals, the draft Treaty establishing a Constitution for Europe envisages European laws to establish measures to provide incentives and support for the action of Member States, but excluding any harmonisation of the laws and regulations of the Member States.

All this suggests that a cautious approach will be taken to harmonising national laws even in areas where the Community is competent to act. This cautious approach is likely to be endorsed by the Irish Government.

PART III (ASYLUM AND REFUGEE LAW)

3.1 Have the Dublin Rules worked satisfactorily and what is expected from the Dublin II Regulation (343/2003) of 18 February 2003?

Ireland has participated in the adoption of, and is subject to and bound by, the Dublin II Regulation. The decision to exercise the option provided for in the Fourth Protocol appears to have been taken with little debate.

The Refugee Act 1996, as amended by the Immigration Act 2003, empowers the Minister to make subsidiary legislation for giving full effect to the Dublin II Regulation. A greater degree of flexibility is provided for, with the Minister able to designate immigration officers at ports of entry to make first instance decisions, with speedier decision-making procedures and with the possibility of short-term detention (although no specific orders have yet been made covering these matters). The fact that appeals against the first instance determination will not have suspensive effect should also result in a speedier process.

3.2 Has the Eurodac Regulation No. 2725/2000 of 11th December 2000 concerning the establishment of Eurodac for the comparison of fingerprints for an effective application of the Dublin Convention, operative since January 15, 2003 resulted in an increase of Dublin cases? Has Eurodac become effective in your country or is it expected to become eventually effective?

The Oireachtas approved Ireland's participation in the Eurodac Regulation in October 1999.

The Immigration Act 1999 introduced a new Section 9A of the Refugee Act 1996 which allowed for the fingerprinting of all asylum applicants over 14 years of age. Such fingerprinting commenced in November 2000. The minimum age limit was removed by the Immigration Act 2003, subject to certain safeguards.

Ireland has introduced a semi-automated system for the transmission of fingerprints to Eurodac in the short term and it is intended as soon as possible to introduce a full electronic fingerprinting system.

3.3 What major changes, if any, will the implementation of the amended proposal of a directive on minimum standards on procedures in Member States for granting and withdrawing refugee status on which the Council has reached political agreement on most points in June 2003, bring for the legislation and practice in your country in particular relating to:
- **rights of applicants in the procedure;**
- **administrative and judicial appeal procedure;**
- **the use of safe third country and safe country of origin concepts;**
- **detainment of asylum seekers;**
- **airport and border procedures?**

Rights of applicants in the procedure

The Refugee Act 1996, as most recently amended by the Immigration Act 2003, contains a series of provisions on the rights (and obligations) of applicants for refugee status. A number of these provisions should be briefly identified in the light of proposed provisions of the Directive covering basic principles and guarantees.

Access to the procedure (draft Art. 5). Provisions in the 1996 Act on access to the procedure are largely consistent with Article 5 of the draft Directive.

Right to remain (draft Art. 6). Provisions on the right to remain are, if anything, more liberal than those of Article 6 of the draft Directive.

Examination of applications (draft Art. 7). Recommendations of the Refugee Applications Commissioner – who is to be treated as the "determining authority" for the purposes of the draft Directive – generally appear to be made on the basis of an "appropriate examination" as specified in Article 7(2) of the draft Directive.

Requirements for a decision by the determining authority (draft Art. 8). The current provisions appear to conform to Article 8 of the draft Directive.

Guarantees for applicants for asylum (draft Art. 9). Except for measures on linguistic assistance, which is to be given where possible, the Irish position generally conforms to the requirements of the draft Directive.

Obligations of applicants for asylum (draft Art. 9A). Amendments to the Refugee Act introduced by the Immigration Act 2003 place increased stress on the obligation of the applicant failure to cooperate with the Commissioner and to furnish relevant information, with breach resulting in withdrawal or affecting the credibility of the application. This appears to be consistent with the draft Directive.

Personal interviews (draft Arts. 10 to 12). The 1996 Act does not contain detailed provisions on personal interviews as envisaged in draft Article 11, though many of the requirements in draft Article 11 appear to be satisfied in practice. The applicant receives information in relation to the interview as part of the report accompanying the first stage recommendation and this conforms to draft Article 12.

Right to legal assistance and representation (draft Art. 13). The 1996 Act specifically provides for the entitlement of the applicant to consult a solicitor. Free legal assistance is made available through the Refugee Legal Service.

Scope of legal assistance and representation (draft Art. 14). The 1996 Act contains no specific provisions on *access* to information on file or to closed areas. Legal representatives will normally be able to observe interviews and make any necessary points at the end.

Unaccompanied minors (draft Arts. 5(2) and 15). The 1996 Act does not provide specific guarantees for unaccompanied minor children as envisaged in draft Article 15.

Procedure in case of withdrawal of application (draft Arts. 19 and 20). Article 11(9) of the 1996 Act now specifically provides for explicit withdrawal of the application and there are a number of cases where withdrawal will be deemed. Under Article 13(2), withdrawal will result in the termination of the application and a recommendation (which cannot be appealed to the Tribunal) that the applicant should not be declared to be a refugee.

The role of the UNHCR (draft Art. 21). The 1996 Act provides for the involvement of the High Commissioner throughout the individual asylum application process. The requirements of the draft Article appear to be met.

Collection of information on individual cases (draft Art. 22). Section 18 of the 1996 Act provides for the protection of identity of applicants and appears to extend beyond the level envisaged in the draft.

Administrative and judicial appeal procedures

The Refugee Act 1996 establishes two bodies which are independent in the performance of their functions:

- the Refugee Applications Commissioner, who is responsible for investigating claims for asylum and for making recommendations to the Minister at first instance;
- the Refugee Appeals Tribunal, responsible for considering appeals from negative recommendations by the Commissioner.

Neither of these bodies formally takes the decision to grant refugee status. The decision is taken by the Minister for Justice who is bound to follow any recommendation by the Commissioner or Tribunal that an applicant be declared to be a refugee but *may* refuse to grant a declaration in the case of a negative recommendation.

Examination procedures (draft Art. 23). Provisions on examination procedures under Section 12 of the 1996 Act are consistent with draft Article 23(3) and some of the relevant matters identified in Section 12 reflect the specific grounds in draft Article 23(4). There are no specific provisions in the 1996 Act allowing for the acceleration of proceedings before the Refugee Applications Commissioner. However, Section 13 of the 1996 Act, as amended by the Immigration Act 2003, provides for foreshortened time limits for appealing to the Refugee Appeals Tribunal in certain cases.

Inadmissible applications (draft Arts. 25 and 26). The 1996 Act does not specifically provide for inadmissible applications as envisaged in the draft Directive.

Cases of unfounded application (draft Art. 29). Provisions on "manifestly unfounded applications" formerly in the 1996 Act were removed by the Immigration Act 2003. They have been replaced by provisions allowing prioritisation of applications, provisions on credibility and provisions reducing the timeframe for lodging an appeal to the Refugee Appeals Tribunal in "undeserving" cases.

Cases of subsequent applications (draft Arts. 33–34). The 1996 Act does not provide for the special procedures which the draft Directive provides that Member States may adopt in cases of subsequent applications.

Withdrawal of refugee status (draft Arts. 36 and 37). Section 21 of the 1996 Act sets out the conditions under which the Minister for Justice may revoke a declaration of refugee status. In broad terms, the procedural provisions are consistent with the requirements of the draft Directive.

The right to an effective remedy before a court or tribunal (draft Art. 38). The 1996 Act provides for an appeal to be made to the Refugee Appeals Tribunal from a negative recommendation by the Refugee Applications Commissioner. As understood in the Irish context, there thus appears to be an effective remedy before a court or tribunal against a decision taken on an asylum application. No specific provision is made for the reopening of cases where there has been an explicit withdrawal or implicit withdrawal/abandonment of the application. In all cases, the effective remedy includes the possibility of an examination on both relevant facts and points of law.

Under Section 5 of the Illegal Immigrants (Trafficking) Act 2000, a right of appeal against a decision to refuse refugee status, on foot of recommendations of the Refugee Applications Commissioner or, on appeal, of decisions of the Refugee Appeals Tribunal, lies *only* to the High Court by way of an application for judicial review. This application must – in contrast to the ordinary time limits for judicial review – ordinarily be made within 14 days of the making of the deportation order, unless the High Court considers that there is good and sufficient reason for extending this period. Leave is to be made by motion on notice, rather than *ex parte*, and is not to be granted unless the High Court is satisfied that there are "substantial grounds for contending that the . . . decision, determination, recommendation . . . concerned is invalid or ought to be quashed". The possibility of a further appeal to the Supreme Court has been severely limited.

The right to remain during review and appeal proceedings (draft Art. 39). Provisions in the 1996 Act on entitlement to remain appear to comply with the requirements of the draft Directive.

Time limits and scope of the examination in review or appeal (draft Art. 40). Section 16 of the 1996 Act and the Refugee Act 1996 (Appeals) Regulations 2003 contain detailed provisions on the time limits and scope of appeals to the Refugee Appeals Tribunal.

The use of safe third country and safe country of origin concepts

Safe third country (draft Arts. 27 to 28). The "safe third country" concept was introduced into the Refugee Act 1996 by the Immigration Act 2003. Under Section 22(5) of the 1/996 Act, the Minister for Justice may designate a country as a safe third country having regard to whether: (a) the country is party to and generally complies with obligations under the Convention against Torture, the ICCPR and, where appropriate, the ECHR; (b) the country has a democratic political system and an independent judiciary; and (c) whether the country is governed by the rule of law. The country concerned and the State must be parties to an agreement containing provisions providing for the prompt transfer of asylum applications made in one of them where the applicant has arrived in that country from the other. Section 22 of the Act provides the basis for secondary legislation in relation to arrangements with safe third countries. The criteria in Annex II of the draft Directive for designating "safe third countries" differ somewhat from those set out in the Refugee Act and the current procedures would have to be reviewed in light of the specific rules on application of the concept (see Article 28 of the draft). In general terms, Ireland would seem to be comfortable with the concept if flexibly applied.

Safe country of origin (draft Arts. 30 to 30B). Under Section 12(4) of the Refugee Act 1996, introduced by the Immigration Act 2003, the Minister for Justice may designate a country as a "safe country of origin". In deciding whether to make an order, the Minister must consider whether: (a) the country is party to and generally complies with obligations under the Convention against Torture, the ICCPR and, where appropriate, the ECHR; (b) the country has a democratic political system and an independent judiciary; and (c) whether the country is governed by the rule of law. The Minister has designated a number of countries – the Accession States, Bulgaria and Romania – as safe countries of origin. The criteria for designating a country as a "safe country of origin" differs from those set out in Annex III of the draft Directive and this may ultimately result in changes to the provisions in the Refugee Act (though the application of the different sets of criteria would tend to the same result).

Detention of asylum seekers

Detention (draft Art. 17). Sections 9 and 10 of the Refugee Act 1996 contain detailed provisions on detention.

The draft Directive contains very sparse provisions in relation to detention. It is clear that Ireland is not able to hold a person in detention for the sole reason that he/she is an applicant for asylum (see Article 17(1) of the draft). The requirement of a possibility of speedy judicial review (in the sense envisaged in Article 17(2) of the draft) seems to be satisfied.

Airport and border procedures

Cases of border procedures (draft Arts. 35 and 35A). There are no "border procedures" as envisaged in Article 35 of the draft Directive in the Refugee

Act 1996. Whilst there is no identified "border procedure", this does not mean that Ireland would not wish to avail of possibilities to refuse entry to applicants at the border in justified cases (for example for the reasons identified in Article 35A of the draft Directive).

3.4 What measures have been undertaken to implement Directive 2003/9 of 27 January 2003 on reception of asylum seekers in your country relating to:
– the flexibility clauses in the Directive;
– restriction of free movement;
– access to the labour market;
– rights of migrant workers under Article 11 § 2 of the Directive?

Ireland is not participating in the Directive. Although it does take part in many of the elements of the Common European Asylum System, it has chosen so far to avail of its opt-out under the Protocol on the position of the UK and Ireland annexed, following the Amsterdam Treaty, to the TEU and the EC Treaty. No official reason has been given for the decision not to participate, though it seems that the access to work issue has been a sticking point. This does not mean that Ireland does not in fact adhere to (or surpass) most of the Directive's standards or to human rights requirements.

The challenge of accommodating asylum seekers is a relatively recent one. Ireland was, until recently, a country of emigration and – located in the periphery of Europe – attracted few asylum seekers. In 1992, there were 39 asylum seekers. By 1997, there had been an increase to 3,883 and, in 2002, 11,634 asylum applications were made.

It may be helpful here to identify some elements of the Irish reception regime.

- The Reception and Integration Agency ("RIA"), a part of the Department of Justice, Equality and Law Reform, has since 2001 been responsible for planning and coordinating the provision of services to asylum seekers and refugees. Leaving aside the costs involved in funding any reception system, there have been problems in sourcing accommodation and in recruiting the people to run it.
- The current system is one of "direct provision" and "dispersal" of asylum seekers to full-board accommodation centres throughout the State. The decision to introduce direct provision was a controversial one, but it was taken in the context of severe housing shortages. It has been claimed that, had such a system not been introduced, "asylum-seekers would have been sleeping in parks and on streets, a situation that no right thinking person would wish to countenance".

- Under the current system, all accommodation costs, together with the cost of meals, heat, light, laundry, etc. are paid directly by the State, which enters into agreements with accommodation providers specifying the standards for the provision of full-board accommodation. Approval to leave direct provision may be given on exceptional social or medical grounds. Asylum seekers in direct provision are paid euro 19.10 per adult and euro 9.60 per child per week (an amount that has been frozen since 1999). Where appropriate, asylum seekers receive Child Benefit (though there have been threats to reduce this), One Parent Family Payment, Disability Allowance and Non-Contributory Old Age Pension. Once-off "exceptional needs payments" may also be made in certain cases.
- The children of asylum seekers enjoy access to primary and post-primary education on the same basis as Irish children. State-funded language training courses are provided free of charge to adults. Access to the health services is on the same basis as the local population, with asylum seekers usually qualifying for a medical card on income grounds.
- Asylum seekers are *not* allowed to work in Ireland whilst awaiting a determination of their asylum applications (Section 9(4)(b) of the 1996 Refugee Act). To allow them to work would, in the view of the Government, operate as a "pull" factor, with any "sudden upsurge" of applicants – trying to gain a foothold in the State for simply economic reasons – quite simply overwhelming the system. The current and effective work permit system would be undermined. Finally, "any extension of the right to work to all applicants, even if it was six months in the determination process, would be portrayed abroad by people traffickers to potential victims as a cast-iron guarantee of a right to work as soon as they arrive in Ireland irrespective of the amount of time they spend in the asylum process".

3.5 What steps have been undertaken to implement Directive 2001/55 on temporary protection in national law? Are there any procedures for burden sharing arrangements? Is there a legal basis for admission of refugees receiving temporary protection in a mass-movement situation?

Under Article 1 of the Protocol on the position of the United Kingdom and Ireland, Ireland did not participate in the adoption of Directive 2001/55. In accordance with Article 4 of the Protocol, Ireland notified the Commission in April 2003 of its intention to accept the Directive. The Commission issued a favourable opinion and, under Article 11(3) of the EC Treaty, on 2 October 2003 adopted Decision 2003/690 applying the Directive to Ireland.

Article 2 of Decision 2003/690 requires Ireland to bring into force the laws, regulations and administrative provisions necessary to comply with the Directive by 31 December 2003 at the latest. Section 24 of the Refugee Act 1996 contains provisions on "programme refugees". The position appears to have been taken that Section 24 – together with appropriate administrative measures to be taken if temporary protection is introduced under Article 4 of the Directive as well as guarantees of due legal process under the Irish Constitution – constitute satisfactory implementation of Directive 2001/55. It is, nonetheless, unfortunate that the fact that Ireland has signed up to the Directive has been all but unacknowledged by "official" Ireland.

Section 24 applies to a "programme refugee", defined in Section 24(1) as "a person to whom leave to enter and remain in the State for temporary protection or resettlement as part of a group of persons has been given by the Government and whose name is entered in a register established and maintained by the Minister for Foreign Affairs, whether or not such a person is a refugee [as defined]". The programme refugee will be entitled to the same level of rights as refugees and may be issued, subject to refusal on national security or public policy ("*ordre public*") grounds, with a travel document identifying the holder as a refugee. Under a new provision, introduced by the Immigration Act 2003, the Minister for Justice may, after consultation with the Minister for Foreign Affairs, enter into agreements with the High Commissioner for the reception and resettlement in the State of refugees.

In addressing the question of liability of carriers, Section 2(9) of the Immigration Act 2003 makes it clear that provisions on such liability are without prejudice to, amongst other provisions, Section 24 of the Refugee Act 1996.

No real acknowledgment of the Irish adoption of Directive 2001/55 has been made. The question of full compliance by Ireland with the Directive will, perhaps, come to be judged only when temporary protection is introduced under the Directive. However, it appears that, in practice, Irish participation in the Directive will not change the current position in Ireland. It has participated in UNHCR initiatives over the years to accommodate groups of programme refugees, including Hungarians (1956), Chileans (1974), Vietnamese (1979), Bosnians (1992) and Kosovars (1999). In the most recent case, in 1999, Ireland responded to the UNHCR request for assistance in offering temporary protection to Kosovars of ethnic Albanian origin. At times of need, Ireland has not up to now been found wanting.

3.6 The Council has reached political agreement on the principles for a directive on minimum standards for the qualification and status of third country nationals as refugees or persons who otherwise need international protection, COM (2001) 510 final (see Council documents of June 2003). What measures are envisaged to implement the Directive, once it is adopted, in your country relating to:

– the definition of refugee

The definition of "refugee" given in Section 2 of the 1996 Act is the same as that given in the draft Directive.

– the definition of persons entitled to subsidiary protection

The term "subsidiary protection" is unknown to Irish law and administrative practice. Although there is thus no specific category of persons seeking "subsidiary protection", persons seeking such protection as understood by that term may seek leave to remain in Ireland: (a) to a failed asylum seeker on a discretionary basis (Section 17(6) of the 1996 Act); (b) to a refugee whose declaration has been revoked (Section 21(7) of the 1996 Act); (c) on "humanitarian grounds", again on a discretionary basis (Section 3 of the Immigration Act 1999); or (d) on the basis of the mandatory prohibition of refoulement (Section 5 of the 1996 Act, Section 4 of the Criminal Justice (UN Convention against Torture) Act 2000).

In implementing the draft Directive in Ireland, it will clearly be necessary to introduce a right-based, as opposed to the current discretion-based, regime to cover persons seeking subsidiary protection as defined in the Directive.

– status of persons entitled to subsidiary protection

Persons currently given leave to remain on "subsidiary protection" grounds do not enjoy the statutory rights given to refugees. They do, however, fall within the general class of legally-resident third-country nationals and enjoy a significant measure of equality with host nationals. Implementation of the Directive will probably require that the statutory rights given to refugees under Section 3 of the 1996 be extended to those entitled to subsidiary protection.

– the issue of internal flight alternative as defined by the Directive

There is no current statutory provision dealing with the issue of internal flight alternative.

– exclusion clauses, particularly issues of terrorism

Exclusion clauses in Section 2 of the 1996 Act are similar to those in the draft Directive. The definition of refugee excludes: (a) a person who is receiving protection or assistance from UN organs or agencies (other than the High Commissioner); or (b) is regarded by the authorities of the country of residence as having the rights and obligations attaching to the possession of nationality of that country. A person will also be excluded where there are serious reasons for considering that he/she: (a) has committed a crime against peace, a war crime or a crime against humanity; (b) has committed a serious non-political crime outside the State prior to arrival; or (c) has been guilty of acts contrary to the purposes and principles of the UN. It will be necessary to amend the legislation if it is sought to make it clear that "particularly cruel actions, even if committed with an allegedly political objective, may be classified as serious non-political crimes" (see Article 14 of the draft Directive).

3.7 In the Commission's Communication of November 22, 2000, COM 2000,755 (see also 2nd Commission Report COM 2003, 152 final) the Commission's concept of a common European asylum procedure and a uniform status for those who are granted asylum valid throughout the Union is set out. Do you consider that the concept is generally in line with your country's asylum policy? Are concerns of refugee organizations such as Amnesty International and other organizations of an undermining of the international regime for the protection of refugees shared in political circles of your country responsible for decision-making?

My impression is that the Irish Government favours a tough approach to asylum seekers, seeking mechanisms to separate the "genuine" refugee from economic migrants exploiting the asylum system. Refugee organisations – including Amnesty and the Irish Refugee Council – have been highly critical of Irish Government policy and tighter refugee legislation.

3.8 The open coordination mechanism as suggested by the Commission provides for a first stage and a second stage legislation in which the flexibility provisions in some of the directives on migration and asylum are to be replaced by a full harmonization. Is this concept discussed in your country and what are the perceptions relating to the gradual establishment of a European asylum policy which eventually might replace national procedures and national decision-making?

I am not aware of any public discussion of the open coordination mechanism and the two-stage approach in Ireland. Public debate has been focused on the effectiveness and fairness of the asylum rules, rather than on the emergence of a future European policy. However, I do not think that there is any objection in principle to the emergence of such a policy.

3.9 The Communication of June 2003 towards a more accessible, equitable and managed asylum system – in reaction to the UK paper – develops some ideas on new approaches to pursue an orderly and managed arrival of persons in need of international protection. What is the political reaction in your country as to the concept of an outside accessed asylum procedure, distribution of refugees and responsibility-sharing and other new concepts and ideas in coping with mass refugee movements?

I am not aware of any public position taken by the Irish government in this regard.

PART IV (TERMINATION OF ILLEGAL RESIDENCE, RETURN AND REPATRIATION)

4.1 How many third country nationals without a valid residence permit are presently according to estimates staying in your country? How many deportations have actually been made in previous years? Is the whole enforcement process considered as acceptable?

No official figures on the number of third-country nationals without a valid residence permit are available. I do not know of any reliable unofficial figures.

Section 3 of the Immigration Act 1999 provides the basis for deportation orders, made on a largely discretionary basis by the Minister for Justice, Equality and Law Reform.

The 2002 Report of the Department of Justice, Equality and Law Reform set out the position with regard to deportations from November 1999 to the end of 2002 as follows:

Year	Deportation Orders Made	Persons Deported	Returned Voluntarily
1999	102	6	37
2000	940	187	248
2001	2025	365	365
2002	2430	521	506

In the same period, 55 other persons left the State before the deportation order could be enforced and 3490 persons evaded deportation or were not at their last known address for the purpose of service.

In 2003, 2,428 orders were made by the Minister and 590 persons actually deported.

The figures suggest that, notwithstanding a number of high profile cases involving multiple deportations (including the deportation of

65 Romanians and Moldovans in mid-February 2004), a large number of persons against whom deportation orders were made have remained in Ireland (or have "voluntarily" moved outside the State). That said, concrete steps are being taken to increase the number of actual deportations. The absence of direct scheduled flights to many destinations – and the costs of escorting police officers on scheduled flights – has resulted in the increased use of charter flights, and the beginnings of cooperation with other EU Member States. In 2002, the Government approved the recruitment of an additional 200 Gardaí (police officers) to allow for an increase in strength of the dedicated Garda National Immigration Bureau to enhance its capacity to combat illegal immigration and enforce deportation orders. The staffing of the repatriation unit of the Department of Justice, Equality and Law Reform has also been increased.

Measures to increase the rate of deportations have not gone unchallenged. Criticisms have been made of "covert" deportations, with individuals allegedly being picked up and sent off on night-time charter flights. The "targeting" of the illegally-resident migrant parents of citizen children has also been subject to widespread criticism.

Mention should also be made of a series of voluntary return projects, undertaken by IOM on behalf of the Department for Justice, covering the parents of Irish-born children, those of all nationalities who do not have the means to fund their own return to their countries of origin and unaccompanied minors.

4.2 What has been undertaken to implement the Directive of November 28, 2002 dealing with the facilitation of unauthorized entry, transit and residence?

Ireland is taking part in the adoption and application of Council Directive 2002/90/EC defining the facilitation of unauthorised entry, transit and residence, as well as the accompanying Council Framework Decision on the strengthening of the penal framework to prevent the facilitation of unauthorised entry, transit and residence.

The deadline for implementing measures under both instruments is 5 December 2004.

The Illegal Immigrants (Trafficking) Act 2000 meets a substantial number of the requirements of the new Community regime. Persons organising or knowingly facilitating the entry into the State of illegal immigrants are liable on conviction on indictment to a fine and/or imprisonment for a term of up to ten years, or to lower penalties on summary conviction.

This does not apply to anything done otherwise than for gain or to assist asylum seekers to employees of a bona fide organisation giving assistance to persons seeking asylum. Vehicles used for committing or facilitating the commission of the offence may be forfeited. Where an offence has been committed by a body corporate, complicit directors and other officers are also guilty of an offence.

4.3 How many illegal applicants have been apprehended at or near the border? How many criminal procedures for human trafficking have been instituted in the last year?

During 2002, 4391 illegal immigrants were refused leave to land – that is, to enter Ireland – and were returned either to their country of origin or the country from which they had arrived.

A number of investigations under the Illegal Immigrants (Trafficking) Act 2000 have been conducted. It has not, however, been possible to establish whether there are likely to be any prosecutions in the near future.

4.4 What efforts have been undertaken in your country concerning the Budapest June 2003 recommendations concerning the harmonization of penalty scales with regard to the crime of smuggling of migrants and trafficking of persons in line with Council Directive 2002/90 of 28 November 2002? Did your country sign the relevant UN protocols on smuggling of migrants?

See, generally, the response in Section 4.2, above. Ireland does not appear to have participated in the Rhodes Conference of 25–26 June 2003.

Ireland signed the Protocol against the Smuggling of Migrants by Land, Sea and Air on 13 December 2003.

4.5 What measures have been taken to implement the Council Directive of 28th May 2001 on the mutual recognition of decisions on the expulsion of third country nationals? What, if any shortcomings or gaps of the Directive should be corrected in a further directive on cooperation on expulsion or deportation of third country nationals?

Article 4 of the Protocol integrating the Schengen *acquis* into the framework of the European Union states that Ireland and the UK, which are not bound by that *acquis*, might at any time request to take part in some or all of its provisions. The Council is to decide on the request with the unanimity of the thirteen Schengen signatories and of the representative of the Government of the State concerned.

In June 2000, Ireland lodged a request to take part in certain elements of the Schengen *acquis* and a supplement to this application was lodged on

1 November 2001. Article 2 of Council Decision 2002/192/EC of 28 February 2002 decided, amongst other matters, that Ireland was to participate in Directive 2001/40.

Decision 2002/192 itself sets no specific date for implementation of this Directive by Ireland. Rather, Article 6(3) provides that Directive 2001/40, amongst other measures, is to take effect for Ireland on the date or dates on which the Council decides – under Article 4 – to put the Article 1 *acquis* into effect for Ireland. It appears to be contemplated that the Article 4 Decision will be adopted only after Ireland has taken the measures necessary to implement the *acquis* and the relevant Directives.

There has been no measure implementing the Directive and no proposals for implementation have been published. However, there appears to be a political commitment to implement Directive 2001/40 at the latest by the end of the Irish Presidency in June 2004, by means of statutory instrument under the European Communities Act 1972.

Pending implementation, it is not possible for Ireland, as an "enforcing Member State", legally to recognise an expulsion decision issued in another Member State and to take measures on this basis. However, the fact that an expulsion decision has been issued in another Member State may be a factor that the Minister may take into account in deciding whether or not to exercise his discretion to allow a person to remain under Section 3 of the Immigration Act 1999. Under Section 3(6), the Minister must, in determining whether to make a deportation order in relation to a person, have regard to a number of factors, including "the common good" and "considerations of national security and public policy", and the fact that an exclusion order has been issued elsewhere would clearly be relevant in this regard. However, no deportation order appears to have been made on this basis, at least in the recent past.

4.6 Do readmission agreements or other international treaties or arrangements with the aim of controlling and curbing illegal immigration and facilitating return exist in your country? Have they functioned satisfactorily?

Ireland has entered into readmission agreements with Romania, Poland,[1] Nigeria[2] and Bulgaria.[3] These agreements, which provide for the readmission of certain categories of persons at the request of a Contracting Party, reflect "the importance of a return and readmission policy

[1] Entered into force on 23 June 2002.
[2] Ratified by Ireland in March 2002.
[3] Ratified by Ireland in March 2002.

as an integral and vital component in the fight against illegal immigration".[4]

4.7 To what extent have EU-standards and recommendations influenced your country's return policy? Have efforts been undertaken to cooperate with other EU Member States in enforcing return decisions by common deportation actions, exchange of information, facilitation of air and land transit, common principles on flight security, etc.?

Efforts have been made to cooperate with the UK and the Netherlands in relation to sharing charter flights for returning illegal immigrants.

4.8 Do you consider a need to elaborate a common legal regime for air deportations (legal status of armed guards on board of the aircrafts, rights of the aircraft commander, legal rules in case of transit stops, applicability of national police law on board of aircraft on flight, etc.)?

I am not aware of these issues being discussed in the Irish context.

[4] Department of Justice, Equality and Law Reform *Annual Report 2002*, p. 54.

ITALY

BRUNO NASCIMBENE*
Professor of Law
University of Milan

FOREWORD

The understanding of Italian law on immigration was greatly facilitated by legislative decree no. 286 of 25th July 1998 entitled "Testo unico delle leggi sull'immigrazione" (Single text of immigration laws, the so called law Turco-Napolitano), which collected in a single text all the provisions in force, in particular Law no. 40 of 6th March 1998 on the conditions of immigration and the legal status of aliens. The law no. 286/1998 was amended in 2002, by the law of 30th July 2002, no. 189 (the so called law Bossi-Fini). Such amendments are aimed essentially at improving the regulation of immigration flows and at tackling the problem of illegal immigration more effectively. In this respect, it has to be noted that the new enforcement regulation, relating to the provisions contained in the above mentioned law, has not been adopted yet and the Decree of the President of the Republic no. 394 of 31st August 1999, remains currently in force. On the base of the single text, a document setting out the programme for immigration policy must be adopted every three years by the Italian Government. The last document (for the years 2001–2004) was adopted by means of the Decree of the President of the Republic of 30th March 2001.

Understanding Italian law on asylum is particularly difficult due to the absence of a single text on Asylum Law. The proposals of laws which were submitted these last years have not been approved. This subject remains therefore regulated by Article 1 of the Law no. 39 of 28th February 1990, as partially amended by Law no. 189/2002, and by Article 10, par. 3 of the Constitution.

* Professor of Law University of Milan, in collaboration with Chiara Favilli, Researcher, University of Florence.

PART I ENTRY, VISA REGIME AND BORDER CONTROL

1.1 What national authorities are competent to deal with visa applications?

The competent authority is the Foreign Office, through the Diplomatic delegations in the applicant's country of residence. In exceptional situations and subject to certain conditions the short term visa and the transit visa can be issued by the border authorities

Are there any procedures to avoid duplication or successive visa applications at different EU consulates?

There is no ban on re-applying for a visa after a refusal. The application may be submitted either to the same Consulate or to another one.

On what substantive criteria other than the Schengen minimum requirements are visas granted or refused?

The foreigner has to show:

a) His means of transport including his return ticket (see the "direttiva" [directive] of the Italian Internal Affairs Office, 1 March 2000, in Official Journal no. 64 of 17 March 2000);
b) His financial resources (see the "direttiva" cit.). For example, a stay of 1 to 5 days requires resources of € 269,60 (for longer periods of stay – 6 to 10 days; 11 to 20; more than 20 days – the resources required include an amount "à forfait" and an amount for each successive day);
c) adequate accommodation.

A Visa can be refused if the foreigner:

- is the subject of an alert issued for the purposes of refusing entry;
- is a threat to public order;
- is condemned for one of the crimes listed in Art. 380, par. 1–2, "c.p.p." (code of criminal procedure);
- is subject to a prohibition on entry following expulsion;

Moreover, Art. 5, par. 4, of the "regolamento" [regulation] no. 394/1999 states that Consulates can require that further conditions be fulfilled if necessitated by the local situation or by decisions agreed with other Schengen countries.

How many visa have been issued or refused?

In 2002, 853,466 visas were issued with an income (corresponding to the fees paid by the applicants) of € 27,000,000.

1.2 Is there a visa tracking procedure in order to identify visa overstayers?

It is not clear if there is a check on expired visas (in any event there is no legal provision for a special procedure). Generally this kind of check is done when the person applies for the issue or the renewal of the permit of stay.

What data are collected from visa-applicants (fingerprints)?

There is not an organised visa database. The personal data requested are those written on the passport or other valid document. Sensitive data are not collected at this stage but later when the foreigner applies for a residence permit.

Admissibility of visa data to alien and police authorities?

The Consulates can consult the security authorities in order to gain more information on applicants but it is not clear if they send the collected data to the police authorities (there is no specific rule on the matter).

1.3 Have courts ever decided on the refusal of a Schengen visa based upon Schengen blacklisting by other Member States?

Consulates check the "World Net Visa" (a digital network of the Italian diplomatic delegations) and the SIS in order to verify if an alert has been issued for the purposes of refusing the applicant's entry.

The visa refusal is not generally appealed to court so there is no significant decision on this subject.

1.4 What measures have been undertaken in the implementation of the action programme for administrative cooperation in the field of external borders, visa, asylum and immigration following the Council Decision of June 13 2002?

No specific measure has been adopted.

1.5 What measures have been undertaken to implement the Directive 2001/51 EC supplementing the Schengen rules concerning carrier sanctions? How often have carrier sanctions been used?

A decree was adopted on 7th April 2003, no. 87 (in Official Journal n. 94 of 23rd April 2003). Carrier sanctions have not (yet) been used.

1.6 According to your judgement, does the visa law and policy of your country live up to EU standards or are adjustments needed?

Italian law on the subject is largely inspired by European law including the Common Manual and Common Consular Instructions. Changes are necessary, in view of the recent European proposals on data collection and particularly on finger prints.

Do you consider that there is need for further EU-harmonization of visa policies concerning
- *common criteria for granting visas aiming at harmonizing visa obligations among states participating in the Budapest Process;*
- *establishment of a European visa identification system (VIS and SIS II)?*

There are several reasons supporting the need for harmonisation in this sector. Actually this is the most harmonised chapter of the immigration and asylum policy.

It is important that VIS and SIS II be combined in a single database: this could initially give rise to complications when setting up the new SIS but in the long run should simplify matters given the need for local authorities to check both systems for the same application. It is however crucial to guarantee transparency, the right to an effective remedy in case of refusal, the individuals right to access and be informed of personal data stored in the database and the right to ask for the removal of data from the database.

To what extent will the EU enlargement process present a chance or danger for tackling issues of illegal entry and border control?

The enlargement should be used as an opportunity to strengthen border control measures: new Member States should be requested to pay special attention to their "new" responsibility in this area.

PART II ADMISSION AND RESIDENCE OF THIRD COUNTRY NATIONALS

2.1 What are the basic principles in Italy concerning

- **Admission of third country nationals for labour purpose or self-employed activities**

a) The system is based on yearly quotas fixing the maximum number of foreigners eligible to enter. It is presumed that the employer and employee signed the work contract before the worker arrived in Italy, before they even knew each other. In practice this is avoided by the foreigner coming as a tourist, contacting the employer and then returning to his home country and then applying for a work visa (this practice was provided for in the past by the so called law Turco-Napolitano, no. 286/98).

The procedures are complex: after the signing of the contract between the employer and employee, the employer asks for that person through the local immigration office. If the application is within the quota limits, the employer can request a visa. Once the employee enters Italy, the employee and employer must sign a contract of stay in which the employer guarantees to provide the employee with accommodation and a return ticket. Then the permit of stay is issued for a limited and variable time depending on the length of the employment contract.

b) For independent activities, workers must always apply within the yearly quotas in respect of the specific rules of the profession/job they want to do.
c) It is not permitted to change a tourism permit to a work permit.
d) Family reunion visas do not fall within the yearly quotas.

Admission of third country nationals for study and vocational training

As regards students there are special yearly decrees adopted by the Minister for Foreign Affairsr concerning the maximum number of students admissible. Each University has to fix the number of foreigners who can enrol. The student's visa is renewable for the duration of the course attended. A system of quotas is applicable even in this case.

Legal status of third country nationals in possession of a long-term residence visa of another Member State

There is no specific law dealing with this issue. It is dealt with by the Directive approved on the 25th November 2003. and consequently national legislation will be adopted in due terms.

To what extent do these principles differ from the European Commission's proposals?

As far as admission to exercise an economic activity is concerned, the main difference with the original proposal concerns the right to ask for a work permit either from the country of origin or directly in the Member States in cases where the applicant is already legally resident (Art. 5, par. 2). However, on this point governments do not agree and the proposal is likely be modified. This is a crucial point which, if confirmed, will entail the amendment of national law and should help (hopefully) to reduce the number of illegal immigrants.

Another difference concerns the limitation, for the first three years, on exercising specific jobs and, in some cases, the requirement to work in a specific Region. This limitation does not exist in Italian law; it seems to be too strict, in particular, considering the flexibility of the job market and the way in which supply and demand function.

2.2 What are the legal requirements and procedures for obtaining a residence permit for third country nationals for the purpose of employment?

Italian migration law seeks to ensure that the stay in Italy is linked to a work contract. This is the reason why the so called law Bossi-Fini, no. 189/2002, has eliminated the right to enter Italy to search for a job and has established the "stay agreement" ("contratto di soggiorno"), signed by employer and worker, which strictly links the permit of stay to the work contract.

Which procedures are used in maintaining the preferred access of EU-Citizens and Turkish nationals (association agreement) to the labour market?

Art. 22 of the law no. 286/1998 as ammended by the law no. 189/2002 states that the request for a foreign worker is disseminated and forwarded by the local office for employment via the internet. Then they have 20 days in which to verify if there is an Italian or European Union citizen suitable for that job. The law does not make explicit reference to Turkish workers.

Do special programmes exist for highly qualified professionals facilitating access to the labour market? To what extent are trade unions and employers involved in such programmes?

The annual quota can take account of different kinds of jobs so permitting the entry of specially qualified workers. Social parties have a right to be heard when quotas are being fixed.

Is there a procedure to calculate the demand for foreign labour? How is the EU-enlargement taken into consideration?

It is not clear if a formal procedure exists; the quotas are determined by one or more decrees over the course of the year by the Ministry of Labour and Welfare. The enlargement has never been explicitly considered in public acts.

To what extent has the recent economic recession and unemployment influenced the concepts on admission of third country nationals?

This factor is taken into account when fixing the yearly quotas of foreigners who can enter Italy to work. The criteria used in fixing quotas are explained generally in Art. 3 of the law no. 286/98 and particularly in the detailed programme issued by the government every three years.

2.3 To what extent do existing laws and practices differ substantially from the approach taken in the Commission's Proposal on admission for the purpose of paid employment and self-employed activities relating to:

– Admission of third country nationals for study and vocational training

The Commission's Proposal COM (2002) 548, and the Italian law on entry and stay for reasons of study or vocational training are inspired by similar principles. However, the Commission's proposal demonstrates a more favourable approach to this kind of immigration than that currently existing in Italy. The main points of the proposal do not diverge from the Italian rules: student permits are not included in the yearly work quota; the permit is renewable each year up until the end of the course; at the end of the course the students can apply for a work permit within the limits of the yearly quota; students can work for a maximum of 20 hours per week. The rules with regard to entry for vocational training purposes in the Proposal are stricter than the corresponding Italian ones as the former are limited to unpaid training positions while the Italian law also permits entry for the purpose of attending traditional vocational training. Changes in Italian law are required regarding the mobility of students between European Union Member States; entry as a volunteer; the applicable procedures and to promote transparency in particular the dissemination of information concerning opportunities available within the European Union.

– on legal status of third country nationals in possession of a long term residence permit of another Member State

To what extent do these principles differ from the European Commission's proposals?

See point 2.6.

2.4 What measures have been taken to implement the Directive of 29th June 2000 implementing the principle of equal treatment between persons irrespective of racial or ethnic origin and Council Directive 2000/78 EC of 27th November 2000 establishing a general framework for equal treatment in employment and occupation? Have legislative changes been undertaken? To what extent is "affirmative action" considered as necessary to promote equal opportunites for migrant workers from third countries?

Two decrees (no. 215 and no. 216 of 9th July 2003, in Official Journal no. 186 of 12th August 2003 and no. 187 of 13th August 2003) have been adopted in order to comply with the obligation of Directive 2000/43 and 2000/78. These decrees broaden what is stated in law no. 286/98 about the notion of racial discrimination and the judicial remedies against acts of discrimination. Of course they extend the legal protection to the other grounds listed in Art. 13 of the EC Treaty. A national body against racial discrimination is to be set up. Positive actions are allowed as prescribed by the directives and as already allowed in relation to acting against discrimination based on sex.

2.5 Concerning the proposal for a directive on the right to family reunion agreed upon by the Council in February 2003:
- **Do you consider the proposed standards below the principles of family reunification valid in your country?**
- **Will the implementation of the directive, once it is adopted, lead to changes in the national law on family reunification downgrading the standard of protection? If so, what changes are envisaged?**

Following four years of negotiations, Directive 2003/86 has been adopted in a very "soft" version. On almost every crucial point it allows Member States to retain their national rules (e.g. family members). Italian national law, although more restrictive pursuant to changes introduced in 2002 (as a consequence of the approval of the so called law Bossi-Fini, no. 189/2002), generally provides for a higher standard of protection: e.g. entitlement to an autonomous permit, exercise of employment activities, length of procedure. It is important to emphasise that the Directive will not result in the lowering of national standards in particular as the right to family union is considered a fundamental right under the Italian Constitution and under the European Convention on Human Rights. In so far as this is permitted by the Directive, the Italian legislator should not modify the existing law. To date there has not been any official or unofficial Governmental position on this issue.

Art. 4, par. 1, of the Directive contains a crucial and critical provision which allows Member States, before authorising the entry and stay of a child aged over 12, to verify whether he or she meets the conditions for integration provided for by its existing legislation on the date of implementation of the Directive (see the infringement action brought by Parliament to the European Court of Justice in December 2003). No similar entry condition is required under Italian Law.

2.6 The proposal for a directive on the rights of long-term third country nationals as agreed upon by the Council on June 5, 2003 provides for a number of rights approximating the standards of long-term residents to the status of EU-citizens. Will the implementation of the Directive involve major legal and policy changes in your country? What are the major points of concern if any, concerning the approximation concept of the directive relating to:
- **non-discrimination in social rights;**
- **the concept of "civic citizenship" (see also extended impact assessment on the Communication on Integration of June 11, 2003);**
- **family reunification and access of family members to the labour market;**
- **security of stay?**

Art. 10 of law no. 286/1998, concerning the "Carta di soggiorno", a special permit of stay, already gives rights to long-term residents which are very similar to those recognised by Directive 2003/109, except for the right to free movement. The only difference is the required length of stay to qualify for the status (6 years under Italian law – 5 years under European Union law). This Directive does not create any particular problems and makes a significant contribution to the integration of third country nationals and to the consolidation of the concept of civic citizenship: a concept still used more as a political slogan than as a legal notion.

2.7 Considering the perspective of a future common migration policy as developed by the Commission in the Open Coordination Communication (COM 2001, 387) and the communication on a migration policy of the European Union (COM 2000, 757 final), how do you assess the role of the Community organs in determining a European migration policy in terms of competences of the Member States to decide on residence rights and admission to the labour market and integration? Should harmonization of legislation go further, and if so, in what respect?

Almost 5 years after the Amsterdam Treaty entered in force it is clear that we are very far from the creation of a common policy on immigration and asylum. The spirit of the Communication cited in the question has never been shared by the Council and seems today to have been also abandoned by the Commission. The Commission's proposals have not followed a coherent design and today we are witnesses to the failure of almost every Commission proposal, just a few months before the end of the 5 year "transitional period". This is particularly true in the case of the rules on entry and stay which are at the core of every migration policy. The fight against illegal immigration is an exception (unanimity has been more easily achieved): this illustrates the lack of political will for making serious progress in the harmonisation of national migration laws. In any event, when that political will exists, the European Commission should write a composite proposal at least regarding the different parts of migration law such as entry, stay and illegal immigration. The European Commission should have a central role in coordinating the national laws. In this respect, the model of the coordination on employment should be followed.

PART III ASYLUM AND REFUGEE LAW

3.1 Have the Dublin Rules worked satisfactorily and what is expected from the Dublin II Regulation No. 343, 2003 of February 18, 2003?

It is not possible to evaluate the impact of the Dublin II Regulation. Taking into account that the criteria have not been substantially changed, it is not expected that there will be any evident change in practice except for stricter time limits in responding to a request. It is interesting to note, however, that in 2002, the amount of requests presented by Italy to other States (1069) was almost the same as the amount of requests presented to Italy (1374). Considering the cost and length of the procedure we think it could be better to concentrate efforts on harmonising procedures and status and introducing a system of cost sharing.

3.2 Has the Eurodac Regulation No. 2725/2000 of 11th December 2000 concerning the establishment of Eurodac for the comparison of fingerprints for an effective application of the Dublin Convention, operative since January 15, 2003 resulted in an increase of Dublin cases? Has Eurodac become effective in your country or is it expected to become eventually effective?

Eurodac is already effective in Italy. It is not clear if it has resulted in an increase in cases. Perhaps it has quickened the pace of the identification procedures (no figures and data are available).

3.3 What major changes, if any, will the implementation of the amended proposal of a directive on minimum standards on procedures in Member States for granting and withdrawing refugee status on which the Council has reached political agreement on most points in June 2003 bring for the legislation and practice in your country in particular relating to:
- **rights of applicants in the procedure;**
- **administrative and judicial appeal procedure;**
- **the use of safe third country and safe country of origin concepts;**
- **detainment of asylum seekers;**
- **airport and border procedures?**

Despite a new law on Asylum passed on July 2002 (the so called law Bossi-Fini, no. 189/2002, Articles 31–32) the European Union proposals have not been taken into account by the Italian Parliament. That new law is not yet operational as there has been a delay in the adoption of a detailed Rule ("regolamento di attuazione"). However that law will have to be modified when the Directives are formally adopted.

As regards administrative and judicial appeal procedures, national law does not provide for the possibility of remaining in Italy once the first request has been rejected even if that rejection is appealed. The Directive allows Member States to keep their national rules if adopted before the Directive. National law does not expressly recognise the right to a legal adviser and does not provide for a maximum period of detention (administrative detention or "retention").

There are no specific rules in Italian law regarding airports controls.

3.4 What measures have been undertaken to implement the Directive 2003/9 of 27 January 2003, on reception of asylum seekers in your country relating to:
- **the flexibility clauses in the directive;**
- **restriction of free movement;**
- **access to the labour market;**
- **rights of migrant workers under Article 11 § 2 of the Directive?**

National Parliament has delegated to the government the task of adopting a decree to implement Directive 2003/9 with the law no. 306 of 31st October 2003. A provision on the access to employment will have to be introduced as it is not currently guaranteed to asylum seekers throughout the procedure.

3.5 What steps have been undertaken to implement the Directive on temporary protection, COM 2001, 55 in national law? Are there any procedures for burden sharing arrangements? Is there a legal basis for the admission of refugees receiving temporary protection in a mass-movement situation?

Last year a decree ("decreto legislative") no. 85 of 7th April on the implementation of Directive 2001/55 was agreed. It refers expressly to Art. 20, law no. 286/1998 regarding extraordinary measures of reception in exceptional circumstances such as armed conflicts, natural disasters or other serious situations. Since 1998, it has been used only once, during the Kosovo conflict in 1999, with a Decree issued on 12 May 1999, giving temporary protection to citizens coming from that region until the 30 June 2000. A repatriation programme was then implemented in conjunction with the UNHCR. Decree 2003/85, gives more details on procedure and on minimum reception conditions in accordance with Directive 2001/55.

As far as burden sharing is concerned, it is not referred to in the national decree. Art. 12 concerning the budget states that resources have to be taken from the special budget chapter dedicated to European policies under Art. 5 of law 16th April 1987, no. 183.

3.6 The Council has reached political agreement on the principles for a directive on minimum standards for the qualification and status of third country nationals as refugees or persons who otherwise need international protection, COM 2001, 510 final (see Council documents of June 2003). What measures are envisaged to implement the directive, once it is adopted, in your country relating to:
– the definition of refugee;
– the definition of persons entitled to subsidiary protection;
– status of persons entitled to subsidiary protection;
– the issue of internal flight alternative as defined by the directive;
– exclusion clauses, particularly issues of terrorism?
To what extent are the refugee policies as reflected in the law and jurisprudence of your country in accordance with the proposal of the directive?

National law will have to be changed in order to implement the articles relating to the definition of refugee and, in particular, the detailed description of persecution; the grounds of persecution; and the 5 years length of the permit of stay issued to refugees and beneficiaries of subsidiary protection. Finally, the directive makes provision for the recognition of the same status to family members entering with the applicant: this provision will have to be implemented in national law.

3.7 In the Commission's Communication of November 22, 2000, COM 2000, 755 (see also 2nd Commission Report COM 2003, 152 final) the Commission's concept of a common European asylum procedure and a uniform status for those who are granted asylum valid throughout the Union is set out. Do you consider that the concept is generally in line with your country's asylum policy? Are concerns of refugee organizations, such as Amnesty International and other organizations, of an undermining of the international regime for the protection of refugees shared in political circles of your country responsible for decision-making?

Political circles in Italy do not appear to be aware of European Union law on migration or asylum. Among those who follow the debate, it is generally agreed that laws providing for harmonisation will be few.

With regard to the new Italian law passed on July 2002, (no. 189/2002) it does not diverge much from European Union law in particular considering the flexible approach adopted by the European legislator.

3.8 The open coordination-mechanism as suggested by the Commission provided for a first stage and a second stage legislation in which the flexibility provisions in some of the directives on migration and asylum are to be replaced by a full harmonization. Is this concept discussed in your country and what are the perceptions relating to the gradual establishment of a European asylum policy which eventually might replace national procedures and national decision-making?

As was stressed in par. 3.7, there is no debate on the subject neither on the political front nor among academics. The European Union asylum directives or proposals have been considered only by the political opposition (left and centre-left) in the debate against the new law in 2002. Perhaps in the second stage, with full harmonisation, more attention will be paid.

3.9 The Communication of June, 2003 towards a more accessible, equitable and managed asylum system – in reaction to the UK paper – develops some ideas on new approaches to pursue an orderly and managed arrival of persons in need of international protection. What is the political reaction in your country to the concept of an outside accessed asylum procedure, distribution of refugees and responsibility-sharing and other new concepts and ideas in coping with mass refugee movements?

The concept of an outside accessed asylum procedure has raised much concern among NGOs. In Italy, Art. 10 of the Constitution must be respected: it recognises the right of persons seeking asylum to enter the territory. It seems odd that this kind of proposal is made by a country that is, as a general rule, out of Title IV of the EC Treaty. The question also arises as to how this could change the provisions adopted to date: introducing rapid changes to proposals that are the culmination of years of work could undermine the credibility of European Institutions. A fundamental right has to be fully and really considered "fundamental" and protected from any kind of possible attack.

PART IV TERMINATION OF ILLEGAL RESIDENCE, RETURN AND REPATRIATION

4.1 How many third country nationals without a valid residence permit are currently, according to estimates, staying in your country? How many deportations have actually been made in previous years? Is the whole enforcement process considered as acceptable?

There are always a large number of people without a valid residence permit in Italy: about 1,000,000, despite the several regularisations held since 1986. In 1995, 256,048 people asked for a regularisation; in 1998 (with the centre-left Government) 250,966; in 2002 (with the centre-right Government) and only 4 years after the previous regularisation, 702,156.

Expulsion orders were systematically ignored (about 85%) until the adoption of law no. 286/98 introducing forced deportation or, when that is not possible, the detention (administrative retention or "trattenimento") of foreigners.

In 2002, 105,808 people were expelled and 44,706 effectively left the country: 17,019 on the basis of readmission agreements. The others are presumed to have stayed in the country irregularly.

4.2 What has been undertaken to implement the Directive of 28 November 2002, dealing with the facilitation of unauthorized entry, transit and residence?

As Art. 12 of law no. 286/98 already includes the crimes defined in Directive 2002/90 and imposes more severe sanctions than those set out in the Framework decision 2002/946/GAI, Italian law does not require much modification.

However, the Italian national Parliament has delegated to the Government the task of adopting a decree to implement Directive 2002/90 with the law no. 306/2003.

4.3 How many illegal applicants have been apprehended at or near the border? How many criminal procedures for human trafficking have been instituted in the last year?

In 2002, 43,795 illegal applicants were apprehended at or near airport, sea and land borders.

4.4 What efforts have been undertaken in your country concerning the Budapest June 2003, recommendations concerning the harmonization of penalty scales with regard to the crime of smuggling migrants and the trafficking of persons in line with Council Directive 2002/90 of 28 November 2002? Did your country sign the relevant UN protocols on the smuggling of migrants?

There is no reference to the Budapest recommendations in official acts or official declarations. Only Directive 2002/90 has been considered (see supra).

With regard to the United Nations Convention against Transnational Organized Crime of 15 November, 2000 and related Protocols, Italy has signed but not yet ratified them.

4.5 What measures have been taken to implement the Council Directive of 28 May 2001 on the mutual recognition of decisions on the expulsion of third country nationals? What, if any shortcomings or gaps of the Directive should be corrected in a further directive on cooperation on expulsion or deportation of third country nationals?

As far as Directive 2001/40 is concerned, Italy is in breach of Community law because it has not yet implemented that Directive. National Parliament has delegated the task to the Government to adopt a decree with the law no. 306/2003.

Further measures in this area should concern the harmonisation of the rules regarding the adoption of expulsion orders and in setting out the minimum rights to be respected during the procedures, in conformity with the ECHR.

4.6 Do readmission agreements or other international treaties or arrangements with the aim of controlling and curbing illegal immigration and facilitating return exist in your country? Have they functioned satisfactorily?

There are several readmission agreements signed between Italy and other countries. The following agreements have been signed and have entered into force: Albania, Austria, Bulgaria, Croatia, Estonia, France, Sri Lanka, Yugoslavia, Latvia, Lithuania, Macedonia, Hungary, Romania, Slovakia, Slovenia, Switzerland, Tunisia (exchange of letters), Greece, Spain. The following have only been signed: Morocco, Cyprus, Germany, Algeria, Georgia, Malta, Moldavia, Nigeria and Pakistan. Negotiations are undergoing with the following countries: Ukraine, Senegal, Egypt, Philippine. Contacts have been taken with: India, Bangladesh, China, Bosnia-Herzegovina, Iran, Libya, Lebanon, Syria, Turkey and Ghana. These agreements are very effective in guaranteeing the execution of expulsion orders, in particular where there are doubts regarding the nationality of the foreigner. In 2002, 17,019 third country nationals were deported on the basis of a readmission agreement.

4.7 To what extent have EU-standards and recommendations influenced your country's return policy? Have efforts been undertaken to cooperate with other EU Member States in enforcing return decisions by common deportation actions, exchange of information, facilitation of air and land transit, common principles on flight security, etc.?

Community measures have not influenced Italian legislation. Co-operation is taking place in the context of a number of pilot projects in order to strengthen mutual aid e.g. in the execution of expulsion orders or in checks of maritime borders (see the so called Nettuno Project). It seems that the European Union approach in this sector is to support the activities of the Member States in order to enable them to be more efficient and to share the costs. This is also proved by the fact that many proposals for either legislative acts or for operational cooperation, have been proposed by Member States under Art. 67 of the EC Treaty.

4.8 Do you consider a need to elaborate a common legal regime for air deportations (legal status of armed guards on board of the aircrafts, rights of the aircraft commander, legal rules in case of transit stops, applicability of national police law on board of aircraft on flight, etc.)?

The creation of common rules in this sector is particularly important because the exercise of force in a foreign land can give rise to many problems especially in view of the fact that illegal entry is not a crime in all Member States (in Italy it is not a crime). It is also important to specify who is liable for the safety of aliens.

LATVIA

RENARS DANELSONS
Press Secretary of European Union Law
Association of the Republic of Latvia

INTRODUCTION

Latvia's response to the questionnaire is as follows.

PART I (ENTRY, VISA REGIME AND BORDER CONTROL)

1.1 What national authorities are competent to deal with visa applications (Schengen visas and long-term visas)? Are there any procedures to avoid duplication or successive visa applications at different EU-consulates? On what substantive criteria other than the Schengen minimum requirements are visas granted or refused? How many visas have been issued or refused?

At the beginning, it should be emphasized that the Republic of Latvia does not issue Schengen visas as it is not a part of the Schengen area. A special decision by the Council is necessary before Latvia can become a Contracting Party to the Schengen Agreement. Such a decision is not likely before 2007.

According to Regulations No. 131 "*Procedures for Issuance of Republic of Latvia Visas*" adopted by the Cabinet of Ministers on April 6 1999, Latvian visas are issued by diplomatic and consular missions of the Republic of Latvia abroad, the Office of Citizenship and Migration Affairs, and the Consular Department of the Ministry of Foreign Affairs.

As Latvia is not a party to the Schengen Agreement, it does not have access to the Schengen Visa Identification System and it is difficult to determine if successive visa applications have been made at different EU missions and at Latvian missions. If a decision has been taken not to issue a visa or to annul the issued visa, a relevant endorsement with a stamp is made in the applicant's travel document.

In addition to the Schengen minimum requirements (traveller's cheques in the amount of 20 lats (30 euros) for each day, a document which certifies the reservation of a certified place of accommodation, a round trip ticket with fixed dates) since May 1 2003, the applicant has to present a valid health and life insurance policy, which guarantees the cover of expenses related to health care in the Republic of Latvia, including the return of the applicant to his/her country of domicile in the case of his/her serious illness or death.

In 2003, 124,249 visas were issued (look at Annex 1) and 563 visas were been refused.

1.2 Is there a visa tracking procedure in order to identify visa overstayers? What data are collected from visa-applicants (fingerprints)? Admissibility of visa data to alien and police authorities?

Visa overstayers are detected in two ways. First of all, the Latvian Visa Information System and Immigration Data Base are interconnected and immigration authorities are able to access the necessary information. Secondly, information is received from the public (mass media, telephone calls, letters etc.).

Of course, information on visa applications is accessible to the secret services.

1.3 Have courts ever decided on the refusal of a Schengen visa based upon Schengen blacklisting by other Member States?

According to Latvian Immigration Law, a decision regarding the refusal to issue a visa may not be appealed and, consequently, there is no court case on visa refusal.

1.4 What measures have been undertaken in the implementation of the action programme for administrative cooperation in the field of external borders, visa, asylum and immigration following the Council Decision of 13 June 2002?

As Latvia is not yet a member of the Schengen area, it is not covered by the ARGO programme, however, co-operation with the member states in the field of external borders, visa, asylum and immigration is very successful. Two PHARE projects provide examples of such success stories – "Development of Integrated Border Administration and Infrastructure" and "System of Migration and Asylum Administration".

1.5 What measures have been undertaken to implement Directive 2001/51 EC supplementing the Schengen rules concerning carrier sanctions? How often have carrier sanctions been used?

The principles contained in Directive 2001/51 have been implemented in the Administrative Offences Code where one of the articles deals with "Carrying of Persons into the Republic of Latvia Without Valid Travel

Documents". There are more significant penalties for carrying persons by air or maritime transport than by road transport. The maximum penalty for carrying persons by air or maritime transport is up to 300 lats (448 euros) for physical persons and up to 5000 lats (7474 euros) for legal persons while the penalty for carrying by road transport is up to 250 lats (374 euros) and up to 2000 lats (2990 euros) respectively.

Carrier sanctions are imposed on average five times per day.

1.6 In your judgement, does the visa law and policy of your country live up to EU standards or are adjustments needed? Do you consider that there is need for further EU-harmonization of visa policies concerning:
- **common criteria for granting visas aiming at harmonizing visa obligations among states participating in the Budapest Process;**
- **establishment of a European visa identification system (VIS and SIS II)?**

To what extent will the EU enlargement process present an opportunity or a challenge for tackling issues of illegal entry and border control?

Generally, analysing migration policy, Latvia is already prepared for integration into the Schengen area and there are no major discrepancies between Latvian and EU standards.

It is absolutely necessary to achieve a further harmonization of visa policy within the European Union. It is vital to have a proper exchange of the so called "black lists" used by the member states. A lot could be achieved so as to avoid duplication or successive visa applications. The establishment of a European visa identification system is a top priority.

Without any doubt there is a danger that EU enlargement will lead to an increase in illegal migration but this is more due to a shortage of finances to tackle the issue rather than unwillingness to cope with it. Therefore the complete integration of the ten new member states into the Schengen area is of crucial importance and it should happen as soon as possible.

PART II (ADMISSION AND RESIDENCE OF THIRD COUNTRY NATIONALS)

2.1 What are the basic principles in your country concerning:
- **admission of third country nationals for labour purpose or self-employed activities**

The Latvian Immigration Law lays down basic rules regarding this issue. Currently the term "third country national" is not used in legislation. Instead, we use the term "alien" which is a person who is neither a Latvian citizen nor a non-citizen of Latvia.[1] Article 23 (points 3, 5, 6) provides that an alien has the right to request a temporary residence permit in connection with their employment. The same is true as regards possible self-employment (Article 23, points 2 and 4). The necessary documents for obtaining a residence permit are enumerated in Regulations of the Cabinet of Ministers (April 29, 2003, No.213) "*Residence Permit Regulations*". If an alien intends to reside in Latvia on the basis of an employment contract or contract for work performance, he/she needs an invitation from Latvia. In other cases where an alien intends to reside in Latvia on account of his/her employment, an invitation is not required and a work permit is issued together with a residence permit. As a consequence, we have a dual system in Latvia where, in some instances, the issuing of a work permit and residence permit is under a single administrative procedure while in others it is not.

On 20 January 2004, the Cabinet of Ministers adopted new regulations "*On work Permits for Aliens*". This new regulation transposes Directives 90/364 and 93/96.

Admission of third country nationals for study and vocational training

Latvian legislation provides that an alien intending to reside in Latvia for the purposes of study or vocational training may do so only if he/she has been granted a temporary residence permit. The Immigration Law also provides that an alien who is a pupil or full time student may request a temporary residence permit for a paid study period. If an alien's residence in Latvia is related to pupil or student exchange, practice or apprenticeship in one of the educational establishments of the Republic of Latvia or in a commercial company registered in the commercial register or the performance of another task, he/she may qualify for obtaining temporary residence for a period of up to one year. Necessary documents for obtaining a residence permit are enumerated in Regulations of the Cabinet of Ministers (April 29, 2003, No.213) "*Residence Permit Regulations*". The Regulations of the Cabinet of Ministers "*On Work Permits for Aliens*" provide that aliens residing in Latvia for the purpose of study or apprenticeship are able to take up employment for up to 20 hours per week.

Legal status of third country nationals in possession of a long-term residence visa of another Member State

[1] This is a category of people (unique only for Latvia) which is characterized by the fact that they have no citizenship of any country whatsoever and at the same time they are not considered and treated as stateless persons.

Currently there are no rules or procedure in Latvia for the purpose of allocating special status to a specific group of third country nationals.

To what extent do these principles differ from the European Commission's proposals?

They do not differ substantially except for the wish to maintain some regulative functionality for member states. As regards the third proposal there are no differences since there are no rules on the subject.

2.2 What are the legal requirements and procedures for obtaining a residence permit for third country nationals for the purpose of employment? Which procedures are used in maintaining the preferred access of EU-citizens and Turkish nationals (association agreement) to the labour market? Do special programmes exist for highly qualified professionals facilitating access to the labour market? To what extent are trade unions and employers involved in such programmes? Is there a procedure to calculate the demand for foreign labour? How is the EU-enlargement taken into consideration? To what extent has the recent economic recession and unemployment influenced the concepts on admission of third country nationals?

Article 23 (points 3, 5, 6) of the Immigration Law provides that an alien has the right to request a temporary residence permit in connection with their employment. Regulations of the Cabinet of Ministers (No.213, April 29, 2003) "*Residence Permit Regulations*" contain detailed rules regarding the documents required in order to obtain a residence permit. If a legal person invites an alien to Latvia, then the former has to submit the documents. In order to obtain or to register for a residence permit an alien has to be invited and the relevant invitation has to be registered with the Office of Citizenship and Migration Affairs. Several documents (for instance, a document affirming the provision of the necessary minimum subsistence cost while residing in Latvia, etc.) for obtaining a residence permit are enumerated in the above regulations as well as further documents (for instance, documents affirming education or qualifications necessary for performing the relevant job, etc.) in each specific case in which residence is connected with an employment.

Currently there is a provision in the Immigration law which states that an alien who wishes to establish legal employment relations by entering into an employment agreement or be employed on the basis of another civil legal contract (including as a member of a capital company's executive body) or be a self-employed person shall need a work permit. However this does not apply to EU nationals, (Article 9(2)5). Nevertheless, currently new amendments are being elaborated in order to comply with the obligations resulting from the Accession Treaty and in particular from transitional periods.[2] The latter Article is also to be amended, although the principle of priority for EU nationals is probably going to be retained. There are no provisions regarding Turkish nationals.

Special programmes, as such, for facilitating the access of highly qualified professionals to the labour market do not exist. There are some provisions on this matter, however. Thus, Regulations of the Cabinet of Ministers "*On Work Permits for Aliens*" provide a simplified procedure for obtaining a work permit for some special occupations (IT leading experts, for instance). Pursuant to that procedure the provision of an invitation for acquiring a work permit is not necessary. The Regulations provide for a specific situation for some occupations where an alien may come to Latvia to perform a specific job (up to 90 days per half year) on the basis of an issued visa (even from countries where visas are not required) or residence permit. This is due to the fact that a residence permit may be acquired within one month while visas may be obtained in three days. This provision substantially improves the necessary service. The Office of Citizenship and Migration Affairs issues work permits corresponding to the period of the visa.

To our knowledge there is no specific procedure for calculating the demand for foreign labour. It is done more or less on the initiative of each relevant sector, as was the case with IT.

The concepts on admission of third country nationals are hardly affected by economic recession or unemployment. Illegal unemployment could have an impact.

2.3 To what extent do existing national laws and practices differ substantially from the approach taken in the Commission's Proposal on admission for the purpose of paid employment and self-employed activities relating to:
– admission of third country nationals for study and vocational training

Latvian Immigration Law is applicable to a larger group of aliens (in comparison with the Directive) who are entitled to get a residence permit for the purpose of education in Latvia. Documents needed for obtaining a residence permit are basically the same (as in the Directive) except for some not very substantial differences in wording. Contrary to the

[2] Currently it is planned to replace the Article with the one saying that aliens coming to Latvia within the framework of posting (Directive 96/71) shall not need work permits if the duration does not exceed 90 days. As regards EU nationals and their family members it is foreseen to issue work permits automatically for statistical purposes.

proposal, Latvian Immigration Law does not provide for the possibility for an alien who does not have a legal reason to reside in Latvia to appeal personally against the decision to refuse or annul a residence permit. In such cases, the person who invited the alien, may appeal against the decision. Immigration Law also does not provide for the possibility of obtaining a residence permit for the purpose of study on account of postponing conditions, i.e. while an alien is being admitted to the relevant educational establishment.

On legal status of third country nationals in possession of a long-term residence permit of another Member State

There are no rules. There is a provision in the Immigration Law delegating the power to the Cabinet of Ministers to adopt relevant regulations (Article 69) as soon as the Directive is in force.

To what extent do these principles differ from the European Commission's proposals?

As regards the first proposal, the government supports the laying down of common principles and criteria at the European level for the purpose of third country nationals' admission in connection with employment. However, there is a view that the proposal should limit itself to setting out general rules, maintaining the balance between providing an option for third country nationals, under certain criteria, to demand a residence permit (work permit) and maintaining a discretion for the member states to review each case individually. As to common administrative procedures for obtaining visas, residence permits and work permits, the governmental view is that it should be kept separate in so far as it would lead to an increased administrative burden. Our point of view is that an excuse which simply seeks to justify the government's inability to organize its activities is not a valid one.

2.4 What measures have been taken to implement the Directive of 29th June 2000 implementing the principle of equal treatment between persons irrespective of racial or ethnic origin and Council Directive 2000/78 EC of 27th November 2000, establishing a general framework for equal treatment in employment and occupation? Have legislative changes been undertaken? To what extent is "affirmative action" considered as necessary to promote equal opportunities for migrant workers from third countries?

Council Directive 2000/78 EC is to be transposed into the Latvian Labour Code. Currently the relevant amendments are before the parliament and it is expected that the law will be amended by approximately

April 1, 2004 at the latest. "Affirmative action" in order to promote equal opportunities for migrant workers from third countries is not considered as necessary whatsoever.

2.5 Concerning the proposal for a directive on the right to family reunion agreed upon by Council in February 2003:
- **Do you consider the proposed standards below the principles of family reunification valid in your country?**

No, in general the provisions of the relevant Directive are in conformity with the principles contained in the Immigration Law and, actually, for the purposes of its implementation only minor wording amendments will be needed.

Will the implementation of the Directive once it is adopted lead to changes in the national law on family reunification downgrading the standard of protection? If so, what changes are envisaged?

No.

2.6 The proposal for a Directive on the rights of long-term third country nationals as agreed upon by the Council on June 5, 2003 provides for a number of rights approximating the standards of long-term residents to the status of EU-citizens. Will the implementation of the Directive involve major legal and policy changes in your country? What are the major points of concern if any, concerning the approximation concept of the directive . . . .

The directive will be of major importance in Latvia in so far as we have a large number of people residing here for a period of more than 5 years who do not have Latvian citizenship. Although initially the directive was meant to cover third country nationals (persons, who are nationals of a country other than the country in which they reside) the Commission pointed out in a specific letter that, as regards Latvia, the term "third country national" shall also include so called non-citizens of Latvia – people who do not have any citizenship and are not stateless persons either. This interpretation could create some uncertainty since in the document entitled "Proposal for a Council Directive concerning the status of third country nationals who are long-term residents" (CELEX Nr.52001PC0127) the Commission, commenting on the concept "third country nationals" expressly refers to "persons having the nationality of a third country" and to "stateless persons within the meaning of the New York Convention of 28 September 1954".[3] Article 1 of the Convention provides that "For the

[3] Convention relating to the Status of Stateless Persons http://www.unhchr.ch/html/menu3/b/ocsp.htm.

purpose of this Convention, the term "stateless person" means a person who is not considered as a national by any State under the operation of its law". Consequently, it is evident that the Directive was not aimed at categories of persons such as non-citizens of Latvia. This is certainly a political issue as well and may become rather sensitive in the future. We believe that the government of Latvia has to take a more strict line on the issue – up to the inclusion of a special reference in the Directive in respect of non-citizens in order to avoid any ambiguities whatsoever. We also believe that very little (or nothing) has been done to clarify the issue to the public. In this regard it should also be mentioned that from the political point of view the proposal is not an unambiguous one since by granting almost equal rights (in respect of free movement of persons) to the non-citizens of Latvia, the process of naturalization could be hampered in so far as there will be no additional motivation for non-citizens to become Latvian (EU) citizens. On the other hand it was extremely important for Latvia to "get" these people "under" the definition of "third country nationals" since otherwise people having or acquiring the citizenship of a third country (not Latvia) would be in a more favourable situation in comparison with non-citizens.

The planned status of "third country nationals" is very similar to the status which is granted to those who have obtained a permanent residence permit (certain social guarantees, access to the labour market, etc.). Consequently, the basic difference between long-term third country nationals within the meaning of the Directive and those with a permanent residence permit is the period for obtaining each respective status – for long-term residents this is 5 years, but for persons with a permanent residence permit it is 10 years (generally in accordance with Immigration Law). In general, the Directive increases residence guarantees. As regards certain aspects within the field of social guarantees some minor improvements could be necessary in respect of persons acquiring the status of long-term residents.

- **non-discrimination in social rights**

Permanent residence permits already provide for access to social assistance and social services, as well as free access to labour markets and education in conformity with the rules provided in the Directive.

- **the concept of "civic citizenship" (see also extended impact assessment on the Communication on Integration of June 11, 2003);**
- **family reunification and access of family members to the labour market**

Already now the Immigration Law provides that a permanent residence permit entails the right to reunite families in Latvia and family members in such circumstances have free access to the labour market as well. Consequently permanent residence permits entail an identical range of rights and guarantees as those in this field.

– **security of stay**

The Directive broadens residence guarantees, in comparison with the Immigration law, in respect of cases where a permanent residence permit is obtained. The Directive provides for the possibility of expulsion solely on the grounds of public security; security of the state and health protection. However, the Immigration Law also provides for the possibility of expulsion in certain cases connected with violations of residence rules taking into account the proportionality of an expulsion order in comparison with the duration of residence.

2.7 Considering the perspective of a future common migration policy as developed by the Commission in the Open Coordination Communication (COM 2001, 387) and the communication on a migration policy of the European Union (COM 2000, 757 final), how do you assess the role of the Community organs in determining a European migration policy in terms of the competences of the Member States to decide on residence rights and admission to the labour market and integration? Should harmonization of legislation go further, and if so, in what respect?

The Community organs have been very active in enacting rules in respect of European migration policy in order to cope with the latest trends. However, we believe that the harmonization process has gone far enough for the present and it should use this opportunity to appraise new situations in order to avoid any disturbances in future.

PART III (ASYLUM AND REFUGEE LAW)

3.1 Have the Dublin Rules worked satisfactorily and what is expected from the Dublin II Regulation No. 343, 2003 of February 18, 2003?

The Republic of Latvia has not ratified and implemented the Dublin Convention. Latvia declared in its position paper for the Accession Negotiations that it realized the importance of the Dublin Convention in the area of asylum and was ready to harmonize its legislation in order to be able to accede to the Convention upon accession to the EU. As there is no longer a need to ratify the Dublin Convention Latvia will now concentrate its efforts on the Dublin II Regulation No. 343.

The Government of Latvia declared in its position paper for the Accession Negotiations that it would take the following measures in order to implement the Dublin Convention:

1) the procedures for the examination of applications for asylum forwarded from the EU Member States, and procedures regulating the forwarding of applications from Latvia to the EU Member States would be elaborated;
2) in addition, the procedures would be prepared for the transfer and admission of persons whose applications are forwarded;
3) special training of involved employees would be provided;
4) additional staff would be allocated.

Since the Dublin II Regulation is based on the same principles as the Dublin I Convention, all the measures envisaged above by the Government of Latvia will apply to Dublin II Regulation. Dublin II Regulation will take effect in Latvia from May 1, 2004.

3.2 Has the Eurodac Regulation No. 2725/2000 of 11th December 2000 concerning the establishment of Eurodac for the comparison of fingerprints for an effective application of the Dublin Convention, operative since January 15, 2003 resulted in an increase of Dublin cases? Has Eurodac become effective in your country or is it expected to become eventually effective?

The Eurodac Regulation is not effective and has not been applied by the responsible institutions, yet. It will only become effective from the time Latvia becomes a member of the EU, i.e. from May 1, 2004.

3.3 What major changes, if any, will the implementation of the amended proposal of a directive on minimum standards on procedures in Member States for granting and withdrawing refugee status on which the Council has reached political agreement on most points in June 2003 bring for the legislation and practice in your country in particular relating to:
- **rights of applicants in the procedure;**
- **administrative and judicial appeal procedure;**
- **the use of safe third country and safe country of origin concepts;**
- **detainment of asylum seekers;**
- **airport and border procedures?**

The Asylum Law, adopted in the Saeima[4] on 7 March 2002, and effective from 1 September 2002, governs procedure for granting and withdrawing

[4] Parliament of the Republic of Latvia.

refugee status in the Republic of Latvia. Since its adoption and to date, the Asylum Law has not been amended. Several provisions of the Asylum Law are implemented by eight Regulations of the Cabinet.[5]

Comparing the amended proposal of a Directive on minimum standards in Member States for granting and withdrawing refugee status (2000/0238 (CNS)) (hereinafter – amended proposal of the directive) with the Asylum Law, it has to be concluded that the provisions of the Asylum Law substantially and generally conform to the provisions of the amended proposal of the Directive.

The amended proposal of the Directive contains many optional provisions (*may provide*), which leave Member States the choice as to whether to implement the respective provision or not. For this reason, it is not possible to say whether the respective provision will be implemented or not in the Asylum Law. However, the amended proposal of the Directive has a number of exhaustive provisions that leave no choice to the Member States. The wording below only refers to the exhaustive provisions.

The following provisions of the amended proposal of the Directive must be implemented in the legislation of the Republic of Latvia, as they are not provided in the current legislation:

1) Article 9 (2);
2) Article 11 (1);
3) Article 12 (2);
4) Article 13 (2);
5) Article 15 (1) (b);
6) Article 15 (2) (b);
7) Article 16 (2);
8) Article 16 (3);
9) Article 17;
10) Article 19;
11) Article 20;
12) Article 25 (e);
13) Article 34 (3) (a);
14) Article 38 (1);
15) Article 41 (2);
16) Annex I;
17) Annex II.

[5] Government of the Republic of Latvia.

3.4 What measures have been undertaken to implement Directive 2003/9 of 27 January 2003, on reception of asylum seekers in your country relating to:
– the flexibility clauses in the directive;
– restriction of free movement;
– access to the labour market;
– rights of migrant workers under Article 11 § 2 of the Directive?

The Asylum Law already conforms substantially with Directive 2003/9. However, several provisions of the Directive have not been implemented under the Asylum Law. On 3 July 2003, the Ministry of Interior announced amendments to the Asylum Law at the meeting of State Secretaries in order to implement the Directive. However, to date neither the Government of Latvia, nor the Parliament of Latvia has adopted the mentioned amendments. In any event, the draft amendments do not implement all requirements of the Directive.

The Asylum Law has already implemented Article 3(4) of the Directive, i.e. the Asylum Law applies the same procedure and rights for persons who do not come under the definition of refugee but nevertheless need international protection. Alongside the granting of refugee status, the Asylum Law sets out the basis for obtaining the alternative status. Persons may receive alternative status if there is reason to believe that (1) that person is under threat of the death penalty, corporal punishment, torture, inhuman or degrading treatment, or degrading punishment in the country of his or her citizenship or, if the person is a stateless person, in the country of his or her former residence; or (2) due to external or internal armed conflict this person needs protection and he or she cannot return to the country of his or her citizenship or, if the person is a stateless person, to the country of his or her former residence.

Neither Asylum Law, nor the draft amendments provide more favourable provisions in the field of reception conditions.

According to the Asylum Law, during the examination of an application, the asylum seeker is accommodated at an accommodation centre where necessary living conditions are provided. The asylum seeker is not accommodated at the accommodation centre for asylum seekers until he or she has a legal basis to reside in the Republic of Latvia. The asylum seeker also has the right to reside outside the accommodation centre for asylum seekers. With regard to this right, a permit is issued in each case by the administration of the accommodation centre for asylum seekers and an entry is made in the personal identity document of the asylum seeker. Neither the Asylum Law, nor any other legal act prescribe that asylum seekers shall not require permission to keep appointments with authorities and courts if his or her appearance is necessary.

Latvia has not implemented, nor do the draft amendments provide a basis for the implementation of, Article 11 of the Directive. Legal acts of Latvia specify that an asylum seeker has no access to the labour market at all. Only persons who obtain refugee or alternative status may work in Latvia. No basis is provided for application of Article 11(2) of the Directive.

3.5 What steps have been undertaken to implement the Directive on temporary protection, COM 2001, 55 in national law? Are there any procedures for burden sharing arrangements? Is there a legal basis for admission of refugees receiving temporary protection in a mass-movement situation?

A considerable part of Directive 2001/55/EC is already incorporated in the Asylum Law. However, a major part of the Directive still needs to be implemented. Since adoption of the Asylum Law, no new measures to implement the Directive have been adopted. The Asylum Law provides a legal basis for protection in case of the mass influx of displaced persons, i.e. the Asylum Law provides temporary protection, which is granted to a group of persons for a specified period of time if such persons need protection and they are or have been forced to leave the country of their citizenship or, if the persons are stateless persons, their country of former residence due to (1) ethnic conflict, or (2) civil war.

The Asylum Law does not provide for the person who obtains temporary protection the right to obtain social security as for refugees or persons of alternative status. The right to decide on accommodation and the amount of subsistence means is left to the Government, which takes an individual decision in each case.

Latvian law does not provide any measure for giving persons granted temporary protection the right to engage in employed or self-employed activities. The Asylum Law does not provide any justifications for refusing to grant temporary protection, the discretion to grant temporary protection is assigned to the Government. The Asylum Law also does not implement Article 4(1) of the Directive; the duration of residence of temporary protected persons is decided by the Government of Latvia.

The procedure provided for in Article 26 of the Directive is not implemented in Latvian law.

3.6 The Council has reached political agreement on the principles for a directive on minimum standards for the qualification and status of third country nationals as refugees or persons who otherwise need international protection, COM 2001,

510 final (see Council documents of June 2003). What measures are envisaged to implement the Directive, once it is adopted, in your country relating to:
– the definition of refugee;
– the definition of persons entitled to subsidiary protection;
– status of persons entitled to subsidiary protection;
– the issue of internal flight alternative as defined by the Directive;
– exclusion clauses, particularly issues of terrorism?
To what extent are the refugee policies as reflected in the law and jurisprudence of your country in accordance with the proposal of the directive?

The definition of refugee specified in the Asylum Law fully conforms with the definition in the draft directive on minimum standards for the qualification and status of third country nationals as refugees or persons who otherwise need international protection. Also, the definition of persons entitled to alternative status specified by the Asylum Law corresponds with the definition of persons entitled to subsidiary protection under the draft directive. Consequently, it will not be necessary to adopt any measures in this regard.

Persons who have obtained alternative status possess equal rights and obligations as refugees, e.g. they both may not be deported or extradited; they both are granted residence permits; they both are given travel documents etc. However, there are differences in relation to access to employment and access to education.

Refugees, after receiving refugee status, are entitled to a permanent residence permit. According to Latvian legislation, the permanent residence permit grants rights of access to employment under the same conditions as Latvian citizens without the need to obtain a work permit and the Latvian Law on Education grants rights to receive education under the general education system.

But persons who have obtained alternative status are only entitled to a temporary residence permit. The temporary residence permit does not grant the rights to access employment under the same conditions as Latvian citizens, i.e. persons of alternative status need to get a work permit: a procedure which is neither cheap nor easy. The government has prepared a new draft regulation which will remove one requirement under the procedure for obtaining a work permit. However, this draft regulation still requires persons of alternative status to obtain a work permit in order to access employment in Latvia. Persons of alternative status have no access to education under the general education system.

The Asylum Law does not recognize the alternative principle of internal protection and does not provide for the possibility of returning a person to another part of the country, i.e. this principle will need to be implemented in the Latvian legal system after the draft directive becomes effective.

The Asylum Law provides the following cases where the provisions for granting refugee status do not apply:

1) where the applicant has committed a crime against peace, a war crime or a crime against humanity, also a crime of genocide within the meaning defined in international documents which have been adopted to carry out measures against crimes of such type;
2) before arrival in the Republic of Latvia the applicant has committed an especially serious non-political crime; or
3) the applicant is guilty of committing acts that are contrary to the principles and purposes of the United Nations.

Under the Asylum Law, alternative status shall not be granted to an asylum seeker if there is cause to believe that the asylum seeker:

1) before arrival in the Republic of Latvia resided in a country where he or she could have requested and received protection;
2) has committed a crime against peace, a war crime or a crime against humanity, also a genocide crime within the meaning defined in international documents which have been adopted to carry out measures against crimes of such kind;
3) is guilty of committing acts which are contrary to the principles and purposes of the United Nations; or
4) poses a threat to the security of the State and the people of Latvia.

The above information shows that the refugee policy of the Republic of Latvia in general conforms to the above mentioned draft directive. However, minor changes will be required to bring Latvian legislation in line with the draft directive.

3.7 In the Commission's Communication of 22 November 2000, COM 2000,755 (see also 2nd Commission Report COM 2003, 152 final) the Commission's concept of a common European asylum procedure and a uniform status for those who are granted asylum valid throughout the Union is set out. Do you consider that the concept is generally in line with your country's asylum policy? Are concerns of refugee organizations, such as Amnesty International and other organizations, of an undermining of the international regime for the protection of refugees shared in political circles of your country responsible for decision-making?

Latvian asylum policy is completely new. The law providing for the procedure for granting asylum entered into effect only as from 1998.

Latvia has little experience in the area of asylum; this is a new sphere of policy for Latvia. For that reason, the asylum system of Latvia was founded on international practice, and especially on the practice of the EU since Latvia undertook political obligation to become a member of the EU. In order to become an EU member, Latvia had to conform with the EU asylum principles. Asylum policy is not an important policy for Latvia because the number of asylum seekers is very low. For example, only 134 persons sought asylum in Latvia from 1998 until the end of 2003; refugee status has been granted to only 8 persons during the operation of asylum policy in Latvia; and alternative status has been granted to only 3 persons from 2002, up until 8 October 2003.

The Government of Latvia is not very active in the area of asylum policy since the number of asylum seekers is minimal and they do not influence the economy of Latvia substantially. Comparing the Commission's concept of a common European asylum procedure and a uniform status for those who are granted asylum with the asylum policy of Latvia, – generally the asylum policy of Latvia conforms to the Commission's concept.

Latvia has a common procedure both for granting refugee status and alternative status: applications for both statuses are reviewed by the same institutions. Persons who are granted refugee status and persons who are granted alternative status receive more or less the same treatment. The responsible officials of the Ministry of the Interior support eliminating "asylum shopping" through the adoption of a common procedure and uniform status throughout the Union.

The Asylum Law does not allow asylum applications to be submitted at diplomatic or consular missions of Latvia abroad. Moreover, the Government of Latvia does not support the admission of asylum seekers through the diplomatic or consular missions.

The Government of Latvia has not expressed its attitude towards the concerns of refugee organizations. However, it is possible to implicitly conclude from the Asylum Law and practice that Latvia supports the principle of "suspensive effect", i.e. that asylum seekers should not be expelled at all during the examination of the asylum application. The Asylum Law does not allow for the expelling of an asylum seeker even if it is manifest that there is no ground for granting asylum in Latvia.

3.8 The open coordination-mechanism as suggested by the Commission provided for a first stage and a second stage legislation in which the flexibility provisions in some of the directives on migration and asylum are to be replaced by a full harmonization. Is this concept discussed in your country and what are the perceptions relating to the gradual establishment of a European asylum policy

which might eventually replace national procedures and national decision-making?

There was discussion concerning two Commission proposals for directives within the first stage of legislation in Latvia, i.e. the Directive on minimum standards on procedures in Member States for granting and withdrawing refugee status; and the Directive on minimum standards for the qualification and status of third country nationals and stateless persons as refugees or as persons who otherwise need international protection. The Government of Latvia adopted a national position concerning these two proposals.

The Government of Latvia considers that a common list of safe third countries would make the asylum procedure more effective and would eliminate the attempts of asylum seekers to choose the country in which to submit the asylum application, so-called "asylum shopping". According to the Asylum law, entry may not be refused for those asylum seekers who arrive directly from safe third countries. Latvia would like it to be possible to reject entry for such asylum seekers in future.

The Government of Latvia has not adopted any position with regard to the gradual establishment of a European asylum policy which might eventually replace national procedures and national decision-making. For that reason it is not possible to determine Latvia's views on this issue.

3.9 The Communication of June, 2003 towards a more accessible, equitable and managed asylum system – in reaction to the UK paper – develops some ideas on new approaches to pursue an orderly and managed arrival of persons in need of international protection. What is the political reaction in your country as to the concept of an outside accessed asylum procedure, distribution of refugees and responsibility-sharing and other new concepts and ideas in coping with mass refugee movements?

The position of Latvia concerning the proposals specified in the UK paper is reserved and cautious.

Concerning the distribution of refugees or quotas for refugees, Latvia supports quotas for the admission of refugees only in emergency situations and situations of crisis. In other cases, the adoption of such decisions should remain within the competence of the member states. The government argues that a quota for the admission of refugees would not diminish the number of asylum seekers. Such situation would create an extra economic and social burden in Latvia and would influence the state budget substantially. It has to be taken into account that in admitting quotas of refugees, assistance must be given promptly to groups which are less socially secure – minors, women and elderly people. It would require a long-term solution for the system of health care, rehabilitation, education, professional re-qualification and of social security. The experience of other Member States shows that integration by the first generation of immigrants is not usually successful and people become dependent on the system of social assistance.

The Government of Latvia does not support the admission of refugees through the diplomatic or consular missions abroad. It argues that this procedure would require substantial extra investments in Latvian diplomatic and consular missions abroad (both human and financial resources). At present, Latvia does not have diplomatic and consular missions in the regions where persons may need international protection or such diplomatic and consular missions have minimal numbers of staff. This procedure would not lessen movements of asylum seekers and it would not provide for procedural guarantees during the examination of the asylum application (problems with accommodation during the residence of persons in third countries; ensuring rights for appeal; would not preclude re-submission of the asylum applications). Latvia would rather support assistance for UNHCR programmes in these areas.

PART IV (TERMINATION OF ILLEGAL RESIDENCE, RETURN AND REPATRIATION)

4.1 How many third country nationals without a valid residence permit are currently, according to estimates, staying in your country? How many deportations have actually been made in previous years? Is the whole enforcement process considered as acceptable?

There are no public data available according to the Office of Citizenship and Migration Affairs as to how many third country nationals without a valid residence permit are currently staying in Latvia. The explanation provided by the authorities is that it is impossible to estimate the number of such persons due to the large number of ex- soviet citizens who continue to reside in Latvia illegally.

1) According to the data collected by the State Border Control, the numbers of deported persons who were escorted to the border during the previous years were as follows:

Year 1997 – 342;
Year 1998 – 346;
Year 1999 – 190;

Year 2000 – 176;
Year 2001 – 238;
Year 2002 – 255;
Year 2003 – 366.

2) The number of persons who were ordered to leave the state but were not escorted to the border was:

Year 1997 – 240;
Year 1998 – 187;
Year 1999 – 122;
Year 2000 – 57;
Year 2001 – 61;
Year 2002 – 131;
Year 2003 – 137.

The total number of deported persons may be obtained by summing up the number of deported persons who were escorted to the border and those who were not:

Year 1997 – 582;
Year 1998 – 533;
Year 1999 – 312;
Year 2000 – 233;
Year 2001 – 537;
Year 2002 – 386;
Year 2003 – 503.

Yes, the enforcement process is considered to be acceptable.

4.2 What has been undertaken to implement the Directive of November 28, 2002 dealing with the facilitation of unauthorized entry, transit and residence?

Directive 2002/90/EC of 28 November 2002, defining the facilitation of unauthorized entry, transit and residence has been implemented since 11.12.2003. when the amendments to the Criminal Law were adopted. Article 285 of the Criminal Law provides for a criminal sanction – deprivation of liberty for a term not exceeding five years – for a person who unlawfully conveys a person across a State border, in violation of provisions regarding border crossing. This sanction is more severe if: such an act is committed repeatedly; if it is committed by a state official utilizing his or her official position; or person is unlawfully conveying a large number of persons, that is, more than five persons at one time.

4.3 How many illegal applicants have been apprehended at or near the border? How many criminal procedures for human trafficking have been instituted in the last year?

During the year 2003, the number of persons apprehended without valid visas or residence permits was 742. Out of those 742 persons, 274 were apprehended on the Latvian/Lithuanian or Latvian/Estonian border. During the year 2003, 118 persons tried to cross the border with counterfeit documents or documents belonging to other persons (in the year 2002, this number was 73).

According to the State Border Guard, no criminal procedures for human trafficking have been instituted during the year 2003 in respect of the illegal trafficking of immigrants. According to the Office of Citizenship and Migration Affairs, several cases regarding the human trafficking of Latvian citizens and non-citizens have been initiated. The Criminal Law was supplemented with an article on human trafficking relatively recently: 25.04.2002. and it entered into force on 23.05.2002.

4.4 What efforts have been undertaken in your country concerning the Budapest June 2003 recommendations concerning the harmonization of penalty scales with regard to the crime of smuggling of migrants and trafficking of persons in line with Council Directive 2002/90 of 28th November 2002? Did your country sign the relevant UN protocols on the smuggling of migrants?

Latvia ratified the UN Convention's Protocol Against the Smuggling of Migrants by Land, Sea and Air, Supplementing the United Nations Convention Against Transnational Organized Crime, G.A. res. 55/25, annex III, 55 UN GAOR Supp. (No. 49) at 65, UN Doc. A/45/49 (Vol. I) on 23 April 2003. During the ratification process, all legislative acts in Latvia were in conformity with the requirements of the protocol. No changes were needed in respect of Criminal Law and Administrative Law.

The Ministry of Interior has elaborated the State Programme for the Prevention of Human Trafficking 2004–2008. Currently this programme has been submitted to the government, but has not yet been adopted. During the elaboration of this programme, experts identified not only international and EU legal acts in the area, which are binding on Latvia, but also those, which belong to the body of soft-law. The Budapest June 2003 recommendations were also taken into account while elaborating this programme.

4.5 What measures have been taken to implement the Council Directive of 28 May 2001, on the mutual recognition of decisions on the expulsion of third country nationals? What, if any shortcomings or gaps of the Directive should be corrected

in a further directive on cooperation on expulsion or deportation of third country nationals?

This Directive has not yet been implemented. According to the information provided by the Office of Citizenship and Migration Affairs, Latvia is not in a hurry to transpose this Directive due to the attitudes of the existing member states towards the relatively vaguely formulated mutual recognition duty. However, the Ministry of Interior is currently drafting the amendments to the Immigration Law for implementing the requirements of this Directive. The amendments have not yet been submitted to the government.

4.6 Do readmission agreements or other international treaties or arrangements with the aim of controlling and curbing illegal immigration and facilitating return exist in your country? Have they functioned satisfactorily?

A number of readmission agreements have been concluded between Latvia and the EU as well as with non-EU states. Please find more detailed information in the table below.

Country	Date of signature	Date of entry into force
Armenia	26.06.2002.	17.05.2003.
Austria	08.06.2000.	01.09.2000.
Baltic States	01.07.1995.	01.07.1995.
Benelux	09.06.1999.	
Bulgaria	05.07.2002.	12.10.2002.
Croatia	21.09.1998.	21.08.1998.
Denmark	18.12.1996.	01.07.1997.
Finland	02.12.1996.	04.05.1997.
France	05.12.1997.	16.06.1998.
Germany	16.12.1998.	01.02.1999.
Greece	17.03.1999.	21.12.2000.
Hungary	17.10.2001.	04.05.2002.
Iceland	18.04.1997.	21.04.1997.
Italy	21.05.1997.	07.11.1997.
Liechtenstein	23.12.1997.	22.01.1998.
Norway	15.05.1997.	01.07.1997.
Portugal	08.11.1999.	
Romania	05.07.2002.	
Slovenia	05.03.1998.	16.10.1998.
Spain	30.03.1999.	01.02.2000.
Sweden	09.04.1997.	01.05.1997.
Switzerland	23.12.1997.	22.01.1998.
Ukraine	17.10.2001.	17.05.1998.

Currently negotiations about the conclusion of readmission agreements are ongoing with Russia, Belarus, Georgia, Moldova, Canada, Azerbaijan, Poland, Kyrgyz Republic, Kazakhstan, Serbia and Montenegro and Albania. The conclusion of a readmission agreement with Russia was suspended due to a stand still in negotiations regarding the border agreement which in its turn happened due to political reasons.

In general, all readmission agreements which have entered into force function satisfactorily. A new readmission agreement among the Baltic States is currently being negotiated, because the previous one has been in existence for almost 10 years and does not cover all the issues which have recently become actual.

4.7 To what extent have EU-standards and recommendations influenced your country's return policy? Have efforts been undertaken to cooperate with other EU Member States in enforcing return decisions by common deportation actions, exchange of information, facilitation of air and land transit, common principles on flight security, etc.?

Up until now, EU standards and recommendations have not had an important influence on Latvia's return policy. Firstly, because Latvia is not yet an EU member state. Secondly, those 4 countries which are the source of the most significant flows of illegal immigration coming to Latvia are not EU member states. These countries are: Lithuania, Russia, Ukraine and Estonia.

Besides, Latvia is not a country which is attractive to legal immigrants as a final destination, nor is it often used for the transit of illegal immigrants. In addition, Latvia is not a significant source of illegal immigrants.

However, Latvia has implemented the recommendation regarding the standard document for the third country national who is to be deported.

4.8 Do you consider that there is a need to elaborate a common legal regime for air deportations (legal status of armed guards on board of the aircrafts, rights of the aircraft commander, legal rules in case of transit stops, applicability of national police law on board of aircraft on flight, etc.)?

Currently, Latvia does not consider that there is a need to elaborate a common legal regime for air deportations because the total number of deportations from Latvia is relatively low and mainly these deportations are land deportations. Besides Riga airport is not used as a transit point for important international flights and the situation will not change in the foreseeable future.

LUXEMBOURG

RAOUL UEBERECKEN
Attaché de Gouvernement
Ministère de la Justice

INTRODUCTION

Le questionnaire est divisé en quatre parties principales qui sont les suivantes:

I L'entrée sur le territoire, le régime des visas et le contrôle aux frontières;
II L'accueil et le droit de séjour des ressortissants de pays tiers;
III La législation relative aux demandeurs d'asile et aux réfugiés;
IV Les procédures visant à mettre fin à une résidence illégale, les procédures de retour et rapatriement.

PARTIE I ENTRÉE SUR LE TERRITOIRE, RÉGIME DES VISAS ET CONTRÔLE AUX FRONTIÈRES

La situation luxembourgeoise se distingue de celle des autres Etats membres de l'Union européenne sur plusieurs points:

- le Luxembourg se situe au cœur de l'espace Schengen avec une absence de frontières extérieures terrestres et maritimes,
- la seule frontière extérieure se trouve à l'aéroport de Luxembourg avec un nombre limité de vols extra-Schengen,
- le réseau diplomatique luxembourgeois est de taille modeste, les seuls postes diplomatiques non-européens sont situés aux Etat-Unis, en Russie, en Chine, en Inde et au Japon.

De ces trois éléments découle que le Luxembourg ne maîtrise que de façon limitée les entrées sur son territoire national. Pour la délivrance des visas il doit en outre souvent recourir aux services d'autres Etats membres tel que cela est prévu dans le cadre du Benelux ou encore, de manière plus limitée, dans le cadre de Schengen.

La législation nationale applicable à l'entrée et séjour des ressortissants de pays tiers est essentiellement la loi modifiée du 28 mars 1972 concernant 1. l'entrée et le séjour des étrangers, 2. le contrôle médical des étrangers, 3. l'emploi de la main d'œuvre étrangère. Les autorités nationales compétentes sont le Ministère de la Justice (entrée et séjour, asile), le Ministère des Affaires étrangères (visa) et la Police grand-ducale (immigration illégale, contrôle aux frontières).

1.1 Quelle sont les autorités nationales compétentes en matière de demandes de visas (dans le cadre de l'espace Schengen et pour les visas de longue durée)? Existe-t-il des procédures permettant d'éviter une duplication des demandes de visas ou d'éviter le dépôt de demandes successives dans les différents consulats dans l'Union européenne? En fonction de quels critères substantiels, autres que les exigences minimum requises dans le cadre de l'espace Schengen, les visas sont-ils accordés ou refusés? Combien de demandes de visas ont été satisfaites, combien ont été rejetées?

L'autorité compétente pour la délivrance des visas est le Ministère des Affaires étrangères. Néanmoins, pour certains types de visas, le Ministère de la Justice a un pouvoir décisionnel (p.ex. visas de long séjour, visas en vue de la délivrance d'un titre de séjour). Dans ces cas, le service compétent du Ministère des Affaires étrangères doit se conformer aux décisions prises au niveau du Ministère de la Justice.

Concernant la possible duplication des demandes de visa, les autorités consulaires sont en principe tenues, en application des règles Schengen, d'apposer dans le document de voyage du demandeur un cachet indiquant qu'une demande a été déposée. Dans le cas où un visa est accordé, la vignette est apposée de sorte à recouvrir le cachet. Dans le cas d'un refus de délivrance, le cachet, en étant visible, donnera une indication aux autres autorités consulaires sur le dépôt d'une demande antérieure.

Les visas ne sont délivrés qu'aux conditions d'entrée définies par les dispositions pertinentes de la Convention d'application de l'Accord de Schengen et en particulier par celles de l'article 5. De plus, les Instructions consulaires communes (ICC) donnent un grand nombre d'indications sur la procédure à suivre pour l'instruction d'une demande de visa.

Outre ces éléments, les autorités luxembourgeoises procèdent à un contrôle approfondi des moyens d'existence et du risque de séjour illégal, par exemple par dépassement de la durée de séjour autorisée. Ce contrôle est effectué notamment grâce à une vérification auprès de la personne de référence indiquée par le demandeur. Lors de cette vérification, les autorités sont guidées par des éléments comme les antécédents de la personne de référence, les buts du voyage ou encore le risque de tentative d'établissement.

Ces contrôles résultent de la pratique administrative, le cadre législatif et réglementaire est constitué par les seules règles découlant de Schengen.

1.2 Existe-t-il une procédure permettant de tracer les personnes dont le visa a expiré? Quel genre de données sont recueillies lors du dépôt d'une demande de visas (empreintes digitales, par exemple)? Les données recueillies peuvent-elles être communiquées aux autorités policières ou étrangères?

Aucune procédure systématique ou automatisée permettant de tracer les personnes dont le visa a expiré n'est en place. Toutefois, la base de donnée nationale permet de vérifier cette donnée au cas par cas. Sur la base de ces informations, le service compétent procède à des contrôles épisodiques, notamment lorsque les renseignements en sa possession permettent de supposer un risque de séjour illégal.

A noter que dans le cadre des discussions en cours au niveau de l'UE pour la mise en place d'un Système d'information visa (VIS), un enregistrement systématique des sorties du territoire Schengen est envisagé.

La demande de visa est recueillie à l'aide du formulaire uniforme Schengen. Les informations recueillies sont en conséquence essentiellement celles contenues sur ce formulaire. Il est par ailleurs toujours loisible aux autorités consulaires et à l'autorité nationale compétente de demander des renseignements complémentaires, s'ils l'estiment nécessaire pour la bonne instruction du dossier. Une prise des empreintes digitales n'est pas effectuée. Toutefois, l'UE a décidé d'inclure ces données à l'avenir sur la vignette uniforme. La banque de donnée luxembourgeoise et le VIS devront en tenir compte.

La législation nationale permet la communication des données relatives aux demandes de visas par le Ministère des Affaires étrangères au Ministère de la Justice, à la Police grand-ducale et au Service compétent pour la sécurité nationale.

En outre, les données sont communiquées aux autorités des Etats parties à Schengen, dans les cas où une consultation est prévue au titre de Schengen.

1.3 Les juridictions se sont-elles déjà prononcées sur un refus de demande de visa dans le cadre de Schengen au motif qu'elle provenait d'un ressortissant d'un pays figurant sur la "liste noire" des Etats membres?

Lors d'une des très rares affaires portées devant les juridictions luxembourgeoises, ces dernières ont retenu que «le refus de l'intéressé de prêter son concours à l'instruction de sa demande justifie le refus d'un visa touristique lorsqu'il met les autorités administratives compétentes dans l'impossibilité de procéder à un examen de sa situation personnelle. Une audition personnelle est justifiée pour éclairer les autorités administratives compétentes relativement aux éléments de fait qui sont apparus lors de la vérification de la situation personnelle et professionnelle de l'intéressé au Luxembourg» (TA 30-5-01, 12475, confirmé par arrêt du 4-12-01, 13713C).

1.4 Quelles ont été les mesures prises afin de mettre en œuvre le programme d'action en matière de coopération administrative dans le domaine du contrôle aux frontières extérieures, des questions de visas, d'immigration et de demandes d'asile en application de la décision du Conseil du 13 juin 2002?

Ce programme d'action, encore dénommé ARGO, est un des programmes classiques offerts par l'UE pour encourager financièrement les Etats membres à réaliser ensemble certaines activités. Par le passé, le Luxembourg n'a pas présenté de projets ou de demandes de financement sous le programme ARGO.

1.5 Quelles démarches ont été entreprises afin de transposer la directive communautaire 2001/51/CE du Conseil du 28 juin 2001 visant à compléter les dispositions de la Convention d'application de l'accord de Schengen relativement aux sanctions imposées aux transporteurs? Ces sanctions ont-elles souvent été appliquées?

Les autorités luxembourgeoises ont entamé des réflexions internes en vue de la transposition de cette directive.

L'article 26 de la Convention d'application de l'Accord de Schengen est transposé en droit luxembourgeois par l'article 33 de la loi modifiée du 28 mars 1972 concernant 1. l'entrée et le séjour des étrangers, 2. le contrôle médical des étrangers, 3. l'emploi de la main d'œuvre étrangère.

Aucun cas d'application de cette sanction n'est connu.

1.6 Selon vous, le droit et les politiques relatifs aux visas en vigueur dans votre pays respectent-ils les exigences de l'Union européenne en la matière ou des ajustements sont-ils nécessaires?

En matière de visas, le droit et les politiques luxembourgeoises respectent les exigences de l'UE. Cela a été par ailleurs confirmé dans le passé par les évaluations Schengen.

Pensez-vous qu'une harmonisation communautaire des réglementations en matière de visas soit indispensable concernant notamment:

- les critères communs d'octroi des visas visant à harmoniser les obligations pesant en ce domaine sur les Etats participant au processus de Budapest;

Concernant le processus de Budapest, les autorités luxembourgeoises ne suivent pas ce processus de manière assidue. Disposant d'une administration publique aux ressources humaines limitées, le Luxembourg se consacre prioritairement aux travaux de l'UE et subsidiairement à ceux du Benelux. Par ailleurs, on est en droit de se poser la question de la relevance du processus de Budapest après l'élargissement de l'UE en juin 2004.

Par rapport aux critères communs d'octroi des visas, une des questions à soulever est celle de l'intégration de l'acquis de Schengen dans le droit communautaire. En effet, la solution trouvée à l'époque pour cette intégration était spécialement conçue, sui generis, et a laissé persister toute une panoplie de textes qui ne correspondent pas à la typologie des actes communautaires. Au premier plan de ces derniers figurent le Manuel commun Schengen pour les gardes frontières et les Instructions consulaires communes (ICC). La Commission européenne réfléchit à une communautarisation de ces textes sous forme de règlements. Tant les ICC que le Manuel commun contiennent un nombre impressionnant de règles pratiques et de détails de procédures indispensables au bon fonctionnement de l'espace Schengen. L'exercice de révision que cette opération implique, fera certainement ressortir les dispositions problématiques, les différences d'interprétation, les règles devenues obsolètes en pratique, et en conséquence les besoins d'harmonisation.

On peut également noter que l'UE a récemment été amenée à régler un certain nombre de situations très spécifiques et de développer des solutions novatrices : création de documents de transit spéciaux pour les personnes transitant entre la Russie et son enclave de Kaliningrad; incorporation du visa dans la carte d'accréditation olympique pour les jeux d'Athènes. La Commission a également soumis une proposition concernant ce qu'on appelle communément le petit trafic frontalier. Ces différentes initiatives n'intéressent certes pas le Luxembourg au premier chef, mais les autorités luxembourgeoises ne négligent pas pour autant les effets indirects que ces textes peuvent avoir étant donné la liberté de circulation qui existe à l'intérieur de l'espace Schengen.

- la création d'un système européen d'identification des visas (VIS et SIS II).

Le bon fonctionnement du VIS présuppose non seulement une réglementation harmonisée, mais encore des pratiques administratives très similaires dans l'application de la réglementation commune. Or, le degré d'harmonisation des pratiques administratives est très difficile à quantifier.

L'espace Schengen, comme l'UE d'ailleurs, se caractérise par des règles communes mais une exécution par des autorités nationales et sous la responsabilité de ces dernières. Le VIS permettra d'uniformiser davantage ces pratiques à travers un instrument informatique commun. Le VIS constituera un outil commun très important pour la gestion de la politique commune des visas.

Il n'est pas à exclure que le développement et la mise en œuvre du VIS (et du SIS II) fasse apparaître des divergences d'interprétation relatives aux règles existantes auxquelles il faudra remédier par des mesures législatives.

1.7 Dans quelle mesure le processus d'élargissement de l'Union européenne représente-t-il une opportunité ou, au contraire, un danger dans la lutte contre l'immigration clandestine et le contrôle des frontières?

A l'élargissement est lié une crainte d'immigration illégale, ou du moins semi-legale, intra-communautaire. Les gouvernements des Etats membres ont réagi face à cette crainte en instaurant des périodes transitoires pour la libre circulation des travailleurs. Seul l'avenir pourra dire si cette crainte est justifiée. Lors de l'élargissement de l'UE à l'Espagne et au Portugal, le Luxembourg avait demandé et obtenu une période transitoire de 10 ans pour les ressortissants portugais à cause de la très grande communauté portugaise présente à Luxembourg. A mi-chemin, donc après 5 ans, le Luxembourg a aboli les restrictions car les craintes qui en étaient à la base ne se sont pas vérifiées.

En ce qui concerne l'immigration clandestine extra-communautaire, certains Etats membres actuels devront faire l'expérience que le Luxembourg a faite lors de la suppression des frontières intérieures : la perte de l'outil de maîtrise des flux migratoires qu'est le contrôle frontalier. On pense ici aux frontières terrestres Est de l'espace Schengen. C'est partiellement la crainte de la perte de la maîtrise de ce pouvoir de contrôle qui est à la base de la dynamique que l'on peut observer actuellement au sein de l'UE concernant la gestion des frontières extérieures.

Certes, certains Etats membres actuels se plaignent du fait qu'étant les plus exposés de part leur situation géographique, ils doivent assumer seul la charge de contrôler les frontières extérieures (communes). De ce fait ils poussent fortement vers une meilleure solidarité entre Etats membres, laquelle devrait être, à leurs yeux, surtout financière.

Conscient du fait que les Etats adhérents assureront le jour de leur participation à l'espace Schengen, le contrôle des frontières extérieures parmi les plus vulnérables en terme d'immigration illégale, les Etats membres actuels mettent tout en œuvre pour que ce contrôle ait lieu selon les règles de l'art et pour qu'ils gardent un droit de regard sur ce qui se passe sur ces nouvelles frontières extérieures. La création de l'Agence pour la coordination du contrôle aux frontières extérieures s'inscrit pleinement dans cette logique.

PARTIE II LES PROCÉDURES D'ACCUEIL ET LE DROIT DE SÉJOUR DES RESSORTISSANTS DES PAYS TIERS

Les règles applicables sont celles de la loi modifiée du 28 mars 1972 concernant 1. l'entrée et le séjour des étrangers, 2. le contrôle médical des étrangers, 3. l'emploi de la main d'œuvre étrangère; du règlement grand-ducal modifié du 28 mars 1972 relatif aux formalités à remplir par les étrangers séjournant au pays; du règlement grand-ducal modifié du 12 mai 1972 déterminant les mesures applicables pour l'emploi des travailleurs étrangers sur le territoire du Grand-Duché de Luxembourg.

La législation luxembourgeoise se caractérise par des règles souvent très générales qui parfois même s'apparentent plus à des principes qu'à de véritables règles législatives ou réglementaires. Ainsi, par exemple, un certain nombre de situations, que la Commission européenne a proposé de réglementer par des textes spécifiques, n'ont jamais été spécifiquement prises en considération par le législateur luxembourgeois : le regroupement familial, l'entrée et le séjour aux fins de l'exercice d'une activité non salariée, le résident de longue durée ou encore l'entrée et le séjour aux fins d'études.

Cet état des choses laisse un pouvoir d'appréciation très (trop ?) élevé à l'administration compétente, ce qui s'accompagne de la possibilité de réagir avec flexibilité à un environnement en pleine évolution. Pour ne prendre que la seule loi de mars 1972, elle n'a fait l'objet que de 8 changements depuis son entrée en vigueur. Il n'y a eu aucune modification entre 1977 et 1993. Les changements des années 90 étaient surtout dûs à la mise en conformité de la législation nationale avec les règles Schengen.

De plus, la législation luxembourgeoise approche la question de l'immigration non pas en déterminant un certain nombre de règles positives applicables à telle ou telle catégorie, mais elle se contente au contraire de dispositions générales prescrivant sous quelles conditions l'entrée et le séjour peuvent être refusés à l'étranger.

A cet égard, l'article 2 de la loi de 1972 est symptomatique en ce qu'il stipule que : «L'entrée et le séjour au Grand-Duché pourront être refusés à l'étranger:

- qui est dépourvu de papiers de légitimation prescrits, et de visa si celui-ci est requis,
- qui est susceptible de compromettre la sécurité, la tranquillité, l'ordre ou la santé publics,
- qui ne dispose pas de moyens personnels suffisants pour supporter les frais de voyage et de séjour.»

Les différentes initiatives communautaires se caractérisent en revanche par des règles précises, par l'énumération de conditions à remplir et droits accordés. La législation luxembourgeois actuelle ne pourra que très difficilement résister à une révision complète lors de la transposition des textes communautaires. Le gouvernement et le législateur auront devant eux, dans un proche avenir, un important chantier législatif et réglementaire.

2.1 Quels sont les principes fondamentaux dans votre pays concernant:
– l'entrée des ressortissants des pays tiers afin d'exercer une activité salariée ou une activité économique indépendante;

L'article 2 précité de la loi de 1972 est complété par des dispositions réglementaires qui précisent que l'étranger qui veut s'établir au pays doit présenter le document sous le couvert duquel il est entré, présenter un certificat médical, produire un extrait récent du casier judiciaire ou un certificat de bonne vie et mœurs, justifier d'un logement adéquat et «justifier de moyens d'existence personnels suffisants ou de la possibilité de les acquérir de manière légale».

Pour le travailleur salarié, la réglementation précise qu'aucun étranger ne peut occuper un emploi sans y être autorisé. Le travailleur étranger doit donc être en possession du permis de travail dont la délivrance est du ressort du Ministre du Travail et de l'Emploi.

Il faut lire cette règle ensemble avec celle qui oblige les employeurs à déclarer toute vacance de poste aux autorités, avec celle qui accorde une priorité à l'embauche aux citoyens européens et aux ressortissants de l'Espace économique européen, ainsi qu'avec celle qui prévoit que l'octroi ou le renouvellement du permis de travail peuvent être refusés au travailleur étranger pour des raisons inhérentes «à la situation, à l'évolution ou à l'organisation du marché de l'emploi».

L'administration luxembourgeoise dispose ainsi de tous les outils réglementaires nécessaires à la régulation de l'entrée et du séjour des travailleurs migrants en fonction de l'offre et de la demande présente sur le marché du travail.

En ce qui concerne l'entrée et le séjour aux fins de l'exercice d'une activité indépendante, l'étranger devra se conformer à la législation applicable aux différents métiers, professions et activités. Ce n'est que lors qu'il disposera d'une autorisation d'établissement en tant qu'indépendant qu'il remplira au yeux de la loi et du Ministère de la Justice le critère de «justifier de moyens d'existence personnels suffisants ou de la possibilité de les acquérir de manière légale».

- l'entrée des ressortissants des pays tiers afin de faire des études ou de suivre une formation professionnelle;

Aucune disposition en droit luxembourgeois ne règle spécifiquement l'entrée et le séjour aux fins d'études. Ici les mêmes règles générales que décrites supra s'appliquent (ressources suffisantes, logement, etc.). En ce qui concerne l'enseignement post-secondaire, le Ministère de la Justice suit de manière générale, les décisions d'inscription académique des établissements d'enseignement. En revanche, pour l'enseignement secondaire, voire primaire, les autorités ont une approche très restrictive. A noter que pour les étudiants admis au pays, il n'ont pas le droit de travailler.

Le législateur devra remédier à ces lacunes de la législation et créer des règles spécifiques aux étudiants d'une part à cause de la directive européenne le jour où elle sera adoptée, et d'autre part, d'un point de vue national, pour tenir compte du nombre plus élevé d'étudiants étrangers qui s'annonce suite à la création en 2003 de la nouvelle Université du Luxembourg.

Les stagiaires et les apprentis sont assimilés à des travailleurs. Les règles décrites sous le tiret précédent leurs sont donc applicables. Sur ce point également, le droit luxembourgeois est en conflit avec la proposition de directive.

- le statut juridique des ressortissants qui bénéficient d'un droit de séjour de longue durée dans un autre Etat membre;

Le droit luxembourgeois ne connaît ni un «statut» spécifique pour les ressortissants de longue durée, ni même la notion de «droit de séjour de longue durée».

Néanmoins, certains éléments d'un tel statut peuvent être trouvés. Ainsi, l'étranger qui entre pour la première fois au Luxembourg en vue d'y séjourner se voit délivrer une autorisation provisoire de séjour d'une durée de validité d'un an. Certaines catégories de personnes se voient délivrer plusieurs autorisations de séjour provisoires successives. En règle générale, l'autorisation de séjour provisoire donne cependant droit à la présentation d'une demande de carte d'identité d'étranger. La durée de validité de cette carte d'identité d'étranger est en principe de 5 ans, renouvelable. Aucun permis de séjour d'une durée plus longue n'est prévu.

Au niveau de l'autorisation de travail, la législation a prévu une progression en étapes. Le permis de base délivré à un nouvel immigrant est le permis A (valable pour un an, une seule profession et un seul employeur). Après une période de résidence et d'occupation d'un an, le travailleur peut prétendre à un permis B (valable 4 ans, pour une seule profession mais pour tout employeur). Après cinq ans de résidence et d'occupation, le travailleur peut prétendre à un permis C (durée de validité non limitée, pour toute profession et tout employeur).

La directive sur les résidents de longue durée, nécessitera d'une part le regroupement de différentes dispositions existantes (également au niveau du droit social) pour en faire les éléments constitutifs d'un nouveau statut, et d'autre part la transposition de certains droits prévus par la directive mais non par la législation nationale.

2.2 Quels sont les exigences juridiques et les procédures requises en vertu du droit national pour obtenir un titre de séjour permettant aux ressortissants des pays tiers de travailler dans le pays d'accueil? Quelles sont les procédures utilisées afin de maintenir la préférence en faveur des citoyens de l'Union européenne et des nationaux de Turquie (en application de l'accord d'association) dans leur accès au marché du travail?

Voir la réponse sous 2.1. premier tiret. A noter que hormis les citoyens européens et les ressortissants des Etats membres de l'EEE, aucun accès préférentiel au marché du travail n'est accordé.

2.2 Existe-t-il des programmes spécifiques en faveur des professionnels qualifiés leur facilitant l'accès au marché du travail? Quelle est le degré d'implication des syndicats et des employeurs dans ce genre de programmes?

A notre connaissance, de tels programmes n'existent pas.

2.2 Y a t il une procédure visant à évaluer la demande pour des travailleurs étrangers?

Tel que décrit sous le point 2.1., c'est la demande de main d'œuvre émanant des employeurs et l'offre de main d'œuvre communautaire déterminent la possibilité pour le recrutement de travailleurs étrangers. Aucune procédure d'évaluation n'est prévue en dehors de ce mécanisme.

2.2 Dans quelle mesure l'élargissement de l'Union européenne est-il pris en considération?

L'élargissement de l'UE n'est pas pris en compte à l'heure actuelle.

2.2 Quel a été l'impact de la récession économique récente et de l'augmentation corrélative du chômage sur le concept de l'admission des ressortissants des pays tiers?

Le ralentissement de l'économie n'a pas eu d'impact sur la législation en matière d'admission des ressortissants de pays tiers aux fins d'emploi. Il n'y a pas eu non plus de discussion politique en ce sens. Ceci est probablement dû au fait que la législation actuelle permet de réguler les flux migratoires en fonction des besoins du marché du travail.

2.3 Dans quelle mesure les droits et pratiques nationaux en vigueur diffèrent-ils substantiellement de l'approche adoptée par la Commission dans sa proposition sur la politique d'admission à des fins de l'exercice d'une activité salariée ou d'une activité professionnelle indépendante, concernant notamment:
- **l'entrée des ressortissants des pays tiers aux fins d'études et de formation professionnelle;**
- **le statut juridique des ressortissants des pays tiers qui ont un titre de séjour de longue durée accorder par un autre Etat membre;**

Dans la mesure où la législation luxembourgeoise en matière d'entrée et de séjour s'applique en relation très étroite avec celle sur l'emploi de la main d'œuvre étrangère, elle est conceptuellement très proche de la proposition de directive de la Commission relative à l'entrée et au séjour aux fins de l'exercice d'une activité salariée.

La différence majeure entre l'approche européenne et la législation luxembourgeoise se situe au niveau administratif. Même si en droit luxembourgeois, droit de séjour et accès au territoire sont très liés, la personne concernée, respectivement son employeur, doit entamer deux procédures distinctes, une auprès du Ministère de la Justice et une auprès du Ministère du Travail. La personne concernée se voit délivrer en fin de procédure deux documents distincts, le permis de séjour et le permis de travail. La Commission en revanche n'envisage qu'un seul document « permis de séjour – travailleur » avec pour le demandeur une « one stop procedure ».

Au niveau des droits accordés, des divergences existent également entre la proposition européenne et les textes nationaux.

Concernant l'entrée et le séjour aux fins d'études et de formation professionnelle, il y a lieu d'indiquer que la législation luxembourgeoise se caractérise de nouveau par l'absence presque totale de dispositions spécifiques. Même si la pratique administrative ne dévie que très peu de l'approche proposée par la Commission, le législateur devra faire un effort considérable de transposition.

La différence majeure avec l'approche européenne tient au champ d'application. Les autorités nationales ne prennent en compte à l'heure actuelle que les demandes d'entrée d'étudiants (niveau universitaire). Sont donc exclus les élèves (enseignement secondaire) et la formation professionnelle. De plus, les échanges d'étudiants ou le volontariat ne sont considérés que sur une base ad hoc. Concernant les étudiants, la législation luxembourgeoise exclut tout accès à une activité salariée, contrairement à la proposition de directive qui prévoit un accès limité.

Concernant les résidents de longue durée, comme expliqué plus tôt ce concept est inconnu des autorités luxembourgeoises à l'heure actuelle.

2.4 Quelles démarches ont été entreprises afin de transposer en droit national la directive du 29 juin 2000 relative au principe de non-discrimination en fonction de la race ou de l'origine ethnique et la directive du Conseil du 27 novembre 2000 établissant un cadre général d'égalité de traitement sur le lieu de travail? Est-ce que des réformes législatives ont été entrepris? Dans quelle mesure le recours à la notion de "discrimination positive" est-il jugé nécessaire afin de promouvoir l'égalité des chances en faveur des travailleurs immigrés en provenance des pays tiers?

Le gouvernement a déposé en date du 21 novembre 2003 un projet de loi portant transposition de la directive 2000/43/CE. L'objectif en est d'adapter la législation en étendant la notion de discrimination tant à la discrimination directe et indirecte, qu'au harcèlement et à l'injonction de pratiquer une discrimination. Pour les affaires en justice, le renversement de la charge de la preuve sera étendu aux cas de discriminations fondées sur la race ou l'origine ethnique.

En outre, le droit de certaines associations d'ester en justice afin de défendre les droits des victimes de discriminations fondées sur la race ou l'origine ethnique sera étendu par le projet de loi.

Aucun recours à la notion de discrimination positive n'est envisagé.

2.5 Concernant la proposition de directive sur le droit au regroupement familial présentée par le Conseil en février 2003,

– pensez-vous que les critères proposés soient en deça des principes relatifs au regroupement familial actuellement en vigueur dans votre pays?
– la mise en œuvre de cette directive, une fois adoptée, va-t-elle conduire à des changements dans votre système juridique national sur le droit au regroupement familial et qui abaissent le niveau de protection existant? Si c'est le cas, quels changements sont envisagés?

Il est difficile de fournir une réponse adéquate à cette question étant donné que premièrement aucune disposition législative nationale ne traite spécifiquement du droit au regroupement familial, tout dépend donc de la pratique, que deuxièmement la directive prévoit une multitude de clauses optionnelles et que troisièmement le gouvernement ne s'est pas encore penché sur la manière dont il entend transposer la directive.

Il est toutefois probable que dans la transposition, le regroupement soit limité à la famille nucléaire et aux ascendants dépendants, ce qui correspond à la pratique actuelle et que l'âge pour le regroupement des enfants soit maintenu à 18 ans. En ce qui concerne le regroupement de partenaires non mariés, actuellement non permis, le débat se posera en des termes différents suite à l'adoption du projet de loi instituant un partenariat enregistré dont le vote est prévu pour le printemps 2004.

La pratique nationale quant à l'accès au marché du travail devra également être revue, en particulier en ce qui concerne le conjoint.

2.6 La proposition de directive sur les droits des résidents de longue durée telle que présentée par le Conseil le 5 juin 2003 prévoit un certain nombre de droits visant à approximer le statut des résidents de longue duré avec celui des citoyens de l'Union européenne. L'application de ce texte communautaire va-t-elle conduire à des réformes juridiques et politiques importantes dans votre pays? Quelles seront les questions essentielles soulevées, le cas échéant, par le processus d'approximation envisagée par la directive à l'égard notamment:
– du principe de non-discrimination dans le domaine des droits sociaux;
– du concept de "citoyen civique" (voir aussi l'évaluation de l'impact de la communication sur l'intégration du 11 juin 2003);
– du droit au regroupement familial et de l'accès des membres de la famille au marché du travail;
– de la garantie du droit de rester sur le territoire.

Quant aux droits sociaux (article 11 de la directive) aucune mesure fondamentale de transposition ne s'avère nécessaire.

En matière de protection contre l'éloignement, la directive introduit des nouveautés quant aux éléments à prendre en compte (article 12.3) et en ce que l'éloignement ne peut intervenir pour des raisons économiques (article 12.2).

Finalement, la nouveauté principale de la directive est le droit de séjourner dans un autre Etat membre, même si ce droit est soumis à des conditions strictes, en particulier en ce qui concerne l'exercice d'une activité économique.

2.7 En ayant à l'esprit la perspective d'une future politique commune en matière d'immigration telle qu'élaborée par la Commission dans sa communication sur la coordination ouverte (COM 2001/387) et sa communication sur la politique de l'immigration de l'Union européenne (COM 2000/757, version finale), comment envisagez-vous le rôle des institutions communautaires dans la définition d'un telle politique concernant notamment les compétences des Etats membres pour décider du droit de séjour, de l'accès au marché du travail et de l'intégration? L'harmonisation des législations nationales doit-elle aller plus loin, et si oui, dans quelle mesure?

Dans une Union sans frontières intérieures et basé sur une communauté économique, le cadre de référence de l'immigration légale, y inclus l'accès au marché du travail, doit être un cadre de référence commun et harmonisé. C'est également là une question de transparence et de lisibilité pour les candidats à l'immigration. Il ne faut pas non plus perdre de vue les risques de mouvements secondaires, d'immigrants et de candidats à l'immigration, entre les Etats membres dus à des différences sensibles dans les conditions d'entrée et de séjour. Vu sa situation géographique, ceci est un problème qui concerne de près le Luxembourg.

Au-delà du cadre de référence, les autorités nationales doivent garder une marge d'appréciation dans les cas individuels qui se présentent à eux pour pouvoir tenir compte de spécificités nationales, voire régionales. Ceci vaut en particulier pour l'accès au marché de l'emploi.

Même si les Etats membres sont assez réticents vis-à-vis d'une politique de coordination ouverte à cause de la charge de travail qu'elle implique, il est néanmoins essentiel qu'au niveau européen on dispose de toutes les informations, des statistiques et autres données, nécessaires à une juste appréciation de la situation. Cela vaut non seulement pour les flux migratoires de ressortissants de pays tiers vers et au départ l'UE, mais également pour les flux au sein de l'UE.

PARTIE III LA RÉGLEMENTATION APPLICABLE AUX DEMANDEURS D'ASILE ET AUX RÉFUGIÉS

3.1 Les règles de Dublin ont-elles fonctionné de facon satisfaisante jusqu'à présent et qu'attend-on du règlement 343/2003 du 18 février 2003 (Dublin II)?

Trop de divergences d'interprétation sont apparues au fil des années dans l'application de la Convention de Dublin par les autorités nationales des Etats membres, chacune essayant trop souvent de faire peser la charge sur l'autre. Le règlement Dublin II a apporté certaines des clarifications attendues et a amélioré les procédures. Un effort notable est également en cours pour moderniser les voies de communication entre les autorités compétentes des Etats membres.

De plus, le règlement Dublin II règle de manière plus équitable la compétence des Etats membres qui sont confrontés aux afflux massifs d'illégaux aux frontières extérieures dont il ont la charge.

3.2 **Le règlement 2725/2000 du Conseil du 11 décembre 2000 relatif à la création du système Eurodac pour la comparaison des empreintes digitales aux fins de l'application efficace de la Convention de Dublin, et en vigueur depuis le 15 janvier 2003, a-t-il eu pour résultat une augmentation des affaires en ce domaine? Eurodac est-il déjà effective dans votre pays ou, sinon, le sera-t-il dans l'avenir?**

Eurodac fonctionne pleinement depuis le 15 janvier 2003. Le Luxembourg a connu une hausse notable des cas d'application de la Convention de Dublin, augmentation supérieure au taux d'augmentation des demandes d'asile.

3.3 **Quels changements significatifs impliquent la transposition de la directive (telle qu'amendée et pour la majorité de quelle le Conseil a obtenu un accord politique en juin 2003) relative aux normes minimales applicables dans le cadre des procédures nationales d'octroi et de retrait du statut de réfugié, pour la législation et la pratique dans votre pays, en termes notamment:**
- **de droits procéduraux des demandeurs;**
- **de recours administratifs ou judiciaires;**
- **d'utilisation des concepts de "safe third country" et "safe country of origin" (Etats tiers ou Etats d'origine garantissant les droits des demandeurs);**
- **de la détention des demandeurs d'asile;**
- **des procédures de contrôle dans les aéroports et aux frontières.**

La proposition de directive sur les procédures d'asile, du moins dans la dernière version sur la table de négociation, implique un changement conceptuel pour le traitement de certaines demandes. Ainsi la distinction entre demandes non fondées et demandes manifestement infondées, telle que prévue par le droit luxembourgeois, serait remplacée par une distinction entre procédure normale et procédure accélérée avec la possibilité de recourir à cette dernière tout au long de la procédure, en fonction d'événements spécifiques.

Au niveau des droits procéduraux, la directive apportera des clarifications en ce qui concerne la notification des décisions ou encore les auditions des demandeurs d'asile. Elle permettra également de revoir le droit à l'assistance judiciaire gratuite.

Concernant les voies de recours, la proposition de directive n'oblige pas en l'état le Luxembourg à revoir sa législation, mais ouvre néanmoins certaines possibilités en direction d'une limitation des voies de recours.

Le concept de pays tiers sûr n'est que très peu appliqué au Luxembourg car il se heurte à des difficultés de preuve et à la question des accords de réadmission. La directive n'y changera rien.

Le concept de pays d'origine sûr ouvrira de nouvelles possibilités en ce sens que les autorités nationales pourront appliquer d'office la procédure accélérée aux personnes originaires des pays d'origine figurant sur la future liste commune européenne.

En ce qui concerne la détention et les procédures de contrôle à la frontière, la directive apportera peu de changements au Luxembourg.

3.4 Quelles ont été les mesures prises dans votre pays afin de transposer la directive communautaire 2003/9/CE du Conseil du 27 janvier 2003 relative à l'accueil des demandeurs d'asile dans les Etats membres? Vous insisterez sur les points particuliers suivants:
- **les clauses de flexibilité dans la directive;**
- **les restrictions à la libre circulation;**
- **l'accès au marché du travail;**
- **les droits des travailleurs immigrés en vertu de l'article 11 paragraphe 2 de la directive.**

Une première série d'articles ayant trait à l'octroi d'une aide sociale aux demandeurs d'asile a été transposée par le règlement grand-ducal du 4 juillet 2002.

Certaines flexibilités ont été utilisées comme par exemple les possibilités de réduction des conditions d'accueil en fonction du comportement de la personne et de sa volonté de coopération avec les autorités. D'autre volets comme les restrictions à la libre circulation ou l'accès au marché du travail n'ont pas encore été transposés. Il n'est pas à exclure que dans ce contexte le gouvernement songe à l'introduction de structures d'accueil fermées pour certaines catégories de demandeurs d'asile, à l'instar de ce qui se fait dans les pays limitrophes.

La politique du Luxembourg étant de ne pas donner d'accès au marché du travail aux demandeurs d'asile, il est peu probable que les autorités aillent au-delà des obligations minimales prévues par la directive.

3.5 Quelles démarches ont été entreprises en droit national afin de transposer la directive 2001/55/CE du Conseil du 20 juillet 2001 relative à l'octroi d'une protection temporaire en cas d'afflux massif de personnes déplacées? Existe-t-il des procédures visant à la répartition des efforts consentis par les Etats membres

en ce domaine? Y-a-t-il un fondement juridique ouvrant droit à des mesures de protection temporaire pour des réfugiés dans le contexte d'une immigration de masse?

La directive 2001/55/UE n'a pas encore été transposée.

La législation luxembourgeoise prévoit depuis mars 2000 un régime de protection temporaire introduit suite à l'afflux massif de demandeurs d'asile dans le contexte de la guerre du Kosovo. Le régime n'a encore jamais été mis en œuvre.

3.6 Les membres du Conseil se sont mis d'un accord politique sur les principes d'une directive relative aux normes minimales requises en matière de qualification et de statut des ressortissants des Etats tiers en tant que réfugiés ou personnes exigeant une protection internationale (proposition COM 2001/510, voir les documents du Conseil de juin 2003). Quelles sont les mesures envisagées au niveau national afin de transposer cette directive en ce qui concerne:
- **la définition du réfugié;**
- **la définition des personnes ayant droit à une protection complémentaire;**
- **le statut des personnes ayant droit à une protection complémentaire;**
- **la question de l'alternative d'un vol interne telle que défini par la directive;**
- **les dispositions relatives aux exceptions, notamment liées au terrorisme (exclusion clause).**

Dans quelle mesure les politiques internes visant les réfugiés telles que reflétées dans le droit et la jurisprudence de votre pays sont-elles conformes à la proposition de directive?

En l'état actuel de la proposition de directive, un effort de transposition attend le Luxembourg. La définition du réfugié n'est pas explicitée outre mesure dans la législation luxembourgeoise qui se contente de renvoyer à la Convention de Genève. Néanmoins les critères retenus par la proposition de directive sont largement en ligne avec ceux consacrés par la jurisprudence nationale. Quelques développements peuvent être attendus au sujet des agents de persécution.

L'introduction d'un statut de protection subsidiaire est une nouveauté totale. Il en va de même pour les clauses d'exclusion, la législation actuelle se référant uniquement à l'article 1.F de la Convention de Genève. En revanche, le traitement de la possibilité de fuite interne n'apportera rien de nouveau.

3.7 Dans la communication de la Commission du 22 novembre 2000 (COM 2000/755; voir aussi le second rapport de la Commission, COM 2003/152), on trouve l'idée d'une procédure communautaire commune d'asile et un statut uniforme à travers l'Union des personnes bénéficiaires d'un droit d'asile. Considérez-vous que cette idée soit généralement en accord avec votre politique nationale en matière de droit d'asile? Les craintes émises par certaines organisations de

protection des droits des réfugiés, telle qu'Amnesty International, concernant une diminution éventuelle du niveau international de protection des réfugiés sont-elles partagées par les cercles politiques chargés de prendre les décisions dans votre pays?

L'idée d'une procédure communautaire commune d'asile et d'un statut uniforme correspond aux attentes du gouvernement luxembourgeois. Ainsi dans une récente intervention le Ministre de la Justice a déclaré: «Dans le domaine de l'asile deux principes sont importants. Premièrement l'attachement de l'Union en tant que communauté de valeurs aux principes de l'asile et de la protection internationale. L'Union est et doit rester une terre d'accueil pour les personnes qui ont besoin de notre protection. Deuxièmement, la question de l'asile et les problèmes d'abus et de flux secondaires doivent recevoir une réponse européenne commune, unique et solidaire. La Constitution parle d'un système européen commun d'asile avec à la clef un statut uniforme valable dans toute l'Union. C'est un grand progrès par rapport au système actuel, caractérisé par de nombreux systèmes nationaux divergents et quelques règles minimales négociées avec difficulté au niveau européen. Le statut d'asile doit devenir un statut européen. La voie de l'harmonisation doit conduire à terme à un système communautaire autonome. C'est par lois et non par lois-cadres qu'il faut progresser.»

Les craintes formulées par certaines organisations comme Amnesty Internationl ne sont pas partagées par les autorités, du moins pas publiquement. En revanche, l'opinion en particulier du HCR a un poids certain.

3.8 La méthode de coordination ouverte telle que suggérée par la Commission prévoyait un premier et un deuxième étape dans le processus d'adoption de la législation au cours desquelles les dispositions offrant une certaine discrétion aux autorités nationales figurant dans certaines des directives sur l'immigration et le droit d'asile devaient être remplacées par une harmonisation totale. Cela est-il discuté dans votre pays et quelle est la perception de la mise en place progressive d'une politique communautaire relative au droit d'asile qui remplacera, au bout du compte, les procédures et les mesures adoptées au niveau national?

Une discussion sur ces points n'a pas vraiment lieu. De l'intervention du Ministre de la Justice reprise ci-dessus, on pourrait tirer la conclusion que le Luxembourg y serait assez favorable.

3.9 La Communication de juin 2003 visant à organiser un système plus accessible et équitable en matière de droit d'asile – en réaction notamment à la proposition britannique – envisage de nouvelles approches afin d'assurer une arrivée mieux

organisée des personnes nécessitant une protection internationale. Quelle a été la réaction politique dans votre pays à l'égard d'une politique d'asile commune, de la répartition des réfugiées entre les Etats membres ainsi que du partage des responsabilités et autres nouvelles approches et idées qu'implique la prise en charge d'un afflux massif de réfugiés?

La réaction aux idées britanniques a été très réservée. Néanmoins, confronté, comme d'autres pays, au problème quasi insoluble des demandeurs d'asile dont une infime minorité se voit accordée le statut de réfugié, le Luxembourg se doit d'être à l'écoute de nouvelles approches en la matière, telle que l'initiative « A revised EU PRONG proposal » du HCR.

PARTIE IV SANCTIONS DES RESSORTISSANTS EN SITUATION IRRÉGULIÈRE, RETOUR ET RAPATRIEMENT

4.1 Combien, selon les estimations fournies, de ressortissants de pays tiers sans titre de séjour valable sont-ils dans votre pays? Combien d'expulsions ont-été ordonnées ces précédentes années? L'ensemble du processus de mise en œuvre de ces mesures est-t-il considéré comme acceptable?

Aucune estimation à cet égard n'est disponible.

En ce qui concerne le retour des demandeurs d'asile déboutés les chiffres s'élèvent à 183 pour 2001, 234 pour 2002 et 708 pour 2003. Pour l'année 2003, s'y ajoutent le retour de 80 personnes qui se trouvaient au Luxembourg en violation de la loi sur le séjour des étrangers.

L'augmentation du nombre de retours ces dernières années est le reflet d'une volonté politique plus déterminée.

Néanmoins comme dans les autres Etats membres, la lutte contre l'immigration illégale et les demandes d'asile manifestement abusives se heurte à des difficultés notables en fin de procédure, c'est-à-dire lors du retour de ces personnes. Le Luxembourg est confronté à des difficultés au niveau de la coopération avec les pays tiers (exécution des rares accords de réadmission, obtention de laissez-passer, etc.). S'y ajoute que vue sa taille, le Luxembourg pèse peu dans les relations bilatérales avec certains grands pays d'origine.

4.2 Quelles démarches ont été entreprises afin de transposer la directive du 28 novembre 2002 relative aux mesures facilitant l'entrée non autorisée sur le territoire, le transit et le droit de séjour?

Aucune démarche en vue de la transposition n'a été entamée.

4.3 Combien de clandestins ont-ils été appréhendés aux frontières ou dans un périmètre proche des frontières? Combien de procédure pour trafic illégal de clandestins ont-elles été mises en œuvre l'année passée?

Ces chiffres ne sont pas connus.

4.4 Quels efforts ont été entrepris dans votre pays concernant les recommandations de Budapest de juin 2003 sur l'harmonisation des échelles de peines applicables aux délits de trafic des immigrés et de traite des êtres humains en accord avec les dispositions de la directive du 28 novembre 2002? Votre pays a-t-il- signé les protocoles des Nations Unies relatifs au trafic des clandestins?

Aucun effort spécifique n'a été entrepris par rapport aux recommandations de Budapest.

4.5 Quelles démarches ont-elles été entreprises afin de mettre en œuvre la directive 2001/40/CE du Conseil du 28 mai 2001 sur la reconnaissance mutuelle des décisions d'éloignement des ressortissants des pays tiers? Quels seraient, le cas échéant, les améliorations à apporter afin de remédier aux défauts et combler les lacunes de la directive en question en vue de l'adoption d'une nouvelle mesure sur la coopération des Etats membres en la matière?

Le gouvernement n'a pas encore pris de mesure de transposition ou déposé de projet de loi à cette fin.

4.6 Existe-t-il dans votre pays des accords de réadmission ou autres arrangements internationaux visant à contrôler et limiter l'immigration clandestine et faciliter le rapatriement? Si c'est le cas, ces accords ont-ils fonctionné de façon satisfaisante?

Très peu d'accords de réadmission ont été conclus par le Luxembourg, encore moins sont en vigueur.

On peut noter que le Luxembourg négocie souvent des accords de réadmission ensemble avec ses partenaires du Benelux.

4.7 Dans quelle mesure les critères et recommandations adoptés dans le cadre de l'Union européenne ont-ils influencé la politique du retour en vigueur dans votre pays? Des efforts de coopération ont-ils été entrepris avec d'autres Etats membres de l'Union européenne afin de mettre en œuvre les mesures d'expulsion et d'éloignement du territoire dans le cadre d'actions communes, d'échanges d'informations, de mesures visant à faciliter le transit aérien ou terrien, de principes communs sur la sécurité dans les avions, etc.?

Une attention accrue a été accordée ces dernières années par les pouvoirs publics aux problèmes liés aux retours.

Des coopérations, souvent informelles, ont lieu avec les autorités des pays voisins. Encore récemment, les ministres du Benelux ont décidé d'étudier l'organisation de retours conjoints dans le cadre de la politique européenne de retour.

4.8 Pensez-vous qu'il soit nécessaire d'élaborer un régime commun juridique de déportation aérienne, avec notamment la nécessité de déterminer le statut juridique des agents de sécurité armés à bord des avions, les droits du pilote de l'avion, les règles applicables en cas d'arrêt de transit, l'applicabilité des règles nationales de police à bord de l'appareil en cours de vol, etc.?

Ces différents points qui conditionnent la mise en œuvre d'une coopération accrue entre les Etat membres et en particulier la réalisation de retours conjoints doivent être résolus, soit au niveau de l'UE, soit à un niveau bilatéral ou régional.

MALTA

DR. KATRINE CAMILLERI LL.D

INTRODUCTION

Malta will become a Member State of the EU in May 2004. The present moment is therefore one of rapid and unprecedented change in various sectors, as Malta strives to bring its laws and policies in line with the *acquis.*

The area of migration and asylum is, without a shadow of doubt, one of those that poses greatest challenges. This is due not only to the fact that significant changes had to be made in national laws and policies in this area as a result of prospective EU membership, but also because, in recent years, there was a dramatic surge in the number of irregular migrants arriving in Malta by boat.[1]

This increase placed considerable pressure on the newly established national structures and procedures for the examination and determination of applications for refugee status, as well as upon domestic immigration laws, policies and structures. It also served to highlight some of the inadequacies of the existing systems and structures, both in the area of asylum and that of immigration, in spite of the recent overhaul carried out in view of EU membership.

At this point in time, the process of adoption of the *acquis* has not yet been fully implemented, it is however envisaged that Malta will be in line by accession in May.

It should be stated at the outset that, in the area of immigration and asylum, there is an almost total absence of clearly formulated policy

[1] During 2002 a total of 21 boats, containing 1686 irregular/undocumented migrants arrived in Malta. All were travelling in an irregular manner, and, from information provided by the Maltese immigration authorities, it would appear that they left from Libya with the intention of travelling to Italy (Seychell, April 11, 2003). In 2003, 497 such migrants arrived in Malta on 11 boats – a significant reduction when compared to the previous year, but still much higher than 2001, when less than 60 migrants arrived in Malta travelling in this manner.

guidelines.[2] Decisions are usually taken on an *ad hoc* basis, and policy is developed piecemeal rather than as a cohesive whole. This lack of clear, written policies made the job of the National Rapporteurs in this area somewhat more difficult.

Most of the information regarding government policy on various issues was obtained from private interviews with the Assistant Commissioner of Police responsible for immigration and the Permanent Secretary at the Ministry for Justice and Home Affairs. NGOs working in the field were also consulted.

Every effort has been made to ensure that the information included in this report is correct.

Entry, visa regime and border control

National legislation regulating various aspects of immigration into Malta was amended and updated a number of times in recent years[3], primarily but not exclusively, in view of Malta's impending EU accession. Among the amendments introduced are the insertion of a provision in the Immigration Act allowing for the imposition of carrier sanctions[4] and the inclusion of provisions in our Criminal Code establishing trafficking in human beings as an offence.[5]

However, although the basic legislative framework is largely in line with the EU *acquis*, the regulations and policies, establishing the procedures and structures necessary for the implementation of national legislation and related EU directives, are still being progressively established.

One significant example is the inclusion of a provision in the Immigration Act[6], authorising the Principal Immigration Officer to impose sanctions upon carriers who transport migrants who are not in possession of

[2] In his report on his visit to Malta, carried out in October 2003, the Council of Europe Human Rights Commissioner, Mr Alvaro Gil-Robles, in fact recommended the drawing up of "a long-term migration policy taking both future challenges and the fundamental rights of migrants into account".

[3] The Immigration Act (Chapter 217 of the Laws of Malta), enacted on September 21, 1970, was amended a number of times in the subsequent years. Many of the more recent amendments, i.e. those brought in by Acts IV and IX of 2000 and Act XXIII of 2002, were introduced in order to align Malta's immigration law with the EU *acquis*.

[4] Section 15 of the Immigration Act.

[5] Section 248A of the Criminal Code, introduced in April 2002.

[6] Introduced by Act XXIII of 2000.

the necessary documentation.[7] To date, the regulations necessary to give effect to this provision have not yet been put in place. Consequently, today, although carriers who transport inadequately documented passengers or passengers using false or fraudulent documents take them back at their own cost, so far none have actually been penalised for doing this.

It is envisaged that, some time before accession, regulations will be put in place to enable the Principal Immigration Officer to impose such sanctions. Only then will we be fully compliant with Directive 2001/51 EC supplementing the Schengen rules concerning carrier sanctions.

To date the system in place for the issue of visas for entry and extensions of stay in Malta is essentially much the same as it has been for the past years. It is envisaged that by accession several significant changes will be introduced, some of which will be briefly outlined in this section. However, in view of the fact that the proposed amendments and/or improvements to existing policy and practice have not been implemented, as well as the fact that clear, detailed and publicly available information regarding the changes to be implemented is limited, it was difficult for the National Rapporteurs to make an accurate assessment of the proposed developments in the light of existing and proposed EU law and policies.

The following is a brief description of the existing laws and procedures in place to regulate the entry and stay of foreign nationals in Malta.

The national authority authorised to deal with visa applications is the Central Immigration Office, within the Immigration Department of the Security Branch of the Malta Police Force. Applications for the issue of visas or extensions of stay in Malta are either made directly to this office or to Maltese embassies abroad. All applications made to embassies are referred to this office via the Consular Office of the Ministry of Foreign Affairs, and record of each such application is kept by the local immigration authorities.

Under the current system, the data collected from a visa applicant essentially includes personal details (name, sex, nationality at birth and at present, profession, etc.), address in Malta and abroad, means of

[7] Section 15(3) of the Immigration Act provides for the imposition of sanctions upon carriers in breach of their obligation not to carry passengers who are not in possession of "any travel document, visa or other special authorisation where required under this Act". Such penalty shall be fixed by the Principal Immigration Officer, but cannot exceed LM5,000 or other maximum sum prescribed by the Minister. In terms of section 25A of the same act, the carrier may appeal from the decision to impose a penalty to the Immigration Appeals Board within a period of 3 working days.

subsistence, duration and purpose of stay, and details relating to the applicant's passport, return visa, etc.[8] The immigration authorities do not keep data such as the fingerprints of visa applicants.

Upon accession the Common Visa Application Form will be introduced, and Malta will follow the Common Consular Instructions on issuing visas.[9]

At present Malta is not a Schengen country and, from the information available,[10] it would seem that it is highly unlikely that Malta will be accepted as such before 2007. Today the only visas issued by the national immigration authorities are those issued in terms of the Immigration Act,[11] i.e. national visas, which are usually valid for one month, with the possibility of extension for further periods. Currently some 45,000 national visas are granted yearly.[12]

Upon accession, although Malta will not yet be a Schengen country, it is possible that Malta will adopt the system used in countries such as the UK: i.e. that of issuing Schengen type visas nationally.

The Central Immigration Office is currently in the process of moving towards a totally computerised system of data collection and recording, which should be fully functioning by the date of accession. To date, in view of the lack of a central database containing relevant and easily accessible information, regarding visas issued for entry and subsequent extensions of stay in Malta, the main methods used to track visa overstayers are field operations and inspections.

It is clear that the efficacy of such methods of control is questionable, especially in view of the relatively limited human resources available to carry out the task. It is practically impossible to estimate the number of migrants with irregular migration status present in Malta at any given time. The immigration authorities' official position is that few, if any, such migrants manage to evade police control for long, particularly in

[8] A copy of the "Visa application form for entry into Malta" is attached to this report in annex 1.

[9] Information provided by Assistant Commissioner of Police, Andrew Seychell, Principal Immigration Officer, during a private interview with the National Rapporteur in December 2003.

[10] Asst. Commissioner Andrew Seychell, December 2003.

[11] Section 8 of the Immigration Act, the national law regulating immigration, and the regulations enacted in terms of this section control the issue of visas for entry and stay in Malta.

[12] Assistant Commissioner Andrew Seychell, December 2003.

view of Malta's small size.[13] Other sources[14] however believe that there are a considerable number of foreign nationals with irregular migration status who manage to evade police controls, often for years.

Certain recent events give an indication of the extent to which foreigners with irregular migration status are present in Malta. One, particularly clear example is the arrest, and subsequent detention, of 146 irregular migrants during a massive manhunt mounted by the local policeforce over a three-day period between July 20 and 23, 2003. This search operation followed the escape of 54 irregular migrants from a detention centre in Floriana, housing a total of 121 irregular migrants, on July 20, 2003. In the course of their operation, in which up to 146 police officers from a number of police departments were involved at any given time, the police managed to round up 24 of the escapees and a total of 122 other migrants with irregular status.[15] It would seem that the majority of the migrants within the latter category had entered legally and drifted into illegality once their permit to stay in Malta expired, and some of them had entered Malta illegally and managed to escape detection.[16]

In this context, it is useful to compare the number of irregular migrants apprehended during this three-day period, as a result of the extraordinary and intensive measures implemented, with the total number of migrants apprehended by the police during 2002, as a result of routine checks and inspections carried out by the immigration police. The statistics for 2002 state that during this year, the police dealt with 700 cases of foreigners who had entered Malta legally but whose stay became illegal once their permission to stay had expired.[17]

These figures indicate that the local immigration authorities, using ordinary means of control and the resources normally available to them, are only managing to apprehend a relatively small number of the migrants with irregular status present in Malta at any given time.

[13] Assistant Commissioner, Andrew Seychell, December 2003.

[14] Information provided by a representative of JRS Malta, a refugee assisting a NGO which has had contact with a considerable number of migrants with irregular migration status over the years.

[15] Information obtained from reports carried in the local media, particularly the Times of Malta and the Malta Independent on July 21, 22, 23 and 24, 2003.

[16] This information was obtained through informal channels. There are no publicly available official statistics on the exact status of these persons.

[17] "Sharing best practice with countries of origin, transit and destination" (Malta's point of view), paper delivered by Assistant Commissioner of Police, Andrew Seychell, Principal Immigration Officer, April 11, 2003.

It is hoped that the introduction of a computerised system of data collection and preservation will make it easier to track visa overstayers. The creation and maintenance of such a system was one of the issues dealt with as part of a Twinning Project between the Maltese, Spanish and UK immigration authorities in the area of immigration and asylum, within the context of the ARGO programme.

This project was mainly directed towards capacity building, and much effort was invested in the strengthening of existing structures and the creation of the new administrative structures necessary for Malta to be able to implement existing EU directives and policies in the area of illegal entry and border control. There was significant input in the area of training of immigration officials, including border personnel.

The project also included the provision of training for staff at the offices of the national authorities responsible for examining and determining asylum claims, and basic training for legal advisors who are providing, or may at some time in the future provide, legal assistance to asylum seekers within the context of procedures for the examination of applications for refugee status.

In recent months, partly but not only as a result of this project, Malta's capacity to deal with issues of illegal entry and border control was directly enhanced through the allocation of more personnel, both at the point of entry and in the area of field operations, and through the purchase and use of enhanced equipment.[18] The improved resources and increased surveillance on the ground have led to a drastic reduction in the incidence of irregular migration from Malta to Italy.[19]

It is clear that adjustments and improvements to the procedures and structures in place in order to control entry to Maltese territory and to curb irregular migration were and still are being made. The basic legislation, the Immigration Act, has been amended, thus creating the necessary legal framework within which the adjustments can take place. The regulations necessary to give effect to the said legal provisions are still in the process of being drawn up and introduced, and the necessary policies, procedures and structures are being created. Although the exact stage which this ongoing process has reached is not clear, local authorities envisage

[18] This includes the installation of a microwave link system for the Armed Forces of Malta, who are responsible for patrolling the marine borders and equipment to detect forged passports. Information obtained from Asst. Commissioner Andrew Seychell, December 2003.

[19] Asst. Commissioner Andrew Seychell, April 11, 2003.

that Malta will be fully compliant with EU standards in this area upon accession.[20]

Admission and residence of third country nationals

Malta's laws and policies regarding the admission and residence of foreign nationals are essentially restrictive and protectionist. Immigration, particularly for employment purposes, is a very sensitive issue politically in view of Malta's limited size and resources. National immigration policies reflect this perception of the local situation: very few migrants are allowed to reside and work in Malta and, even then, they are usually not allowed to remain in Malta indefinitely.[21]

To date Malta's laws and policies regarding the admission and residence of foreign nationals for labour or study purposes or for vocational training have remained largely unchanged in spite of Malta's upcoming EU accession.

Currently the only way in which a foreign national may be admitted to Malta for labour purposes is on the basis of a visa granted on the strength of an employment licence, authorising the prospective employer to employ the migrant concerned in a particular capacity, which is commonly known as a work permit. An employment licence is granted by the Department of Citizenship and Expatriate Affairs within the Ministry of Justice and Home Affairs.

In order for such a work permit to be issued, the post must be one that cannot be filled by a Maltese national. Such permits are usually issued for jobs requiring particular skills or experience not usually available in the Maltese labour market, and are often granted on the express condition that the person employed trains members of the local workforce to do the job. They are never granted for unskilled labour or for posts where there is a high rate of mobility of the workforce, no matter how

[20] Information provided by Dr Godwin Grima, Permanent Secretary, Ministry of Justice and Home Affairs, during a private interview with the National Rapporteur in December 2003.

[21] During an interview with the National Rapporteurs in December 2003, Mr Andrew Seychell stated that: "As a matter of policy we do not allow non-nationals to reside in Malta for extended or indefinite periods . . . It is not envisaged that the policy will change in the near future." Dr Godwin Grima too stated that: "Over the years we have observed a strict limit on the number of non-nationals allowed to reside in Malta and the length of time for which they have been allowed to stay. This policy is dictated by the limitation of resources available and is unlikely to change with regard to third country nationals even after EU accession."

long a particular post is vacant for. This category would include posts such as those held by domestic workers, jobs in the catering business requiring little or no particular skill, such as waiters or dishwashers, unskilled labourers in the construction business and seasonal agricultural work.

Work permits are normally granted for a maximum period of one year, and are usually renewable. The exact length of time for which the permit is granted will essentially depend on the nature of the work for which the permission to employ the foreign national is being granted. For example, in the case of people coming to Malta with a travelling funfair or circus, the permit will be granted only for the duration of the period during which the said attraction will be in Malta. In certain cases a work permit has been granted for more than one year, e.g. the case of company directors where a certain amount of continuity is required.

Just for the record, our law does not allow for foreign nationals to engage in self-employed activities. This restriction is usually circumvented through the establishment of a limited liability company in Malta, which then employs the individual concerned, usually in a managerial post.

Under the present system it is possible for a foreign national to gain admission into Malta on a tourist visa, and to change the purpose of his stay in Malta while he is here. This would happen in cases where the individual concerned finds a job while he is in Malta, and his employer manages to obtain an employment licence to be able to employ him. It is however envisaged that upon EU accession such change of purpose of visit will no longer be possible.[22]

Foreign nationals who provide proof that they have been accepted as students at a recognised educational institution, have paid the fees for the current year and have the means to sustain themselves during their stay here, are granted a visa to gain admission into Malta and reside here. Such visa is usually extended for the duration of the course, provided the necessary evidence is produced. Foreign students are not allowed to undertake employment in Malta, as a general rule.

Third country nationals in possession of a long-term residence permit in an EU Member State, should they come to Malta, are currently not granted any special status in Malta or any rights of residence or employment. Upon accession, as we will not be part of Schengen, it would seem that their position will remain essentially unchanged.

[22] Asst. Commissioner Andrew Seychell, December 2003.

We were informed that prior to accession in May 2004, regulations will have to be drawn up in terms of the Immigration Act, in order to bring Malta's policy and procedures in line with existing EU directives in this area.[23] The exact content of the proposed regulations is yet unknown, as they are still under discussion and there is no publicly available information in this regard, however it would seem that, among other things, they will regulate matters such as the right of EU citizens to enter, stay and work in Malta, and the rights of third country nationals lawfully in the territory of Member States.[24]

It would however seem that, even following accession, Malta's position on issues relating to the admission and residence of third country nationals for labour purposes, self-employment, study and vocational training, even if they have long-term residence in an EU Member State, will remain essentially restrictive.[25]

In this context it is worth noting that, even with regard to EU citizens[26] and Turkish nationals, who will have the right of preferred access to the labour market upon accession, Malta will be able to apply safeguards, effectively limiting their right to work in Malta for a period of seven years after membership.

It is envisaged that, even after accession, Malta will retain the existing work permit system. Under normal circumstances, the Maltese authorities will grant permits to EU citizens as a matter of course, but in case of a threat of disruption of its labour market, which is of an urgent and exceptional nature, Malta will be able to withhold the granting of work permits to EU citizens, either across the board or in particular sectors. The decision to refuse or withhold work permits during the first seven years will essentially rest with the Maltese government, who may act unilaterally and subsequently inform the competent EU institutions of the action taken and the reasons for such a decision.

[23] Assistant Commissioner Andrew Seychell (Principal Immigration Officer) and Dr Godwin Grima (Permanent Secretary, Ministry for Justice and Home Affairs), December 2003.

[24] Assistant Commissioner Andrew Seychell, Principal Immigration Officer, December 2003, informed the National Rapporteurs that discussions are underway regarding the proposed amendments, but could not provide any information regarding the details of such proposals.

[25] See footnote 21 above.

[26] Section 4A of the Immigration Act, which was added by Act XXIII of 2002, provides for the enactment of regulations to grant and regulate the right of EU citizens and their dependants to enter, remain, reside and work in Malta.

This mechanism is intended as a safeguard, to allow Malta to take timely remedial action in the event of sudden or high influxes of additional labour into Malta or in case of a threat thereof. At any time following this initial seven-year period, in case of a disproportionate influx of EU workers which threatens to disrupt the local labour market, Malta may seek a remedy through EU institutions, rather than unilaterally. It is envisaged that this agreement will be confirmed by a joint declaration which will be annexed to Malta's Treaty of Accession.[27]

This special arrangement requested by the Maltese authorities during negotiations regarding the issue of Free Movement of Persons, gives a clear indication of the manner in which issues relating to admission of third country nationals, for whatever reason, will be dealt with even after EU accession.

The European Commission's proposals on these issues are significantly more liberal than the current arrangements. Moreover, whereas in certain areas such as the admission of third country nationals for the purpose of education, the differences between the current government policy and the EU Commission's proposals are not so wide, in other areas, such as the admission of third country nationals for the purposes of employment or self employment the divergence in approach is far greater.

The major issue is essentially that of access to the local labour market, which is perceived as limited and vulnerable in spite of the relatively low rate of unemployment.[28] For example, there has always been strong resistance to the idea of foreign students being allowed to work in Malta while they are studying here. Dependent family members, including the spouse, of a foreign national who is in Malta for employment purposes, are granted a visa to live in Malta, but they are hardly ever allowed to undertake employment.

Even when it comes to the granting of a "residence permit – worker" to third country nationals, the criteria laid down in Article 6 of the EU Commission's proposal are significantly wider than those currently used in Malta to determine whether a particular post should be filled by a foreign national. Under current government policy employers are never granted a licence to employ a migrant worker for certain categories of jobs, particularly those which do not require any special skills. This remains

[27] Malta-EU Information Centre, Aggornament, Special Edition No 3, August 2001.

[28] The latest statistics on employment in Malta published by the Employment and Training Corporation and quoted in the Times of Malta of Thursday February 5, 2004, stated that the registered rate of unemployment stood at 5.5%. Most local commentators, including most unions, agree that such figures are always somewhat inflated, as they will inevitably include a number of people who work while they are registering for unemployment benefits.

true even if the post remains vacant for a significant length of time. Even when an employer is allowed to employ a foreign national, the employment licence is usually only for a period of one year, although it may be renewed. Should the foreign national no longer remain employed by the said employer in that particular post, the said licence is no longer valid.

Again, when it comes to the admission of foreign nationals for the purposes of vocational training the problem is usually that, although they may gain admittance to the academic or other institution offering the training, they have significant difficulties in completing the practical part of such courses as this necessitates the ability to work in Malta.[29]

As may be seen, Malta's policies and practices in the area of allowing non-nationals access to the local labour market are essentially premised on the fact that Malta is a tiny country with limited resources. As such economic recession *per se* does not unduly influence such polices, which are highly restrictive in the first place.

This position is somewhat ironic in view of the fact that it is rumoured, quite consistently, that a, not insignificant, number of migrants, including some with irregular migration status, are employed in an irregular manner in various sectors, such as the construction and the catering industries. There are no reliable statistics available on the true extent of such practices, however, reports carried in the local media from time to time highlight the continued relevance of this issue.

Unfortunately there are no procedures in place to calculate the demand for foreign labour. On a political level unemployment is a major issue, and the general assumption seems to be that there is no scope for such an evaluation within the context of the local job market.[30] Local unions too, who are more or less divided along partisan political lines, have an attitude which is for the most part protectionist and there is little or no discussion regarding the existence or otherwise of a demand for foreign labour within certain sectors. The fact that foreign nationals are being

[29] One category of migrants who faced this problem was a group of minor asylum seekers who were granted "humanitarian protection", a form of subsidiary protection, in Malta. As this status does not confer upon them the right to work in Malta they met with significant difficulties as the authorities concerned refused to allow them to attend the practical part of the course as they could not be registered as workers, so they could not undergo an apprenticeship with a local company or business.

[30] Both Dr Godwin Grima (Permanent Secretary, Ministry for Justice and Home Affairs) and Assistant Commissioner Andrew Seychell (Principal Immigration Officer), during private interviews with the National Rapporteurs, stated categorically that there is no scope for employment of foreign workers in Malta, in view of the limitations of the local job market.

employed, often in an irregular manner, to do certain jobs is seen as a threat to Maltese nationals' livelihoods, rather than a sign that Maltese nationals are unwilling or unable to take jobs in certain sectors and that this may be an indication of a demand for foreign labour in these areas.

Malta's essentially restrictive approach towards the admission of foreign nationals to live and work in Malta, is also mirrored in our legal provisions regarding family reunion. Currently, the dependent family members[31] of a person granted a residence permit[32] in Malta or in favour of whom an employment licence has been issued[33] may apply for permission for their spouse and dependants to be authorised to enter and reside in Malta. Such authorisation is normally granted, however these people usually cannot work while they are in Malta.

With regard to refugees, the Refugees Act 2000, the national legislation dealing with the recognition and protection of refugees, does not specifically provide for a right of family reunification, even for recognised refugees. Section 11(2) of the Act simply states that: "Dependent members of the family[34] of the person declared to be a refugee, if they are in Malta at the time of the declaration or if they join him in Malta, enjoy the same rights and benefits as the refugee." As may be seen this provision falls short of a right to family reunification. In practice, refugees are usually granted the necessary authorisation to bring the members of their immediate family over to Malta. On the other hand, persons granted "humanitarian protection"[35] in terms of the Refugees Act are not afforded the same benefits, and in practice people with this status face significant difficulties when trying to bring even the members of their immediate family over to Malta.

[31] Section 2 of the Immigration Act defines "dependent" family members of an individual as: "the child or step-child of such person, if the child or the step-child is under the age of 21 years; an adopted child under the age of 21 years, having been adopted by such person in a manner authorized by law; a parent or grandparent of such person who proves to the satisfaction of the Principal Immigration Officer that he is wholly maintained by the said person; any other member of the family as may be prescribed by the Minister".

[32] Section 7 of the Immigration Act provides for the issue of residence permits.

[33] The granting of an employment licence is regulated in terms of Section 11 of the Immigration Act.

[34] Section 2 of the Refugees Act, defines dependent members of the family as "the spouse of the refugee, provided the marriage is subsisting on the date of the refugee's application, and the children of the refugee who on the date of the refugee's application are under the age of 18 years and are not married".

[35] "Humanitarian protection" is a form of subsidiary protection, defined as "special leave to remain in Malta until such time when the person concerned can return safely to his country of origin or otherwise resettle safely in a third country" (Section 2, Refugees Act).

In view of the fact that no category of migrants in Malta, even recognised refugees, have the automatic right to bring dependent members of their immediate family to Malta, the proposal for a Council directive, which grants a right, albeit limited, to family reunion, is significantly wider than Malta's current law and policy in this area.

In our view, it is regrettable that the Commission's Proposal does not make it obligatory to extend the right of family reunion to "unmarried partners . . . with whom the applicant is in a duly attested long term relationship", but simply leaves it within the discretion of Member States to include such a provision.

Reference is made to the considerable body of jurisprudence of the European Court of Human Rights and the Commission, which, in interpreting the term "family life" contained in Article 8 of the European Convention on Human Rights, have consistently held that "the question of existence or non-existence of 'family life' is essentially a question of fact depending upon the real existence in practice of close personal ties . . ." (*K v UK (1986)*) and not exclusively upon the existence or otherwise of a formal matrimonial union.

However, the proposed directive contains provisions which, if implemented, will confer rights and benefits which go way beyond the scope of existing legislation and practice in Malta. One example is the obligation to grant an unaccompanied minor refugee's first-degree relatives in the ascending line the right to join him/her in the country of asylum. Other examples are those found in Article 14, which will grant at least some members of the applicant's family who join him/her in the Member State, the same rights as the applicant in terms of education, employment or self-employed activity and vocational training or re-training.

Asylum and refugee law

Although Malta signed the 1951 Convention on the Status of Refugees and the 1967 Protocol to the said Convention in 1971, domestic legislation providing for the recognition and protection of refugees was only enacted in 2000.

The Refugees Act, 2000[36] is a relatively basic piece of legislation, in line with the current practice of adopting "skeleton" legislation, which is then supplemented by copious regulations. It provides for the creation of the Office of the Refugee Commissioner,[37] responsible for examining

[36] Chapter 420 of the Laws of Malta.

[37] Section 4 of the Refugees Act, 2000.

and determining applications for refugee status at first instance, and for the creation of the Refugee Appeals Board,[38] responsible for hearing and determining appeals from decisions of the Refugee Commissioner.

The Act provides basic procedural rights for asylum seekers, including the right to a private interview within one week, where necessary with the assistance of an interpreter,[39] guarantees of confidentiality of all information related to the asylum application,[40] the right to consult the UNHCR and to have legal assistance at all stages of the proceedings for the examination of their application for protection.[41] Free legal assistance is only provided at the appeal stage of the proceedings.[42] The Act places an obligation on the immigration officer to provide an applicant with information regarding the procedures and his/her rights and obligations.[43] It also states that the decision of the Refugee Commissioner "shall be in writing and shall state the reasons supporting it",[44] however there is no similar requirement for decisions of the Appeals Board. The Act seeks to limit asylum seekers' right to seek judicial review, by stating that the decision of the Appeals Board is "final and conclusive, and may not be challenged and no appeal may lie therefrom, before any court of law".[45]

Asylum seekers are entitled to enter and remain in Malta until their application for refugee status is finally determined in terms of the Act,[46] i.e. until their appeal, if they choose to appeal a negative decision at first instance, is decided by the Board.

The Act provides for a form of "accelerated procedures",[47] which to date have never been used. The procedure is actually quite cumbersome, and whether or not it would qualify as accelerated, either in theory or in practice, is open to question. The Act provides for basic procedural guarantees in the context of these proceedings, including the assistance of an interpreter during the interview, the assistance of a lawyer and access to the UNHCR representative.

In terms of the Act, an applicant may be granted either refugee status, essentially granted to those who fulfil the criteria of the refugee definition contained in the Act,[48] which is practically identical to that found in the 1951 Convention, or a form of subsidiary protection called "humanitarian protection". This protection is defined as "special leave to remain in Malta

[38] Sections 5, 6 and 7 of the Refugees Act, 2000.
[39] Section 8(2) of the Refugees Act, 2000.
[40] Section 8(3) of the Refugees Act, 2000.
[41] Section 8(1) of the Refugees Act, 2000.
[42] Section 7(5) of the Refugees Act, 2000.
[43] Section 8(1) of the Refugees Act, 2000.
[44] Section 8(5) of the Refugees Act, 2000.
[45] Section 7(9) of the Refugees Act, 2000.
[46] Section 10(1) of the Refugees Act, 2000.
[47] Section 18 of the Refugees Act.
[48] Section 2 of the Refugees Act, 2000.

until such time when the person concerned can return safely to his country of origin or otherwise resettle safely in a third country".[49] In practice, to date, this form of protection has only been granted to people coming from countries where there is violent and widespread civil conflict.[50]

The Act lays down the rights of asylum seekers[51] and people granted refugee status.[52] It makes no mention of the rights or benefits, to which people granted humanitarian protection are entitled.

It should be stated that the structures and procedures established in terms of the Refugees Act, 2000, which have been functioning for slightly over two years now, are still somewhat basic, and as a result the protection provided to asylum seekers and refugees leaves much to be desired.

Major areas of concern include asylum seekers' lack of access to independent, reliable information about the proceedings, their rights and obligations, the legal framework within which their application will be examined, as well as regarding the conduct of the proceedings for the examination of their application for refugee status. The procedures at appeal stage are also questionable, as the Board meets in private (i.e. without the presence of the appellant or his legal advisor) and does not give reasons for its decisions. Moreover, although the Board is authorised to hold oral hearings if it deems necessary, to date it has never done so, and all appeals from decisions of the Refugee Commissioner have been rejected as manifestly unfounded. In addition to this, in spite of the fact that asylum seekers have a right to legal aid at appeal stage, in practice it has proved extremely difficult not to say impossible for asylum seekers to obtain such assistance.[53]

The Office of the Refugee Commissioner conducts a thorough examination of each application for refugee status, based on an interview with each applicant. However, in spite of the fact that the law requires the Commissioner to interview asylum seekers within a week from the date of their application, in practice it has proved impossible for this office to do so. This is mainly due to the fact that it is ill equipped to deal with the huge caseload it has had to process since its inception. This delay, which is hardly the fault of this office, is worrying primarily because all asylum

[49] Section 2 of the Refugees Act, 2000.

[50] Asylum seekers from Somalia, Liberia, DRC, Ivory Coast and West Sudan, among others, have been granted this form of protection.

[51] Section 10 of the Refugees Act, 2000. [52] Section 11 of the Refugees Act, 2000.

[53] For more information see JRS Malta Recommendations for the improved protection of asylum seekers in Malta, November 2002, and the Report by Mr Alvaro Gil-Robles, Council of Europe Commissioner for Human Rights on his visit to Malta, December 18, 2003.

seekers who enter Malta in an irregular manner are detained. Such detention is indefinite and lasts until their application is finally determined, or until they are removed from Malta, in case of rejected asylum seekers or immigrants who do not apply for protection.[54]

As may be seen, local structures and procedures for the determination of asylum applications, particularly at appeal stage, are still quite rudimentary and totally unsophisticated in comparison to those existing in other jurisdictions. However, a cursory examination of the amended Proposal of a Directive on Minimum Standards on Procedures in Member States for Granting and Withdrawing Refugee Status reveals that, once implemented, it will do little to enhance the quality of protection provided to refugees and asylum seekers in Malta.

Regarding the rights of applicants throughout the procedures, it is not envisaged that the implementation of the said proposal would necessitate major changes in domestic law, as it stands at present. It should be stated, however, that currently a bill containing a number of amendments to the Refugees Act, 2000 has been tabled in Parliament. Among the changes proposed is one requiring an application for protection under the Act to be submitted within two weeks of the asylum seeker's arrival in Malta for it to be valid.[55] This proposed amendment runs counter to Article 5 of the Commission's proposal, which states that asylum applications should not be rejected or excluded from examination on the sole ground that they have not been made as soon as possible.

One area where the proposal for a Directive would substantially improve the level of protection is that relating to judicial review and appeal to a court of law on points of fact or of law. In addition to the fact that, in practice, the procedure for the determination of appeals raises a number of serious concerns, the Act specifically rules out recourse to a court of law, i.e. judicial review. The only exceptions are actions based on the European Convention for the Protection of Human Rights and Fundamental Freedoms, which is part of domestic law, or the human rights provisions in the Constitution of Malta.

Moreover, where applications for refugee status are assigned to the accelerated procedures, the law does not allow an appeal either to the Appeals Board, which is an administrative tribunal, or to a court of law. In terms of the proposal it is clear that even in such cases there would be a

[54] For more information see JRS Malta report on Detention of asylum seekers in Malta: a human rights perspective, July 2003.

[55] Section 4 of the Bill, entitled an Act to amend the Refugees Act, 2000.

right to an effective remedy before a court of law. This would significantly upgrade the protection provided, as long as, in practice, the applicant is able to gain effective access to the courts and to obtain the necessary legal assistance to be able to do so.

The notions of "safe third country" and "safe country of origin" are already incorporated in domestic legislation,[56] however there is a difference in the legal context in which they are employed. The actual legal content of both these terms, though not totally identical, is substantially the same. In terms of the Refugees Act as it stands today, these concepts are to be employed simply as a procedural tool in order to determine whether an application should be examined in the regular or the accelerated procedures.[57] It should be stated, however, that in terms of the bill mentioned earlier, the notion of "safe country of origin" would be used to bar access to the asylum procedures for those applicants coming from countries deemed to be safe.

The other category of applications, which would be assigned to accelerated procedures under existing local legislation, is that of applications deemed "manifestly unfounded".[58] The definition of this term includes the criteria found in the proposal and others that the proposal describes as "inadmissible" rather than manifestly unfounded.

Our law does not provide for border or airport procedures, and it is not clear whether or not such procedures will be introduced at any stage in the near or distant future.

One of the major concerns regarding the standard of protection which asylum seekers receive is the fact that the majority are detained throughout the time it takes to complete the process for the determination of their application for refugee status. Detention not only causes undue and often totally unnecessary hardship for the asylum seekers concerned, but also significantly affects the quality of the process for the determination of their application for protection. In practice being detained usually means inadequate access to reliable information, inability to obtain access to basic rights, such as medical treatment or legal assistance, difficulties in obtaining documents necessary to substantiate claims, problems filing an appeal and difficulties in obtaining information about the conduct of the proceedings.

Moreover, the manner in which the policy of detention is implemented raises concerns of arbitrariness. All asylum seekers who enter

[56] See section 2 for definitions of these terms.

[57] Section 18(1) of the Refugees Act, 2000.

[58] Section 18(1) of the Refugees Act, 2000.

Malta without leave, be they men, women or children, are detained upon arrival.[59] The decision to detain is, essentially, an administrative one, which is not based on an examination of the individual circumstances of each case, nor is it subject to any form of judicial review. Asylum seekers are usually held in detention until their application for refugee status is determined, or until they are deported, if their application for protection is rejected. This process can, and often does, take months.

The safeguards provided in Article 17 of the proposal, though somewhat minimal, would serve to impose a measure of restraint upon the current government policy of blanket and indefinite detention. Improvements would include, the requirement that detention is objectively necessary in the individual case, the prohibition on detention for the sole reason that an asylum seeker's application needs to be examined and the requirement that detention is subject to initial judicial review and subsequent regular judicial reviews.

Many organisations and institutions, both local[60] and international,[61] have recommended that more substantial reforms be implemented, including the adoption of specific legislation on the detention of irregular migrants in order to limit its length and clarify the competence of the judiciary in this area. With regard to asylum seekers, it has been recommended that the law state specifically that detention should only be resorted to in exceptional circumstances where non-custodial measures have proved ineffective, after an examination of the particular circumstances of the individual case, and that vulnerable asylum seekers should never be detained.[62]

It is uncertain whether the law or the current government policy on this matter will be modified in the near future,[63] with the exception of one specific issue. The bill currently tabled in parliament will allow for

[59] Section 5(1) and section 10 of the Immigration Act.

[60] See JRS Malta report on Detention of asylum seekers in Malta: a human rights perspective, July 2003 and comments by the Peace Lab, a local NGO which lobbies on behalf of asylum seekers in detention and immigration detainees.

[61] See report by Mr Alvaro Gil-Robles, Council of Europe Commissioner for Human Rights on his visit to Malta, December 18, 2003.

[62] See JRS Malta report on Detention of asylum seekers in Malta: a human rights perspective, July 2003 and the report by Mr Alvaro Gil-Robles, Council of Europe Commissioner for Human Rights on his visit to Malta, December 18, 2003.

[63] In an article carried in the Times of Malta, of February 11, 2004, entitled "Detention centres inadequate to house human beings: Gil Robles", the Minister for Justice and Home Affairs was quoted as saying that "illegal immigrants will continue to be detained for the interest of the nation".

a detainee to challenge his/her detention if he/she deems it to be unreasonable, by means of an application to the Immigration Appeals Board, an administrative tribunal. This amendment, though welcome, is insufficient to guarantee the rights of asylum seekers and other immigration detainees in terms of the ECHR, primarily because the reasons when detention would be considered reasonable are not specifically stated and the manner in which it will be interpreted is far from clear.

Beyond the procedures for the examination of applications for refugee status and the issues raised by the policy of detention *per se*, there is currently a total lack of administrative and other structures for the reception of asylum seekers or to facilitate the integration of refugees in Malta.

The law provides that asylum seekers will be entitled to access state educational and medical services free of charge. Apart from this there is no provision for any form of financial or other assistance in kind, and asylum seekers are not allowed to work. The only accommodation the state provides for asylum seekers is in detention centres. In addition to the fact that residence in these necessarily centres involves deprivation of liberty, the conditions in these centres are basic at best and in many cases fall far short of internationally recognised standards.[64] Currently none of the NGOs that operate in Malta provide accommodation to asylum seekers.

It should be stated that there is a relatively small number of asylum seekers who are not detained, as they either enter Malta legally and apply for refugee status, or they apply before they are apprehended by the police because of their irregular stay. These asylum seekers must either depend on charity to survive or else resort to working illegally, with all the consequent risks of exploitation and abuse. Local NGOs have recorded instances of asylum seekers sleeping in the street or living in other totally inadequate conditions.[65]

It would also seem that, if an asylum seeker is unable to maintain him/herself, that person could find himself considered a "prohibited immigrant" in terms of the Immigration Act[66] and therefore end up detained by the immigration authorities.[67]

[64] See report by Mr Alvaro Gil-Robles, Council of Europe Commissioner for Human Rights on his visit to Malta, December 18, 2003, the JRS Malta report on Detention of asylum seekers in Malta: a human rights perspective, July 2003 and the report by the same organisation on the conditions in Floriana detention centre, July 2003.

[65] Information provided by a representative of JRS Malta.

[66] Section 5 of the Immigration Act.

[67] Information provided by JRS Malta.

The Directive on Minimum standards for the reception of asylum seekers will therefore necessitate major changes in Malta's law and policy in this area, which is almost totally unregulated. The changes must cover issues as diverse as information provided to the applicant, the provision of documents certifying the legal status of the asylum seeker, the conditions regulating asylum seekers' access to the labour market, and the provision and modalities of adequate material conditions of reception for asylum seekers, among other things. To date there do not seem to be any proposed amendments in this regard.

With regard to the Directive on temporary protection, to date there have been no legislative or other measures introduced in order to implement this directive in national law. It is unclear at this stage what measures will be taken. However it is clear that existing legislation is insufficient to provide the protection envisaged by the directive, which necessitates an examination of each individual application for refugee status before any protection can be granted under the Act.

It is also pertinent to note that so far the Dublin Convention is not applicable, however it will be operative in Malta as from May 1, 2004, i.e. upon EU accession.

With reference to the proposed Directive on minimum standards for the qualification and status of third country nationals as refugees or persons who otherwise need international protection, to our knowledge there are as yet no amendments to law or policy envisaged at this stage. It is clear that, if and when this proposal becomes a directive, a number of amendments will have to be introduced.

One major change would be the definition of "subsidiary protection". At present, the only form of subsidiary protection granted in terms of the Refugees Act, humanitarian protection, is only granted to applicants falling within the scope of Article 15(c) of the proposed directive. Persons fearing torture or inhuman and degrading treatment or punishment or other serious violations of their human rights under international law are not granted protection in terms of existing legislation. This in spite of the fact that the definition of humanitarian protection contained in the Act[68] implies that all who cannot return safely to their country should be granted such protection.

In practice, in order to be able to obtain the protection to which they are entitled such persons would have to institute proceedings, before the local

[68] Section 2 of the Refugees Act.

courts or the appropriate international institution, in order to challenge their deportation. This is particularly difficult for many asylum seekers to do, as many are detained so they do not have access to free legal assistance or sufficient funding to secure the assistance of a private lawyer. In view of this, there is serious concern that persons in need of protection, other than that which can be obtained in terms of the Refugees Act, will slip through the net and will not be granted the protection to which they are entitled.[69]

In addition to this, any proceedings under one of the human rights instruments, to which Malta is a party, are usually instituted only after the conclusion of the asylum proceedings. In practice this often means after the asylum seeker has been detained for months, as a minimum, and usually for well over a year. In view of this, the concept of a two-tier or two-stage system for examining applications for protection is far from ideal, particularly in view of the inaccessibility of the second stage for most asylum seekers and the length of time such proceedings will inevitably take.[70]

It should also be stated that even if rejected asylum seekers are granted some sort of protection from forced return, they are not granted any formal legal status, not even humanitarian protection. This essentially means that these people are forced to live outside the protection of the law, without even the most basic protection of their rights.

Under the current system, people granted humanitarian protection have lesser rights than those granted to recognised refugees. It would seem that, even if the definition of humanitarian protection is extended, the difference in the level of protection provided to these people as opposed to recognised refugees will remain.[71]

[69] A case in point is that of a group of Eritrean asylum seekers who arrived in Malta in March 2002. All of them applied for refugee status and the vast majority had their applications for protection rejected. A group of approximately 47 people filed a human rights case before the local courts claiming that their human rights in terms of the European Convention on Human Rights would be violated if they were to be returned to Eritrea. The rest of the group did not, and they were eventually deported in September/October 2002. The deportations were followed by a wave of reports that the deported asylum seekers were subjected to arbitrary detention and other forms of ill-treatment following their return to Eritrea. These reports have received unofficial confirmation from a number of extremely credible international organizations, leading to fears that the current system is insufficient to ensure that all who need protection are in fact granted the protection they need.

[70] See European Court of Human Rights decisions in *Kadem* and in *Sabeur Ben Ali* vs *Malta*.

[71] Dr Godwin Grima, Permanent Secretary, Ministry for Justice and Home Affairs, December 2003.

One final word in relation to both the issue of the existence of "internal flight options" and the issue of the interpretation of the exclusion clauses. It is clear that both of these concepts are applied by decision-makers in asylum proceedings. However, in view of the fact that there is no published case law locally, it is very difficult to determine the exact manner in which they are interpreted.

In conclusion it is pertinent to state that, at this stage in Malta debate is largely focused on bringing Malta's laws and policies in line with existing EU standards. The issue of harmonisation at EU level and its effect on the quality of protection provided to refugees, has not yet become a subject of public debate and it is doubtful whether it will ever be. There is the stated political will to provide protection to all who need it, however, in practice there are major concerns regarding Malta's limited resources. There is, among local authorities, a desire to see some consideration for these "special circumstances", particularly through the development of mechanisms for burden-sharing that are worthy of the name.

Termination of illegal residence, return and repatriation

There are no publicly available and accurate statistics regarding the number of third country nationals staying in Malta without a valid residence permit.[72] Hundreds of deportations are carried out every year, with 590 being carried out in 2003 and 767 in 2002.[73] Many of these deportations are voluntary, however there have been a couple of notable exceptions, particularly the deportation and repatriation of 233 Eritrean nationals in September and October 2002.[74]

Currently most deportations are carried out either via commercial flights or, particularly where large numbers of deportees are involved, on a chartered flight using the national airline. Both options prove to be rather expensive, especially when considered that, particularly in the case of involuntary removal, there must be two soldiers or security personnel on board for every deportee.[75]

There are no legal rules or regulations regarding air deportations currently applicable in Malta, moreover it is very difficult, not to say

[72] See pages 270 and 271 above.

[73] Statistics obtained from the Ministry of Justice and Home Affairs on January 9, 2004.

[74] See page 287 above, in particular footnote 69.

[75] Dr Godwin Grima, Permanent Secretary, Ministry for Justice and Home Affairs, December 2003.

impossible, to assess the manner in which these deportations are carried out. Deportation or removal is not subject to any independent scrutiny and it is therefore very difficult to arrive at any hard and fast conclusion in this regard.

The authorities concerned stated that we do not have particular difficulties when it comes to repatriating foreign nationals, even without re-admission agreements.[76] The only country with which we have a re-admission agreement is Italy, and this agreement is thought to have functioned satisfactorily.[77]

The majority of irregular migrants apprehended at or near the border arrived by boat, travelling in an irregular manner. During 2002 there were 21 irregular landings involving some 1686 such migrants, while in 2003 we had a total of 11 landings involving a total of 497 people.[78] There are always a number of illegal immigrants who are apprehended at the air and seaports, but over the past two years these have been the minority.[79]

We are not aware of any criminal proceedings for human trafficking instituted in the past year in Malta.

[76] Dr Godwin Grima, Permanenet Secretary, Ministry for Justice and Home Affairs.

[77] Assistant Commissioner Andrew Seychell, December 2003.

[78] Statistics obtained from the local immigration authorities.

[79] Assistant Commissioner Andrew Seychell, December 2003.

THE NETHERLANDS

THOMAS SPIJKERBOER
Professor
Vrije Universiteit Amsterdam

PART I (ENTRY, VISA REGIME AND BORDER CONTROL)

1.1 What national authorities are competent to deal with visa applications (Schengen visa and long-term visa)? Are there any procedures to avoid duplication or successive visa applications at different EU- consulates? On what substantive criteria other than the Schengen minimum requirements are visas granted or refused? How many visas have been issued or refused?

The Minister of Foreign Affairs is competent to issue short-term Schengen visas and long-term visas. The agency which processes visa applications is the *Visadienst*, which in fact is a part of the *Immigratie en Naturalisatiedienst*. Usually, information concerning applications for Schengen visas is exchanged between the consulates of Schengen countries in the country where the application is submitted. The most frequent ground for refusing a Schengen visa, apart from the criteria mentioned in Article 5 SIA, is the risk that the applicant will remain in the country after the expiry of the validity of the visa. Data about long-term visas are publicly available.[1] 57% of all applications are granted.

1.2 Is there a visa tracking procedure in order to identify visa overstayers? What data are collected from visa-applicants (fingerprints)? Admissibility of visa data to alien and police authorities?

There is no systematic visa tracking procedure to detect overstayers. The use of biometrical data to identify incoming travellers is under investigation in the Netherlands.

1.3 Have courts ever decided on the refusal of a Schengen visa based upon Schengen blacklisting by other Member States?

Case law about Schengen visas is scarce. The following decisions were found:

[1] Tweede Kamer 2003–2004, 19 637, nr. 787.

Rechtbank's-Gravenhage zp Amsterdam 19 May 1998, *Jurisprudentie Vreemdelingenrecht* 1998/151

Article 5(1)(c) SIA only empowers the administration to ask for the documents in that provision if there are concrete circumstances which justify doubt as to whether the alien's statements about the aim of his travel and the circumstances under which he will reside are credible or sufficiently concrete. Entry cannot be refused on the sole ground that the alien cannot indicate in detail what he intends to do and does not have documents which show that he has decided beforehand about his travels and residence.

President Rechtbank's-Gravenhage zp Haarlem 16 April 1999, *Jurisprudentie Vreemdelingenrecht* 1999/S157

The alien's passport which contained a valid Schengen visa, contained falsified in and out stamps of Benin and Nigeria. However, it was held that, as the passport had not lost its probative power entry could not be refused.

There is case law about aliens seeking to be removed from the Schengen Information System: this case law is predominantly procedural in nature.

1.4 What measures have been undertaken in the implementation of the action programme for administrative cooperation in the field of external borders, visa, asylum and immigration following the Council Decision of June 13, 2002?

I have not been able to trace implementation measures following this action programme, which suggests that they have not been taken under that rubric.

1.5 What measures have been undertaken to implement Directive 2001/51 EC supplementing the Schengen rules concerning carrier sanctions? How often have carrier sanctions been used?

A bill to implement Directive 2001/51 has been introduced in Parliament.[2] No reasons for the transgression of the term for implementation were given. The bill proposes minor changes in the Dutch Aliens Act in order to eliminate minor differences between existing Dutch law and the standard proposed by the Directive.[3]

[2] Tweede Kamer 2002–2003, 29 016, nrs. 1–2, 28 August 2003.

[3] See in more detail K. M. Zwaan: Implementation of Council Directive 2001/51/EC of 28 June 2001 supplementing the provisions of Article 26 of the Convention implementing the Schengen Agreement of 14 June 1985 (OJ L 187/45 of 10 July 2001) in the Netherlands, to be published in the Yearbook on European Immigration and Asylum Law (ed. Philippe De Bruycker).

PART II (ADMISSION AND RESIDENCE OF THIRD COUNTRY NATIONALS)

2.1 What are the basic principles in your country concerning:
– admission of third country nationals for labour purposes or self-employed activities;
– admission of third country nationals for study and vocational training;
– legal status of third country nationals in possession of a long-term residence permit of another Member State;
To what extent do these principles differ from the European Commission's proposals?

Third country nationals (hereafter TCNs) can be admitted as labour migrants if they fulfil the following basic requirements, laid down in Article 3.31 Aliens Decree 2000 (Vb 2000):

- a work permit should have been granted, which in practice normally means that there is no labour supply for the vacancy concerned on the national labour market;
- the applicant must have been granted a long-term visa, except if s/he belongs to a category of aliens exempted from this requirement;
- the applicant must be in possession of a valid travel document;
- the applicant must earn a wage at least equal to the social minimum
- the applicant must be willing to under go a health test
- the applicant must not be a danger to public order or national security.

TCNs can be admitted for purposes of self-employed activities if they fulfil the following basic requirements, laid down in Article 3.30 Vb 2000:

- the self-employed labour must be in the national interest in the opinion of the Minister of Immigration
- the applicant must earn a permanent and sufficient independent income from these activities
- the applicant must fulfil the requirements for engaging in the particular economic activity (possession of relevant permits etc.)
- the requirements of possession of a long-term visa, a valid travel document, undergoing a health test, and public order/national security are not explicitly set out in Article 3.30 Vb 2000, but do apply on the basis of general provisions.

Despite the legalisation of prostitution, no residence permit can be granted to a TCN for (self-employed) labour as a prostitute (Article 3.32 Vb 2000).

TCNs can be admitted for the purposes of study or vocational training if they fulfil the following basic requirements (Article 3.41 Vb 2000):

- the applicant studies full time at a Dutch university or polytechnic; or s/he studies full time at a Dutch institute for vocational training, provided the Netherlands is the most obvious country for doing so and the Minister of Immigration is of the opinion that the alien in this way will make a positive contribution to the development of the country of origin
- the university or school has given a written statement to the effect that the applicant enrolled in a full time study programme there
- the Minister of Immigration is of the opinion that the applicant's departure is reasonably guaranteed
- the applicant has sufficient income (specified in Article 3.42 Vb 2000).

TCNs can be admitted for a *stage* (i.e. traineeship in the framework of a study) if a working permit (which is always required for this) has been granted (Article 3.39 Vb 2000). The circumstances in which a working permit will be granted are stipulated in par. 24 of the *Uitvoeringsregels Wet Arbeid Vreemdelingen* (Implementation Rules Act Labour Foreigners). A working permit will be granted provided that this is an ordinary and necessary part of the studies the alien is pursuing. The *stage* should not take longer than one year. If the applicant is studying abroad, it is required that s/he has already had sufficient training to qualify for this vocational training. There should not be more than 10% of trainees at one employer, and no less than two. If the applicant is studying at a Dutch institution and has a residence permit for this purpose, the maximum 10%, minimum of two-rule does not apply.

There are no provisions privileging TCNs in possession of long-term residence permits of another Member State. They are treated in the same way as other TCNs. This is a marked difference from the Commission's proposals on the subject.

2.2 What are the legal requirements and procedures for obtaining a residence permit for third country nationals for the purpose of employment? Which procedures are used in maintaining the preferred access of EU-citizens and Turkish nationals (association agreement) to the labour market? Do special programmes exist for highly qualified professionals facilitating access to the labour market? To what extent are trade unions and employers involved in such programmes? Is there a procedure to calculate the demand for foreign labour? How is EU-enlargement

taken into consideration? To what extent has the recent economic recession and unemployment influenced the concepts on the admission of third country nationals?

The main legal requirements for obtaining a residence permit for TCNs for the purpose of employment have been laid out above. A complication arises because, on the one hand, Article 3.31 par. 1 Vb 2000 states that a residence permit can only be granted if a working permit has been granted. However, Article 8(1)(c)(1) of the Act on Labour of Foreigners (*Wav*) stipulates that a working permit can only be granted if a residence permit has been granted, or has been applied for, or a long-term visa has been applied for. In practice, the procedure is as follows. The applicant first applies for a long-term visa, thus fulfilling the requirement of Article 8(1)(c)(1) of the Act on Labour of Foreigners. S/he then applies for a working permit. If a working permit is granted, the long-term visa can be granted. Once the visa has been granted, the applicant can travel to the Netherlands, and apply for a residence permit. This will normally be granted.

In order to ensure that the preferred labour supply of nationals and EU citizens is used to fill vacancies, the employer is required to report a vacancy to the Labour Office at least five weeks before applying for a working permit for that vacancy. If the Labour Office has not been able to refer the employer to unemployed who qualify for the job within five weeks, an employer can apply for a permit with some likelihood of the permit being granted.

For employees at the top of the labour market, there are no general special substantive rules. However, there is a fast track procedure for getting them visas and work permits.

2.3 To what extent do existing laws and practices differ substantially from the approach taken in the Commission's Proposal on admission for the purpose of paid employment and self-employed activities relating to:
- **admission of third country nationals for study and vocational training;**
- **on legal status of third country nationals in possession of a long-term residence permit of another Member State;**

To what extent do these principles differ from the European Commission's proposals?

Present Dutch practice would not have to be altered dramatically if the Commission's proposal for a Directive on admission for study etc. were to be adopted.

2.4 What measures have been taken to implement the Directive of 29th June 2000, implementing the principle of equal treatment between persons irrespective of racial or ethnic origin and Council Directive 2000/78 EC of 27th November 2000, establishing a general framework for equal treatment in employment and occupation? Have legislative changes been undertaken? To what extent is "affirmative action" considered as necessary to promote equal opportunities for migrant workers from third countries?

In order to implement Directives 2000/43/EC and 2000/78/EC, the government submitted a bill proposing amendments to, mainly, the General Act on Equal Treatment.[4] The bill, which at present is pending in the First Chamber of parliament and which will be adopted soon, contains a number of detailed refinements of present anti-discrimination legislation. Two relatively major changes are the introduction of a prohibition on discrimination in membership of employers' organisations and trade unions, and introduction of a prohibition on discrimination on account of race in social security.

Affirmative action is allowed under Dutch law (it is excepted from the prohibition of discrimination), but it is not mandatory. An act inspired by the Canadian Employment Equity Act, requiring employers to register their employees as to ethnicity and to develop an action plan for equal opportunities, has had limited effect.[5]

2.5 Concerning the proposal of a directive on the right to family reunion agreed upon by Council in February 2003:
- **Do you consider the proposed standards below the principles of family reunification valid in your country?**
- **Will the implementation of the Directive once it is adopted lead to changes in the national law on family reunification downgrading the standard of protection? If so, what changes are envisaged?**

The family reunification Directive seems to be below the standards set by Dutch law: international law is a full part of Dutch law in as far as it is directly applicable, at some points. First, Article 5(5) of the Directive stipulates that *due regard* shall be had to the best interests of minor children. This seems to be a formulation falling short of the formulation of Article 3 ICRC, which provides that the interests of the child shall be *a primary consideration.*

Second, the combination of Article 8 (waiting period of two or three years), with Article 4 last subparagraph (integration requirement for

[4] TK 2002–2003, 28 770.

[5] P. Jonkers: *Diskwalificatie van wetgeving. De totstandkoming en uitvoering van de Wet bevordering evenredige arbeidsdeelname allochtonen*, Aksant, Amsterdam 2003.

children over 12) and/or Article 4(6) (apply before the child is 15) may lead to a situation in which an immigrant first has to wait for two or three years; than a child is over 12 years and has to pass an integration test; then may have turned 15 and be too old to apply. These measures may lead to a prolonged, and sometimes permanent separation of families, which may well fall short of obligations under Article 8 ECHR. At present, Dutch law does have a provision requiring aliens who themselves entered as family members to reside three years before they can be a sponsor (Article 3.15 par. 2 Vb 2000). A proposal to introduce integration requirements in Dutch immigration law is pending, in time to meet the implementation deadline set out in Article 4(1), last subparagraph. Dutch immigration law does not limit reunification with older children as envisaged in Article 4(6).

One would expect the Dutch government to introduce legislation in order to make integration a requirement for children over 12, and possibly to exclude the possibility of children over 14 applying for family reunification.

2.6 The proposal for a directive on the rights of long-term third country nationals as agreed upon by the Council on June 5, 2003 provides for a number of rights approximating the standards of long-term residents to the status of EU-citizens. Will the implementation of the Directive involve major legal and policy changes in your country? What are the major points of concern if any, concerning the approximation concept of the directive relating to:
- **non-discrimination in social rights;**
- **the concept of "civic citizenship" (see also extended impact assessment on the Communication on Integration of June 11, 2003);**
- **family reunification and access of family members to the labour market;**
- **security of stay?**

The Directive on long-term third country nationals will not lead to major changes in Dutch immigration law. Long-term TCNs have equal access to social security and other social rights. They have voting rights in local elections. They are treated equally to Dutch nationals in matters of family reunification, and their family members have free access to the labour market. The permanent residence permit to which long-term TCNs are entitled can only be withdrawn in the following circumstances: if they move their domicile outside the Netherlands; if they submitted false information leading to the grant of the permanent residence permit; if they are a danger to national security; or on grounds of public order. The public order ground can be applied when the alien has been sentenced for a criminal offence for which a prison term of three years or more is possible. This ground will be applied according to criteria relating the length of the legal residence to the unconditional part of the prison term imposed in the alien's case.[6] The table looks as follows:

Residence permit may be withdrawn

if the legal residence lasted	and the unconditional prison term imposed was equal to or more than
less than 1 year	1 month
1–2 years	3 months
2–3 years	6 months
3–4 years	9 months
4–5 years	12 months
5–6 years	24 months
6–7 years	30 months
7–8 years	36 months
8–9 years	45 months
9–10 years	54 months
10–15 years	60 months
15–20 years	96 months

There are more detailed rules for the second generation, and for aliens whose legal residence has lasted longer than 10 or 15 years.

The Directive will not require major amendments to legislation governing the position of long-term TCN's.

PART III (ASYLUM AND REFUGEE LAW)

3.1 Have the Dublin Rules worked satisfactorily and what is expected from the Dublin II Regulation No. 343, 2003 of February 18, 2003?

The Dublin rules have not led to an equitable distribution of asylum applicants between the Member States. It does assist in preventing multiple applications. It has led to an extensive pre-procedure, in which the issue is which country is responsible for the examination of an asylum application. After the responsible country has been identified – which can take months and even more than one year – a substantive asylum procedure has to be undertaken, in which it is not assured however that the asylum claim itself will be addressed. It is possible that the substantive asylum procedure will lead to the removal of the applicant to a third country for status determination. The extensiveness and complicated nature

[6] Article 3.98 jo. 3.86 Vb 2000.

of the pre-procedure, combined with the absence of a guarantee that the responsible Member State will itself examine the claim to asylum, is a considerable drawback of the Dublin system, and is at odds with the preamble of the Dublin Convention and the Dublin Regulation.

3.2 Has the Eurodac Regulation No. 2725/2000 of 11th December 2000 concerning the establishment of Eurodac for the comparison of fingerprints for an effective application of the Dublin Convention, operative since January 15, 2003 resulted in an increase of Dublin cases? Has Eurodac become effective in your country or is it expected to become eventually effective?

Eurodac became effective in early 2003. Data are available up until 1 July 2003. These do not indicate a clear increase in the number of Dublin claims.[7] Even if a change existed in the number of claims, the question would arise as to whether this change resulted from Eurodac.

3.3 What major changes, if any, will the implementation of the amended proposal of a directive on minimum standards on procedures in Member States for granting and withdrawing refugee status, on which the Council reached political agreement on most points in June 2003, bring for the legislation and practice in your country in particular relating to:
– rights of applicants in the procedure;
– administrative and judicial appeal procedure;
– the use of safe third country and safe country of origin concepts;
– detainment of asylum seekers;
– airport and border procedures?

The proposal on minimum standards for asylum procedures at this moment is in such a state of flux that it is hard to draw any clear conclusions as to the consequences it will have for Dutch legal practice. In general, it does not seem to propose standards which are above the present level of legal protection of asylum applicants in the Netherlands. Of course, it is conceivable that the Dutch level of legal protection will be adapted downwards in order to reach the lowest possible level according to the directive, but this is speculative at this moment.

The one point on which Dutch legislation would have to be adapted is on the point of the accelerated procedure. At present, Dutch law does not contain any criteria specifying in which cases the accelerated procedure can be used. Article 23(4) as it stands (I have relied on ASILE 66, 4 December 2003) seems to provide that the accelerated procedure may only be used in the cases specified in that provision. This would require that Member States specify the cases in which the accelerated procedure

[7] Tweede Kamer 2003–2004, 19 637, nr. 787, p. 31.

can be used: presently, Dutch law does not do so. However, an extra provision in the Aliens Act implementing Article 23(4) would not lead to substantive changes in Dutch legal practice, as the grounds on which the accelerated procedure can be used are defined so broadly in the Draft Directive that they would be unlikely to exclude cases in which it is being used in present day Dutch legal practice.

3.4 What measures have been undertaken to implement Directive 2003/9 of 27 January 2003, on the reception of asylum seekers in your country relating to:
- **the flexibility clauses in the Directive;**
- **restriction of free movement;**
- **access to the labour market;**
- **rights of migrant workers under Article 11 § 2 of the Directive?**

As yet, no implementation measures have been undertaken with regard to Directive 2003/9 on the reception of asylum seekers. Implementation has been announced. One of the issues to be addressed is the fact that presently, asylum applicants submitting a second application are excluded from reception facilities without an individual examination of their circumstances, even if they belong to vulnerable groups. This is at odds with Article 16(4) of the Directive.

3.5 What steps have been undertaken to implement the Directive on temporary protection, COM 2001, 55 in national law? Are there any procedures for burden sharing arrangements? Is there a legal basis for admission of refugees receiving temporary protection in a mass-movement situation?

In order to implement Directive 2001/55 on temporary protection, a bill has been introduced.[8] It is proposed to adopt a new Article 43a Aliens Act 2000. The proposed article provides that, if the Council decides to grant temporary protection to a group of persons, a decision on the asylum application has to be taken within six months after temporary protection ends. Normally, a decision has to be taken within the six months after the application is submitted. Temporarily protected persons will be treated as asylum applicants. No burden sharing arrangements have been adopted.

3.6 The Council has reached political agreement on the principles for a directive on minimum standards for the qualification and status of third country nationals as refugees or persons who otherwise need international protection, COM 2001, 510 final (see Council documents of June 2003). What measures are envisaged to implement the Directive, once it is adopted, in your country relating to:

[8] Tweede Kamer 2002–2003, 29 031, nrs. 1–2, 8 September 2003.

– the definition of refugee;
– the definition of persons entitled to subsidiary protection;
– status of persons entitled to subsidiary protection;
– the issue of internal flight alternative as defined by the Directive;
– exclusion clauses, particularly issues of terrorism?
To what extent are the refugee policies as reflected in the law and jurisprudence of your country in accordance with the proposal of the directive?

As the Directive on qualification has not yet been adopted, no public debate has taken place about its implementation, nor have concrete implementation measures been envisaged. The present version would not require changes in Dutch legal practice.

3.7 In the Commission's Communication of November 22, 2000, COM 2000,755 (see also 2nd Commission Report COM 2003, 152 final) the Commission's concept of a common European asylum procedure and a uniform status for those who are granted asylum valid throughout the Union is set out. Do you consider that the concept is generally in line with your country's asylum policy? Are concerns of refugee organizations, such as Amnesty International and other organizations, of an undermining of the international regime for the protection of refugees shared in political circles of your country responsible for decision-making?

The concept of a common European asylum procedure is not in line with the Dutch asylum procedure, because a common European asylum procedure does not yet exist. In Dutch law, there is only one single asylum status, with identical secondary rights regardless of the ground on which it has been granted. The grounds on which the single status may be granted are:

- the alien is a Convention refugee;
- expulsion of the alien would be contrary to Article 3 ECHR or Article 3 CAT;
- in the opinion of the Minister of Aliens affairs, it cannot be reasonably required that the alien returns to the country of origin on account of compelling reasons of a humanitarian nature which are related to the reasons for which the alien left that country;
- in the opinion of the Minister of Aliens affairs, expulsion would be unduly harsh on account of the general situation in the country of origin.

There have been concerns about undermining the Convention regime. However, because case law now focuses to a great extent on procedural issues, it is hard to evaluate the single status system on this point.

3.8 The open coordination-mechanism as suggested by the Commission provided for a first stage and a second stage legislation in which the flexibility provisions in some of the directives on migration and asylum are to be replaced by a full harmonization. Is this concept discussed in your country and what are the perceptions relating to the gradual establishment of a European asylum policy which eventually might replace national procedures and national decision-making?

There are no policy papers giving clear indications about the perspective of the Dutch government on the second phase of harmonisation. The Advisory on Aliens affairs a couple of days ago released an advice on the future of European migration law.[9]

3.9 The Communication of June 2003, towards a more accessible, equitable and managed asylum system – in reaction to the UK paper – develops some ideas on new approaches to pursue an orderly and managed arrival of persons in need of international protection. What is the political reaction in your country as to the concept of an outside accessed asylum procedure, distribution of refugees and responsibility-sharing and other new concepts and ideas in coping with mass refugee movements?

The Dutch government participates in the group of Member States cooperating in the further elaboration of the UK proposals. The political reactions were mixed, but the coalition parties fully consented to further cooperation.

PART IV (TERMINATION OF ILLEGAL RESIDENCE, RETURN AND REPATRIATION)

4.1 How many third country nationals without a valid residence permit are presently according to estimates staying in your country? How many deportations have actually been made in previous years? Is the whole enforcement process considered as acceptable?

One of the few serious studies on the number of illegal aliens in the Netherlands finds that their estimated number is between 112,000 and 163,000.[10] In 2002, 2276 rejected asylum applicants were actually removed, as well as 9739 other illegal aliens.[11] The general notion is that expulsion is the least developed part of immigration policy. Recently, the Minister of Aliens affairs announced new, ambitious plans, envisaging

[9] Adviescommissie voor Vreemdelingenzaken: *Voorbij de horizon van "Amsterdam"*, The Hague, February 2004.

[10] G. Engbersen et al.: *Illegale vreemdelingen in Nederland*, Risbo, Rotterdam 2002.

[11] Tweede Kamer 2003–2004, 19 637, nr. 787, p. 41–42.

the deportation of 26,000 rejected asylum applicants who are still in the Netherlands.

4.2 What has been undertaken to implement the Directive of November 28, 2002 dealing with the facilitation of unauthorized entry, transit and residence?

4.4 What efforts have been undertaken in your country concerning the Budapest June 2003 recommendations concerning the harmonization of penalty scales with regard to the crime of smuggling of migrants and trafficking of persons in line with Council Directive 2002/90 of 28th November 2002? Did your country sign the relevant UN protocols on the smuggling of migrants?

In order to implement this Directive and the UN protocols, which were signed by the Netherlands, a bill has been introduced envisaging amendments to the Criminal Code on the point of trafficking and illegal entry.[12] The proposed changes are rather technical and detailed.

4.3 How many illegal applicants have been apprehended at or near the border? How many criminal procedures for human trafficking have been instituted in the last year?

No data are available on the number of persons apprehended at or near the border. On prosecution for trafficking, the most recent data concern 2001. In that year, the public prosecutor was involved in 132 cases. In 63% of these cases, actual prosecution followed. In 2001, 86 cases were judged by the courts. In 87% of these cases, the suspect was found guilty.[13]

4.5 What measures have been taken to implement the Council Directive of 28th May 2001 on the mutual recognition of decisions on the expulsion of third country nationals? What, if any shortcomings or gaps of the Directive should be corrected in a further directive on cooperation on expulsion or deportation of third country nationals?

The Minister of Aliens affairs has published a notification stating that Directive 2001/40 does not need implementation because Dutch legislation is fully in line with it.[14]

4.6 Do readmission agreements or other international treaties or arrangements with the aim of controlling and curbing illegal immigration and facilitating return exist in your country? Have they functioned satisfactorily?

[12] Tweede Kamer 2003–2004, 29m 291, nrs. 1–2, 12 November 2003.

[13] A. G. Korvinus: *Mensenhandel. Aanvullende kwantitatieve gegevens*, Bureau Nationaal Rapporteur Mensenhandel, The Hague 2003, p. 89.

[14] *Staatscourant* 25 October 2002, nr. 206, p. 10.

Readmission agreements exist between the Netherlands (sometimes as part of the Benelux) and Belgium/Luxembourg (in the framework of the Benelux), Bulgaria, Germany, Estonia, France, Hungary, Croatia, Latvia, Lithuania, Austria, Poland, Romania, Slovakia, Slovenia, Switzerland, and Yugoslavia. No data are published about their actual use.

4.7 To what extent have EU-standards and recommendations influenced your country's return policy? Have efforts been undertaken to cooperate with other EU Member States in enforcing return decisions by common deportation actions, exchange of information, facilitation of air and land transit, common principles on flight security, etc.?

Return policy does not seem to have been influenced to a great extent by EU standards. There has been co-operation on the issue of mass expulsions (common charter flights and the like), but this seems to have been done on an ad hoc basis.

4.8 Do you consider that there is a need to elaborate a common legal regime for air deportations (legal status of armed guards on board of the aircrafts, rights of the aircraft commander, legal rules in case of transit stops, applicability of national police law on board of aircraft on flight, etc.)?

I doubt whether an elaborate common legal regime would contribute much to return policy in terms of efficiency and/or human dignity. The problems Member States are facing seem to be of a primarily practical rather than of a legal nature.

NORWAY

HENRIK BULL
Associate Professor
Centre for European Law
University of Oslo

INTRODUCTORY REMARK

As is generally known, Norway is not a member of the EU, but has two agreements of interest with regard to migration and asylum law:

The EEA Agreement covers free movement of EU citizens and the citizens of Iceland and Liechtenstein – and their family members even if third country citizens – in accordance with Community law (pre-Maastricht). A revision of the EFTA Convention extends these rules to Switzerland, in parallel with Switzerland's agreements with the EU.

Together with Iceland, Norway has a cooperation agreement with the EU on the "Schengen cooperation". The association agreement provides for open borders between Iceland, Norway and the "EU Schengen States", as well as a common regime for control at the outer borders, including participation in the Schengen Information System (SIS) and the Dublin II Regulation. However, EU cooperation with regard to the application of the Refugee Convention, so-called secondary protection and the content of migration policy in general does not form part of the agreement. On the other hand, with open borders, it is obvious that EU developments in these fields have a significant impact on the Norwegian policy.

Further clarifications will follow from the answers given below.

PART I ENTRY, VISA REGIME AND BORDER CONTROL

1.1 What national authorities are competent to deal with visa applications (Schengen visas and long-term visas)? Are there any procedures to avoid duplication or successive visa applications at different EU-consulates? On what substantive criteria, other than the Schengen minimum requirements, are visas granted or refused? How many visas have been issued or refused?

Unless delegated, visa applications are decided upon by the National Immigration Directorate. However, Norwegian embassies and (some) consulates have been delegated powers to issue 3 month visitors' visas with the exception of "hard cases", which are referred to the Directorate for decision. Refusals to issue a visa may be appealed administratively to the Directorate if the decision has been made by an embassy or consulate, and to a special Appeals Board if the initial decision was made by the Directorate (and further appealed in court, which is impractical in visa cases).

To avoid duplication and successive visa applications, embassies and consulates confer with their local Schengen counterparts. In addition, the date of application is stamped in the passport upon application. If a visa is issued, the visa "sticker" is placed on top of the stamp. If the application is rejected, the stamp will remain visible to other authorities that may get an application from the same person. As of yet there is no national electronic register of all visa applications.

As an associate participant in the Schengen cooperation, Norway adheres to the Schengen rules on the substantive criteria for issuing visas. In addition, there is a couple of "national visas" which only are valid for travels to Norway. Firstly, job-seekers may get a special "job-seeking visa", cf. below in part II where this is further commented upon. Secondly, when a foreigner has been granted a residence permit, he will get a visa valid for seven days, during which he must report to the police to be issued formally with the document containing the residence permit.

In 2002 the National Immigration Directorate issued 4,419 visas and rejected 5,490 applications. Embassies and consulates issued 61,313 visas and rejected 7,058 applications.

1.2 Is there a visa tracking procedure in order to identify visa overstayers? What data are collected from visa-applicants (fingerprints)? Admissibility of visa data to alien and police authorities?

There is no special "visa tracking procedure". Visa overstayers are usually found out upon leaving, as a result of the police checking foreigners' identity in the streets, when the foreigner applies for another type of permission to stay on in Norway, or in connection with inspections at construction sites etc. to check whether the contractors use illegal foreign labour.

The following data are collected from visa applicants: Name, date of birth, address, citizenship, occupation, marital status, name of close relatives in the applicant's home state, purpose of visit, economic means for staying in Norway and travelling back. In addition, the applicant must submit a photo, but so far not fingerprints. Applicants from areas with ethnic tensions and a potential for producing asylum seekers, such as some areas in the Balkans, may be asked to state their ethnic identity.

The applicant himself has full access to the information in the file established for his application, unless special rules, e.g. on national security, bar access. If the police are asked to verify information given by the applicant with regard to persons, e.g. relatives, living in Norway, the police will also get the information. Apart from this, neither the police nor the National Immigration Directorate will get access to the information in connection with visas issued by embassies or consulates.

1.3 Have courts ever decided on the refusal of a Schengen visa based upon Schengen blacklisting by other Member States?

There seem to be no court cases in Norway on the refusal of Schengen visas based upon blacklisting by Schengen Member States.

1.4 What measures have been undertaken in the implementation of the action programme for administrative cooperation in the field of external borders, visa, asylum and immigration following the Council Decision of 13 June 2002?

Reference is made to the introductory remarks above. The Council Decision of June 13, 2002 illustrates the position of Norway (and Iceland) quite well: As far as the decision concerns external border control and visas, Norway implements the action programme. However, with regard to immigration and asylum (except "Dublin matters"), the decision does not apply to Norway.

1.5 What measures have been undertaken to implement the Directive 2001/51 EC supplementing the Schengen rules concerning carrier sanctions? How often have carrier sanctions been used?

There have been no specific implementation measures with regard to directive 2001/51, the national provisions already covering Article 26 of the Schengen Convention being sufficient. No nationwide statistics seem to be readily available, but at the Oslo Airport, which in this context is by far the most important, there seem to be about five fines being issued a year.

1.6 In your judgement, does the visa law and policy of your country live up to EU standards or are adjustments needed? Do you consider that there is need for further EU-harmonization of visa policies concerning:
- **common criteria for granting visas aiming at harmonizing visa obligations among states participating in the Budapest Process;**
- **establishment of a European visa identification system (VIS and SIS II)?**

To what extent will the EU enlargement process present an opportunity or challenge for tackling issues of illegal entry and border control?

Generally Norwegian policy lives up to Schengen standards.

A further harmonisation of the criteria for issuing visas would seem to be a natural consequence of having "Schengen visas" in the first place. With regard to visas providing access to the whole Schengen area, the criteria ought to be the same regardless of which country issues the visa. However, a possibility of issuing "national visas" should be kept as a "safety valve", in particular with regard to Norway and Iceland, since these states do not participate in all aspects of EU immigration and asylum policies.

As mentioned in 1.1, there is no national register of visa applications. This is a problem, and a common European visa identification system would provide a solution.

The enlargement is probably both an opportunity and a danger for tackling issues of illegal entry and border control. Some new external borders will probably be more difficult to control than those which exist today. On the other hand, moving the external borders closer to those areas which produce illegal immigrants could also present new opportunities for tackling the problem.

PART II ADMISSION AND RESIDENCE OF THIRD COUNTRY NATIONALS

2.1 What are the basic principles in your country concerning:
- **admission of third country nationals for labour purposes or self-employed activities;**
- **admission of third country nationals for study and vocational training;**
- **legal status of third country nationals in possession of a long-term residence permit of another Member State?**
- **To what extent do these principles differ from the European Commission's proposals?**

Admission of third country nationals for labour purposes or self-employed activities

The basic principle in operation since 1975 is a moratorium on immigration for economic purposes from third countries. However, there are several exceptions.

The most important exception concerns people with "specialist competence". This includes anyone with vocational training of three or more years, or professional skills equivalent to that obtained through practical experience, with the exception of some professions where higher education is required (currently religious leaders and cooks specialising in national cuisines). In order to obtain a residence permit, the applicant must demonstrate that he has a firm offer of employment (not part-time) from a Norwegian employer who needs the applicant's special skills, with a salary and other employment benefits equivalent to those offered to Norwegian employees in similar positions. In principle he must also demonstrate that he has a place to live which the health authorities find satisfactory, but in reality this is not subject to any regular control. Many categories of "specialists" are subject to a quota arrangement which means that as long as the quota is not filled, there is no individual assessment of whether the post could be filled by Norwegian job-seekers. The quotas are so generous that they are unlikely to be filled. Outside the quota arrangement an individual assessment takes place, but in practice it is limited to announcing the post vacant for two weeks in Norway and other EEA countries through the employment authorities. If nobody applies for the job as a result of this, the third country national may take it.

In 2002, 1,676 "specialist" permits were issued. Up until October 2003, 979 permits were issued that year.

People falling within the "specialist" category may apply for a residence permit after they have arrived in Norway. Foreign "specialists" needing a visa to visit Norway may obtain a special "job-seeking visa" (which is a national visa, not a Schengen visa) in order to come to Norway and look for a job. However, visas may be denied for "immigration policy reasons". This means that if the immigration authorities, based i.e. on previous experience with people from the applicant's country, deem it likely that the foreigner will not leave voluntarily should he not find a job (but for example apply for asylum), a visa will not be issued.

Self-employed persons from third countries may in principle also obtain residence permits, provided that immigration and labour market authorities find, based on the applicant's detailed plans, that there is a need for this kind of activity and that it is economically viable. Any licence which may be needed in order to engage in the particular trade or profession must be obtained beforehand. The rules may seem liberal, but in fact it is quite hard to convince the authorities. An application may not be submitted while the applicant is in Norway, and there is no special visa arrangement as there is for job-seekers.

Both for "specialists" and self-employed persons the residence permit is issued for one year. Provided the foreigner is still at work, the permit will be renewed twice for one year at a time, and after three years he will normally be entitled to a permanent residence permit, with no limitations with regard to type of work, employer etc.

Apart from this there are some schemes which apply to people seeking non-skilled work, such as seasonal work, e.g. helping out in harvesting crops, au-pairs etc. Generally permits are issued for the time the work is likely to last, which could be only a few months, and they do not provide a basis for obtaining permanent residence permits. The same conditions with regard to salary and a place to live apply here as for "specialists". There is a general requirement that Norwegian workers or workers in other EEA states cannot be found. Permits are usually tied to working for a particular employer.

In addition there are of course rules applicable to guest scientists at universities etc. To the extent these categories fall under the more generous "specialist" rules, the applicant is issued with a "specialist" residence permit instead.

Outside the particular schemes that cover unskilled labour there is no possibility for third country nationals to obtain a residence permit in order to do unskilled work.

Admission of third country nationals for study and vocational training

As a general rule, residence permits for studies and vocational training are only issued to people who have obtained a place at a university or other academic institution. There is no general possibility for third country nationals to come to Norway for their high school education or their non-academic vocational training, but some special schemes apply, tied to cultural agreements with other states etc.

Legal status of third country nationals in possession of a long-term residence permit of another Member State

There are no special rules for third country nationals in possession of a long-term residence permit of a EU Member State or of EFTA states.

Comparison to Commission proposals

The proposed directives would fall outside Norway's agreements with the EU.

Except for some differences with regard to the formalities in connection with applications etc., the main difference between the proposals and current Norwegian legislation would seem to be

- More liberal treatment proposed in the directives for studies, vocational training and voluntary service.
- It would also seem that the proposal on paid employment and self-employed activities would be more liberal with regard to unskilled labour: In principle there should be a general opportunity also for unskilled labour, which may be restricted through quotas and otherwise. Under current Norwegian legislation, a third country national seeking unskilled work must qualify under one of the specific categories enumerated in the legislation, if not, there is no possibility, not even in principle.
- Third country nationals with a residence permit in another EEA state have no privileged position under current Norwegian legislation with regard to obtaining a residence permit in Norway.

2.2 What are the legal requirements and procedures for obtaining a residence permit for third country nationals for the purpose of employment? Which procedures are used in maintaining the preferred access of EU-citizens and Turkish nationals (association agreement) to the labour market? Do special programmes exist for highly qualified professionals facilitating access to the labour market? To what extent are trade unions and employers involved in such programmes? Is there a procedure to calculate the demand for foreign labour? How is the EU-enlargement taken into consideration? To what extent has the recent economic recession and unemployment influenced the concepts on admission of third country nationals?

Reference is made to the answers above, in particular with regard to skilled labour. The quotas that apply to skilled labour seem deliberately to be set higher than the likely demand. The economic downturn has not so far led to restrictions, and the accession of the ten new Member States to the EU – and the EEA – does not seem to lead to restrictions on third country nationals. However, it could perhaps be said that the economic downturn and the enlargement of the EU and the EEA have quelled a debate that was starting on whether Norway was in need of more non-skilled labour from third countries.

Trade unions and employers' organisations are not formally involved in programmes.

The association agreement with Turkey does not apply to Norway.

2.3 To what extent do existing national laws and practices differ substantially from the approach taken in the Commission's Proposal on admission for the purpose of paid employment and self-employed activities relating to:
- **admission of third country nationals for study and vocational training;**
- **on legal status of third country nationals in possession of a long-term residence permit of another Member State?**

To what extent do these principles differ from the European Commission's proposals?

Reference is made to the answers to 2.1.

2.4 What measures have been taken to implement the Directive of 29th June 2000, implementing the principle of equal treatment between persons irrespective of racial or ethnic origin and Council Directive 2000/78 EC of 27th November 2000, establishing a general framework for equal treatment in employment and occupation? Have legislative changes been undertaken? To what extent is "affirmative action" considered as necessary to promote equal opportunities for migrant workers from third countries?

Directive 2000/78 does not form part of the EEA Agreement.

2.5 Concerning the proposal for a directive on the right to family reunion agreed upon by the Council in February 2003:
- **Do you consider the proposed standards below the principles of family reunification applicable in your country?**
- **Will the implementation of the Directive, once it is adopted, lead to changes in the national law on family reunification downgrading the standard of protection? If so, what changes are envisaged?**

The proposed directive will not apply to Norway.

2.6 The proposal for a directive on the rights of long-term third country nationals as agreed upon by the Council on 5 June 2003, provides for a number of rights approximating the situation of long-term residents to the status of EU-citizens. Will the implementation of the Directive involve major legal and policy changes in your country? What are the major points of concern if any, concerning the approximation concept of the directive relating to:
- **non-discrimination in social rights;**
- **the concept of "civic citizenship" (see also extended impact assessment on the Communication on Integration of June 11, 2003);**
- **family reunification and access of family members to the labour market;**
- **security of stay?**

The proposed directive will not apply to Norway.

2.7 Considering the perspective of a future common migration policy as developed by the Commission in the Open Coordination Communication (COM 2001, 387) and the Communication on a Migration policy of the European Union (COM 2000, 757 final), how do you assess the role of the Community organs in determining a European migration policy in terms of competencies of the Member States to decide on residence rights and admission to the labour market and integration? Should harmonization of legislation go further, and if so, in what respect?

A common migration policy will not apply to Norway.

PART III ASYLUM AND REFUGEE LAW

3.1 Have the Dublin Rules worked satisfactorily and what is expected of the Dublin II Regulation No. 343, 2003 of 18 February 2003?

The "old" Dublin regime worked quite slowly – so slowly, in fact, that the case could often be dealt with more quickly by making a decision on the substance of the asylum application in Norway rather than wait for another Dublin country to assume responsibility for the case. However, this has improved with Regulation No 343/2003.

3.2 Has the Eurodac Regulation No. 2725/2000 of 11th December 2000, concerning the establishment of Eurodac for the comparison of fingerprints for an effective application of the Dublin Convention, operative since January 15, 2003, resulted in an increase of Dublin cases? Has Eurodac become effective in your country or is it expected to become effective eventually?

Eurodac has resulted in a marked increase in Dublin cases among the asylum applications to Norwegian authorities. Since Eurodac became operative on 15 January 2003 and until the end of 2003 there were 1,789 hits. This should be compared to the following figure: between 01.01.03 and 30.09.03, the National Immigration Directorate decided upon 12,100 asylum cases, which is an increase of 1,300 cases over the same period in 2002. Of those 12,100 cases, 2000 were Dublin cases. The Directorate expects the "Dublin share" of the total number of cases to increase further, since most asylum seekers arriving in Norway probably have come through another "Dublin country", but have disposed of their ID papers before they approach Norwegian authorities and ask for asylum.

3.3 What major changes, if any, will the implementation of the amended proposal for a directive on minimum standards on procedures in Member States for granting and withdrawing refugee status, on which the Council has reached political agreement on most points in June 2003, bring for the legislation and practice in your country in particular relating to:
- **rights of applicants in the procedure;**
- **administrative and judicial appeal procedures;**
- **the use of safe third country and safe country of origin concepts;**
- **detainment of asylum seekers;**
- **airport and border procedures?**

The proposed directive on minimum standards on procedures for granting and withdrawing refugee status seems to correspond well with current Norwegian practice, with one exception: Under current Norwegian practice, an asylum seeker is granted the benefit of the doubt with regard to the assessment of whether he is in need of protection under Article 33(1) of the Refugee Convention. However, in deciding whether the asylum seeker should be granted the status of "refugee", rather than a residence permit "on humanitarian grounds" (which has slightly less generous terms with regard to rights and benefits), it would seem that only those applicants whose stories really seem convincing are granted status as "refugees". The rest of those who are allowed to stay because of Article 33(1) are granted a residence permit on "humanitarian grounds". It may perhaps be argued that such a practice would be contrary to the proposed directive, which deals with refugee status, and in Article 16 sets out the principle of the benefit of the doubt.

3.4 What measures have been undertaken to implement Directive 2003/9 of 27 January 2003, on reception of asylum seekers in your country relating to:
- **the flexibility clauses in the Directive;**
- **restriction of free movement;**
- **access to the labour market;**
- **rights of migrant workers under Article 11 § 2 of the Directive?**

Directive 2003/9 on the reception of asylum seekers is not binding for Norway. However, Norwegian procedures for the reception of asylum seekers fulfil the requirements of the directive. Asylum seekers are required to stay in a designated facility until they have been interviewed by representatives of the National Immigration Directorate and undergone a health check. After this interview they are offered boarding in special facilities, but may choose to find somewhere to live on their own, provided they can pay for it out of their own means. All applicants receive a temporary working permit if they so wish. Recently an "express procedure" has been introduced for asylum seekers from countries thought of as safe – their applications should be dealt with within 48 hours. During that period their freedom of movement is restricted.

3.5 What steps have been undertaken to implement the Directive on temporary protection, COM 2001, 55 in national law? Are there any procedures for burden sharing arrangements? Is there a legal basis for the admission of refugees for the purposes of receiving temporary protection in a mass-movement situation?

The directive does not apply to Norway, but there is a special procedure for temporary protection in mass-movement situations: People falling under this procedure, which is declared applicable to special groups when a special situation arises, are granted a residence permit with the right to work for up to three years without any individual assessment of their need for protection. If the reasons why mass protection was afforded still exist after three years, a one year renewal is offered. If, after four years, the members of the group can still not go back, they receive a permanent residence permit.

The assessment of any individual application for asylum is put on hold for up to three years for members of the group. When three years have lapsed, or if the reasons for offering mass protection disappear before that, the applicant is informed that he must expressly ask for the application to be assessed at that time. Immigration authorities will not handle it ex officio at that stage.

3.6 The Council has reached political agreement on the principles for a Directive on minimum standards for the qualification and status of third country nationals as refugees or persons who otherwise need international protection, COM 2001, 510 final (see Council documents of June 2003). What measures are envisaged to implement the Directive, once it is adopted, in your country relating to:
- **the definition of refugee;**
- **the definition of persons entitled to subsidiary protection;**
- **status of persons entitled to subsidiary protection;**
- **the issue of internal flight alternative as defined by the Directive;**
- **exclusion clauses, particularly issues of terrorism?**

To what extent are the refugee policies as reflected in the law and jurisprudence of your country in accordance with the proposal for the directive?

A commission is presently drafting a new Immigration Act, including provisions on asylum and temporary protection. Although the directive on minimum standards for the qualification and status of third country nationals as refugees or persons who are otherwise in need of international protection will not be binding on Norway, the commission will have to assess whether it would still be useful to reflect the text of the directive more closely in the new act than is the case with the existing act. This would not necessarily lead to many changes in who is allowed to stay, but it might lead to some reclassifications with regard to who is qualified as a "refugee" and who is granted a residence permit formally on other grounds, cf. in this respect 3.3 above.

3.7 In the Commission's Communication of 22 November, 2000, COM 2000, 755 (see also 2nd Commission Report COM 2003, 152 final) the Commission's concept of a common European asylum procedure and a uniform status for those who are granted asylum valid throughout the Union is set out. Do you consider that the concept is generally in line with your country's asylum policy? Are the concerns of refugee organizations, such as Amnesty International and other organizations, of an undermining of the international regime for the protection of refugees shared in the political circles responsible for decision-making of your country?

3.8 The open coordination-mechanism, as suggested by the Commission, provided for first stage and second stage legislation in which the flexibility provisions in some of the directives on migration and asylum are to be replaced by full harmonization. Is this concept discussed in your country and what are the perceptions relating to the gradual establishment of a European asylum policy which might eventually replace national procedures and national decision-making?

3.9 The Communication of June 2003, towards a more accessible, equitable and managed asylum system – in reaction to the UK paper – develops some ideas on new approaches to pursue an orderly and managed arrival of persons in need of international protection. What is the political reaction in your country to the concept of an outside accessed asylum procedure, distribution of refugees and responsibility-sharing and other new concepts and ideas in coping with mass refugee movements?

Norway's position as a non-member of the EU – and the initiatives mentioned in 3.7–3.9 not being formally part of Norway's association agreements with the EU – means that these initiatives do not influence Norwegian asylum policy debate in the same way as in the EU. However, Norway is of course directly affected by EU policies in this area: Norwegian policies that are – or are perceived by asylum seekers to be – more liberal than those of EU Member States, will probably lead to an increase in the number of people applying for asylum in Norway.

As the influx of asylum seekers to Norway has gone up over the last years, there has been a shift in the prevailing attitude towards asylum seekers. Whereas the political community some years back very much concentrated on what was perceived by many to be an unnecessarily strict policy, focus is now more on what to do with asylum seekers without sufficient grounds for their application – how to speed up the handling of their application, how to repatriate them quickly after their application has been rejected and so on.

The practice described under 3.3 above has also tended to complicate the debate, since it could give the impression that a smaller proportion of those who are allowed to stay are in need of protection than is actually the case.

PART IV TERMINATION OF ILLEGAL RESIDENCE, RETURN AND REPATRIATION

4.1 How many third country nationals without a valid residence permit are currently, according to estimates, staying in your country? How many deportations have actually been made in previous years? Is the whole enforcement process considered as acceptable?

By the third quarter of 2003, 1,900 asylum seekers who had received a final rejection of their applications and for that reason should have gone back to their country of origin still remained in boarding facilities. A new and controversial policy has recently been instituted whereby such persons may no longer remain in the facilities, and they also loose subsistence allowances.

There are no reliable figures on how many foreigners live and work in Norway without any permit (and excluding asylum seekers waiting for their case to be decided). The police estimate that in the greater Oslo area, where presumably most of these foreigners are, there may be around 20,000 of them. However, the police consider that the number may also be only half of this, or considerably higher. (In comparison, the greater Oslo area has less than one million inhabitants, and the total population of Norway is around 4.5 million.)

People expelled with a ban on return (for a certain time or for ever): 914 in 2002 (excluding asylum seekers).

People expelled without a ban on return (also excluding asylum seekers): 2,009 in 2002. 2,002 of these cases concern people who are refused entry at the border for not fulfilling entry requirements, for instance not having a visa when they need one, or not having sufficient means to cover their stay in Norway and the return to their home country.

There is no readily available number on deported asylum seekers in previous years. The number is probably quite low. A new national police unit for deportation has recently been established in order to increase efficiency. However, the traditional problems remain: Lack of proper ID papers, and the asylum seekers' refusal to cooperate in obtaining such papers from the authorities of what Norwegian authorities believe to be their home state, makes deportation very difficult to carry out.

4.2 What has been undertaken to implement the Directive of 28 November 2002, dealing with the facilitation of unauthorized entry, transit and residence?

At the end of January 2004, a ministerial consultation letter with proposals for implementation of directive 2002/90 was still being considered by interested parties. In the opinion of the ministry, Norwegian legislation already fulfils most of the requirements of the directive. The only amendment would be to remove the requirement that wilful assistance to persons in illegally entering the Schengen area must be offered for economic gain in order to be a criminal offence.

4.3 How many illegal applicants have been apprehended at or near the border? How many criminal procedures for human trafficking have been instituted in the last year?

There seem to be no readily available statistics on how many illegal immigrants have been apprehended at or near the border. It must be borne in mind that except for a short border with Russia, which is heavily policed on both sides and mainly runs in the middle of a large river or in mountainous terrain, all Norwegian land borders are with other Schengen states. These borders are not subject to regular border controls.

As mentioned under 4.1, 2,002 persons were stopped at the borders in 2002 for not fulfilling entry requirements (excluding asylum seekers, whose applications are of course always subject to a more thorough examination).

The police estimate that as many as 80% of all asylum seekers who reach Norway have been assisted by traffickers at some point. In 2002 there were 61 criminal proceedings against people charged with assisting foreigners in illegally entering Norway. In 2003 there were 63 cases.

4.4 What efforts have been undertaken in your country regarding the Budapest June 2003 recommendations concerning the harmonization of penalty scales with regard to the crime of the smuggling of migrants and trafficking of persons, in line with Council Directive 2002/90 of 28th November 2002? Did your country sign the relevant UN protocols on the smuggling of migrants?

The consultation letter mentioned under 4.2 also deals with the implementation of framework decision 2002/946, which is considered to constitute the implementation of the Budapest June 2003 recommendations. Only one amendment to existing legislation is deemed necessary: an increase in the penalty for those whose assistance for personal gain to persons illegally entering the Schengen area has put the life of those persons in danger. In order to remain in line with normal Norwegian sentencing practises, the upper limit is proposed to be six years' imprisonment.

Norway has signed the relevant UN protocols on smuggling of migrants.

4.5 What measures have been taken to implement the Council Directive of 28 May 2001, on the mutual recognition of decisions on the expulsion of third country nationals? What, if any shortcomings or gaps of the Directive should be corrected in a further directive on cooperation on expulsion or deportation of third country nationals?

Directive 2001/40 is binding upon Norway under the agreement with the EU on participation in the Schengen cooperation. The directive has led to two new provisions in the Immigration Act, one implementing Article 3(b) of the directive and another making it possible for Norwegian authorities to cooperate with their colleagues in other Schengen states also in cases concerning expulsion regardless of professional secrecy obligations. For the rest, Norwegian legislation was considered already to be in compliance. However, some doubts must linger, because the commission mentioned in 3.6 has been asked to take a second look at whether or not Article 3(a), second alternative, ought to lead to an amendment as well.

4.6 Do readmission agreements or other international treaties or arrangements with the aim of controlling and curbing illegal immigration and facilitating return exist in your country? Have they functioned satisfactorily?

In December 2003 Norway and Sweden signed an agreement on the simplification of procedures and shortening of time limits when applying the Dublin II regulation.

4.7 To what extent have EU-standards and recommendations influenced your country's return policy? Have efforts been undertaken to cooperate with other EU Member States in enforcing return decisions by common deportation actions, exchange of information, facilitation of air and land transit, common principles on flight security, etc.?

see answer to 4.8

4.8 Do you consider that there is a need to elaborate a common legal regime for air deportations (legal status of armed guards on board of the aircrafts, rights of the aircraft commander, legal rules in case of transit stops, applicability of national police law on board of aircraft on flight, etc.)?

Norway takes part in the so-called "Expulsion Group" under the Schengen cooperation and implements decisions made as a result of EU cooperation in this field, such as rules on transit during air deportations, joint flights etc. Norway also endeavours to conclude readmission agreements with third countries parallel to the EU. Joint flights and transit during deportations would seem to necessitate a certain minimum of common rules on the application of national police law on board aircrafts, armed guards etc., although in particular the question of armed guards tend to be delicate in Norway, whose police officers, like British police officers, are not normally armed.

THE REPUBLIC OF POLAND

DR. MICHAL KOWALSKI
Department of Public International Law Jagiellonian University

INTRODUCTION

The conversion of the Polish political system – from totalitarian to democratic – in 1989 led to substantial changes in the whole legal order obviously including migration and asylum law. In fact, the creation of a totally new system must have begun. Among other aspects, the obligations under international law deriving from newly adhered to international agreements such as the 1951 Refugee Convention had to be taken into account. Moreover, the future EU accession requirements gradually become a determinant in the process.

The first comprehensive regulation was adopted only in 1997 when the Alien Act covering both migration and asylum issues was adopted. However, the deficiencies which appeared in practice, as well as the accelerating process of adjusting Polish migration and asylum regulations to the EU standards which formally began in 1999 led to major amendment of the Aliens Act in April 2001. The evolution of the migration and asylum law within the EU led to further major changes. In 2003 the new Aliens Act was adopted jointly with the Act on granting protection to aliens within the territory of the Republic of Poland both of 13 June 2003 (*Journal of Laws 2003, No. 128, item 1175 and 1176 respectively*; hereafter referred to as the AA and the APA respectively). Both acts entered into force on 1 September 2003. Earlier the Act on principles and conditions of entry and residence of nationals of Member States of the European Union and their family members within the territory of the Republic of Poland of 27 July 2002 (*Journal of Laws 2002, No. 141, item 1180, as amended*), which will enter into force on the day of accession, was adopted. The two latter acts are of *lex specialis* character in relation to the AA. One should also mention the Act on Repatriation of 9 November 2000 (*Journal of Laws 2000, No. 106, item 1118, as amended*).

However, taking into account the EU developments, the process of establishing the Polish migration and asylum law system continues. New amendments aimed at further adjustment to the EU standards are planned. Due to the dynamic evolution of the EU regulations the adjusting process must be assessed as especially difficult. It has been informally labelled as a "shooting at a moving target" activity. Nevertheless, it seems that a more critical approach by the Polish authorities towards the EU standards, which very often cause serious concerns as far as conformity with international law standards is concerned, would be much more desirable. Yet, a passive approach has definitely prevailed so far.

The creation process of Polish migration and asylum law as such has been strictly linked with EU developments. Thus, it is hardly possible to answer the question what Polish migration and asylum law would be like without the adjustment process and, in consequence, to credibly assess the influence of EU standards on the Polish regulations.

PART I ENTRY, VISA REGIME AND BORDER CONTROL

1.1 What national authorities are competent to deal with visa applications (Schengen visas and long-term visas)? Are there any procedures to avoid duplication or successive visa applications at different EU-consulates? On what substantive criteria, other than the Schengen minimum requirements, are visas granted or refused? How many visas have been issued or refused?

Visa regulations of the 2003 AA which have significantly changed the previous ones were introduced in order to improve the effectiveness and coherence of the Polish visa system and to ensure its compatibility with the EU standards.

The AA identifies the following visa categories: airport visa, transit visa, entry visa, residence visa, diplomatic visa, service visa, courier visa, transit diplomatic visa.

Generally, a consul is the competent authority to deal with a visa application (Art. 46.1 AA). Additionally, in specified situations, other authorities are competent. They include: a voivod (*wojewoda*; a local representative of government; Poland is divided into 16 regions /*województwo*/), a commanding officer of the Border Guard checkpoint, the minister competent with respect to foreign affairs; a head of a Polish diplomatic mission and a person appointed by the minister competent with respect to foreign affairs to perform consular functions.

The extraordinary residence visa provided for in Art. 33 AA, may be issued even if the general conditions justifying visa refusal apply. It may be issued or refused, alternatively by a consul or by a voivod competent with respect to the place of the alien's residence. Issuing such a visa is subject to the prior consent of the Head of the Repatriation and Aliens Office (Art. 46.3 AA).

The residence visa provided in Art. 34.1–2 AA for a minor alien born on the territory of Poland or, alternatively, for a person representing a minor whose travel document lists the minor concerned is issued or refused by a voivod competent with respect to the place of residence of the person representing the minor (Art. 46.4 AA).

Diplomatic visas, service visas, courier visas and transit diplomatic visas are issued or refused by the minister competent with respect to foreign affairs, a head of a Polish diplomatic mission or a person appointed by the minister competent with respect to foreign affairs to perform consular functions (Art. 46.5.1–2 AA). In particularly justified cases they may be also issued by a commanding officer of the Border Guard checkpoint (Art. 46.5.3 AA).

A commanding officer of the Border Guard checkpoint is also entitled to issue an extraordinary residence visa under Art. 47 AA. Such a visa may be issued to an alien proving exceptional and urgent grounds justifying his or her entry to, residence in or transit through Poland and that he or she was unable to be issued with a visa from a consul for unforeseeable and imperative reasons. The competence of a commanding officer of the Border Guard checkpoint to issue an extraordinary residence visa under Art. 47 AA will cease at the moment of accession to the EU (Art. 165.2 AA).

The AA, in comparison with previous regulations, limits the visa competences of authorities other than a consul and sets out these competences in a more detailed manner.

A visa refusal decision is final except for a visa issued by a voivod (Art. 46.8 AA).

1.2 Is there a visa tracking procedure in order to identify visa overstayers? What data are collected from visa-applicants (fingerprints)? Admissibility of visa data to alien and police authorities?

No special visa tracking procedure exists in order to find out visa overstayers. Generally, the legality of an alien's residence in Poland is controlled when an alien is justifiably believed to reside illegally or violates public order (Art. 85–87 AA and the Minister of Interior Regulation on the legality control procedures with respect to aliens residence within the territory of the Republic of Poland, *Journal of Laws 2003, No. 143, item 1426*). The pending reform of the Polish Border Guard including, *inter alia*, the extension of competences to control aliens within the whole territory of Poland should be also mentioned in this context.

Data which may be collected from aliens in procedures covered by the AA are stipulated in Art. 12.1 AA. They include: first name(s); surname; former surname; surname at birth; sex; father's first name; mother's first name and surname at birth; date of birth or age; place and country of birth; description including height in centimetres, colour of the eyes and distinctive features; fingerprints; citizenship; ethnic origin; marital status; education; current occupation; place of employment; place of residence or stay; information on criminal record, judicial or administrative decisions and pending criminal proceedings. Additionally, data on an alien's state of health may be collected in visa, admission and residence procedures (Art. 12.2 AA).

However, under the AA fingerprints are only collected in the following situations: illegal entry, save in situations where an alien entered unintentionally and subsequently was immediately escorted to the border (Art. 14.2 AA); issuing an expulsion decision (Art. 93 AA); detaining an alien to whom the premises of expulsion apply or who does not comply with an expulsion decision (Art. 101 AA). Additionally, fingerprints are collected from aliens seeking protection under the APA.

Visa applications (visa prolongation application) must include: an alien's personal data, as well as the data of children whom the application covers, as well as data of other persons listed in an alien's travel document; data on an alien's travel document; information relating to travelling and residing abroad within the previous five years; the purpose of the residence planned. An alien is obliged to justify the application and to enclose documents confirming information stated in the application as well as photographs of persons covered by the application (Art. 45 AA).

Visa data including the above mentioned data on visa applicants, as well as detailed data on particular visa procedures (applications, administrative decisions, judgements) form the Visa Register which is a part of the general aliens data system under the AA, known as the Residence System (*System Pobyt*). All data from the Residence System, as well as from the separate Register of Aliens' Fingerprints are available under Art. 133 AA to the following authorities: the Commandant in Chief of the Police; the Commandant in Chief of the Border Guard; the Chief of the Internal Security Agency; the Chief of the Intelligence Agency; the Minister of National Defence; the minister competent with respect to public finances; the minister competent with respect to internal affairs; the Refugee Council;

a court; the Supreme Administrative Court; a prosecutor; a voivod; a consul. Data included in the Residence System may be transferred abroad under relevant international agreements (Art. 134 AA).

1.3 Have courts ever decided on the refusal of a Schengen visa based upon Schengen blacklisting by other Member States?

n/a

1.4 What measures have been undertaken in the implementation of the action programme for administrative cooperation in the field of external borders, visa, asylum and immigration following the Council Decision of 13 June 2002?

According to the information from the Repatriation and Aliens Office no special measures of administrative co-operation are in operation so far.

1.5 What measures have been undertaken to implement the Directive 2001/51 EC supplementing the Schengen rules concerning carrier sanctions? How often have carrier sanctions been used?

Carrier sanctions have been effectively used in practice since they were introduced to the Polish legal system by the 1997 Aliens Act. Currently, carrier sanctions are regulated in Chapter 12 of the 2003 AA (Art. 135–140). Regulations of the AA have significantly changed the previous regulations. New regulations were introduced in order to meet the EU standards.

The regulations of Chapter 12 of the AA cover all standards specified in the Directive of 28 June 2001 which supplement the provisions of Article 26 of the Convention implementing the Schengen Agreement of 14 June 1985 (2001/51/EC), including: carrier obligations on aliens in transit; the financial responsibility of a carrier which is unable to effect the return of an alien; the amount of penalties (according to Art. 138 AA the penalty amounts to the PLN equivalent of not less than EUR 3,000, – up to EUR 5,000, – for each person and not more than EUR 500,000, – in total; other penalties are not provided); as well as carriers' effective rights of defence and appeal with respect to penalties.

However, provisions on carrier sanctions apply only to air and sea carriers. According to Art. 165.1 AA they will also be applied to land carriers following the accession.

Moreover, the case-law of the Supreme Administrative Court (NSA), referring mainly to the scope of a carriers' control obligation, has been taken into account. Consequently new regulations precisely delimit the obligation of a carrier to control travel documents and visas.

1.6 In your judgement, does the visa law and policy of your country live up to EU standards or are adjustments needed? Do you consider that there is need for further EU-harmonization of visa policies concerning:
- **common criteria for granting visas aiming at harmonizing visa obligations among states participating in the Budapest Process;**
- **establishment of a European visa identification system (VIS and SIS II)?**

To what extent will the EU enlargement process present an opportunity or challenge for tackling issues of illegal entry and border control?

Polish migration law, including visa regulations, has been intensively adjusted to the EU standards. Definitely, the 2003 AA marked significant progress in this respect. However, the process is still on-going.

PART II ADMISSION AND RESIDENCE OF THIRD COUNTRY NATIONALS

2.1 What are the basic principles in your country concerning:
- **admission of third country nationals for labour purposes or self-employed activities;**
- **admission of third country nationals for study and vocational training;**
- **legal status of third country nationals in possession of a long-term residence permit of another Member State?**

To what extent do these principles differ from the European Commission's proposals;

2.2 What are the legal requirements and procedures for obtaining a residence permit for third country nationals for the purpose of employment? Which procedures are used in maintaining the preferred access of EU-citizens and Turkish nationals (association agreement) to the labour market? Do special programmes exist for highly qualified professionals facilitating access to the labour market? To what extent are trade unions and employers involved in such programmes? Is there a procedure to calculate the demand for foreign labour? How is the EU-enlargement taken into consideration? To what extent has the recent economic recession and unemployment influenced the concepts on admission of third country nationals?

2.3 To what extent do existing national laws and practices differ substantially from the approach taken in the Commission's Proposal on admission for the purpose of paid employment and self-employed activities relating to:
- **admission of third country nationals for study and vocational training;**
- **on legal status of third country nationals in possession of a long-term residence permit of another Member State?**

To what extent do these principles differ from the European Commission's proposals?

2.4 What measures have been taken to implement the Directive of 29th June 2000, implementing the principle of equal treatment between persons irrespective

of racial or ethnic origin and Council Directive 2000/78 EC of 27th November 2000, establishing a general framework for equal treatment in employment and occupation? Have legislative changes been undertaken? To what extent is "affirmative action" considered as necessary to promote equal opportunities for migrant workers from third countries?

The residence visa is issued for the following purposes listed in Art. 26.1.4. However, the catalogue is not of *numerus clausus* character. The residence visa may be of short-term (for a maximum of three months) or long-term character (for a maximum of one year). Long-term residence visas may be issued for the listed purposes (tourism; visits, participation in sports events; self-employment; cultural activity or participation in international conferences; performing service obligations by representatives of foreign states or international organisations; asylum procedure – which is distinct from refugee status procedure; see Part III below – ; employment – pursuing economic activity – ; education, training, didactic – other than economic activity; enjoying temporary protection) in circumstances which require residence for a period longer than three months. The residence period is determined according to the relevant circumstances. Residence visas for the purpose of employment may be issued to an alien who provides a document certifying that an employment permit will be issued or – if such a permit is not required – a document issued by an employer certifying the intention to employ an alien. Residence visas may be prolonged once within the maximum validity period of one year only if each of the following conditions is met: the alien has important professional or personal interests for staying or humanitarian grounds occur; the reasons for visa prolongation are of unforeseeable and imperative character; the purpose of residence is not distinct from the declared one; established grounds for visa refusal (Art. 42.2–7) do not apply.

The AA provides two forms of residence permits: residence permits and settlement permits.

A residence permit is granted to an alien if circumstances justify his or her residence for a period exceeding three months and one of the following is met:

a) an alien provides a document certifying that an employment permit will be issued or prolonged or – if such a permit is not required – a document issued by an employer certifying the intention to employ the alien concerned;

b) an alien is self-employed and the activity pursued is in the interest of Poland and he or she possesses sufficient financial means for covering residence within Polish territory;
c) an alien is an established artist intending to continue his or her activity in Poland;
d) an alien participates in training and vocational training in the framework of the EU programmes;
e) an alien intends to join a migrant worker in accordance with the provisions of the European Social Charter of 18 October 1961;
f) an alien is a spouse of a Polish national;
g) an alien intends to come or has come to Poland for family reunification;
h) an alien is a minor born within Polish territory being a child of an alien with a residence permit (Art. 53.1 AA).

Moreover, a residence permit may be granted to an alien if: he or she proves that circumstances justifying his or her residence for a period exceeding three months other than those listed in Art. 53.1 AA occur and he or she possesses sufficient financial means to cover residence within Polish territory; or an alien intends to begin or to continue university education being able to provide a relevant document of confirmation, as well as possesses sufficient financial means to cover residence within Polish territory (Art. 53.3 AA). The residence permit is also granted to a person enjoying temporary protection (Art. 110.2 APA). Moreover, the premisses of residence permit refusal are provided in Art. 57.1 AA.

It is assumed that an alien possesses sufficient financial means to cover residence within Polish territory if they cover the costs of accommodation, living and health care of the alien concerned and his or her dependant family members without recourse to the social assistance system (Art. 53.4 AA).

The settlement permit is granted:

a) to an alien who proves that: he or she has established family or economic links with Poland; and possesses accommodation and means of support in Poland; and was continuously residing within the territory of Poland directly before applying for a settlement permit for a period of minimum five years under visas, a residence permit or refugee status or for a minimum of three years under residence permits issued for the purpose of family reunification;
b) to a minor born within the territory of Poland who is a child of an alien if at least one of his or her legal representatives has been issued a settlement permit;

c) to an alien married to a Polish national for at least three years if he or she was residing within the territory of Poland directly before applying for a settlement permit for a continuous period of two years minimum;
d) to an alien who is not covered by the situations listed above and who was residing within the territory of Poland directly before applying for a settlement permit for a continuous period of a minimum of ten years under visas, a residence permit, tolerated stay leave or of a minimum of eight years under refugee status;
e) to a child of a Polish national if the latter enjoys parental authority.

The grounds for refusing a settlement permit are provided in Art. 66 AA and they are in line with the relevant regulations of the Directive of 25 November 2003 concerning the status of third country nationals who are long-term residents (2003/109/EC).

As a general rule, an alien may be employed (pursue economic activity) subject to the alien possessing an employment permit. However, aliens who have been granted a settlement permit, refugee status, tolerated residence leave or temporary protection are exempted from the requirement of possessing an employment permit. Following the day of accession the exemption will be extended to nationals of the EU Member States and their family members (Art. 50.1 of the Act on employment and preventing unemployment of 14 December 1994, *Journal of Laws 2003, No. 58, item 514, as amended* in conjunction with Art. 1.2 of the Act on amending the Act on employment and preventing unemployment of 26 April 2002, *Journal of Laws 2002, No. 74, item 675, as amended*). Some further categories of aliens pursuing determined economic activities are also exempted from the requirement of possessing an employment permit.

An employment permit is issued by a voivod. An application for an employment permit is preceded by the issuing of a document certifying the intention to employ an alien. Such a document is issued by a voivod on the request of an employer and is the basis for an alien to apply for a residence visa for the purpose of employment or for a residence permit. Issuing employment permits to aliens who have already been issued with a relevant visa or residence permit is not preceded by issuing a document certifying the intention to employ an alien.

There are no special programmes facilitating access to the labour market for highly qualified professionals.

2.5 Concerning the proposal for a directive on the right to family reunion agreed upon by the Council in February 2003:

- **Do you consider the proposed standards below the principles of family reunification applicable in your country?**
- **Will the implementation of the Directive, once it is adopted, lead to changes in the national law on family reunification downgrading the standard of protection? If so, what changes are envisaged?**

The principles of the AA on family reunification are generally in line with the Directive of 22 September 2003 on the right to family reunification (2003/86/EC) as they were modelled on the basis of the draft directive. Thus, it is hard to assess whether further implementation of the Directive standards – if needed – would lead to the downgrading of the family reunification standards under the AA. Nonetheless, this cannot be excluded. For instance, restrictions upon family members' access to employment and self-employment might be introduced in accordance with Art. 14.2–3 of the Directive. Yet, the AA requires the sponsor – save a person granted refugee status – to have stayed lawfully in the territory for a period of three years before becoming entitled to reunite with family members (Art. 54.1 AA). This is a standard lower than the one contained in the general rule set out in Art. 8 of the Directive which limits such a requirement to a maximum period of two years. Some of the family reunification standards of the AA based on the Directive model (e.g. the scope of family members entitled to reunite) cause serious concerns regarding their conformity with the established international law standards of family protection such as Art. 8 of the European Convention on Human Rights.

2.6 The proposal for a directive on the rights of long-term third country nationals as agreed upon by the Council on 5 June 2003, provides for a number of rights approximating the situation of long-term residents to the status of EU-citizens. Will the implementation of the Directive involve major legal and policy changes in your country? What are the major points of concern if any, concerning the approximation concept of the directive relating to:
- **non-discrimination in social rights;**
- **the concept of "civic citizenship" (see also extended impact assessment on the Communication on Integration of June 11, 2003);**
- **family reunification and access of family members to the labour market;**
- **security of stay?**

The status of long-term residents (enjoying a settlement permit) in Poland under the AA seems generally in line with the Directive of 25 November 2003 concerning the status of third country nationals who are long-term residents (2003/109/EC) including the approximation of certain rights to the status of Polish nationals. No major legal changes seem to be necessary save implementation of regulations on the terms of residence in Member States other than the one which conferred long-term status.

2.7 Considering the perspective of a future common migration policy as developed by the Commission in the Open Coordination Communication (COM 2001, 387) and the Communication on a Migration policy of the European Union (COM 2000, 757 final), how do you assess the role of the Community organs in determining a European migration policy in terms of competences of the Member States to decide on residence rights and admission to the labour market and integration? Should harmonization of legislation go further, and if so, in what respect?

No official position concerning the perspectives of a future common migration policy exists.

PART III ASYLUM AND REFUGEE LAW

Poland acceded to the 1951 Refugee Convention only in 1991. Since then the creation process of the comprehensive Polish asylum system has begun. The process reflects the increasing number of persons seeking protection in Poland, as well as the EU accession requirements. Thus, the impact of EU asylum legislation and policies may be regarded as decisive. As such, it has given rise to major concerns concerning the conformity of some of the EU standards and policies with the 1951 Refugee Convention system and other relevant human rights standards.

The 1997 Constitution guarantees in Art. 56 that aliens may be granted asylum in Poland and those seeking protection from persecution may be granted refugee status. The APA of 2003 provides that four forms of protection may be granted to aliens within the territory of Poland: a) asylum; b) refugee status; c) subsidiary protection (known as tolerated residence); d) temporary protection.

The institution of asylum in Polish law originates from legal traditions prior to the accession to the 1951 Refugee Convention in 1991. Asylum may be granted when an alien is in need of protection and cumulatively granting asylum is in the best interest of Poland. The institution is of a highly discretional character. The appeal procedure is limited to challenging expulsion only. The practical importance of the institution is marginal.

3.1 Have the Dublin Rules worked satisfactorily and what is expected of the Dublin II Regulation No. 343, 2003 of 18 February 2003?

The future application of the Dublin II Regulation of 18 February 2003 (343/2003) will undoubtedly lead to an increase in the number of asylum-seekers in Poland which will be a challenge for the effectiveness of the Polish asylum system. Moreover, the below mentioned inconsistencies with the EU standards cause special concern in this respect.

3.2 Has the Eurodac Regulation No. 2725/2000 of 11th December 2000, concerning the establishment of Eurodac for the comparison of fingerprints for an effective application of the Dublin Convention, operative since January 15, 2003, resulted in an increase of Dublin cases? Has Eurodac become effective in your country or is it expected to become effective eventually?

A special workgroup has been established within the Repatriation and Aliens Office in order to ensure the effective participation of Poland in Eurodac following the accession.

3.3 What major changes, if any, will the implementation of the amended proposal for a directive on minimum standards on procedures in Member States for granting and withdrawing refugee status, on which the Council has reached political agreement on most points in June 2003, bring for the legislation and practice in your country in particular relating to:
- **rights of applicants in the procedure;**
- **administrative and judicial appeal procedures;**
- **the use of safe third country and safe country of origin concepts;**
- **detainment of asylum seekers;**
- **airport and border procedures?**

As far as the rights of applicants in the refugee procedure are concerned, they are generally compatible with the proposed Directive. The rights include: the right to be informed in an understandable language about the procedure and applicant's rights and obligations (Art. 22 APA); the right to be interviewed (Art. 27.2 APA); and the right to communicate with the UNHCR and other refugee organisations (Art. 23.1 APA). Moreover, extensive guarantees for unaccompanied minors, violence victims and disabled asylum-seekers are provided (Art. 47–55 APA). Also, the special status of the UNHCR is guaranteed (Art. 23.2–8 APA).

The right to be interviewed is generally limited to the obligation of the determining authority to interview an applicant. The lack of further statutory guarantees on the right to an interview – save the guarantees for unaccompanied minors, victims of torture and disabled asylum-seekers – is significant in the light of the proposed Procedure Directive standards in this respect. However, the standards are generally met in practice.

Also, problems may arise in the context of the right to legal assistance and representation. Free legal assistance to asylum-seekers is effectively offered by NGOs and other relevant entities such as university legal clinics which asylum-seekers are free to consult. However, there is no formal obligation for authorities to ensure such assistance. The problem becomes especially important in the case of detained asylum-seekers. The problem is currently being debated.

The determining authority at first instance of the refugee procedure is the Head of the Repatriation and Aliens Office. The appeal authority body of second instance is the Refugee Council which is an independent administrative body of quasi-judicial character. The Refugee Council is entitled to examine both points of law and facts. An applicant is allowed to remain on the territory during the appeal procedure before the Refugee Council. From the decision of the Refugee Council an appeal to an administrative court may be lodged. Lodging an appeal to the court does not result in leave to remain on the territory but such leave may be granted by both the Refugee Council (*ex officio* or on request) or the court (on request). Since 1 January 2004 and following the reform of the Polish administrative judicial system the administrative judicial procedure consists of two instances. The administrative courts are not entitled to make decisions on the merits of a case. The procedure is compatible with the proposed Procedure Directive requirements. However, taking into account the four-instance refugee procedure and the cassational character of administrative courts' judgements, ensuring that the procedure results in a final decision within a reasonable time seems to be a challenge.

It seems that the concepts of "safe third countries" and "safe countries of origin" are good illustrations of the difficulties faced in adopting the EU measures to the Polish legal system. Art. 35.3 of the 1997 Aliens Act in its original version stated that access to the asylum procedure is to be denied if an asylum-seeker "*has arrived in the territory of the Republic of Poland from a safe country of origin or a safe third country and the application lodged by him/her is manifestly unfounded*". Thus, it was not in conformity with the EU soft law measures, or with international refugee law standards. The Polish regulation was changed in this respect by the 1997 Aliens Act's amendment of April 2001 and the lists of "safe third countries" and "safe countries of origin" have been abolished. The issue of whether an asylum-seeker came from a "safe third country" was determined in an admissibility decision by the relevant determining authority (the Head of the Repatriation and Aliens Office). As regards the "safe countries of origin" concept, if the relevant authority determined – while examining an application – that an asylum-seeker had come from a "safe country of origin", it was a ground to recognise an application as manifestly unfounded and refuse the granting of refugee status (accelerated procedure applied here). The regulation on "safe countries of origin" has been incorporated in the 2003 Aliens Act. However, the same rule was extended to the "safe third country" concept as well (Art. 14.1.3). *De lege lata*, both coming from a "safe country of origin" and a "safe third country" constitute a ground for recognising an application as manifestly unfounded and refusing the grant of refugee status (accelerated procedure applies here). Such a regulation is far from the approach taken in this respect by the Commission in the proposed Procedure Directive. However, the pending debate within the Council must also be taken into account. As far as the definitions of the "safe country of origin" and the "safe third country" concepts are concerned, they are defined in Art. 2.2 and 2.3 of the AA respectively.

The 2003 APA has introduced regulations on the detainment of asylum-seekers (Chapter : Art. 40–46 APA). The regulation is based on the internationally recognised principle that generally asylum-seekers should not be detained. Yet, it allows for far reaching exceptions. An asylum-seeker is to be detained and placed in a guarded centre or in a deportation centre if he or she: submits an application at the border being not entitled to enter; submits an application while staying illegally within the territory; illegally entered or attempted to enter before submitting an application; was issued a decision obliging him or her to leave or a decision on expulsion before submitting an application; was issued a decision on expulsion after submitting an application (Art. 40 APA). Asylum-seekers who are unaccompanied minors, disabled or victims of torture must not be detained (Art. 47.5 and Art. 54.3 APA respectively). Asylum-seekers are detained upon a court's decision and a subsequent court review is also provided. According to the authorities, the regulations on detention were introduced in order to stop the abuse of the refugee procedure (e.g. an alien not entitled to enter submits a refugee application and subsequently disappears within the territory). Nevertheless, the extensive character of detention causes serious concerns. The problem of the detained asylum-seekers' rights, such as the right to be informed of one's own legal status (the APA is silent in this respect) or the right of access to effective legal assistance and representation (the APA regulation is limited to providing free contact with the UNHCR or refugee organisation representatives), seems especially important in the context of Art. 5 of the European Convention on Human Rights. Yet, as far as the proposed Procedure Directive is concerned, the implementation of the provisions on the detention of asylum-seekers, which are rather ambiguous, does not seem to require any changes.

There are no special airport and border procedures regarding refugee procedures (save the above mentioned regulations on detention). An application may be lodged at the border to a commanding officer of the Border Guard checkpoint and subsequently must be transferred to the determining authority (the Head of the Repatriation and Aliens Office) within 48 hours.

3.4 What measures have been undertaken to implement Directive 2003/9 of 27 January 2003, on reception of asylum seekers in your country relating to:
- **the flexibility clauses in the Directive;**
- **restriction of free movement;**
- **access to the labour market;**
- **rights of migrant workers under Article 11 § 2 of the Directive?**

As far as minimum standards for the reception of asylum-seekers are concerned, the relevant regulations of the 2003 APA are based on the Directive of 27 January 2003 laying down minimum standards for the reception of asylum-seekers (2003/9/EC). Generally, the standards of the Reception Directive are met. However, according to Polish regulations asylum-seekers do not enjoy access to the labour market. Amendments adjusting the regulation to the requirements of Art. 11 of the Reception Directive will be necessary. The APA does not provide any limitations upon asylum-seekers' freedom of movement save those detained.

3.5 What steps have been undertaken to implement the Directive on temporary protection, COM 2001, 55 in national law? Are there any procedures for burden sharing arrangements? Is there a legal basis for the admission of refugees for the purposes of receiving temporary protection in a mass-movement situation?

The institution of temporary protection was introduced into the Polish legal system for the first time only in the 2001 amendment of the 1997 Aliens Act. The previous lack of relevant regulations was significant especially in 1999 when it impeded the process of granting protection to the Kosovars. The 2003 APA introduced an extensive regulation on temporary protection in Chapter 3 (Art. 106–118). The regulation is based on the Temporary Protection Directive of 20 July 2001 (2001/55/EC). Till the accession to the EU the temporary protection regime has been introduced by the Council of Ministers of the Republic of Poland (Art. 108.1–3 APA in conjunction with Art. 146.3 APA). Following the accession the temporary protection regime will be introduced in accordance with the decision of the Council of the EU. Additionally, the Council of Ministers of the Republic of Poland will retain the competence to grant temporary protection to those not covered by the decision of the Council of the EU (Art. 107 APA in conjunction with Art. 146.1 APA).

However, it is worth noticing that the APA establishes the duration of temporary protection for one year. Further, the temporary protection regime may be extended by two six-month periods for a maximum of one year (Art. 106.2–3 APA). This regulation is in conformity with Art. 4.1 of the Temporary Protection Directive. It seems, however, that it falls under the competences of the Council of Ministers of the Republic of Poland only. The duration of temporary protection introduced by the Council of the EU is to be determined independently in its decision. Remarkably, in consequence the maximum duration of the temporary protection regime introduced by the Council of the EU will be three years (Art. 4.1–2 of the Temporary Protection Directive), whereas the maximum duration of the temporary protection regime introduced by the Council of Ministers of the Republic of Poland will be two years.

Moreover, certain minor inconsistencies between the APA regulation and the Temporary Protection Directive may be identified. Art. 9 of the Temporary Protection Directive clearly requires that persons enjoying temporary protection are to be informed about their legal status in writing. Art. 111 of the APA formulates the same requirement but it is silent as far as the form is concerned.

Other standards of the Temporary Protection Directive have been met in the APA. The right to apply for refugee status of persons enjoying temporary protection is not suspended. No special procedures for burden sharing arrangements exist.

3.6 The Council has reached political agreement on the principles for a Directive on minimum standards for the qualification and status of third country nationals as refugees or persons who otherwise need international protection, COM 2001, 510 final (see Council documents of June 2003). What measures are envisaged to implement the Directive, once it is adopted, in your country relating to:
- **the definition of refugee;**
- **the definition of persons entitled to subsidiary protection;**
- **status of persons entitled to subsidiary protection;**
- **the issue of internal flight alternative as defined by the Directive;**
- **exclusion clauses, particularly issues of terrorism?**

To what extent are the refugee policies as reflected in the law and jurisprudence of your country in accordance with the proposal for the directive?

According to Art. 13.1 APA refugee status *is* granted to an alien covered by the definition of refugee contained in the 1951 Refugee Convention and the 1967 New York Protocol. This is a significant change in comparison to the previous regulations. According to the previous regulations under the 1997 Aliens Act (both before and after the amendment of 2001) refugee status only *might* be granted to those covered by the convention definition. Note that Art. 56.2 of the 1997 Constitution states that refugee status may be granted to an alien seeking protection from persecution within the territory of Poland according to binding international agreements. It is questionable whether the new provision of Art. 13.1 APA is in conformity with the further APA provisions providing for grounds for the refusal of refugee status additional to those set out in the convention definition, such as: coming from a safe country of origin; coming from a safe third country; responsibility under an international agreement to examine an application by another State-Party to the 1951 Refugee Convention (in all three cases applications are to be regarded as manifestly unfounded and refused; Art. 14.1.3–4); or being granted refugee status in another state (Art. 15.3).

The interpretation of the definition of refugee in the convention concerning such issues as agents of persecution, nature of persecution, refugees *sur place*, etc., is not statutorily established save the regulation on the internal flight alternative (see below). Yet, a restrictive interpretive approach has prevailed in the case-law of the determining authorities so far.

The subsidiary protection has been comprehensively introduced to the Polish legal system only by the 2003 APA. This form of protection, subsidiary to refugee status, is known as tolerated residence (*pobyt tolerowany*).

According to Art. 97 APA a tolerated residence leave is granted – in the refugee status procedure or in the context of the expulsion procedure – to an alien who must not be expelled because an expulsion:

a) would lead to the violations of rights defined in Arts. 2–7 of the European Convention on Human Rights;
b) may not be put into effect for independent grounds;
c) would be contrary to a judicial decision on the inadmissibility of the expulsion or to a decision of the Minister of Justice denying expulsion;
d) would be based on grounds other than being a threat to national security or defence or to public security and order and an alien is a spouse of a Polish national or an alien who has been granted a residence permit.

This regulation causes some concern. The criteria of selecting only some human rights seem to be unclear. It is also unclear why only international obligations under the European Convention on Human Rights have been taken into account.

The status of persons enjoying tolerated residence leave generally approximates to that of recognised refugees. However, the former are not issued with a travel document and are not entitled to receive means of support and integration facilities.

Until the entry into force of the 2003 APA, the internal flight alternative was a ground for recognising an application as manifestly unfounded and for refusing the grant of refugee status (accelerated procedure applied here). The APA changed this approach: the internal flight alternative constitutes a ground for refusing the grant of refugee status (Art. 15.1.1 APA). However, an asylum-seeker must not be refused refugee status on the sole ground of an internal flight alternative if it would not be reasonable to expect him or her to move to another part of the country of origin (Art. 15.2 APA). Thus, the regulation of the APA generally reflects the approach of the proposed Qualification and Status Directive. However, a strong presumption against the internal flight alternative if an agent of persecution is associated with the national government is not statutorily established under the APA.

There are no special exclusion regulations. Art. 15.1.2 provides that refuge status is to be refused if the exclusion clauses of the 1951 Refugee Convention apply.

3.7 In the Commission's Communication of 22 November, 2000, COM 2000, 755 (see also 2nd Commission Report COM 2003, 152 final) the Commission's concept of a common European asylum procedure and a uniform status for those who are granted asylum valid throughout the Union is set out. Do you consider that the concept is generally in line with your country's asylum policy? Are the concerns of refugee organizations, such as Amnesty International and other organizations, of an undermining of the international regime for the protection of refugees shared in the political circles responsible for decision-making of your country?

3.8 The open coordination-mechanism, as suggested by the Commission, provided for first stage and second stage legislation in which the flexibility provisions in some of the directives on migration and asylum are to be replaced by full harmonization. Is this concept discussed in your country and what are the perceptions relating to the gradual establishment of a European asylum policy which might eventually replace national procedures and national decision-making?

The concept of a common European asylum procedure and a uniform status for those who are granted asylum seems to be accepted in Poland and may be regarded in line with the Polish asylum policy which is aimed at adjusting to the EU standards. However, it must be stressed that there is no public debate concerning asylum policy. Neither are the political circles actively involved in the process. Thus, such concepts as a common European asylum system or an open co-ordination mechanism are debated to a very limited extent within expert circles only.

3.9 The Communication of June 2003, towards a more accessible, equitable and managed asylum system – in reaction to the UK paper – develops some ideas on new approaches to pursue an orderly and managed arrival of persons in need of international protection. What is the political reaction in your country to the concept of an outside accessed asylum procedure, distribution of refugees and responsibility-sharing and other new concepts and ideas in coping with mass refugee movements?

There are no official political positions concerning such concepts as outside accessed asylum procedures, distribution of refugees and responsibility-sharing, etc.

PART IV TERMINATION OF ILLEGAL RESIDENCE, RETURN AND REPATRIATION

An expulsion decision is issued if the following circumstances provided in Art. 88 AA are fulfilled:

a) illegal residence;
b) illegal employment or self-employment;
c) lack of sufficient financial means;
d) an alien's data are in the register of aliens undesirable within the territory of Poland;
e) an alien's further stay would be a threat to national safety or security or the protection of public security and order or would be contradictory to national interests;
f) illegal entry or an attempt to enter illegally;
g) non-compliance with a decision obliging an alien to leave the territory of Poland voluntarily;
h) non-compliance with fiscal obligations towards Poland;
i) completion of an imprisonment sentence for an intentional criminal offence or fiscal offence.

A decision obliging an alien to leave the territory of Poland voluntarily within seven days may be issued in the circumstances listed under a–c above (Art. 97.1 AA).

4.1 How many third country nationals without a valid residence permit are currently, according to estimates, staying in your country? How many deportations have actually been made in previous years? Is the whole enforcement process considered as acceptable?

There are no official figures on the estimated number of aliens residing illegally within the territory of Poland. According to the data delivered by the Polish Border Guard in 2002 *4836* expulsions took place. *1172* of them were due to illegal residence within the territory of Poland.

The 2003 AA introduced special provisions aimed at decreasing the number of aliens residing in Poland illegally. First, Art. 154 AA provided for the possibility of legalising the situation of illegal residence of aliens within the territory of Poland under determined conditions (known as the large abolition). An application for the legalisation of an illegal stay might be submitted till 31 December 2003. Secondly, Art. 155 AA provides for the possibility for aliens residing illegally to leave the territory of Poland without being listed in the relevant registers (known as the small abolition). To benefit from this regulation an alien must have registered, within two months since the AA entered into force, to the Police or the Border Guard and must have left the territory of Poland in accordance with the subsequent decision obliging him or her to leave. No relevant statistical data is available yet.

4.2 What has been undertaken to implement the Directive of 28 November 2002, dealing with the facilitation of unauthorized entry, transit and residence?

The standards of the Directive of 28 November 2002 defining the facilitation of unauthorised entry, transit and residence (2002/90/EC) are met in the relevant criminal law regulations (Art. 264 of the Criminal Code of 6 June 1997, *Journal of Laws 1997, No. 88, item 553, as amended*).

4.3 How many illegal applicants have been apprehended at or near the border? How many criminal procedures for human trafficking have been instituted in the last year?

According to the data delivered by the Polish Border Guard in 2002 *5372* persons were apprehended at or near the border while entering the territory of Poland illegally (*660* of whom were apprehended on the eastern borders with Russia, Lithuania, Belarus and Ukraine). This is a decrease of 13.14% in comparison with 2001 when *6186* persons were apprehended (*790* on the eastern border).

As far as criminal proceedings for human trafficking are concerned, only two proceedings were instituted in 2002 according to the data delivered by the Polish Border Guard.

4.4 What efforts have been undertaken in your country regarding the Budapest June 2003 recommendations concerning the harmonization of penalty scales with regard to the crime of the smuggling of migrants and trafficking of persons, in line

with Council Directive 2002/90 of 28th November 2002? Did your country sign the relevant UN protocols on the smuggling of migrants?

In 2002 the governmental National Programme on Combating and Preventing Human Trafficking was adopted. The National Programme is in line with the obligations of Poland under the UN Protocol on preventing, combating and punishment of human trafficking of 2002 to which Poland is a State-Party. The programme is of a comprehensive character and provides for various measures such as education (including special training programmes for the Border Guard), victim protection schemes, media co-operation etc. As far as legal developments are concerned, the National Programme provides for:

a) Introducing the definition of human trafficking to the Criminal Code. Human trafficking is penalised by the Criminal Code (Art. 253), however, it has not been defined which results in differentiated interpretations by courts. The human trafficking definitions of the 2002 Protocol and the Council Framework Decision on combating human trafficking of 19 July 2002 (2002/629/JAI) are to be implemented. The relevant amendment of the Criminal Code is planned by 1 May 2004.
b) Introducing special short-term residence permits for victims of human trafficking who co-operate with the authorities. The relevant amendment of the AA is planned for the first half of 2004.
c) Adhering to the UN Optional Protocol to the Convention on the Rights of the Child concerning the Sale of Children, Child Prostitution and Child Pornography. This will occur in the first half of 2004.

4.5 What measures have been taken to implement the Council Directive of 28 May 2001, on the mutual recognition of decisions on the expulsion of third country nationals? What, if any shortcomings or gaps of the Directive should be corrected in a further directive on cooperation on expulsion or deportation of third country nationals?

No measures implementing the Directive of 28 May 2001 on the mutual recognition of decisions on the expulsion of third country nationals (2001/40/EC) have been adopted so far.

4.6 Do readmission agreements or other international treaties or arrangements with the aim of controlling and curbing illegal immigration and facilitating return exist in your country? Have they functioned satisfactorily?

Readmissions agreements concluded by Poland are generally considered to function satisfactorily. According to the data delivered by the Polish Border Guard *4836* persons were readmitted from Poland to other states in 2002 (in comparison: *5954* in 2001) and *5281* persons were readmitted to Poland (*3452* Polish nationals and *1856* aliens; in comparison: *7623* persons /*5399* Polish nationals and *2224* aliens/ in 2001).

4.7 To what extent have EU-standards and recommendations influenced your country's return policy? Have efforts been undertaken to cooperate with other EU Member States in enforcing return decisions by common deportation actions, exchange of information, facilitation of air and land transit, common principles on flight security, etc.?

According to the Repatriation and Aliens Office, no co-operation with the EU Member States in enforcing return decisions by common deportation actions, facilitation of transit, etc., has taken place so far.

4.8 Do you consider that there is a need to elaborate a common legal regime for air deportations (legal status of armed guards on board of the aircrafts, rights of the aircraft commander, legal rules in case of transit stops, applicability of national police law on board of aircraft on flight, etc.)?

No official position exists concerning a need to elaborate a common legal regime for air deportation.

PORTUGAL

NUNO PIÇARRA
Professeur à la Faculté de Droit
de la Universidade Nova de Lisboa

Partie I – Entrée dans le territoire, régime des visas et contrôle aux frontières

1.1 Quelle sont les autorités nationales compétentes en matière de demandes de visas (dans le cadre de l'espace Schengen et pour les visas de longue durée)? Existe-t-il des procédures permettant d'éviter une duplication des demandes de visas ou d'éviter le dépôt de demandes successives dans les différents consulats dans l'Union européenne? En fonction de quels critères substantiels, autres que les exigences minimum requises dans le cadre de l'espace Schengen, les visas sont-ils accordés ou refusés? Combien de demandes de visas ont été satisfaites, combien ont été rejetées?

L'article 30 de l'ordonnance n° 244/98 du 8 août, relative aux conditions d'entrée, séjour, sortie et éloignement d'étrangers du territoire portugais, telle que modifiée en dernier lieu par ordonnance n.° 34/2003, du 25 février (ci-après «ordonnance n° 244/98»[1]) attribue aux postes consulaires de carrière portugais la compétence pour accorder tous les types de visa énoncés par l'article 27, à savoir, (a) le visa d'escale, (b) le visa de transit, (c) le visa de courte durée, (d) le visa de résidence, (e) le visa d'études, (f) le visa de travail (g) le visa de séjour temporaire. Les ambassades portugaises sont également compétentes pour accorder des visas d'escale, de transit et de courte durée lorsqu'ils sont demandés par les titulaires de passeports diplomatiques, de service, officiels ou spéciaux, ou de documents de voyage émis par des organisations internationales.

Aux termes de l'article 47, les visas de transit et de courte durée peuvent être aussi accordés, à titre exceptionnel, dans les postes de frontière extérieure, ainsi que le visa spécial. Dans ces cas, en vertu de

[1] L'ordonnance (*Decreto-Lei*) est un acte de nature législative adopté par le gouvernement sur la base d'une autorisation parlementaire lorsqu'il s'agit d'un domaine relevant de la réserve de compétence relative du parlement en vertu de l'article 165 de la Constitution, comme celui sur lequel porte ordonnance n° 244/98 (paragraphe 1, sous *b*), du même article). Le gouvernement utilise aussi le *Decreto-Lei* pour exercer sa compétence législative propre.

l'article 50, l'autorité nationale compétente est le directeur général du Service d'étrangers et de frontières (ci-après «SEF»), qui peut déléguer cette compétence au directeur général central de frontières et aux directeurs régionaux, lesquels peuvent, à leur tour, la sous-déléguer.

Il découle des dispositions combinées des articles 28, paragraphe 1, et 48, paragraphe 3, que les visas d'escale, de transit et de courte durée doivent en principe être valables pour tout l'espace Schengen. Par contre, il résulte des dispositions combinées des articles 28, paragraphe 2, et 49, paragraphe 2, que les visas de résidence, d'études, de travail et de séjour temporaire, ainsi que le visa spécial, ne peuvent être valables que pour le territoire portugais.

Les trois types de «visa Schengen» sont normalement accordés par les autorités nationales compétentes une fois réunies les conditions prévues par l'acquis Schengen. Les quatre autre types, étant des visas de longue durée valables exclusivement pour le territoire national, ne relèvent pas de cet acquis et par conséquent ne sont pas soumis aux conditions y prévues, mais à celles établies par l'ordonnance n° 244/98[2].

Le droit portugais ne prévoit pas de procédures permettant d'éviter une duplication des demandes de visas ou le dépôt de demandes successives dans les différents postes consulaires de carrière des États membres de l'Union européenne. Le système de concession de visas Schengen permet néanmoins de détecter certains cas de duplication de demandes de visa[3].

D'après les statistiques obtenues auprès des services compétents, en 96.939 demandes de visas, 82.435 ont été satisfaites, 9.376 ont été rejetées, 1.587 ont été radiées et 3.590 sont encore pendantes

1.2 Existe-t-il une procédure permettant de tracer les personnes dont le visa a expiré? Quel genre de données sont recueillies lors du dépôt d'une demande de visas (empreintes digitales, par exemple)? Les données recueillies peuvent-elles être communiquées aux autorités policières ou étrangères?

Le droit portugais ne prévoit pas une procédure spéciale permettant de tracer les personnes dont le visa a expiré. Ce tracement peut néanmoins être fait notamment au travers d'un contrôle mené par le SEF à l'adresse indiquée par le demandeur de visa, une fois expirée la période de validité de celui-ci.

[2] Les conditions requises par ordonnance n° 244/98 pour l'octroi d'un visa de travail et d'un visa d'études seront examinées à la Partie II, 2.1. et 2.2.

[3] Voir notamment le point 8.2. de l'Instruction consulaire commune destinée aux missions diplomatiques et aux postes consulaires de carrière.

Le décret réglementaire n° 5-A/2000, du 26 avril 2000, tel que modifié en dernier lieu par le décret réglementaire n° 9/2001, du 31 mai 2001, portant sur les modalités d'application de l'ordonnance n° 244/98, ne prévoit pas que des empreintes digitales des demandeurs de visa puissent être recueillies lors du dépôt d'une telle demande. Les données dont l'acquisition par l'autorité compétente est prévue sont les suivants: des photos, l'identification complète du demandeur de visa, l'identification du document de voyage, l'objet et la période de séjour pour lesquels le visa est demandé, des certificats de conditions de logement et d'existence de moyens de subsistance, ainsi que des certificats médicaux et de casier judiciaire.

Il n'y a pas dans l'ordonnancement portugais une base juridique expresse qui permette de communiquer les données recueillies lors du dépôt d'une demande de visa aux autorités policières ou autres. Cette communication doit se faire, en tout état de cause, dans les limites de la législation nationale en matière de protection des données personnelles.

1.3 Les juridictions se sont-elles déjà prononcées sur un refus de demande de visa dans le cadre de Schengen au motif qu'elle provenait d'un ressortissant d'un pays figurant sur la "liste noire" des Etats membres?

Aucune décision juridictionnelle nationale n'a été trouvée qui se soit prononcée sur une mesure administrative de rejet d'une demande de visa Schengen, fondée sur la circonstance qu'elle a été introduite par un ressortissant d'un pays figurant sur la liste de ceux dont les ressortissants ont besoin de visa pour franchir les frontières des Etats membres.

1.4 Quelles ont été les mesures prises afin de mettre en œuvre le programme d'action en matière de coopération administrative dans le domaine du contrôle aux frontières extérieures, des questions de visas, d'immigration et de demandes d'asile en application de la décision du Conseil du 13 juin 2002?

Le programme d'action en matière de coopération administrative dans le domaine du contrôle aux frontières extérieures, des questions de visas, d'immigration et de demandes d'asile (ARGO), établi par la décision du Conseil du 13 juin 2002, n'a pas donné lieu jusqu'à présent à des mesures d'application au Portugal. Cependant, au mois de mars 2004 (du 1er au 12), aura lieu à Lisbonne le VIII Séminaire d'experts en documents de sécurité, financé par ce programme et organisé conjointement par les Pays-Bas, le Royaume Uni et le Portugal.

1.5 Quelles démarches ont été entreprises afin de transposer la directive communautaire 2001/51/CE du Conseil du 28 juin 2001 visant à compléter les dispositions

de la Convention d'application de l'accord de Schengen relativement aux sanctions imposées aux transporteurs? Ces sanctions ont-elles souvent été appliquées?

La directive communautaire 2001/51/CE du Conseil, du 28 juin 2001, visant à compléter les dispositions de la Convention de Schengen en ce qui concerne les sanctions imposées aux transporteurs a été transposée par les articles 21, 141 et 142 de l'ordonnance n° 244/98. Cependant, l'article 21 ne couvre pas tous les cas de refus d'entrée de l'étranger dans le territoire portugais, mais seulement les cas où celui-ci ne réunit pas les conditions formelles d'entrée. De leur côté, les montants minimaux et maximaux des sanctions pécuniaires à appliquer aux transporteurs, fixés par les articles 141 et 142, sont inférieurs à ceux imposées par la directive. Par contre, la variation de ces montants en fonction de la qualité de personne physique ou de personne juridique des transporteurs, établie par ces dispositions, bien qu'elle ne soit pas prévue par la directive, peut être considérée comme relevant du pouvoir d'appréciation que cet instrument octroie au législateur national.

Les sanctions prévues par ces dispositions sont fréquemment appliquées aux transporteurs.

1.6 **Selon vous, le droit et les politiques relatifs aux visas en vigueur dans votre pays respectent-ils les exigences de l'Union européenne en la matière ou des ajustements sont-ils nécessaires? Pensez-vous qu'une harmonisation communautaire des réglementations en matière de visas soit indispensable concernant notamment:**
- **les critères communs d'octroi des visas visant à harmoniser les obligations pesant en ce domaine sur les Etats participant au processus de Budapest;**
- **la création d'un système européen d'identification des visas (VIS et SIS II).**

A mon avis, le droit et les politiques en matière de visas existantes au Portugal peuvent être considérés comme respectant en substance les exigences de l'Union européenne en la matière. C'est surtout au niveau de la pratique d'octroi de visas aux postes consulaires de carrière qu'il faudra procéder à certains ajustements. Je pense, par exemple, aux conditions de sécurité dans lesquelles y sont gardés les vignettes de visa et d'autres documents y afférents.

Un texte communautaire fixant les critères communs d'octroi des visas en vue d'harmoniser les obligations qui incombent en ce domaine aux États participant au processus de Budapest, ainsi que la création d'un système européen d'identification des visas (VIS et SIS II) s'avèrent sans doute nécessaires. Les justifications qu'en donne la Commission au point 1.1. de sa communication au Parlement européen et au Conseil, concernant le développement d'une politique commune en matière d'immigration clandestine, de trafic illicite et de traite d'êtres humains, de frontières extérieures et de retour des personnes en résidence irrégulière, de juin 2003, le démontrent à suffisance.

1.7 Dans quelle mesure le processus d'élargissement de l'Union européenne représente-t-il une opportunité ou, au contraire, un danger dans la lutte contre l'immigration clandestine et le contrôle des frontières?

Le processus d'élargissement de l'Union européenne représente une opportunité plutôt qu'un danger dans la lutte contre l'immigration clandestine et le contrôle des frontières. Plusieurs raisons peuvent être invoquées pour justifier cette affirmation.

Tout d'abord, les frontières des États candidats qui deviendront leurs frontières extérieures au moment de l'adhésion se trouveront considérablement renforcées à la suite de la préparation qui a été faite au cours des dernières années en coopération avec la Commission et les quinze États membres actuels, ayant impliqué des investissements d'envergure dans les domaines de la formation du personnel et de l'équipement de contrôle indispensable. Par ailleurs, les nouveaux États membres, à partir du moment où ils intègreront l'espace de liberté, de sécurité et de justice, seront soumis au droit commun de l'Union en la matière et donc aux mêmes obligations de lutter contre l'immigration clandestine qui incombent aux États membres actuels, ainsi que d'entreprendre des actions en commun. Enfin, toute activité des futurs États membres dans cet espace sera soumise aux mécanismes de contrôle et d'évaluation mutuels en vigueur, en vue de maintenir l'indispensable confiance réciproque entre tous.

Partie II – Les procédures d'accueil et le droit de séjour des ressortissants des pays tiers

2.1 Quels sont les principes fondamentaux dans votre pays concernant:
- **l'entrée des ressortissants des pays tiers afin d'exercer une activité salariée ou une activité économique indépendante;**
- **l'entrée des ressortissants des pays tiers afin de faire des études ou de suivre une formation professionnelle;**
- **le statut juridique des ressortissants qui bénéficient d'un droit de séjour de longue durée dans un autre Etat membre;**
- **dans quelles mesure ces principes diffèrent-t-ils des propositions de la Commission européenne?**

Les principes fondamentaux en vigueur au Portugal concernant l'entrée des ressortissants des pays tiers afin d'exercer une activité salariée ou une activité économique indépendante sont prévus par l'ordonnance n° 244/98. Cette entrée dépend de l'obtention *préalable* d'une *autorisation* sous forme de «visa de travail» ou de «visa de résidence». Le premier est valide pour des entrées multiples et le second pour deux entrées. Ces visas permettent à leur titulaire d'exercer temporairement, jusqu'à un an avec la possibilité de prorogation jusqu'à deux ans[4], dans le premier cas, ou jusqu'à six mois prorogeables, une activité professionnelle, subordonnée ou non.

Aux termes de l'article 37, le visa de travail comprend quatre types, à savoir, (a) le visa de travail I, pour l'exercice d'une activité professionnelle dans le domaine du sport ou des spectacles; (b) le visa de travail II, pour l'exercice d'une activité de recherche scientifique ou présupposant une connaissance technique hautement qualifiée, dûment certifiées, dans les deux cas, par un organisme public compétent; (c) le visa de travail III, pour l'exercice d'une activité professionnelle indépendante dans le domaine d'une prestation de services; (d) le visa de travail IV, pour l'exercice d'une activité professionnelle subordonnée.

Pour ce qui est de l'entrée des ressortissants des pays tiers désireux de faire des études ou de suivre une formation professionnelle, le principe fondamental, prévu par l'article 35 de l'ordonnance n° 244/98, est celui de l'obtention préalable obligatoire d'un «visa d'études», valide pour de multiples entrées et pour un séjour jusqu'à un an, renouvelable, qui permettra à son titulaire de (a) suivre un programme d'études dans un établissement d'enseignement reconnu officiellement; (b) réaliser des travaux de recherche scientifique en vue d'obtenir un degré académique ou d'intérêt scientifique certifié par un établissement d'enseignement reconnu officiellement; (c) fréquenter un stage complémentaire d'études conclus au Portugal ou à l'étranger; (d) fréquenter des stages dans des entreprises, services publics ou centres de formation qui ne soient pas considérés des établissements officiels d'enseignement. Le titulaire d'un visa d'études peut exercer une activité professionnelle à titre complémentaire tant qu'il poursuivra avec succès l'activité pour laquelle le visa a été accordé.

Quant au statut juridique des ressortissant de pays tiers bénéficiant d'un droit de séjour de longue durée dans un autre État membre, le droit portugais ne fixe aucun principe fondamental spécifique. Ne trouvent

[4] En vertu de l'article 53, paragraphe 6, de l'ordonnance, dans des cas dûment motivés, une prorogation de séjour peut être accordé outre la prorogation-limite de deux ans prévue par le paragraphe 1, sous *e)*, du même article.

donc à s'appliquer que les articles 21 et suivants de la Convention de Schengen, qui accordent à ces étrangers le droit de circuler librement au Portugal (comme dans tout autre État membre intégralement lié par l'acquis Schengen), pendant une période maximale de trois mois, dans les conditions y prévues. Cela signifie notamment que si un étranger résident de longue durée dans un autre État membre veut résider ou travailler au Portugal, il tombe dans le champ d'application de l'ordonnance n° 244/98, tout comme n'importe quel autre étranger ayant la même intention.

Les différences entre ces principes et ceux proposés par la Commission européenne sont substantielles dans ce troisième cas, dans la mesure où le droit portugais n'accorde pas aux ressortissants des pays tiers résidents de longue durée dans un autre État membre un statut différent de celui accordé à tous les restants ressortissants de ces pays, alors que la directive 2003/109/CE du Conseil, du 25 novembre 2003, relative au statut des ressortissants des pays tiers résidents de longue durée, établit pour ceux-ci un statut qu'on pourrait considérer comme «à mi-chemin» entre le statut du citoyen de l'Union et celui du ressortissant d'un pays tiers qui n'est pas un résident de longue durée[5].

Dans les deux premiers cas susmentionnés, les différences entre les principes en vigueur dans l'ordre juridique portugais et ceux envisagés par la Commission, respectivement dans la proposition de directive du Conseil relative aux conditions d'entrée et de séjour des ressortissants des pays tiers aux fins d'un emploi salarié ou de l'exécution d'une activité économique indépendante, et dans la proposition de directive sur les conditions d'entrée et de séjour des ressortissants des pays tiers aux fins d'études, de formation professionnelle ou de volontariat, sont d'un autre ordre. Il s'agit moins de l'énoncé des conditions requises pour l'entrée et pour le séjour à ces fins (bien que la Commission cherche à les énoncer d'une façon plus précise) que du type de pouvoir administratif accordé aux autorités nationales en la matière.

En effet, selon les propositions de la Commission, les États membres devraient, dans des délais impartis, accorder un droit d'entrée et de séjour aux étrangers réunissant toutes les conditions juridiquement requises pour exercer dans leurs territoires une activité salariée ou indépendante

[5] À cet égard, il convient de noter que le droit portugais ne distingue pas, en termes de statut, les ressortissants des pays tiers en fonction de leur condition de résidents de longue durée ou non dans son propre territoire. Les deux catégories de ressortissants sont soumises au même droit des étrangers.

(y compris, le cas échéant, l'existence de vacance d'emploi conformément au quota fixé) ou pour y faire des études ou suivre une formation professionnelle. En d'autres mots, il s'agirait pour les États membres, dans ce contexte, de l'exercice d'un pouvoir plutôt lié (sans préjudice de la prévision de clauses dérogatoires), alors que l'ordonnance n° 244/98 attribue aux autorités administratives compétentes pour autoriser l'entrée dans ces cas un pouvoir essentiellement discrétionnaire, vis-à-vis duquel l'entrée et le séjour des ressortissants des pays tiers ne sauraient être considérés comme un droit subjectif. Dans une autre perspective, il est enfin à remarquer que le champ matériel d'application de la dernière directive mentionnée est plus ample que celui de l'article 35 de ordonnance n° 244/98, lequel ne couvre pas le volontariat.

2.2 Quels sont les exigences juridiques et les procédures requises en vertu du droit national pour obtenir un titre de séjour permettant aux ressortissants des pays tiers de travailler dans le pays d'accueil? Quelles sont les procédures utilisées afin de maintenir la préférence en faveur des citoyens de l'Union européenne et des nationaux de Turquie (en application de l'accord d'association) dans leur accès au marché du travail? Existe-t-il des programmes spécifiques en faveur des professionnels qualifiés leur facilitant l'accès au marché du travail? Quelle est le degré d'implication des syndicats et des employeurs dans ce genre de programmes? Y a t il une procédure visant à évaluer la demande pour des travailleurs étrangers? Dans quelle mesure l'élargissement de l'Union européenne est-il pris en considération? Quel a été l'impact de la récession économique récente et de l'augmentation corrélative du chômage sur le concept de l'admission des ressortissants des pays tiers?

L'acquisition d'un titre de séjour permettant à un ressortissant d'un pays tiers de travailler au Portugal dépend d'une condition fondamentale prévue par l'article 35 de l'ordonnance n° 244/98, à savoir, que la «limite maximale annuelle impérative» d'entrées de ressortissants d'Etats tiers pour l'exercice d'une activité professionnelle n'ait pas encore été dépassée. L'activité que le ressortissant d'un pays tiers souhaiterait exercer doit être comprise dans la prévision des opportunités de travail et des secteurs d'activité où celles-ci ont été constatées. Cette prévision figure dans un rapport élaboré chaque deux ans par le gouvernement sur avis de l'institut de l'emploi et de la formation professionnelle (IEFP) et après audition de l'inspection générale du travail, de l'association nationale des municipes portugais, des confédérations de patrons et de syndicats, ainsi que du haut commissaire pour l'immigration et les minorités ethniques. L'élaboration de ce rapport doit prendre en considération: (a) les besoins du marché en général, (b) les besoins de main-d'œuvre dans les secteurs fondamentaux pour l'économie nationale, (c) les besoins de main-d'œuvre pour les activités saisonnières et (d) la pondération géographique des opportunités de travail pour des étrangers conformément à la capacité d'accueil de chaque district.

Cette approche plus restrictive de l'admission des ressortissants des pays tiers, en résultat de la dernière modification de ordonnance n° 244/98, reflet clairement l'impact de la récession économique récente et de l'augmentation corrélative du chômage.

L'octroi des visas de travail III (pour l'exercice d'une activité professionnelle indépendante de prestation de services) et IV (pour l'exercice d'une activité professionnelle subordonnée) est obligatoirement précédé de consultation au SEF[6]. Par ailleurs, le visa de travail IV ne peut être accordé sans l'avis favorable de l'inspection générale du travail, auprès de laquelle une demande à cette fin doit être introduite par l'employeur.

L'article 41 précise que l'offre d'emploi est prioritairement satisfaite par des travailleurs communautaires, ainsi que par des travailleurs non communautaires résidant légalement au Portugal. Il échoit à l'IEFP d'élaborer trimestriellement un rapport identifiant, par activité professionnelle, le nombre de postes de travail déjà occupés et de procéder à une évaluation de l'exécution du rapport biannuel du gouvernement susmentionné, ainsi que de sa correspondance avec les opportunités de travail existantes. Il lui échoit aussi de vérifier si les destinataires des propositions de travail sur lesquelles des avis ont été émis occupent effectivement les postes correspondants.

Lorsque l'offre d'emploi est essentielle à l'économie nationale ou revêt une nature hautement qualifiée ou d'intérêt scientifique, artistique ou social important pour le pays, mais n'est pas prévue par le rapport gouvernemental susmentionné ou excède le nombre de postes de travail y prévus, cette offre pourra néanmoins être prise en compte si elle a fait l'objet d'un avis favorable de l'IEFP, assurant que la préférence en faveur des citoyens de l'Union et des ressortissants de pays tiers résidant légalement au Portugal a été respectée. Par ailleurs, l'IEFP, en articulation avec le Ministère des affaires étrangères et le SEF, est chargé de mettre en place les mécanismes nécessaires pour répondre aux offres de travail non satisfaites à niveau national et communautaire, lorsque l'employeur manifeste un intérêt pour le recrutement de travailleurs ressortissants de pays tiers.

[6] La consultation du SEF peut cependant être dispensée dans des cas urgents et dûment justifiés (article 40, paragraphe 2).

L'élargissement de l'Union est implicitement pris en considération par ces dispositions, dans la mesure où, d'une part, la préférence communautaire qu'elles prévoient s'étendra aux ressortissants des nouveaux États membres conformément aux actes d'adhésion et, d'autre part, les «offres de travail non satisfaites à niveau communautaire» se référeront à celles de l'Union élargie le moment venu.

2.3 Dans quelle mesure les droits et pratiques nationaux en vigueur diffèrent-ils substantiellement de l'approche adoptée par la Commission dans sa proposition sur la politique d'admission à des fins de l'exercice d'une activité salariée ou d'une activité professionnelle indépendante, concernant notamment:
- **l'entrée des ressortissants des pays tiers aux fins d'études et de formation professionnelle;**
- **le statut juridique des ressortissants des pays tiers qui ont un titre de séjour de longue durée accorder par un autre Etat membre;**

Le droit et les pratiques portugais envisagent le pouvoir exercé par les autorités compétentes s'agissant de permettre l'entrée des ressortissants des pays tiers aux fins d'études et de formation professionnelle comme un pouvoir essentiellement discrétionnaire, alors que l'approche adoptée par la Commission dans sa proposition sur la politique d'admission en vue de l'exercice d'une activité salariée ou d'une activité professionnelle indépendante va dans le sens de conditionner plus intensément et à plusieurs égards (y compris les délais de décision) ce pouvoir des États membres, en vue d'accorder un vrai droit d'entrée à ces ressortissants, lorsqu'il peut être constaté objectivement qu'ils réunissent toutes les condition requises à cet effet et ne tombent pas dans le champ d'application d'une clause dérogatoire.

En ce qui concerne le statut juridique des ressortissants des pays tiers ayant un titre de séjour de longue durée accordé par un autre État membre, le droit et les pratiques portugais ne distinguent, à aucune fin, ces ressortissants de ceux qui ne possèdent pas un tel titre de séjour, alors que la directive 2003/109/CE relative à ce statut vise à l'approximer, sous certains aspects, du statut des citoyens de l'Union.

2.4 Quelles démarches ont été entreprises afin de transposer en droit national la directive du 29 juin 2000 relative au principe de non-discrimination en fonction de la race ou de l'origine ethnique et la directive du Conseil du 27 novembre 2000 établissant un cadre général d'égalité de traitement sur le lieu de travail? Est-ce que des réformes législatives ont été entrepris? Dans quelle mesure le recours à la notion de "discrimination positive" est-il jugé nécessaire afin de promouvoir l'égalité des chances en faveur des travailleurs immigrés en provenance des pays tiers?

Moins d'un an avant l'adoption par le Conseil de la directive 2000/43/CE, du 29 juin 2000, visant à appliquer le principe d'égalité de traitement sans distinction d'origine sociale ou ethnique, le Portugal a adopté la Loi n° 134/99, du 28 août 1999, «interdisant des discriminations dans l'exercice des droits pour des raisons basées sur la race, la couleur, la nationalité ou l'origine ethnique». Aux termes de son article 1er, cette loi «vise à prévenir et à interdire la discrimination raciale sous toutes ses formes et à sanctionner la pratique d'actes se traduisant par des violations de droits fondamentaux, ou par le refus ou le conditionnement de l'exercice des droits économiques, sociaux ou culturels par une personne, en raison de son appartenance à une certaine race, couleur, nationalité ou origine ethnique». L'article 3, paragraphe 1, définit la notion de discrimination raciale, et l'article 4 énonce une série de pratiques discriminatoires interdites. Le paragraphe 3 de l'article 3 admet la discrimination positive vis-à-vis de certains groupes défavorisés, avec l'objectif de garantir l'exercice des droits en conditions d'égalité. La loi crée une instance d'accompagnement de son application – la commission pour l'égalité et contre la discrimination raciale – et établit un régime de sanctions pécuniaires frappant les actes discriminatoires, développé par le *Decreto-Lei* n° 111/2000, du 4 juillet. Les auteurs de ces actes peuvent, sans préjudice de leur éventuelle responsabilité civile, se voir infliger des amendes par une autorité administrative.

La Loi n° 134/99 et le *Decreto-Lei* n° 111/2000 restent en deçà, sous certains aspects (*v. g.* en matière de protection juridictionnelle contre la discrimination et de charge de la preuve de discrimination), de l'ensemble normatif formé par la directive 2000/43/CE, susmentionnée, et la directive 2000/78/CE du Conseil du 27 novembre 2000, établissant un cadre général d'égalité de traitement dans l'emploi et l'activité professionnelle. Ces directives n'ont pas été formellement transposées dans l'ordre juridique portugais dans le délai y imparti.

La notion de «discrimination positive», juridiquement prévue au Portugal, peut se révéler un instrument important pour promouvoir l'égalité des chances en faveur des travailleurs immigrés en provenance des pays tiers. Elle pourra aussi être mise en œuvre en faveur des enfants de ces travailleurs, notamment en ce qui concerne leur accès à l'éducation et à la formation professionnelle. L'article 4, paragraphe 1, sous *i)*, de la Loi n° 134/99 l'admet implicitement, en conformité, d'ailleurs, avec l'article 74, paragraphe 2, sous *j)*, de la Constitution, aux termes duquel il incombe à l'État, dans la réalisation de la politique d'éducation, de garantir aux enfants des immigrés un appui adéquat afin de rendre effectif leur droit à l'enseignement.

2.5 Concernant la proposition de directive sur le droit au regroupement familial présentée par le Conseil en février 2003,
- **pensez-vous que les critères proposés soient en deça des principes relatifs au regroupement familial actuellement en vigueur dans votre pays?**
- **la mise en œuvre de cette directive, une fois adoptée, va-t-elle conduire à des changements dans votre système juridique national sur le droit au regroupement familial et qui abaissent le niveau de protection existant? Si c'est le cas, quels changements sont envisagés?**

Les principes établis par la Directive 2003/86/CE du Conseil, du 22 septembre 2003, sur le droit au regroupement familial restent en deçà des principes fixés dans ce domaine par ordonnance n° 244/98. Quelques exemples peuvent être avancés: (a) le champ d'application personnel de cette ordonnance, défini par l'article 57, est plus ample que celui défini par l'article 4 de la directive; (b) l'article 57 ne prévoit pas la condition imposée par l'article 3, paragraphe 1, de la directive au requérant du regroupement de devoir posséder, outre son permis de résidence, une «perspective fondée d'obtenir un droit de résidence permanente»; (c) la loi portugaise ne prévoit pas dans ce contexte la mise en œuvre de «mesures d'intégration» envisagées par l'article 7, paragraphe 2, de la directive; (d) la période d'attente pour le regroupement est d'un an, aux termes de l'article 56 de la loi portugaise, alors que l'article 8 de la directive permet aux États membre de fixer des périodes d'attente pouvant aller jusqu'à trois ans; (e) l'article 58, paragraphe 2, de la loi portugaise n'exige qu'une période de deux ans à compter de l'émission du premier permis de résidence pour que les membres de la famille regroupée aient droit à un permis de résidence autonome, alors que l'article 15, paragraphe 1, de la directive permet aux États membres de fixer à cette fin une période pouvant aller jusqu'à cinq ans.

Sans préjudice de cette constatation, il convient d'observer que la loi portugaise, lors de sa dernière modification, intervenue le 25 février 2003, a pris expressément en considération la proposition de directive du Conseil relative au droit de regroupement familial dont le texte venait de faire l'objet d'un accord politique.

La directive 2003/86/CE peut être considérée comme transposée dans l'ordre juridique portugais. Dès lors qu'elle n'établit que des «normes minimales» en la matière, permettant aux États membres «d'adopter ou de maintenir des dispositions plus favorables» (article 3, paragraphe 5), et que la loi portugaise actuellement en vigueur va au-delà de ces normes minimales, aucune modification de ordonnance n° 244/98 ne s'avère nécessaire en vertu de la directive. En tout cas, on ne saurait exclure qu'un gouvernement présent ou futur, en articulation avec la majorité parlementaire qui l'appuie, se fonde sur la directive pour abaisser le niveau de protection existant.

2.6 La proposition de directive sur les droits des résidents de longue durée telle que présentée par le Conseil le 5 juin 2003 prévoit un certain nombre de droits visant à approximer le statut des résidents de longue duré avec celui des citoyens de l'Union européenne. L'application de ce texte communautaire va-t-elle conduire à des réformes juridiques et politiques importantes dans votre pays? Quelles seront les questions essentielles soulevées, le cas échéant, par le processus d'approximation envisagée par la directive à l'égard notamment:
- **du principe de non-discrimination dans le domaine des droits sociaux;**
- **du concept de "citoyen civique" (voir aussi l'évaluation de l'impact de la communication sur l'intégration du 11 juin 2003);**
- **du droit au regroupement familial et de l'accès des membres de la famille au marché du travail;**
- **de la garantie du droit de rester sur le territoire.**

Le fait que la loi portugaise ne connaît pas, ainsi qu'il a déjà été indiqué, la catégorie des «ressortissants des pays tiers résidents de longue durée», telle que définie par la directive 2003/109/CE, ne signifie pas que la transposition de cette directive dans l'ordonnancement portugais y exigera des réformes juridiques et politique importantes. En effet, aux termes de l'article 15 de la Constitution, «les étrangers et les apatrides se trouvant ou résidant au Portugal jouissent des droits et sont soumis aux devoirs du citoyen portugais», à l'exception de certains droits politiques, de l'exercice des fonctions publiques n'ayant pas un caractère principalement technique et des droits et devoirs réservés par la Constitution et la loi exclusivement aux ressortissants portugais (paragraphes 1 e 2). Par ailleurs, aux termes du paragraphe 4 du même article, la loi peut attribuer aux étrangers résidents dans le territoire national, sous conditions de réciprocité, le droit d'élire et d'être élu dans le cadre des élections locales. Selon la loi relative aux communautés locales, un étranger acquiert le droit de vote pour les élections locales après trois ans de résidence et le droit d'être élu après quatre ans.

L'approximation du statut des résidents de longue durée à celui des citoyens de l'Union prétendue par la directive ne posera donc aucune question essentielle au Portugal à l'égard du de principe non-discrimination dans le domaine des droits sociaux et du concept de «citoyenneté civique». Quant au droit au regroupement familial, y compris l'accès des membres de la famille regroupée au marché de travail, l'article 94 de l'ordonnance n° 244/98 le prévoit déjà pour tous les étrangers résidents au Portugal depuis un an. Enfin, pour ce qui est de la protection contre l'expulsion du territoire national, le régime actuellement prévu par l'article 33, paragraphe 2, de la Constitution et par les dispositions combinées des articles 109, 99, paragraphe 1, sous *b)* à *e)*, et 101, est parfaitement compatible avec ce que dispose l'article 12 de la directive 2003/109/CE, voire plus favorable que celle-ci.

2.7 En ayant à l'esprit la perspective d'une future politique commune en matière d'immigration telle qu'élaborée par la Commission dans sa communication sur la coordination ouverte (COM 2001/387) et sa communication sur la politique de l'immigration de l'Union européenne (COM 2000/757, version finale), comment envisagez-vous le rôle des institutions communautaires dans la définition d'un telle politique concernant notamment les compétences des Etats membres pour décider du droit de séjour, de l'accès au marché du travail et de l'intégration? L'harmonisation des législations nationales doit-elle aller plus loin, et si oui, dans quelle mesure?

Une future politique commune en matière d'immigration cessera d'avoir une base juridique dans la mesure où elle dépassera les domaines prévus par l'article 63, premier alinéa, points 3 e 4, du traité CE[7], à savoir, (a) les conditions d'entrée et de séjour, (b) les procédures de délivrance par les États membres de visas et de titres de séjour de longue durée, y compris aux fins de regroupement familial, (c) l'immigration clandestine et le séjour irrégulier, y compris le repatriement et (4) les droits de séjour des ressortissants des pays tiers résidents de longue durée dans un État membre dans les autres États membres. Cette base juridique pour une politique commune en matière d'immigration a été maintenue, en substance, par l'article III-168 du projet de traité établissant une constitution pour l'Europe.

Dans ces conditions, une telle politique ne pourra en aucun cas modifier, en contradiction avec le traité, ni le rôle des institutions communautaires dans sa définition et ni les compétences décisionnelles des États membres concernant le droit de séjour, l'accès au marché de travail et l'intégration. Il en va de même pour l'harmonisation des législations nationales en la matière. Outre qu'elle est délimitée par l'article 63 du traité CE, la politique commune en matière d'immigration doit respecter les principes de subsidiarité et de proportionnalité, ainsi que ceux prévus par l'article 6 du traité sur l'Union européenne et notamment celui du

[7] Sans préjudice, le cas échéant, d'un recours à l'article 308 du traité.

respect des droits de l'homme et des libertés fondamentales, si sensible dans ces domaines. C'est surtout à l'égard de ce dernier qu'il faudra poser la question de savoir si l'harmonisation des législations nationales ne devrait aller plus loin dans certains aspects. Le regroupement familial n'en est qu'un exemple parmi d'autres.

Partie III – La réglementation applicable aux demandeurs d'asile et aux réfugiés

3.1 Les règles de Dublin ont-elles fonctionné de facon satisfaisante jusqu'à présent et qu'attend-on du règlement 343/2003 du 18 février 2003 (Dublin II)?

Il est assez consensuel parmi les responsables portugais de l'application de la Convention de Dublin que celle-ci n'a pas fonctionné de façon satisfaisante. On parle de l'inefficacité pratique des dispositions sur la procédure de transfert des demandeurs d'asile, en fonction de la détermination de l'État membre responsable du traitement de la demande respective, de l'absence de mécanismes plus contraignants susceptibles d'engager les États membres dans le respect effectif des obligations qui leur incombaient en vertu de cette convention, etc.

Le fait que la matière en question fait maintenant l'objet du règlement n° 343/2003, du 18 février 2003, est considéré positif dans la mesure où cet instrument est doté d'une efficacité juridique accrue et il permet l'intervention de la Commission, en tant que gardienne du traité, dans le contrôle de son application. Mais ce règlement n'échappe pas à la critique, surtout en ce que son contenu ne représente pas un vrai changement qualitatif par rapport à la Convention de Dublin, notamment en ce qui concerne les pouvoirs discrétionnaires octroyés aux autorités administratives chargées de son application.

3.2 Le règlement 2725/2000 du Conseil du 11 décembre 2000 relatif à la création du système Eurodac pour la comparaison des empreintes digitales aux fins de l'application efficace de la Convention de Dublin, et en vigueur depuis le 15 janvier 2003, a-t-il eu pour résultat une augmentation des affaires en ce domaine? Eurodac est-il déjà effective dans votre pays ou, sinon, le sera-t-il dans l'avenir?

Le système Eurodac, crée par le règlement n° 2725/2000 du Conseil, du 11 décembre 2000, pour la comparaison des empreintes digitales aux fins d'une application efficace des règles sur la responsabilité des États membres pour le traitement des demandes d'asile introduites auprès d'eux, est déjà effectif au Portugal, et ce depuis le 15 janvier 2003.

Le SEF est le seul organisme national qui opère avec le système Eurodac, sans préjudice de l'accès à ce système garanti à la Commission nationale pour la protection des données personnelles dans le domaine de ses compétences en tant qu'autorité nationale de contrôle. Le cabinet de l'asile et des réfugiés du SEF est le département qui opère le plus couramment dans le système Eurodac. Les postes de frontière jouent un rôle dans la prise d'empreintes digitales des ressortissants des pays tiers qui sont détectés à l'occasion du franchissement illégal des frontières extérieures portugaises mais ne peuvent pas être éloignés, situation rare selon les prévisions.

A la suite de la mise en fonctionnement du système Eurodac, aucune augmentation du volume d'affaires dans ce domaine n'a été constatée.

3.3 Quels changements significatifs impliquent la transposition de la directive (telle qu'amendée et pour la majorité de quelle le Conseil a obtenu un accord politique en juin 2003) relative aux normes minimales applicables dans le cadre des procédures nationales d'octroi et de retrait du statut de réfugié, pour la législation et la pratique dans votre pays, en termes notamment:
- **de droits procéduraux des demandeurs;**
- **de recours administratifs ou judiciaires;**
- **d'utilisation des concepts de "*safe third country*" et "*safe country of origin*" (Etats tiers ou Etats d'origine garantissant les droits des demandeurs);**
- **de la détention des demandeurs d'asile;**
- **des procédures de contrôle dans les aéroports et aux frontières.**

Au Portugal, la procédure d'octroi et de retrait du statut de réfugié est réglée par la Loi n° 15/98, du 22 mars, établissant un nouveau régime juridique en matière d'asile et de réfugiés. Aux fins de cette loi, la demande d'asile est définie comme celle par laquelle un étranger sollicite à un État la protection garantie par la Convention de Genève de 1951, en invoquant la qualité de réfugié au sens de l'article 1er de cette convention, telle que modifiée par le Protocole de New York.

Les droits procéduraux, y compris les recours administratifs et judiciaires dont disposent les demandeurs d'asile, sont les suivants: (a) le droit d'être entendu par l'autorité compétente (le SEF) dans un délai de cinq jours compté de la présentation de la demande (article 11, paragraphe 4, de la Loi n° 15/98); (b) le droit d'être informé, lors de la notification pour comparaître devant le SEF afin d'être entendu, de ses droits et obligations (article 11, paragraphe 5), (c) le droit de requérir la réappréciation de la décision d'irrecevabilité de la demande d'asile, avec effet suspensif, auprès du commissaire national pour les réfugiés, lequel peut entendre le demandeur d'asile s'il l'estime nécessaire et doit se prononcer dans un délai de quarante-huit heures (article 16, paragraphe 1)[8]; (d) le droit de recours contentieux, sans effet suspensif, contre la décision du commissaire national pour les réfugiés (article 16, paragraphe 2); (e) le droit de se prononcer sur la teneur du projet de proposition motivée d'octroi ou de refus d'asile élaboré par le commissaire national pour les réfugiés (article 23, paragraphe 3); (f) le droit à ce que ses observations soient prises en considération par ce commissaire (article 23, paragraphe 4); (g) le droit de recours contentieux, avec effet suspensif, contre la décision de refus d'asile prise par le ministre des affaires intérieures, à introduire dans le délai de vingt jours, à compter de la notification de cette décision (article 24).

S'agissant de la procédure de retrait du droit d'asile ou du statut de réfugié, l'intéressé a le droit d'être entendu par l'autorité compétente et de lui présenter des moyens de preuve (article 42), ainsi que le droit de recours contentieux ou juridictionnel contre la décision de retrait ou de perte du statut de réfugié (article 47)[9].

L'article 12 de la Loi n° 15/98 dispose que la présentation d'une demande d'asile fait obstacle à l'ouverture, contre le demandeur ou les personnes qui l'accompagnent, d'une procédure administrative ou criminelle pour cause d'entrée irrégulière dans le territoire portugais. Cela signifie donc que ces personnes ne pourront pas être détenues même si les infractions éventuellement commises imposaient cette détention. Elles ne peuvent être détenues non plus en raison de leur condition de demandeurs d'asile.

Finalement, l'article 13, paragraphe 1, sous *b)*, prévoit qu'une demande d'asile est irrecevable si elle est introduite par un ressortissant ou résident habituel d'un pays tiers susceptible d'être considéré comme «pays sûr» ou «pays tiers d'accueil», notions qui correspondent en substance à celles de «*safe third country*» et «*safe country of origin*». Le paragraphe 3 du même article définit sous *a)* le pays sûr comme celui par rapport auquel

[8] Dans l'hypothèse où la demande d'asile est présentée auprès d'un poste de frontière par un étranger qui ne remplit pas les conditions juridiques requises pour entrer dans le territoire national, le délai prévu pour la demande de réappréciation de la décision d'irrecevabilité, avec effet suspensif, est de vingt-quatre heures (article 19, paragraphe 1). Le recours contentieux contre la décision confirmant l'irrecevabilité de la demande d'asile n'ayant pas d'effet suspensif, le requérant peut demander que son éloignement soit reporté d'un délai maximal de quarante-huit heures afin de transmettre à un avocat les éléments nécessaires à l'introduction ultérieure d'un recours contentieux (article 20, paragraphe 4).

[9] Les cas où la décision de retrait ou de perte du droit d'asile/statut de réfugié peut être prise par le ministre des affaires intérieures et les cas où elle doit être prise par une juridiction sont prévus par les dispositions combinées des articles 38 et 36.

il est possible d'établir avec sûreté, de façon objective et vérifiable, qu'il ne donne origine à aucun réfugié, ou par rapport auquel il est possible de déterminer que les circonstances que, auparavant, pouvaient justifier l'application de la Convention de Genève ont cessé d'exister, compte tenu notamment des éléments suivants: respect des droits de l'homme, existence et fonctionnement normal des institutions démocratiques, stabilité politique. La même disposition définit sous *b)* le pays tiers d'accueil comme celui dans lequel il est certain que le requérant d'asile ne fera pas l'objet de menaces à sa vie et liberté, au sens de l'article 33 de la Convention de Genève, ni sera soumis à des tortures ou à un traitement inhumain ou dégradant, et où il a obtenu protection ou a eu l'opportunité, à la frontière ou à l'intérieur du territoire, de contacter les autorités de ce pays pour demander protection ou dans lequel il a été admis, y bénéficiant d'une protection réelle contre le refoulement, au sens de la Convention de Genève.

Telles étant les dispositions juridiques en vigueur au Portugal, il s'ensuit que la transposition de la directive relative aux normes minimales applicables dans le cadre des procédures nationales d'octroi et de retrait du statut de réfugié n'impliquera aucun changement significatif du régime juridique en matière d'asile et de réfugiés en vigueur, ni en général, ni pour ce qui est, en particulier, des droits procéduraux des demandeurs de ce statut, des recours administratifs et judiciaires, ou des notions de *safe third country* et de *safe country of origin.* Les dispositions de la directive concernant la possibilité de détention des demandeurs d'asile en raison même de cette qualité étant facultatives, il n'est pas prévisible que le législateur portugais les transpose dans l'ordre juridique national.

3.4 Quelles ont été les mesures prises dans votre pays afin de transposer la directive communautaire 2003/9/CE du Conseil du 27 janvier 2003 relative à l'accueil des demandeurs d'asile dans les Etats membres? Vous insisterez sur les points particuliers suivants:
- **les clauses de flexibilité dans la directive;**
- **les restrictions à la libre circulation;**
- **l'accès au marché du travail;**
- **les droits des travailleurs immigrés en vertu de l'article 11 paragraphe 2 de la directive.**

La directive communautaire 2003/9/CE du 27 janvier 2003, relative à l'accueil des demandeurs d'asile dans les États membres n'a pas encore été formellement transposée dans l'ordre juridique portugais.

Nonobstant, les dispositions obligatoires de cette directive peuvent être considérées comme contenues dans les articles 49 et suivants de la Loi n° 15/98, en ce qui concerne notamment l'accès au marché de travail et aux droits découlant de l'article 11, paragraphe 2, de la directive en question. Aucune des restrictions à la libre circulation, prévues à titre facultatif par la directive, n'est imposée aux demandeurs d'asile au Portugal, et il n'est pas probable que ces restrictions soient consacrées lors d'une prochaine modification du régime légal en matière d'asile et de réfugiés.

3.5 Quelles démarches ont été entreprises en droit national afin de transposer la directive 2001/55/CE du Conseil du 20 juillet 2001 relative à l'octroi d'une protection temporaire en cas d'afflux massif de personnes déplacées? Existe-t-il des procédures visant à la répartition des efforts consentis par les Etats membres en ce domaine? Y-a-t-il un fondement juridique ouvrant droit à des mesures de protection temporaire pour des réfugiés dans le contexte d'une immigration de masse?

La directive 2001/55/CE du Conseil du 20 juillet 2001, relative à l'octroi d'une protection temporaire en cas d'afflux massif de personnes déplacées a été transposée dans l'ordre juridique portugais par la Loi n° 67/2003, du 23 août.

Cette loi prévoit dans son chapitre V, dont le titre est «solidarité et coopération», que pendant la période de protection temporaire l'Etat portugais coopère avec les autres États membres en ce qui concerne le transfert de la résidence des bénéficiaires, sous réserve de l'existence d'un intérêt de ceux-ci pour ce transfert (article 26, paragraphe 1). Aux termes du paragraphe 5 du même article, les personnes transférées d'un autre État membre se verront accorder le régime de protection temporaire au Portugal.

L'article 4, paragraphe 3, de la Loi n° 67/2003 permet d'adopter des mesures de protection temporaire à caractère exclusivement national dans le contexte d'un afflux massif de personnes déplacées, moyennant une résolution du gouvernement considérant en chaque situation les risques que courent les personnes déplacées, *l'urgence e nécessité de protection temporaire* et les conséquences pour l'ordre public et la sécurité national.

Avant la transposition de la directive 2001/55/CE, l'ordre juridique portugais contenait déjà une disposition susceptible de servir de base à l'octroi de protection temporaire dans ce type de situations. C'était l'article 9 de la Loi n° 15/98, lequel a été substitué précisément par la Loi n° 67/2003.

3.6 Les membres du Conseil se sont mis d'un accord politique sur les principes d'une directive relative aux normes minimales requises en matière de qualification et de statut des ressortissants des Etats tiers en tant que réfugiés ou personnes exigeant une protection internationale (proposition COM 2001/510, voir les

documents du Conseil de juin 2003). Quelles sont les mesures envisagées au niveau national afin de transposer cette directive en ce qui concerne:
- **la définition du réfugié;**
- **la définition des personnes ayant droit à une protection complémentaire;**
- **le statut des personnes ayant droit à une protection complémentaire;**
- **la question de l'alternative d'un vol interne telle que défini par la directive;**
- **les dispositions relatives aux exceptions, notamment liées au terrorisme (*exclusion clause*).**

Dans quelle mesure les politiques internes visant les réfugiés telles que reflétées dans le droit et la jurisprudence de votre pays sont-elles conformes à la proposition de directive?

Le droit portugais définit la notion de réfugié par renvoi exprès à l'article 1er, point A, de la Convention de Genève. C'est ce que prévoit l'article 2, sous *e)*, de la Loi n° 67/2003, conformément à la directive 2001/55/CE susmentionnée. De son côté, l'article 6 de la Loi n° 15/98 en matière d'asile, dont le titre est «statut du réfugié», dispose que le réfugié jouit des droits et est soumis aux devoirs des étrangers au Portugal, dans la mesure où ces devoirs ne contrarient pas les dispositions de cette loi et celles de la Convention de Genève et du Protocole de New York. Le réfugié a droit, aux termes de la Convention, à un titre d'identité certifiant sa qualité, accordé par le ministre de l'intérieur et «doit, notamment, respecter les lois et règlements, ainsi que les mesures destinées au maintien de l'ordre public.

Pour ce qui est de la définition et du statut des personnes ayant droit à une protection subsidiaire, l'article 8 de la Loi n° 15/98, dont le titre est «permis de résidence pour des raisons humanitaires», impose à l'autorité compétente d'accorder ce permis «aux étrangers et apatrides qui ne réunissent pas les conditions pour se voir accorder un droit d'asile, mais qui sont empêchés ou se sentent dans l'impossibilité de retourner au pays d'où ils sont ressortissants ou ont une résidence habituelle, pour cause de grave insécurité due à des conflits armés, ou à la violation systématique des droits fondamentaux y constatée». Le permis de résidence est accordé par le ministre de l'intérieur sur proposition du commissaire national pour les réfugiés, pour une période maximale de cinq ans, renouvelable après une analyse de l'évolution de la situation dans le pays d'origine. Il résulte de l'article 26 que le requérant de protection subsidiaire doit disposer, dans le cadre de la procédure prévue à cette fin, de droits procéduraux et de recours administratifs et judiciaires assimilables à ceux dont dispose le requérant d'asile. Par ailleurs, l'interprétation correcte de la Loi n° 15/98 mène à la conclusion que les droits prévus dans son chapitre VI pour les requérants d'asile, à commencer par le droit d'accès au marché de travail, sont à étendre aux requérants de protection subsidiaire. Enfin, les clauses d'exclusion de l'asile prévues par l'article 3 et notamment la commission de crimes contre la paix, crimes de guerre ou crimes contre l'humanité, ainsi que la pratique d'actes contraires aux finalités et aux principes des Nations Unies, doivent, par interprétation extensive, empêcher également l'octroi d'une protection subsidiaire. Le terrorisme rentre, bien-entendu, dans le champ d'application de ces clauses.

Dans ces conditions, il faut conclure que la transposition de la future directive relative aux normes minimales requises en matière de qualification et de statut des ressortissants des États tiers en tant que réfugiés ou personnes exigeant une protection internationale (subsidiaire) ne posera pas des difficultés au Portugal. En plus, le droit national en vigueur peut être facilement interprété et appliqué en conformité avec la proposition de directive, y compris l'obligation d'examiner si le requérant de protection subsidiaire peut être renvoyé raisonnablement à une autre partie du pays où il se trouve, dans laquelle il n'existe aucun motif pour craindre d'être persécuté ou de subir d'autres offenses graves et injustifiées.

3.7 Dans la communication de la Commission du 22 novembre 2000 (COM 2000/755; voir aussi le second rapport de la Commission, COM 2003/152), on trouve l'idée d'une procédure communautaire commune d'asile et un statut uniforme à travers l'Union des personnes bénéficiaires d'un droit d'asile. Considérez-vous que cette idée soit généralement en accord avec votre politique nationale en matière de droit d'asile? Les craintes émises par certaines organisations de protection des droits des réfugiés, telle qu'Amnesty International, concernant une diminution éventuelle du niveau international de protection des réfugiés sont-elles partagées par les cercles politiques chargés de prendre les décisions dans votre pays?

Le traité CE dans son article 63, point 1, charge le Conseil d'adopter jusqu'au premier mai 2004 plusieurs «mesures relatives à l'asile, conformes à la Convention de Genève du 28 juillet 1951 et au Protocole du 31 janvier 1967, relatifs au statut des réfugiés ainsi qu'aux autres traités pertinents», à savoir, (a) les critères et mécanismes de détermination de Etat membre responsable de l'examen d'une demande d'asile présentée dans l'un des États membres par un ressortissant d'un pays tiers et (b) des «normes minimales» (i) régissant l'accueil des demandeurs d'asile dans les États membres; (ii) concernant les conditions que doivent remplir les ressortissants des pays tiers pour pouvoir prétendre au statut de réfugié; (iii) concernant la procédure d'octroi ou de retrait du statut de réfugié.

Le traité n'attribue donc pas à la Communauté compétence pour régler l'ensemble que constitue une politique d'asile. Il s'est limité à permettre à la Communauté d'adopter des mesures concernant quatre aspects spécifiques de cette politique. On est donc loin de pouvoir dire que la Communauté est devenue compétente pour régler la politique d'asile dans les mêmes conditions qu'elle règle les politiques prévues aux autres titres de la troisième partie du traité. Qui plus est, le Conseil n'est chargé d'adopter que des «normes minimales» dans ces domaines, notion qui a été interprétée officiellement comme exigeant que, dans un premier temps, le régime communautaire ne reflète que «les plus petits dénominateurs communs» accordés par les États membres. Des solutions tendant à refléter «les plus grands dénominateurs communs» ne pourraient être adoptées que dans un second temps. À cela il faudra ajouter que ces dernières solutions ne pourront être adoptées qu'après une révision du traité, selon la procédure y prévue, qui supprime la notion de «normes minimales»[10].

Dans ces conditions, l'établissement d'une procédure communautaire commune d'asile ainsi qu'un statut uniforme des bénéficiaires d'un droit d'asile ne trouvent pas une base juridique claire dans le traité. Mais même admettant que l'article 63, premier alinéa, point 1, du traité, en constitue une base juridique suffisante, le fait que cette politique commune et ce statut soient en train d'être établis à partir de «normes minimales», dont la fonction principale a été jusqu'à présent celle de «légitimer» les législations nationales les moins protectrices, rend justifiées les craintes émises par certaines organisations de protection des droits des réfugiés à l'égard d'une diminution éventuelle du niveau international général de protection de ces droits. En effet, les États membres dont la législation en la matière est plus avancée ou généreuse seront tentés de la réviser «vers le bas», afin d'éviter que les conséquences du maintien de cette législation ne deviennent trop onéreuses.

Quoi qu'il en soit, l'idée d'une procédure communautaire commune d'asile et d'un statut uniforme pour les réfugiés ne saurait être considérée incompatible avec la politique portugaise en la matière, laquelle a été conçue et est exécutée sans avoir connu jusqu'à présent des afflux de demandeurs d'asile comparables à ceux qui pèsent sur d'autres États

[10] Il convient de remarquer que le projet de traité établissant une constitution pour l'Europe a effectivement procédé à la suppression de la notion de «normes minimales» dans le domaine de la politique commune d'asile et de protection temporaire, ainsi que l'atteste l'article III-168.

membres. Mais compte tenu des dispositions de droit communautaire entre-temps élaborées en la matière, on ne saurait exclure que certains cercles politiques portugais s'engagent à réviser vers le bas la législation en vigueur.

3.8 La méthode de coordination ouverte telle que suggérée par la Commission prévoyait un premier et un deuxième étape dans le processus d'adoption de la législation au cours desquelles les dispositions offrant une certaine discrétion aux autorités nationales figurant dans certaines des directives sur l'immigration et le droit d'asile devaient être remplacées par une harmonisation totale. Cela est-il discuté dans votre pays et quelle est la perception de la mise en place progressive d'une politique communautaire relative au droit d'asile qui remplacera, au bout du compte, les procédures et les mesures adoptées au niveau national?

Pour les mêmes raisons avancées en réponse à la question précédente, il manque dans le traité une base juridique suffisante pour une «harmonisation totale» en matière d'immigration et d'asile et, à plus forte raison, pour une politique communautaire relative au droit d'asile qui remplacerait les procédures et mesures au niveau national. La question a été débattue notamment lors de la conférence européenne sur l'asile qui a eu lieu à Lisbonne, sous la présidence portugaise du Conseil de l'Union européenne, en juin 2000. Je me permets de renvoyer à ce que j'ai dit à l'époque, croyant exprimer la perception majoritaire au Portugal:

«Le modèle adopté par le traité CE pour la politique commune en matière d'asile est loin d'être un modèle fédéral. En effet, dans une structure de ce type, tout droit d'asile 'intrafédération' ou, ce qui revient au même, entre États fédérés est exclu. En outre, la compétence pour octroyer un droit d'asile à des ressortissants de pays tiers appartient à la fédération et est exercée par une instance centrale, ainsi que le démontrent, parmi d'autres, les cas de l'Allemagne, de l'Autriche ou des États Unis. Dans le cadre de l'Union européenne, par contre, les États membres sont les protagonistes de la définition et de l'exécution tant d'une 'politique d'asile interne'[11] que d'une 'politique d'asile externe commune'.

Une option hypothétique pour le modèle fédéral de la politique d'asile dans le cadre de l'Union européenne n'exigerait seulement une révision des traités sur lesquels elle est fondée. Cette option exigerait aussi la révision de la Convention de Genève et du Protocole de New York – instruments qui n'admettent que des États en tant que Parties Contractantes – et

[11] Ainsi que le confirme clairement le protocole relatif au droit d'asile des ressortissants des Etats membres de l'Union européenne, annexé au traité CE par le traité d'Amsterdam.

celle de plusieurs constitutions des États membres, où l'asile est consacré comme droit fondamental. De surcroît, on ne saurait exclure qu'une modification de ces constitutions dans le sens de priver les États membres respectifs de leur compétence en matière d'asile s'avère incompatible avec les limites matérielles établies pour leur propre révision».

3.9 La Communication de juin 2003 visant à organiser un système plus accessible et équitable en matière de droit d'asile – en réaction notamment à la proposition britannique – envisage de nouvelles approches afin d'assurer une arrivée mieux organisée des personnes nécessitant une protection internationale. Quelle a été la réaction politique dans votre pays à l'égard d'une politique d'asile commune, de la répartition des réfugiées entre les Etats membres ainsi que du partage des responsabilités et autres nouvelles approches et idées qu'implique la prise en charge d'un afflux massif de réfugiés?

Ainsi qu'il a déjà été mentionné, le Portugal a été jusqu'à présent très épargné par des afflux massifs de requérants d'asile. L'octroi du droit d'asile, prévu par la Constitution elle-même, ou du statut de réfugié, n'ont jamais été une question politique ou budgétaire de première importance. Le nombre réduit de demandeurs d'asile (quatre-vingt-huit au cours de l'an 2003) n'a pas exigé jusqu'à présent la création d'infrastructures particulières ni l'affectation d'un grand nombre de fonctionnaires.

Dans ces circonstances, l'idée d'une politique commune d'asile, de répartition des réfugiés entre les États membres ainsi que d'un partage des responsabilités semble être envisagée avec une certaine réserve par la plupart des cercles politiques nationaux.

Partie IV – Sanctions des ressortissants en situation irrégulière, retour, repatriement

4.1 Combien, selon les estimations fournies, de ressortissants de pays tiers sans titre de séjour valable sont-ils dans votre pays? Combien d'expulsions ont-été ordonnées ces précédentes années? L'ensemble du processus de mise en œuvre de ces mesures est-t-il considéré comme acceptable?

Le nombre de ressortissants des pays tiers se trouvant au Portugal sans titre de séjour valable est estimé en cinquante mille par le gouvernement et en deux cents mille par certaines ONG's.

En ce qui concerne la procédure d'expulsion, l'article 33, paragraphe 2, de la Constitution statue qu'elle doit revêtir une nature juridictionnelle lorsqu'elle est ouverte à l'encontre d'un ressortissant d'un pays tiers qui (a) est entré et demeure régulièrement dans le territoire national, (b) a obtenu un permis de résidence ou (c) a introduit une demande d'asile non refusée.

L'expulsion du territoire national en tant que peine accessoire doit aussi être décidée dans le cadre d'une procédure juridictionnelle (article 101 de ordonnance n° 244/98). La décision juridictionnelle d'expulsion peut faire l'objet d'un recours sans effet suspensif (article 116).

En revanche, le ressortissant d'un pays tiers en situation illégale dans le territoire national peut être expulsé par décision du directeur général du SEF. Dans le cadre de la procédure administrative d'expulsion, il est assuré à ce ressortissant le droit d'être entendu, ainsi que toutes les garanties de défense. La décision administrative d'expulsion lui est formellement notifiée et peut faire l'objet d'un recours contentieux sans effet suspensif (articles 117 et suivants).

À l'égard du principe de l'Etat de droit et de son corollaire constitué par le droit à une protection juridictionnelle effective contre les actes d'autorité, le seul point problématique de ces procédures est l'absence d'effet suspensif soit du recours juridictionnel dans le premier cas, soit du recours contentieux dans le second cas.

Au cours de l'an 2003 ont été exécutées quatre-vingt-onze expulsions judiciaires, quatre cents vingt expulsions administratives e soixante acheminements à la frontière. 2.054 procédures d'expulsion administrative ont été ouvertes.

4.2 Quelles démarches ont été entreprises afin de transposer la directive du 28 novembre 2002 relative aux mesures facilitant l'entrée non autorisée sur le territoire, le transit et le droit de séjour?

La directive 2002/90/CE du Conseil, du 28 novembre, relative à la définition de l'aide á l'entrée, au transit et à la résidence irréguliers, a été transposée dans l'ordre juridique portugais par les articles 134 et suivants de ordonnance n° 244/98, tels que modifiés en dernier lieu par ordonnance 34/2003. Cela a été fait en moins de trois mois après l'entrée en vigueur de la directive et bien avant l'expiration du délai fixé pour sa transposition (5 décembre 2004).

Les mêmes dispositions de ordonnance n° 244/98 ont également transposé la décision-cadre du Conseil, du 28 novembre 2002, relative au cadre pénal pour la prévention de l'aide à l'entrée, au transit et à la résidence irréguliers. La transposition de ces deux instruments peut être considérée, quant à l'essentiel, comme correcte.

4.3 Combien de clandestins ont-ils été appréhendés aux frontières ou dans un périmètre proche des frontières? Combien de procédure pour trafic illégal de clandestins ont-elles été mises en œuvre l'année passée?

Selon les données fournies par les organismes compétents, au cours de l'an 2003, il y a eu 3.700 cas de refus d'entrée aux postes de frontière extérieure aériens et maritimes.

Selon les mêmes données, le nombre de procédures ouvertes pour trafic illégal de clandestins et infractions connexes a été jusqu'à présent de trois cents vingt-cinq.

4.4 Quels efforts ont été entrepris dans votre pays concernant les recommandations de Budapest de juin 2003 sur l'harmonisation des échelles de peines applicables aux délits de trafic des immigrés et de traite des êtres humains en accord avec les dispositions de la directive du 28 novembre 2002? Votre pays a-t-il- signé les protocoles des Nations Unies relatifs au trafic des clandestins?

Ayant transposé correctement la directive et la décision-cadre mentionnées au point 4.2., l'Etat portugais a correspondu simultanément à une partie des recommandations de Budapest de juin 2003, sur l'harmonisation des échelles de peines applicables aux crimes de trafic d'immigrés et de traite d'êtres humains.

Le Portugal a signé les protocoles des Nations unies relatifs au trafic de clandestins. La procédure de ratification de ces protocoles est en cours.

4.5 Quelles démarches ont-elles été entreprises afin de mettre en œuvre la directive 2001/40/CE du Conseil du 28 mai 2001 sur la reconnaissance mutuelle des décisions d'éloignement des ressortissants des pays tiers? Quels seraient, le cas échéant, les améliorations à apporter afin de remédier aux défauts et combler les lacunes de la directive en question en vue de l'adoption d'une nouvelle mesure sur la coopération des Etats membres en la matière?

La directive 2001/40/CE du Conseil, du 28 mai 2001, relative à la reconnaissance mutuelle des décisions d'éloignement de ressortissants de pays tiers a été transposée dans l'ordre juridique portugais par la Loi n° 53/2003. Il s'agit cependant d'un cas particulièrement évident de mauvaise transposition. Pour ne citer que deux exemples, le législateur n'a pas distingué clairement Etat portugais en sa qualité d'auteur d'une décision d'éloignement de celle d'exécuteur d'une telle décision. Par ailleurs, il s'est permis d'imposer des obligations à d'autres États membres en leur qualité d'auteurs d'une décision d'éloignement.

Outre qu'elle doit être complétée par des dispositions en matière de compensation des déséquilibres financiers qu'elle est susceptible de provoquer, cette directive doit être amendée de façon à établir un cadre obligatoire pour la reconnaissance mutuelle de toutes les décisions de retour.

4.6 Existe-t-il dans votre pays des accords de réadmission ou autres arrangements internationaux visant à contrôler et limiter l'immigration clandestine et faciliter le rapatriement? Si c'est le cas, ces accords ont-ils fonctionné de façon satisfaisante?

Le Portugal est signataire d'accords de réadmission visant à contrôler et limiter l'immigration clandestine et à faciliter le repatriement. Parmi d'autres, on peut citer les accords bilatéraux avec l'Espagne et la France, parmi les États membres, avec la Roumanie, parmi les Etats candidats, conclu en 2002, et avec El Salvador, parmi les Etats tiers, conclu en 2003.

D'après les organismes compétents pour leur application, la plupart de ces accords a fonctionné jusqu'à présent de façon satisfaisante.

4.7 Dans quelle mesure les critères et recommandations adoptés dans le cadre de l'Union européenne ont-ils influencé la politique du retour en vigueur dans votre pays? Des efforts de coopération ont-ils été entrepris avec d'autres Etats membres de l'Union européenne afin de mettre en œuvre les mesures d'expulsion et d'éloignement du territoire dans le cadre d'actions communes, d'échanges d'informations, de mesures visant à faciliter le transit aérien ou terrien, de principes communs sur la sécurité dans les avions, etc.?

L'ordonnance n° 34/2003 a introduit dans ordonnance n° 244/98 un nouvel article 126-A, dont le titre est «appui au retour volontaire». Aux termes de son paragraphe 1, l'Etat portugais pourra appuyer le retour volontaire aux pays d'origine des étrangers remplissant les conditions requises, et ce dans le cadre de programmes de coopération établis avec l'organisation internationale pour les migrations.

S'agissant, par ailleurs, de l'exécution de mesures d'expulsion et d'éloignement du territoire, le Portugal coopère avec d'autres États membres et principalement avec l'Espagne et la France dans le cadre d'actions en commun, d'échanges d'informations et de la facilitation du transit aérien ou terrien.

4.8 Pensez-vous qu'il soit nécessaire d'élaborer un régime commun juridique de déportation aérienne, avec notamment la nécessité de déterminer le statut juridique des agents de sécurité armés à bord des avions, les droits du pilote de l'avion, les règles applicables en cas d'arrêt de transit, l'applicabilité des règles nationales de police à bord de l'appareil en cours de vol, etc.?

L'adoption d'un régime juridique commun de déportation aérienne, comprenant notamment le statut juridique des agents de sécurité à bord et du personnel de bord s'avère d'un intérêt certain. Ce régime doit cependant être soigneusement pondéré à l'égard tant du principe de subsidiarité que du principe de proportionnalité.

SPAIN

MANUEL PEREZ GOMEZ

PART I (ENTRY, VISA REGIME AND BORDER CONTROL)

1.1 What national authorities are competent to deal with visa applications (Schengen visas and long-term visas)? Are there any procedures to avoid duplication or successive visa applications at different EU-consulates? On what substantive criteria, other than the Schengen minimum requirements, are visas granted or refused? How many visas have been issued or refused?

The national authorities competent to deal with visa applications are Consulates and the General Directorate for Consular Affairs.

The procedure used to avoid duplicate or successive visa applications at different EU-consulates is to check if the applicant has the stamp of another EU-consulate in his passport. That stamp is proof that a previous visa application was rejected.

Where a passport contains a stamp, the relevant consulate verifies with the consulate which stamped the passport as to the reason for the refusal of the previous visa application.

Criteria which are taken into account, other than the Schengen minimum requirements, for granting or refusing a Schengen visa are economic resources and the guarantee of return to the country of origin. In the case of a long term visa the previous report of the competent authority permitting residence in Spain is taken into consideration.

The total number of issued visas (Schengen and long term visas) during 2002, was 651,698 (519,328 Schengen visas and 132,370 long term visas). In the first semester of 2003, the number was 286,061 (211,878 Schengen visas and 74,183 long term visas. There is no record of the number of visa refusals.

1.2 Is there a visa tracking procedure in order to identify visa overstayers? What data are collected from visa-applicants (fingerprints)? Admissibility of visa data to alien and police authorities?

The only procedure for identifying visa overstayers is the information provided by the carriers regarding persons who do not use their return tickets to their country of origin.

The following data are collected from visa-applicants: name; date and place of birth; nationality; passport number; validity of the passport; certificate of criminal record and certificate of health. Finger prints are not collected.

Visa data is available to the police authorities. In the case of the alien authorities it is possible to make information available to them in accordance with the Common Consular Instruction of Schengen.

1.3 Have courts ever decided on the refusal of a Schengen visa based upon Schengen blacklisting by other Member States?

Yes, courts have decided on the refusal of Schengen visas based upon Schengen blacklisting by another Member State and the courts support the decision of the Consulate.

1.4 What measures have been undertaken in the implementation of the action programme for administrative cooperation in the field of external borders, visa, asylum and immigration following the Council Decision of 13 June 2002?

In the context of implementing the action programme for administrative cooperation in the field of external borders, visa, asylum and immigration, Spain has organised "Ulysses", which is a joint operation for coordinating the control of maritime external borders in the Mediterranean area in the first half of 2003, and in the Canary Islands in the second half of 2003.

1.5 What measures have been undertaken to implement the Directive 2001/51 EC supplementing the Schengen rules concerning carrier sanctions? How often have carrier sanctions been used?

Directive 2001/51 EC has been implemented by the Law 14/2003, which was approved on 29 October 2003, and entered into force on 22 December, 2003. As this law has only recently become effective, no carrier sanctions have been imposed to date.

1.6 In your judgement, does the visa law and policy of your country live up to EU standards or are adjustments needed? Do you consider that there is need for further EU-harmonization of visa policies concerning:
- **common criteria for granting visas aiming at harmonizing visa obligations among states participating in the Budapest Process;**
- **establishment of a European visa identification system (VIS and SIS II)?**

To what extent will the EU enlargement process present an opportunity or challenge for tackling issues of illegal entry and border control?

Spanish visa law and policy does not require any adjustment to EU standards.

There is a need for further EU-harmonization of the visa policies of those Member States participating in the Budapest Process and to establish a European visa identification system.

The EU enlargement process could facilitate cooperation between Member States and accession countries in combating illegal entry. However, measures must be taken to ensure better control over the external borders of the accession countries. Without such measures, there will be an increase in illegal immigration to EU Member States over the coming years.

PART II (ADMISSION AND RESIDENCE OF THIRD COUNTRY NATIONALS)

2.1 What are the basic principles in your country concerning:
- **admission of third country nationals for labour purposes or self-employed activities;**
- **admission of third country nationals for study and vocational training;**
- **legal status of third country nationals in possession of a long-term residence permit of another Member State?**

To what extent do these principles differ from the European Commission's proposals?

Foreign workers are authorised to enter Spain on condition that public employment services have previously established that there are no available workers (Spanish nationals or resident third country nationals) in the territory of Spain in the productivity sector referred to in the employer's application.

Authorisation for carrying out activities on a self-employed basis is only granted if those activities will give rise to financial investment and the creation of jobs.

In so far as the admission of third country nationals for the purposes of studies or vocational training is concerned, it must be established that the relevant academic institution is duly accredited for that purpose and that the third country national has economic means for the intended period of stay in Spain.

Third country nationals holding the status of long term resident in another Member State of the European Union are not treated differently from third country nationals residing in their country of origin. However, in accordance with the Schengen Agreement, they are allowed to circulate through the territory of Spain for up to three months.

In the case of the admission of third country nationals for paid employment, the difference between the principles of Spanish legislation and the

Commission proposal lies in the fact that the latter considers the above mentioned market test on the basis of the availability of workers in the whole of the European Union, not only in Spain.

As for students, the principles that inspire Spanish legislation are not basically different from the proposals put forward by the European Commission.

Regarding long term residents, there is a substantial difference between the approach adopted by the Commission and that adopted in Spain. Pursuant to Spanish legislation, third country nationals holding the status of long term residents in another EU Member State are not permitted to take up residence in the territory of Spain.

2.2 What are the legal requirements and procedures for obtaining a residence permit for third country nationals for the purpose of employment? Which procedures are used in maintaining the preferred access of EU-citizens and Turkish nationals (association agreement) to the labour market? Do special programmes exist for highly qualified professionals facilitating access to the labour market? To what extent are trade unions and employers involved in such programmes? Is there a procedure to calculate the demand for foreign labour? How is the EU-enlargement taken into consideration? To what extent has the recent economic recession and unemployment influenced the concepts on admission of third country nationals?

The legal requirements for obtaining a residence permit for third country nationals for the purpose of employment include the following: an offer of employment produced by an employer, a favourable report by public employment services for the admission of the applicant and proof that the applicant holds no judicial records that may constitute grounds for refusing the employment application.

The preferred access of EU-citizens and Turkish nationals to the Spanish labour market is maintained by the requirement that public employment services will consider this preference in their report before authorising entry to any third country nationals for the purpose of employment.

There are no special programmes for facilitating the access of highly qualified professionals to the labour market.

There is a procedure to calculate the annual demand for foreign labour which will determine the quota of third country nationals required by the labour market for the following year. The procedure takes account of labour required in specific sectors of activity.

The EU-enlargement is not taken into consideration in calculating the demand for foreign labour.

The recent economic recession has not influenced the admission of third country nationals for the purpose of employment to Spain; the number of foreign workers admitted to Spain has risen in recent years.

2.3 To what extent do existing national laws and practices differ substantially from the approach taken in the Commission's Proposal on admission for the purpose of paid employment and self-employed activities relating to:
– admission of third country nationals for study and vocational training;
– on legal status of third country nationals in possession of a long-term residence permit of another Member State?
To what extent do these principles differ from the European Commission's proposals?

The Commission's Proposal on the admission of third country nationals for the purpose of study or vocational training does not substantially differ from Spanish legislation. There is, however, a particular aspect which is a novelty as regards the existing legislation in Spain, that is the concept of the admission of third country nationals for the purpose of voluntary service. This is not envisaged in Spanish legislation.

Spanish legislation and practice do not contemplate the possibility of allowing entry for the purpose of employment to a long term resident of another EU Member State: legislative changes will be needed to provide for this possibility.

2.4 What measures have been taken to implement the Directive of 29th June 2000, implementing the principle of equal treatment between persons irrespective of racial or ethnic origin and Council Directive 2000/78 EC of 27th November 2000, establishing a general framework for equal treatment in employment and occupation? Have legislative changes been undertaken? To what extent is "affirmative action" considered as necessary to promote equal opportunities for migrant workers from third countries?

The Directive of 29th June 2000 and Council Directive 2000/78 EC of 27 November 2000, have been incorporated into Spanish legislation by means of a Law passed by the Spanish Parliament on 23rd December 2003, which will be published in the Official Journal before its entry into force.

The notion of "positive discrimination" has not been included in the new law as it was not considered necessary in order to promote equal opportunities for third country workers.

2.5 Concerning the proposal for a directive on the right to family reunion agreed upon by the Council in February 2003:
– Do you consider the proposed standards below the principles of family reunification applicable in your country?
– Will the implementation of the Directive, once it is adopted, lead to changes in the national law on family reunification downgrading the standard of protection? If so, what changes are envisaged?

Directive 2003/86, of 22nd September 2003, on the right to family reunification is pending incorporation in Spain. The incorporation will not substantially affect the principles which currently regulate the protection of this right under Spanish law.

2.6 The proposal for a directive on the rights of long-term third country nationals as agreed upon by the Council on 5 June 2003, provides for a number of rights approximating the situation of long-term residents to the status of EU-citizens. Will the implementation of the Directive involve major legal and policy changes in your country? What are the major points of concern if any, concerning the approximation concept of the directive relating to:
- **non-discrimination in social rights;**
- **the concept of "civic citizenship" (see also extended impact assessment on the Communication on Integration of June 11, 2003);**
- **family reunification and access of family members to the labour market;**
- **security of stay?**

Incorporating the Directive on long term residents, recently adopted by the Council, will require the existing law to be modified. In this respect, the most important question which will have to be considered is that of the access to resident status of third country nationals who are long term residents of another EU Member State.

2.7 Considering the perspective of a future common migration policy as developed by the Commission in the Open Coordination Communication (COM 2001, 387) and the Communication on a Migration policy of the European Union (COM 2000, 757 final), how do you assess the role of the Community organs in determining a European migration policy in terms of competences of the Member States to decide on residence rights and admission to the labour market and integration? Should harmonization of legislation go further, and if so, in what respect?

Once the five year period established by the Amsterdam Treaty has elapsed, the role of the EU institutions, and particularly that of the Commission, will be fundamental in order to determine European Union migration policy. However, Member States will maintain competences in this matter and a total transfer of these competences in favour of EU institutions cannot be foreseen.

The harmonisation of national legislation in this respect must focus on fundamental principles leaving Member States with the capacity to specify the terms of the main principles established by the European Union.

PART III (ASYLUM AND REFUGEE LAW)

3.1 Have the Dublin Rules worked satisfactorily and what is expected of the Dublin II Regulation No. 343, 2003 of 18 February 2003?

Generally, the application of the Dublin Rules has been satisfactory. However, it is necessary to establish a common interpretation of several concepts, such as "the taking in charge" and "readmission".

3.2 Has the Eurodac Regulation No. 2725/2000 of 11th December 2000, concerning the establishment of Eurodac for the comparison of fingerprints for an effective application of the Dublin Convention, operative since January 15, 2003, resulted in an increase of Dublin cases? Has Eurodac become effective in your country or is it expected to become effective eventually?

The establishment of Eurodac has not resulted in an increase in Dublin cases. Generally, its application has become effective, although it is necessary to solve several problems of interpretation, such as the persons to be included under category 1.

3.3 What major changes, if any, will the implementation of the amended proposal for a directive on minimum standards on procedures in Member States for granting and withdrawing refugee status, on which the Council has reached political agreement on most points in June 2003, bring for the legislation and practice in your country in particular relating to:
- **rights of applicants in the procedure;**
- **administrative and judicial appeal procedures;**
- **the use of safe third country and safe country of origin concepts;**
- **detainment of asylum seekers;**
- **airport and border procedures?**

In its current form, the final approval of the Directive on minimum standards on procedures in Member States for granting and withdrawing refugee status will not give rise to substantial changes in the Spanish legislation regarding the rights of applicants in the procedure, the administrative and judicial appeal procedure, the detention of asylum seekers, and airport and border procedures.

As far as the list of safe third countries and safe countries of origin is concerned, it is not presently included in Spanish legislation and will have to be incorporated. In any case, the list will only be used in an indicative way, since Spanish legislation requires the individual analysis and solution of each application.

3.4 What measures have been undertaken to implement Directive 2003/9 of 27 January 2003, on reception of asylum seekers in your country relating to:
- **the flexibility clauses in the Directive;**
- **restriction of free movement;**
- **access to the labour market;**
- **rights of migrant workers under Article 11 § 2 of the Directive?**

The deadline for the transposition of Directive 2003/9 of 27 January 2003, is 6 February 2005. Consequently measures necessary for its adoption are still being considered.

However, Spanish legislation already provides for the compulsory obligations contained in the Directive, the possibility of restricting free movement, as well as access to the labour market after six months from the application date.

3.5 What steps have been undertaken to implement the Directive on temporary protection, COM 2001, 55 in national law? Are there any procedures for burden sharing arrangements? Is there a legal basis for the admission of refugees for the purposes of receiving temporary protection in a mass-movement situation?

The Real Decree 1325/2003, of 24 October has incorporated the Directive on temporary protection into Spanish law. No procedure is provided for burden sharing arrangements. There is a legal basis for the admission of refugees receiving temporary protection in a mass-movement situation.

3.6 The Council has reached political agreement on the principles for a Directive on minimum standards for the qualification and status of third country nationals as refugees or persons who otherwise need international protection, COM 2001, 510 final (see Council documents of June 2003). What measures are envisaged to implement the Directive, once it is adopted, in your country relating to:
- **the definition of refugee;**
- **the definition of persons entitled to subsidiary protection;**
- **status of persons entitled to subsidiary protection;**
- **the issue of internal flight alternative as defined by the Directive;**
- **exclusion clauses, particularly issues of terrorism?**

To what extent are the refugee policies as reflected in the law and jurisprudence of your country in accordance with the proposal for the directive?

Measures for the adoption of the Directive on the qualification of refugees and other ways of protection are presently under consideration and awaiting final approval of the Directive.

The Spanish legislation has to be adapted to the definitions of "refugee", "subsidiary protection" and "internal flight" contained in the proposal of the Directive. Regarding the exclusion clauses, the text of the Directive does not differ from Spanish legislation.

3.7 In the Commission's Communication of 22 November, 2000, COM 2000, 755 (see also 2nd Commission Report COM 2003, 152 final) the Commission's concept of a common European asylum procedure and a uniform status for those who are granted asylum valid throughout the Union is set out. Do you consider that the concept is generally in line with your country's asylum policy? Are the concerns of refugee organizations, such as Amnesty International and other organizations, of

an undermining of the international regime for the protection of refugees shared in the political circles responsible for decision-making of your country?

National policy on asylum is in accordance with the results of the debates held by the Council of Ministers when reaching final agreement on the Commission's proposals.

The responsible politicians in that matter do not share the concerns of refugee organisations regarding a decrease in the level of protection.

3.8 The open coordination-mechanism, as suggested by the Commission, provided for first stage and second stage legislation in which the flexibility provisions in some of the directives on migration and asylum are to be replaced by full harmonization. Is this concept discussed in your country and what are the perceptions relating to the gradual establishment of a European asylum policy which might eventually replace national procedures and national decision-making?

It is understandable that once the first phase is completed, progress can be made towards greater harmonisation. Nevertheless, the first phase must be completed before planning the next, more ambitious phase.

3.9 The Communication of June 2003, towards a more accessible, equitable and managed asylum system – in reaction to the UK paper – develops some ideas on new approaches to pursue an orderly and managed arrival of persons in need of international protection. What is the political reaction in your country to the concept of an outside accessed asylum procedure, distribution of refugees and responsibility-sharing and other new concepts and ideas in coping with mass refugee movements?

The reaction to the Communication of June 2003, is that of caution, considering the absence of an EU legal basis to deal with the subjects contained in that Communication. From the Spanish perspective, the Communication does not reflect the real situation as regards refugee distribution. In particular, account needs to be taken of immigrants as well as refugees and the discussion should concern the distribution of immigrants.

PART IV (TERMINATION OF ILLEGAL RESIDENCE, RETURN AND REPATRIATION)

4.1 How many third country nationals without a valid residence permit are currently, according to estimates, staying in your country? How many deportations have actually been made in previous years? Is the whole enforcement process considered as acceptable?

It is impossible to determine the number of persons in an irregular situation by reason of that irregularity.

The total number of repatriations in 2002 was of 77,113 persons; while from January 1 to December 26, 2003, the total number was 92,457.

The procedure for the implementation of such repatriation measures is considered acceptable although improvements could be made.

4.2 What has been undertaken to implement the Directive of 28 November 2002, dealing with the facilitation of unauthorized entry, transit and residence?

Law 14/2003, which entered into force on 22 December 2003, has incorporated Directive 90/2002, of 28 November 2003, into Spanish law.

4.3 How many illegal applicants have been apprehended at or near the border? How many criminal procedures for human trafficking have been instituted in the last year?

The number of persons apprehended at or close to the border in 2002, was 64,954, while from January 1 to December 26, 2003, the number was 78,340.

The number of illegal immigration networks involved in court procedures in 2002, was 777; while from January 1 to December 16, 2003, the number was 677.

4.4 What efforts have been undertaken in your country regarding the Budapest June 2003 recommendations concerning the harmonization of penalty scales with regard to the crime of the smuggling of migrants and trafficking of persons, in line with Council Directive 2002/90 of 28th November 2002? Did your country sign the relevant UN protocols on the smuggling of migrants?

Spain has incorporated into its legislation all the Budapest June 2003, recommendations concerning the harmonisation of penalties with regard to the crime of the smuggling of migrants and trafficking of persons in line with Council Directive 2002/90 of November 28, 2002.

Spain has also signed the UN protocols on the smuggling of migrants.

4.5 What measures have been taken to implement the Council Directive of 28 May 2001, on the mutual recognition of decisions on the expulsion of third country nationals? What, if any shortcomings or gaps of the Directive should be corrected in a further directive on cooperation on expulsion or deportation of third country nationals?

Directive 40/2001, of 28 May 2001, has been incorporated into Spanish legislation by the Law 14/2003, which entered into force on 22 December 2003, allowing for the expulsion of a third country national pursuant to a legal ruling of any EU Member State.

As the legislation has only recently entered into force it is not yet possible to assess its defects or gaps.

4.6 Do readmission agreements or other international treaties or arrangements with the aim of controlling and curbing illegal immigration and facilitating return exist in your country? Have they functioned satisfactorily?

Spain has signed an important number of agreements with EU Member States and with third countries, mainly from Africa, America and Eastern Europe, regarding the control of illegal immigration and to facilitate the readmission of their nationals.

Most of those agreements work satisfactorily, although some of them, such as that signed with Morocco do not work in so far as the readmission of their nationals is concerned.

4.7 To what extent have EU-standards and recommendations influenced your country's return policy? Have efforts been undertaken to cooperate with other EU Member States in enforcing return decisions by common deportation actions, exchange of information, facilitation of air and land transit, common principles on flight security, etc.?

The criteria and recommendations adopted by the EU are helpful in order to establish the basic criteria of the Spanish return policy.

Spain has make progress in cooperating with other countries of the European Union, such as France, Germany, Italy, United Kingdom and Portugal on information exchange, through liaison officials, and through the organisation of joint flights for repatriations to third countries.

4.8 Do you consider that there is a need to elaborate a common legal regime for air deportations (legal status of armed guards on board of the aircrafts, rights of the aircraft commander, legal rules in case of transit stops, applicability of national police law on board of aircraft on flight, etc.)?

The elaboration of a common legal regime for air deportations is only necessary if its purpose is to facilitate deportations. Spain does not consider the elaboration of a regime which makes deportations more difficult to be either necessary or desirable.

Madrid, 29 December 2003.

SWEDEN

OLA HENRIKSON

PART I ENTRY, VISA REGIME AND BORDER CONTROL

1.1 What national authorities are competent to deal with visa applications (Schengen visas and long-term visas)? Are there any procedures to avoid duplication or successive visa applications at different EU- consulates? On what substantive criteria other than the Schengen minimum requirements are visas granted or refused? How many visas have been issued or refused?

The main responsibility lies with the Migration Board however, the Board may authorise missions abroad both to grant and deny visas. All authorised missions may both grant and deny visas. A number of cases are still referred to the Migration Board.

There is local cooperation between Member/Schengen States in order to avoid duplication or successive visa applications in different consulates.

The Migration Board sets out guidelines on the granting or refusal of visas. The guidelines are individual to different third countries.

In 2003, approximately 129,500 visas were granted and 19,000 refused.

1.2 Is there a visa tracking procedure in order to identify visa overstayers? What data are collected from visa-applicants (fingerprints)? Admissibility of visa data to alien and police authorities?

Overstayers are mostly detected at exit controls. There is also a possibility for the police to control people on the territory. Information on visas granted and denied is transferred from the missions abroad to the Migration Board.

Personal data such as name, date of birth, address, purpose of the visit, etc., has to be filled in on the application form. No biometric data are collected.

The data are admissible to the Migration Board and to the police, upon request.

1.3 Have courts ever decided on the refusal of a Schengen visa based upon Schengen blacklisting by other Member States?

No. There is no right of appeal in cases concerning visa applications.

1.4 What measures have been undertaken in the implementation of the action programme for administrative cooperation in the field of external borders, visa, asylum and immigration following the Council Decision of June 13, 2002?

The competent authorities are taking part in relevant council working groups and are responsible for the implementation of the action programme.

1.5 What measures have been undertaken to implement Directive 2001/51 EC supplementing the Schengen rules concerning carrier sanctions? How often have carrier sanctions been used?

The Government presented a bill containing draft legislation to Parliament on 22 January 2004. The new legislation is due to come into force on 1 July 2004.

1.6 According to your judgement, does the visa law and policy of your country live up to EU standards or are adjustments needed? Do you consider that there is need for further EU-harmonization of visa policies concerning:
- **common criteria for granting visas aiming at harmonizing visa obligations among states participating in the Budapest Process;**
- **establishment of a European visa identification system (VIS and SIS II)?**

To what extent will the EU enlargement process present an opportunity or danger for tackling issues of illegal entry and border control?

Yes, in my view Sweden lives up to the relevant EU-standards. I think there is a further need to harmonise visa policy both concerning criteria for granting visas and the establishment of VIS.

PART II ADMISSION AND RESIDENCE OF THIRD COUNTRY NATIONALS

2.1 What are the basic principles in your country concerning:
- **admission of third country nationals for labour purpose or self-employed activities;**
- **admission of third country nationals for study and vocational training;**
- **legal status of third country nationals in possession of a long-term residence permit of another Member State?**

To what extent do these principles differ from the European Commission's proposals?

The basic principle concerning admission and residence for all third country nationals is that the person concerned should apply for the relevant permits before entering the country. Applications are made at a Swedish mission abroad, where an application form is filled out and, if necessary, an interview is carried out. The case is then referred to the Migration Board.

Concerning applications for labour purposes, an assessment is first made as to whether the vacancy can be filled by an EEA-national and second as to whether there is a need to allow for labour immigration in the particular case.

Regarding self-employed activities an assessment is made if the business the applicant is going to engage in is likely to be sufficiently profitable for the applicant to make a living out of it.

There is no special status awarded to third country nationals in possession of a long-term residence permit of another Member State. This will be changed when the Directive on long-term residents is transposed into national legislation.

2.2 What are the legal requirements and procedures for obtaining a residence permit for third country nationals for the purpose of employment? Which procedures are used in maintaining the preferred access of EU-citizens and Turkish nationals (association agreement) to the labour market? Do special programmes exist for highly qualified professionals facilitating access to the labour market? To what extent are trade unions and employers involved in such programmes? Is there a procedure to calculate the demand for foreign labour? How is EU-enlargement taken into consideration? To what extent has the recent economic recession and unemployment influenced the concepts on admission of third country nationals?

See 2.1. A labour market assessment is carried out. EU-Citizens do not have to apply before entering the country.

No special programmes exist for highly qualified professionals.

There is no special nationwide procedure to calculate the demand for foreign labour. However an assessment is carried out by the Migration Board and the County Labour Board when a third country national applies for a work permit in order to determine whether the vacancy can be filled by EEA-nationals.

The Government will propose that transitional rules are applied when it comes to the free movement for workers. The details will be presented by the Government in March.

The number of third country nationals admitted for labour purposes has been rather low for some decades so it cannot be said that economic development during recent years has had an impact in this field.

2.3 To what extent do existing laws and practices differ substantially from the approach taken in the Commission's Proposal on admission for the purpose of paid employment and self-employed activities relating to:

- admission of third country nationals for study and vocational training;
- on legal status of third country nationals in possession of a long-term residence permit of another Member State?

To what extent do these principles differ from the European Commission's proposals?

The Commission was asked by the Council, at the end of 2003, to redraft its proposal. The new draft directive has not been presented yet.

2.4 What measures have been taken to implement the Directive of 29th June 2000 implementing the principle of equal treatment between persons irrespective of racial or ethnic origin and Council Directive 2000/78 EC of 27th November 2000 establishing a general framework for equal treatment in employment and occupation? Have legislative changes been undertaken? To what extent is "affirmative action" considered as necessary to promote equal chances for migrant workers from third countries?

Both Directives have been implemented in the new anti-discrimination law and through amendments in other laws on anti-discrimination.

2.5 Concerning the proposal for a directive on the right to family reunion agreed upon by Council in February 2003:
- Do you consider the proposed standards below the principles of family reunification valid in your country?
- Will the implementation of the Directive once it is adopted lead to changes in the national law on family reunification downgrading the standard of protection? If so, what changes are envisaged?

To some degree the standards of the Directive are below national principles, namely when it comes to age limits and integration conditions but also concerning same sex partners and unmarried couples.

It will probably lead to minor changes in the national legislation. When it comes to maintenance obligations as a condition, changes may be made.

2.6 The proposal for a directive on the rights of long-term third country nationals as agreed upon by the Council on 5 June 2003, provides for a number of rights approximating the standards of long-term residents to the status of EU-citizens. Will the implementation of the directive involve major legal and policy changes in your country? What are the major points of concern if any, concerning the approximation concept of the directive relating to:
- non-discrimination in social rights;
- the concept of "civic citizenship" (see also extended impact assessment on the Communication on Integration of June 11, 2003);
- family reunification and access of family members to the labour market;
- security of stay?

There will be changes to national legislation since the underlying principles of the Directive are new to our legal system. The Government has appointed a committee that will present draft legislation and other possible measures by the end of 2004.

According to the Swedish view, when it comes to family reunification and access of family members to the labour market, it is vital that family members should be in a position to earn their living.

2.7 Considering the perspective of a future common migration policy as developed by the Commission in the Open Coordination Communication (COM 2001, 387) and the communication on a migration policy of the European Union (COM 2000, 757 final), how do you assess the role of the Community organs in determining a European migration policy in terms of competences of the Member States to decide on residence rights and admission to the labour market and integration? Should harmonization of legislation go further, and if so, in what respect?

In the foreseeable future, the competence to decide on residence rights and admission to the labour market and integration must lie with national authorities. However, those authorities must apply relevant Community law including decisions of the Court of Justice of the European Communities. But when it comes to considering the individual applications, this must be dealt with at the national level both from an efficiency perspective and in the light of the principle of subsidiarity. There is a room for further harmonisation, the legal acts already adopted by the Council show that the Commission's initial proposals have not survived fully.

PART III ASYLUM AND REFUGEE LAW

3.1 Have the Dublin Rules worked satisfactorily and what is expected from the Dublin II Regulation No. 343, 2003 of February 18, 2003?

The Dublin rules have not worked altogether satisfactorily. The procedures to establish the Member State responsible for trying applications for asylum are too lengthy. The time limits laid down in the Convention are too long. Due to lack of travel documents and other documentation among asylum seekers it has in many cases been cumbersome to apply the Convention. The Dublin Regulation has been applied since September 2003, and it is an improvement compared to the Convention especially when it comes to time limits.

3.2 Has the Eurodac Regulation No. 2725/2000 of 11th December 2000 concerning the establishment of Eurodac for the comparison of fingerprints for an effective application of the Dublin Convention, operative since January 15, 2003 resulted in an increase of Dublin cases? Has Eurodac become effective in your country or is it expected to become effective eventually?

The Eurodac system has increased the number of Dublin cases. The Migration Board has found more than 1,000 matching fingerprints. It has become effective.

3.3 What major changes, if any, will the implementation of the amended proposal for a directive on minimum standards on procedures in Member States for granting and withdrawing refugee status, on which the Council has reached political agreement on most points in June 2003, bring for the legislation and practice in your country in particular relating to:
- **rights of applicants in the procedure;**
- **administrative and judicial appeal procedure;**
- **the use of safe third country and safe country of origin concepts;**
- **detainment of asylum seekers;**
- **airport and border procedures?**

The draft Directive will not require any major changes concerning the rights of applicants in the procedure. Sweden already applies standards similar to most of the provisions proposed in the draft.

When it comes to appeal procedures, the implementation of the draft will mean one major change to the current system. The Migration Board and the Aliens Appeals Board will no longer have the possibility to refer cases to the Government. Today, the authorities have this possibility under certain conditions.

The current legislation contains rules on the safe third country and safe country of origin concepts. The basic principle when applying those concepts is that every case has to be tried individually on its own merits. There is no use of lists of safe third countries or safe countries of origin, at least not apart from the Dublin Regulation and the Protocol on asylum for EU-nationals.

The draft is not very specific when it comes to rules on the use of detention. There are no major differences between the draft and current legislation.

The current Swedish legislation does not contain any specific provisions on airport or border procedures. The provisions on accelerated procedures are of a more general kind.

3.4 What measures have been undertaken to implement Directive 2003/9 of 27 January 2003 on reception of asylum seekers in your country relating to:
- **the flexibility clauses in the directive;**
- **restriction of free movement;**
- **access to the labour market;**
- **rights of migrant workers under Article 11 § 2 of the Directive?**

The government is currently preparing a bill containing draft legislation to be presented to parliament during May 2004.

3.5 What steps have been undertaken to implement the Directive on temporary protection, COM 2001, 55 in national law? Are there any procedures for burden sharing arrangements? Is there a legal basis for admission of refugees receiving temporary protection in a mass-movement situation?

The Directive is implemented in national legislation through amendments to the Aliens Act.

3.6 The Council has reached political agreement on the principles for a directive on minimum standards for the qualification and status of third country nationals as refugees or persons who otherwise need international protection, COM 2001, 510 final (see Council documents of June 2003). What measures are envisaged to implement the Directive, once it is adopted, in your country relating to:
– the definition of refugee;
– the definition of persons entitled to subsidiary protection;
– status of persons entitled to subsidiary protection;
– the issue of internal flight alternative as defined by the Directive;
– exclusion clauses, particularly issues of terrorism?
To what extent are the refugee policies as reflected in the law and jurisprudence of your country in accordance with the proposal for the directive?

There will be changes to the current legislation.

The definition of refugee will be wider. Today persecution because of gender or sexual orientation does not qualify for refugee status.

In the current legislation there is a definition of "other persons in need of protection" which in many ways is similar to the definition of subsidiary status in the draft directive. However, there is no clear provision in the current legislation stating that non-state agents of persecution may qualify for subsidiary status.

Internal flight is not defined in the current legislation: it is defined by interpretation of the travail preparatoire and through practice.

The current legislation contains provisions on exclusion from refugee status based on Article 1 F of the Geneva Convention. There are no provisions on exclusion from subsidiary status.

3.7 In the Commission's Communication of November 22, 2000, COM 2000, 755 (see also 2nd Commission Report COM 2003, 152 final) the Commission's concept of a common European asylum procedure and a uniform status for those who are granted asylum valid throughout the Union is set out. Do you consider that the concept is generally in line with your country's asylum policy? Are concerns of refugee organizations, such as Amnesty International and other organizations, of an undermining of the international regime for the protection of refugees shared in the political circles of your country responsible for decision-making?

From a medium to long time perspective, the concept of a common European asylum procedure and a uniform status would be in line with Swedish asylum policy. This will of course also depend on the contents of individual legal acts, who will be granted asylum and pursuant to what procedures. The idea of a uniform status valid throughout the EU would be in line with Swedish policy, not least since it would have a positive impact on the possibility for refugees to move between Member States. The concerns of Amnesty International and other organisations are shared by some persons in political circles. Parliamentarians have on many occasions voiced criticism of EU-policy in the field of asylum: there is a view that Commission proposals have been watered down during negotiations in the Council. The majority though would be in favour of a more harmonised EU-policy.

3.8 The open coordination-mechanism as suggested by the Commission provided for a first stage and a second stage legislation in which the flexibility provisions in some of the directives on migration and asylum are to be replaced by full harmonization. Is this concept discussed in your country and what are the perceptions relating to the gradual establishment of a European asylum policy which eventually might replace national procedures and national decision-making?

There is really not much of a discussion on the open coordination-mechanism. Discussions tend to focus on the draft directives and draft regulations and the impact those will have on national legislation.

3.9 The Communication of June, 2003 towards a more accessible, equitable and managed asylum system – in reaction to the UK paper – develops some ideas on new approaches to pursue an orderly and managed arrival of persons in need of international protection. What is the political reaction in your country as to the concept of an outside accessed asylum procedure, distribution of refugees and responsibility-sharing and other new concepts and ideas in coping with mass refugee movements?

The ideas put forward in the Communication were heavily criticised by all parties in Parliament and by the minister responsible for migration. However, Sweden has a long tradition of receiving refugees in yearly resettlement programmes managed in close cooperation with the UNHCR and would like to see more EU-cooperation in the field of resettlement.

PART IV TERMINATION OF ILLEGAL RESIDENCE, RETURN AND REPATRIATION

4.1 How many third country nationals without a valid residence permit are presently, according to estimates, staying in your country? How many deportations have actually been made in previous years? Is the whole enforcement process considered as acceptable?

It is not possible to estimate the number of third country nationals staying in Sweden without valid residence permits. There are figures on asylum seekers (the lack of valid residence permits), on persons having absconded when expulsion orders should have been carried out (it is very hard to know how many of those are actually still on the territory). Apart from this, there are of course a number of overstayers (no estimations have been made) and persons who enter illegally and do not apply for asylum or residence permits on other grounds (no estimations have been made).

In 2003, approximately 12,000 persons left the country after having received a final expulsion order: more than 9,000 of those left voluntarily. In the same year almost 13,000 absconded after having received a final expulsion, Many of those might very well have left the country.

The enforcement process is considered to be acceptable, that is to say the way in which enforcement is carried out. There is occasional criticism in individual cases, but this must be considered to be exceptional. There are, of course, problems when it comes to actually implementing expulsion orders. One major problem is that approximately 90% of asylum applicants do not present any travel documents. Another problem is that a number of countries do not readmit their own citizens and a third problem is the number of persons absconding.

4.2 What has been undertaken to implement the Directive of November 28, 2002 dealing with the facilitation of unauthorized entry, transit and residence?

A government bill containing amendments to current legislation was presented to Parliament in December 2003. The draft legislation is supposed to enter into force on 1 September 2004.

4.3 How many illegal applicants have been apprehended at or near the border? How many criminal procedures for human trafficking have been instituted in the last year?

Swedish legislation does not contain the concept of an illegal applicant or anything similar. The number of criminal procedures instituted in 2003, was 16.

4.4 What efforts have been undertaken in your country concerning the Budapest June 2003 recommendations concerning the harmonization of penalty scales with regard to the crime of smuggling of migrants and trafficking of persons in line with Council Directive 2002/90 of 28th November 2002? Did your country sign the relevant UN protocols on the smuggling of migrants?

Sweden has signed the protocol on the smuggling of migrants (Palermo). It has not yet been ratified by Parliament.

4.5 What measures have been taken to implement the Council Directive of 28th May 2001 on the mutual recognition of decisions on the expulsion of third country nationals? What, if any, shortcomings or gaps of the Directive should be corrected in a further directive on cooperation on expulsion or deportation of third country nationals?

Amendments to the Aliens Act were adopted by Parliament in 2002. A Council decision regarding the sharing of costs when implementing the directive was adopted in 2003. More common rules and more cooperation in the field of expulsion and deportation will come in the future.

4.6 Do readmission agreements or other international treaties or arrangements with the aim of controlling and curbing illegal immigration and facilitating return exist in your country? Have they functioned satisfactorily?

Sweden has signed 11 bilateral agreements on readmission (Bulgaria, Croatia, Estonia, France, Germany, Latvia, Lithuania, Poland, Romania, Serbia and Montenegro and Switzerland). There are provisions on readmission in the convention on the Nordic Passport Union. Some bilateral agreements have worked fairly well and in some cases there has been no need to implement the agreements. There have been major problems in reaching agreements on readmission with some third countries, from which large numbers of asylum seekers who have had their applications turned down originate. The convention on the Nordic Passport Union worked very well for decades.

4.7 To what extent have EU-standards and recommendations influenced your country's return policy? Have efforts been undertaken to cooperate with other EU Member States in enforcing return decisions by common deportation actions, exchange of information, facilitation of air and land transit, common principles on flight security, etc.?

Sweden has used the EU-prototype when signing readmission agreements with third countries. Efforts have been undertaken to cooperate with other Member States in enforcing return decisions, especially regarding the exchange of information between relevant authorities.

4.8 Do you consider that there is a need to elaborate a common legal regime for air deportations (legal status of armed guards on board of the aircrafts, rights of the aircraft commander, legal rules in case of transit stops, applicability of national police law on board of aircraft on flight, etc.)?

Yes, maybe in order to have clear cut rules on who is responsible for what and in order to make life easier for the staff carrying out expulsion orders.

SWITZERLAND

Le rapprochement de la Suisse à la politique européenes en matière d'asile et d'immigration

CHRISTINE KADDOUS
Professeure de droit européen
Directrice du Centre d'études juridiques européennes de l'Université de Genève
(www.unige.ch/ceje)

RUTE VICENTE
Collaboratrice scientifique
Centre d'études juridiques européennes (www.unige.ch/ceje)

INTRODUCTION

Dans le cadre de la réalisation de «l'espace de liberté, de sécurité et de justice», les Etats membres de l'Union européenne se sont fixé pour objectif de mettre en place une politique commune en matière d'immigration jusqu'en mai 2004. L'Accord de Schengen de 1985[1], sa Convention d'application de 1990[2] et la Convention de Dublin de 1990[3] constituèrent les premières règles communes en la matière. Mais depuis l'entrée en vigueur du traité d'Amsterdam, des étapes importantes ont été franchies en vue de la coordination et de l'harmonisation des législations nationales dans les domaines de l'immigration et de l'asile, et ce afin de parvenir à une gestion plus efficace des flux migratoires, à l'intégration des ressortissants

[1] Accord entre les gouvernements des Etats de l'Union économique Benelux, de la République fédérale d'Allemagne et de la République française relatif à la suppression graduelle des contrôles aux frontières communes, signé à Schengen le 14 juin 1985, JO n° L 239 du 22.09.2000, p. 13, in: Christine KADDOUS, *Union européenne. Communauté européenne. Recueil de textes*, LGDJ/Stämpfli (Paris/Berne), 2e édition, 2003, p. 537.

[2] Convention d'application de l'Accord de Schengen du 14 juin 1985 entre les gouvernements des Etats de l'Union économique Benelux, de la République fédérale d'Allemagne et de la République française relatif à la suppression graduelle des contrôles aux frontières communes, JO n° L 239 du 22.09.2000, p. 19, in: Christine KADDOUS, op cit, p. 543. Ci-après: Convention d'application.

[3] Convention relative à la détermination de l'Etat responsable de l'examen d'une demande d'asile présentée dans l'un des Etats membres des Communautés européennes, signée à Dublin le 15 juin 1990, JO n° C 254 du 19.09.1997, p. 1, aujourd'hui abrogée et remplacée par le règlement 343/2003, voir *supra* (note 93).

de pays tiers en situation régulière, et, dans le domaine l'asile, à l'établissement d'un régime commun d'asile européen conforme aux dispositions de la Convention de Genève relative au statut des réfugiés de 1951[4].

En Europe, la Suisse est l'un des pays qui connaît le pourcentage le plus élevé de la population résidante de nationalité étrangère (près de 20% de la population). C'est un chiffre deux fois supérieur à n'importe quel autre Etat membre de l'Union européenne, à l'exception du Luxembourg[5]. En ce qui concerne l'asile, la Suisse fait également partie des pays de l'OCDE dont les autorités ont enregistré, ces dernières années, le plus grand nombre de demandes en proportion avec le nombre d'habitants[6]. Aussi, la législation relative à l'immigration, actuellement en révision, est un pilier essentiel de la politique suisse.

Entourée presque exclusivement par des Etats membres de l'Union européenne, la Suisse ne peut que suivre avec intérêt l'évolution de l'harmonisation européenne en matière d'immigration et d'asile. Nous nous proposons, dans le cadre de la présente contribution, d'analyser les similitudes et les différences entre les deux systèmes[7]. Les récents Accords bilatéraux, et notamment l'Accord sur la libre circulation des personnes[8], ont démontré l'importance du rapprochement entre la Suisse et l'Union européenne. Mais la volonté de coopérer ne s'arrête pas là,

[4] Convention du 28 juillet 1951 relative au statut des réfugiés, RS 0.142.30; disponible sur http://www.unhchr.ch/french/html/menu3/b/o_c_ref_fr.htm. Ci-après: Convention de Genève de 1951.

[5] Pour l'année 2001, c'est le Luxembourg qui, parmi les Etats membres de l'Union européenne, connaît le taux le plus élevé de population étrangère (37,5%), suivi de l'Autriche (9,4%), de l'Allemagne (8,9%), de la Belgique (8,2%) et de la France (5,6%). Sources: Statistiques de la population active: 1982–2002, OCDE, Paris, 2003.

[6] Pour l'année 2002, plus de 26'000 demandes d'asile ont été enregistrées en Suisse. Au sein de l'Union européenne, c'est le Royaume-Uni qui compte le plus de demandes, suivi de l'Allemagne et de la France. Sources: UNHCR, mars 2003.

[7] Les questions relatives à l'entraide judiciaire internationale ne sont pas traitées dans le présent rapport, dans la mesure où le questionnaire du rapporteur général, le Prof. Kail Hailbronner, n'en fait pas mention et que ces questions relèvent prioritairement de l'espace pénal européen, traitées dans le sujet n° 1 du Congrès FIDE 2004.

[8] Sept accords sectoriels ont été signés le 21 juin 1999 entre, d'une part, la Suisse et, d'autre part, la Communauté européenne et ses Etats membres et sont entrés en vigueur le 1er juin 2002. Ces accords portent sur la libre circulation des personnes, le transport aérien, le transport terrestre, la reconnaissance mutuelle en matière d'évaluation, les marchés publics, l'agriculture ainsi que la coopération scientifique et technologique. Pour un commentaire des Accords bilatéraux, voir Daniel Felder/Christine Kaddous (éd.), *Accords bilatéraux Suisse-UE, Commentaires. Bilaterale Abkommen Schweiz-EU, Erste Analysen*, Collection des Dossiers de droit européen, Helbing & Lichtenhahn/Bruylant (Bâle, Genève, Munich/Bruxelles), 2001.

puisqu'elle tente aujourd'hui de s'étendre également aux questions d'asile et d'immigration. Des négociations pour une association de la Suisse au système de Schengen et Dublin sont en cours[9].

I Entrée sur le territoire, visas et contrôles aux frontières

Avec l'adoption de l'Accord de Schengen en 1985[10], puis de sa Convention d'application en 1990[11], les Etats membres de l'Union européenne (à l'exception du Royaume-Uni et de l'Irlande[12]) supprimèrent entre eux les contrôles aux frontières intérieures, créant ainsi «l'espace Schengen»[13]. Des règles communes en matière de visas et de contrôles aux frontières extérieures furent adoptées afin de gérer au mieux les problèmes liés aux flux migratoires.

La Suisse ne participe pas au régime mis en place par Schengen. Ses frontières avec les principaux voisins, la France, l'Italie, l'Allemagne et l'Autriche, sont dès lors considérées comme des «frontières extérieures»

[9] Les thèmes des négociations des accords bilatéraux II entre la Suisse et l'Union européenne portent sur la fiscalité de l'épargne, la lutte contre la fraude, le renforcement de la coopération en matière de justice, de police, d'asile et de migration (Schengen/Dublin), les produits agricoles transformés, l'éducation/formation professionnelle/jeunesse, les médias, les statistiques, l'environnement et les pensions des fonctionnaires retraités de l'Union européenne.

[10] Voir *supra* (note 1). [11] Voir *supra* (note 2).

[12] Le Royaume-Uni et l'Irlande n'ont pas souscrit à l'acquis de Schengen (voir les art. 4 et 5 du Protocole intégrant l'acquis de Schengen dans le cadre de l'Union européenne, le Protocole sur l'application de certains aspects de l'article 14 du Traité instituant la Communauté européenne au Royaume-Uni et à l'Irlande et le Protocole sur la position du Royaume-Uni et de l'Irlande, annexés au Traité sur l'Union européenne et au Traité instituant la Communauté européenne). Ces deux Etats peuvent toutefois participer à tout ou partie des dispositions de l'acquis de Schengen après un vote du Conseil à l'unanimité des treize Etats parties aux accords et du représentant du gouvernement de l'Etat concerné. A ce jour, ils ont demandé à participer à certains aspects de la coopération basée sur Schengen comme la coopération policière et judiciaire en matière pénale, la lutte contre les stupéfiants et le système d'information SIS (voir la décision 2000/365 du Conseil du 29 mai 2000 relative à la demande du Royaume-Uni de Grande-Bretagne et d'Irlande du Nord de participer à certaines dispositions de l'acquis de Schengen, JO n° L 131 du 01.06.2000, p. 43, et la décision 2002/192 du Conseil du 28 février 2002 relative à la demande de l'Irlande de participer à certaines dispositions de l'acquis de Schengen, JO n° L 64 du 07.03.2002, p. 20). La situation du Danemark est régie par l'art. 3 du Protocole intégrant l'acquis de Schengen dans le cadre de l'Union européenne.

[13] L'espace Schengen s'étend également à la Norvège et à l'Islande depuis le 25 mars 2001, en vertu de l'Accord du 18 mai 1999 conclu par le Conseil de l'Union européenne la République d'Islande et le Royaume de Norvège sur l'association de ces deux Etats à la mise en œuvre, à l'application et au développement de l'acquis de Schengen, JO n° L 176 du 10.07.1999, p. 36, in: Christine KADDOUS, *Union européenne. Communauté européenne. Recueil de textes*, LGDJ/Stämpfli (Paris/Berne), 2e édition, 2003, p. 603.

au sens de la Convention d'application, avec toutes les conséquences qui en découlent et que nous examinerons ci-après[14].

a. Politique et délivrance des visas au sein de l'Union européenne et en Suisse

Les Etats membres participant au système Schengen se sont engagés à adopter une politique commune en matière de visa sur la base de l'art. 62 § 2 CE. Il a donc été établi un *visa uniforme (le visa Schengen)*, valable sur le territoire de l'ensemble des etats members pour une durée de trois mois[15]. En outre, le règlement 539/2001[16] fixe la liste des pays dont les ressortissants doivent être munis d'un visa lors du franchissement des frontières extérieures de l'Union européenne (Annexe I du règlement), ainsi que la liste des pays dont les ressortissants sont exemptés du visa (Annexe II du règlement)[17]. Les Etats membres de l'Union européenne ne sont donc plus en droit de déterminer de manière unilatérale le régime applicable aux ressortissants de pays tiers.

Les visas sont délivrés selon des critères uniformes sur la base de l'instruction consulaire commune (ICC)[18]. Est compétente pour délivrer le visa la représentation de destination unique ou principale du voyage

[14] Le Liechtenstein a exprimé, dans une lettre du 12 octobre 2001 à la Commission, l'intérêt qu'il porte à être associé, parallèlement à la Suisse, à la mise en œuvre de l'acquis de Schengen et à celle de la législation en matière d'asile (Bulletin UE 6–2002, registre du Conseil, doc. 10024/02). La Commission a été chargée de préparer un mandat de négociation.

[15] Règlement 1683/95 du Conseil du 29 mai 1995 établissant un modèle type de visa, JO n° L 164 du 14.07.1995, p. 1, adopté sur la base de l'exart. 100 c § 3 CE tel que modifié par le règlement 334/2002 du Conseil du 18 février 2002 qui lui a été adopté sur la base de l'art 62 § 2 CE, JO n° L 53 du 23.02.02, p. 7.

[16] Règlement 539/2001 du Conseil du 15 mars 2001 fixant la liste des pays tiers dont les ressortissants sont soumis à l'obligation de visa pour franchir les frontières extérieures des Etats membres et la liste de ceux dont les ressortissants sont exemptés de cette obligation, JO n° L 81 du 21.03.2001, p. 1, tel que modifié par le règlement 2414/2001 du Conseil du 7 décembre 2001, JO n° L 327 du 12.12.2001, p. 1, par l'Acte relatif aux conditions d'adhésion à l'Union européenne de la République tchèque, de la République d'Estonie, de la République de Chypre, de la République de Lettonie, de la République de Lituanie, de la République de Hongrie, de la République de Malte, de la République de Pologne, de la République de Slovénie et de la République slovaque, et aux adaptations des traités sur lesquels est fondée l'Union européenne, JO n° L 236 du 23.09.2003, p. 718, et par le règlement 453/2003 du Conseil du 6 mars 2003, JO n° L 69 du 13.03.2003, p. 10.

[17] En outre, avec l'entrée en vigueur de l'Accord bilatéral sur la libre circulation des personnes le 1er juin 2002, la Suisse a été supprimée de la liste de l'Annexe II; voir le règlement 453/2003 *supra* (note 16).

[18] Décision du Comité exécutif du 28 avril 1999 concernant les versions définitives du Manuel commun et de l'Instruction consulaire commune, JO n° L 239 du 22.10.2000, p. 317.

ou, cas échéant, celle de l'Etat de première entrée. Le demandeur doit en principe se présenter personnellement pour exposer les motifs de sa demande. Avant de délivrer un visa, les autorités consulaires et diplomatiques vérifient que les conditions prévues par la Convention d'application sont bien remplies: documents valables, documents justifiant l'objet et les conditions du séjour envisagé, moyens de subsistance suffisants, pas de signalement aux fins de non-admission au Système d'information Schengen (SIS), et ne pas être considéré comme pouvant compromettre l'ordre public, la sécurité nationale ou les relations internationales de l'Etat[19]. Une fois délivré, le visa Schengen permet à son titulaire d'entrer et de circuler sur le territoire des autres Etats membres de l'espace Schengen.

La *politique suisse en matière de visas* coïncide largement avec celle de l'Union européenne, puisque dans l'ensemble, les normes relatives aux conditions et modalités de délivrance des visas figurant dans l'ICC et dans les décisions du Comité exécutif ne sont pas très différentes de celles figurant dans la législation suisse. En principe, le ressortissant d'un pays tiers qui entre en Suisse doit être muni d'un visa. Il dépose sa demande auprès de la représentation suisse à l'étranger compétente, accompagnée de tous les documents nécessaires[20]. En principe, l'ambassade ou le consulat sont seuls compétents pour délivrer le visa; dans certains cas, l'autorisation du Département fédéral de justice et police ou celle du Département fédéral des affaires étrangères sera nécessaire[21]. Le visa sera refusé lorsque l'étranger ne remplit pas les conditions d'entrée prévues dans l'*Ordonnance concernant l'entrée et la déclaration d'arrivée des étrangers*[22], à savoir qu'il présente un danger pour la sécurité du pays, ou fait l'objet d'une interdiction d'entrée ou d'une mesure d'expulsion; ou qu'il ne présente pas les garanties nécessaires en vue d'une sortie de Suisse dans les délais impartis; ou enfin, qu'il ne dispose pas de moyens suffisants pour subvenir à ses besoins durant le transit ou le séjour en Suisse, ou qu'il n'est pas en mesure de se les procurer légalement[23]. Le visa sera également refusé lorsque l'étranger ne présente pas les justificatifs demandés, lorsqu'il fournit des données inexactes ou présente des

[19] Art. 5 Convention d'application.

[20] Art. 10 de l'Ordonnance concernant l'entrée et la déclaration d'arrivée des étrangers du 14 janvier 1998 (OEArr), RS 142.211. Sont nécessaires les documents de voyage et les justificatifs prouvant le but et les modalités du séjour ou du transit. La législation suisse est accessible sur internet: http://www.admin.ch/ch/f/rs/rs.html.

[21] Art. 16–18 OEArr. Cela concerne les séjours de plus de trois mois ou effectués à d'autres fins que le tourisme, visite, affaires et traitements médicaux.

[22] Voir *supra* (note 20). [23] Art. 1 OEArr.

justificatifs faux ou falsifiés, ou lorsqu'il existe des doutes fondés quant à l'identité du requérant ou le but de son séjour[24].

La durée de validité du visa est fixée en fonction des besoins du requérant et de la durée de validité de son document de voyage, mais pour trois ans au plus[25]. En cas de refus du visa, la représentation à l'étranger communique la décision au requérant d'une manière informelle et l'informe qu'une décision susceptible de recours peut être requise de la part des autorités fédérales, moyennant le prélèvement d'une taxe[26].

Les autorités suisses délivrent en moyenne entre 600'000 à 700'000 visas par an[27]. Pour la plupart, il s'agit de visas pour touristes ou hommes d'affaires, en provenance majoritairement d'Inde, de Russie, de Chine, de Turquie ou encore d'Arabie Saoudite. La non-participation de la Suisse au régime des visas applicable dans l'Union européenne oblige les ressortissants de pays tiers à se procurer un second visa s'ils souhaitent se rendre en Suisse et sur le territoire de l'Union européenne. La Suisse facilite toutefois l'entrée sur son territoire, sur une base unilatérale, aux ressortissants d'Arabie saoudite, de Bahreïn, des Emirats arabes unis, du Koweit, d'Oman, du Quatar, de Thaïlande et de Taïwan lorsqu'ils sont titulaires d'un visa Schengen, ainsi qu'aux ressortissants de pays tiers titulaires d'une autorisation de séjour durable délivrée par un Etat Schengen, en leur permettant de circuler librement en Suisse pendant une durée de trois mois[28].

b. *Mesures visant à contrôler les entrées illégales*

Les Etats parties doivent assurer un contrôle efficace aux frontières extérieures de l'espace Schengen[29]. La responsabilité en matière de contrôles aux frontières extérieures est d'autant plus importante aujourd'hui que l'Union européenne est sur le point de réaliser un élargissement conséquent[30]. La coopération entre les services nationaux est fondamentale. C'est la raison pour laquelle le Conseil a adopté, en 2002,

[24] Art. 14 al. 2 OEArr. [25] Art. 12 OEArr. [26] Art. 14 al. 4 et 27 OEArr.

[27] Minh Son Nguyen, *Droit public des étrangers*, Stämpfli (Berne), 2003, p. 313.

[28] Art. 4 al. 2 lit. c à e OEArr.

[29] Bien qu'il n'y ait plus de contrôles aux frontières intérieures, les Etats membres sont toutefois libres d'instaurer un contrôle mobile à l'intérieur même de leur territoire, voire même, si la sécurité l'exige, de rétablir provisoirement les contrôles aux frontières (par exemple lors du sommet du G8 en juin 2003 à Evian). Art. 2 al. 2 Convention d'application.

[30] Les Etats adhérents participeront à Schengen et Dublin aux conditions fixées dans les Traités d'adhésion, voir *infra* (note 36).

un *programme d'action concernant la coopération administrative dans les domaines des frontières extérieures, des visas, de l'asile et de l'immigration*[31]. Un tel cadre communautaire est nécessaire pour uniformiser les pratiques des Etats membres lorsqu'ils appliquent les règles communautaires en la matière.

L'idée d'une gestion commune des frontières extérieures n'implique pas encore la mise sur pied d'un corps de gardes-frontières européen. Pour de nombreux Etats membres, le contrôle aux frontières doit rester une tâche nationale. Il n'en reste pas moins vrai que la mise en place d'un système de coordination des opérations favoriserait une meilleure efficacité des contrôles[32].

Sur le plan européen, l'efficacité des contrôles aux frontières est assurée en premier lieu par un système d'information commun, le *Système d'information Schengen (SIS).* Cette base de données informatisée permet aux autorités chargées du contrôle aux frontières de vérifier si le ressortissant d'un pays tiers désirant entrer sur le territoire Schengen fait l'objet d'un signalement aux fins de non-admission[33]. Si tel est le cas, l'étranger se verra refuser l'entrée. Aussi, le SIS constitue un outil efficace, voire même le pilier de base du bon fonctionnement du système Schengen.

Il est prévu de compléter le système SIS par un *Système d'information Schengen de deuxième génération* (*SIS II*)[34]. La mise sur pied de ce nouveau système est rendue nécessaire par le besoin d'une stratégie de sécurité commune et intégrée dans un espace de libre circulation. Le système actuel n'a pas été conçu pour traiter les requêtes de plus de 18 pays participants[35]. Aussi, un des objectifs du SIS II est de mettre en place un système permettant la connexion des nouveaux Etats membres, condition impérative de

[31] Décision du Conseil du 13 juin 2002 portant adoption d'un programme d'action concernant la coopération administrative dans les domaines des frontières extérieures, des visas, de l'asile et de l'immigration (programme ARGO), JO n° L 161 du 19.06.2002, p. 11.

[32] Charles Elsen, *Le Conseil européen de Thessalonique. Un nouveau pas vers une politique commune en matière d'asile, d'immigration et de contrôle aux frontières*, Revue du Marché commun et de l'Union européenne, n° 471, septembre 2003, p. 516–518, p. 517.

[33] Pour la liste des autorités compétentes autorisées à interroger directement les données du SIS, voir doc. 6265/1/03 rev 1 du Conseil du 9 octobre 2003 sur le registre du Conseil.

[34] Voir la Communication de la Commission au Conseil et au Parlement européen – Le développement du système d'information Schengen II et les synergies possibles avec un futur système d'information sur les visas (VIS), COM (2003) 771 final. Le calendrier initial prévoyait que le système SIS II devait être opérationnel fin 2006, mais il semble que cette date sera repoussée. Voir aussi les Conclusions du Conseil JAI des 5/6 juin 2003 concernant le développement du système d'information sur les visas (VIS).

[35] Le SIS fonctionne actuellement dans les 13 Etats Schengen, ainsi qu'en Islande et en Norvège. Il devrait devenir partiellement opérationnel pour le Royaume Uni et l'Irlande.

l'abolition des contrôles aux frontières intérieures[36]. Cette nouvelle base de données permettra d'introduire de nouveaux types d'informations, notamment des données biométriques. En outre, il est également prévu d'établir une base de données relative aux visas: le *Système d'information visas (VIS)*. Il s'agit d'un système commun proposé pour l'échange de données concernant les visas entre les Etats membres de l'Union européenne. Le SIS II pourra être consulté avant la délivrance d'un visa et le VIS permettra de contrôler l'authenticité d'un visa à la frontière.

Outre le système d'échanges d'informations, la Convention d'application prévoit d'autres mesures pour décourager les abus dans le domaine de l'immigration, notamment l'obligation pour les Etats parties de prévoir des *dispositions relatives à la responsabilité du transporteur*[37]. Ils sont tenus d'introduire dans leur droit interne l'obligation pour le transporteur de prendre toutes les mesures nécessaires pour s'assurer que l'étranger transporté par voie aérienne ou maritime est bien en possession des documents de voyage requis pour l'entrée sur leurs territoires[38]. Ils s'engagent également à prévoir des sanctions à l'encontre des transporteurs qui acheminent par voie aérienne ou maritime d'un Etat tiers vers leur territoire, des étrangers qui ne sont pas en possession des documents

[36] La suppression des contrôles aux frontières intérieures pour les ressortissants des Etats adhérents ne se fera pas immédiatement. Conformément à l'art. 3 al. 2 de l'Acte relatif aux conditions d'adhésion à l'Union européenne de la République tchèque, de la République d'Estonie, de la République de Chypre, de la République de Lettonie, de la République de Lituanie, de la République de Hongrie, de la République de Malte, de la République de Pologne, de la République de Slovénie et de la République slovaque, et aux adaptations des traités sur lesquels est fondée l'Union européenne, JO n° L 236 du 23.09.2003, p. 33, les dispositions de l'acquis de Schengen qui ne figurent pas à l'Annexe I du traité d'adhésion, bien qu'elles soient contraignantes pour les nouveaux Etats membres à compter de la date d'adhésion, ne s'appliquent dans un nouvel Etat membre qu'à la suite d'une décision du Conseil à cet effet, après qu'il a été vérifié, conformément aux procédures d'évaluation de Schengen applicables en la matière, que les conditions nécessaires à l'application de toutes les parties concernées de l'acquis sont remplies dans ce nouvel Etat membre, et après consultation du Parlement européen.

[37] Nathalie Berger, *La politique européenne d'asile et d'immigration. Enjeux et perspectives*, Bruylant (Bruxelles), 2000, p. 98–100. L'auteur considère que le système de la responsabilité du transporteur est critiquable à plusieurs égards. En premier lieu, aucune disposition ne prescrit comment le transporteur doit procéder à la vérification de l'authenticité des documents. Ensuite, mettre en place un tel système de responsabilité conduit à charger le transporteur du contrôle de l'immigration, tâche en principe réservée aux autorités policières et douanières nationales. Enfin, le contrôle des documents et le refus éventuel du transport peuvent constituer une entrave au droit d'asile et violer aussi la Convention de Genève de 1951.

[38] Art. 26 al. 1 lit. b Convention d'application.

de voyage requis[39], ainsi que l'obligation pour le transporteur de prise en charge immédiate et de réacheminement lorsque l'étranger qu'il a amené à la frontière extérieure par voie aérienne, maritime ou terrestre se voit refuser l'entrée sur le territoire de l'une des parties contractantes[40]. L'adoption de la *directive 2001/51*[41] vient renforcer ce dispositif. Elle tend à harmoniser autant que possible les sanctions pécuniaires prévues par les Etats membres en cas de violation des obligations de contrôle qui incombent aux transporteurs.

A l'instar de l'Union européenne, la Suisse a également prévu, dans le cadre de la révision de la *loi fédérale sur le séjour et l'établissement des étrangers*[42], d'introduire des *sanctions contre les transporteurs*[43]. Le projet de loi soumet expressément les entreprises de transport aérien au devoir de diligence et au devoir de prise en charge des frais. Le projet prévoit également la possibilité d'étendre cette obligation à d'autres entreprises de transport (terrestre ou maritime)[44]. L'introduction de telles mesures en droit suisse aura des effets sur les cantons, et plus particulièrement sur les cantons frontaliers ou disposant d'un aéroport dans la mesure où cela nécessitera un renforcement de l'appareil administratif et judiciaire[45].

c. *Perspectives de coopération entre la Suisse et l'Union européenne*

En cas d'association à Schengen, la Suisse pratiquerait la même politique que la Communauté européenne en matière de visas de courte durée. Elle reconnaîtrait de manière automatique les visas Schengen et pourrait à son

[39] Art. 26 al. 2 Convention d'application. [40] Art. 26 al. 1 lit. a Convention d'application.

[41] Directive 2001/51 du Conseil du 28 juin 2001 visant à compléter les dispositions de l'article 26 de la Convention d'application de l'Accord de Schengen, JO n°L 187 du 10.07.2001, p. 45.

[42] Loi fédérale du 26 mars 1931 sur le séjour et l'établissement des étrangers (LSEE), RS 142.20.

[43] Art. 87 à 90 du projet de loi fédérale sur les étrangers, FF 2002 3604. Pour des informations complémentaires, voir le site de l'IMES (Immigration Migration Intégration Suisse), http://www.bfa.admin.ch.

[44] Dans l'hypothèse d'une association de la Suisse à Schengen, il faudrait veiller à étendre la responsabilité du transporteur également aux entreprises de transport terrestre et maritime, afin que la législation suisse soit euro-compatible.

[45] L'obligation de prévoir des mesures contre les transporteurs découle également du Protocole contre le trafic illicite de migrants par terre, air et mer, additionnel à la Convention des Nations Unies contre la Criminalité transnationale organisée. La Suisse a signé la Convention en décembre 2002 et ses deux protocoles (dont le Protocole contre le trafic illicite de migrants par terre, air et mer) en avril 2002. Ces textes ne sont pas encore en vigueur pour la Suisse; les instruments sont en procédure de consultation depuis décembre 2003 et devront être encore ratifiés par le Parlement suisse.

tour délivrer de tels visas valables dans tout l'espace Schengen et sur le territoire suisse[46]. Une telle perspective améliorerait de manière fondamentale la sécurité sur l'ensemble des territoires concernés et aurait des répercussions positives en particulier sur le tourisme, les voyages d'affaires, et le commerce. En revanche, la délivrance de visas de longue durée demeurerait soumise au droit suisse exclusivement.

En outre, les cas de refus d'entrée prononcés en Suisse seraient intégrés dans le SIS et pris en compte par les autres Etats participants, garantissant ainsi une observation à l'échelle européenne. La Suisse assure actuellement, avec ses propres moyens, les contrôles aux frontières. Le contrôle des passeports aux points de passages routiers, ainsi que dans le trafic fluvial et dans les trains régionaux, est assuré exclusivement par les autorités douanières de la Confédération (le Corps des gardes-frontières)[47]; les polices cantonales assurent uniquement le contrôle des personnes dans les gares et les aéroports internationaux. Une association de la Suisse au système de Schengen impliquerait la suppression des contrôles aux frontières avec les voisins européens (ces frontières deviendraient des «frontières intérieures»), et le maintien des contrôles aux entrées et sorties aux frontières extérieures (aéroports internationaux et port fluvial du Rhin)[48].

La Suisse a passablement renforcé la coopération bilatérale transfrontalière avec ses voisins, en particulier dans le domaine de la coopération policière[49], partie centrale du dispositif de Schengen, et des

[46] En cas d'association à Schengen, la Suisse devrait également reprendre intégralement le règlement 539/2001 (*supra*, note 16), ce qui impliquerait pour les autorités suisses de soumettre certains ressortissants de pays tiers à l'obligation de visa (ressortissants de l'Afrique du Sud, Bahamas, Barbade, Dominique, Grenade, Jamaïque, Kiribati, Saint-Kitts-et-Nevis, Sainte-Lucie, Sainte-Vincent-et-les-Grenadines, Iles Salomon, Trinité-et-Tobago, et Tuvalu). Récemment, la Suisse a procédé à la levée de l'obligation de visas pour les ressortissants de Bulgarie (22.10.2003) et de Roumanie (15.12.2003), marquant ainsi une étape supplémentaire en vue de l'harmonisation de la politique en matière de visas entre la Suisse et l'Union européenne.

[47] Art. 59 loi fédérale sur les douanes, RS 631.0.

[48] Les ports et aéroports sont à la fois des frontières extérieures et intérieures selon que le navire ou l'avion provient d'un pays tiers ou d'un pays Schengen. Dans les aéroports par exemple, il faudrait veiller à la mise en place d'une séparation des flux «intra-Schengen» et «extra-Schengen».

[49] Voir Accord du 27 avril 1999 entre la Confédération suisse et la République fédérale d'Allemagne relatif à la coopération transfrontalière en matière policière et judiciaire, RS 0.360.136.1; Accord du 27 avril 1999 entre la Confédération suisse, la République d'Autriche et la Principauté de Liechtenstein concernant la coopération transfrontalière des autorités compétentes en matière de sécurité et de douane, RS 0.360.163.1; Accord du 11 mai 1998 entre le Conseil fédéral suisse et le Gouvernement de la République française

accords de réadmission. En bref, les accords de coopération policière conclus par la Suisse avec ses Etats voisins reprennent sur une base bilatérale des pans entiers de la coopération policière sous Schengen (poursuite et observation sans limitation dans l'espace et le temps, sauf avec l'Italie; livraisons surveillées et enquêtes sous couverture avec l'Allemagne; échange d'informations spontané et sur demande). Ces accords ont même été concrétisés, en 2002, par des centres de coopération commune avec l'Italie à la frontière de Chiasso et avec la France à Genève[50].

L'élargissement de l'Union européenne aura incontestablement des répercussions sur la politique migratoire. Une nouvelle infrastructure sera créée afin de permettre une gestion efficace des contrôles aux frontières. Au 1er mai 2004, ce sont potentiellement 27 Etats[51] qui coopèreront sur la base du système de Schengen et Dublin, ce qui, en soit, peut s'avérer être une coopération très efficace. La suppression des contrôles aux frontières pour les nouveaux Etats membres ne se fera toutefois pas immédiatement[52]. Pour la Suisse, l'élargissement de l'Union européenne signifie également une extension éventuelle du champ d'application de l'Accord sur la libre circulation des personnes. Les termes de cette extension font actuellement l'objet de négociations entre la Suisse et l'Union européenne.

II Procédures d'accueil et droit de séjour des ressortissants de pays tiers

La politique européenne d'immigration doit veiller à ce que les ressortissants de pays tiers puissent s'intégrer au mieux dans le pays d'accueil. Cela suppose notamment la mise en place de règles communes relatives à l'accueil et au séjour de ces personnes dans l'Union européenne afin de leur assurer un traitement aussi équitable que possible.

relatif à la coopération transfrontalière en matière judiciaire, policière et douanière, RS 0.360.349.1; Accord du 10 septembre 1998 entre la Confédération suisse et la République italienne relatif à la coopération entre les autorités de police et de douane, RS 0.360.454.1.

50 Pour la France, voir le protocole additionnel du 28 janvier 2002 à l'Accord du 11 mai 1998 entre le Conseil fédéral suisse et le Gouvernement de la République française relatif à la coopération transfrontalière en matière judiciaire, policière et douanière; pour l'Italie, voir le protocole du 17 septembre 2002 «protocollo tra la Confederazione svizzera e la Repubblica italiana relativo all'istituzione di centri di cooperazione di polizia e doganale».

51 Les treize Etats Schengen, le Royaume-Uni, l'Irlande et le Danemark partiellement, les dix Etats adhérents participant à terme, ainsi que la Norvège et l'Islande.

52 Voir *supra* (note 36).

L'adoption de la *directive 2003/86 sur le regroupement familial*[53] constitue une avancée majeure dans le processus de la définition d'une politique commune en matière d'immigration. Il s'agit du premier texte qui traite de l'intégration des ressortissants de pays tiers en situation régulière. D'autres *projets de directives* sont en discussion: la proposition de directive relative au statut des ressortissants de pays tiers résidents de longue durée[54]; la proposition de directive relative aux conditions d'entrée et de séjour des ressortissants de pays tiers aux fins d'études, de formation professionnelle ou de volontariat[55]; et la proposition de directive relative aux conditions d'entrée et de séjour des ressortissants de pays tiers aux fins d'un emploi salarié ou de l'exercice d'une activité économique indépendante[56].

En Suisse, *la loi fédérale sur le séjour et l'établissement des étrangers*[57] constitue, avec l'*Ordonnance limitant le nombre des étrangers*[58], le pilier de l'actuelle politique relative aux ressortissants de pays tiers. Cette législation est sur le point d'être remplacée par une nouvelle loi fédérale sur les étrangers[59]. Compte tenu du nombre élevé de ressortissants de pays tiers en Suisse, une importance particulière est accordée à la politique d'intégration, qui doit avant tout viser à instaurer l'égalité des chances d'accès aux ressources sociales et économiques. L'actuelle révision de la loi sur les étrangers est, par ailleurs, guidée par l'idée directrice d'intégration et de simplification des procédures. Les dispositions

[53] Directive 2003/86 du Conseil du 22 septembre 2003 relative au droit au regroupement familial, JO n° L 251 du 03.10.2003, p. 12. A noter le dépôt d'un recours en annulation, le 22 décembre 2003, du Parlement européen, au motif d'une violation par certaines dispositions (art. 4 § 1 et § 6, art. 8) des droits fondamentaux, notamment du droit à la vie familiale et du droit à la non-discrimination.

[54] Proposition de directive du Conseil relative au statut des ressortissants de pays tiers résidents de longue durée, COM (2001) 127 final. Ci-après: proposition relative au séjour longue durée.

[55] Proposition de directive du Conseil relative aux conditions d'entrée et de séjour des ressortissants de pays tiers aux fins d'études, de formation professionnelle ou de volontariat, COM (2002) 548 final. Ci-après: proposition relative au séjour aux fins d'études et formation professionnelle.

[56] Proposition de directive du Conseil relative aux conditions d'entrée et de séjour des ressortissants de pays tiers aux fins d'un emploi salarié ou de l'exercice d'une activité économique indépendante, COM (2001) 386 final. Ci-après: proposition relative au séjour aux fins d'emploi.

[57] Voir *supra* (note 42).

[58] Ordonnance du 6 octobre 1986 limitant le nombre des étrangers (OLE), RS 823.21.

[59] Voir notamment le Message relatif au projet de loi sur les étrangers du 8 mars 2002, FF 2002 3469.

touchant à l'intégration des ressortissants de pays tiers ont été considérablement étendues[60].

a. *Vers une politique d'intégration européenne*

L'harmonisation de la politique d'intégration des ressortissants de pays tiers en situation régulière telle qu' envisagée par l'Union européenne se veut progressive. En effet, l'immigration est une donnée sensible de la politique nationale et les Etats membres connaissent une réglementation souvent très détaillée en la matière.

La question du regroupement familial a été le premier thème sur lequel les Etats membres de l'Union européenne sont parvenus à un accord. Le regroupement familial est un moyen fondamental pour contribuer à l'intégration dans l'Etat d'accueil. La *directive 2003/86 relative au droit au regroupement familial* a pour objectif de fixer les conditions matérielles pour l'exercice de ce droit. Seuls sont en principe concernés le conjoint et les enfants mineurs du ressortissant d'un pays tiers résidant légalement sur le territoire des Etats membres[61]. Les conditions du regroupement familial ne diffèrent pas beaucoup de celles prévues pour le regroupement familial des ressortissants des Etats membres de l'Union européenne, à savoir un logement considéré comme normal, une assurance-maladie couvrant l'ensemble des risques ainsi que des ressources stables, régulières et suffisantes pour vivre. En outre, les membres de la famille reçoivent un titre de séjour et peuvent accéder à l'éducation, à une activité salariée ou indépendante, ainsi qu'à l'orientation, à la formation au perfectionnement et au recyclage professionnel[62]. Les Etats membres rejetteront toutefois la demande de regroupement familial lorsque des raisons d'ordre public, de sécurité publique ou de santé publique l'exigent[63].

La *proposition de directive relative aux conditions d'entrée et de séjour des ressortissants de pays tiers aux fins d'un emploi salarié ou de l'exercice d'une activité économique indépendante* présentée en 2001 a, quant à elle,

[60] Art. 51 à 57 du projet de loi fédérale sur les étrangers, FF 2002 3604.

[61] Art. 4 directive 2003/86. Les Etats membres seront toutefois libres de décider s'ils souhaitent autoriser le regroupement familial pour les ascendants en ligne directe, les enfants majeurs célibataires, les partenaires non mariés ou enregistrés et, dans le cas de mariages polygames, les enfants mineurs d'une autre épouse. Mais ils ne pourront autoriser le regroupement familial d'un autre conjoint s'il y a déjà un conjoint vivant avec le regroupant sur le territoire d'un Etat membre.

[62] Art. 13 et 14 directive 2003/86.

[63] Art. 6 directive 2003/86.

pour but de fixer les conditions communes concernant la procédure de demande et l'octroi d'un permis unique de travail et de séjour. Le projet couvre les travailleurs, les indépendants, les saisonniers, les frontaliers, les personnes transférées à l'intérieur de leur entreprise et les stagiaires. L'accès à une activité lucrative ne sera vraisemblablement pas inconditionnel dans la mesure où il faut prouver, pour les activités salariées, que le poste déterminé ne peut être pourvu sur le marché du travail intérieur (priorité du travailleur indigène), et, pour les activités indépendantes, que cette activité constituerait une valeur ajoutée pour l'emploi ou pour le développement économique de l'Etat d'accueil[64].

Souvent, les ressortissants de pays tiers s'installent dans l'Etat d'accueil pour une longue durée, voire même de manière définitive. Il a alors paru judicieux de prévoir un régime commun relatif aux longs séjours. Aussi, *la proposition de directive relative au statut des ressortissants de pays tiers résidents de longue durée* de 2001 vise à établir un permis de séjour longue durée. Le statut de résident longue durée devrait être accordé au ressortissant d'un pays tiers qui réside depuis cinq ans de manière légale et ininterrompue sur le territoire d'un Etat membre de l'Union européenne. Ce statut est permanent (sous réserve d'un éventuel retrait[65]), d'une durée de validité de dix ans, et est renouvelable. Il permettra par ailleurs de reconnaître à leur titulaire l'égalité de traitement dans plusieurs domaines de la vie économique et sociale. Une fois l'autorisation de séjour de longue durée délivrée par un Etat membre, le ressortissant d'un pays tiers pourra en principe exercer son droit de séjour sur le territoire des autres Etats membres de l'Union européenne, pour une période dépassant trois mois, aux fins d'un emploi ou d'études, à condition toutefois de disposer de ressources suffisantes pour vivre et d'une assurance-maladie couvrant l'ensemble des risques dans le deuxième Etat membre[66].

Enfin, afin de compléter les initiatives présentées en vue de la mise en place d'un cadre juridique complet régissant l'admission de ressortissants de pays tiers en fonction de l'objet de leur séjour, la Communauté européenne entend également harmoniser le séjour des étudiants et des bénévoles. Les *séjours aux fins d'études, de formation professionnelle ou de volontariat* ont une caractéristique bien particulière: ce sont

[64] Art. 6 et 19 proposition relative au séjour aux fins d'emploi.
[65] Art. 7 proposition relative au séjour longue durée.
[66] Art. 15 et suivants proposition relative au séjour longue durée.

des séjours temporaires et indépendants de la situation du marché du travail de l'Etat d'accueil. La proposition de directive, présentée en 2002, distingue quatre catégories de bénéficiaires: les étudiants, les élèves, les stagiaires non rémunérés et les volontaires[67]. Outre les conditions générales d'admission (notamment les ressources suffisantes pour pouvoir subvenir à leurs besoins), la proposition de directive définit des conditions spécifiques à chacune de ces catégories, à savoir, respectivement, l'admission dans un établissement d'enseignement, la participation à un programme d'échanges d'élèves, la signature d'une convention de formation professionnelle ou la participation à un programme de volontariat. Par ailleurs, les étudiants, élèves, stagiaires et volontaires devraient pouvoir exercer une activité salariée ou indépendante dans l'Etat membre d'accueil, à raison de 10 à 20 heures par semaine[68].

b. La politique suisse d'intégration des ressortissants de pays tiers

La politique suisse d'immigration vise également à intégrer, dans les meilleures conditions possibles, les ressortissants de pays tiers résidant légalement sur son territoire, notamment grâce au *regroupement familial* tel que prévu par la *loi fédérale sur le séjour et l'établissement*[69], et conformément à l'art. 8 CEDH[70]. Sont couverts par le regroupement familial le conjoint et les enfants célibataires jusqu'à l'âge de 18 ans qui vivent avec le couple. La loi n'autorise toutefois que les ressortissants de pays tiers «établis» en Suisse[71] à demander le regroupement familial[72]. La jurisprudence tend toutefois vers une certaine souplesse dans la mesure

[67] Pour les volontaires, le fait qu'ils ne soient ni travailleurs, ni étudiants peut leur créer quelques difficultés à obtenir un titre de séjour; la proposition de directive tend notamment à remédier à ce problème.

[68] Art. 18 proposition relative au séjour aux fins d'études et formation professionnelle.

[69] Art. 17 al. 2 LSEE, art. 38–39 OLE.

[70] Convention européenne de sauvegarde des droits de l'homme et des libertés fondamentales du 4 novembre 1950, RS 0.101, STE 005.

[71] C'est-à-dire, un ressortissant d'un pays tiers qui est titulaire d'une autorisation d'établissement en Suisse.

[72] Le regroupement familial est exclu pour certaines catégories de ressortissants de pays tiers, notamment les titulaires d'une simple autorisation de séjour ou les saisonniers (art. 38 al. 2 OLE). Ces restrictions ont souvent été critiquées. C'est pourquoi, le projet de loi fédérale sur les étrangers prévoit l'amélioration du statut juridique du ressortissant d'un pays tiers dans le domaine du regroupement familial, notamment en vue de faciliter son intégration. Pour une distinction entre l'autorisation d'établissement et l'autorisation de séjour, voir *infra* (note 75).

où elle entend protéger le plus possible l'unité de la famille conformément à la CEDH[73]. Le regroupant doit disposer d'un logement suffisamment grand et de ressources financières lui permettant d'entretenir sa famille[74]. En cela, les conditions sont semblables à celles posées par la directive communautaire sur le regroupement familial de 2003.

Tout comme la proposition de directive relative aux conditions d'entrée et de séjour des ressortissants de pays tiers aux fins de l'exercice d'une activité économique salariée ou indépendante, la Suisse n'autorise des ressortissants de pays tiers à entrer et à séjourner sur son territoire pour y *exercer des activités salariées* que si une autorisation de séjour[75] leur a été délivrée, ainsi qu'une autorisation de travail. L'autorisation de travail doit être établie conformément aux règles relatives aux priorités dans le recrutement. L'admission des ressortissants de pays tiers est limitée aux travailleurs qualifiés qui sont indispensables (système binaire d'admission)[76]. Le ressortissant d'un pays tiers ne pourra travailler que

[73] Le Tribunal fédéral suisse fait découler de l'art. 8 CEDH un droit au permis de séjour dès lors que le refus de l'octroi ou du renouvellement de l'autorisation pourrait remettre en cause le droit au respect de la vie familiale du ressortissant d'un pays tiers. Ce véritable droit au regroupement familial présuppose que la vie de famille soit effectivement vécue avec une personne résidant en Suisse de manière stable. Giorgio MALINVERNI, *Le droit des étrangers*, in «Droit constitutionnel suisse», édité par Daniel THÜRER/Jean-François AUBERT/Jörg Paul MÜLLER, Schulthess (Zürich), 2001, p. 986. Voir aussi Michel HOTTELIER et Hanspeter MOCK, *Le Tribunal fédéral suisse et la «discrimination à rebours» en matière de regroupement familial*, Revue trimestrielle des droits de l'homme, octobre 2003, pp. 1275–1304. A mentionner encore un arrêt récent du Tribunal fédéral suisse du 4.11.2003 (2A.91/2003), où le Tribunal fédéral, se fondant sur une jurisprudence récente de la Cour de justice des Communautés européennes (arrêt du 23 septembre 2001, aff. C-109/01) a retenu que dans le cadre du regroupement familial, les ressortissants d'Etats tiers pouvaient se prévaloir de l'accord sur la libre circulation des personnes uniquement si, avant le dépôt de la demande de regroupement familial, ils étaient en possession d'une autorisation de séjour ordinaire dans un Etat de la Communauté européenne ou de l'AELE.

[74] Art. 39 al. 1 OLE.

[75] Il est utile de préciser ici que la Suisse distingue plusieurs sortes d'autorisation de séjours, notamment l'autorisation de séjour (art. 5 LSEE; d'une durée limitée à une année, elle peut être conditionnelle), l'autorisation d'établissement (art. 6 LSEE; d'une durée indéterminée, elle est inconditionnelle), ou encore l'autorisation de courte durée (art. 20 OLE) et l'autorisation pour les frontaliers (art. 23 OLE). Selon le type d'autorisation reçue, les droits et avantages accordés aux ressortissants de pays tiers varient.

[76] Avant le 1er novembre 1998, l'ordre de priorité du recrutement était établi sur la base du système des «trois cercles»: d'abord le cercle intérieur (Union européenne et AELE), puis le cercle médiant (USA, Canada, Australie, Nouvelle-Zélande, Monaco, Andorre et la Cité du Vatican), et enfin le cercle extérieur (le reste du monde). Depuis le 1er novembre 1998, le système binaire s'applique: d'un côté, les ressortissants des Etats membres de l'Union européenne et de l'AELE, de l'autre, le reste du monde.

si aucun travailleur indigène[77] capable et désireux d'exercer cette activité aux mêmes conditions ne peut être trouvé[78]. En outre, le Conseil fédéral suisse décide du nombre de ressortissants de pays tiers pouvant être admis (contingentement)[79]. L'autorisation de travail ne sera délivrée que si les conditions de salaire et de travail en usage dans la localité et la profession sont respectées[80]. Enfin, il faut ajouter à cela la condition du logement convenable[81]. Aussi, la politique suisse en matière d'admission des ressortissants des pays tiers actifs est double: protéger les travailleurs ressortissants de pays tiers contre les conditions de travail abusives et lutter contre le dumping social[82].

D'un point de vue procédural, il convient d'observer que l'exécution des dispositions légales relatives aux ressortissants de pays tiers incombe avant tout aux cantons. La Confédération ne peut contraindre un canton à délivrer une autorisation à moins qu'une base légale formelle ne confère au ressortissant de pays tiers un tel droit[83]. Une voie de recours contre les décisions négatives de la police des étrangers est prévue à l'échelon cantonal. Lorsque le ressortissant d'un pays tiers peut se prévaloir d'un droit de séjour en Suisse, il peut déposer, en dernière instance, un recours de droit administratif auprès du Tribunal fédéral suisse.

Il y a lieu également de préciser que le titulaire d'une autorisation de séjour (par opposition au titulaire d'une autorisation d'établissement) ne jouit pas de la liberté économique telle que garantie par l'art. 27 de la Constitution fédérale suisse, et de ce fait ne peut s'installer en tant qu'indépendant.

La Suisse reconnaît également aux ressortissants de pays tiers un *statut de résident longue durée* par l'octroi de l'autorisation d'établissement[84]. Dans la mesure où cette autorisation est de durée indéterminée et n'est soumise à aucune condition, elle permet à son titulaire de bénéficier du statut le plus stable et le plus favorable en matière de séjour et d'activité

[77] Il faut entendre par «travailleurs indigènes» non seulement les citoyens suisses, mais également les titulaires d'une autorisation d'établissement, les réfugiés et apatrides reconnus, les membres étrangers de la famille de ressortissants suisses ou encore les jeunes étrangers venus avec leurs parents ayant effectué leur scolarité en Suisse.

[78] Art. 7 OLE. [79] Art. 12 OLE. [80] Art. 9 OLE. [81] Art. 11 OLE.

[82] Minh Son Nguyen, *op. cit.*, p. 209–210.

[83] Le ressortissant d'un pays tiers peut invoquer un droit à une autorisation sur la base de la loi sur le séjour et l'établissement des étrangers, de la loi fédérale sur l'asile (*infra*, note 95), de la CEDH, ou encore de l'Accord entre la Communauté européenne et ses Etats membres d'une part et la Suisse d'autre part sur la libre circulation des personnes, (publié au RS 0.142.112.681 et au JO n° L 114 du 30.04.2002, p. 6).

[84] Art. 6 LSEE; voir *supra* (note 75).

lucrative (aucune restriction relative au marché du travail par exemple). En d'autres termes, elle lui permet d'être pratiquement sur un pied d'égalité avec les ressortissants suisses, à l'exception du droit de vote et d'éligibilité[85]. Une autorisation d'établissement n'est accordée en général qu'après un séjour ininterrompu de dix ans en Suisse. Mais sur la base d'accords internationaux, de nombreux résidents d'Etats tiers obtiennent l'autorisation d'établissement après avoir résidé en Suisse avec une autorisation de séjour pendant seulement cinq ans[86].

Enfin, de nombreux ressortissants de pays tiers viennent en Suisse pour y *poursuivre des études ou y suivre une formation professionnelle.* L'Ordonnance limitant le nombre des étrangers opère une distinction entre l'élève (qui suit une formation dans une école publique ou privée reconnue et qui dispense un enseignement général ou professionnel à plein temps) de l'étudiant (qui suit une formation dans une université ou un institut de formation supérieure)[87]. Outre le fait de venir seul et de présenter un programme d'études, l'élève et l'étudiant doivent disposer des moyens financiers nécessaires[88]. Ils ont le droit d'exercer une activité lucrative dans la mesure où cette activité reste marginale et accessoire car la formation doit constituer le but principal de leur présence en Suisse. Les étudiants n'ont pas le droit au regroupement familial[89]. Mais en pratique, les autorités examinent les requêtes avec bienveillance dans la mesure où les conditions légales sont remplies[90].

c. Perspectives d'évolution des politiques européenne et suisse en matière d'intégration

A bien des égards, la politique suisse en matière d'immigration, et plus particulièrement en matière d'intégration des ressortissants de pays tiers en situation régulière, correspond aux lignes directrices établies au sein de l'Union européenne.

Dans le cadre de l'actuelle révision de la législation suisse, il est notamment proposé d'améliorer le statut juridique des ressortissants de pays tiers et de simplifier les procédures administratives afin de

[85] Giorgio Malinverni, *op. cit.*, p. 984.

[86] Par exemple pour les ressortissants d'Etats membres de l'Union européenne et de l'AELE.

[87] Art. 31 et 32 OLE.

[88] Les art. 31 et 32 OLE énoncent les conditions d'admission des élèves et étudiants.

[89] Art. 38 al. 2 OLE.

[90] Art. 38 et 39 OLE, à savoir un séjour et une activité lucrative suffisamment stables, un logement convenable, des ressources financières suffisantes.

favoriser l'intégration des ressortissants de pays tiers séjournant en Suisse, d'accélérer les procédures pour les employeurs et les autorités, et d'assurer une application uniformisée de la loi.

Au niveau communautaire, il y a lieu de souligner que les Etats membres de l'Union européenne se sont efforcés d'élargir autant que possible le cercle des ressortissants de pays tiers bénéficiaires des facilités d'intégration. Toutefois, la réglementation actuelle ne vise pas le séjour des ressortissants de pays tiers à d'autres fins que l'exercice d'une activité économique ou les études puisqu'il semble que leur nombre ne soit pas très élevé. Ces situations continuent donc à être régies par la législation nationale des Etats membres de l'Union européenne.

III Réglementation applicable aux demandeurs d'asile et aux réfugiés

L'harmonisation de la réglementation applicable aux demandeurs d'asile fait partie de la construction d'un espace européen de liberté, de sécurité et de justice. La Convention de Dublin sur le pays de premier asile, conclue en 1990[91], constitua la première étape dans la mise en place progressive d'une politique commune européenne en matière d'asile[92]. Aujourd'hui, la Convention de Dublin a été remplacée par un instrument de droit

[91] Voir *supra* (note 3).

[92] Comme pour l'espace Schengen, certains Etats membres de l'Union européenne n'ont pas souhaité participer pleinement au système de Dublin. Il s'agit du Royaume-Uni, de l'Irlande et du Danemark (voir le Protocole sur l'application de certains aspects de l'article 14 du Traité instituant la Communauté européenne au Royaume-Uni et à l'Irlande, le Protocole sur la position du Royaume-Uni et de l'Irlande et le Protocole sur la position du Danemark, annexés au Traité sur l'Union européenne et au Traité instituant la Communauté européenne). Le Danemark ne participe pas à l'adoption des nouveaux actes communautaires dans le domaine de l'asile. Il n'est notamment pas soumis au règlement 343/2003. Toutefois, le Conseil a autorisé en mai 2003 la Commission à négocier avec le Danemark la conclusion d'un accord relatif aux critères et aux mécanismes permettant de déterminer l'Etat responsable de l'examen d'une demande d'asile introduite au Danemark ou dans un autre Etat membre de l'Union européenne et à négocier avec l'Islande et la Norvège la conclusion d'un protocole au titre de l'art 12 de l'accord entre la Communauté européenne, la République d'Islande et le Royaume de Norvège relatif aux critères et aux mécanismes permettant de déterminer l'Etat responsable de l'examen d'une demande d'asile introduite dans un Etat membre, en Islande ou en Norvège. En ce qui concerne le Royaume-Uni et l'Irlande, ces deux Etats notifient leur souhait de participer ou non aux différents actes communautaires en la matière. Conformément à l'art 3 du protocole sur la position du Royaume-Uni et de l'Irlande annexé au Traité sur l'Union européenne et au Traité instituant la Communauté européenne, le Royaume-Uni et l'Irlande ont notifié, par une lettre du 30 octobre 2001, leur souhait de participer à l'adoption et à l'application du règlement 343/2003.

communautaire: le *règlement 343/2003* (Dublin II), adopté sur la base de l'art. 63 al. 1 point 1a) CE[93]. Ce mécanisme de détermination de l'Etat responsable de la demande d'asile permet d'éviter que les réfugiés ne puissent demander asile successivement dans plusieurs Etats membres, tout en garantissant l'examen des demandes. Dans le cadre de la mise en œuvre de la Convention de Dublin, la *directive Eurodac,*[94] fixe quant à elle, les bases d'une banque de données européenne permettant d'enregistrer et d'échanger les empreintes des demandeurs d'asile et immigrés clandestins.

Le processus d'harmonisation impliquait toutefois que les Etats membres veillent également à mettre en place un régime de protection temporaire et à coordonner leurs législations en relation avec la procédure d'asile et les garanties minimales accordées aux demandeurs d'asile, afin d'éviter la «concurrence» entre les procédures d'asile nationales.

De par sa longue tradition humanitaire, la Suisse a développé une politique des réfugiés et de l'asile accordant une large protection aux personnes persécutées. Jusque dans les années quatre-vingt-dix, les règles en matière d'asile faisaient partie de la loi sur le séjour et l'établissement des étrangers. La *loi fédérale sur l'asile*[95] est entrée en vigueur le 1er janvier 1981, et fut révisée totalement en 1999[96]. Pour la Suisse, la mise en œuvre d'une telle politique nécessite une étroite coordination et collaboration avec les autres Etats, et notamment avec les Etats membres de l'Union européenne. Aussi, elle vise à se rapprocher des dispositions légales et de la pratique européennes en la matière[97]. Des négociations avec l'Union européenne

[93] Règlement 343/2003 du Conseil, du 18 février 2003, établissant les critères et mécanismes de détermination de l'Etat membre responsable de l'examen d'une demande d'asile présentée dans l'un des Etats membres par un ressortissant d'un pays tiers, JO n° L 50 du 25.02.2003, p. 1, in: Christine Kaddous, *Union européenne. Communauté européenne. Recueil de textes,* LGDJ/Stämpfli (Paris/Berne), 2e édition, 2003, p. 651.

[94] Règlement 2725/2000 du Conseil, du 11 décembre 2000, concernant la création du système «Eurodac» pour la comparaison des empreintes digitales aux fins de l'application efficace de la Convention de Dublin, JO n° L 316 du 15.12.2000, p. 1, in: Christine Kaddous, *Union européenne. Communauté européenne. Recueil de textes,* LGDJ/Stämpfli (Paris/Berne), 2e édition, 2003, p. 667.

[95] Loi fédérale sur l'asile (LAsi) du 26 juin 1999, RS 142.31.

[96] Une nouvelle révision de la loi est actuellement en discussion. Il est notamment proposé d'introduire des modifications concernant la reconnaissance des Etats tiers sûrs, la suppression du renvoi préventif, la procédure d'asile et les possibilités de recours dans les centres d'enregistrement et dans les aéroports. Voir le Message concernant la modification de la loi sur l'asile, FF 2002 6359.

[97] Suisse-Union européenne, Rapport sur l'intégration du 3 février 1999, p. 236; Message relatif au projet de loi sur les étrangers, FF 2002 3469. Voir kay Hailbronner, *kompatibilität des Schweiz Asylver Fahrens mit Harmonisierungbestrebungen im Asylrecht der Europaïschen Union,* Schulthess/Stämpfli (Zurich/Berne), 2000.

sont en cours en vue d'une éventuelle association au système de Dublin dans le cadre de la deuxième série des accords bilatéraux. La Suisse remplit en grande partie les critères minimaux établis au niveau européen. Des différences existent cependant en ce qui concerne les modalités du droit de recours et la réglementation relative à l'octroi de la protection temporaire.

a. *Admission des demandeurs d'asile, statut de réfugié et procédure d'asile au sein de l'Union européenne*

L'admission des demandeurs d'asile, le déroulement de la procédure d'asile ainsi que la question du statut de réfugié sont trois éléments-clé de la définition d'un régime commun en matière d'asile.

La *directive 2003/9 relative à des normes minimales pour l'accueil des demandeurs d'asile*[98] constitue une étape indispensable à la mise en place du régime commun. Il était en effet nécessaire de fixer des normes minimales d'accueil suffisantes à leur garantir un niveau de vie digne dans tous les Etats membres de l'Union européenne. La directive couvre tous les ressortissants de pays tiers et apatrides qui déposent une demande d'asile à la frontière ou sur le territoire d'un Etat membre tant qu'ils sont autorisés à demeurer sur le territoire en qualité de demandeurs d'asile, ainsi qu'aux membres de leur famille couverts par la demande d'asile[99]. Par le biais de cette directive, un large éventail de droits et de garanties leur est accordé: droit à l'information relative aux avantages dont ils peuvent bénéficier et des obligations qu'ils doivent respecter eu égard aux conditions d'accueil; octroi d'un certificat à leur nom attestant leur statut de demandeurs d'asile ou attestant qu'ils sont autorisés à demeurer sur le territoire des Etats; libre circulation sur le territoire de l'Etat membre d'accueil ou à l'intérieur d'une zone qui leur est fixée par cet Etat; préservation de l'unité familiale; droit pour les enfants mineurs d'accéder au système éducatif dans des conditions analogues à celles qui sont prévues pour les ressortissants de l'Etat membre d'accueil; accès à la formation professionnelle; et garantie d'accès aux conditions matérielles d'accueil (logement) et aux soins de santé (au minimum les soins urgents et le traitement essentiel des maladies)[100]. Une question importante était celle de l'accès des demandeurs d'asile à l'exercice d'une activité lucrative. La

[98] Directive 2003/9 du Conseil du 27 janvier 2003 relative à des normes minimales pour l'accueil des demandeurs d'asile dans les Etats membres, JO n° L 31 du 06.02.3003, p. 18.

[99] Art. 3 directive 2003/9.

[100] Art. 5 à 8, 10, 12, et 13 à 15 directive 2003/9.

directive a laissé la liberté aux Etats membres de fixer une période pendant laquelle l'exercice d'une telle activité économique pourra être refusée aux demandeurs d'asile[101].

A l'heure actuelle, l'attribution du *statut de réfugié* s'effectue dans tous les Etats membres de l'Union européenne en application de la Convention de Genève de 1951. Toutefois, son interprétation et son application varient selon les Etats, ce qui rend nécessaire une définition commune de la notion de réfugié utile à l'édification d'un statut européen[102].

A cet effet, le Conseil a adopté une position commune concernant l'application harmonisée de la définition du terme de réfugié au sens de l'art. 1er de la Convention de Genève[103] qui établit les principes conducteurs pour la détermination de la qualité de réfugié. L'élément central de la définition repose sur la notion de «crainte de la persécution». Par conséquent, cela suppose évidemment de parvenir à une définition commune de la notion de persécution! La *proposition de directive concernant les normes minimales relatives aux conditions que doivent remplir les ressortissants des pays tiers et les apatrides pour pouvoir prétendre au statut de réfugié ou de personne qui, pour d'autres raisons, a besoin d'une protection internationale, et relative au contenu de ces statuts* de 2001[104] vise à combler cette lacune. Conformément à ce projet de directive, le statut de réfugié devrait être accordé à tout ressortissant d'un pays tiers qui, parce qu'il craint avec raison d'être persécuté du fait de sa race, de sa religion, de sa nationalité, de ses opinions politiques ou de son appartenance à un certain groupe social, se trouve hors du pays dont il a la nationalité et qui ne peut, ou ne veut, se réclamer de la protection de ce pays[105]. Afin que la protection soit évaluée et accordée de manière égale dans tous les Etats membres, le projet fixe les critères d'évaluation de la crainte du demandeur d'être persécuté ou de subir d'autres atteintes graves et injustifiées. En outre, l'attribution d'une «protection subsidiaire» permet à ceux qui ne remplissent pas les conditions d'octroi du statut de réfugié, mais qui, pour d'autres raisons,

[101] Art. 11 directive 2003/9. [102] Nathalie Berger, *op. cit.*, p. 156–157.

[103] Position commune 96/196/JAI du 4 mars 1996 définie par le Conseil sur la base de l'article K.3 du traité sur l'Union européenne, concernant l'application harmonisée de la définition du terme «réfugié» au sens de l'article 1er de la Convention de Genève du 28 juillet 1951 relative au statut des réfugiés, JO n° L 63 du 13.03.1996, p. 2.

[104] Proposition de directive concernant les normes minimales relatives aux conditions que doivent remplir les ressortissants des pays tiers et les apatrides pour pouvoir prétendre au statut de réfugié ou de personne qui, pour d'autres raisons, a besoin d'une protection internationale, et relative au contenu de ces statuts, COM (2001) 510 final. Ci-après: proposition relative au statut de réfugié.

[105] Art. 1 proposition relative au statut de réfugié.

satisfont aux règles concernant la protection internationale au sens de la directive, de bénéficier de la protection internationale[106].

Enfin, s'agissant du déroulement de la procédure d'asile, la *proposition de directive relative à des normes minimales concernant la procédure d'octroi et de retrait du statut de réfugié dans les Etats membres* de 2002[107] veille à établir les garanties et les droits procéduraux que les Etats membres doivent prévoir dans leur droit national, la résolution du Conseil du 20 juin 1995 sur les garanties minimales pour les procédures d'asile[108] n'étant plus suffisante. Les demandes d'asile visées sont celles qui sont déposées à la frontière, dans une zone de transit portuaire ou aéroportuaire ou sur le territoire des Etats membres[109]. Les demandeurs d'asile doivent pouvoir rester sur le territoire de l'Etat membre aussi longtemps que l'autorité responsable de la détermination ne s'est pas prononcée[110]. Le projet énonce ensuite les conditions auxquelles est soumis l'examen des demandes, les conditions auxquelles est soumise la décision de l'autorité responsable de la détermination, ainsi que les garanties accordées aux demandeurs d'asile pendant la procédure, le droit à un entretien personnel, le droit à l'assistance judiciaire et à la représentation. Ce large éventail de droits et garanties est conforme à l'esprit de l'art. 6 CEDH.

La proposition de directive de 2002 prévoit notamment la possibilité d'une procédure accélérée lorsque les demandes se révèlent irrecevables ou manifestement infondées. Cela est notamment le cas lorsque le ressortissant d'un pays tiers a transité par un pays considéré comme le «premier pays d'asile» ou comme un «pays tiers sûr»[111], ou lorsque le demandeur provient d'un «pays d'origine sûr»[112].

[106] Art. 2 let. e, et 15 à 17 proposition relative au statut de réfugié. Il faut distinguer la protection subsidiaire de la protection temporaire. La protection temporaire, telle que définie par la directive 2001/55 (*infra*, note 129), est une procédure de caractère exceptionnel assurant, en cas d'afflux massif de personnes déplacées une protection immédiate et temporaire. La protection subsidiaire est une forme de protection internationale destinée aux personnes qui ne remplissent pas les conditions d'octroi du statut de réfugié, mais qui, pour d'autres raisons, ont besoin d'une telle protection.

[107] Proposition de directive relative à des normes minimales concernant la procédures d'octroi et de retrait du statut de réfugié dans les Etats membres COM (2000) 578 final, telle que modifiée; voir COM (2002) 326. Ci-après: proposition relative aux normes minimales de la procédure d'asile.

[108] Résolution du Conseil du 20 juin 1995 sur les garanties minimales pour les procédures d'asile, JO n° C 274 du 19.09.1996, p. 13.

[109] Art. 3 proposition relative aux normes minimales de la procédure d'asile.

[110] Art. 6 proposition relative aux normes minimales de la procédure d'asile.

[111] Art. 25 lit. b et c proposition relative aux normes minimales de la procédure d'asile.

[112] Art. 29 lit. c proposition relative aux normes minimales de la procédure d'asile.

Les notions de "*pays tiers sûr*"[113] et de "*pays d'origine sûr*"[114] ne sont pas nouvelles dans le droit de l'Union européenne. La résolution des ministres de l'Immigration, adoptée à Londres les 30 novembre et 1er décembre 1992 sur les demandes d'asile manifestement infondées, prévoyait déjà que si un Etat membre décidait que dans un pays donné, il n'existe en règle générale pas de risque sérieux de persécution, la demande d'asile pouvait être automatiquement rejetée. Selon la résolution de 1995, la notion de «pays où en général il n'existe pas de risque sérieux de persécution» peut désigner le pays d'origine du demandeur ou un pays par lequel il a transité pour arriver sur le territoire de l'Etat de la demande. En d'autres termes, l'asile devrait être demandé dans le premier pays sûr que le demandeur a pu atteindre.

Le projet de directive de 2002 reprend le même concept. Les annexes I et II proposées déterminent les principes permettant de désigner un pays comme un pays tiers sûr ou comme un pays d'origine sûr. Pour l'essentiel, le pays doit observer systématiquement les normes de droit international relatives à la protection des réfugiés ainsi que les normes fondamentales du droit international relatives aux droits de l'homme. Les Etats membres de l'Union européenne sont sur le point de constituer une liste commune des pays qu'ils considèrent sûrs. Les discussions en cours semblent toutefois révéler des divergences entre les Etats membres, tant sur le concept de pays tiers sûr lui-même que sur une éventuelle liste commune européenne[115].

La définition des pays considérés comme suffisamment sûrs pour réadmettre leurs ressortissants qui auraient déposé une demande d'asile dans l'un des Etats membres de l'Union européenne, ainsi que l'établissement d'une liste commune sont deux éléments importants de la mise en œuvre de la politique européenne commune en matière d'asile. Ils font toutefois l'objet de vives critiques, notamment par le Haut Commissariat pour les Réfugiés et Amnesty International. En effet, ils pourraient, selon eux, constituer des instruments dangereux, notamment en ce qui concerne le concept de pays tiers sûr car le renvoi dans un pays qualifié comme tel peut être à la source de renvois successifs jusqu'à l'Etat

[113] Art. 27–28 proposition relative aux normes minimales de la procédure d'asile.

[114] Art. 30–31 proposition relative aux normes minimales de la procédure d'asile.

[115] Les discussions au sein de l'Union européenne ont été agendées à 2004. Par exemple, la plupart des Etats membres sont d'accord pour inclure les USA et le Japon dans la liste des pays tiers sûrs, mais certains indiquent que ces deux pays pratiquent la peine de mort.

que le réfugié fuit, et ainsi entraîner une violation du principe de non-refoulement[116].

De manière générale, l'ensemble de ces actes tend également à harmoniser les *voies de recours nationales*[117]. Les Etats membres doivent veiller à ce qu'un droit de recours effectif devant une juridiction nationale soit assuré. S'agissant notamment de la procédure d'asile, ils doivent autoriser le demandeur d'asile qui intente soit un recours administratif soit un recours juridictionnel à rester sur leur territoire dans l'attente de l'issue du recours.

b. Admission des demandeurs d'asile, statut de réfugié et procédure d'asile en Suisse

La procédure d'asile permet en Suisse de déterminer s'il existe un droit à la protection d'après des critères établis par la loi sur l'asile. En effet, il apparaît qu'un certain nombre de requérants n'appartiennent ni à la catégorie des réfugiés, ni à celle des personnes déplacées par la guerre.

Pour *obtenir l'asile en Suisse*, le requérant peut déposer sa demande à l'étranger auprès des autorités consulaires et diplomatiques (ce que ne prévoit pas le système communautaire), à la frontière, ou à l'aéroport. Les étrangers vivant déjà officiellement en Suisse (titulaires donc une autorisation de séjour valable) peuvent déposer une demande d'asile directement auprès de la police des étrangers de leur canton de domicile si, suite à des changements politiques intervenus dans leur pays, ils courent le risque d'être exposés à des persécutions politiques à leur retour. Enfin, la majorité des demandes d'asile sont déposées par des personnes entrées illégalement en Suisse. Celles-ci peuvent se rendre dans l'un des quatre centres d'enregistrement de l'Office fédéral des réfugiés (ODR)[118] pour y déposer leur requête. Cette façon de procéder leur permet d'éviter le risque d'être renvoyées à la frontière, puisque si la personne est arrêtée dans la zone frontalière au moment de franchir illégalement la frontière, elle sera immédiatement remise aux autorités de l'Etat voisin où elle aura la possibilité de demander l'asile[119]. Seuls font exceptions les cas dans

[116] Nathalie Berger, *op. cit.*, p. 185–186. Le principe de non-refoulement est consacré aux art. 33 de la Convention de Genève de 1951 et 3 CEDH. L'art. 25 de la Constitution fédérale suisse garantit également le principe de non-refoulement; voir *infra* (note 150).

[117] Art. 21 directive 2003/9 et art. 38–41 proposition relative aux normes minimales de la procédure d'asile.

[118] Chiasso, Bâle, Genève ou Kreuzlingen.

[119] Art. 24 LAsi.

lesquels un proche du demandeur d'asile vit déjà officiellement en Suisse. Pour les situations dans lesquelles il n'est pas possible de démontrer de quel pays le requérant est venu, une procédure d'asile lui sera garantie en Suisse.

Le demandeur d'asile est en principe attribué à un canton[120]. Il reçoit une autorisation de séjour valable 6 mois, renouvelable de 6 en 6 mois. Ce document ne confère toutefois aucun droit de présence, et il ne lui est pas permis de franchir la frontière, sauf autorisation de l'ODR. L'assistance des demandeurs d'asile relève de la compétence des cantons qui sont chargés de leur verser des prestations d'assistance (frais d'assistance, frais d'hébergement et frais d'assurances maladie). Pendant les trois premiers mois qui suivent le dépôt de sa demande d'asile, le requérant n'a pas le droit d'exercer d'activité lucrative; à l'échéance de ce délai, il devra se conformer aux dispositions relatives à l'exercice d'une activité lucrative[121]. Si une décision négative est rendue en première instance avant l'expiration de ce délai, le canton peut lui refuser l'autorisation d'exercer une activité lucrative pendant trois mois de plus.

La définition de *la notion de réfugié* est assez restrictive, de manière à faire une sélection entre les personnes qui sont vraiment menacées et les migrants économiques. L'art. 3 de la loi fédérale sur l'asile définit les «réfugiés» comme étant les personnes qui, dans leur Etat d'origine ou dans le pays de leur dernière résidence, sont exposées à de sérieux préjudices ou craignent à juste titre de l'être en raison de leur race, de leur religion, de leur nationalité, de leur appartenance à un groupe social déterminé ou de leurs opinions politiques (al. 1). Sont notamment considérées comme de sérieux préjudices la mise en danger de la vie, de l'intégrité corporelle ou de la liberté, de même que les mesures qui entraînent une pression psychique insupportable, et il y a lieu de tenir compte des motifs de fuite spécifiques aux femmes (al. 2). Cette définition est parfaitement conforme à la Convention de Genève de 1951, et va même au-delà dans la mesure où elle englobe les pressions psychologiques. Pour justifier sa demande d'asile, l'intéressé doit prouver que, dans son Etat d'origine ou dans le pays de sa dernière résidence, il est exposé à de sérieux préjudices ou craint à juste titre de l'être. La notion de persécution s'analyse essentiellement en fonction de l'intensité de la persécution qui doit être imputable à l'Etat, du caractère ciblé de la persécution, des motifs de persécution, de la crainte fondée de la persécution, et de l'absence de possibilité de refuge

[120] Le changement de canton est possible à condition que le canton d'accueil l'accepte.

[121] Art. 43 LAsi. Il sera notamment assujetti au principe de la priorité du travailleur indigène. Il ne peut donc être employé que s'il y a pénurie de main d'œuvre.

interne. Les motifs économiques ne sont en aucune manière suffisants pour obtenir le statut de réfugié politique. Le ressortissant d'un pays tiers qui est placé dans la situation d'un réfugié exclu de l'asile bénéficie de l'admission provisoire[122].

Pendant la procédure, le requérant d'asile qui a déposé sa demande en Suisse est autorisé à rester sur le territoire national[123]. Un renvoi préventif est toutefois envisageable si la poursuite de son voyage dans un Etat tiers est possible et licite, et qu'elle peut raisonnablement être exigée de lui[124]. La jurisprudence de la Commission suisse en matière de recours a toutefois démontré l'inefficacité d'une telle réglementation et l'actuelle révision de la loi tend à corriger ce problème. La *notion de «pays sûr»* n'est donc pas inconnue du droit suisse. Au contraire, la Suisse a été le premier Etat à introduire la réglementation concernant les pays réputés sûrs en 1981[125]. Outre la question du renvoi préventif pendant la procédure, le fait que le requérant provienne d'un Etat où il ne risque pas d'être persécuté est une cause de non-entrée en matière sur la demande déposée par un requérant d'asile. Depuis le 1er août 2003, la Suisse rejette toutes les demandes d'asile déposées par des ressortissants de l'Union européenne, de l'AELE, des futurs Etats membres de l'Union européenne, de Bosnie-Herzégovine et de Macédoine. L'Albanie, la Roumanie, la Bulgarie, la Lituanie, la Gambie, le Ghana, le Sénégal, l'Inde et la Mongolie figuraient déjà dans cette liste. Les demandes formulées par les ressortissants de ces Etats sont considérées comme *a priori* manifestement infondées et rejetées dans le cadre d'une procédure accélérée. S'il apparaît toutefois que la demande d'asile pourrait être recevable, le dossier devrait être instruit. Il convient de souligner que 11,3% des 26'125 personnes qui ont déposé une demande d'asile en Suisse en 2002 proviennent de pays désormais considérés comme sûrs.

Au niveau fédéral, c'est la *Commission pour les recours en matière d'asile* (CRA) qui contrôle l'application du droit d'asile par l'ODR et garantit une jurisprudence cohérente en la matière. La CRA, autorité judiciaire indépendante, est en fonction depuis le 1er avril 1992. Ses décisions sont définitives[126]. Il n'y a donc pas de recours possible au Tribunal fédéral suisse. Toutefois, un recours de droit administratif au Tribunal fédéral est

[122] Art. 44 al. 2 LAsi et art. 14a al. 1 LSEE : «Si l'exécution du renvoi ou de l'expulsion n'est pas possible, n'est pas licite ou ne peut pas être raisonnablement exigée, l'Office fédéral des réfugiés décide d'admettre provisoirement l'étranger». La notion de l'admission provisoire en droit suisse correspond à la notion de protection subsidiaire prévue par la proposition relative au statut de réfugié.

[123] Art. 42 al. 1 LAsi. [124] Art. 42 al. 2 LAsi.

[125] Art. 34 LAsi. [126] Art. 105 al. 1 LAsi.

ouvert contre les décisions des autorités fédérales (ODR) et cantonales lorsque sont en cause des questions notamment en rapport avec le lieu de séjour, l'accès à la vie économique, et l'assistance.[127]

Pour l'année 2002, 1'729 décisions positives sur 25'185 demandes d'asile ont été rendues et 4'172 demandeurs d'asile ont été admis provisoirement, soit un total de 23,5% de réponses favorables. En 2003, 27'200 demandes d'asile ont été traitées avec 1'638 octrois d'asile. Seuls environ 10% des demandeurs d'asile sont reconnus comme réfugiés.

c. Le régime de la protection provisoire dans l'Union européenne et en Suisse

L'idée de la protection temporaire est de fournir une protection à des personnes qui en principe ne souhaitent pas s'établir de manière définitive dans le pays d'accueil, mais seulement y trouver refuge pour une période limitée[128].

La *directive 2001/55 relative à des normes minimales pour l'octroi d'une protection temporaire en cas d'afflux massif de personnes déplacées*[129] a été adoptée en juillet 2001. Elle vise les personnes déplacées ne pouvant rentrer dans leur pays d'origine. C'est une définition large, qui englobe les victimes d'agents de persécution non-étatique, non-protégées par la Convention de Genève de 1951. Les Etats membres de l'Union européenne sont autorisés à élargir, en vertu de leur droit national, le cercle des bénéficiaires de la protection temporaire à des catégories de personnes, déplacées pour les mêmes raisons, dans la mesure où elles ne seraient par couvertes par la directive.

En *Suisse*, le *concept de protection provisoire* a été introduit par la *loi fédérale sur l'asile.* Bénéficient de cette protection les personnes exposées

[127] Par exemple, le Tribunal fédéral sera compétent dans le cas où l'étranger a droit à une autorisation (Arrêt du Tribunal fédéral, du 26 février 1997 ATF 123 II 145) ou qu'il y a un problème au niveau de la prise en charge des différences de tarif d'une hospitalisation des requérants d'asile hors canton (Arrêt du Tribunal fédéral, du 26 août 1998 ATF 124 II 489).

[128] Benjamin Katabuka, *La compatibilité du droit suisse sur l'asile à la Convention de Dublin, dans l'hypothèse d'une éventuelle participation*, Revue de droit administratif et fiscal 2003, p. 31–60, p. 50.

[129] Directive 2001/55 du Conseil du 20 juillet 2001 relative à des normes minimales pour l'octroi d'une protection temporaire en cas d'afflux massif de personnes déplacées et à des mesures tendant à assurer un équilibre entre les efforts consentis par les Etats membres pour accueillir ces personnes et supporter les conséquences de cet appareil, JO n° L 212 du 07.08.2001, p. 12.

à un danger général grave notamment pendant une guerre, une guerre civile ou lors de situations de violence généralisée[130]. Aussi, la protection provisoire tend à offrir un statut temporaire aux personnes qui ne tombent pas dans la définition de la notion de réfugié parce qu'elles ne subissent pas une persécution individuelle, dans leur pays[131].

En ce qui concerne le champ d'application personnel, le droit suisse est compatible avec la directive communautaire. En outre, les deux réglementations prévoient des clauses similaires d'exclusion de la protection provisoire et garantissent le droit au regroupement familial, à l'emploi, à la sécurité sociale, ainsi qu'à d'autres prestations[132].

La différence majeure entre les deux systèmes de protection temporaire tient à la question de la reconnaissance de la qualité de réfugié faite par les personnes bénéficiant de la protection temporaire. Comme le droit communautaire considère la protection temporaire comme une forme de protection subsidiaire par rapport à la Convention de Genève de 1951, ses bénéficiaires ont la possibilité de présenter une demande de reconnaissance du statut de réfugié[133]. En revanche, le droit suisse n'autorise pas le cumul entre la protection provisoire et la reconnaissance de la qualité de réfugié puisque l'octroi de la protection provisoire suspend la procédure de demande d'asile[134].

La durée maximale de la protection temporaire fixée par la directive 2001/55 est de deux ans. Il incombe aux Etats membres de réglementer, au niveau national, la situation des personnes bénéficiant de la protection temporaire au-delà de la durée maximale de deux ans. Il y a lieu toutefois de se demander si cette durée n'est pas trop courte. Le droit suisse ne prévoit pas de durée maximale. La protection est accordée aussi longtemps que les personnes sont exposées à un «danger général grave». Après cinq ans de résidence en Suisse, la personne protégée peut passer sous le régime normal de séjour et d'établissement, c'est-à-dire être soumise à la loi sur le séjour et l'établissement des étrangers.

d. Perspectives de coopération entre la Suisse et l'Union européenne

La politique suisse en matière d'asile ne peut être considérée indépendamment de l'évolution européenne. Au fur et à mesure que la coopération entre les Etats membres de l'Union européenne progresse, la dépendance de la Suisse à son égard semble s'accentuer. En restant en

[130] Art. 4 LAsi. [131] Giorgio Malinverni, *op. cit.*, p. 990.
[132] Art. 12, 13 et 15 directive 2001/55; art. 71, 75, et 80–84 LAsi.
[133] Art. 17 directive 2001/55. [134] Art. 69 al. 3 LAsi; Benjamin Katabuka, *op.cit.*, p. 56.

dehors du système mis en place au niveau européen, la Suisse risque de devenir le pays-cible des demandeurs d'asile déboutés puisque le refus d'une demande d'asile par un Etat membre de l'Union européenne exclut toute nouvelle demande à l'intérieur de ce même territoire. Aussi, une association au système de Dublin permettrait à la Suisse de se décharger de l'examen d'une demande d'asile qui serait déposée deux fois et pour l'examen de laquelle un Etat membre de l'Union européenne serait responsable. Cela permettrait également de contenir l'augmentation de l'immigration illégale vers la Suisse. D'autre part, les Etats voisins resteraient obligés, sur la base des accords de réadmission conclus avec la Suisse, de reprendre les immigrants illégaux qui auraient pénétré depuis leur territoire en Suisse[135].

Une association à Eurodac permettrait également une coopération plus efficace en matière d'asile et d'immigration illégale. Avec le système Eurodac, l'Union européenne s'est dotée d'une base de données permettant aux Etats membres (et plus particulièrement à l'Etat membre responsable de la demande d'asile) de vérifier que la personne concernée n'a pas déjà déposé une demande d'asile auprès d'un autre Etat membre de l'Union européenne. Y sont enregistrés les requérants d'asile, les étrangers appréhendés lors du franchissement illégal d'une frontière extérieure et les étrangers en séjour irrégulier.

Les autorités fédérales gèrent actuellement une banque de données pour l'enregistrement des empreintes digitales ainsi que des photographies des demandeurs d'asile et des personnes appréhendées franchissant illégalement la frontière afin de pouvoir comparer les nouvelles empreintes avec les empreintes déjà enregistrées. Cette comparaison permet de lutter contre les demandes d'asile multiples, sous différentes identités[136]. Une participation de la Suisse à Eurodac serait très profitable puisque

[135] Accord du 20 décembre 1993 entre le Conseil fédéral suisse et le Gouvernement de la République fédérale d'Allemagne relatif à la réadmission de personnes en situation irrégulière, RS 0.142.111.368; Accord du 3 juillet 2000 entre le Conseil fédéral suisse, le Gouvernement fédéral autrichien et la Principauté de Liechtenstein relatif à l'admission des personnes en situation irrégulière, RS 0.142.111.639; Accord du 28 octobre 1998 entre le Conseil fédéral suisse et le Gouvernement de la République française relatif à la réadmission des personnes en situation irrégulière, RS 0.142.113.499; Accord du 10 septembre 1998 entre la Confédération suisse et la République italienne relatif à la réadmission des personnes en situation irrégulière, RS 0.142.114.549.

[136] Voir Ordonnance 3 sur l'asile relative au traitement de données personnelles (Ordonnance 3 sur l'asile, OA 3) du 11 août 1999, RS. 142.314; voir aussi Benjamin Katabuka, *op.cit.*, p. 49.

le contrôle pourrait se faire à l'échelle européenne. Elle ne poserait par ailleurs aucun problème majeur au regard du droit suisse.

Les négociations en cours entre la Suisse et la Communauté européenne pour une association au système de Schengen et Dublin, permettraient de couvrir la participation de la Suisse au règlement Dublin II et à la directive Eurodac. En revanche, l'accord d'association envisagé ne prévoit pas une coopération plus large couvrant les autres aspects de la politique d'asile européenne, en particulier les mesures d'harmonisation et les normes minimales.

IV Sanctions contre les ressortissants de pays tiers en situation irrégulière, retour et rapatriement

Une politique d'immigration reste inefficace et incomplète lorsqu'il n'est pas prévu de mesures sanctionnant les comportements illégaux. Les ressortissants de pays tiers qui n'ont pas ou plus de statut juridique leur permettant de rester, doivent quitter le territoire de l'Union européenne. Une telle mesure est essentielle afin de ne pas compromettre la politique d'admission des ressortissants de pays tiers. Pour l'heure, la question des sanctions demeure de la responsabilité des Etats membres, bien que certaines mesures aient été prises au niveau communautaire[137].

En Suisse, les autorités fédérales ont recensé dans les années quatre-vingt-dix entre 50'000 et 100'000 ressortissants de pays tiers en situation irrégulière[138]. Ces chiffres importants peuvent s'expliquer du fait de la politique restrictive de l'Union européenne, dans la mesure où la Suisse peut constituer un second choix pour les personnes en provenance d'un pays tiers qui ne remplit pas les conditions d'admission dans l'Union européenne[139]. Il importe de ce fait d'assurer une certaine coordination des mesures.

[137] Notons l'adoption de la directive 2002/90 du Conseil du 28 novembre 2002 définissant l'aide à l'entrée, au transit et au séjour irréguliers, JO n° L 328 du 05.12.2002, p. 17. La Commission devrait présenter en 2004 une proposition de directive relative à des normes minimales pour les procédures de retour et la reconnaissance mutuelle des décisions en matière de retour.

[138] Est en situation irrégulière: celui qui demeure sur le territoire d'un Etat alors qu'il n'est plus au bénéfice d'un droit de présence; celui qui entre en qualité de touriste et qui ne quitte pas le territoire à l'échéance du visa; le requérant d'asile qui fait l'objet d'une décision négative et exécutoire; et enfin celui qui est entré illégalement sur le territoire national.

[139] Voir notamment Minh Son Nguyen, *op. cit.*, p. 578.

a Sanctions, retour et rapatriement

L'expulsion est la sanction classique en matière de séjour illégal. Au sein de l'Union européenne, les décisions d'expulsions sont encore prises par les Etats membres, de manière discrétionnaire[140]. La *directive 2001/40 relative à la reconnaissance mutuelle des décisions d'éloignement des ressortissants de pays tiers*[141] fixe les règles de base à respecter pour pouvoir rendre une décision d'expulsion, afin que celle-ci soit reconnue et exécutable par les autres Etats membres.

La question du retour est particulièrement délicate dans le domaine de l'asile. En effet, une politique efficace pour le retour des personnes déboutées de leur demande de protection internationale est indispensable pour sauvegarder l'intégrité d'un régime d'asile commun[142]. Un des soucis majeurs dans ce domaine est de garantir que le retour se fasse en conformité avec le principe de non-refoulement. De manière générale, les procédures d'expulsions et reconduites à la frontière doivent respecter les droits de l'homme et offrir des possibilités suffisantes de recours devant un tribunal[143].

En Suisse, l'immigration clandestine et le trafic de migrants sont réprimés par la *loi fédérale sur le séjour et l'établissement des étrangers.* Si le ressortissant d'un pays tiers est pris en flagrant délit d'entrée illégale sur territoire suisse, il sera reconduit à la frontière. Lorsqu'il n'est plus ou pas au bénéfice d'un quelconque droit de présence (pour cause de rejet de la demande d'autorisation de séjour ou d'échéance/caducité de l'autorisation), la police des étrangers prononce à son encontre une décision de renvoi[144]. Cette décision est une mesure administrative par laquelle l'autorité signifie au ressortissant d'un pays tiers qu'il doit quitter la Suisse et lui fixe un délai pour le faire.

La décision d'expulsion sanctionne toujours un comportement répréhensible du ressortissant d'un pays tiers[145]. L'expulsion peut être

[140] L'expulsion doit être effectuée conformément au respect des obligations internationales des Etats membres en matière de droits fondamentaux: CEDH, bonne foi et motivation raisonnable; CJCE, arrêt *Pereira Roque c. Jersey* du 16 juillet 1998, aff. C-171/96, Rec. 1998, p. I–4607.

[141] Directive 2001/40 du Conseil du 28 mai 2001 relative à la reconnaissance mutuelle des décisions d'éloignement des ressortissants de pays tiers, JO n° L 149 du 02.06.2001, p. 34.

[142] Voir le Livre vert relatif à une politique communautaire en matière de retour des personnes en séjour irrégulier, COM (2002) 175.

[143] Art. 6 CEDH. [144] Art. 12 LSEE.

[145] L'art. 10 LSEE énonce les motifs d'expulsion; Giorgio Malinverni, *op. cit.*, p. 987.

d'ordre politique, judiciaire[146] ou administrative. En pratique, l'expulsion administrative n'est jamais prononcée contre les clandestins; elle est plutôt réservée aux titulaires d'une autorisation de séjour ou d'établissement. Le ressortissant d'un pays tiers en situation irrégulière peut se voir infliger une décision d'éloignement assortie d'une interdiction d'entrée, voire même être l'objet de mesures de contrainte comme la détention préparatoire ou la détention en vue du refoulement[147]. En outre, l'entrée, le séjour et l'exercice d'une activité lucrative illégaux constituent des infractions pénales[148] et les peines prévues peuvent s'accompagner de l'expulsion judiciaire (ce qui implique des poursuites pénales, voire même une détention préventive). Un réfugié ne peut être expulsé que s'il compromet gravement la sûreté intérieure ou extérieure de la Suisse ou s'il a porté gravement atteinte à l'ordre public[149]. La Constitution suisse prohibe l'expulsion et l'extradition de réfugiés sur le territoire d'un Etat dans lequel ils sont persécutés[150], et nul ne peut être refoulé sur le territoire d'un Etat dans lequel il risque la torture ou tout autre traitement ou peine cruels et inhumains[151].

La législation suisse réprimant le trafic des migrants est desservie par des peines relativement légères en comparaison avec la décision-cadre de l'Union européenne qui invite les Etats membres à prévoir la réclusion pour huit ans au plus dans les cas de trafic professionnel de migrants ou lorsque l'infraction est commise dans le cadre d'une organisation criminelle[152].

Etant donné que l'immigration clandestine et le trafic de migrants concernent plusieurs domaines (sécurité aux frontières, migration, asile, police et justice), les compétences sont réparties entre plusieurs départements, et il est difficile d'obtenir des statistiques consolidées dans

146 Il s'agit d'une mesure pénale accessoire. Art. 55 CP (Code pénal suisse du 21 décembre 1937, RS 311.0).

147 Art. 13a ss LSEE. 148 Art. 23 ss LSEE. 149 Art. 65 LASi.

150 Art. 25 al. 2 Cst (Constitution fédérale de la Confédération suisse du 18 avril 1999, RS 101); voir également l'art. 5 LAsi.

151 Art. 25 al. 3 Cst.

152 2002/629/JAI: Décision-cadre du Conseil du 19 juillet 2002 relative à la lutte contre la traite des êtres humains, JO n° L 203 du 01.08.2002, p. 1; voir aussi 2002/946/JAI: Décision-cadre du Conseil du 28 novembre 2002 visant à renforcer le cadre pénal pour la répression de l'aide à l'entrée, au transit et au séjour irréguliers, JO n° L 328 du 05.12.2002, p. 1. Actuellement, en Suisse, la peine la plus élevée qui peut être prononcée est l'emprisonnement (trois ans maximum) et l'amende, ce qui range le trafic de migrants dans la catégorie des délits. Le projet de loi fédérale sur les étrangers prévoit un durcissement des dispositions pénales (emprisonnement jusqu'à une année ou d'une amende de 20'000 francs).

ce domaine. A titre indicatif, le nombre d'immigrés clandestins arrêtés par les gardes-frontières suisses a varié entre 8'500 et 15'800 en 1993 et 1998 en raison des guerres en Bosnie et au Kosovo. Un minimum se situe aux alentours de 5'000 pour les années 1991 et 2001. Au cours de l'année 2002, il y a eu près de 7'400 arrestations. Enfin, on peut comptabiliser entre 7'000 et 9'000 condamnations par an.

Sur le plan international, la Suisse a signé, en avril 2002, les protocoles additionnels à la Convention de l'ONU sur la criminalité transnationale organisée relatifs à la traite des êtres humains et au trafic de migrants, s'associant ainsi aux efforts internationaux menés dans la lutte contre ces fléaux[153].

b. Accords de réadmission

Le succès d'une politique en matière de retour est subordonné à l'existence d'une coopération fructueuse avec les pays d'origine ou de transit, notamment par le biais d'accords de réadmission.

Le principe selon lequel les Etats doivent réadmettre leurs nationaux sur leur territoire est généralement admis dans la pratique contractuelle du droit international public. Le principe a été reconnu de droit international coutumier. Depuis les années 90, la tendance s'est accentuée de renforcer l'obligation faite aux Etats de réadmettre leurs nationaux et d'instaurer une coopération interétatique en la matière. Les accords de réadmission contiennent des dispositions d'entraide administrative réglementant l'établissement de l'identité, la nationalité ainsi que le transit des personnes à rapatrier sur le territoire des parties contractantes. Les personnes tenues de quitter le territoire sont protégées par le principe de non-refoulement et les dispositions relatives à la protection des données. Ces accords entendent garantir la réadmission rapide et en toute sécurité des personnes tenues de quitter le territoire.

La *Communauté européenne et ses Etats membres* ont développé une stratégie d'action commune qui vise à conclure, avec les Etats tiers[154], des accords bilatéraux relatifs à la réadmission de leurs nationaux et à placer l'obligation de réadmission au centre ou en contrepartie d'aides ou avantages économiques (notamment par l'insertion de clauses de réadmission dans les accords de coopération et d'association)[155]. Des

[153] Voir *supra* (note 45).

[154] Voir notamment les accords conclus avec les pays de l'Europe centrale et orientale.

[155] La Commission a présenté, en juillet 2003, une proposition de décision établissant un programme de coopération avec les pays tiers et en juin 2003 une proposition de règlement

accords multilatéraux ont également été conclus[156]. Les accords de réadmission multilatéraux permettent une coopération globale et avancée entre les Etats; le modèle bilatéral offre, quant à lui, plus de flexibilité et de souplesse, notamment dans sa mise en œuvre[157]. Lorsque la Communauté conclut des accords de réadmission, elle introduit une clause dans une déclaration commune encourageant l'Etat tiers en question à négocier un accord du même type avec les Etats associés au système Schengen (actuellement la Norvège et l'Islande, demain peut-être la Suisse).

Bien qu'aucune règle internationale n'impose aux Etats d'admettre sur leur territoire des personnes autres que leurs nationaux, tous les accords avec des Etats tiers comprennent des dispositions relatives à la réadmission de tiers, à l'exception des accords passés avec la Roumanie[158]. En outre, les Etats membres de l'Union européenne ont conclu entre eux des accords de réadmission de ressortissants de pays tiers en situation irrégulière, lorsqu'ils ont pénétré sur le territoire d'un Etat par une frontière commune, lorsqu'ils résident habituellement dans un Etat contractant ou lorsqu'ils sont titulaires d'un titre de séjour sur le territoire de l'Etat contractant[159]. En effet, dans l'espace Schengen, la réadmission des étrangers entre les parties contractantes est considérée comme une mesure compensatoire à la suppression des contrôles aux frontières intérieures[160].

établissant un programme d'assistance technique et financière 2003, dont l'objectif est d'aider les pays tiers à satisfaire leurs obligations en matière de réadmission à l'égard de l'Union et des Etats membres.

156 Les Etats Schengen ont conclu un accord de réadmission avec la Pologne en mars 1991. Actuellement, l'Union européenne met en place une stratégie plus globale de conclusion d'accords de réadmission entre la Communauté européenne et des pays tiers. Elle a signé un accord de réadmission avec Hong Kong et Macao, paraphé un accord avec le Sri Lanka et achevé les négociations avec l'Albanie. Elle est en cours de négociations avec la Russie, le Maroc et l'Ukraine. Elle entend ouvrir des négociations avec la Turquie, la Chine, le Pakistan et l'Algérie au premier semestre 2004.

157 Voir notamment la Recommandation du Conseil du 30 novembre 1994 concernant un accord type bilatéral de réadmission entre un Etat membre et un pays tiers, JO n° C 274 du 19.09.1996, p. 2.

158 Par exemple, l'Accord entre la Communauté européenne et le gouvernement de la région administrative spéciale de Hong Kong de la République populaire de Chine concernant la réadmission des personnes en séjour irrégulier, JO n° L 17 du 24.01.2004, p. 25, qui prévoit, à son art. 3, l'obligation de réadmettre les "personnes relevant d'une autre juridiction".

159 Par exemple, l'Accord entre la France et l'Espagne relatif à la prise en charge des personnes à la frontière, du 8 janvier 1988, l'Accord entre la France et l'Italie sur à la prise en charge des personnes à la frontière, du 6 décembre 1990, ou l'Accord entre la France et le Portugal, du 8 mars 1993.

160 Art. 23 al. 2 Convention d'application. Nathalie Berger, *op. cit.*, p. 140. Par exemple, France-Allemagne, France-Italie, Autriche-Allemagne, Convention Benelux (Belgique,

Depuis plusieurs années, la *Suisse* développe une politique de conclusion d'accords de réadmission avec un grand nombre de pays de provenance et de transit. Elle tend à appliquer également le principe de la conditionnalité, à savoir qu'elle fait dépendre ses prestations (notamment économiques) en faveur de pays tiers de leur coopération dans le domaine de la migration. Les accords de réadmission passés par la Suisse avec les pays de provenance et de transit s'inscrivent dans la droite ligne des accords de réadmission et des clauses de réadmission figurant dans les accords d'association et de coopération conclus par la Communauté européenne et ses Etats membres avec bon nombre de pays tiers, et des accords de réadmission conclus récemment. La Suisse a conclu des accords de réadmission et de transit avec plusieurs Etats membres de l'Union européenne, notamment avec la France, l'Italie, l'Autriche, la Suède, en dernier lieu le Bénélux (mars 2003) et l'Espagne (novembre 2003)[161], afin de réglementer les questions du statut des agents d'escorte et des responsabilités qu'ils assument, appliquant ainsi par analogie les dispositions prévues par la Convention d'application de 1990 qui visent à protéger les personnes à rapatrier et les agents d'escorte, de même que les tiers qui participeraient éventuellement au bon déroulement du transit.

En janvier 2003, la Suisse a finalisé un nouveau type d'accord avec le Sénégal. Cet accord de transit aurait pu permettre aux autorités suisses de transférer momentanément au Sénégal des requérants d'asile déboutés en provenance de l'Afrique occidentale aux fins de vérifier l'identité et d'obtenir les documents nécessaires au retour dans les pays d'origine; de là, ils auraient été rapatriés dans leur pays d'origine, la Suisse s'obligeant à les reprendre si leur identité ne pouvait être établie. Pour des raisons de politique intérieure, le Sénégal n'a pas soumis l'accord à son Parlement pour ratification. Mais l'idée véhiculée par cet accord sera poursuivie dans le cadre de discussions avec d'autres Etats de la région. Pour le reste, la Suisse est très active dans la négociation d'accords de réadmission avec les Etats tiers[162].

Luxembourg, Pays-Bas), Union nordique des passeports, Benelux-Allemagne, Benelux-France, Benelux-Autriche, . . . etc.

161 Voir *supra* (note 135).

162 Un accord a été conclu avec l'Albanie en septembre 2000; plus récemment, avec l'Arménie, en octobre 2003. La Suisse a finalisé les négociations avec la Moldova (novembre 2003), le Nigéria (janvier 2003) et l'Ukraine (juillet 2003) et poursuit les discussions avec de nombreux autres Etats tiers.

Conclusion

La Suisse et l'Union européenne ont développé une politique d'immigration favorable à une intégration dynamique et progressive des ressortissants de pays tiers en situation régulière en vue de leur assurer un traitement comparable à celui des ressortissants nationaux sur le territoire de l'Etat d'accueil. Sur le plan législatif, il est à noter que l'ordre juridique suisse s'inspire largement du droit et des politiques de l'Union européenne. Depuis 1988, la Suisse tend à aménager sa législation dans une optique favorable à une intégration européenne en s'efforçant d'assurer dans la mesure du possible la compatibilité de son droit avec celui de l'Union européenne dans les domaines ayant une dimension transfrontalière («autonomer Nachvollzug»). Cette approche ne compense cependant pas l'absence d'instruments de coopération.

Le renforcement de la sécurité intérieure en Europe, la gestion efficace et équitable des demandes d'asile, ainsi que la lutte contre la criminalité internationale sont des tâches qui ne peuvent être menées à bien que de manière concertée, à travers la coopération interétatique. La Suisse s'emploie à coopérer largement au sein des enceintes internationales et européennes et a ratifié de nombreux traités multilatéraux. Néanmoins, ses relations avec l'Union européenne, malgré l'objectif à terme de l'adhésion, se fondent pour l'instant sur une approche bilatérale. Après l'entrée en vigueur, le 1er juin 2002 d'un ensemble d'accords, dont un réglant la circulation des personnes sur la base des principes de l'acquis communautaire, la Suisse a entamé des négociations en vue d'être associée au système de Schengen et Dublin et de renforcer la lutte contre la fraude aux intérêts financiers.

Les négociations en vue de la participation de la Suisse à Schengen et Dublin revêtent à cet égard une importance cruciale. L'association à l'espace Schengen permettrait d'établir une coopération efficace en ce qui concerne la délivrance des visas, les contrôles aux frontières, la coopération judiciaire et la coopération policière qui reposent essentiellement sur l'échange d'informations par le biais du SIS, et contribuerait ainsi grandement au renforcement de la sécurité intérieure, pour le bénéfice mutuel de toutes les parties.

Tout comme la coopération Schengen, la coopération dans le domaine de l'asile est primordiale. En ne participant pas au système de Dublin et d'Eurodac, la Suisse risque de devenir, en Europe, le «pays de la dernière chance» pour les demandeurs d'asile déboutés dans un Etat membre de l'Union, et la lutte contre les abus et l'«asylum shopping» serait rendue plus difficile.

Une association de la Suisse aux systèmes de Schengen et Dublin constitue un premier rapprochement essentiel à la politique d'asile et d'immigration européenne. Le cadre de coopération restera néanmoins limité aux domaines couverts par ces deux accords, le champ d'application ne couvrant pas les autres aspects du développement de l'espace de liberté, de sécurité et de justice qui se met progressivement en place dans l'Union européenne. Ces développements du droit de l'Union européenne ne manqueront pas d'avoir une influence sur la Suisse, même si, pour l'heure, elle devra se contenter de les observer de l'extérieur.

THE UNITED KINGDOM

DR. BERNARD RYAN
Senior Lecturer
University of Kent

INTRODUCTION

This report is concerned with the place of Britain[1] within the migration law of the European Union as it has developed since the Treaty of Amsterdam came into force on 1 May 1999. In approaching that question, an account will first be offered of the Amsterdam provisions concerning Britain and migration law. Subsequent sections then consider Britain's participation in three areas: immigration control, legal migration and asylum.[2] The report as a whole documents the extent to which, notwithstanding Britain's non-participation in the Schengen border-free area, it has taken an active part in EU migration law other than that concerning legal migration.

1 The Treaty of Amsterdam

The special provisions of the Treaty of Amsterdam concerning migration law and Britain are in several parts. Firstly, under the Protocol on the application of Article 14 EC to Britain and Ireland, immigration controls are permitted on persons travelling between continental member states on the one hand, and Britain and Ireland on the other.[3] That Protocol also confirmed the right of Britain and Ireland to maintain "arrangements . . . relating to the movement of persons", under what is termed the "common travel area". The co-operation with Ireland is quite different from the Schengen system, however: the arrangements are administrative rather than treaty-based, they are not inherently reciprocal, and there is

[1] Throughout this report, the term "Britain" is used as a synonym for the United Kingdom.
[2] The first part of the questionnaire on entry, and the fourth part on enforcement measures, have therefore been treated together.
[3] OJ 1997 C 340/1, p. 97.

no provision for those who legally enter or reside in one of the states to travel to the other.[4]

Secondly, under the Schengen Protocol, the Schengen states can agree with Britain that they will participate in elements of the Schengen *acquis.*[5] That option was taken up by Council Decision 2000/365, with effect from 2 June 2000.[6] While the Decision was mainly concerned with the Schengen *acquis* on policing, it also extended two parts of the Schengen Implementing Convention concerning immigration to Britain: Article 26 SIC on carriers' obligations, and Article 27 on the facilitation of breaches of immigration laws.

Thirdly, under the Protocol on the position of Britain and Ireland, Britain has the right to opt in to any migration measure adopted under Title IV EC.[7] One possibility is for Britain to opt in to the discussion of a measure within three months of a proposal being made to the Council. Where Britain has opted in, the other states then have the right after a "reasonable period" to proceed without Britain. Alternatively, Britain has an unlimited right to opt in to a measure after it has been adopted.

Finally, what of the small number of measures concerning migration law adopted under Title VI EU? If these are classified as "building upon the Schengen *acquis*", then Article 5 of the Schengen Protocol gives Britain a choice as to whether to participate in the discussions or not. Where Britain does not opt in, the other states are allowed to proceed without it after a "reasonable period". In this case, any later participation will require the agreement of all the Schengen states. By contrast, if the measure is *not* one which 'builds upon the Schengen *acquis*,' then British participation is indispensable.

2 Immigration Control

Britain is not covered by the Schengen/EU rules concerning entry. In particular, it does not have mutual recognition of visas with the Schengen states, and is not covered by the common visa lists under Council Regulation 539/2001.[8] Britain has nevertheless been considerably affected

[4] See generally B. Ryan, "The Common Travel Area between Britain and Ireland" (2001) 64 *Modern Law Review* 855.

[5] Protocol on the integration of the Schengen *acquis* into the framework of the European union, OJ 1997 C 340/1, p. 93, Article 4.

[6] OJ 2000 L 131/43. [7] OJ 1997 C 340/1, p. 99.

[8] Council Regulation 539/2001 determining the third countries whose nationals must be in possession of visas when crossing the external borders of the Member States, OJ 2001 L 81/1.

by the removal of border controls among Schengen states, simply because of the greater possibility for those who wish to enter Britain irregularly to reach channel ports. That phenomenon was reflected most obviously in the intermittent presence after 1998 of persons in the Calais area wishing to enter Britain irregularly, which was itself the reason for the operation of the Red Cross camp in Sangatte between September 1999 and December 2002.[9]

The practical implications of the Schengen system have led to important developments in British policy as regards border control.[10] In the first place, Britain has strengthened its controls *vis-à-vis* continental states. In particular, Britain has developed "juxtaposed controls" with France – that is, reciprocal arrangements under which each state is permitted to operate frontier controls on the territory of the other. Provisions of this kind were initially applied from August 1993 to persons travelling by motor vehicle through the Channel Tunnel. More recently, juxtaposed controls have been extended by international agreement to Eurostar stations (May 2001), and to sea travel between Dover and Calais and Dunkerque (February 2004).[11] A key provision in these two more recent agreements is that asylum applications made before departure are the responsibility of the state of departure. In addition, Britain has participated in a number of operational measures aimed at reducing irregular migration across the external EU/Schengen border. These have included British immigration officials' co-operation with counterparts in Bosnia-Herzegovina, Serbia and Montenegro, and the participation of British air and sea forces in "Operation Ulysses" in the western Mediterranean and off the Canary Islands in 2003. Pursuant to the same policy, Britain opted in to the discussions which led to the Council

Between 1996 and 2001, Britain was covered by the earlier legislation on a common visa list: Council Regulation 2317/95 (1995 OJ L 234/1) and its replacement, Council Regulation 574/1999 (1999 OJ L 72/2).

9 On the Sangatte centre, see L. Schuster, "Asylum Seekers: Sangatte and the Tunnel" (2003) 56 *Parliamentary Affairs* 506 and C. Phuong, 'Closing Sangatte: The Legal Implications of the Asylum Dispute between France and the UK" (2003) 17 *Immigration Asylum and Nationality Law* 157.

10 See generally B. Ryan, "The European Dimension to British Border Control", forthcoming (2004) 18 *Immigration Asylum and Nationality Law.*

11 Additional Protocol to the Sangatte Protocol, *Cm.* 5015 (2000) and Treaty between United Kingdom and France concerning the Implementation of Frontier Controls at the Sea Ports of Both Countries on the Channel and North Sea, *Cm.* 5832 (2003). The 2003 Treaty permits the establishment of juxtaposed controls in any commercial port from which there is sea travel between the two states.

Regulation establishing a network of immigration liaison officers in third countries.[12]

In addition to bilateral and operational measures, Britain has participated in much of the legislation aimed at strengthening immigration control and enforcement throughout the EU/Schengen area. These measures are discussed in the remainder of this section.

Visa and residence permit formats

Britain has participated in the policy laying down a uniform format for visas and residence permit formats at the EU level since it began in 1995,[13] and opted in to the Regulations in 2002 which provide for the inclusion of a photograph in visas and residence permits.[14] The Government's view is that participation in uniform formats is advantageous, since they "enhance the security of documents used for third country nationals entering the UK, without affecting the Government's ability to control third country nationals".[15] The full introduction of a uniform format visa without a photograph was scheduled for September 2003. Visas with photographs are likely to be introduced in 2004, while residence permits with photographs are likely in 2005.[16]

Britain is also favourable to the proposed Council Regulation for the inclusion of biometric data (high-resolution facial images and digital fingerprints) in visas and residence permits, albeit that it does not appear to have opted in to the discussions.[17] EU developments in relation to biometric identifiers would fit with recent developments in British policy. While applicants for British visas or entry clearance are not ordinarily required to provide biometric data, legislation in 2002 empowered the

[12] For the agreed text of the Regulation, see Council doc 15813/03 (7 January 2004).

[13] Council Regulation 1683/95 laying down a uniform format for visas (OJ 1995 L 164/1), Joint Action 97/11/JHA concerning a uniform format for residence permits (OJ 1997 L 7/1).

[14] Council Regulation 334/2002 amending Regulation 1683/95, OJ 2002 L 53/7 and Council Regulation 1030/2002 laying down a uniform format for residence permits for third-country nationals, OJ 2002 L 157/1.

[15] Letter of 11 December 2001 of Home Office Minister Angela Eagle, in House of Commons European Scrutiny Committee, Twelfth Report 2001–02, para 14.3.

[16] Memorandum of 20 October 2003 of Home Office Minister Caroline Flint, summarised in House of Commons European Scrutiny Committee, Thirty-Fifth Report 2002–03, para 7.4.

[17] The proposal is in COM (2003) 558, and was made in September 2003. The British view is in the memorandum of 20 October 2003, above n 16.

Secretary of State to require them to provide "specified information" about their "external physical characteristics".[18] Relying on that power, a trial of compulsory fingerprinting of visa applicants began in Sri Lanka in July 2003, and the Government indicated in August 2003 its desire to extend the principle to other states.[19]

Carriers' obligations

We have already seen that Britain is covered by the provision for carriers' obligations in Article 26 SIC. It has also participated in Council Directive 2001/51, which supplemented Article 26.[20] These EU-level measures firstly require member states to oblige carriers to take responsibility for non-EU nationals who have been refused entry. In British law, the Immigration Act 1971 contains a similar power for immigration officers to give directions to the owners, agents or captain of the ship or aircraft for the removal of a person refused entry.[21] The EU measures also require member states to oblige carriers to check the travel documents of third country nationals, and to impose penalties upon carriers who bring third country nationals without the necessary documents. In Britain, provision for carriers' sanctions was first made by the Immigration (Carriers' Liability) Act 1987, and is now in the Immigration Act 1999.[22] The charge of £2000 per passenger in Britain is consistent with Directive 2001/51, which requires such a penalty to be of at least €3000 per person.[23]

Further EU developments in this area can be anticipated from a proposal under discussion that carriers should be obliged to provide basic data to immigration authorities concerning the passengers they bring to

[18] Nationality Immigration and Asylum Act 2002, s 126.

[19] Immigration (Provision of Physical Data) Regulations 2003, SI 2003 No. 1875 and "Biometric Technology to Tackle Immigration Abuse," Home Office press release, 28 August 2003.

[20] OJ 2001 L 187/45. Britain specifically opted in to the discussions on the measure: see Council doc 12751/00 (27 October 2000). It is arguable however that it was anyway covered by the supplementary measure, since Article 8(2) of Decision 2000/365, states that Britain "shall be deemed irrevocably to have notified . . . that it wishes to take part in all proposals and initiatives which build upon the Schengen acquis referred to . . ."

[21] Immigration Act 1971, Schedule 2, para 8.

[22] Section 40 of the Immigration Act 1999, as substituted by Schedule 8 of the Nationality, Immigration and Asylum Act 2002.

[23] The relevant rate of exchange is that in the Official Journal of 10 August 2001, which was €1 = £0.6269. €3000 per person therefore equates to £1881.

the EU.[24] Britain has opted in to the discussions on this proposal at the Council of Ministers.[25] This too is already provided for in British law. Since the Immigration Act 1999, an immigration officer is permitted to require certain passenger information from carriers, including each passenger's name, nationality and the number of their travel document.[26]

Reference may also be made here to the so-called "civil penalty" which has been imposed since April 2000 upon carriers found to have transported clandestine entrants to Britain.[27] Under the scheme, a penalty of up to £2000 may be imposed upon those in whose vehicles clandestine entrants are found to have been transported, and there is a power for the vehicle to be impounded as security against its payment. The civil penalty scheme is another example of a response to the changed circumstances of British immigration control after the Schengen arrangements came into force. It is at the same time a system which is unique to Britain.

Facilitation

Article 27 SIC requires participating states to impose penalties on those who, for financial gain, assist irregular entry to or residence on the territory of the participating states. The member states' obligations as regards facilitation are to be extended by Directive 2002/90 and Framework Decision 2002/946, which come into force on 5 December 2004.[28] As we saw in section 1, the Schengen *acquis* which is applicable to Britain includes Article 27 SIC. Britain also participated in the negotiation of the two measures on facilitation adopted in 2002.[29] Its objective in co-operation in

[24] The initial proposal is at OJ 2003 C 82/23.

[25] Council doc 10952/03 (27 June 2003).

[26] Immigration Act 1971, s 27B, inserted by Immigration and Asylum Act 1999, s 18. Further detail is in the Immigration (Passenger Information) Order 2000, SI 2000 No. 912.

[27] Part II of the Immigration and Asylum Act 1999, as amended by Sch 8 of the Nationality Immigration and Asylum Act 2002. The amendments were made necessary by the decision of the Court of Appeal in *International Transport Roth and others v Secretary of State for the Home Department* [2002] 3 WLR 344, which doubted the compatibility of aspects of the scheme with the right to a fair trial in Article 6 ECHR and the right to peaceful enjoyment of property under Article 1 of its First Protocol.

[28] Council Directive 2002/90 defining the facilitation of unauthorised entry, transit or residence, OJ 2002 L 328/17 and Council Framework Decision 2002/946/JHA of 28 November 2002 on the strengthening of the penal framework to prevent the facilitation of unauthorised entry, transit and residence, OJ 2002 L 328/1.

[29] Here too, it is arguable that Britain was bound to participate because of the terms of Article 8(2) of Council Decision 2000/365 (see above, n 20). Britain formally opted in only to the discussions on Directive 2002/90 (Council doc 12951/00, 3 November 2000).

this field has been to achieve a more restrictive regime in other member states, so as to reduce the likelihood of onward irregular migration to Britain.[30]

Directive 2002/90 requires member states to impose sanctions upon those who (i) intentionally assist third country nationals to enter or transit illegally through a participating state, irrespective of financial gain, or (ii) intentionally assist third country nationals to reside illegally in a participating state, provided that that is done for financial gain. Member states are however permitted to provide an exception where "the aim of the behaviour is to provide humanitarian assistance to the person concerned". Framework Decision 2002/946 requires member states to have *criminal* penalties for these infringements referred to in the directive which are "effective, proportionate and dissuasive". Where the offence was committed for gain, and was either committed by a criminal organisation or endangered the lives of the persons being smuggled, the maximum penalty must normally be a minimum of eight years. As regards jurisdiction, it is provided that the criminal offences must cover actions committed wholly or partly within the territory of a given member state, and that, where a state does not extradite its own nationals, it must also apply the offences to the actions of its own nationals.

Britain has long had an offence of facilitation, and has strengthened it on a number of occasions over the past decade. Under section 25(1) of the Immigration Act 1971, it was an offence to assist illegal entry to Britain. Two additions were made to that offence by the Asylum and Immigration Act 1996: assisting an individual to obtain leave to remain in Britain by deception, and assisting the entry (irrespective of illegality) of an asylum applicant to Britain. In this last case only, there was an exception for those who did not act for gain, or who acted in the course of employment by a "bona fide organisation" which assisted asylum applicants. In all cases, the maximum custodial sentence was initially seven years, but was increased to ten years by the Immigration and Asylum Act 1999.[31]

Article 27 SIC and the subsequent measures contributed to a further tightening of British law by the Nationality Immigration and Asylum Act 2002.[32] It is now an offence in Britain to assist a breach of the immigration laws of *any* member state. The offence applies to acts done in Britain, and also to acts done by British nationals elsewhere. There is also an offence

[30] See the comments of Home Office Minister Lord Filkin, HL Debates, 23 July 2002, cols 286–287.

[31] Section 29 of the 1999 Act.

[32] Sections 143 and 144 of the 2002 Act.

of assisting entry for the purposes of an asylum application. For each of the offences set out in the 2002 Act, the maximum custodial sentence was increased to fourteen years. It is striking that, after the 2002 Act, British law goes well beyond the EU requirements in many key respects. These include: the absence of a requirement of gain for the offence of assisting irregular entry; the application of the offence of assisting a breach of immigration laws to British nationals even where extradition to another state is possible; the fact that it is an offence to assist an asylum applicant to enter Britain, even where no breach of immigration law has occurred; the confining of the humanitarian exception to cases of organisations which assist asylum applicants; and, the severity of the maximum sentence.

Trafficking

Britain's participation in the Council Framework Decision 2002/629 on trafficking in human beings was indispensable, as it was a Title VI measure which was not deemed to build on the Schengen *acquis.*[33] Under the Framework Decision, member states are required to prohibit action aimed at trafficking an individual for the purposes of sexual or labour exploitation. Member states are required to have criminal penalties for the infringements referred to in the directive which are "effective, proportionate and dissuasive". Some offences are of an aggravated kind: those which endanger the life of the victim, are committed against someone "particularly vulnerable", involve the use of serious violence, or are committed by a criminal organisation. In those cases, the maximum penalty must be a minimum of eight years. The offence(s) must cover actions committed wholly or partly within the territory of the given member state, and the actions of a state's nationals where they cannot be extradited. The Framework Decision comes into force on 1 August 2004.

Specific legislation on trafficking is a new development in Britain. The first such offence was in sections 145 and 146 of the Nationality Immigration and Asylum Act 2002, and applied to trafficking into Britain for the purposes of prostitution. Those sections were then repealed by the Sexual Offences Act 2003, which created wider offences of "intentionally arranging or facilitating" travel into, within or out of Britain for the purposes of sexual exploitation.[34] A more general offence of trafficking for

[33] Council Framework Decision 2002/629/JHA of 19 July 2002, OJ 2002 L 203/1.

[34] Sexual Offences Act 2003, ss 57–60.

exploitation has now been included in recent legislative proposals.[35] The proposed notion of "exploitation" includes a breach of the prohibition on slavery or forced labour in Article 4 ECHR. It also includes a situation in which an individual is "subjected to force, threats or deception to induce him (i) to provide services of any kind, (ii) to provide another person with benefits of any kind, or (iii) to enable another person to acquire benefits of any kind". The offences set out in the 2003 Act and proposed in the 2004 Bill can be committed either by actions within Britain or alternatively by British nationals elsewhere. The maximum penalty is fourteen years' imprisonment.

A final point is that Britain chose not to opt into the directive on short-term residence permits for victims of facilitation or trafficking who cooperate with member state authorities, which was agreed by the Council of Ministers in 2003.[36] The Government's argument has been that it does not wish to establish a general right to a residence permit in this way. It prefers instead its pre-existing approach, which is to grant leave to remain in appropriate individual cases on a discretionary basis, outside of the Immigration Rules.[37]

Mutual recognition of expulsion decisions

Directive 2001/40 requires participating states to be able to enforce each other's expulsion decisions taken against third country nationals (other than the family members of EU citizens). Enforcement must be possible where an individual is the subject of an expulsion decision because of "a serious and present threat to public order or to national security and safety", and either (i) they have been convicted for an offence punishable by imprisonment of at least one year, or (ii) there is evidence that they have committed, or intend to commit "serious criminal offences" in another member state. Enforcement must also be possible where the individual is "the subject of an expulsion decision based on failure to comply with national rules on the entry or residence of aliens".

Britain opted in to the discussions on Directive 2001/ 40, and more recently on the Council Decision concerning the financial imbalances

[35] Clauses 4 and 5 of the Asylum and Immigration (Treatment of Claimants, etc.) Bill 2004.

[36] Council doc 14994 (17 December 2003).

[37] Memorandum of 8 March 2002 of Home Office Minister Angela Eagle, in House of Commons Select Committee on European Scrutiny, 2001–02, *Twenty-Second Report*, para 15.10.

which follow from it.[38] Britain's reasons for participation are less than clear, however, given that it and the Schengen states maintain immigration controls towards one another. Britain does not though appear to have changed its law or policy as a result of the directive. Previously, the Government indicated that in order to comply with the directive, it would be necessary to legislate to permit removal because of an expulsion order made in another Member State.[39] It may be that the view is now taken that the existing provision for deportation in the Immigration Act 1971 is sufficient: it authorises deportation of an individual in any case where the Secretary of State deems that "conducive to the public good".[40]

3 Legal migration

Legislation on the admission and residence of third country nationals is an area of EU-level action in which Britain has consistently refused to participate since the coming into force of the Treaty of Amsterdam. British practice as regards legal migration is probably at least as open as that of other member states. What Britain has sought to retain however is flexibility in admissions policy, and discretion in relation to individuals.

Employment and self-employment

Britain elected not to participate in the discussions on the 2001 Commission proposal for a Directive on entry and residence for the purposes of employment and self-employment.[41] It did so in order to maintain control over the procedure and content of its admission policy.[42]

The Commission proposal and British practice are consistent in the system of preference they establish.[43] The Commission proposal would give preference to (i) EU citizens, (ii) third country nationals with a right to work by virtue of Community law or under an international agreement,

[38] Council doc 12534/00 (19 October 2000) and Council doc 14698/03 (3 December 2003).

[39] Letter from Home Office minister Barbara Roche, 11 May 2001, reported in House of Lords Select Committee on the European Union *First Report* 2001–02, Annex C.

[40] Immigration Act 1971 s 3(5), as substituted by Sch 14 para 44 of the Immigration and Asylum Act 1999.

[41] COM (2001) 386.

[42] Letter of 3 January 2002 of Home Office Minister Angela Eagle, in House of Commons Select Committee on European Scrutiny, 2002–2003, *Fifteenth Report*, para 3.4.

[43] Article 6(1) and (2) of the Commission proposal, and paras 1 and 44 of the Work Permits UK, *Guidance Notes for Employers on How to Apply for a Business and Commercial Work Permit* (September 2003 version).

and (iii) third country nationals who have a right to work under national law or who have worked and lawfully resided in that state for three of the previous five years. The British approach is similar in that it favours EEA nationals and third-country nationals who are "settled" (ordinarily resident) in the United Kingdom. There is also similarity in the requirement as regards the publicity to be given to job offers before a work permit can be issued. In the Commission proposal, it would have to be "demonstrated" that a vacancy could not be filled. That formulation appears consistent with the British approach, which is to require that the publications or other media used to advertise a post be "readily available throughout the EEA". The British practice in relation to self-employment is also broadly consistent with the Commission proposal. The basic requirements in Britain are that the individual has £200,000 to invest and that their investment will result in at least two new full-time posts.[44] While not identical, these requirements are similar in effect to those in the Commission proposal that "the self-employed economic activities . . . will have a beneficial effect on employment in the member State or on the economic development of that Member State".[45]

There are however some significant differences between the Commission proposal and British practice. One difference concerns the Commission proposal for a single application for both work permit and residence permit. In Britain the two are separate: work permits are issued by the Work Permits UK section of the Home Office's Immigration and Nationality Directorate, while applications for leave to enter and remain are dealt with by the immigration authorities, including consular officials and immigration officers at ports. A second difference is that the Commission proposal envisages an application for a work permit being made by the employee, and applying to a specific professional activity or field of activities. By contrast, the British system is that employers apply for work permits for a specified person for a specified job.

The Commission proposal also differs from British practice in relation to exceptions to the need for individual assessment of whether there is a preferred worker available. In the Commission proposal, member states would be allowed to dispense with the need for individual assessment only "for a specific number of jobs, in a specific sector, for a limited time period". That approach is more restrictive than at least three schemes of economic migration in Britain. The first is the Highly Skilled Migrant

[44] Immigration Rules, paras 201 to 203.

[45] Article 19 of the Commission proposal.

Programme, which is a points based system which enables highly qualified individuals to come to Britain without a work permit. The second is the British list of 'shortage occupations', including the medical profession, teachers and several categories of engineer, with respect to which a full individual assessment is not needed. The third is the working holidaymaker scheme, under which Commonwealth citizens under 30 are permitted to have a "working holiday" in Britain for up to two years. Since the scheme is not based on an international agreement, it does not appear to be covered by the Commission proposal.

Students, trainees and volunteers

Britain also declined to participate in the Commission proposal concerning the admission of students, trainees and volunteers.[46] Here too, its objective was to retain freedom of action as to its approach to third country students.[47] The rationale for such a position is not hard to find, given the relatively high number of third country students in the United Kingdom. Indeed, a Commission-funded comparative study which preceded the proposed directive found that in 1999 that were 222,800 such students in Britain, as against 31,500 in France and 23,526 in Germany.[48] It is quite possible that Britain has more third country students than the rest of the EU put together.

One specific reservation with respect to the proposal concerned the proposed right of mobility for students admitted to other countries.[49] A second reservation was that Britain did not wish to allow in-country applications for admission to student status, since British practice is ordinarily to require that entry clearance be obtained from the state in which an individual is permanently "living".[50] In other respects, however, the Commission proposal was not especially onerous for Britain. In particular, Britain already has the kind of employment regime for third country students contemplated by the proposal, in that it gives permission to

[46] COM (2002) 548.

[47] Letter of 6 January 2003 from Home Office Minister Lord Filkin, in House of Lords Select Committee on European Scrutiny, 2002–2003, *Seventh Report*, para 16.4.

[48] International Centre For Migration Policy Development, Admission of Third Country Nationals to an EU Member State for the Purposes of Study or Vocational Training and Admission of Persons Not Gainfully Employed (2000), p. 43.

[49] Article 7 of the Commission proposal.

[50] Article 19 of the Commission proposal.

engage in paid employment for up to 20 hours a week during term, and without limit outside term time.[51]

Long-term residents

The long-term residents' directive has two aspects: it sets out minimum standards for the treatment of third country nationals who have been resident in a member state for five years, and gives such persons the right to move to other member states.[52] British policy in relation to the acquisition of "indefinite leave to remain" is broadly consistent with the first aspect of the directive. Those who are in Britain in an employed or self-employed capacity are eligible for indefinite leave to remain after four years' residence.[53] Other persons are eligible after 10 years' lawful residence, while those who have been continuously resident for 14 years are eligible to apply even if some of the period of residence was not lawful.[54] Where British policy differs from the directive is that the award of indefinite leave to remain is discretionary, whereas the directive treats it as an entitlement to which there is a public policy exception.

It is possible that Britain would have participated in the directive had it only been concerned with the first of these questions. In the event, however, the British Government declined to take part in the measure because it did not wish to create legal rights of admission for third country nationals resident in other member states.[55] Britain has also refused to agree to short-term rights of travel for third country nationals resident in other member states. When the Commission proposed that Britain participate in this part of the Schengen *acquis*, the Government's response was that to do so "would be to remove the UK's ability to operate a full immigration control".[56] The result is not just that resident third country

[51] Article 18 of the Commission proposal.

[52] Council Directive 2003/109 concerning the status of third-country nationals who are long-term residents, OJ 2004 L 16/44.

[53] Paras 134 and 209 of the Immigration Rules.

[54] Paras 276A–276D of the Immigration Rules.

[55] See the explanation given by Home Office Minister Bob Ainsworth, HC Debates, European Standing Committee B, 1 July 2002, cols 4–5.

[56] See Commission Opinion on the request by the United Kingdom to take part in certain provisions of the Schengen *acquis*, SEC (1999) 1198, para 11, reproduced in House of Lords Select Committee on the European Union, *Fifth Report* 1999–2000, Appendix 3. The Government's explanation is out in a letter of 24 November 1999 of Home Office Minister Barbara Roche: *ibid.*, Appendix 4.

nationals in other member states have no EU right to travel to Britain, but that third country nationals resident in the UK have no EU right to travel to continental states either.

Family reunification

Britain also declined to participate in the discussions on the Family Reunification Directive.[57] The Government's concern was that to have participated might have "remove[d] the UK's ability to formulate and adjust policies in relation to family reunification as a matter of domestic law". At the same time, it indicated that it did not intend to be "seriously out of line with our European partners in this important area of immigration policy".[58]

In the event, the relatively weak standards contained within the Family Reunification Directive mean that British policy is consistent with it. The Directive applies to migrants who have a residence permit of at least one year and who have a reasonable prospect of obtaining permanent residence. In relation to those persons, the core obligation is that participating states admit the spouse and unmarried minor children of the primary migrant. British policy goes further than the directive's requirements in several respects. In the first place, it admits the spouses and unmarried minor children of persons other than those referred to in the directive, including those on short-term work permits and students.[59] British policy is also to admit the family members of both same-sex and opposite-sex couples with a relationship akin to marriage of at least two years' standing.[60] By contrast, the directive creates no obligations in that regard.[61] In relation to spouses, British policy is that the sponsor must be at least 18 and the spouse at least 16, whereas the directive allows states to retain minimum age requirements of up to 21.[62] Similarly, in relation to children, there is nothing in British policy similar to the possibilities under the directive for member states to retain an integration test for children over 12 who arrive independently

57 Council Directive on the Right of Family Reunification, OJ 2003 L 251/12.

58 Letter of 26 April 2000 of Home Office Minister Barbara Roche, in House of Commons Select Committee on European Scrutiny, *Eighteenth Report* 1999–2000, para 2.3.

59 Paras 76, 79, 194 and 197 of the Immigration Rules.

60 Paras 295AA to 295O of the Immigration Rules.

61 Article 4(3) of the directive gives participating states the option of admitting unmarried partners and their children.

62 Compare para 177 of the Immigration Rules and Article 4(5) of the directive.

of the rest of the family, or a restriction on the admission of children over 15.[63]

Turkish nationals

Turkish nationals have a number of directly effective rights deriving from Turkey's association agreement with the European Union. The position of Turkish employees is governed by Decision 1/80 of the EEC-Turkey Association Council. Under that instrument, Turkish nationals have in particular the right to change employers after three years' employment, the right to take any employment after four years' employment, and their family members have the right to take any employment after five years' lawful residence. Admission for self-employment is governed by Article 41 of the 1970 Additional Protocol to the Turkish Association Agreement. In *Savas*, the Court of Justice held that, because of Article 41, Turkish nationals who wish to be admitted to Britain for the purposes of self-employment should not be subject to a more restrictive regime than that which operated when Britain joined the EU on 1 January 1973.[64]

While the legal entitlements of Turkish nationals are likely to be enforceable under the European Communities Act 1972, they are not however specifically set out in statute, statutory instrument or the Immigration Rules. Conflicts between British policy and the requirements of Decision 1/80 in relation to Turkish *workers* are unlikely to arise frequently in practice, since, after four years' residence based on employment, an individual and their family are anyway eligible for indefinite leave to remain. As regards admission for *self-employment*, however, British policy has been to give the benefit of Article 41 of the Additional Protocol only to those who apply while lawfully in Britain, while applying the contemporary and more restrictive policy to those in Britain irregularly, or outside Britain.[65] This distinction derives from an ambiguity in the *Savas* judgment, but was rejected by the High Court in *Tum and Dari* in November 2003.[66] It is not yet clear however what the consequence of that litigation will be.

[63] Article 4(1), third paragraph, and Article 4(6) of the directive.

[64] *R* v. *Secretary of State for the Home Department ex p Savas*, Case C-37/98, [2000] ECR I-2927.

[65] See Chapter 5, Section 10 of the Immigration Directorate Instructions, published at http://www.ind.homeoffice.gov.uk/default.asp?PageId=856.

[66] *R* v. *Secretary of State for the Home Department ex p Tum and Dari*, judgment of 19 November 2003 (Davis J).

The 2004 enlargement

British policy as regards the 1 May 2004 enlargement is that it will give unrestricted access to the labour market to nationals of the eight new member states where it has an option (i.e. those other than Cyprus and Malta). The European Union (Accessions) Act 2003 accordingly confers on the Government the power to allow the nationals of those eight states to work from 1 May 2004.[67] There is however the power in the Act to withdraw or modify that right to work for some or all accession state nationals at a later date. One question is what will happen if after two years the British labour market remains open to all nationals of accession states. Under the Accession Treaty, Britain will at that point have to decide whether it wishes to continue with national measures (for up to a further five years) in relation to nationals of the eight states in question. While the Government has not made an announcement on the point, it may well seek to preserve national control after the two year period, even if the labour market remains open to nationals of the eight states in question.

Discrimination

Directive 2000/43 requires all member states to prohibit discrimination on grounds of "racial or ethnic origin" in employment, self-employment, social provision and access to goods and services.[68] In practice, the Race Relations Act 1976 goes further than the Directive in also prohibiting discrimination on grounds of national origin, nationality and colour. The Race Relations Act 2000 moreover extended the reach of the 1976 Act to the police and other public authorities. For these reasons, the changes required in British law by the directive were concerned above all with the concept of discrimination rather then the extent of its application. The changes made included a modified definition of indirect discrimination, an explicit statutory prohibition on harassment, a new definition of a "genuine occupational requirement", an explicit prohibition on discrimination after the end of an employment relationship, and provision for the shifting of the burden of proof to respondents where a *prima facie*

[67] European Union (Accession) Act 2003, s 2.

[68] Council Directive 2000/43 implementing the principle of equal treatment between persons irrespective of racial or ethnic origin, OJ 2000 L 180/22.

case has been made out.[69] Because the 2003 amendments were made as regulations under the European Communities Act 1972, they were confined to implementing the directive, and as a result were narrower than the original Race Relations Act. In particular, the changes do not apply to discrimination on grounds of nationality or colour, and do not apply to decisions of public authorities outside the fields of employment and social provision.

4 Asylum

Britain has been an active participant in Title IV developments relating to asylum since 1999. It has opted in to the discussions on all of the measures proposed in the area, and has been quite successful in influencing their content. The reason for British activity in this area is its belief that effective EU action will lead to a reduction in the level of asylum applications in Britain, whether because other states are obliged to take responsibility for applications, or because other states are obliged to raise standards. The British enthusiasm for EU level action has taken place against the background of a comparatively high level of applications in recent years. In absolute terms, it had more asylum applications than any other EU state in the each of the years 2000–2002, and in 2002 was fourth of the fifteen EU states in applications by population.[70]

Dublin II Regulation

The original Dublin Convention proved of only limited usefulness as a mechanism by which Britain could transfer responsibility for asylum applications to other states,[71] even though many asylum applicants would necessarily have transited through other member states. It was for that reason that Britain favoured both the strengthening of the content of the Dublin Convention, and its conversion into the "Dublin II"

[69] The amendments are in the Race Relations Act 1976 (Amendment) Regulations 2003, SI 2003 No 1626.

[70] See, UNHCR, *Asylum Applications Lodged in Industrialized Countries: Levels and Trends, 2000–2002* (March 2003), Table 1.

[71] Commission figures show that in 1998 and 1999 only 4.0% of asylum applications in Britain gave rise to a Dublin application, and that in only 1.5% of cases did an actual transfer occur: European Commission, *Staff Working Paper: Evaluation of the Dublin Convention*, SEC (2001) 756, Annex III.

Regulation.[72] Britain was especially supportive of the treatment of "tolerated illegal presence" in the Regulation, with responsibility for an asylum application now upon a state where an applicant has stayed irregularly for five months or longer.[73] Britain also supported the lowering of the evidential standards necessary for responsibility to be transferred in the case of irregular migration. Whereas the Dublin Convention required that it be "proved" that an individual had entered a given state irregularly, the Regulation instead states that irregular entry or presence need only be "established, on the basis of proof or circumstantial evidence".[74]

In British law, the Dublin arrangements have been reflected in the provisions on "safe third countries". The Asylum and Immigration Act 1996 provided for the removal of asylum applicants to safe third countries on the basis of certification by the Secretary of State that the Geneva Convention would not be breached in relation to that individual. If the safe third country was a member state, then there would be no in-country right of appeal against the transfer. The courts decided however that the Secretary of State was not permitted to certify a member state which gave a narrower interpretation to the Geneva Convention.[75] It is in order to circumvent that authority that section 11 of the Immigration and Asylum Act 1999 now provides that, where an asylum applicant is removed to a member state under "standing arrangements", there is a statutory presumption that the member state is compliant with the Geneva Convention.[76] As before, there is no in-country right of appeal against a Dublin removal.[77] Further

72 See Council Regulation 343/2003 establishing the criteria and mechanisms for determining the Member State responsible for examining an asylum application lodged in one of the Member States, OJ 2003 L 50/1. The British Government's general view can be found in a memorandum of 23 October 2001 in House of Lords Select Committee on the European Union, Nineteenth Report, 2001–02, Part II, pp. 12–14.

73 Article 10(2) of Regulation 343/2003.

74 Compare Article 6 of the Dublin Convention (1997 OJ C 254/1) with Article 10(1) and 10(2) of Regulation 343/2003.

75 *R* v. *Secretary of State for the Home Department, ex parte Gashi* [1999] Imm AR 415 (CA) and *R* v. *Secretary of State for the Home Department, ex parte Adan and others* [2001] 2 AC 477 (HL).

76 Immigration and Asylum Act 1999, s 11, now as substituted by Nationality Immigration and Asylum Act 2002, s 80. Note that the 2002 version added a definition of "standing arrangements": "arrangements in force between two or more member states for determining which State is responsible for considering applications for asylum". This formulation covers bilateral arrangements with other member states.

77 There is by contrast the possibility of an in-country challenge to removal on ECHR grounds. An ECHR argument can itself be certified as "manifestly unfounded" by the

changes in this area are proposed in the Bill before Parliament at the time of writing. If approved, it would mean that all member states, together with Iceland and Norway, were deemed safe countries under the Geneva Convention and ECHR, and that all appeals against their removal would be precluded.[78]

Reception Conditions

Britain also participated in the negotiation of the directive on reception conditions.[79] It saw in it the possibility to improve reception standards in other member states, and thereby reduce the level of asylum applications in Britain. In the words of one minister, the directive had "clear benefits for the United Kingdom", since "introducing a more level playing field for the living conditions to which asylum seekers are entitled should reduce secondary migration and the disproportionate burden on some member states".[80]

Britain has though worsened its reception conditions for asylum applications in several respects in recent years, and these changes came to influence the content of Directive 2003/9. One example concerns the provision of asylum support in the form of vouchers. From April 2000, payments to asylum applicants, which are set at roughly 70% of the general level of income support, were provided primarily through vouchers. The original Commission proposal was consistent with that British policy in the permission it gave for material reception conditions to be provided in kind or by vouchers.[81] In Britain, however, after criticism of the restrictiveness of vouchers, and of their making asylum applicants identifiable, payment by cash was reintroduced in April 2002.

The possibility to deny support for applicants deemed to apply late is a second example of British influence. Article 16(2) of the directive

Secretary of State, in which case – unless the certificate is quashed – that claim cannot frustrate removal either: see now Nationality Immigration and Asylum Act 2002, s 93.

[78] Clause 12 and Sch 3 of the Asylum and Immigration (Treatment of Claimants, etc.) Bill 2004. Note that at present section 11 of the 1999 Act is defective in not providing for removal for Iceland and Norway. Although parties to the Dublin arrangements, these are not EU member states.

[79] Council Directive 2003/9 on the minimum standards for the reception of asylum seekers, OJ 2003 L 31/ 18.

[80] Immigration Minister Beverley Hughes, *HC Debates*, European Standing Committee B, 17 July 2002, col. 4.

[81] See Article 15(3) of the Commission proposal, COM (2001) 181 and Article 13(5) of the directive.

authorises member states to deny support to applicants who fail "to demonstrate that the asylum claim was made as soon as reasonably practicable after arrival in the Member State". This clause was inserted into the directive on a British proposal at the final stage of the negotiations in November 2002.[82] The change reflects a new policy in Britain, contained in section 55 of the Nationality Immigration and Asylum Act 2002. Under that section, persons who have applied for asylum since 8 January 2003 have been denied welfare and accommodation benefits where they have failed to satisfy the authorities that their application was "made as soon as reasonably practicable after . . . arrival in the United Kingdom". Since the consequence of this provision has been to leave many asylum applicants entirely destitute and homeless, it has been the subject of widespread criticism.[83] Some litigants have succeeded in quashing decisions to the effect that they did not claim asylum as soon as reasonably practicable.[84] That led on 17 December 2003 to a new policy that applications for support would be allowed if, but only if, an application for asylum could be shown to have been made within three days of arrival. Case law has also established that the prohibition on inhuman or degrading treatment in Article 3 ECHR requires the provision of support if an individual is otherwise unable to fend for themselves.[85] The British approach under section 55 of the 2002 Act shows that Article 16 severely weakens the minimum guarantee provided by the directive.

Accommodation centres are a third example. Provision was made in the 2002 Act for the establishment of such centres within which it would be compulsory for asylum applicants who wished support to live.[86] The final text of the directive is permissive of accommodation centres, in that it allows member states "to make provision of the material reception conditions subject to actual residence by the applicant in a specific place", while

[82] See Council doc. 14658/02, 22 November 2002, footnote to Article 16.

[83] For judicial criticism, see the statement of Maurice Kay J in *R (Q, D and others)* v. *Secretary of State for the Home Department*, High Court, 24 October 2003. He indicated that at that time there were 800 asylum support cases before the Administrative Court, and that such cases had amounted to one-quarter of all cases taken to the Administrative Court since the beginning of 2003 (para 2).

[84] *R (S, D and T)* v. *Secretary of State for the Home Department*, High Court (Maurice Kay J), 31 July 2003.

[85] See the Court of Appeal decisions in *R (Q and others)* v. *Secretary of State for the Home Department* [2003] 2 All ER 905 and *R (T)* v. *Secretary of State for the Home Department*, Court of Appeal, 23 September 2003.

[86] At the time of writing, planning approval has been given for only one centre, but is the subject of a legal challenge.

permitting the education of minors to be provided in accommodation centres.[87] These provisions were not included in the original Commission proposal.[88]

A final point concerns the provision made for the employment of asylum applicants. The directive provides that member states "shall decide the conditions for granting access to the labour market" where an initial decision has not been taken within twelve months of an application.[89] The British Government was initially unhappy with this aspect of the directive, since that was a longer period than the six months then required in Britain.[90] Even before the directive was finalised, however, Britain had removed the possibility for asylum applicants to work.[91] It appears that Britain will therefore need to reinstate some form of entitlement to employment for asylum applicants when the directive comes fully into force on 6 February 2005.

Asylum Procedures

Britain opted in to the discussions on the proposed directive on asylum procedures.[92] It has supported the proposed directive because of its "hope that procedural standards in some member States will be raised" and also because it sees the proposal as a first step to a common asylum procedure.[93]

Here too, Britain has also had some success in securing changes to the proposal which reflect its existing provision. One example concerns the provisions in the Commission proposal which defined the circumstances in which an asylum applicant could be detained.[94] Some asylum applicants in Britain are detained solely in order to expedite the consideration of their claims, and the Government's intention was to ensure that that practice

[87] Article 7(4) and Article 10(1) of the directive.

[88] For British Government support for the change with respect to the education of minors, see memorandum of 8 April 2002 of Home Office Minister Angela Eagle, in House of Commons Select Committee on European Scrutiny, 2001–2002, *Twenty-Fourth Report*, para 3.7.

[89] Article 11 of the directive.

[90] Home Office Minister Angela Eagle, above n 88, para 3.8.

[91] Home Office press release, "Faster asylum decisions – historical employment concession ended", 23 July 2002.

[92] (COM (2000) 578, 20 September 2000) and Article 17 of its amended proposal (COM (2002) 326, 3 July 2002).

[93] Government response in House of Lords Select Committee on European Union, *Second Report* 2001–2002, para 7.

[94] See Article 11 of the Commission's original proposal, and Article 17 of its amended proposal.

would be consistent with any directive which was agreed.[95] In the event, the proposal was changed to state simply that "Member States shall not hold a person in detention for the sole reason that he/she is an applicant for asylum, but without specifying the grounds on which detention would be allowed."[96] It appears that that approach is acceptable to the British Government.[97]

The provision in the proposed directive for the availability of publicly funded legal assistance and representation for appeal or review has also been altered to Britain's benefit. The change in question would allow member states to require that an appeal or review be "likely to succeed" before granting assistance/representation.[98] The Government indicated in September 2003 that the amended provision "reflects the current provision in the UK law",[99] under which there are merits tests for public funding of appeals and review proceedings.[100]

Qualification

The British Government has supported the proposed directive on the qualification and status of persons as refugees or as otherwise needing international protection.[101] In its view, "a close degree of harmonisation is generally desirable in the asylum field in order to reduce disparities between Member States and so reduce secondary migration".[102] At the same time, it takes the view that any directive would be unlikely to make a significant difference to its existing law.[103]

95 Memorandum of 24 September 2002 of Home Office Minister Lord Filkin, in House of Commons Select Committee on European Scrutiny, 2001–02, *Forty-First Report*, para 8.6.

96 See for example Article 17(1) of the proposal in Council doc 9947/03 (28 May 2003).

97 Letter of 12 September 2003 of Home Office Minister Caroline Flint, in House of Commons Select Committee on European Scrutiny, 2002–03, *Thirty-Third Report*, para 20.9.

98 Compare Article 13 of the Commission's amended proposal (COM (2002) 326, 3 July 2002) and of the version of the proposal in Council doc 15198/03 (4 December 2003).

99 Letter of Caroline Flint, above n 97, para 20.7.

100 The British Government has recently proposed to limit legal aid for initial asylum determinations to five hours in most cases: see Department of Constitutional Affairs, *Proposed Changes to Publicly Funded Immigration and Asylum Work* (June 2003) and the statement by Minister for Constitutional Affairs David Lammy, HC Debates, 27 November 2003, cols 37–40WS. Since the proposed directive contemplates an entitlement to representation only after the initial determination, it does not appear to conflict with this proposal.

101 The Commission proposal is at COM (2001) 510 (12 September 2001).

102 Home Office memorandum of 4 December 2001, in House of Lords Select Committee on the European Union, *Twenty-Eighth Report*, 2001–2002, at para 12.

103 *Ibid.*, para 14.

Within the negotiations on the directive, Britain has sought to argue for a high level of protection. For example, in relation to international protection *sur place*, the Commission proposal had permitted the exclusion of protection where "activities were engaged in for the sole purpose of creating the necessary conditions for making an application for international protection".[104] Britain supported a change in that provision, so that there would only be a presumption against protection in such circumstances.[105] It did so because it wished an outcome closer to the British position, whereby such activities "though clearly damaging to credibility, have to be judged on the effect they have, and whether or not they place the applicant at risk".[106]

The British Government has also sought to defend the view that protection should be available to those at risk of persecution or serious harm from non-state actors.[107] As is well known, Britain takes the more common view on that question that protection should be available, while France and Germany take a more restrictive approach, based on state accountability. In relation to the directive, the Government view is therefore that "the UK's interest would be best served by the broader majority interpretation because it is a key factor in establishing a level playing field for asylum applications and will help ensure the effectiveness of the Dublin Convention and its successor".[108]

Conclusion

This report has shown that Britain has been a full participant in key elements of EU migration law since May 1999. It has consistently taken part in measures aimed at strengthening immigration control or at the laying down of rules concerning asylum. Conversely, it has consistently refused to participate in measures associated with the relaxation of internal border controls, or which relate to the admission of third country nationals.

Two critical observations may be offered by way of conclusion. In the first place, one may question the logic of British participation in at least some of the measures to do with immigration control – including those on carriers' obligations, facilitation and mutual recognition of expulsion

[104] Article 8(2) of the Commission proposal.

[105] See for example Article 8 of the proposal in Council doc 10576/03 (19 June 2003).

[106] Memorandum of 27 November 2002 of Home Office Minister Lord Filkin, in House of Commons Select Committee on European Scrutiny, 2002–2003, *Fourth Report*, para 6.22.

[107] Article 9 of the Commission proposal.

[108] Memorandum of 4 December 2001, above n 102, para 18.

decisions – given that these are essentially commitments as among states between which border controls have been abolished. A second point concerns the present arrangements whereby Britain is permitted to choose whether to opt in to individual measures, and may elect to do so either at the proposal stage or after adoption. Arguments of both transparency and principle suggest that it would be preferable if Britain were instead obliged to participate in competences rather than measures. This question may become especially important with the extension of qualified majority decision-making within EU migration law. If Britain's response to the possibility of qualified majorities is to avoid opting in until after adoption, while relying on a *de facto* capacity to participate in negotiations, other member states may be tempted to question the precise terms of its special position.

GENERAL RAPPORT

PROFESSOR DR. KAY HAILBRONNER, L. L. M.
AND IMELDA HIGGINS BL

INTRODUCTION

The purpose of this General Report is to examine critically national laws and policies in the area of migration and asylum as compared with EU law and policy in this area. The information in the Report is derived from responses received to a questionnaire which was circulated to National Rapporteurs from twenty five European countries: twenty of those countries responded. These countries can be loosely divided into: 1) EU Member States who also participate in Schengen, namely Austria, Germany, Greece, Italy, Luxembourg, the Netherlands, Spain, Sweden, and Portugal, 2) EU Member States who partially participate in Schengen: Denmark, Ireland, and the UK, 3) EU Accession countries: Estonia, Hungary, Latvia, Malta, and Poland, 4) EEA Member States: Norway and Switzerland, 5) Others: Croatia.

The objective of this General Report differs somewhat from those of the national reports in so far as it is confined to considering issues of particular relevance to EU law and policy. Consequently, not all questions raised in the questionnaire are considered in this Report and in particular those aimed at obtaining information on national structures or procedures.

This General Report will follow the same structure as the questionnaire which was divided into four parts. Part 1 of the General Report, therefore, relates to entry, visa regime and border control. Part 2 deals with admission and residence of third country nationals. Part 3 is concerned with asylum and refugee law. Part 4 pertains to termination of illegal residence, return and repatriation.

In the context of each of the four parts, particular emphasis is placed on the following points:

- implementation of existing EU legislation in the field of migration and asylum law;
- compatibility of national migration and asylum law and policies with pending EC directives and regulations, particularly on asylum procedure, legal status of third country nationals and definition of refugees;

- Prospects and conflicts concerning draft directives and communications of the European Commission on the future development of a European migration and asylum law;
- Long term perspective of EU legislation in the field of migration and asylum law and policy.

PART I ENTRY, VISA REGIME AND BORDER CONTROL

The focus of this part of the General Report is on measures taken against the illegal entry and stay of third country nationals relating to the EU-visa regime and the Schengen rules on border control and the issuance of Schengen visas.

The system of issuing visas is central to the control of illegal entry. In relation to this system, two issues are of particular relevance from an EU perspective. Firstly, control over successive or duplicate visa applications and, secondly, the applicable substantive criteria for issuing or refusing visas.

Procedures for avoiding duplicate or successive visa applications at different EU-consulates

With regard to controlling successive or duplicate visa applications, in so far as Schengen countries are concerned, the Common Consular Instructions on issuing visas require competent authorities to afix a stamp on travel documents when a visa application is made to a Schengen Member State. Where such a stamp is affixed, this constitutes a clear sign to other competent authorities that an applicant has previously submitted an application and may serve to prevent duplicate or successive visa applications. However, one of the weaknesses of the system lies in the fact that, in many cases, migrants do not have travel documents or any other means of identification. Moreover, even where travel documents do exist, the existence of a stamp does not always bar an applicant from making another visa application in another country. Thus, according to the Italian National Report, there is no ban on re-applying for a visa after a refusal.

Aside from afixing a stamp pursuant to the Common Consular Instructions, none of the National Reports indicate any other way of ascertaining whether an applicant has made successive or duplicate applications. Moreover, some countries outside the Schengen area only record the decision to issue or refuse a visa in the travel documents rather than an application per se[1]. It therefore appears, that, until a decision is made on the application there is no way of knowing how many other applications have been submitted by the relevant applicant.

Some National Reports indicate difficulties in controlling successive or duplicate visa applications in the same country. It appears that, while some countries have either systematic[2] or ad hoc checks[3] on whether successive or duplicate visa applications have been made to other competent authorities of that country e.g. to a number of consulates, others do not.

It is likely that the effective implementation of Eurodac will facilitate the more effective identification of duplicate or successive visa applications.

Substantive criteria for granting/refusing visas

In so far as the requirements for issuing visas are concerned, while the Schengen minimum requirements[4] have harmonised the law in this area to some degree, a number of National Reports indicate that other requirements are also imposed[5]. Of these, the most common concerns appears to be those of ensuring that the applicant does not overstay the period for which the visa is granted[6] and has health insurance[7].

[1] See the Latvian National Report.

[2] Estonia has a common visa register which avoids the possibility of duplicate or successive visa applications at different Estonian missions.

[3] Hungary has regional consular checking sections to prevent duplicate or successive visa applications. Hungary's N-VIS is able to check attempts at national level.

[4] Article 5

1. For visits not exceeding three months entry into the territories of the Contracting Parties may be granted to an alien who fulfils the following conditions:
   - (a) in possession of a valid document or documents permitting them to cross the border, as determined by the Executive Committee;
   - (b) in possession of a valid visa if required;
   - (c) if applicable, submits documents substantiating the purpose and the conditions of the planned visit and has sufficient means of support, both for the period of the planned visit and to return to their country of origin or to travel in transit in a Third State, into which their admission is guaranteed, or is in a position to acquire such means legally;
   - (d) has not been reported as a person not to be permitted entry;
   - (e) is not considered to be a threat to public policy, national security or The international relations of any of the Contracting Parties.

[5] See e.g. the Netherlands Report, the Luxembourg Report, the Spanish Report, the Danish Report, and the Austrian Report.

[6] See e.g. the Netherlands Report; the Luxembourg Report, the Spanish Report, the Danish Report.

[7] See e.g. the Austrian Report, the Latvian Report.

Visa tracking procedures

In contrast to the situation with regard to the issuing of visas, which appears to be subject to systematic rules and procedures in all countries, few countries have any systematic procedure for identifying visa overstayers. Consequently, staying in a country illegally appears to be much easier than entering that country illegally in the first place. In this respect, it appears from the National Reports that most countries depend on adhoc procedures for identifying visa overstayers such as: random identify checks; inspection of premises; information received from the general public; checks on applications for renewal or at exit controls. However, some countries are making attempts to improve the identification of visa overstayers, particularly through the construction of centralised data banks[8].

Collection of Biometric Data

To date[9] it appears that no country ordinarily[10] collects biometric data from visa applicants, such as fingerprints[11].

Schengen Blacklisting

The National Reports contain very little information on the issue of the refusal of Schengen Visas due to blacklisting by other Schengen Member States: only the Spanish report indicates the existence of such a decision. The absence of information on this point would appear to indicate that such refusals are not common, although the dearth of information may be

[8] See e.g. the Maltese Report.

[9] The Netherlands is currently investigating the collection of biometrical data to identify incoming travellers.

[10] Poland, under the Alien Act 1997, may collect finger prints in the following circumstances: illegal entry, save in situations where an alien entered unintentionally and subsequently was immediately escorted to the border; issuing an expulsion order; and detaining an alien who does not comply with an expulsion order or who is a situation justifying expulsion. In addition, fingerprints are collected from aliens seeking protection under the Aliens Act 2003.

[11] According to the UK Report, while applicants for British visas or entry clearance are not ordinarily required to provide biometric data, s. 126 of the Nationality Immigration and Asylum Act 2002 empowered the Secretary of State to provide "specified information" about their "external physical characteristics". Relying on that power, a trial of compulsory fingerprinting of visa applicants began in Sri Lanka in July 2003, and the Government indicated in August 2003 its desire to extend the principle to other states.

due to the fact that decisions on this issue are not being published. Clearly, the successful prevention of duplicate or successive visa applications is dependent on the various member states respecting decisions taken by other Member States on visa applications. The alternative is wide spread visa shopping and a wasteful use of resources as investigations carried out in one Member State are repeated by another.

Action programme for administrative co-operation in the field of external borders, visa, asylum and immigration

The action program of administrative co-operation in the field of external borders, visa, asylum and immigration (Argo) essentially offers the Member States the possibility of having co-operation programmes co-financed by the Community. Programmes between Member States and between Member States, accession countries and third countries are all eligible. In so far as Member States are concerned, neither Italy nor Luxembourg appear to have taken advantage of the Argo programme. However, Germany, Greece, Austria and Spain all have programmes in place which are financed by Argo[12].

As was to be expected, the type of programmes carried out within the Argo framework varies widely. Germany has established a central border within its' Ministry for the Interior in which common action on the part of border police is co-ordinated. For example, mixed nationality teams may inspect busses in Germany, Austria, and Italy. At the beginning of 2003, there were in total 17 projects with the aim of harmonising the working procedures of border police. Greece has been the leader country for two projects. These projects concerned, respectively, an operation on migration pressure at the Eastern external land borders of the EU and an operation on sea border control in the South-eastern Mediterranean. Greece has also participated in a series of other projects led by other Member States. Moreover, Greece has submitted a proposal for the establishment of a Joint Sea Borders Co-ordination Centre in Greece. Spain has organised "Ulysses", which is a joint operation for co-ordinating the control of maritime external borders in the Mediterranean area in the first half of 2003, and in the Canary Islands in the second half of 2003.

While neither Portugal nor the Netherlands have any on-going cooperation programmes under ARGO, both those countries together with the

[12] The Swiss Report also refers to co-operation programmes but it is not altogether clear to what extent, if any this co-operation takes place within the context of Argo.

UK have organised a seminar which will took place in March 2004 and which was financed by ARGO.

With regard to the non-Member States, Malta is involved in a Twinning project between the Maltese, Spanish and UK immigration authorities which has as one of its objectives, the creation and maintenance of a computerised system of data collection and preservation to make it easier to track visa overstayers.

From some of the responses given in the National Reports it appears that at least some countries appear to believe that Argo is only of relevance to Schengen Member States[13].

Carrier Sanctions

Directive 2001/51 EC concerns the imposition of obligations on carriers and sanctions for breach of such obligations and extends the obligations imposed on Member States pursuant to Article 26(1)(a) of the Schengen Convention. The date for implementation of that Directive was the 11 February 2003. The Directive was to have been implemented by each of the Schengen member states, Denmark, the UK, Ireland and Norway. The Directive is also of relevance to accession countries. In so far as the member states are concerned, the Directive has been implemented by Austria, Denmark, Germany, Greece, Spain, Italy, Ireland, Portugal[14], the UK and Norway. However, neither Norway nor Denmark have adopted any specific implementation measures as they consider that their existing legislation already complies with the provisions of the Directive. Sweden has adopted legislation which will come into force on 1 July, 2004. Neither Luxembourg nor the Netherlands have implemented the Directive as of yet. In so far as the Accession countries are concerned, Estonia, Poland, and Latvia have all taken measures to implement the Directive. Hungary also imposes carrier sanctions, as does Croatia.

There appears to be little information regarding the application of the Directive. However, a number of countries already applied carrier sanctions under national law and these countries appear to have achieved some success in the implementation of the same[15].

[13] See e.g. the following National Reports: Ireland, Latvia, and Hungary.

[14] Although there appear to be some disparities between the Directive and the implementing legislation.

[15] See e.g. the Polish Report, the Danish Report, the Lithuanian Report and the German Report.

Compatibility of National law and policy regarding Visas with EU Standards

No National Report identifies any significant degree of incompatibility between national law and policy and EU standards. Moreover, all National Rapporteurs appear to consider that there is a clear need for further harmonisation of visa obligations. Regarding the establishment of the European Visa Identification System (VIS and SIS II), while most Rapporteurs were enthusiastic some adopted a more cautious approach. Thus, the German Report identifies certain difficulties such a system may present for data protection law. Similarly, the Italian Report emphasises the need to ensure transparency, the right of access to and information about personal data stored in the data base and the right to ask for the removal of data from the database.

Impact of Enlargement

The extent to which the EU enlargement process is considered as positive or negative seems to turn largely on whether or not the respondent considers that it will be possible to institute effective control over the new external borders. Thus many National Rapporteurs welcome enlargement as a means of strengthening controls in areas which are perceived as currently vulnerable (FN). On the other hand, some consider that enlargement will increase rather than eliminate the impact of this vulnerability on the Schengen area (FN).

PART II ADMISSION AND RESIDENCE OF THIRD COUNTRY NATIONALS

This subject deals with the rules of admission and residence of third country nationals, in particular with regard to the following:

- entry and residence for the purpose of paid employment and self employed activities
- entry and residence for the purpose of studies, vocational training or voluntary service
- the status of third country nationals who are long term residents
- entry and residence for the purpose of family reunion.

Each of these issues is currently either the subject of a Commission proposal or of a recent directive.

Admission of third country nationals for labour purposes or self-employed activities

With regard to the admission of third country nationals for labour purposes or self-employed activities, the most important development at EU level is clearly the Proposal for a Directive on conditions of entry and residence of third country nationals for the purpose of paid employment and self-employed activities[16]. This Proposal pursues a number of aims including the following:

1. laying down common definitions, criteria and procedures regarding the conditions of entry and residence of third-country nationals for the purpose of paid employment and self-employed economic activities, based on concepts, which have already been successfully applied in Member States;
2. laying down common criteria for admitting third-country nationals to employed activities and self-employed economic activities ("economic needs test" and "beneficial effects test") and opening different options for demonstrating compliance with these criteria;
3. providing procedural and transparency safeguards, in order to assure a high level of legal certainty and information for all interested actors on Member State rules and administrative practice in the field of entry and residence of third-country nationals for the purpose of paid employment and self-employed economic activities;
4. providing a single national application procedure leading to one combined title, encompassing both residence and work permit within one administrative act, in order to simplify and harmonise the diverging rules currently applicable in Member States;
5. providing rights to third-country nationals whilst respecting Member States discretion to limit economic migration.

Ireland has opted in to the Proposed Directive, while the UK has opted out in order to maintain control over the procedure and content of its admission policy[17].

It is clear from the National Reports that should this Proposal be adopted, it will require a number of changes in the various national laws, particularly with regard to admission for labour purposes. In this respect, the main changes, which will be required by the Proposal, relate to the following provisions: the provision of a single application procedure for

[16] COM 2001, 386 final. [17] See the UK Report.

entry for the purpose of paid emploment: the right of the migrant to apply for the work permit him/herself; the right of the migrant to apply for a work permit from within the country concerned; the right to change employers; the ability to limit work permits to certain regional districts.

With regard to application procedures, Article 4(1) of the Proposal provides that Member States shall only authorise third-country nationals to enter and reside in their territory for the purpose of exercising activities as an employed person where a "residence permit – worker" has been issued by the competent authorities of the Member State concerned in accordance with this Directive. The Proposal therefore envisages a single permit for the purpose of entry, residence, and employment. According to the National Reports of Luxembourg, the Netherlands, Greece, Ireland, United Kingdom, and Latvia[18] these rights are currently subject to two or more separate procedures and separate application procedures are applied.

Article 5(1) of the Proposal provides that, in order to obtain a "residence permit – worker", a third-country national intending to exercise activities as an employed person in a Member State shall themselves apply to the competent authority of the Member State concerned. The future employer of a third-country national is also given the right to submit an application on behalf of the third-country national applicant. Currently, pursuant to the laws applicable in a number of countries, it appears that a third-country national does not him/herself have the right to submit the application[19].

Article 5(2) of the Proposal provides that Article 5 applications for a "residence permit – worker" may be submitted directly in the territory of the Member State concerned, if the applicant is already resident or legally present there. According to the Italian National Report, legally resident or present applicants do not have a right to submit an application directly in Italy. This is also the situation in Greece.

Pursuant to Article 8 of the Proposal, a "residence permit – worker" shall initially be restricted to the exercise of specific professional activities or fields of activities. It may also be restricted to the exercise of activities as an employed person in a specific region. Neither Italian nor Greek law currently provide for either of the latter restrictions. However a number of States only issue work permits for specified persons for a specified jobs[20].

[18] According to the Latvian National Report, sometimes the issuing of a work permit and residence permit is under a single administrative procedure while sometimes it is not.

[19] Italy, Greece, UK, Malta, Croatia.

[20] See e.g. Ireland and the UK.

In contrast, the Directive reflects the situation in most member states whereby a post can only be fulfilled by a third country national after a thorough assessment of the domestic labour market situation[21].

With regard to the entry and residence of third country nationals for self-employed activities, it appears from the National Reports that fewer changes will be required in national law in order to implement the Commission's proposals in this respect.

Admission of third country nationals for study and vocational training

In so far as the Commission's proposal on the admission of third country nationals for study and vocational training is concerned, Ireland has also opted in to that Proposal while the UK has again opted out so as to retain freedom of action in its approach to third country students. According to the UK National Report, Britain attracts considerably more third country students than other Member States of comparative size. Britain had specific reservations concerning the proposed right of students admitted in other countries. A second reservation was that Britain did not wish to allow in-country applications for admission to student status. On the other hand, in common with the proposal, Britain does permit third country students to engage in paid employment for up to 20 hours a week during term and without limit outside term time.

From the National Reports, it appears that the most significant difference between the Commission's Proposal and national legislation lie in the following factors:

- permitting students to engage in limited employment (Luxembourg, Germany, Greece, Malta)
- entry as a volunteer (Italy, Portugal, Spain, Estonia)
- mobility provisions for third country nationals studying in other Member States.

Legal status of third country nationals in possession of a long term residence permit of another Member State

With regard to the legal status of third country nationals in possession of a long term residence of another Member State, the proposal for a Directive focuses on two central issues. Firstly, the terms for conferring

[21] See e.g. Luxembourg, Denmark, Portugal, Sweden, Austria, Spain, Greece, the Netherlands.

and withdrawing long-term resident status granted by a Member State in relation to third-country nationals legally residing in its territory, and the rights pertaining thereto. Secondly, the terms of residence for third country nationals enjoying that status in Member States other than the one which conferred long-term status on them. Both the UK and Ireland have opted out of the Proposal.

It appears from the National Reports that implementation of this Directive will require substantial modifications in national laws. Currently a significant proportion of countries do not accord any specific rights to third country nationals in possession of a long term residence permit of another Member State[22].

The Right to Family Reunion

In contrast, it appears that the standards contained in the Proposal for a directive on the right to family reunion agreed by the Council in February 2003 are either similar[23] to or lower[24] than those which currently apply in many countries. Nevertheless it appears that the Directive may have a positive impact on some aspects of national law regarding e.g. the minimum age of sponsors and spouses, the spouse's right to work[25], spouses access to vocational education and training[26]; limitation on the administration's discretionary powers[27], period of lawful residence of sponsor.

With regard to the higher standards of protection provide under national law, the following issues were mentioned in the National Reports:

- Scope of application of the right to family reunion is broader in national law than under the Directive (UK, Portugal, Croatia)
- The Directive permits countries to retain minimum age requirements of up to 21, under national law the minimum age is 18 for the sponsor and 16 for the spouse (UK)
- No possibility under national law to apply an integration test for children over 12 who arrive independently of the rest of the family: States have the option of applying such a test under the Directive (UK, Italy, Portugal, the Netherlands)

[22] Austria, Germany, Greece, Italy, the Netherlands, Portugal, Spain, Sweden, Norway, Hungary, Latvia, Estonia, Malta, Ireland.

[23] Austria, Germany (?), Luxembourg, Greece, Spain, Poland, Hungary, Latvia, Estonia.

[24] Sweden, Netherlands, Portugal, Italy, UK, Croatia.

[25] Luxembourg. [26] Greece. [27] Greece.

- No restriction on the admission of children over 15 (UK, the Netherlands)
- Period of lawful residence under national law less than the maximum permitted by the Directive (Portugal, Croatia)
- Directive permits Member States to subject the right of a spouse to an autonomous residence period to a longer waiting period than that envisaged under national law (Portugal)
- Under Article 5(5) of the Directive, Member States are required to have 'due regard' to the best interests of minor children whereas national law requires their interests to be a 'primary consideration' (the Netherlands).

Of those countries whose national law applies a higher standard protection for families, it appears that the majority do not envisage that the Directive will result in a lowering of these standards[28]. However, the position is not yet clear in some countries[29] and some National Reports do reflect the concern that the Directive may lead to such a lowering of standards[30]. Moreover, some National Reports raise concerns regarding the compatibility of the Directive with established international standards of family protection such as Article 8 of the European Convention on Human Rights[31].

Both the UK and Irish National Reports indicate that those countries do not intend to implement the Directive. In this respect, it appears that the UK government feared that participation in the Directive might have "removed the UK's ability to formulate and adjust policies in relation to family reunification as a matter of domestic law". The Directive is also subject to the Danish reservation under the 1997 Protocol. Were Denmark to participate in the Directive a number of amendments in Danish law would be required.

Rights of long-term third country nationals

With regard to the proposal for a Directive on the rights of long-term third country nationals, agreed upon by the Council on 5 June 2003, while the national legislation of some countries is largely compatible[32], others have indicated that implementation of the proposal will require significant changes in national law as some or all of the principles underlying the

[28] Germany, Austria, Estonia, Latvia, Hungary.

[29] According to the Italian National Report there is of yet no government position on this issue.

[30] Portugal, the Netherlands, Poland.

[31] Netherlands, Poland.

[32] Portugal, Netherlands, Latvia, Estonia, Poland.

Directive are new[33]. In so far as changes required in national law by the Directive are concerned, the Reports refer, in particular to the following

- Reasons for which expulsion may be ordered (Luxembourg, Greece)
- factors taken into account with regard to expulsion (Luxembourg, Greece)
- right of residence in another EU Member State (the vast majority of countries)
- the concept of civic citizenship and the integration of third country nationals (Italy, Greece).

The Latvian National Report raises significant concerns regarding the issue of whether or not Latvian "non-citizens" are covered by the Directive. While the Directive refers to third country nationals, the Commission pointed out in a specific letter that, as regards Latvia, the term "third country national" includes persons who do not have citizenship. This is a very sensitive and political issue in Latvia, and it is feared that the inclusion of non citizens within the scope of the Directive could hamper the process of naturalisation be removing the incentive for such persons to acquire Latvian citizenship.

Denmark, Ireland and the UK are not participating in this Directive.

Role of Community Organs in determining a European Migration Policy

With regard to the role of the Community organs in determining a European migration policy in terms of competencies of the Member States to decide on residence rights and admission to the labour market and integration, most National Reports adopt a very cautious approach to this issue. In this respect, questions were raised regarding the legal basis for such a role: the Portugese Report points out that the competencies of the Community are limited by Article 63 of the Treaty of Amsterdam and by the principles of proportionality and subsidiarity. Moreover there appears to be a lack of political will towards making progress in harmonisation in this area with much emphasis on the need for countries to retain competence[34]. However, some enthusiasm for further harmonisation in specific areas is evident[35]. In particular, according to the Luxembourgish Report, some level of harmonisation is necessary to deter migrants from country shopping[36].

[33] Sweden, Luxembourg, Italy, Denmark, Greece, Spain, Hungary.

[34] Italy, Germany, Latvia, Hungary, Greece.

[35] Portugal, Italy, Sweden.

[36] Luxembourg.

PART III ASYLUM AND REFUGEE LAW

This Part primarily concerns the impact of EU asylum legislation upon national laws and practices. Three major topics arise from the directives that have been adopted or are pending, namely: reception of asylum seekers; asylum procedures; and exclusive competence and burden sharing.

The Dublin Rules

In so far as the Dublin Rules are concerned the following problems were identified

- the procedures to establish the Member State responsible for assessing an asylum application are too long (Germany, Sweden, Denmark, Norway, Portugal, Netherlands)
- the time limits set out in the Convention are too long (Germany, Sweden, Denmark)
- the proofs for establishing competence (Germany, UK)
- the Rules do not assist in preventing multiple applications (Netherlands)
- Interpretative difficulties (Germany, Luxembourg, Spain).

The following expectations exist with regard to the Dublin II Regulation No 343/2004,

- faster decision making procedures (Germany, Sweden, Norway, Greece)
- stricter time limits (Italy)
- clarification regarding several interpretative issues (Germany, Luxembourg)
- improved burden sharing (Luxembourg)
- relaxation of proofs required (UK).

Some National Reports mention that the new procedure is regarded as being too complicated[37], that it does not introduce any qualitative change in the Convention procedure and leaves administrative authorities too much discretion[38]. However, most expect that it will be an improvement compared to the Convention. National Reports from the Accession countries indicate that they expect that implementation of the Dublin rules will lead to an increase in asylum applications[39].

[37] Germany. [38] Portugal. [39] Poland, Estonia, Hungary.

Eurodac

It appears that Eurodac is now effective in most Member States[40] and some EEA countries[41]. While some national reports indicate a marked increase in Dublin cases as a result[42], others do not see any clear link[43]. Eurodac will become effective in the Accession countries after accession and according to the National Reports, preparations are already under way in Estonia, Lativa, and Poland. Croatia is in the process of making its system compatible with Eurodac.

Minimum Standards on Procedures for Granting and Withdrawing Refugee Status

With regard to the amended proposal for a directive on minimum standards on procedures in Member States for granting and withdrawing refugee status, while many countries already, for the most part, comply with the Directive it appears that implementation will nevertheless require a number of changes[44]. In particular, the following areas of national legislation may be affected: rights of applicants in the procedure; administrative and judicial appeal procedures; the use of safe third country and safe country of origin concepts; detainment of asylum seekers; airport and border procedures.

the rights of applicants in the procedure:

- ensuring the asylum seeker's right to be informed regarding his rights and duties in a language known to him (Germany, Malta)
- Linguistic assistance (Ireland)
- the implementation of procedural time limits (Germany)
- Introduction of normal and accelerated procedures or amendments to legislation providing for such procedures (Luxembourg, Netherlands)
- Application of the principle of the benefit of the doubt contained in Article 16 of the Proposal (Norway, Estonia)
- Income (Malta)
- Right to work (U.K.).

[40] With the exception of Denmark. [41] Norway.
[42] Norway, Luxembourg, Sweden, Germany, Austria, Greece.
[43] The Netherlands, Portugal, Italy, Spain. [44] Germany, Sweden.

Administrative and judicial appeal procedures

- elimination of the possibility of referring a case to the Government[45]
- introduction of the possibility of staying in the country pending determination of an appeal (Italy, Estonia)[46]
- No express recognition of the right to a legal advisor (Italy, Austria)
- Right of access to national courts (Denmark, Malta, Greece).

use of safe third country and safe country of origin concepts

The vast majority of countries already apply these concepts. However, according to the Luxembourgish National Report, the concept of a safe third country is not often applied due to difficulties relating to proof and the question of re-admission agreements. The Directive will not change this. Nevertheless, the fact that the Directive includes a list of safe countries of origin will enable countries to apply the accelerated procedure to applicants from those countries[47].

Detainment of Asylum seekers

- restraints on the government's right to detain asylum seekers – Malta

Airport and Border procedures

It appears that the vast majority of countries do not provide for the application of specific procedures at airports and borders

Reception of Asylum Seekers

With regard to the implementation of Directive 2003/9, a substantial majority of countries have not yet implemented the Directive or have only partially done so, namely: Austria, Greece, Portugal, the Netherlands, Italy, Luxembourg, Spain, and Sweden. National Reports from these countries indicate the following areas of incompatibility:

- asylum seekers submitting a second application are excluded from reception facilities without any individual examination of their circumstances: this appears contrary to Article 16(4) of the Directive (Netherlands)
- no right of access to the labour market (Italy, Luxembourg)

[45] Sweden.

[46] Member States are permitted to keep their national rules if adopted before the Directive.

[47] Luxembourg.

Norway, Denmark, and Ireland do not intend to implement the Directive. Norwegian law generally corresponds with the Directive. In so far as Denmark and Ireland are concerned the main point of difference seems to relate to access to the labour market.

In so far as the accession countries are concerned, while many National Reports[48] indicate that national law is generally compatible with the Directive there are some differences, principally concerning the issue of access to the labour market[49]. Some National Reports indicate that implementation of the Directive will necessitate major changes[50] in National law.

Temporary Protection

The Directive on temporary protection has been implemented in a number of countries[51]. However, even those Member States which have not implemented the Directive yet or which do not intend to implement the Directive have national provisions for temporary protection[52]. None of the National Reports identified the existence of provisions relating to burdensharing either in existing or in pending legislation.

With regard to the accession countries, a number intend to implement the Directive by the time of accession or shortly thereafter[53]. As is the case with EU/EEA Member States, many accession countries already have provisions relating to temporary protection[54]. However, the establishment of temporary protection measures has also been identified as a priority area in a number of countries[55].

Minimum Standards for the qualification and status of third country nationals as refugees or persons otherwise in need of international protection

In so far as the principles for a directive on minimum standards for the qualification and status of third country nationals as refugees or persons who otherwise need international protection, a number of National Reports indicate that as they now stand, these principles will require few changes in national law[56]. Other National Reports indicate that the

48 Poland, Latvia, Estonia. 49 Poland, Latvia, Malta, Hungary, Estonia.
50 Malta. 51 Sweden, Italy, Portugal, Austria, Spain (?).
52 Norway, Luxembourg, Denmark, Germany, Greece, Ireland.
53 Estonia, Hungary. 54 Hungary, Latvia, Poland. 55 Estonia, Malta.
56 The Netherlands, Portugal, Latvia, Hungary.

following differences exist between the situation under national law and the Proposal

- the definition of refugee (Italy, Luxembourg, Norway, Sweden, Spain)
- the concept and definition of persecution and particularly the issue of non-state persecution (Italy, Germany, Estonia)
- the existence and scope of the status of subsidiary protection (Luxembourg, Sweden, Greece, Ireland, Denmark, Spain, Malta, Estonia, Croatia)
- the recognition of refugee status to family members (Italy)
- the length of the permit of stay issued to refugees and beneficiaries of subsidiary protection (Italy)
- exclusion clauses (Luxembourg, Sweden (?))
- the question of internal flight (Spain)
- recognition of refugee status to a person benefiting from temporary protection (Switzerland).

Common European Asylum Procedure and Uniform Status for Asylum Seekers

The Commission's concept of a common European asylum procedure and uniform status for those who are granted asylum valid throughout the Union seems to be regarded with a certain degree of enthusiasm by Member States[57] provided it does not lead to a relaxing of Member State laws in this field[58]. Few national governments appear to share the concerns of refugee organisations that such a policy would lead to an undermining of the international regime for refugee protection[59]. However, in this respect, the Portuguese National Rapporteur points out that the tendency of the European Union to-date has been to confine itself to establishing minimum standards in this area. This has to some degree legitimises the protective approach adopted by some Member States. Moreover, it also encourages Member States who have previously adopted a more generous approach to harmonise down the level of protection afforded to asylum seekers. Consequently, the fears of refugee organisations appear justified with regard to current EU policy.

[57] Germany, Sweden, Luxembourg, Portugal, Greece, Latvia, Poland.
[58] Germany.
[59] The Green party in Germany has such concerns as does the Dutch government.

Open Co-ordination Mechanism

With regard to the open coordination-mechanism suggested by the Commission, providing for first stage and second stage legislation ultimately leading to full harmonisation, there appears to be little discussion of this suggestion. The Portugese Report indicates that, in any event, the Union currently lacks the legal basis necessary for moving towards full harmonisation. Moreover, along with requiring an amendment of the Treaty, full harmonisation would require the revision of the Geneva Convention and the New York Protocol as these only permit states to be contracting parties.

Development of an accessible, equitable and managed asylum system

The reaction to the UK paper also appears somewhat muted. In those countries in which the paper was discussed, the response seems to have been largely unfavorable[60], although the proposals contained in the paper have not all been rejected out of hand[61]. In addition, as might be expected the enthusiasm with which concepts such as e.g. burden sharing are welcomed by a country depends to a large extent on its popularity as a destination for asylum seekers[62]. The Greek National Report reports concerns that the proposal will lead to the disappearance of the notion of territoriality in asylum matters and the non application of the Geneva Convention.

PART IV TERMINATION OF ILLEGAL RESIDENCE, RETURN AND REPATRIATION

This Part of the questionnaire focuses on the national measures concerning sanctions against illegal entry, other measures against illegal trafficking, problems related to the termination of residence of third country nationals not disposing of a valid residence permit, and co-operation with other EU Member States in return and expulsion issues.

Third Country nationals without a valid residence permit

With regard to the existence of third country nationals without a valid residence permit in the national territory, all National Reports indicate

[60] Germany, Sweden, Luxembourg, Portugal, Italy, Greece.

[61] It does appear, however, that Germany is completely against the idea of externally located asylum camps.

[62] Contrast, in this respect, the German and Portuguese Reports.

the presence of such nationals, although, as might be expected, few could give reliable figures on the numbers of such nationals. National Reports indicate the following difficulties with regard to national enforcement procedures

- lack of identification papers (Norway, Sweden)
- lack of re-admission agreements (Sweden, Luxembourg, Hungary)
- the number of persons absconding (Sweden, Ireland).

Facilitation of unauthorised entry, transit and residence

With regard to the Directive of 28 November 2002, dealing with the facilitation of unauthorised entry, transit and residence, so far, only Germany, Spain and Portugal, Lativa and Poland have fully transposed this Directive. However a number of National Reports indicate that only minor amendments will be required in national law in order to fully implement the Directive[63]. The Croatian National Report indicates that Croatian Law also substantially corresponds to the Directive.

Penalties for smuggling and trafficking

Concerning the harmonisation of penalty scales for the crime of smuggling migrants and trafficking of persons in line with the Budapest June 2003 recommendations and Council Directive 2002/90, as mentioned, only Germany, Spain, Portugal, Lativa and Poland have implemented the Directive. The following countries have signed relevant UN protocols on the smuggling of migrants: Norway, Spain, Ireland, Italy, Sweden, Portugal, Greece, Switzerland, Poland, and Latvia. A number of the National Reports indicate that although signed, the protocols have not yet been ratified: Italy, Sweden, Portugal, and Greece.

Mutual Recognition of Expulsion Decisions

Council Directive of 28 May 2001 on the mutual recognition of decisions on the expulsion of third country nationals has been implemented by Portugal, Denmark, Sweden, the Netherlands, Norway, Spain, and Hungary. However, the Portugese Report raises certain concerns regarding the manner in which the Directive has been transposed by that Member State.

[63] Greece, Ireland, Norway, Italy.

In particular, it appears that the implementing legislation has failed to distinguish between Portugal as the author of an expulsion decision and the state responsible for implementing such a decision.

The following suggestions were made regarding shortcomings of the Directive which should be corrected in a further directive on co-operation on the expulsion or deportation of third country nationals:

- provision of compensation for sharing of costs when implementing the Directive (Portugal)
- establishment of an obligatory framework for the mutual recognition of all decisions to return (Portugal)
- harmonisaton of the rules regarding the adoption of expulsion orders (Italy)
- setting out of minimum rights to be respected during the procedures, in conformity with the ECHR (Italy).

Re-admission Agreements

Attitudes toward re-admission agreements appear to vary. While the majority of countries have concluded such agreements some National Reports indicate that difficulties have been encountered in their conclusion[64]. On the other hand, re-admission agreements are viewed as an effective way of guaranteeing the execution of expulsion orders which in itself a critical part of a functioning immigration policy[65]. However, according to the Maltese National Report, Malta has only entered into one re-admission agreement, with Italy, but nevertheless does not encounter any particular difficulties when repatriating foreign nationals.

Influence of EU Standards and recommendations on national return policies

With regard to the influence of EU-standards and recommendations on national return policies, the following areas of influence were identified:

- raising the profile of issues (Luxembourg)
- use of the EU-prototype when signing re-admission agreements (Sweden, Hungary)
- establishing the basis of national return policy (Spain).

[64] Luxembourg, Norway.

[65] Italy, Germany, Portugal, Ireland, Spain, Portugal, Latvia, Hungary.

The following National Reports indicate that EU standards and recommendations have not influenced their national return policies either at all or substantially: Germany, Italy, Netherlands, Latvia.

Co-operation Agreements

The establishment of co-operation agreements with other countries appears to be widespread, see e.g. the following National Reports: Austria, Luxembourg, Sweden, Germany, Italy, Norway, Spain, Ireland, Portugal.

Many National Reports[66] indicated a need to establish common rules regarding, e.g.: the legal status of armed guards on board of the aircrafts, rights of the aircraft commander, legal rules in case of transit stops, applicability of national police law on board of aircraft on flight, etc. However, the Dutch National Report indicates that such rules might be of little use given that problems in these areas tend to be more practical than legal. Moreover, the German National Report raises the question as to whether the establishment of minimum standards in these areas would be compatible with the principle of subsidiarity. This issue is also raised in the Portuguese National Report.

[66] Norway, Italy, Sweden, Luxembourg, Austria, Portugal, Hungary.

For EU product safety concerns, contact us at Calle de José Abascal, 56–1°, 28003 Madrid, Spain or eugpsr@cambridge.org.

www.ingramcontent.com/pod-product-compliance
Lightning Source LLC
LaVergne TN
LVHW090256210926
848480LV00001B/41